CW00430416

PHILIP'S

STREET ATLAS
Buckinghamshire
and Milton Keynes

www.philips-maps.co.uk
First published in 1990 by
Philip's, a division of
Octopus Publishing Group Ltd
www.octopusbooks.co.uk
Carmelite House
50 Victoria Embankment
London EC4Y 0DZ
An Hachette UK Company
www.hachette.co.uk

Fifth edition with interim revision 2017
First impression 2017
BUCEA

ISBN 978-1-84907-450-6 (spiral)

© Philip's 2017

Contents

III   **Key to map symbols**

IV   **Key to map pages**

VI   **Route planning**

VIII   Major administrative and Postcode boundaries

1   **Street maps** at 3½ inches to 1 mile

214   **Index** of towns, villages, streets, hospitals, industrial estates, railway stations, schools, shopping centres, universities and places of interest

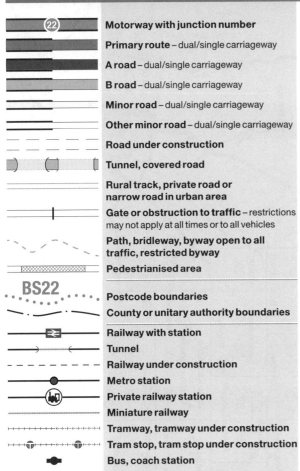

	Motorway with junction number
	Primary route – dual/single carriageway
	A road – dual/single carriageway
	B road – dual/single carriageway
	Minor road – dual/single carriageway
	Other minor road – dual/single carriageway
	Road under construction
	Tunnel, covered road
	Rural track, private road or narrow road in urban area
	Gate or obstruction to traffic – restrictions may not apply at all times or to all vehicles
	Path, bridleway, byway open to all traffic, restricted byway
	Pedestrianised area
BS22	Postcode boundaries
	County or unitary authority boundaries
	Railway with station
	Tunnel
	Railway under construction
	Metro station
	Private railway station
	Miniature railway
	Tramway, tramway under construction
	Tram stop, tram stop under construction
	Bus, coach station

Abbreviations

Acad	Academy	Meml	Memorial
Allot Gdns	Allotments	Mon	Monument
Cemy	Cemetery	Mus	Museum
C Ctr	Civic centre	Obsy	Observatory
CH	Club house	Pal	Royal palace
Coll	College	PH	Public house
Crem	Crematorium	Recn Gd	Recreation ground
Ent	Enterprise		
Ex H	Exhibition hall	Resr	Reservoir
Ind Est	Industrial Estate	Ret Pk	Retail park
IRB Sta	Inshore rescue boat station	Sch	School
		Sh Ctr	Shopping centre
Inst	Institute	TH	Town hall / house
Ct	Law court	Trad Est	Trading estate
L Ctr	Leisure centre	Univ	University
LC	Level crossing	W Twr	Water tower
Liby	Library	Wks	Works
Mkt	Market	YH	Youth hostel

	Ambulance station
	Coastguard station
	Fire station
	Police station
	Accident and Emergency entrance to hospital
H	Hospital
+	Place of worship
i	Information centre – open all year
	Shopping centre, parking
P&R / PO	Park and Ride, Post Office
	Camping site, caravan site
	Golf course, picnic site
Church / ROMAN FORT	Non-Roman antiquity, Roman antiquity
Univ	Important buildings, schools, colleges, universities and hospitals
	Woods, built-up area
River Medway	Water name
	River, weir
	Stream
	Canal, lock, tunnel
	Water
	Tidal water

Adjoining page indicators and overlap bands – the colour of the arrow and band indicates the scale of the adjoining or overlapping page (see scale below)

The dark grey border on the inside edge of some pages indicates that the mapping does not continue onto the adjacent page

The small numbers around the edges of the maps identify the 1-kilometre National Grid lines

The map scale on the pages numbered in blue is 3½ inches to 1 mile
5.52 cm to 1 km • 1:18 103

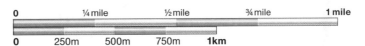

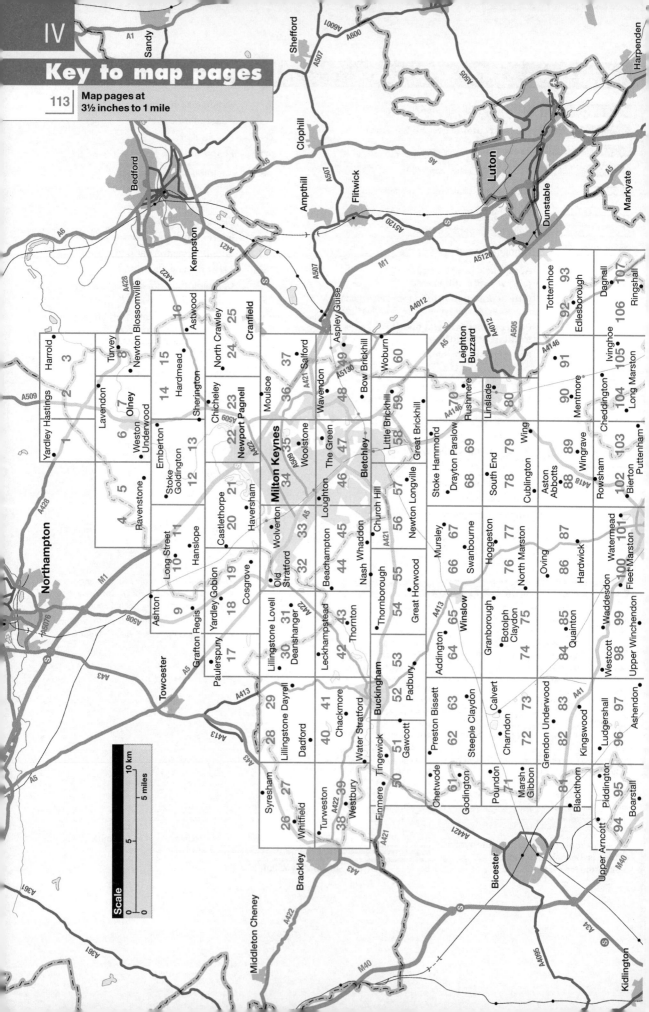

IV

Key to map pages

113 Map pages at
3½ inches to 1 mile

St Albans

Redbourn

Radlett

Hemel Hempstead

Kings Langley

Watford

Bushey

Harrow

Ruislip

Southall

Brentford

Ealing

Hounslow

Feltham

Ashford

Staines

Rickmansworth

Felden **146**
Bovingdon

Flaunden **156**
Chenies

Chorleywood **167**

Maple Cross **178**

South Harefield **190**

Uxbridge **201**

Cowley

Yiewsley

West Drayton **208**

Harmondsworth

Colnbrook **213**

Stanwell

Egham

Northchurch **134** Berkhamsted **135**

Ashley Green **145**
Botley **144**

Chesham **155**
Latimer **155**
Amersham **154**

Chalfont St Giles **167**
A413

Chalfont St Peter **177**

Gerrards Cross **188**

Higher Denham **189**

Iver Heath **200**

Iver **207**

Datchet **212**

Old Windsor **211**

Aldbury **120** Little Gaddesden **121**

Wilstone Green **118** Tring **119** Wigginton

Hastoe **132** Cholesbury **133** St Leonards

Lee Common **142** Chartridge **143**

Great Missenden **152** Little Missenden **153**

Amersham Old Town **164**
Winchmore Hill **165**

Seer Green **176**
Hedgerley **187**

Farnham Common **198** Wexham Street **199**

Slough **205**
Upton **206**

Windsor **210** Clewer Green **209**

Boveney A308

Aston Clinton **116** Weston Turville **117**

Wendover **130** Ellesborough **131**

Wendover Dean **140** Little Hampden **141**

Prestwood **150** Speen **151**

Cryers Hill **162** Hazlemere **163**

Loudwater **174** Beaconsfield **175**

Wooburn Common **186**

Cookham **196** Burnham **197**
Taplow

Maidenhead **204** Eton Wick **205**
Bray **203**

Aylesbury

Stone **114** Bishopstone **115**

Ford **128** Little Kimble **129**

Longwick **138** Princes Risborough **139**

Lacey Green **148** Rout's Green **149**

Naphill **160** West Wycombe **161**

High Wycombe **172** Booker **173**

Flackwell Heath **184** Little Marlow **185**

Cookham Rise **195**

Bisham **194**

Binfield

Bracknell

Upper Pollicott **110** Chilton **111**

Cuddington **112** Chearsley **113** Westlington

Haddenham **126** Kingsey **127**

Henton **137** Chinnor **147** Crowell

Bledlow Ridge **158** Stokenchurch **159**

Lane End **170** Frieth **171**

Marlow Bottom **182** Lower Woodend **183**
Marlow

Hurley **193**

Mill End **192**

Twyford

Wokingham

Brill **110** Long Crendon **124** Thame **125**

Worminghall **122** Ickford **123**

A418 Shabbington

Tiddington **136** Milton Common

Lewknor **157** Turville **169**

Christmas Common **168**

Fawley **180** Hambleden **181**

Maidensgrove **179**

Lower Assendon **191** Henley-on-Thames

Sonning Common

Reading

Horton-cum-Studley Oakley **122**

Wheatley

Oxford

Wallingford

Goring

Didcot

Abingdon-on-Thames

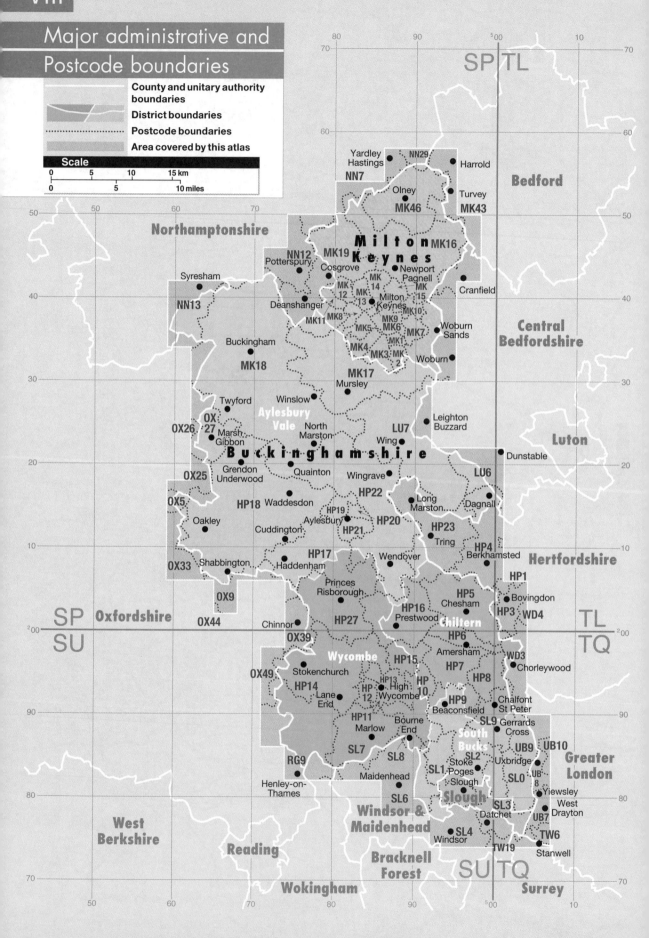

Major administrative and Postcode boundaries

County and unitary authority boundaries
District boundaries
Postcode boundaries
Area covered by this atlas

Scale

0 5 10 15 km
0 5 10 miles

SP TL

Bedford

Northamptonshire

Central Bedfordshire

Luton

Buckinghamshire

Aylesbury Vale

Milton Keynes

Hertfordshire

Oxfordshire

SP
SU

Chiltern

TL
TQ

Wycombe

South Bucks

Greater London

West Berkshire

Windsor & Maidenhead

Slough

Reading

Bracknell Forest

SU TQ

Wokingham

Surrey

Yardley Hastings
NN29
Harrold
NN7
Olney
Turvey
MK46
MK43
MK16
NN12
Potterspury
MK19
Cosgrove
Newport Pagnell
Cranfield
MK 12
MK 14
MK 13
MK 15
Milton Keynes
MK10
NN13
Deanshanger
Woburn Sands
MK11
MK8
MK9
MK5
MK6
MK7
Syresham
MK4
MK1
MK3
MK 2
Woburn
Buckingham
MK18
MK17
Mursley
Twyford
Winslow
Leighton Buzzard
OX 27
Marsh Gibbon
North Marston
LU7
Wing
OX26
Grendon Underwood
Quainton
Wingrave
Dunstable
OX25
HP22
LU6
Long Marston
Dagnall
OX5
HP18
Waddesdon
HP19
Oakley
Aylesbury
HP20
HP23
HP21
Tring
Cuddington
HP4
Berkhamsted
OX33
Shabbington
HP17
Haddenham
Wendover
HP1
Princes Risborough
HP5
Chesham
Bovingdon
OX9
HP16
Prestwood
HP3
WD4
Chinnor
HP27
HP6
WD3
Chorleywood
OX44
OX39
HP15
Amersham
OX49
Stokenchurch
HP7
HP14
HP13
HP 10
HP8
Chalfont St Peter
Lane End
HP 12
High Wycombe
HP9
Beaconsfield
SL9
Gerrards Cross
HP11
Marlow
Bourne End
UB9
UB10
Uxbridge
Marlow
SL7
SL8
SL2
Stoke Poges
SL1
SL0
UB 8
Yiewsley
RG9
Maidenhead
Slough
SL3
Datchet
West Drayton
Henley-on-Thames
SL6
Windsor & Maidenhead
UB7
TW6
SL4
Windsor
TW19
Stanwell
Slough

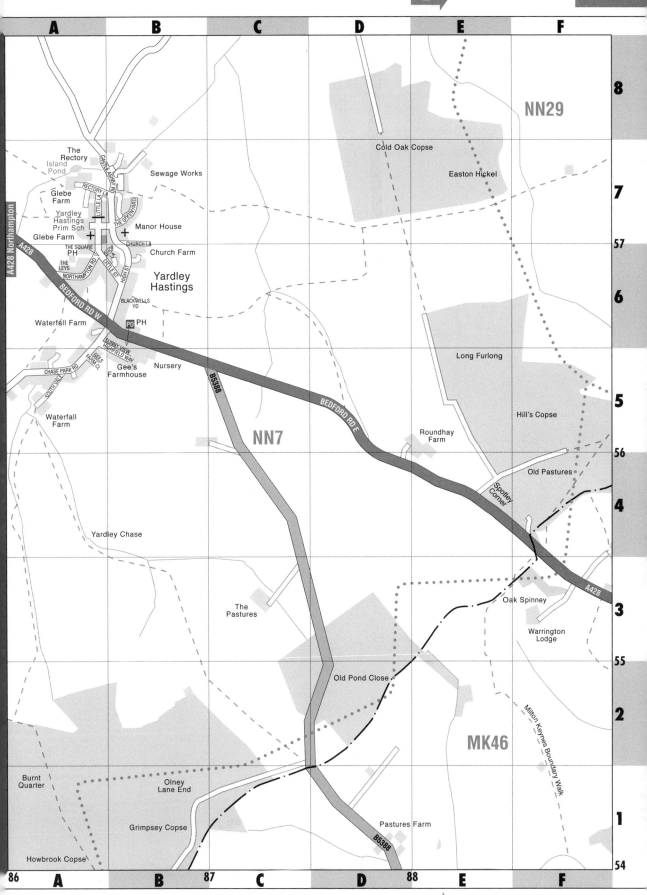

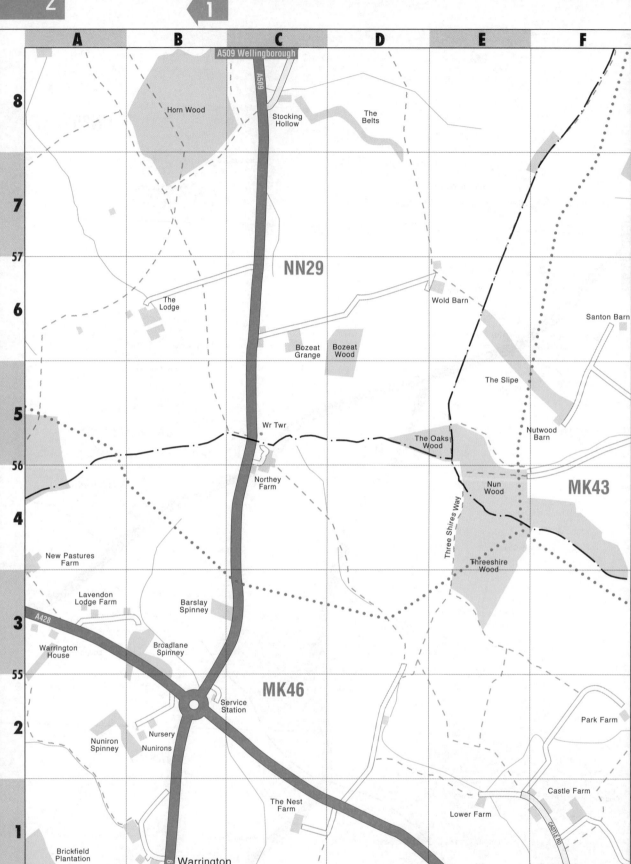

A B C D E F

8

Park
Wood

Austin's
Spinney

Allot
Gdns

New
Buildings

Allot
Gdns

WOOD RD

7

Templegrove
Spinney

ORCHARD LA

BROOK LA

The Mansion

57

Manor
Farm

DICKENS CL 1
BRAMLEY CT 2

CT 1

Harrold

MANSION LA

EAGLE WAY

Harrold
Lower Sch

6

NEW RD

HIGH ST

MOWHILLS

Harrold
Priory
Mid Sch

Priory
Farm

Coldharbour
Hill

Cracknell Hill
House

Cracknell
Hill

5

Middle
Farm

56

MK43

4

River Great Ouse

Millholme
Island

Marsh
Farm

Harrold Lodge
Farm

3

Lavendon
Wood

55

Spring Close
Farm

Church
Farm

Southfields
Farm Cottage

Tollgate
House

TURVEY RD

Valley View
Farm

2

MK46

Snelson
Wood

Snelson
Cottages

Carlton Hall
Farm

Snelson

Carltonhall
Wood

Snelson
Cobs

HARROLD RD

CARLTON RD

1

54

92 A B 93 C D 94 E F

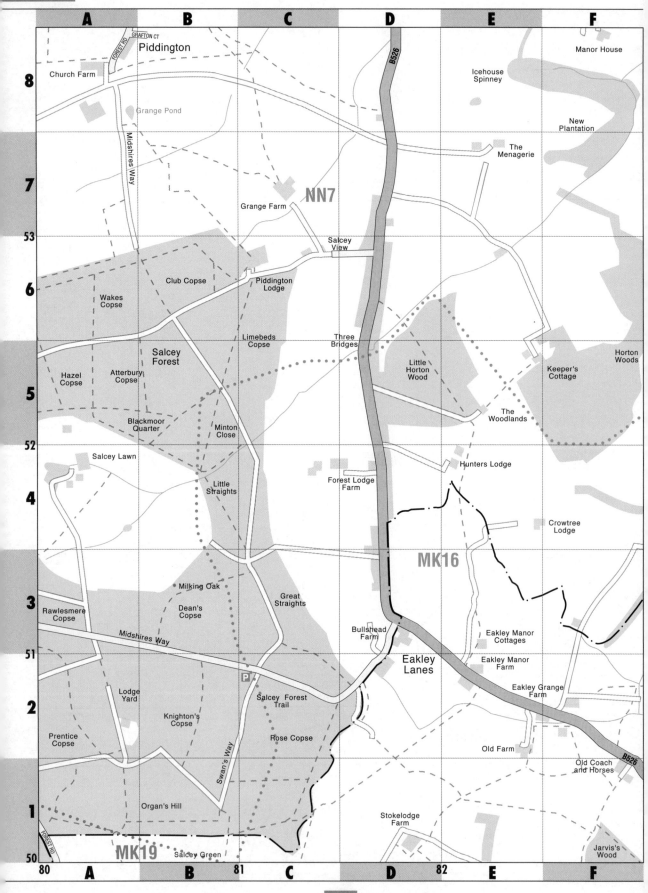

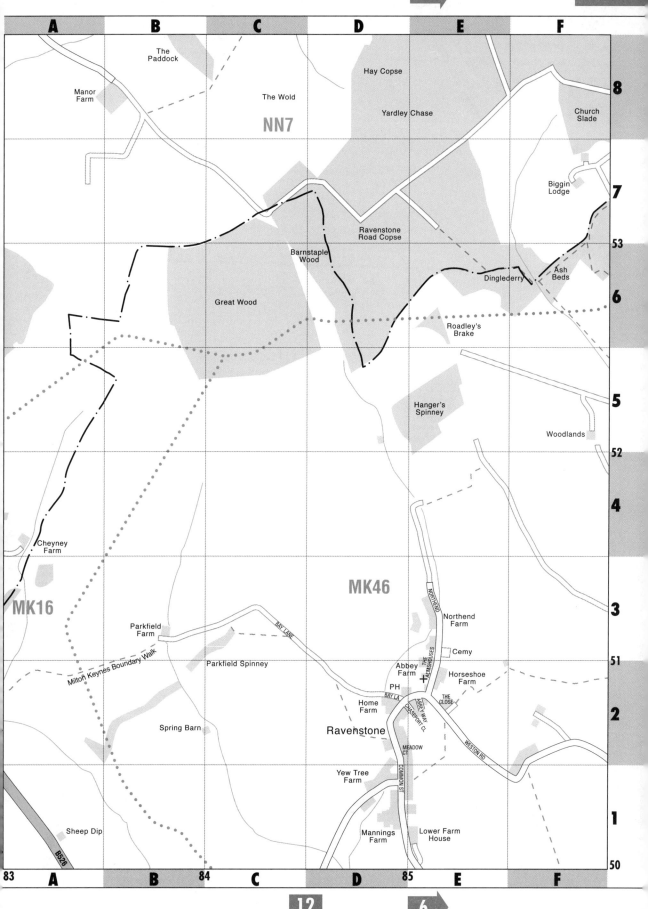

A   B   C   D   E   F

The Paddock

Manor Farm

The Wold

Hay Copse

NN7

Yardley Chase

Church Slade

8

Biggin Lodge

7

53

Ravenstone Road Copse

Barnstaple Wood

Dinglederry

Ash Beds

6

Great Wood

Roadley's Brake

Hanger's Spinney

5

Woodlands

52

4

Cheyney Farm

MK46

MK16

NORTHEND

Northend Farm

Cemy

3

Parkfield Farm

BAY LANE

THE ALMSHOUSES

51

Parkfield Spinney

Abbey Farm

Horseshoe Farm

Milton Keynes Boundary Walk

PH

THE CLOSE

Home Farm

BAY LA

ABBEY WAY

CHASEPORT CL.

2

Spring Barn

Ravenstone

MEADOW CT

WESTON RD

COMMON ST

Yew Tree Farm

1

Sheep Dip

B526

Mannings Farm

Lower Farm House

50

83   A   84   B   C   D   85   E   F

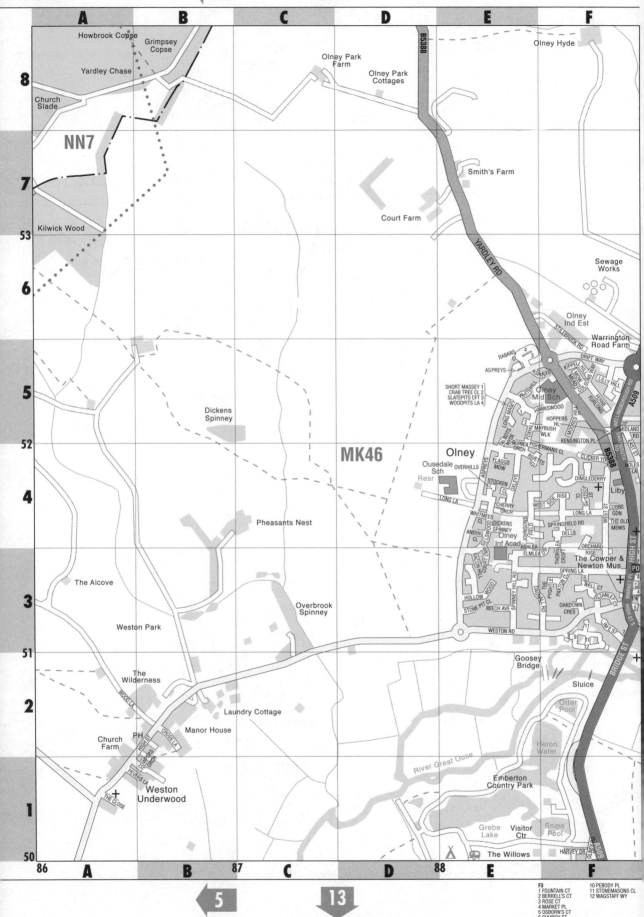

F3
1 FOUNTAIN CT
2 BERRELL'S CT
3 ROSE CT
4 MARKET PL
5 OSBORN'S CT
6 CHURCH ST
7 PEMBROKE HO
8 CHANTRY RI
9 CLAY PIT LA
10 PEBODY PL
11 STONEMASONS CL
12 WAGSTAFF WY

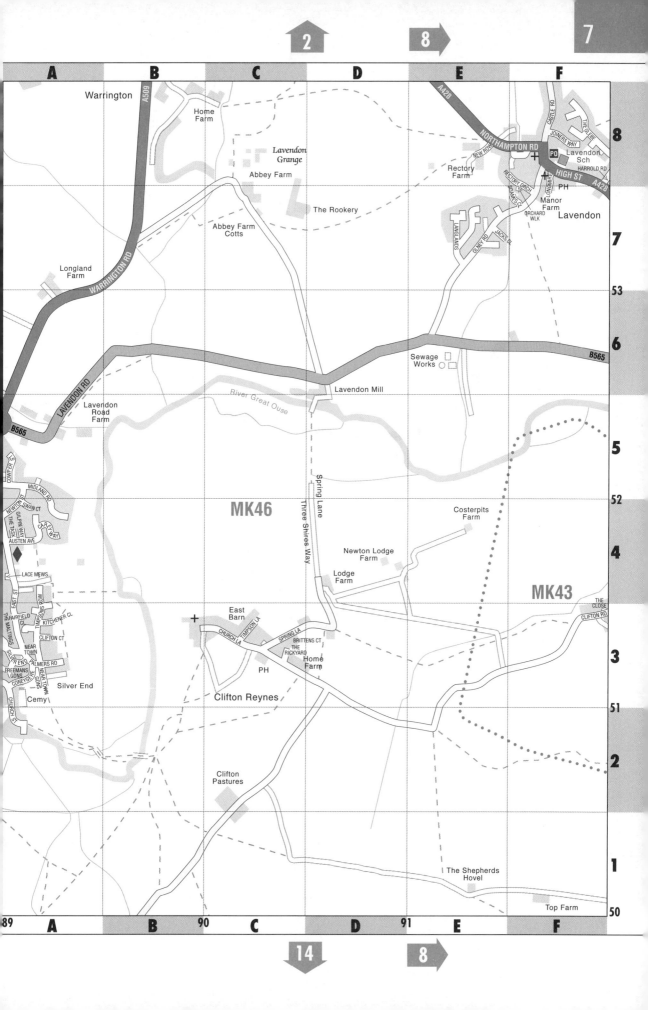

A   B   C   D   E   F

8

Snip
Wood

New Barn

Copymoor

THE GLEBE

HARROLD RD

Uphoe Manor
Farm

Cemy

A428

CARLTON RD

7

53

MK46

New Park

Cricket
Ground

Cemy

New Gains
Farm

6

B565

THE ROW

BEDFORD RD

Turvey
House

Turvey
Lower
Sch

Chantry Farm

HAWTHORN
CL

MAY RD

GROVE CT

NORFOLK RD

Turvey

A428 Bedford

CHURCH
TERR

VINE
ROW

THE PORTLIO

GROVE CL

BAMFORDS LA

MORDAUNT
CL

Cold
Brayfield

Waterfield
Farm

Brayfield
Farm

THE ROW

PO

LAWS

BAKER
BARN

SOFTEYS

ELMWS

ABBEY SQ

Turvey
Bridge

CRANES
CL

HIGH ST

A428

5

BRAYFIELD
HO

BRIDGE ST

TURVEY MILL

MILL LA

TANDYS CL

THE GREEN

NEWTON RD

LADYBRIDGE
TERR

BAMFORDS
YD

JACK'S LA

Turvey
Abbey

Ford

52

MILL
GN

BAKERS CL

Lodge

Long Belt

Abbey
Farm

4

Newton
Blossomville

PH

CLIFTON RD

HARDMEAD RD

Newton Blossomville
CE Sch

BROOK LA

THE ROW

River Great Ouse

Turvey
Cottage

Top Lodge

Woodside
Cottage

Mossy Bank
Wood

Westfields
Barn

MK43

New
Wood

3

Home
Farm

Keepers
Cottage

51

Turvey
Hall

2

Newton Park

Gullet
Wood

Clifton
Spinney

Two
Chimneys

Sheepwalks
Spinney

1

Mast

Newton
Wood

Turvey Lodge
Farm

50

92   A   93   B   C   93   D   94   E   F

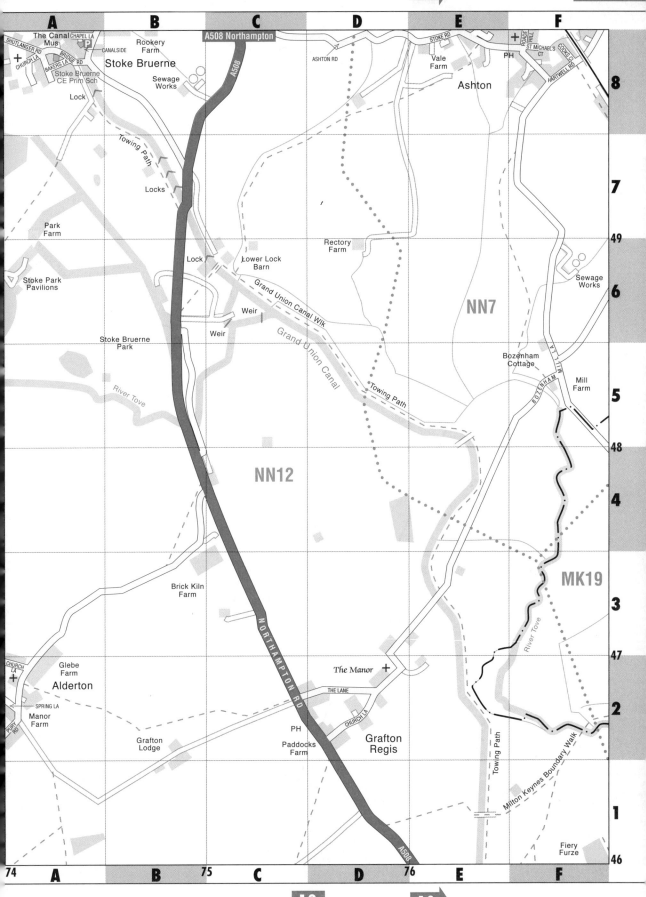

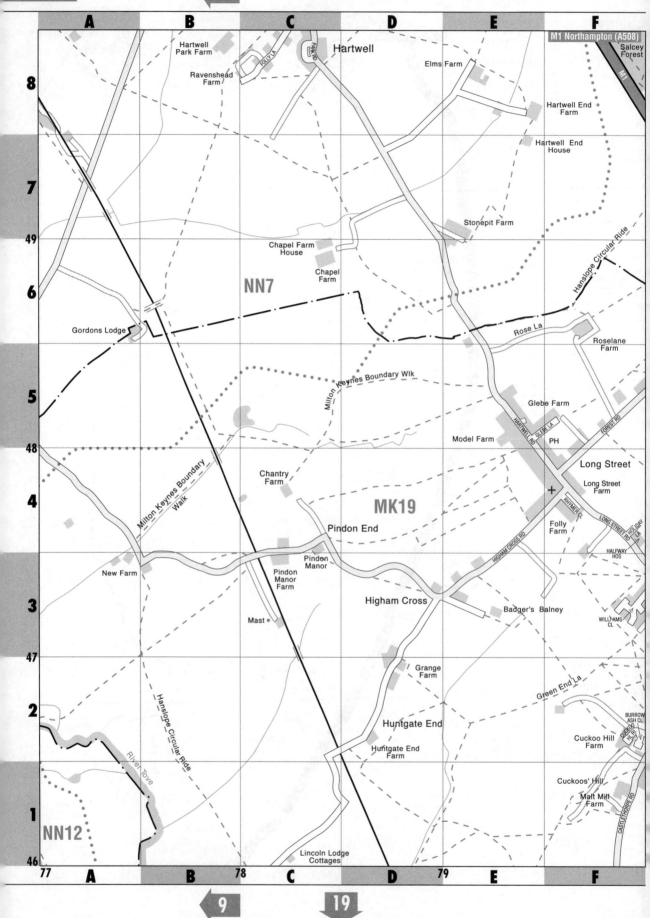

A   B   C   D   E   F

M1 Northampton (A508)

Salcey
Forest

8

Hartwell
Park Farm

Ravenshead
Farm

FOLLY LA

PARK RD

Hartwell

Elms Farm

Hartwell End
Farm

Hartwell End
House

M1

7

49

Chapel Farm
House

Chapel
Farm

Stonepit Farm

NN7

Hanslope Circular Ride

6

Gordons Lodge

Rose La

Roselane
Farm

5

Milton Keynes Boundary Wlk

Glebe Farm

HARTWELL RD

GLEBE LA

FOREST RD

48

Model Farm

PH

Long Street

4

Milton Keynes Boundary
Walk

Chantry
Farm

MK19

Pindon End

Long Street
Farm

RHYMER CT

LONG STREET RD

PRIOLOGY LA

Folly
Farm

HALFWAY
HOS

New Farm

Pindon Manor
Farm

Pindon
Manor

HIGHAM CROSS RD

3

Higham Cross

Badger's Balney

WILLIAMS
CL

Mast

47

Hanslope Circular Ride

Grange
Farm

Green End La

2

River Tove

Huntgate End

BURROW
ASH CL

Cuckoo Hill
Farm

CUCKOO
HILL

Cuckoos' Hill

CASTLETHORPE RD

1

NN12

Huntgate End
Farm

Malt Mill
Farm

46

77   A   78   B   C   79   D   E   F

Lincoln Lodge
Cottages

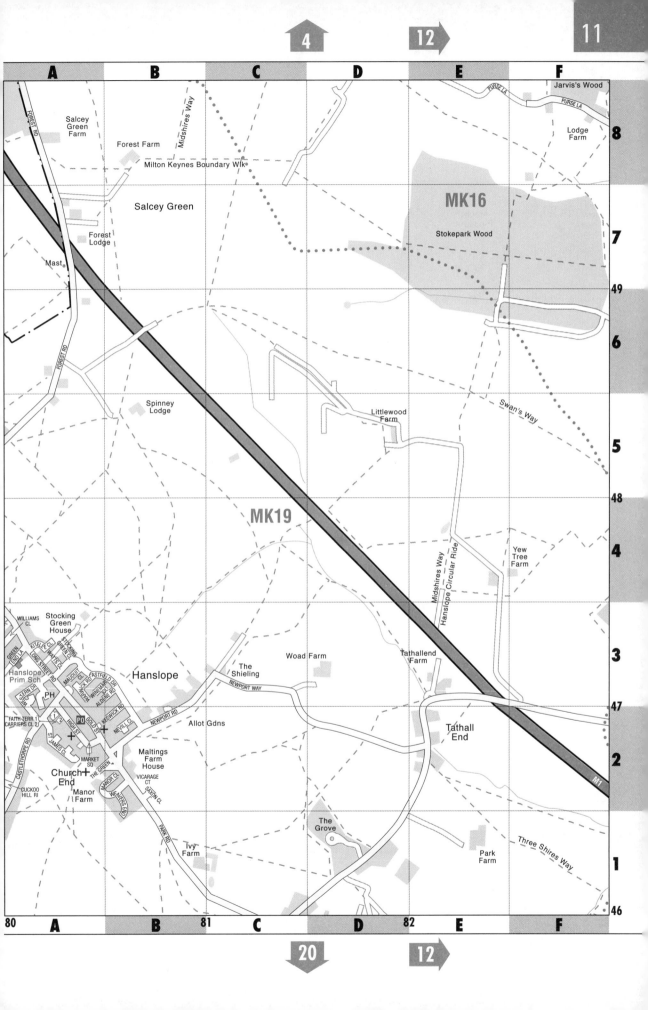

A B C D E F

PURSE LA

B526

Church Farm

CHURCH LANE

✠

Mount
Pleasant

SPRINGBANK
CT

DAG LA

ORCHARD WAY

Old Park
Farm

DAG LANE

HIGH ST

MOUNT PLEASANT

MALTING CL

PH

P

GEORGE
INN CT

Stoke
Goldington

ESKELEY CL

DOVEHOUSE
MEWS

LEASIDE

WESTSIDE LA

Stoke Goldington
CE Fst Sch

RAM ALLEY

Hotel

Ram Alley

CLARKES
ORCH

BAKERS CL

TOWN
END CRES

Ram Alley

RAVENSTONE MILL RD

Field Barns

MK46

Sewage
Works

Ravenstone
Mill

Harley Field Barn

MK16

MK19

Gothurst House

River Great Ouse

Park Farm

Longland's
Wood

The
Wilderness

Tyringham Hall

BACK DR

Tyringham

Bunsty Farm

Bath
House

Gayhurst
Spinney

Bunsty Wood

Digby's
Walk

Gayhurst

Tyringham
Bridge

✠

Gayhurst Wood

M1

New
Plantation

Gayhurst
House

✠

Sir
Francis
Drake
(PH)

Three Shires Way

B526

M1

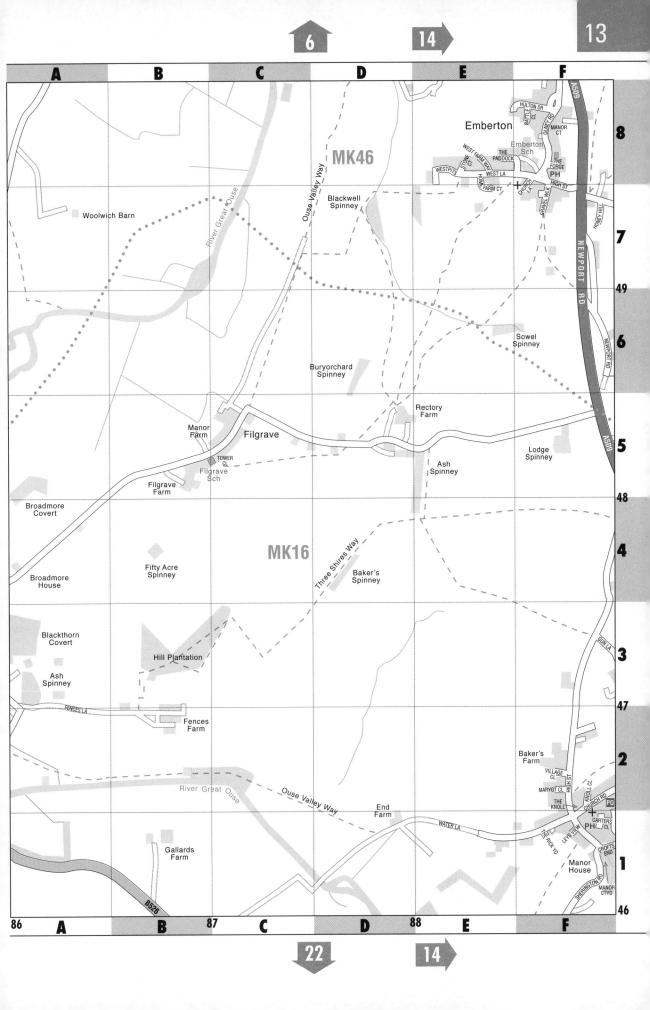

A B C D E F

8

MK46

Emberton

HULTON DR

BATTLE CL

OLNEY RD

MANOR CT

Emberton Sch

WEST FARM WAY

THE PADDOCK

STONE CL

THE FORGE

WESTPITS

WEST LA

PH

HOME FARM CT

HIGH ST

Woolwich Barn

River Great Ouse

Blackwell Spinney

GRAVEL WLK

CHURCH LA

HONEY HILL

A509

NEWPORT RD

7

49

Sowel Spinney

6

NEWPORT RD

Buryorchard Spinney

Manor Farm

Filgrave

TOWER CL

Filgrave Sch

Rectory Farm

Ash Spinney

Lodge Spinney

A509

5

Filgrave Farm

48

Broadmore Covert

MK16

Three Shires Way

4

Broadmore House

Fifty Acre Spinney

Baker's Spinney

GUN LA

Blackthorn Covert

Hill Plantation

3

Ash Spinney

47

FENCES LA

Fences Farm

Baker's Farm

2

VILLAGE CL

MARYOT CL

HIGH ST

KNOLL CL

CHURCH RD

PO

River Great Ouse

Ouse Valley Way

THE KNOLL

CARTERS CL

THE PUCK YD

PH

Gallards Farm

End Farm

WATER LA

LEYS VIEW

CROFTS END

Manor House

1

B526

SHERINGTON RD

MANOR CTYD

46

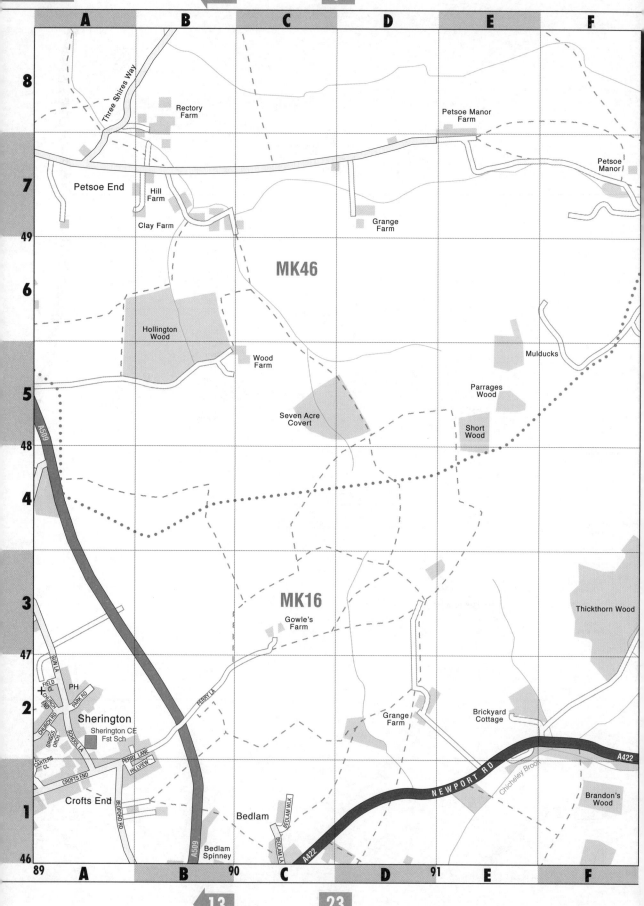

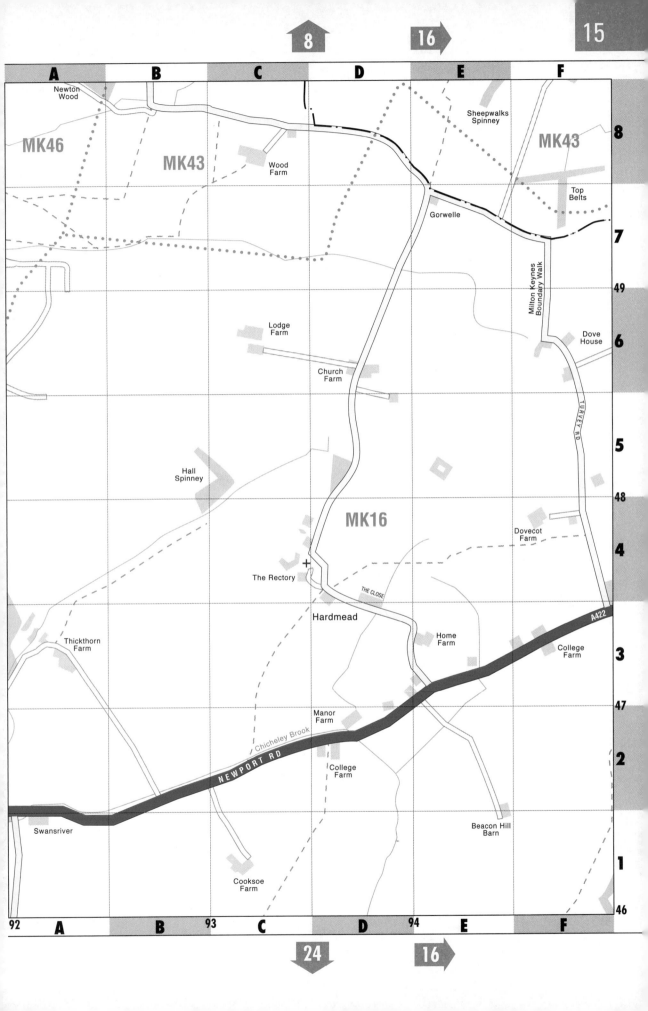

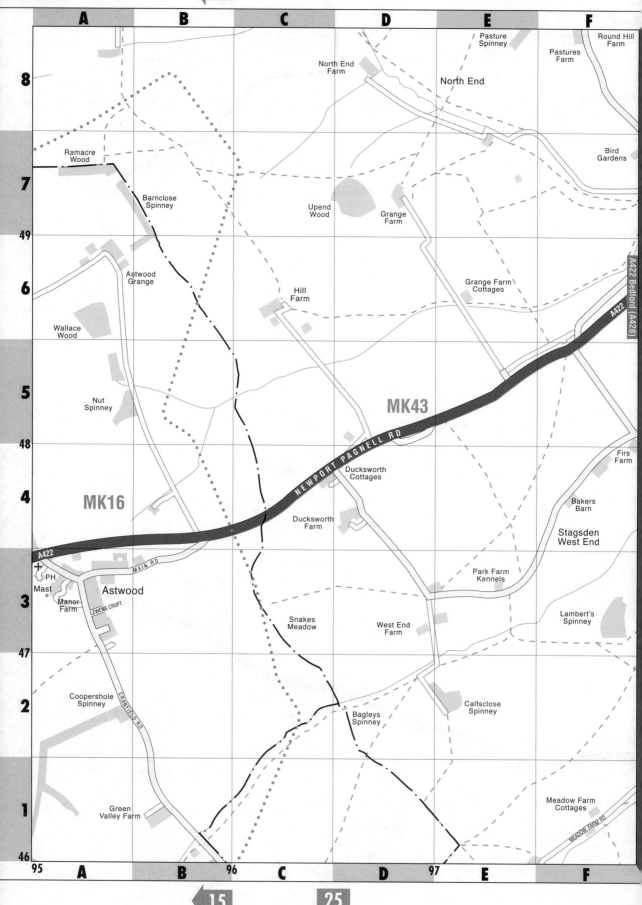

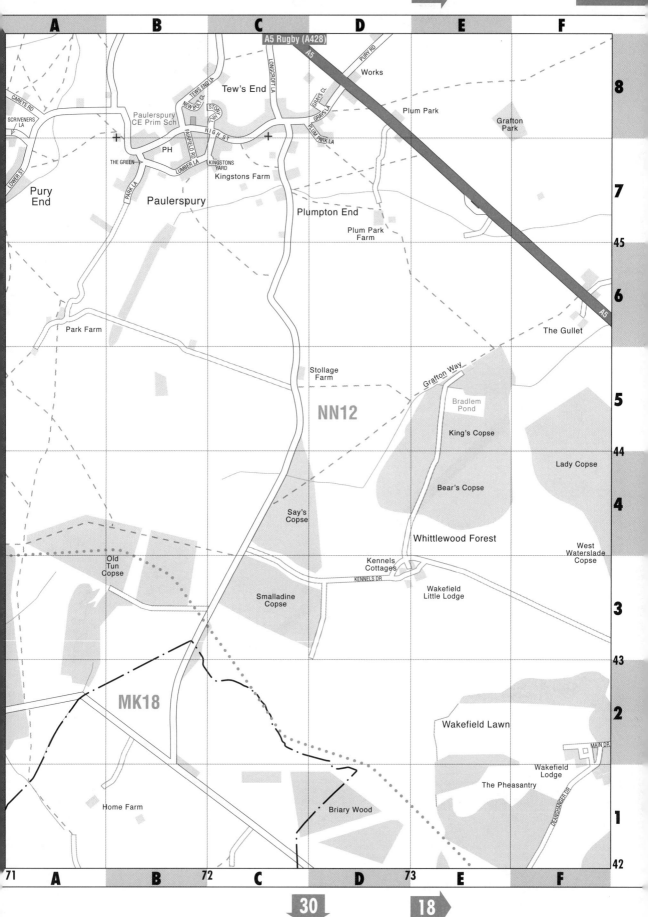

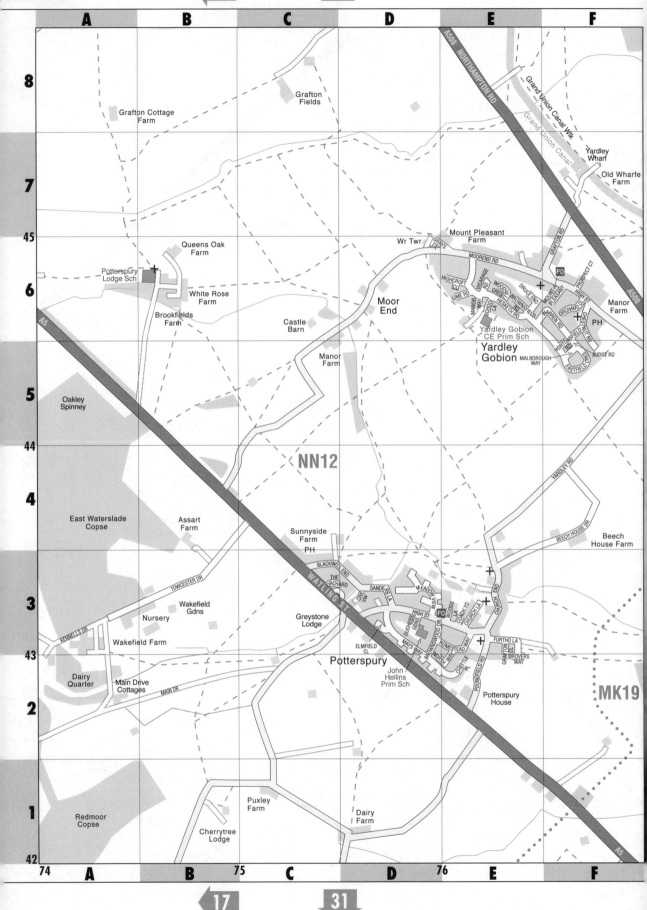

8

Grafton Cottage Farm

Grafton Fields

Grand Union Canal Wlk

Grand Union Canal

A508 NORTHAMPTON RD

Yardley Wharf

7

Old Wharfe Farm

45

Wr Twr

GRAY'S

Mount Pleasant Farm

Queens Oak Farm

MOOREND RD

GRAFTON RD

PO

PROSPECT CT

6

Potterspury Lodge Sch

White Rose Farm

HIGHCROFT CL

VICARAGE RD

WOODHILL

DRUCE END

BROWNSFIELD

CREST HILL

MOUNT PLEASANT

HIGH ST

Manor Farm

Brookfields Farm

Castle Barn

Moor End

LIME RD

MANOB WAY

SCHOOL LA

HESKETH RD

WARREN RD

ORCHARD LA

CHESTNUT RD

A508

Manor Farm

Yardley Gobion CE Prim Sch

HORTONSFIELD RD

PH

Yardley Gobion

MALBOROUGH WAY

BUDGE RD

CASTFIELD

Oakley Spinney

5

44

NN12

4

East Waterslade Copse

Assart Farm

Sunnyside Farm PH

BLACKWELL END

BEECH HOUSE DR

Beech House Farm

TOWCESTER DR

THE ORCHARD

WATLING ST

OAK WY

SANDE-RS LA

M EADOW VIEW

CHURCH END

3

Wakefield Gdns

Greystone Lodge

HIGH ST

WOODS

COACH YD

CHURCH LA

KENNELLS DR

Nursery

Wakefield Farm

DUCHESS GDNS

BROWNSWOOD DR

PO

WAY

FURTHO LA

DROVERS WAY

43

ELMFIELD CL

MAY'S WAY

HOMESTEAD

CHETTLE PL

GRAFTON WAY

Potterspury

John Hellins Prim Sch

POUNDFIELD RD

Dairy Quarter

Main Drive Cottages

MAIN DR

Potterspury House

MK19

2

Redmoor Copse

Puxley Farm

Dairy Farm

1

Cherrytree Lodge

42

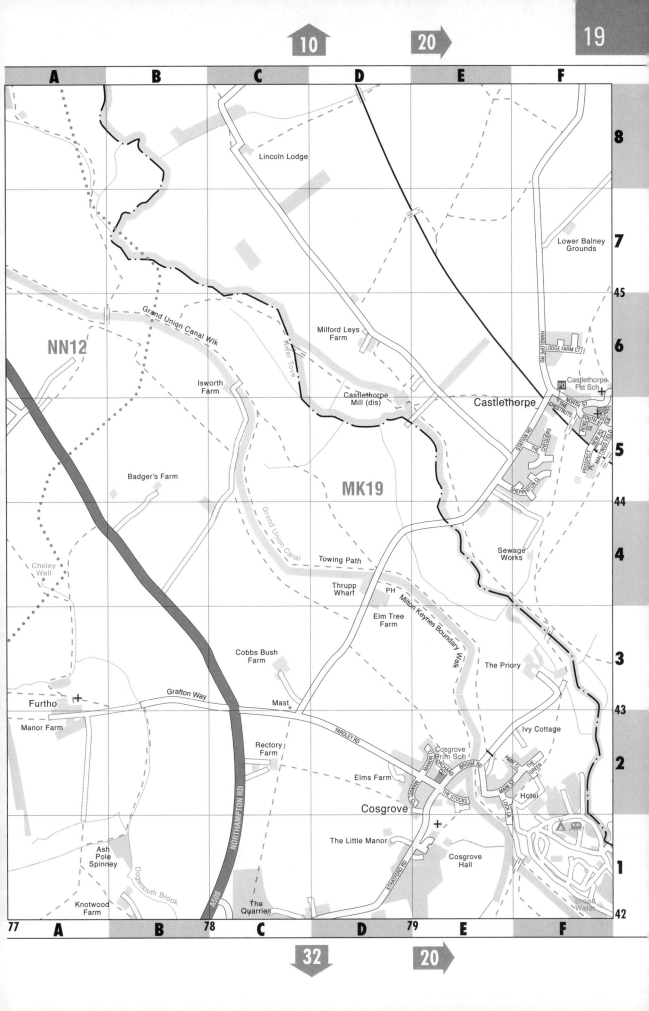

19
11

A **B** **C** **D** **E** **F**

8

Manor Farm

Long Plantation

Mast

Park House

Narrow Leys

Swan's Way
Midshires Way

MK16

Hanslope Park

7

Hanger Quarter

Bullington End

45

Glenmore Farm

Hanslope Lodge

New Buildings

6

BULLINGTON END RD

THRUPP CL

Castlethorpe

NORTH ST

SOUTH ST

FOX COVERT LA

TYRELL CL

PADDOCK CL

Maltings Farm

Leamington Farm

Pineham Farm

Swan's Way
Midshires Way

5

WOLVERTON RD

Hanslope Circular Ride

44

MK19

Pikes Farm

Field House Farm

Otley Farm

4

Water Tower

Fox Covert

Haythorn Spinney

3

Lodge Farm Bsns Ctr

Crossroads Farm

THE STABLES

43

Haversham

PH

2

CHALMERS AVE

ROMAN DR

KEPPEL AVE

Haversham Village Sch

MANOR DR

Haversham Manor

+

BROOKFIELD RD

THE CRESCENT

BEECH TREE CL

HAVERSHAM RD

HIGH ST

1

River Great Ouse

MK12

P

MK13

42

80 **A** 81 **B** **C** 82 **D** **E** **F**

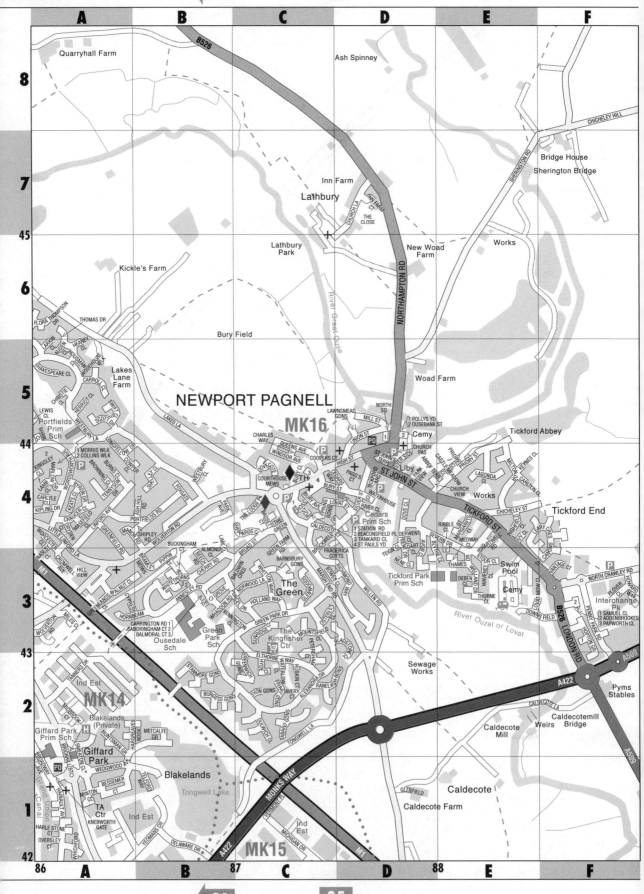

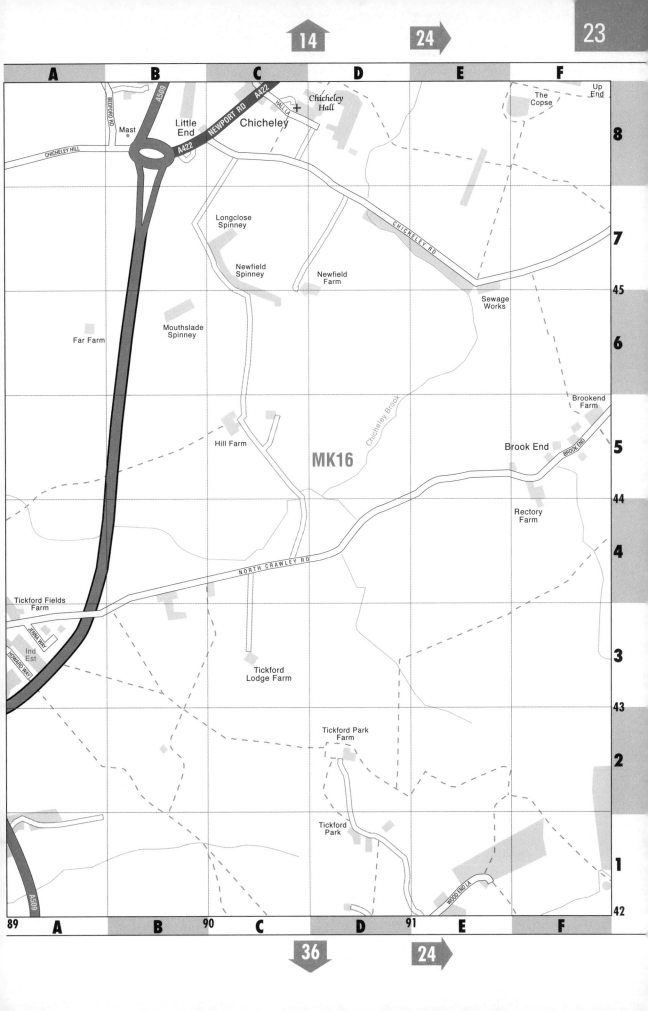

A   B   C   D   E   F

8

Up End

Little Crawley Farm

Horncastle Farm

Chicheley Brook

Dollars Grove Farm

Dollars Grove

7

Old Moat Farm

CHICHELEY RD

Gumbrills Farm

POUND LA

East End Farm

45

ORCHARD WAY

HACKETT PL

Quaker's Farm

6

North Crawley

BRYANT CL

ST THOMAS CL

WELLS CL

VALPIN GDNS

BROOK END

HIGH ST

PH

Crawley Grange

Rookery Farm

Manor Farm

East End

North Crawley CE Sch

CHURCH WLK

CHEQUERS LA

Church Farm

Broadmead

Ford

FOLLY LA

MK16

Lodge Farm

Ringtail Farm

5

44

Ring Croft Farm

SHIRE LANE

4

Hurstend Farm

Murtland's Farm

Rings Wharley Farm

Hurst End

Sewage Works

Wharley Farm

3

FEDDEN HO

Moulsoe Old Wood

WEST RD

ROYCE RD

THE DRIVE

EAST RD

PRINCE PHILIP AVE

HENSON CL

REYNOLDS CL

HANDLEY PAGE CL

MITCHELL RD

DUNCAN RD

Conference Ctr

MERCHANT LA

43

THE CRESCENT

THE GREEN

COLLEGE RD

2

LANCHESTER RD

PO

CENTRAL AVE

Cranfield Univ

MK43

The Cottage

Wharley End

Liby

Cranfield Airport

Chapelclose Spinney

UNIVERSITY WAY

Wharley End Farm

1

42

92   A   B   93   C   D   94   E   F

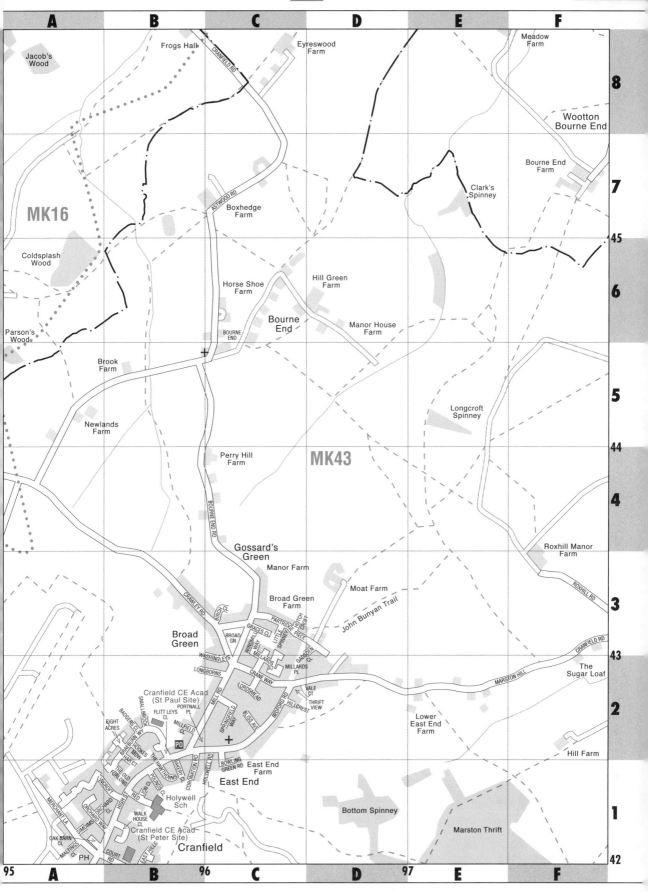

A B C D E F

8

Jacob's Wood

Frogs Hall

Eyreswood Farm

Meadow Farm

Wootton Bourne End

CRANFIELD RD

MK16

7

ASTWOOD RD

Boxhedge Farm

Clark's Spinney

Bourne End Farm

45

Coldsplash Wood

Horse Shoe Farm

Hill Green Farm

6

BOURNE END

Bourne End

Manor House Farm

Parson's Wood

BOURNE END RD

Brook Farm

5

Newlands Farm

Longcroft Spinney

44

Perry Hill Farm

MK43

4

Gossard's Green

Roxhill Manor Farm

Manor Farm

Moat Farm

ROXHILL RD

CRAWLEY RD

Broad Green Farm

John Bunyan Trail

3

BIRCH CL

GRACES CL

LITTLE SPINNEY

HOTCH CROFT

CRANFIELD RD

Broad Green

PARTRIDGE PIECE

The Sugar Loaf

43

BROAD GN

WINDMILL WAY

MILLARDS

GADSDEN CL

MARSTON HILL

WASHINGLEYS

MILLARDS PL

Longborns

CRANE WAY

VALE CT

LORDSMEAD

2

Cranfield CE Acad (St Paul Site)

MILL RD

SPRINGFIELD WAY

BLISS AVE

BROAD RD

HILLCREST

THRIFT VIEW

Lower East End Farm

SMALLBROOK

PORTNALL PL

FLITT LEYS CL

EIGHT ACRES

BADGERS CL

BRAEBURN WAY

MILLFIELD

PO

Hill Farm

HART CT

THE HAWTHORNS

POUND CL

CORONATION RD

HOLDWELL RD

BOWLING GREEN RD

East End Farm

MERCHANT LA

LINGCROFT

THE OLD FURLONG

ORCHARD WAY

HIGH ST

BAKERS CL

East End

Holywell Sch

1

OAK BARN CL

SIMPSONS CL

WALK HOUSE CL

Cranfield CE Acad (St Peter Site)

Bottom Spinney

Marston Thrift

MALTINGS CL

PH

COURT RD

EAST HILLS

Cranfield

42

95 A B 96 C D 97 E F

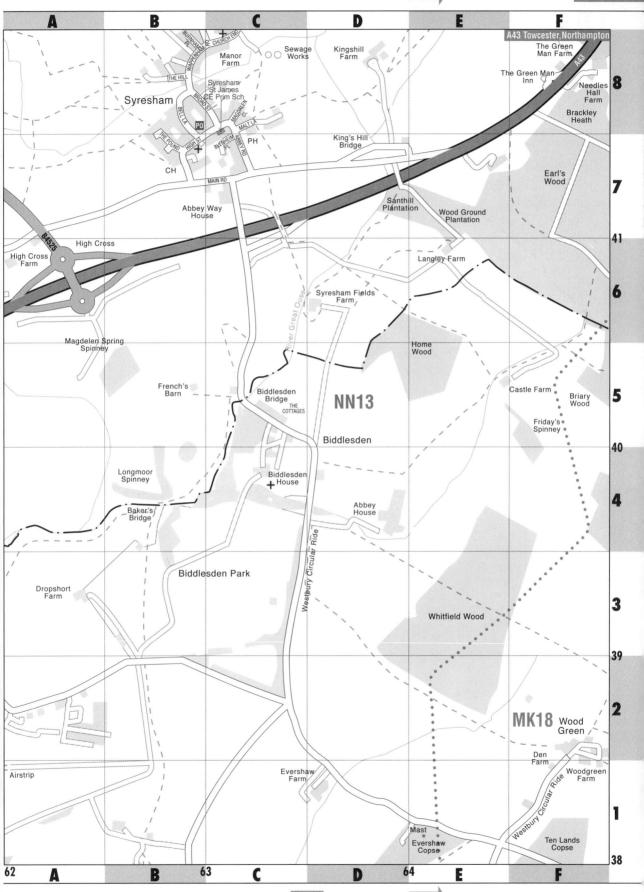

27

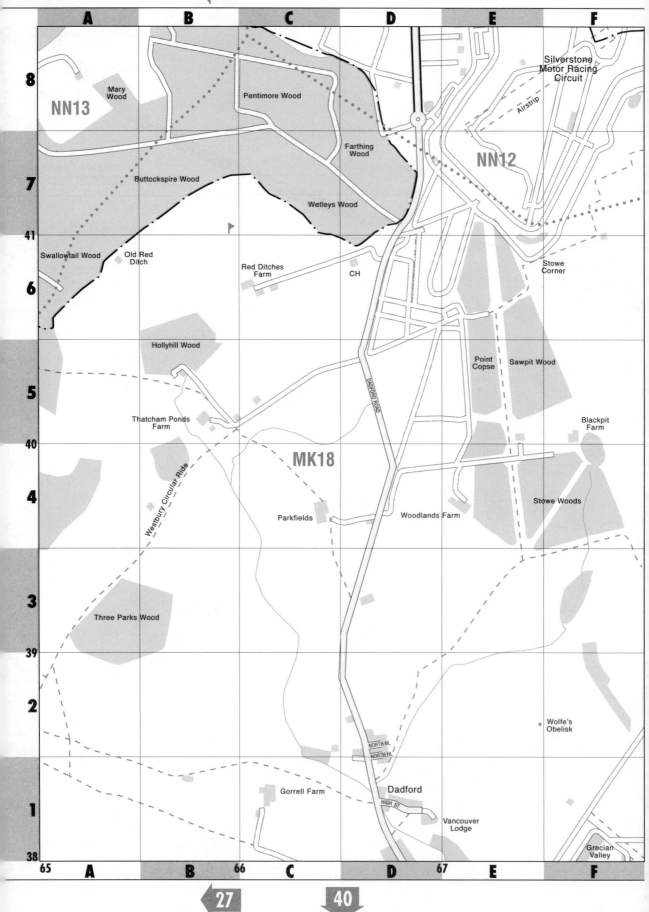

NN13

Mary Wood

Pentimore Wood

Farthing Wood

Buttockspire Wood

Wetleys Wood

NN12

Silverstone Motor Racing Circuit

Airstrip

Stowe Corner

Swallowtail Wood

Old Red Ditch

Red Ditches Farm

CH

Hollyhill Wood

Point Copse

Sawpit Wood

Thatcham Ponds Farm

Blackpit Farm

MK18

Westbury Circular Ride

Parkfields

DADFORD ROAD

Woodlands Farm

Stowe Woods

Three Parks Wood

Wolfe's Obelisk

NORTH HL

NORTH HL

Gorrell Farm

Dadford

HIGH ST

Vancouver Lodge

Grecian Valley

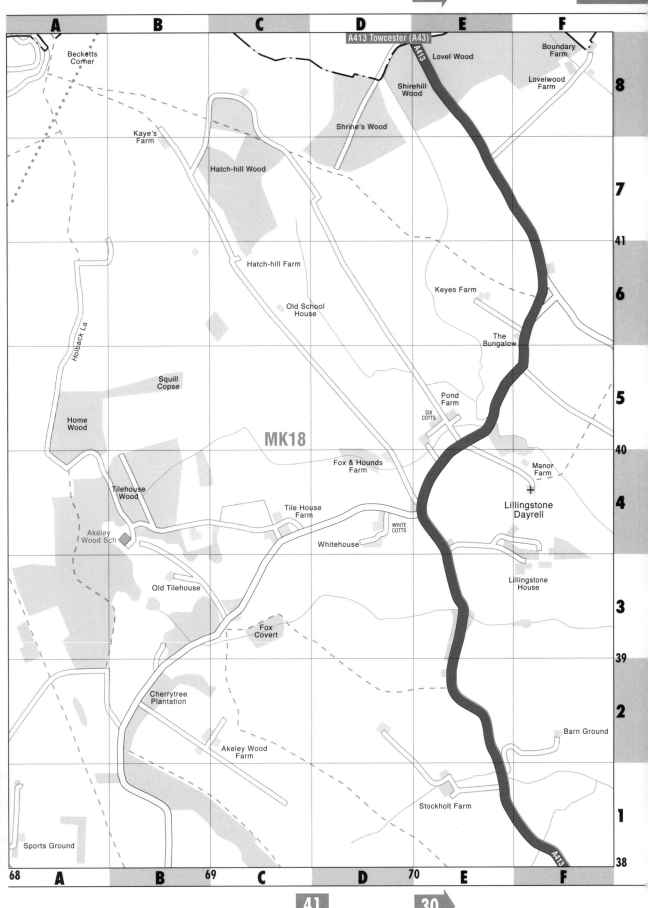

A B C D E F

Beckett's Corner

Kaye's Farm

Lovel Wood

Boundary Farm

Lovelwood Farm

Shirehill Wood

Shrine's Wood

8

Hatch-hill Wood

7

41

Hatch-hill Farm

Keyes Farm

6

Old School House

The Bungalow

Holback La

Squill Copse

Pond Farm

SIX COTTS

5

40

Home Wood

MK18

Fox & Hounds Farm

Manor Farm

Lillingstone Dayrell

Tilehouse Wood

Tile House Farm

WHITE COTTS

4

Akeley Wood Sch

Whitehouse

Lillingstone House

Old Tilehouse

3

Fox Covert

39

Cherrytree Plantation

2

Barn Ground

Akeley Wood Farm

Stockholt Farm

1

Sports Ground

38

68 A B 69 C D 70 E F

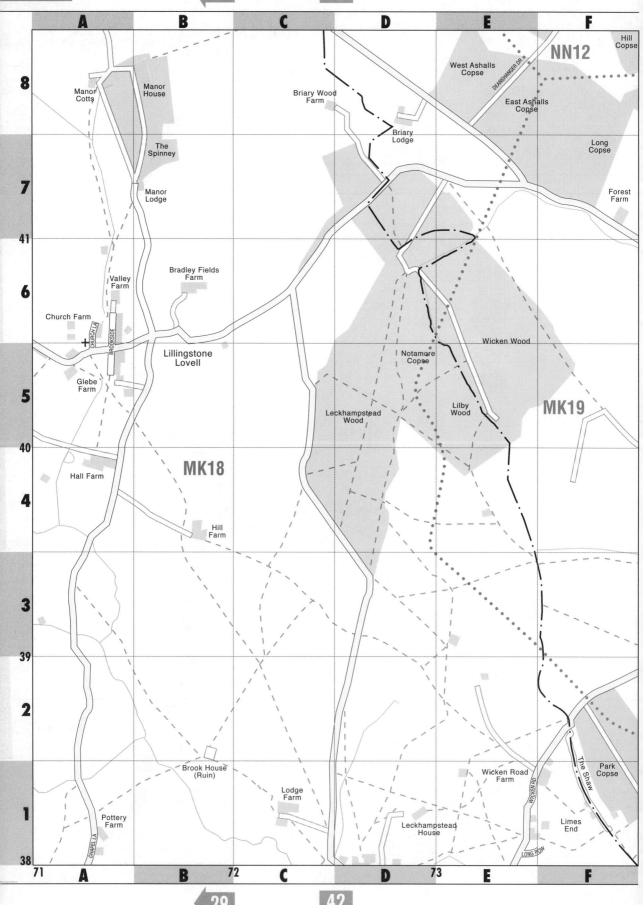

A B C D E F

8

7

41

6

5

40

4

3

39

2

1

38

71 72 73

NN12

Hill Copse

West Ashalls Copse

East Ashalls Copse

DEANSHANGER DR

Long Copse

Forest Farm

Manor Cotts

Manor House

The Spinney

Manor Lodge

Briary Wood Farm

Briary Lodge

Valley Farm

Bradley Fields Farm

Church Farm

CHURCH LA

BROOKSIDE

Lillingstone Lovell

Glebe Farm

Wicken Wood

Notamore Copse

Lilby Wood

MK19

Leckhampstead Wood

MK18

Hall Farm

Hill Farm

Brook House (Ruin)

Lodge Farm

Wicken Road Farm

WICKEN RD

The Shaw

Park Copse

Limes End

Leckhampstead House

LONG ROW

CHAPEL LA

Pottery Farm

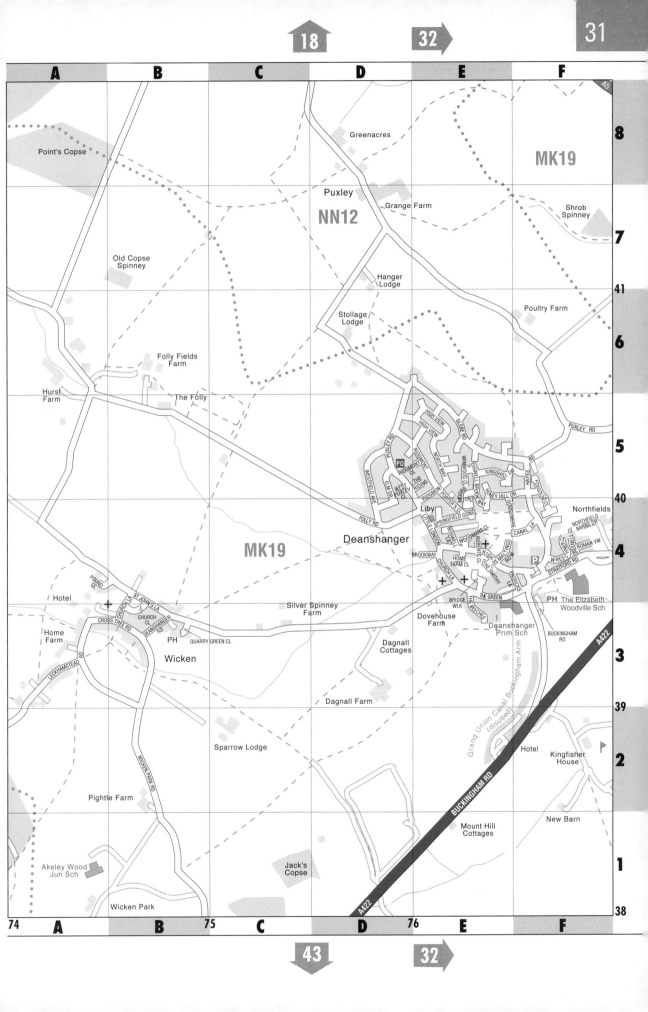

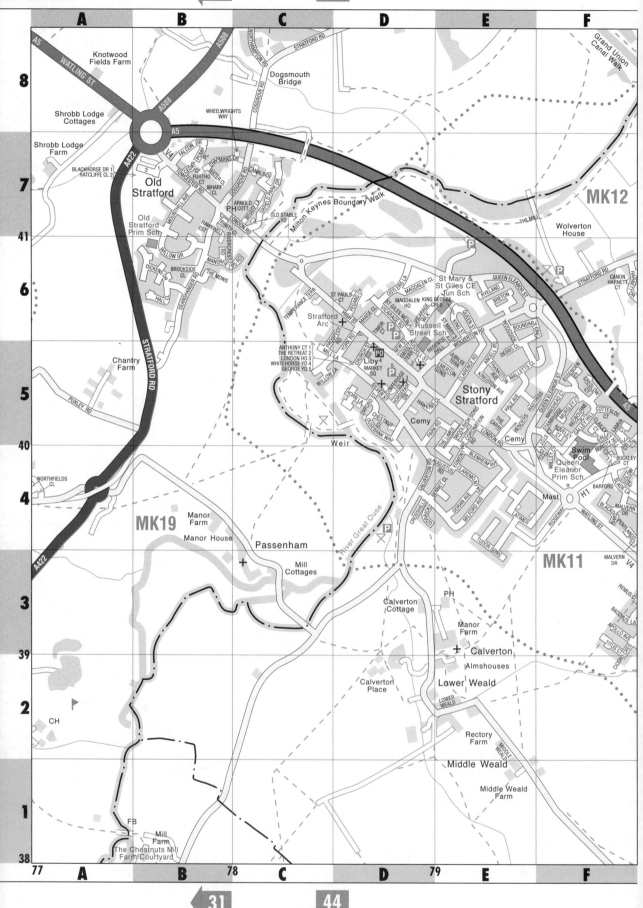

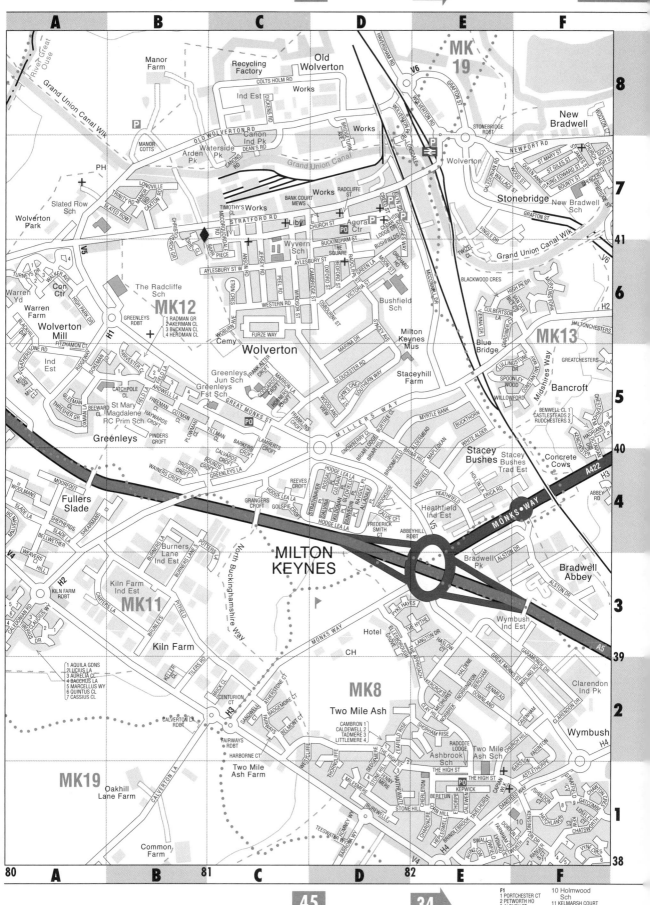

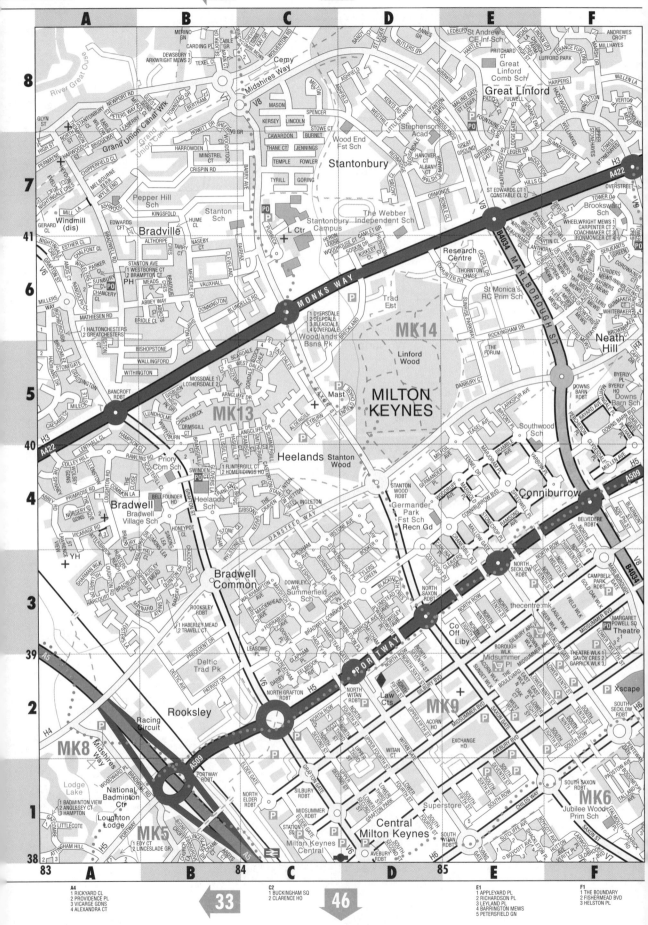

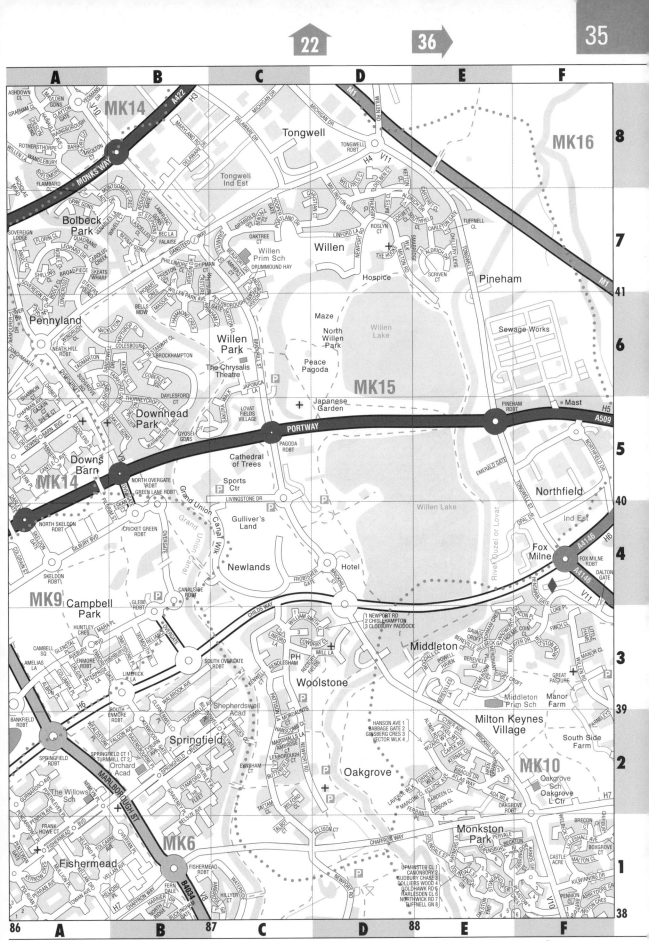

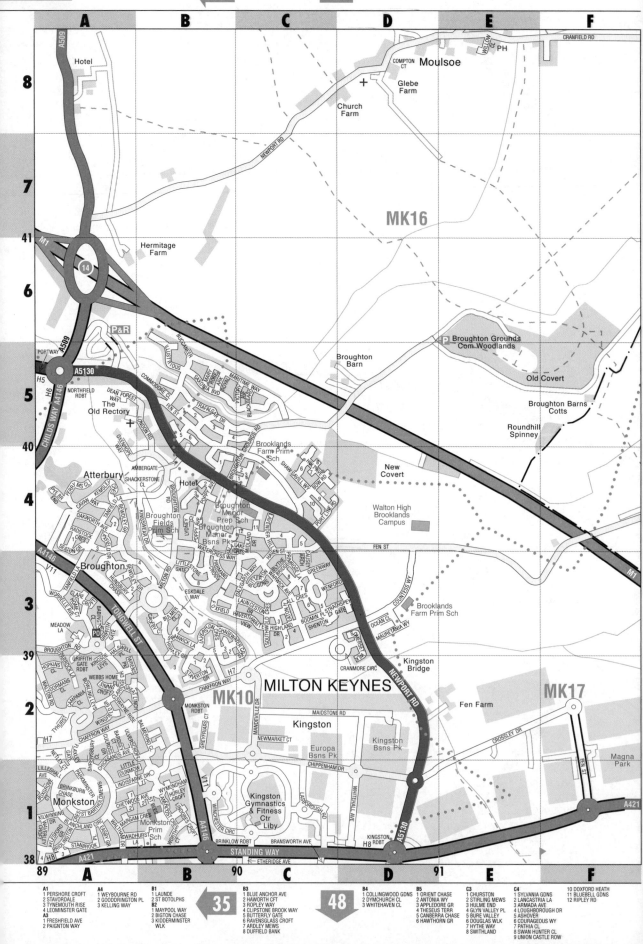

A1
1 PERSHORE CROFT
2 STAVORDALE
3 TYNEMOUTH RISE
4 LEOMINSTER GATE
A3
1 FRESHFIELD AVE
2 PAIGNTON WAY

A4
1 WEYBOURNE RD
2 GOODDRINGTON PL
3 KELLING WAY

B1
1 LAUNDE
2 ST BOTOLPHS
B2
1 MAYPOOL WAY
2 BIGTON CHASE
3 KIDDERMINSTER WLK

B3
1 BLUE ANCHOR AVE
2 HAWORTH CFT
3 ROPLEY WAY
4 CLIPSTONE BROOK WAY
5 BUTTERFLY GATE
6 RAVENSGLASS CROFT
7 ARDLEY MEWS
8 DUFFIELD BANK

B4
1 COLLINGWOOD GDNS
2 DYMCHURCH CL
3 WHITEHAVEN CL

B5
1 ORIENT CHASE
2 ANTONIA WY
3 APPLEDORE GR
4 THESEUS TERR
5 CANBERRA CHASE
6 HAWTHORN GR

C3
1 CHURSTON
2 STIRLING MEWS
3 HULME END
4 GLYN VALLEY PL
5 BURE VALLEY
6 DOUGLAS WLK
7 HYTHE WAY
8 SWITHLAND

C4
1 SYLVANIA GDNS
2 LANCASTRIA LA
3 ARMADA AVE
4 LOUGHBOROUGH DR
5 ASHOVER
6 COURAGEOUS WY
7 PATHIA CL
8 SWAN HUNTER CL
9 UNION CASTLE ROW

10 DOXFORD HEATH
11 BLUEBELL GDNS
12 RIPLEY RD

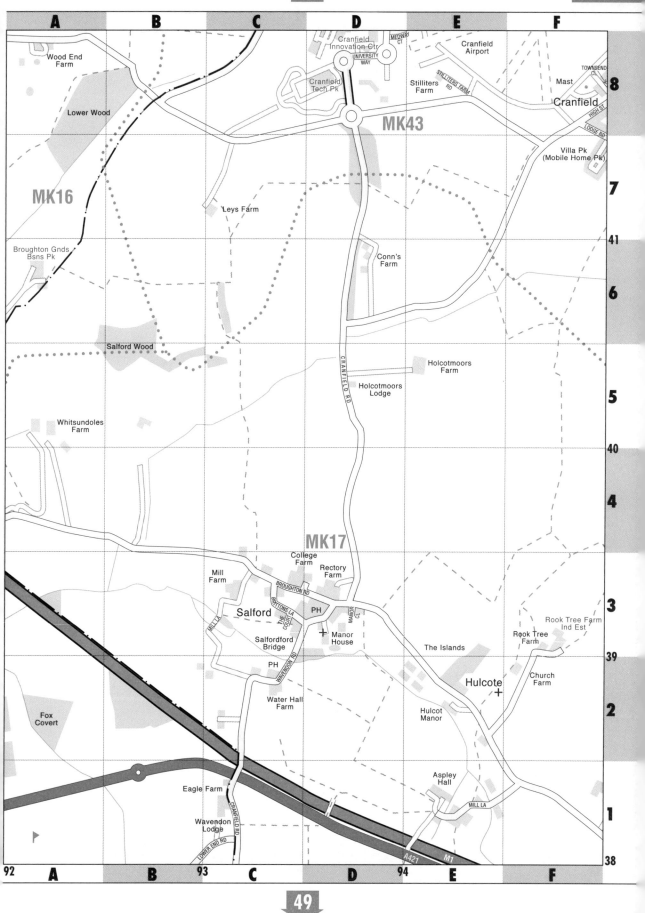

A B C D E F

Wood End
Farm

Cranfield
Innovation Ctr
MEDWAY
CT
Cranfield
Airport
TOWNSEND
CL.
Mast
UNIVERSITY
WAY
Cranfield
Tech Pk
Stilliters
Farm
STILLITERS FARM RD
Cranfield

Lower Wood

MK43
HIGH ST
LODGE RD

Villa Pk
(Mobile Home Pk)

MK16
8

Leys Farm
7

41

Conn's
Farm

Broughton Gnds
Bsns Pk
6

Salford Wood

CRANFIELD RD
Holcotmoors
Farm

Holcotmoors
Lodge
5

Whitsundoles
Farm

40

4

MK17

College
Farm
Rectory
Farm

Mill
Farm
BROUGHTON RD
Rook Tree Farm
Ind Est

BRITTONS LA
Salford
PH
MANOR CL.
Rook Tree
Farm
3

THE COURT
Manor
House
The Islands
39

PH
WAVENDON RD
Salfordford
Bridge

Church
Farm

Hulcote
MILL LA
Water Hall
Farm
Hulcot
Manor
2

Fox
Covert

Aspley
Hall

Eagle Farm
MILL LA
1

CRANFIELD RD
Wavendon
Lodge

LOWER END RD
A421
M1
38

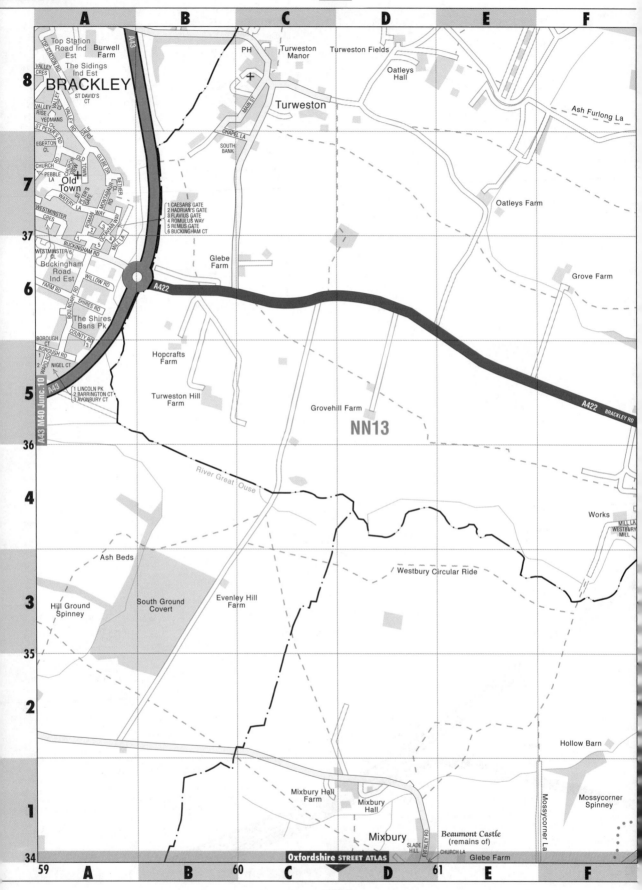

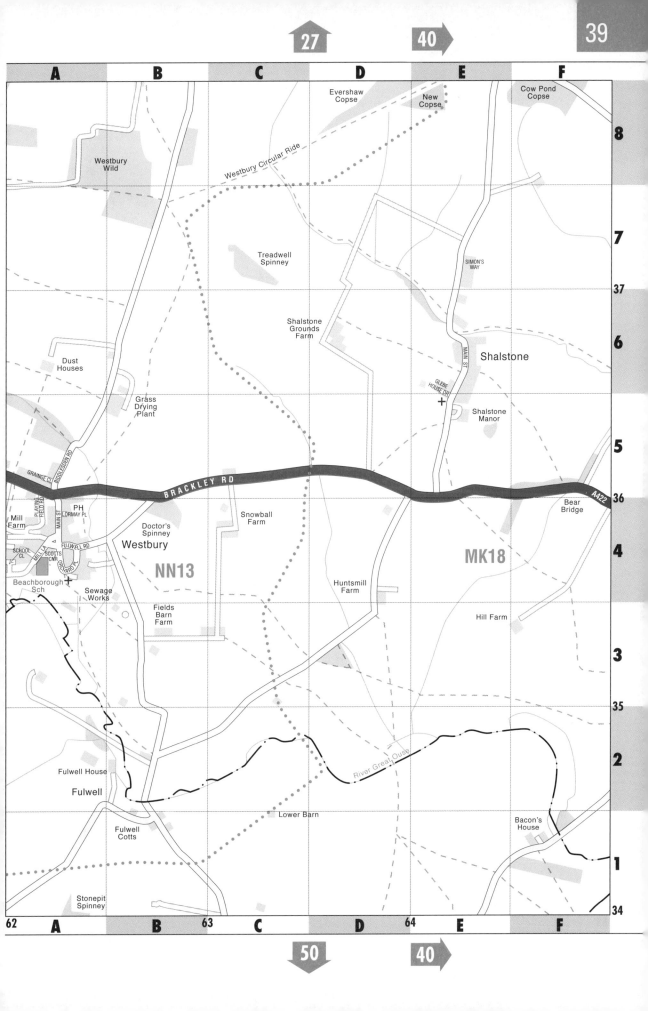

A B C D E F

8

Hill Gate
Spinney

Boycott Manor
Farm

Home Farm

Grecian
Valley

Mon

Temple

Kiln
Spinney

Stowe
Sch

Shell Bridge

7

Boycott Manor

Stowe
Landscape
Gardens

37

CH

Stowe Park

The Lake

6

Welsh Lane
Farm

Boycott
Manor Lodge

Weir

Temple

Oxford
Water

Ashmore Farm

5

Water
Stratford
Wood

MK18

Boycott Farm

36

A422

Park Farm

4

Grounds Farm

Stonepit Hill
Spinney

WELSH LA

Guernsey Hill
Spinney

Ford

3

Spinney Hill
Farm

PH

Buffler's Holt

35

Manor Farm

Manor Farm
Buildings

2

A422

Town
Farm

WATER STRATFORD RD

Water
Stratford

1

Rectory Farm

Tingewick Mill

Radclive Grange

34

65   66   67

A B C D E F

8 Bourbon Tower Home Farm Hillside Farm St James & St John CE Prim Sch Infant Site CEDARS CL A413 CHAPEL LA THE SQUARE CHURCH HILL PH Lodge Akeley Wood Sch CORONATION COTTS Akeley MAIN ST LECKHAMPSTEAD RD

Lamport MANOR RD CAPEL CL

7 Palladian Bridge

37

6 New Inn Stowe, Visitor Ctr Bycell Farm BYCELL RD Longs Wood Foxcote Resr

STOWE AVE

5

36 Dance Farm NEW COLLEGE CT THE MALTINGS MAIN ST PH St James & St John CE Prim Sch Junior Site Chackmore Farm Spinney Chackmore Farm MK18 Maids Moreton House Vitalograph Bsns Pk

4 Chackmore Maids Moreton PH THE PIGHTLE THE LEYS MANOR PK MAIN ST FOSCOTE RD Wellmore TOWCESTER RD SCOTTS FARM CL WALNUT DR

Maids Moreton CE Sch DUCK LAKE SCOTTS LA DUCK LAKE CL THE PADDOCK SOUTH HALL HALL CL GLEBE CL CHURCH ST GLEBE TERR

3 Park Manor Industries STOWE AVE PINE CL GRANGE CL AVENUE RD

35 Castle Fields BUCKINGHAM WHITEHOUSE WY TEMPLE CL VILLIERS CL MANOR GDNS The Manor Buckingham Prim Sch

2 MORETON RD GLEBE FT SCOTT RD LTN COLN BRADFIELD AVE HOLTON BEECH CL HIGHLANDS RD CRISBROOKE WATCHCROFT DR KING CHARLES HUTCHINGS CL MATTOW GDNS MAD FORD RD Page Hill 1 CHETWODE CL 2 NIGHTINGALE PL 3 CROPREDY CT 4 DE CLARE CT 5 BARTLETT PL A422

PIGHTLE CRES NASEBY CROMWELL KEYES CATHERINE EDMONDS CL FLEET A413

1 BRACKLEY RD Cemy STOWE CL A422 STOWE RISE Buckingham Chantry Chapel GRENVILLE RD WESTERN AVE ADAMS CL OVENN AVE OVENN CL COBHAM CL THE PIGHTLE MINSTER CL ORCHARD IRENE ADDINGTON ADDINGTON TERR Nat Res Buckingham Com Old Gaol Mus MARY MACHAM CL PAYNES CT HIGH ST CORNWALL PL WHARF SIDE SANDMARTIN CL LOWER WHARF WHARF VIEW PAGE HILL AVE GIFFORD PL BUSBY CL WITTMILLS OAK GREENWAY WLK PITCHFORD WLK STRATFORD RD A413

River Great Ouse PATEMAN CL GLYNSWOOD RD A422 WEST ST H P PO Liby MEADOW WLK MEADOW ROW

34

D1
1 NORTHEND CT
2 NORTHEND SQ
3 CORNWALLS MDW
4 MEADOW SH CTR
5 MARKET SQ
6 VERNEY CL
7 CECILS YARD
8 BUCKINGHAM CTR

D2
1 HILL RADNOR
2 HEBRIDEAN
3 TEESWATER

D3
1 SHETLAND
2 CASTLEMILK

E3
1 RONALDSAY
2 TWICKENHAM RD
3 LONGLAND RD
4 DE ANGELI CL
5 JELL CL
6 WHEELER PL
7 SKELTON RD
8 ROGERS LA

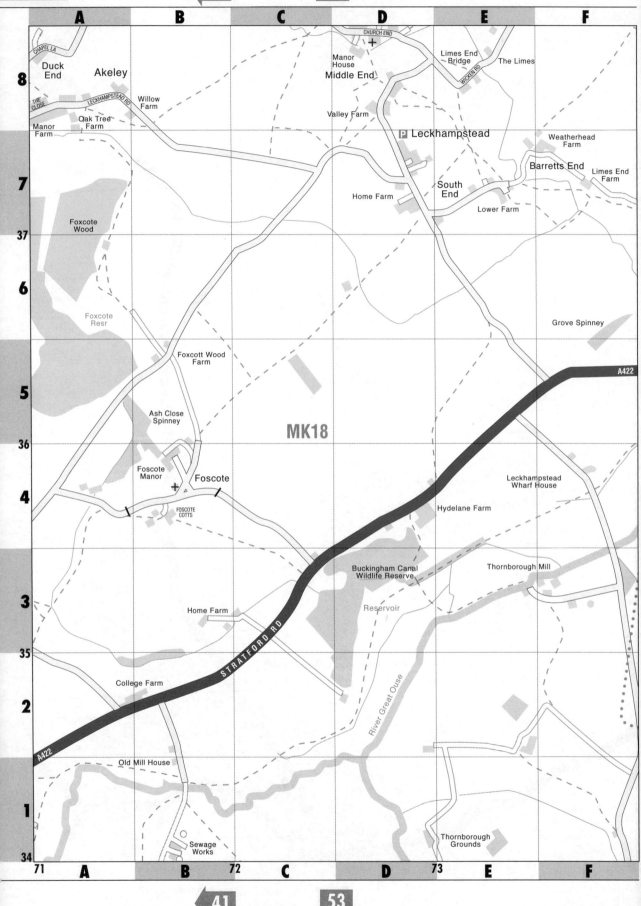

A B C D E F

8

CHAPEL LA

Duck
End

Akeley

THE
CLOSE

Manor
Farm

Oak Tree
Farm

LECKHAMPSTEAD RD

Willow
Farm

CHURCH END

Manor
House

Middle End

Limes End
Bridge

The Limes

WICKEN RD

7

Foxcote
Wood

Valley Farm

P Leckhampstead

Weatherhead
Farm

Barretts End

Limes End
Farm

37

Home Farm

South
End

Lower Farm

6

Foxcote
Resr

Grove Spinney

5

Foxcott Wood
Farm

A422

Ash Close
Spinney

MK18

36

Foscote
Manor

Foscote

4

FOSCOTE
COTTS

Leckhampstead
Wharf House

Hydelane Farm

3

Home Farm

STRATFORD RD

Buckingham Canal
Wildlife Reserve

Reservoir

Thornborough Mill

35

College Farm

2

A422

Old Mill House

River Great Ouse

1

Thornborough
Grounds

34

Sewage
Works

71 A B 72 C D 73 E F

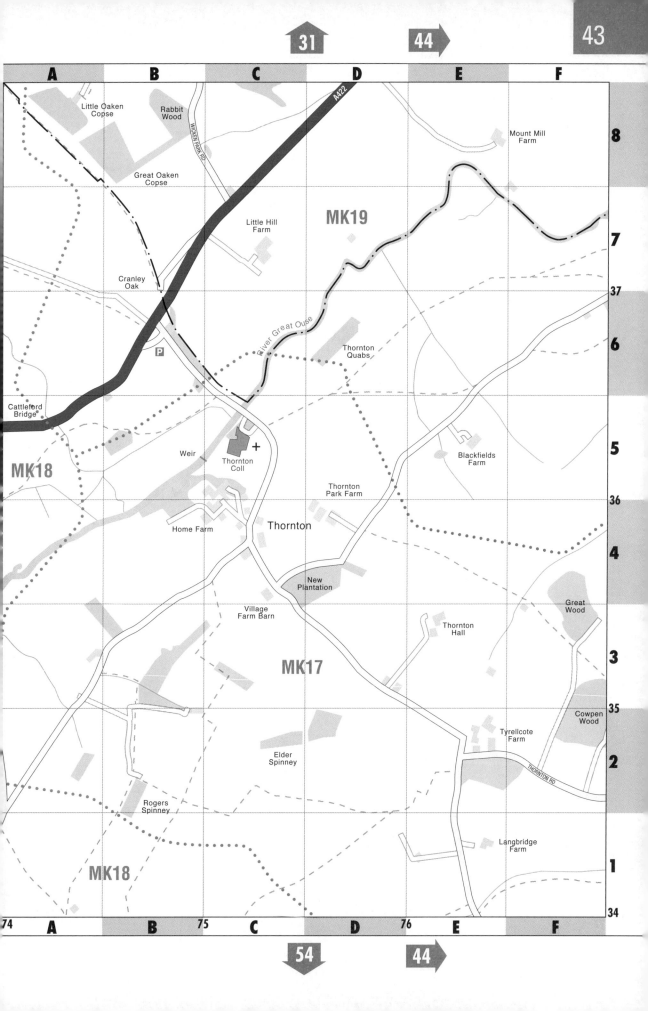

A B C D E F

8

Little Oaken
Copse

Rabbit
Wood

WICKEN PARK RD

A422

Mount Mill
Farm

Great Oaken
Copse

Little Hill
Farm

MK19

7

37

Cranley
Oak

River Great Ouse

Thornton
Quabs

6

P

Cattleford
Bridge

Weir

Thornton
Coll

Thornton
Park Farm

Blackfields
Farm

5

MK18

36

Home Farm

Thornton

New
Plantation

4

Village
Farm Barn

Thornton
Hall

Great
Wood

MK17

3

35

Cowpen
Wood

Elder
Spinney

Tyrellcote
Farm

THORNTON RD

2

Rogers
Spinney

Langbridge
Farm

1

74 A B 75 C D 76 E F 34

43
32

A   B   C   D   E   F

8

River Great Ouse

Blacon
Spinney

Upper
Weald

Beachampton
Hall

7

Manor
Farm

Hill Farm

Milton Keynes Boundary Walk

37

Beachampton

PH

MK19

Home Farm

6

ELMERS CL

MAIN ST

WATERY LA

Red
House
Farm

Beachampton
Grove

Grove Farm

Grange
Farm

5

School
Furze

The Oaks

36

4

Beachampton
Bsns Pk

Potash
Farm

Furzenfield
Farm

3

35

Elm
Farm

2

MK17

Yew Tree
Farm

Basshill
Farm

NASH RD

WHADDON RD

Town
End

THORNTON RD

PANTERS CL

North Buckinghamshire Way

Holywell Farm

Holywell
Cottages

The
Hill

Nash

1

STRATFORD RD

HIGH ST

THORNBOROUGH RD

OLD ENGLISH CL

WINSLOW RD

Barnhill
Farm

34

77   A   B   78   C   D   79   E   F

43
55

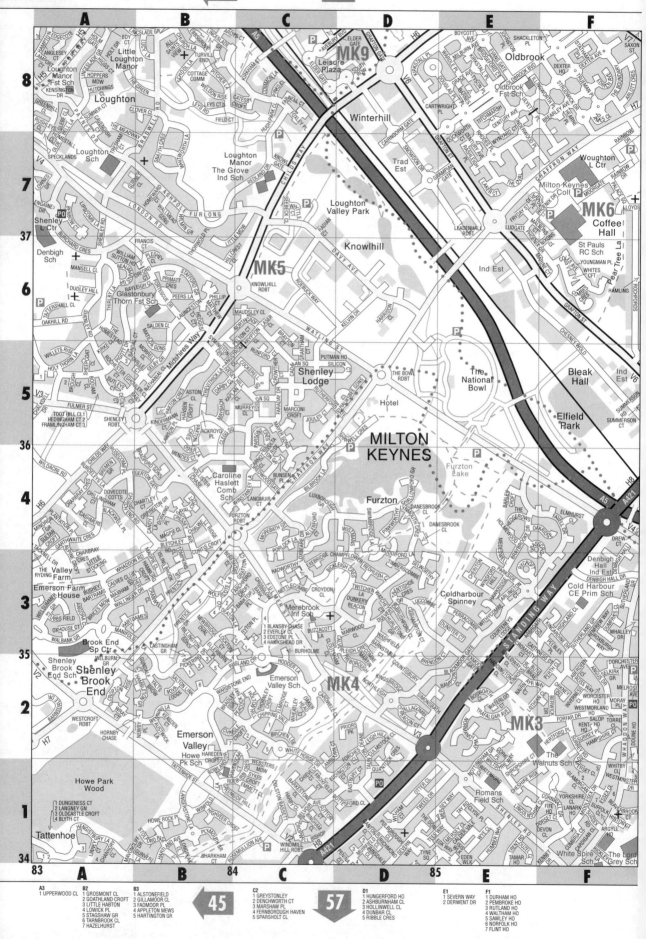

45 34 45 57

A3
1 UPPERWOOD CL

B2
1 GROSMONT CL
2 GOATHLAND CROFT
3 LITTLE HABTON
4 LOWICK PL
5 STAGSHAW GR
6 TARNBROOK CL
7 HAZELHURST

B3
1 ALSTONEFIELD
2 GILLAMOOR CL
3 FADMOOR PL
4 APPLETON MEWS
5 HARTINGTON GR

C2
1 GREYSTONLEY
2 DENCHWORTH CT
3 MARSHAW PL
4 FERNBOROUGH HAVEN
5 SPARSHOLT CL

D1
1 HUNGERFORD HO
2 ASHBURNHAM CL
3 HOLLINWELL CL
4 DUNBAR CL
5 RIBBLE CRES

E1
1 SEVERN WAY
2 DERWENT DR

F1
1 DURHAM HO
2 PEMBROKE HO
3 RUTLAND HO
4 WALTHAM HO
5 SAWLEY HO
6 NORFOLK HO
7 FLINT HO

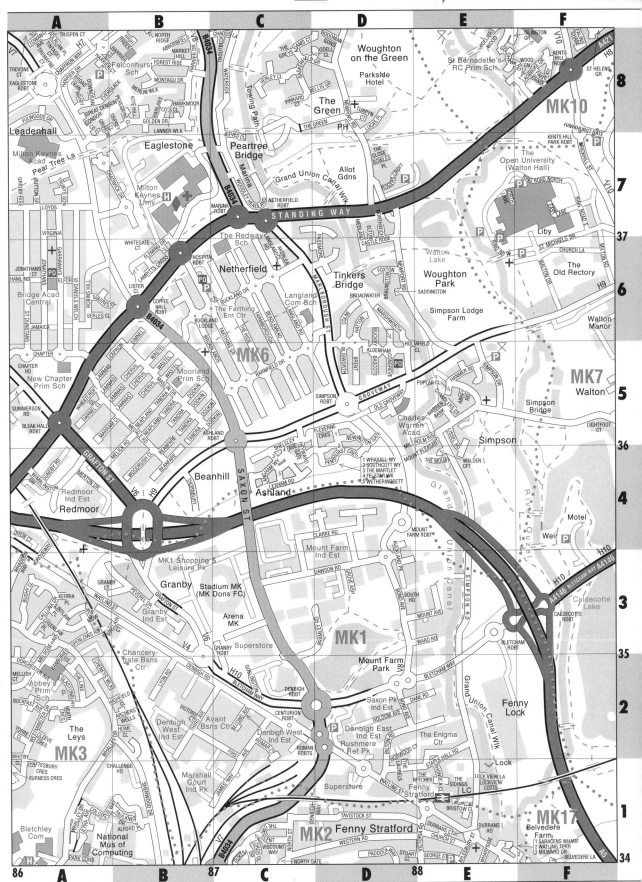

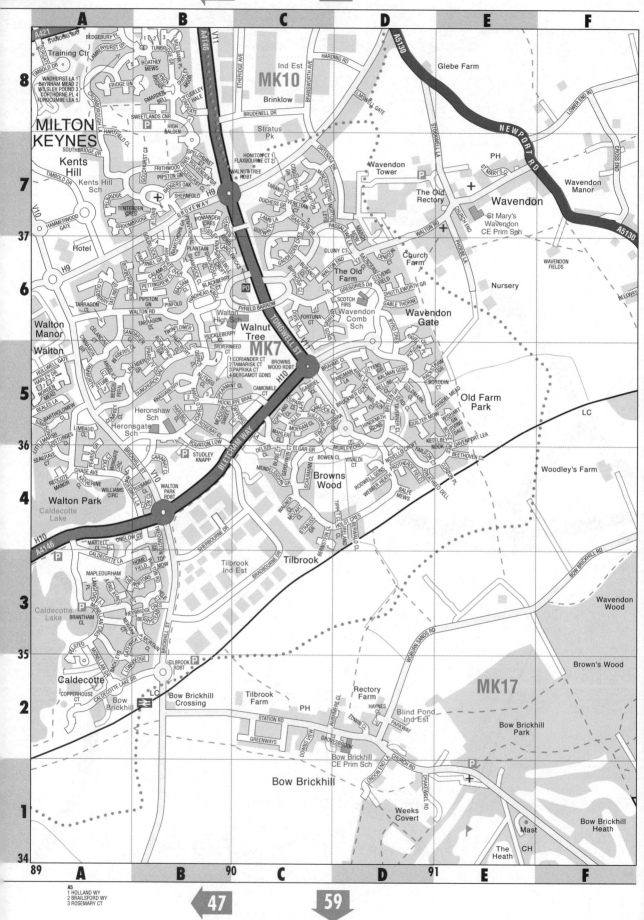

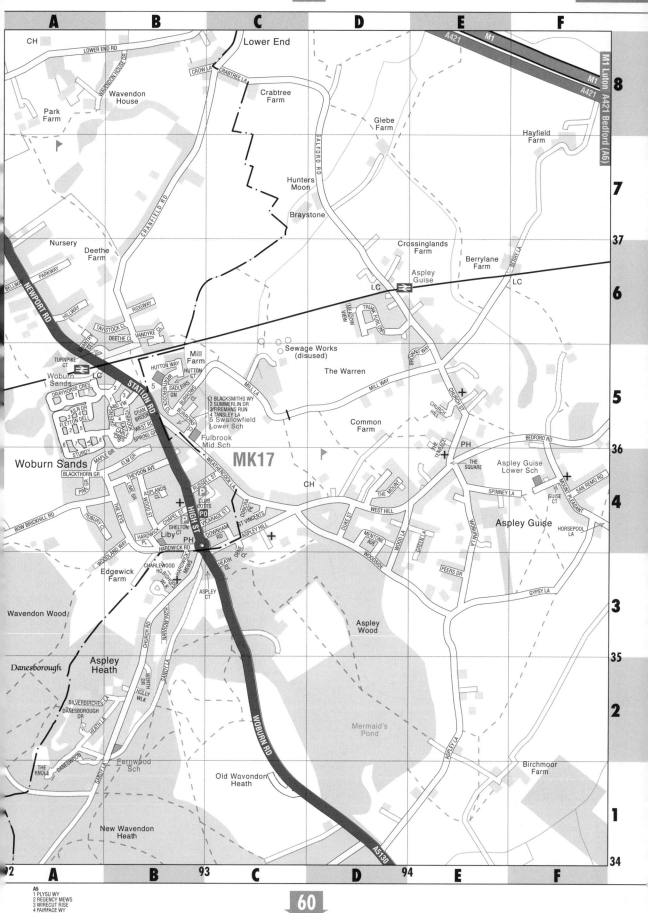

MK17

Woburn Sands

Aspley Guise

Aspley Heath

Danesborough

1 BLACKSMITHS WY
2 SUMMERLIN DR
3 FIREMANS RUN
4 TANSLEY LA
5 Swallowfield Lower Sch

A5
1 PLYSU WY
2 REGENCY MEWS
3 WIRECUT RISE
4 FAIRFACE WY
5 CLAY GDNS
6 EASTAFF CROFT
7 BADGERS HOLT
8 WILKIE CT

60

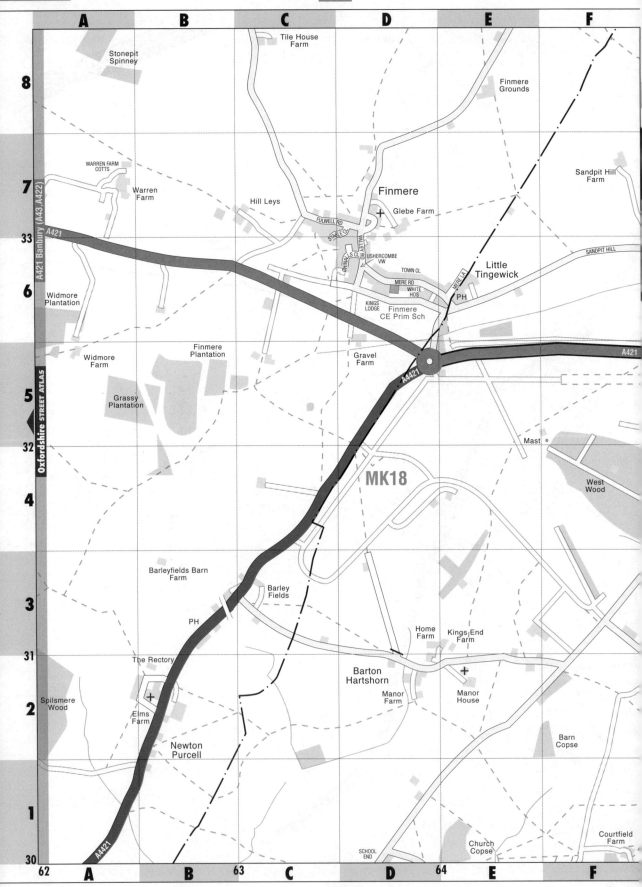

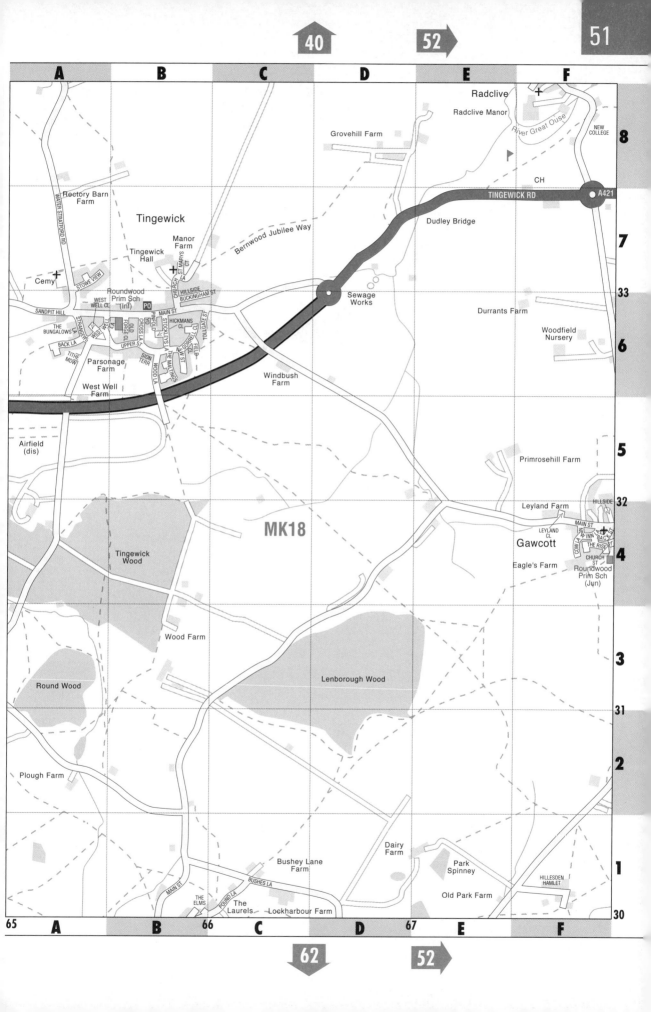

A B C D E F

8
7
33
6
5
32
4
3
31
2
1
30

Radclive
Radclive Manor
River Great Ouse
NEW COLLEGE
CH
TINGEWICK RD
A421
Grovehill Farm
Dudley Bridge
Rectory Barn Farm
WATER STRATFORD RD
Tingewick
Manor Farm
Bernwood Jubilee Way
Tingewick Hall
STOWE VIEW
Cemy
CHURCH LA
ST MARY'S CT
Roundwood Prim Sch (Inf)
WEST WELL CL
Hillside
BUCKINGHAM ST
PO
Sewage Works
Durrants Farm
Woodfield Nursery
SANDPIT HILL
MAIN ST
THE BUNGALOWS
STRANGERS
WEST WELL
HICKMANS CL
STOCKLEY'S LA
GORRELL CL
FIELD
TOLLGATE ST
BACK LA
TITHE MDW
OLD FORGE CL
UPPER ST
SION TERR
WOOD LA
THE MALTINGS
CROSS LA
Windbush Farm
Parsonage Farm
West Well Farm
Airfield (dis)
Primrosehill Farm
Leyland Farm
HILLSIDE
32
LEYLAND CL
MAIN ST
NEW INN
BACK
COW LA
THE RISE
Gawcott
CHURCH ST
Eagle's Farm
Roundwood Prim Sch (Jun)
MK18
Tingewick Wood
Wood Farm
Round Wood
Lenborough Wood
Plough Farm
Dairy Farm
Park Spinney
HILLESDEN HAMLET
Bushey Lane Farm
MAIN ST
BUSHES LA
THE ELMS
POUND LA
The Laurels
Lockharbour Farm
Old Park Farm

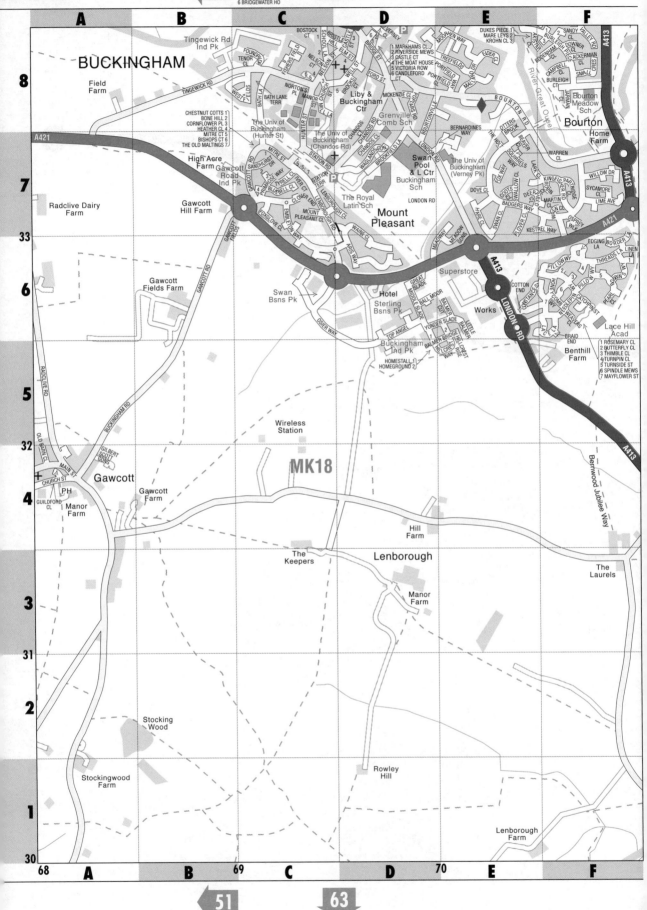

C8
1 OLD SCHOOL CT
2 THE MOORINGS
3 ST RUMBOLD'S LA
4 MILL HO
5 BARHAM LODGE
6 BRIDGEWATER HO

BUCKINGHAM

Tingewick Rd Ind Pk

Field Farm

CHESTNUT COTTS 1
BONE HILL 2
CORNFLOWER PL 3
HEATHER CL 4
MITRE CT 5
BISHOPS CT 6
THE OLD MALTINGS 7

High Acre Farm

Gawcott Road Ind Pk

Radclive Dairy Farm

Gawcott Hill Farm

Gawcott Fields Farm

Swan Bsns Pk

Osier Way

Hotel Sterling Bsns Pk

Buckingham Ind Pk

HOMESTALL 1
HOMEGROUND 2

Wireless Station

MK18

Gilbert Scott Gdns

Gawcott

Gawcott Farm

Manor Farm

Stocking Wood

Stockingwood Farm

The Keepers

Hill Farm

Lenborough

Manor Farm

Rowley Hill

Lenborough Farm

The Laurels

Bernwood Jubilee Way

The Univ of Buckingham (Hunter St)

The Univ of Buckingham (Chandos Rd)

Liby & Buckingham Ctr

Grenville Comb Sch

Swan Pool & L Ctr

The Royal Latin Sch

Mount Pleasant

Buckingham Sch

The Univ of Buckingham (Verney Pk)

Superstore

Works

Bernardines Way

London Rd

Bourton Meadow Sch

Bourton

Home Farm

Lace Hill Acad

1 ROSEMARY CL
2 BUTTERFLY CL
3 THIMBLE CL
4 TURNPIN CL
5 TURNSIDE ST
6 SPINDLE MEWS
7 MAYFLOWER ST

Benthill Farm

1 MARKHAMS CL
2 RIVERSIDE MEWS
3 CASTLE CT
4 THE MOAT HOUSE
5 VICTORIA ROW
6 CANDLEFORD

DUKES PIECE 1
MARE LEYS 2
KROHN CL 3

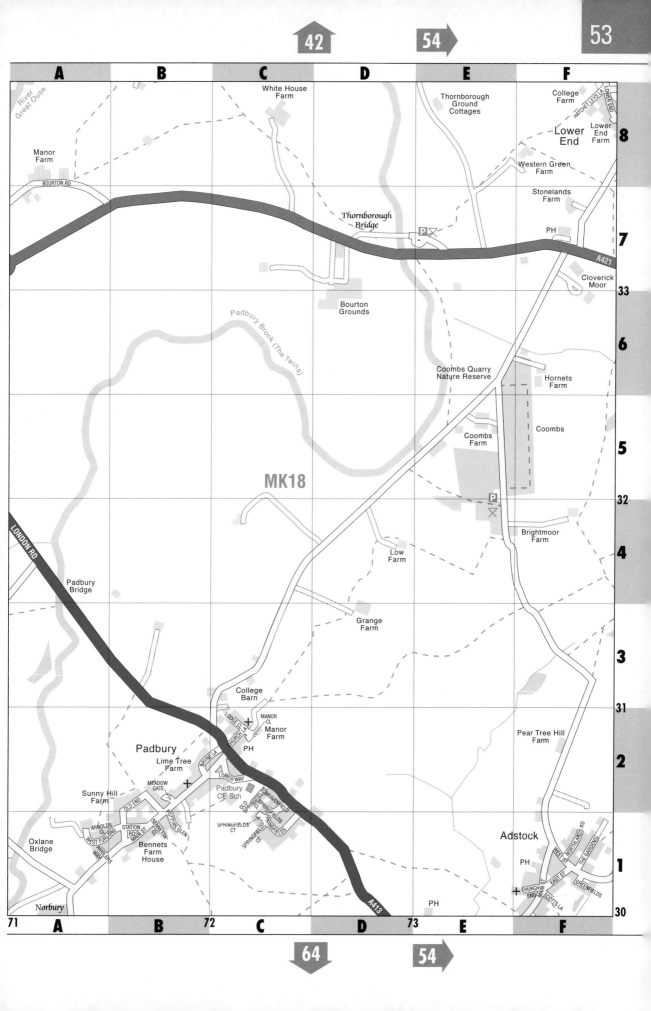

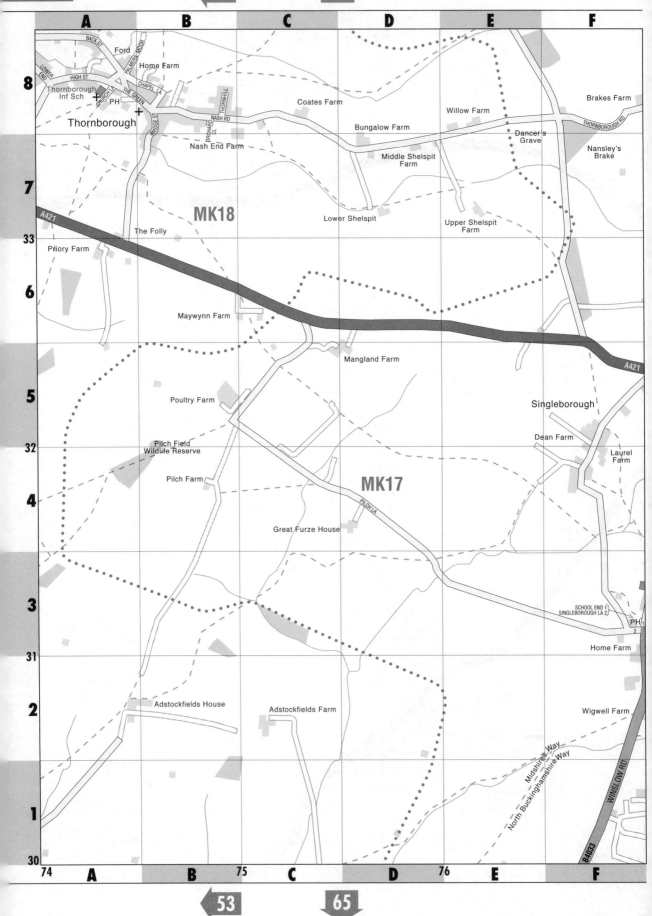

A B C D E F

8

Back St
Ford
Home Farm
Lower End
High St
Thornborough Inf Sch
PH
Palmers Moor
The Green
Chapel La
Coates Farm
Willow Farm
Brakes Farm
Thornborough
Thornhill
Nash Rd
Bungalow Farm
Dancer's Grave
Thornborough Rd
Nansley's Brake
Bridge St
Orchard Cl
Nash End Farm
Middle Shelspit Farm

7

MK18
Upper Shelspit Farm
Lower Shelspit

33

A421
The Folly
Priory Farm

6

Maywynn Farm
Mangland Farm

5

Poultry Farm
A421
Singleborough

32

Pilch Field Wildlife Reserve
Dean Farm
Laurel Farm

4

Pilch Farm
MK17
Pilch La
Great Furze House

3

School End 1
Singleborough La 2
PH
Home Farm

31

Adstockfields House
Adstockfields Farm
Wigwell Farm

2

Midshires Way
North Buckinghamshire Way
Winslow Rd

1

B4033

30

74 A B 75 C D 76 E F

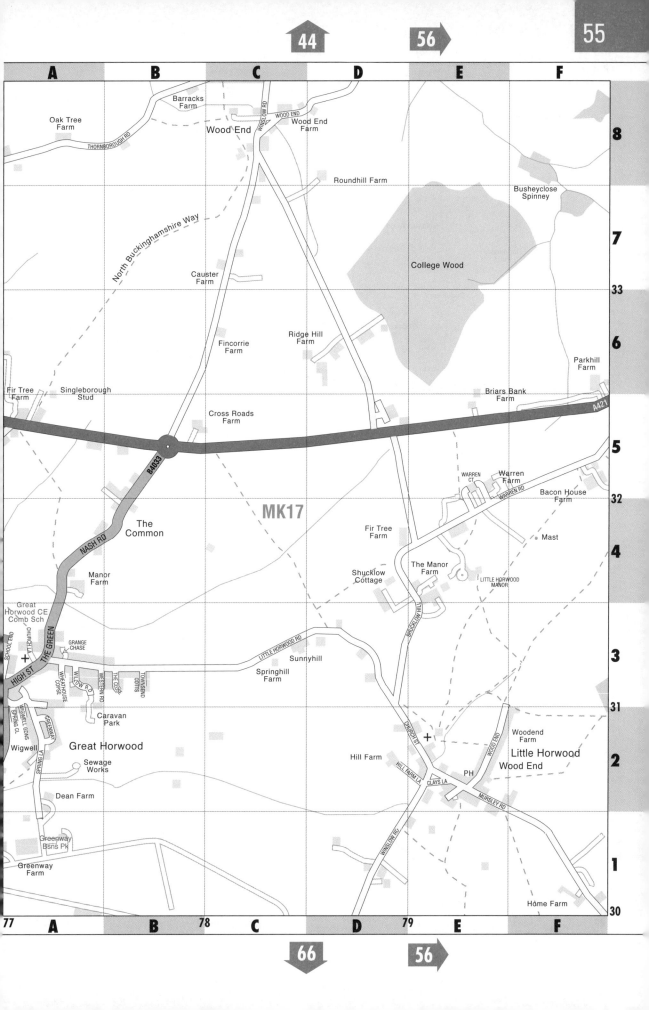

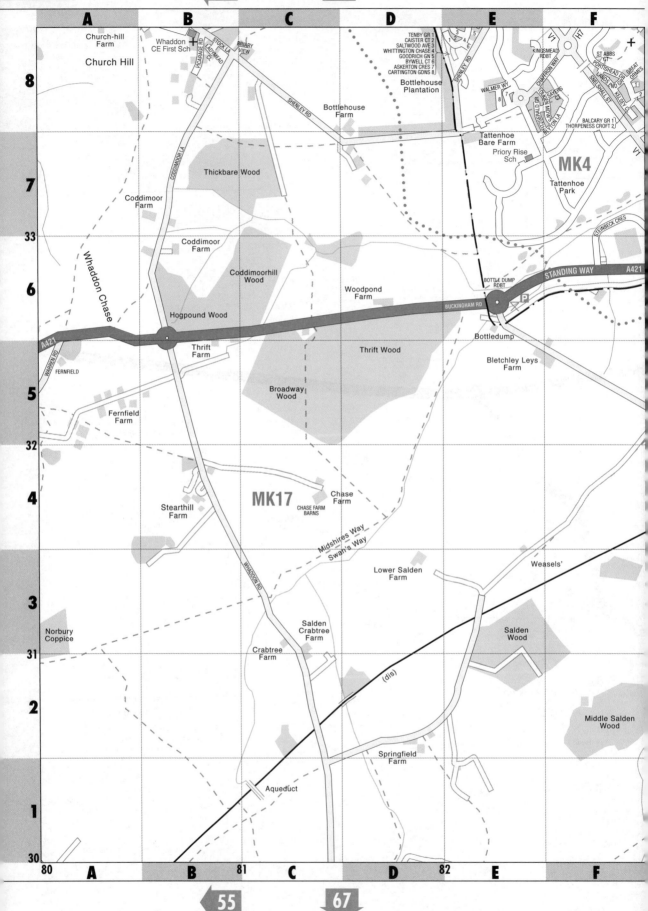

55
45

A B C D E F

8

Church-hill
Farm

Church Hill

Whaddon
CE First Sch

VICARAGE RD
STOCK LA
LADYMEAD CL
BRIARY
VIEW

SHENLEY RD

Bottlehouse
Farm

TENBY GR 1
CAISTER CT 2
SALTWOOD AVE 3
WHITTINGTON CHASE 4
GOODRICH GN 5
BYWELL CT 6
ASKERTON CRES 7
CARTINGTON GDNS 8

Bottlehouse
Plantation

SHENLEY RD

Kingsmead
RDBT

CHAPERON WAY

CHINGFORD GR
FITZGERALD GR
SNOWDEN CT
SAYERS
BLYTON LA

ST ABBS
GT

PORTISHEAD DR
LANDS END GR
SNELSHALL ST
KELSEY CL

GREAT
ORMES

BALCARY GR 1
THORPENESS CROFT 2

WALMER WY

7

Thickbare Wood

Coddimoor
Farm

CODDIMOOR LA

Coddimoor
Farm

Tattenhoe
Bare Farm

Priory Rise
Sch

MK4

Tattenhoe
Park

33

Whaddon Chase

Coddimoor
Farm

Coddimoorhill
Wood

STEINBECK CRES

6

Woodpond
Farm

STANDING WAY   A421

A421

Hogpound Wood

BUCKINGHAM RD

BOTTLE DUMP
RDBT

Bottle DUMP
RDBT

P

WARREN RD

Thrift
Farm

Thrift Wood

Bottledump

Bletchley Leys
Farm

FERNFIELD

5

Broadway
Wood

Fernfield
Farm

32

MK17

Chase
Farm

Stearthill
Farm

CHASE FARM
BARNS

Midshires Way

Swan's Way

Weasels'

4

WHADDON RD

Lower Salden
Farm

Salden
Wood

3

Norbury
Coppice

Salden
Crabtree
Farm

(dis)

31

Crabtree
Farm

2

Middle Salden
Wood

Springfield
Farm

1

Aqueduct

30

80   A   81   B   C   81   D   82   E   F

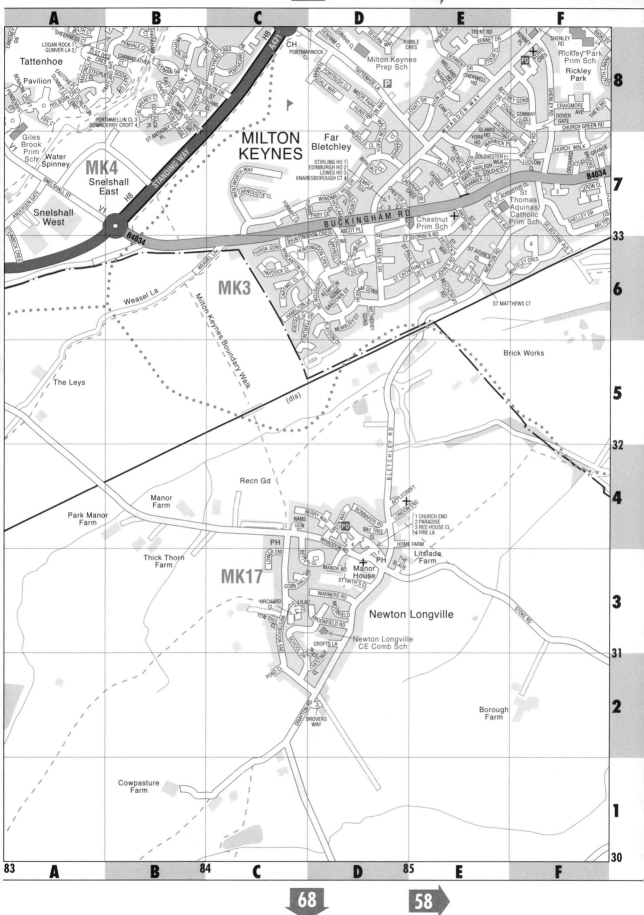

46

58

F7
1 TENNYSON GR
2 KEATS WAY
3 HUGHES CROFT

F8
1 Cambian
Bletchley
Pk Sch

57

A B C D E F

Tattenhoe

Pavilion

Giles Brook Prim Sch

Water Spinney

MK4

Snelshall East

Snelshall West

MK3

MILTON KEYNES

Far Bletchley

STANDING WAY

BUCKINGHAM RD

Chestnut Prim Sch

St Thomas Aquinas Catholic Prim Sch

Milton Keynes Prep Sch

Rickley Park Prim Sch

Rickley Park

Milton Keynes Boundary Walk

The Leys

(dis)

Brick Works

St Matthews Ct

Manor Farm

Recn Gd

Park Manor Farm

Thick Thorn Farm

MK17

Newton Longville

Newton Longville CE Comb Sch

1 CHURCH END
2 PARADISE
3 RED HOUSE CL
4 FIRE LA

Litslade Farm

Manor House

HOME FARM

Borough Farm

Cowpasture Farm

DROVERS WAY

← 57

47

C8
1 ALEXANDER HO
2 LEE HO
3 CHRISTINE HO
4 WOODWARD HO
5 CAWKWELL WY
6 THE CONCOURSE

7 Agora Ctr

D8
1 BOWLING GREEN CL
2 KNIGHTS CRES
3 MARQUESS DR

MK17

MK3

MILTON
KEYNES

Bletchley Com
Bletchley Park
Bletchley
Milton Keynes Coll
War Meml
Holne Chase Prim Sch
Bletchley
Blue Lagoon Nature Reserve
Blue Lagoon Park
Bletchley Bsns Campus
Water Eaton Ind Est
Bishop Parker Catholic Sch
Clay Pit

Council Offices
Brunel Ctr
Knowles Prim Sch
Bletchley L Ctr
Elizabeth Sq
The Premier Acad
Drayton Park Sch
Sir Herbert Leon Acad
Leon L Ctr
Bramley Grange
Water Hall Prim Sch
MK2
Water Eaton
Hebrides Gate

BUCKINGHAM RD
B4034
Grand Union Canal Wlk
River Ouzel
Grand Union Canal
Eaton Leys Farm
Galleylane Spinney
Willowbridge Boat Yard
Stoke House
Towing Path
Hotel
Watling Terr
Belvedere La
Dropshort Farm
V4

A4146

The Old Dairy Farm
Mill La
Southlands Farm
Sewage Works

MK17

BARBADOS ROW 1
ASCENSION GDNS 2
TASMANIA GR 3

1 TOBAGO DR
2 SUMATRA CRES
3 CAYMAN WK
4 HANAN DR
5 BONAIRE GRANGE
6 CYPRUS WY

LANGKAWI LA 1
LAPUTA WY 2
SHETLAND MDWS 3
GUYANA LA 4
MONTSERRAT CT 5

1 HOPKINS RD
2 KING CL
3 GEARY MEWS
4 HARRIS CL
5 LARNER CL
6 HOWE MEWS
7 HALL GN
8 MARTINIQUE MDWS
9 SANTA MARIA LA
10 MARGARITA GDNS

1 GWYNANT CT
2 DIDDINGTON CL

Chadwell Farm
Proctor Mews
Rectory Farm
Burnell Farm

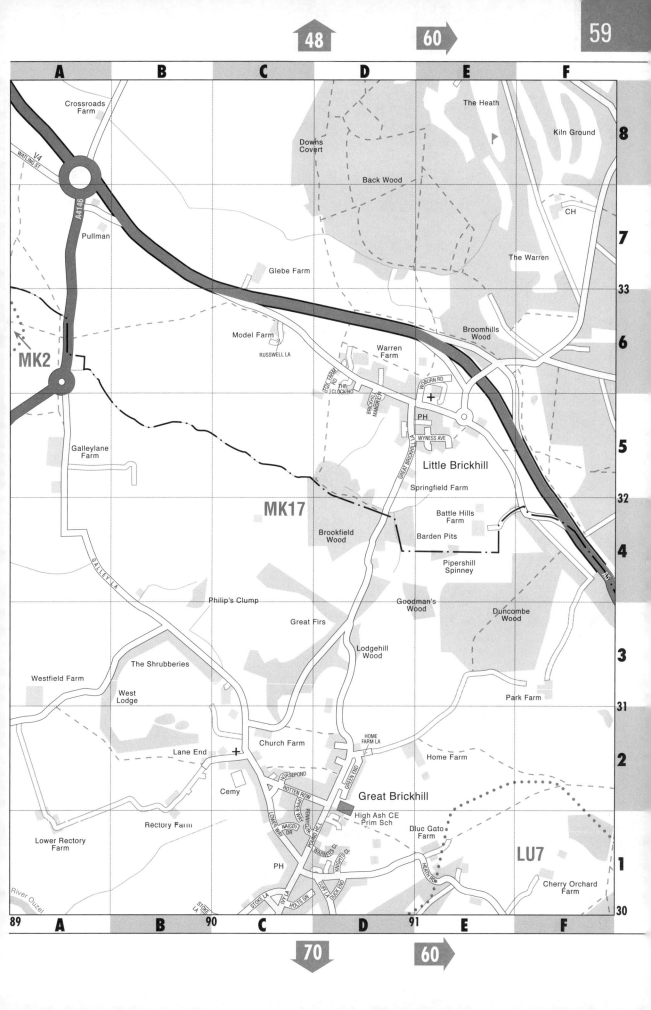

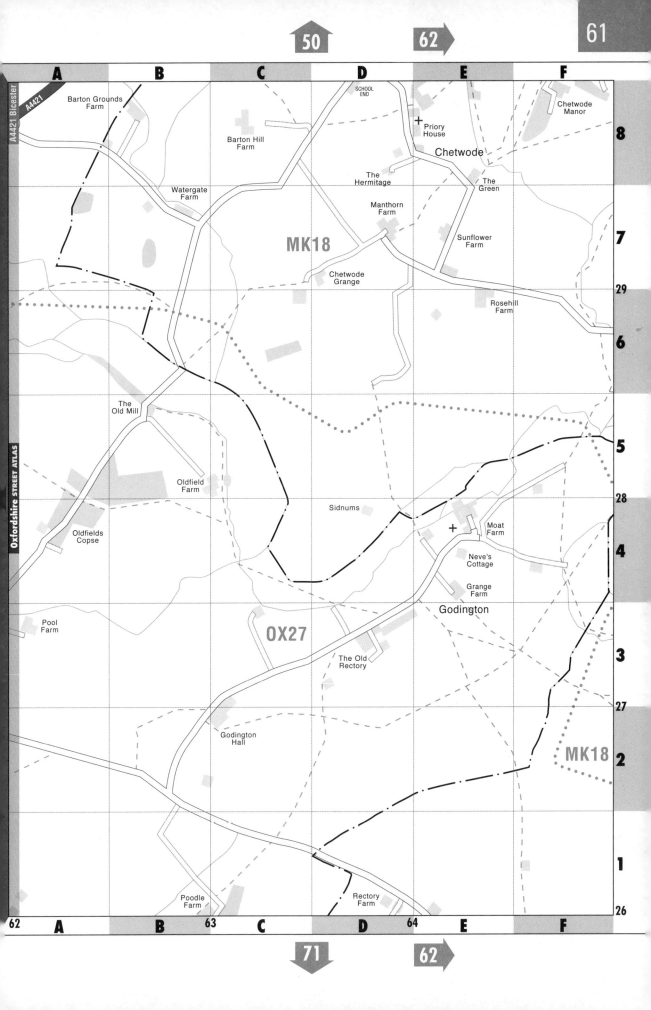

A B C D E F

A4421 Bicester
A4421

Barton Grounds Farm

SCHOOL END

Chetwode Manor

+ Priory House

Barton Hill Farm

Chetwode

The Hermitage

The Green

Watergate Farm

Manthorn Farm

MK18

Sunflower Farm

Chetwode Grange

Rosehill Farm

The Old Mill

Oldfield Farm

Sidnums

Moat Farm

+

Oldfields Copse

Neve's Cottage

Grange Farm

Pool Farm

OX27

Godington

The Old Rectory

MK18

Godington Hall

Poodle Farm

Rectory Farm

8
7
29
6
5
28
4
3
27
2
1
26

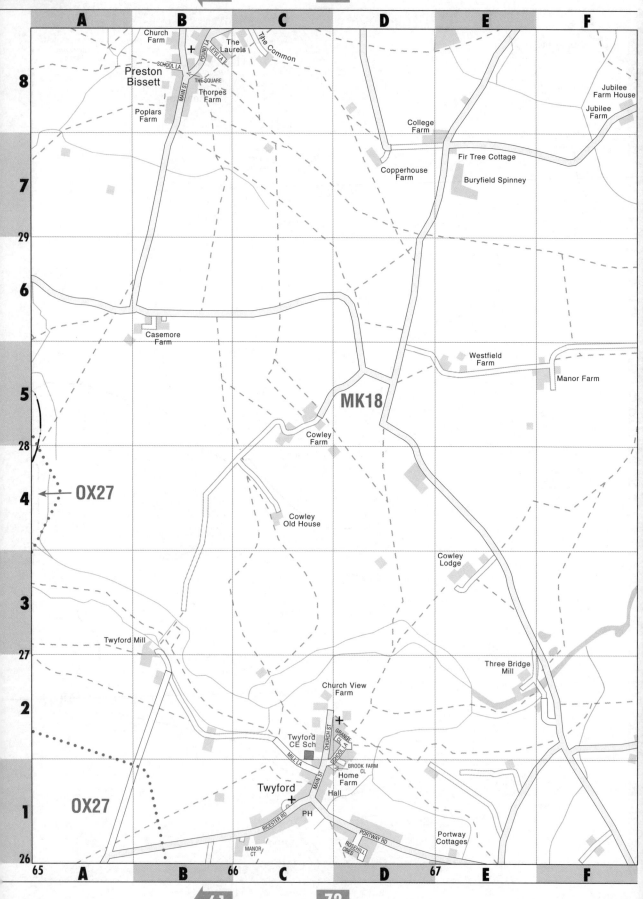

A B C D E F

8

Preston
Bissett

Church
Farm
SCHOOL LA
POUND LA
EYS LA
The Laurels
The Common
THE SQUARE
Thorpes
Farm
MAIN ST
Poplars
Farm

College
Farm

Jubilee
Farm House
Jubilee
Farm

7

Copperhouse
Farm
Fir Tree Cottage
Buryfield Spinney

29

6

Casemore
Farm

Westfield
Farm
Manor Farm

5

MK18

Cowley
Farm

28

OX27

4

Cowley
Old House

Cowley
Lodge

3

Twyford Mill

27

Three Bridge
Mill

Church View
Farm

2

Twyford
CE Sch
MILL LA
MAIN ST
CHURCH ST
GRANGE CL
SCHOOL LA
Brook Farm
CL
Home
Farm

OX27

Twyford
Hall
PH
BICESTER RD
PORTWAY RD
Portway
Cottages

1

MANOR
CT
ROSEHILL
CRES

26

65 A B 66 C D 67 E F

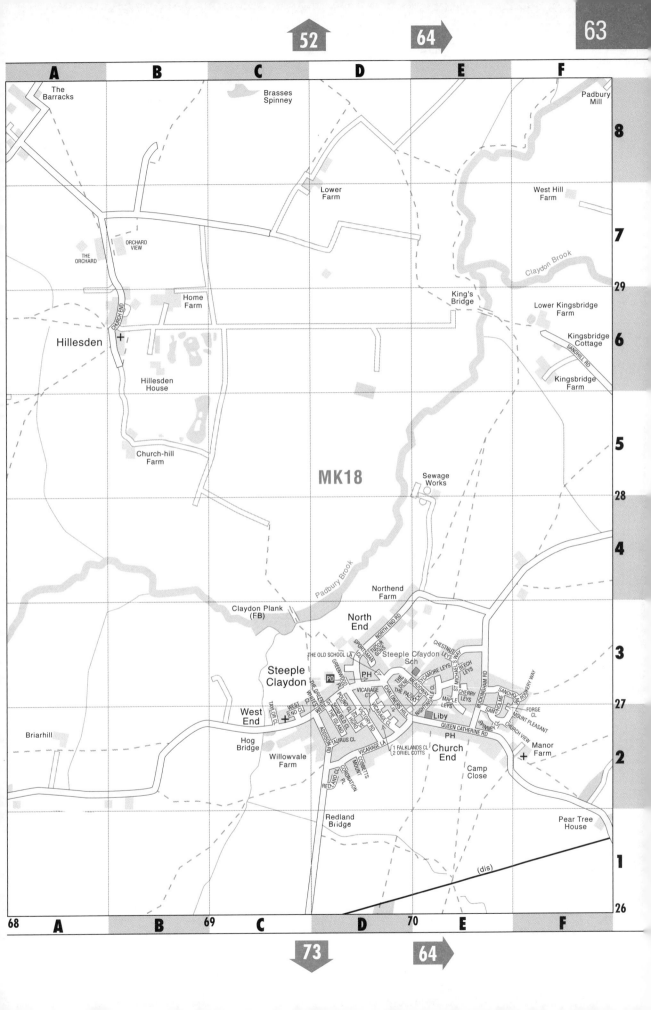

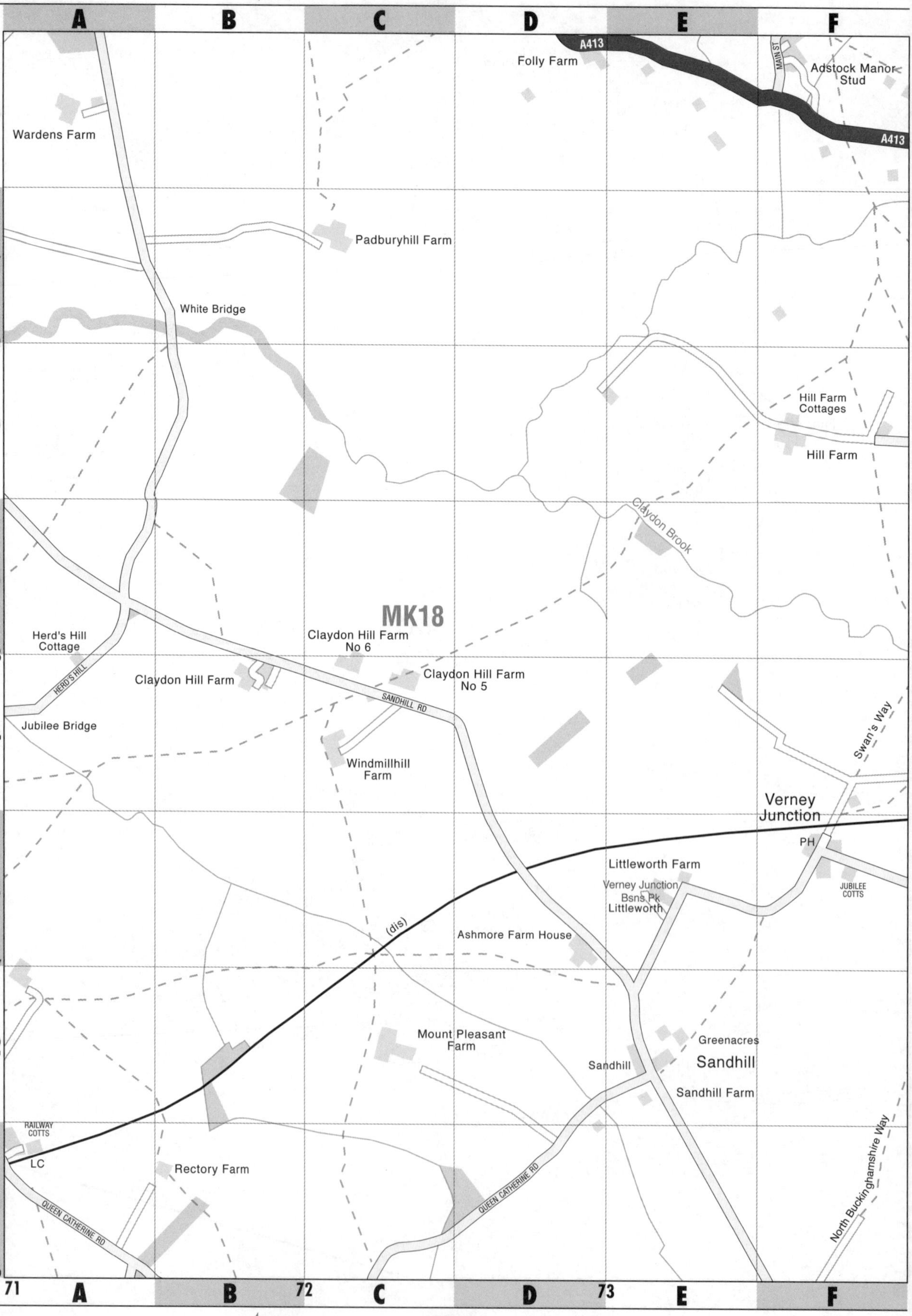

← **63**
53 ↓

	A	B	C	D	E	F

8
Wardens Farm
Folly Farm
A413
A413
Adstock Manor Stud
MAIN ST

7
Padburyhill Farm
White Bridge

29
Hill Farm Cottages

6
Hill Farm

Claydon Brook

5
MK18

28
Claydon Hill Farm No 6
Herd's Hill Cottage
Claydon Hill Farm
Claydon Hill Farm No 5
SANDHILL RD
Swan's Way

4
Jubilee Bridge
Windmillhill Farm
HERD'S HILL
Verney Junction
PH

3
Littleworth Farm
Verney Junction Bsns Pk
Littleworth
JUBILEE COTTS

(dis)
Ashmore Farm House

27

2
Mount Pleasant Farm
Sandhill
Greenacres
Sandhill
Sandhill Farm

RAILWAY COTTS
LC
Rectory Farm
North Buckinghamshire Way

1
QUEEN CATHERINE RD
QUEEN CATHERINE RD

26

← **63**
74 ↓

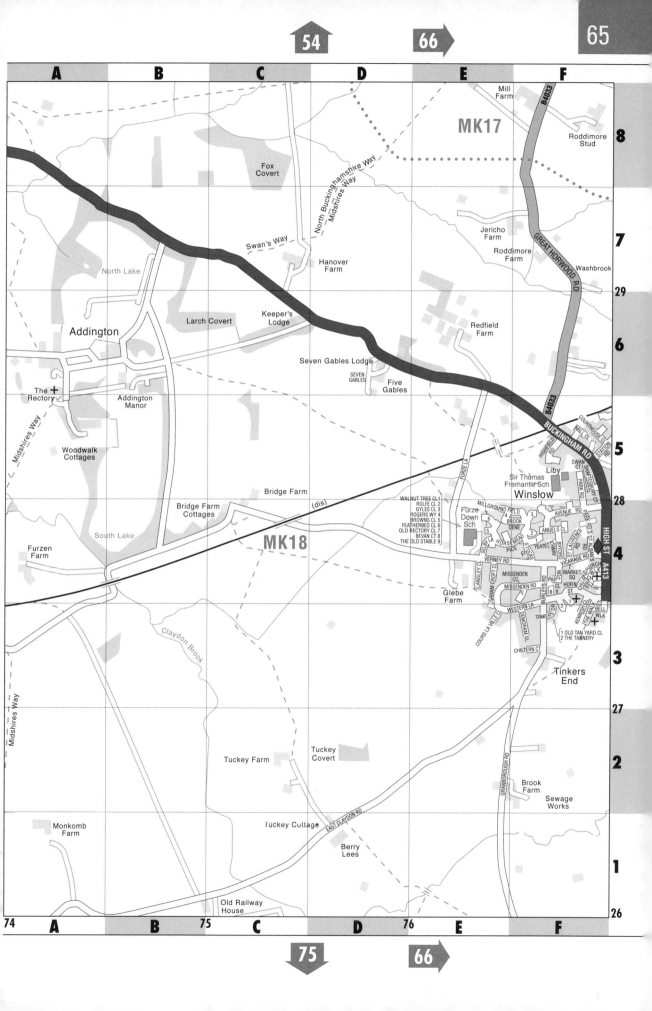

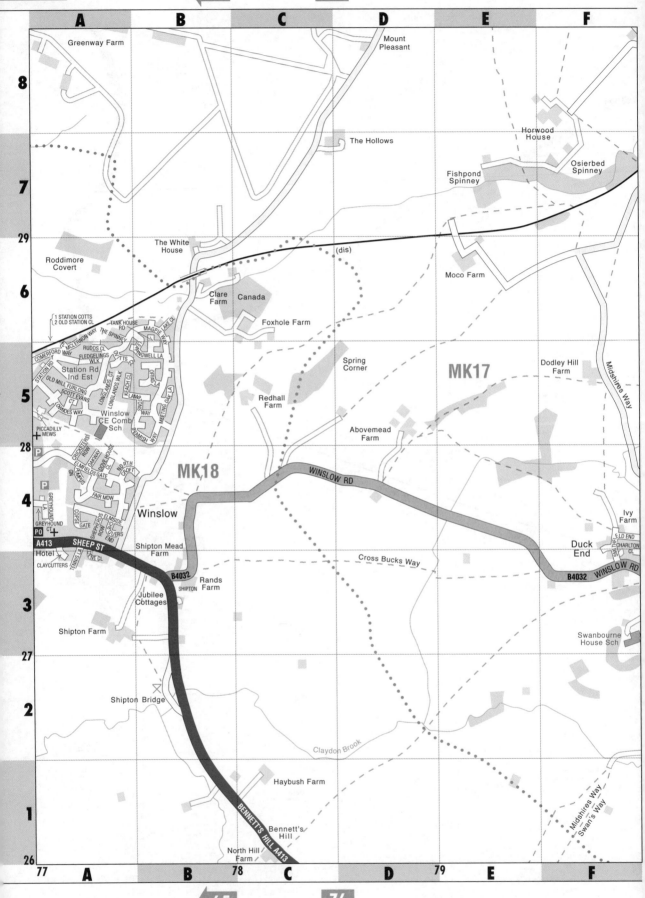

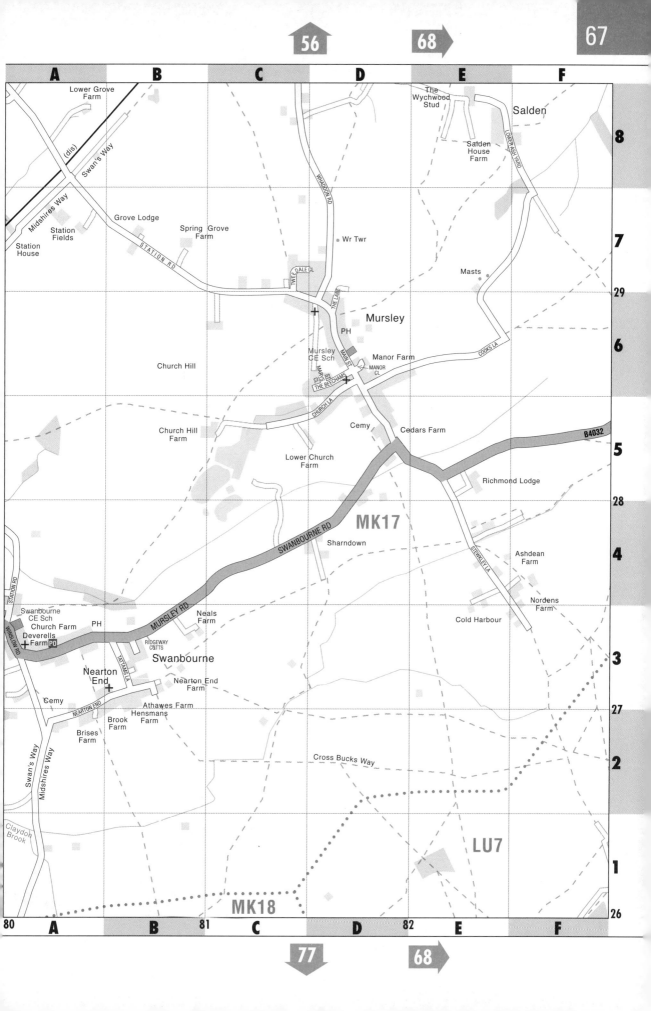

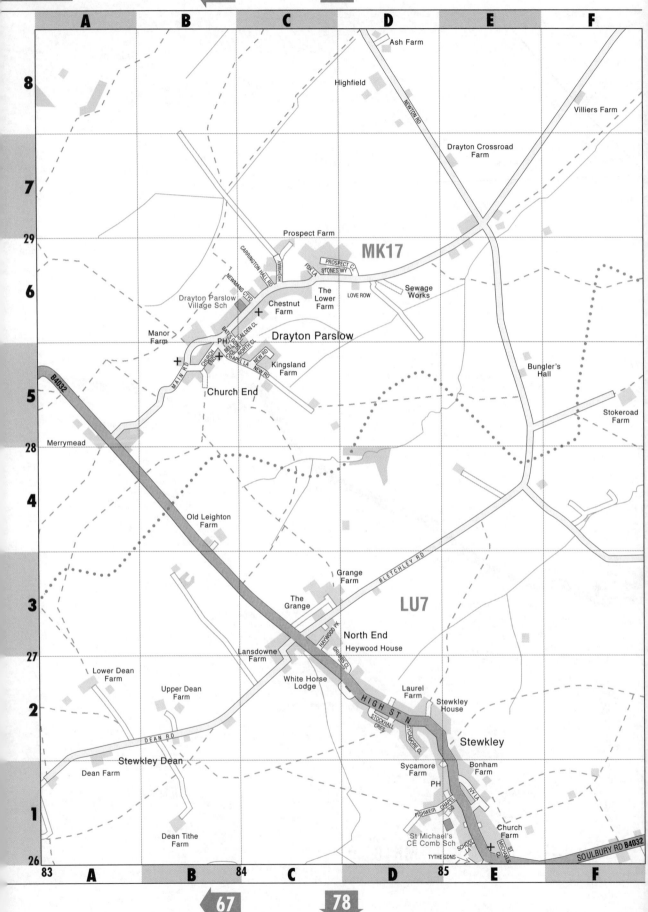

A   B   C   D   E   F

8

7

29

6

MK17

Prospect Farm

Ash Farm

Highfield

Villiers Farm

Drayton Crossroad Farm

NEWTON RD

CARRINGTON HALL RD

HIGHWAY

FOX LA

PROSPECT C
STONES WY

NEWMANS CTYD

Drayton Parslow Village Sch

Chestnut Farm

The Lower Farm

LOVE ROW

Sewage Works

Manor Farm

Drayton Parslow

PH

BATES CL
BELL CL
SALDEN CL
NORTH CL
CHAPEL LA   NEW RD
NEW RD

Kingsland Farm

Bungler's Hall

B4032

Merrymead

CHURCH END
MAIN RD

Church End

Stokeroad Farm

5

28

4

Old Leighton Farm

Grange Farm

BLETCHLEY RD

LU7

The Grange

HAYWOOD PK

North End

Heywood House

3

27

Lansdowne Farm

GRUBBS CL

Lower Dean Farm

Upper Dean Farm

White Horse Lodge

Laurel Farm

Stewkley House

2

HIGH ST N

Stewkley

STOCKHALL CRES

SYCAMORE CL

DEAN RD

Stewkley Dean

Dean Farm

Sycamore Farm

PH

Bonham Farm

IVY LA

1

Dean Tithe Farm

FISHWEIR
CHAPEL
SQ

St Michael's CE Comb Sch

SCHOOL LA

Church Farm

ST MICHAELS CL

SOULBURY RD B4032

26

TYTHE GDNS

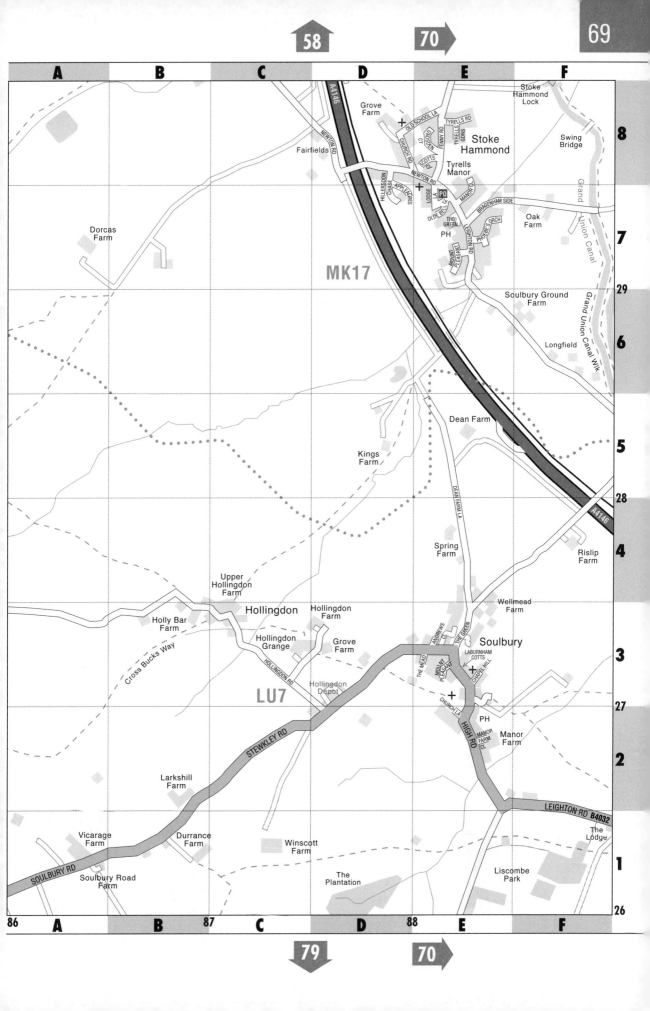

8

7

29

6

5

28

4

3

27

2

1

26

MK17

Grove Farm

Fairfields

Stoke Hammond Lock

Swing Bridge

OLD SCHOOL LA

TYRELLS RD

TYRELLS GDNS

FENNY RD

Stoke Hammond

CHURCH RD

SCOTTS CL

NEWTON RD

Tyrells Manor

HILLERSDON CHASE

APPLEACRES

LODGE LA

OLDE BELL CL

PO

THE GREEN

PH

MOUNT PLEASANT

LEIGHTON RD

PHEBE ORCH

MANOR CL

BRAGENHAM SIDE

Oak Farm

Grand Union Canal

Soulbury Ground Farm

Longfield

Grand Union Canal Wlk

Dorcas Farm

Dean Farm

Kings Farm

DEAN FARM LA

Spring Farm

Rislip Farm

A4146

NEWTON RD

A4146

Upper Hollingdon Farm

Hollingdon

Holly Bar Farm

Cross Bucks Way

Hollingdon Grange

HOLLINGDON RD

Hollingdon Farm

Grove Farm

Wellmead Farm

ANDREWS CL

THE GREEN

Soulbury

LABURNHAM COTTS

THE MEAD

MOUNT PLEASANT

CHAPEL HILL

CHURCH LA

PH

HIGH RD

MANOR FARM CL

Manor Farm

LU7

Hollingdon Depot

STEWKLEY RD

Larkshill Farm

Winscott Farm

LEIGHTON RD B4032

The Lodge

Vicarage Farm

Durrance Farm

SOULBURY RD

Soulbury Road Farm

The Plantation

Liscombe Park

A B C D E F

8

7

River Ouzel

Paper Mill

MK17

29

Partridge Hill

Furze Hill

Partridge House

STRAWBERRY FIELDS

CH

6

Red Bridge

Bragenham Farm

Bragenham

Upper Kiln Farm

Kiln Farm

PH

Stapleford Mill

Stapleford Farm

5

P

28

Grand Union Canal

River Ouzel

Ludley Cottage

BRAGENHAM LA

LU7

4

A4146

Grand Union Canal Wlk

Nares Gadley Farm

Rushmere

Chelmscote Manor Farm

Broad Oak

Cross Bucks Way

Grange Mill

3

27

Manor Gt

P

Old Linslade Manor

Old Linslade

2

B4032

LEIGHTON RD

Dollar Farm

Corbettshill Farm

LEIGHTON BUZZARD

PH

1

STOKE RD

Linslade Wood

Sewage Works

26

Valley Farm

A4146

89 A B 90 C D 91 E F

Stoke La

Ivy Lane Farm

IVY LA

Sewage Works

Stockgrove Farm

Greensand Ridge Wlk

Oak Wood

Alders Farm

Stockgrove Park Ho

P

Visitor Ctr

Stockgrove Country Park

Shire Oak

Rushmere Park

LINSLADE RD

OLD LINSLADE RD

THE HEATH

HEATH DUKES RIDE

CH

Greensand Ridge Wlk

PLANTATION RD

SANDY LA

REDWOOD GLADE

TALL PINES

OXENDON CT

TAYLORS RIDE

ROBINSWOOD CL

WOODLAND AVE

RED GLOVE

DINGLE DELL

GLOBE LA

BOSSINGTON LA

THE MARTINS

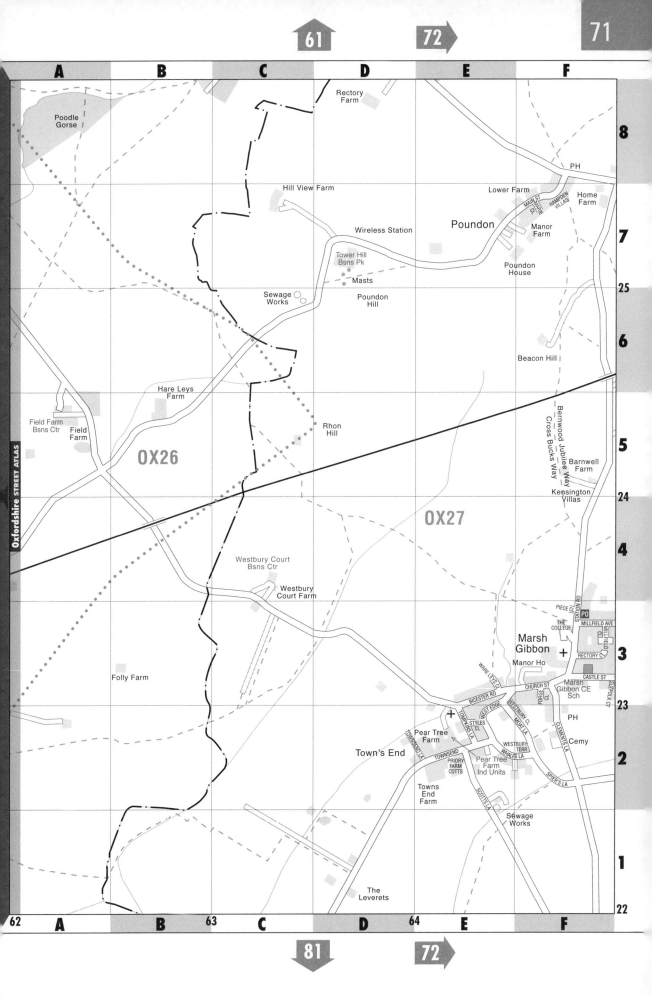

Oxfordshire STREET ATLAS

Poodle Gorse

Rectory Farm

Hill View Farm

Wireless Station

Poundon

Lower Farm

Home Farm

PH

MAIN ST

MARIE CL

HAMPDEN VILLAS

Manor Farm

Poundon House

Tower Hill Bsns Pk

Masts

Poundon Hill

Sewage Works

Beacon Hill

Hare Leys Farm

Field Farm Bsns Ctr

Field Farm

Rhon Hill

OX26

Bernwood Jubilee Way

Cross Bucks Way

Barnwell Farm

Kensington Villas

OX27

Westbury Court Bsns Ctr

Westbury Court Farm

Folly Farm

PIECE CL

STATION RD

PO

THE COLLEGE

MILLFIELD AVE

MILLFIELD CL

Marsh Gibbon

RECTORY C...

Manor Ho

CASTLE ST

Marsh Gibbon CE Sch

SUFFOLK CT

WARE LEYS CL

CHURCH ST

FORGE CL

WESTBURY CL

BICESTER RD

WEST EDGE

PH

CLEMENTS LA

Cemy

Pear Tree Farm

STYLES CL

TOMPKINS LA

MOAT LA

WESTBURY TERR

WHALES LA

Town's End

TOWNSEND LA

TOWNSEND

PRIORY FARM COTTS

Pear Tree Farm Ind Units

SPIER'S LA

Towns End Farm

SCOTTS LA

Sewage Works

The Leverets

8 7 25 6 5 24 4 3 23 2 1 22

62 63 64

A B C D E F

8

Red Furlong Farm

MK18

Rosehill
Farm

PORTWAY
RD

Portway
Farm

Twyford
Lodge

7

Grebe Lake

25

Lawn Farm

CHESHIRE
COTTS

6

Windmill Hill

BARCLAY
CL

HAMPDEN
HILL

Charndon

SCHOOL
HILL

Station House

WOOTTON GN
BEATRICE
CL

Charndon
Grounds

SPENCER
GDNS

Middle
Farm

Valley
Farm

MAIN ST

5

OX27

Hill Farm

MK18

24

4

LITTLE MARSH RD

Gubbinshole Ditch

3

SWAN LA

Swan
Farm

SCOTTS CL

Little Marsh

CASTLE ST

23

CASTLE CL

Leopold Farm

ST MICHAELS
CL

Rectory Farm

2

Summerstown

HP18

PYRELLA
CL

Edgcott

New Swan
Farm

Gubbin's Hole

LEONARDO
CL

BUCKINGHAM RD

1

Gubbins
Hole Farm

Lower Farm

GRENDON RD

LAWN
HOUSE LA

22

65

A

66

B C

67

D E F

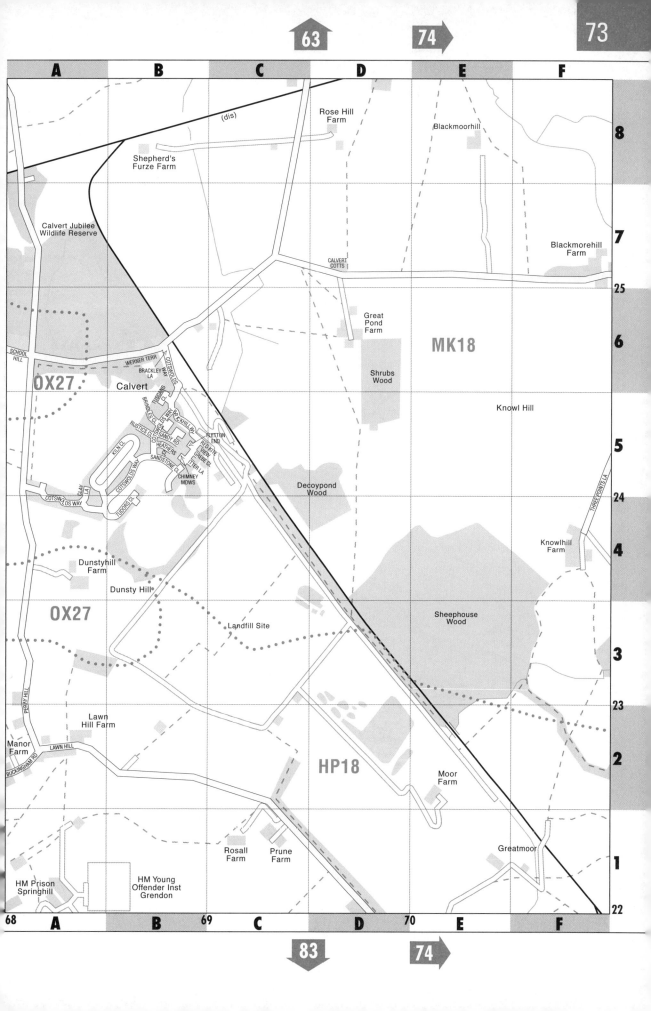

A B C D E F

8

Rose Hill
Farm

(dis)

Blackmoorhill

Shepherd's
Furze Farm

Calvert Jubilee
Wildlife Reserve

7

Blackmorehill
Farm

CALVERT
COTTS

25

SCHOOL
HILL

Great
Pond
Farm

MK18

6

WERNER TERR

BRACKLEY LA

COTSWOLDS

OX27

Calvert

Shrubs
Wood

TUSCANS CL

Knowl Hill

BRINDLES CL

SWOLDS WAY

BLACKHILL WY

SANDY RD

RUSTICS CL

FLETTON
END

KILN CL

HEATERS
CL

REDKITE

GREBE CL

OTTER LA

VIEW

SANDSTONE CL

CHIMNEY
MDWS

5

CLAY LA

COTSWOLDS WAY

Decoypond
Wood

THREE POINTS LA

COTSW DS WAY

TUDORS CL

24

Knowlhill
Farm

4

Dunstyhill
Farm

Dunsty Hill

Sheephouse
Wood

OX27

Landfill Site

3

23

Lawn
Hill Farm

PERRY HILL

Manor
Farm

LAWN HILL

HP18

Moor
Farm

2

BUCKINGHAM RD

Rosall
Farm

Prune
Farm

Greatmoor

1

HM Prison
Springhill

HM Young
Offender Inst
Grendon

22

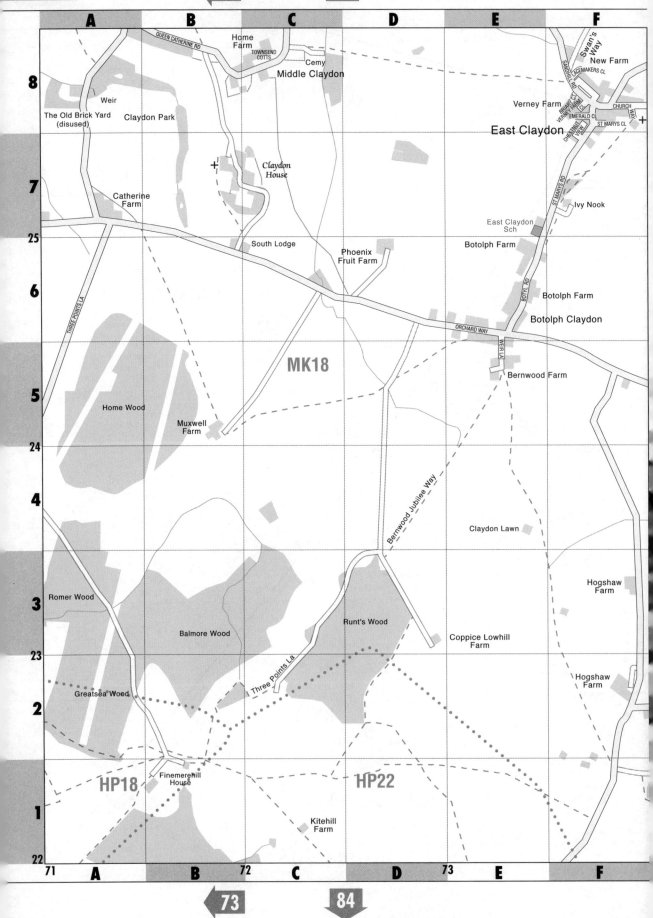

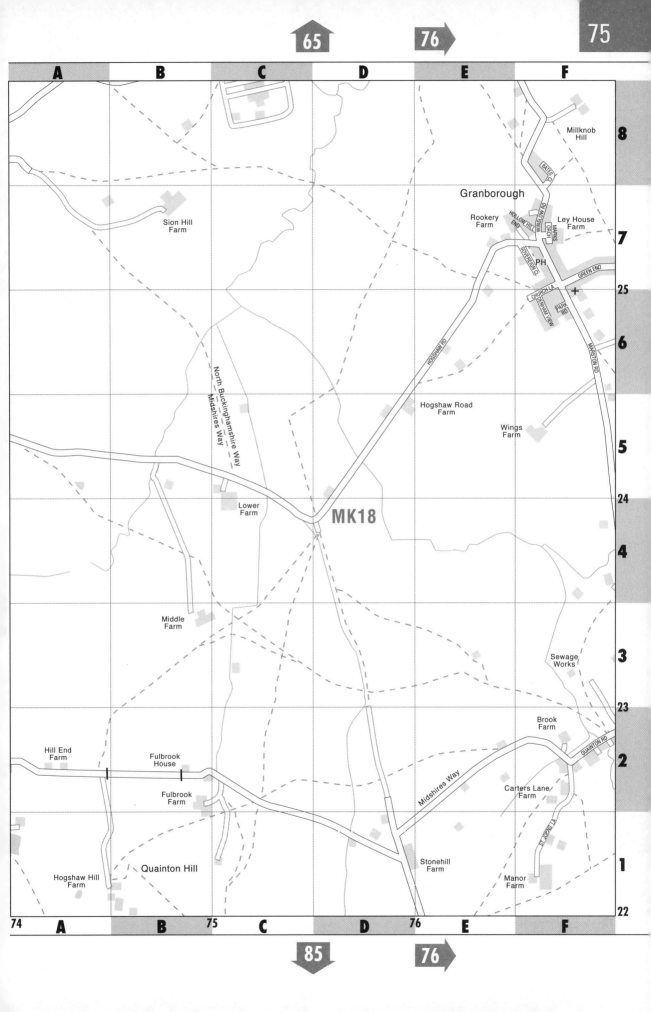

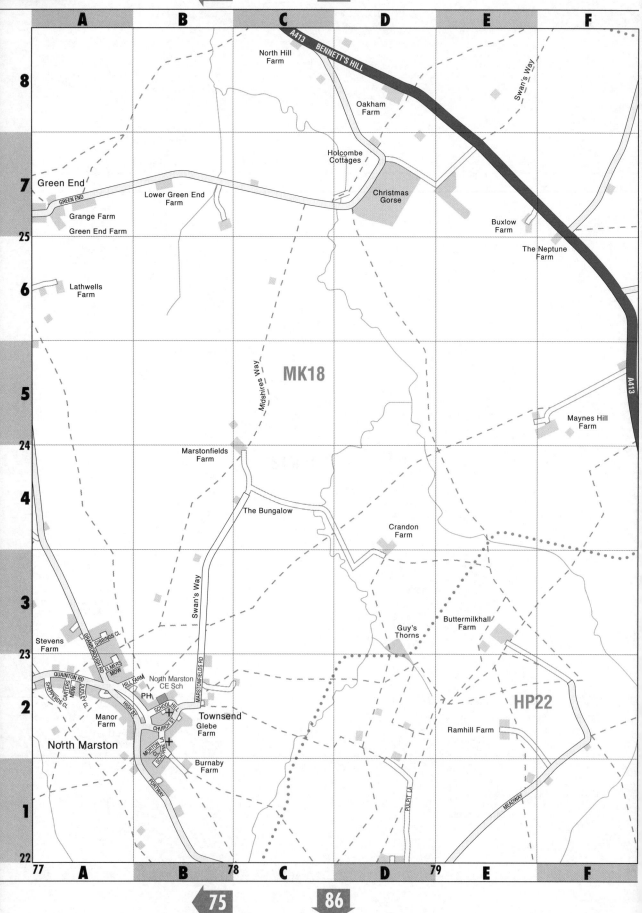

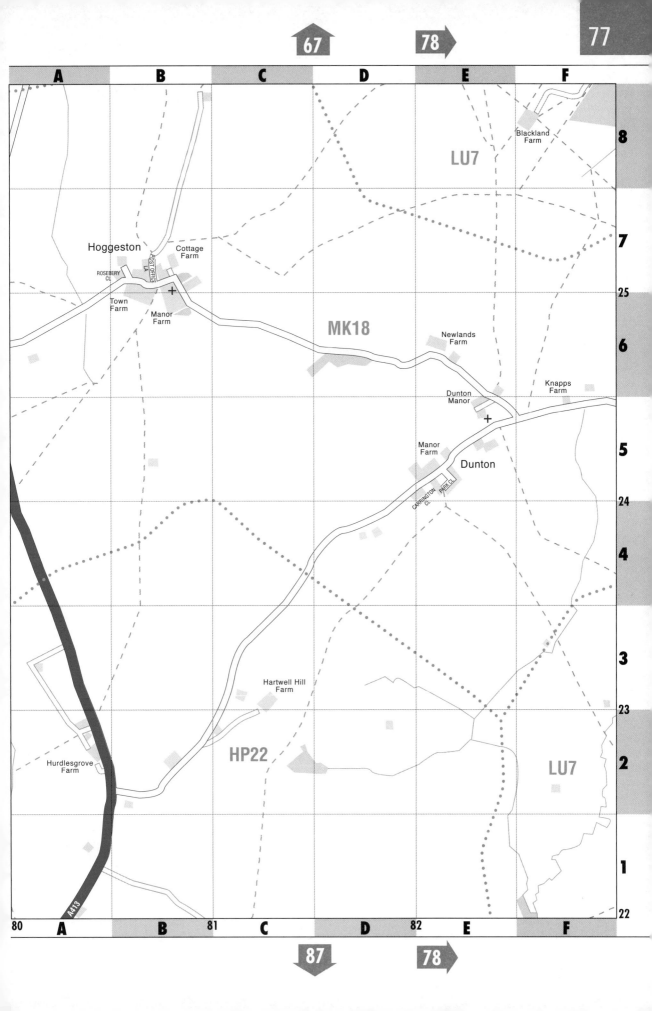

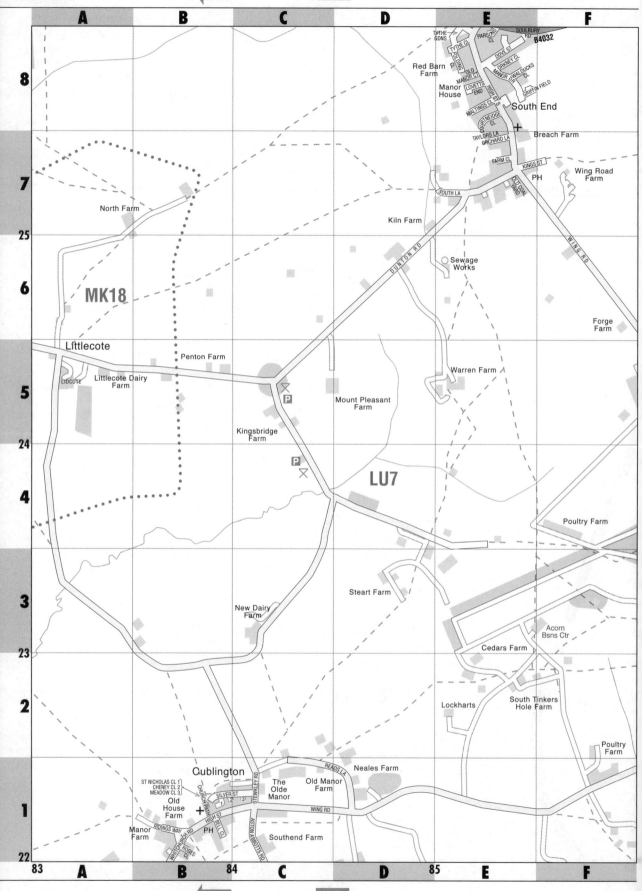

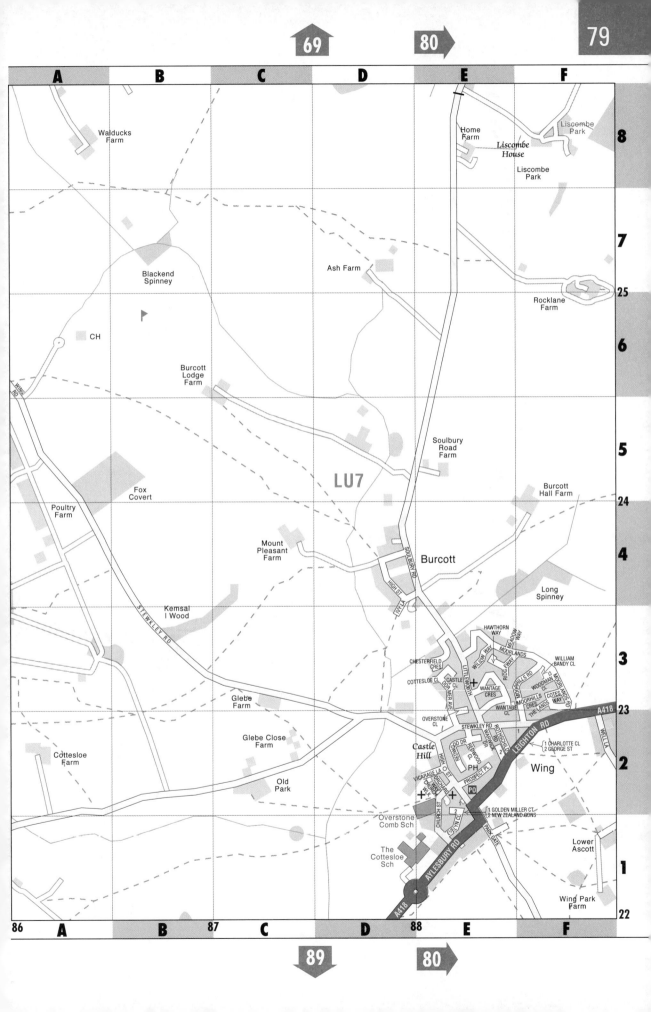

A **B** **C** **D** **E** **F**

8

Walducks Farm

Home Farm

Liscombe House

Liscombe Park

Liscombe Park

7

Blackend Spinney

Ash Farm

25

Rocklane Farm

CH

6

Burcott Lodge Farm

Soulbury Road Farm

5

LU7

Burcott Hall Farm

Fox Covert

Poultry Farm

24

Mount Pleasant Farm

4

Burcott

Long Spinney

Kemsal I Wood

STEWKLEY RD

HIGH ST

SOULBURY RD

HAWTHORN WAY

MEADOW WAY

3

WILLOW WAY

MOORLANDS

CHESTERFIELD CRES

LITTLEWORTH

THE FWAY

MOORHILLS RD

WILLIAM BANDY CL

COTTESLOE CL

CASTLE CL

DORMER AVE

WANTAGE CRES

WOODMAN CL

MOORHILLS CRES

THE LANDS

MOORLANDS RD

COTES WAY

Glebe Farm

WANTAGE CL

OVERSTONE CL

STEWKLEY RD

ROTHSCHILD

A418

23

Glebe Close Farm

LEIGHTON RD

WELL LA

Cottesloe Farm

Castle Hill

OLD DR

CONDUIT

REDWOOD CL

WALLACE

2

PROSPECT PL

1 CHARLOTTE CL
2 GEORGE ST

Wing

Old Park

VICARAGE LA

ORCHARD

CHURCH WK

PH

PO

The Cottesloe Sch

HIGH ST

CHURCH ST

DUFTON CL

PARK GATE

1 GOLDEN MILLER CT
2 NEW ZEALAND GDNS

Overstone Comb Sch

Lower Ascott

1

AYLESBURY RD

A418

Wing Park Farm

22

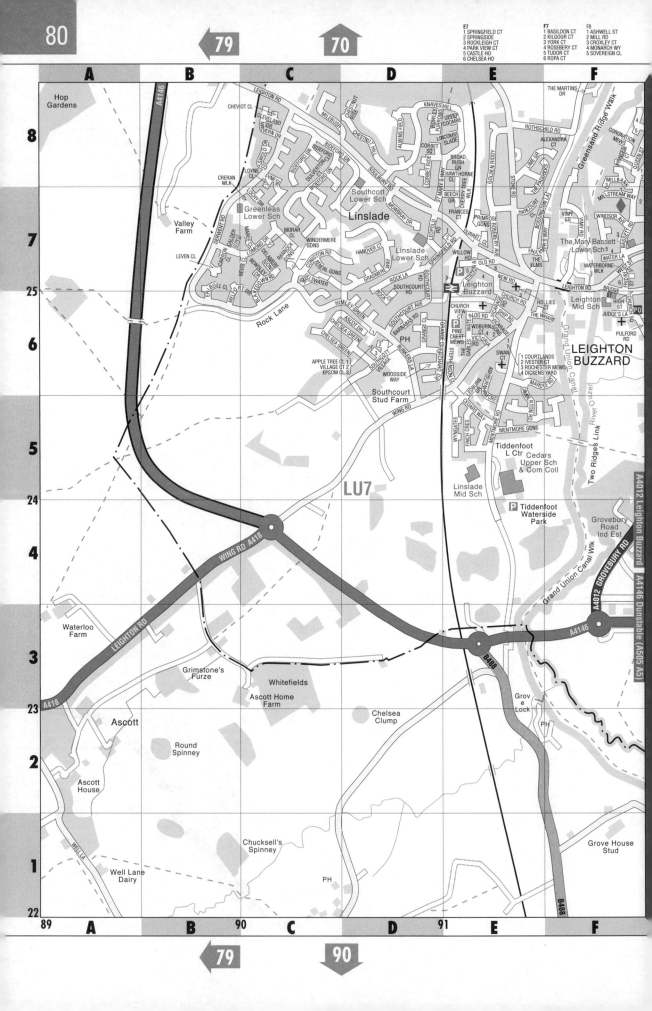

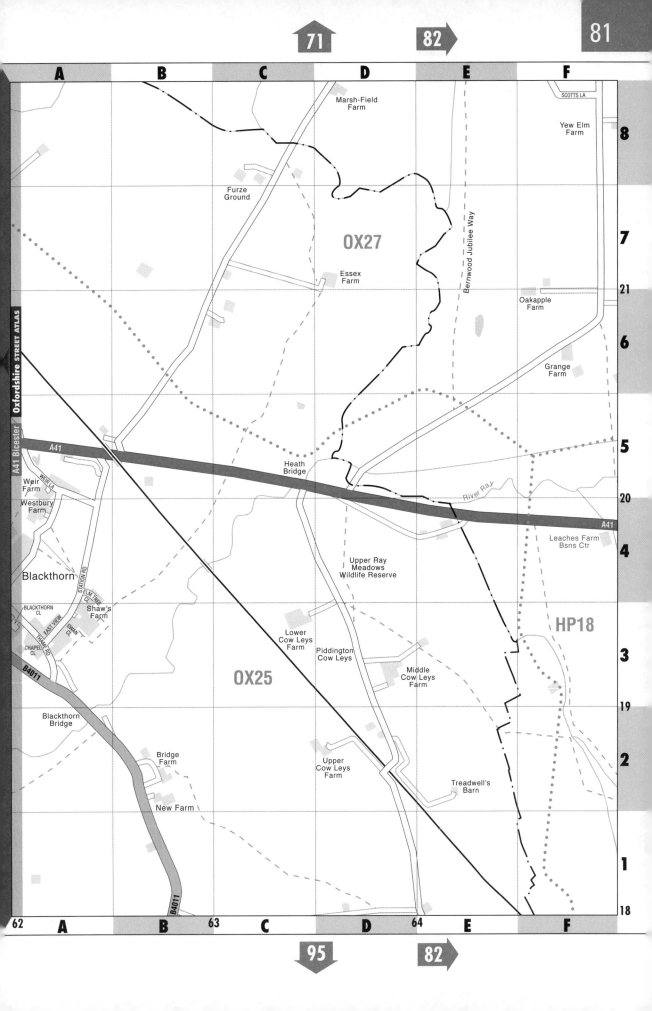

A B C D E F

Marsh-Field Farm

SCOTTS LA

Yew Elm Farm

8

Furze Ground

OX27

7

Bernwood Jubilee Way

Essex Farm

21

Oakapple Farm

6

Grange Farm

A41 Bicester

A41

5

Weir Farm

WEIR LA

Westbury Farm

Heath Bridge

River Ray

A41

20

Leaches Farm Bsns Ctr

4

Blackthorn

STATION RD

ELM TREE CL

Upper Ray Meadows Wildlife Reserve

HP18

BLACKTHORN CL

Shaw's Farm

EAST VIEW CL

SWAN CL

Lower Cow Leys Farm

Piddington Cow Leys

Middle Cow Leys Farm

3

THAME RD

CHAPEL CL

OX25

19

B4011

Blackthorn Bridge

Bridge Farm

Upper Cow Leys Farm

Treadwell's Barn

2

New Farm

1

B4011

18

A B C D E F

8

Yew Elm Farm

MARSH GIBBON RD

PARK RD

SPRINGHILL RD

MON VIEW

Dunmead Farm

Gubbinshole Ditch

Tudor Farm

OX27

HALL CLOSE

7

EDGCOTT RD

21

Manor Farm

MIDSUMMER DR

MILLERS CL

THE BROADWAY

RUMPTONS PADDOCK

MAIN ST

SHAKESPEARE ORCH

SNYE & SELECH

River Ray

6

Shakespeare Farm

Three Points

5

Winding Brook

20

HP18

White House Farm

Tetchwick Brook

A41

4

Cub Pond

Gallow's Bridge

A41

3

Tetchwick Farm

19

Tetchwick

2

New Barn Farm

Sewage Works

1

Tittershall Wood

18

65 A B 66 C D 67 E F

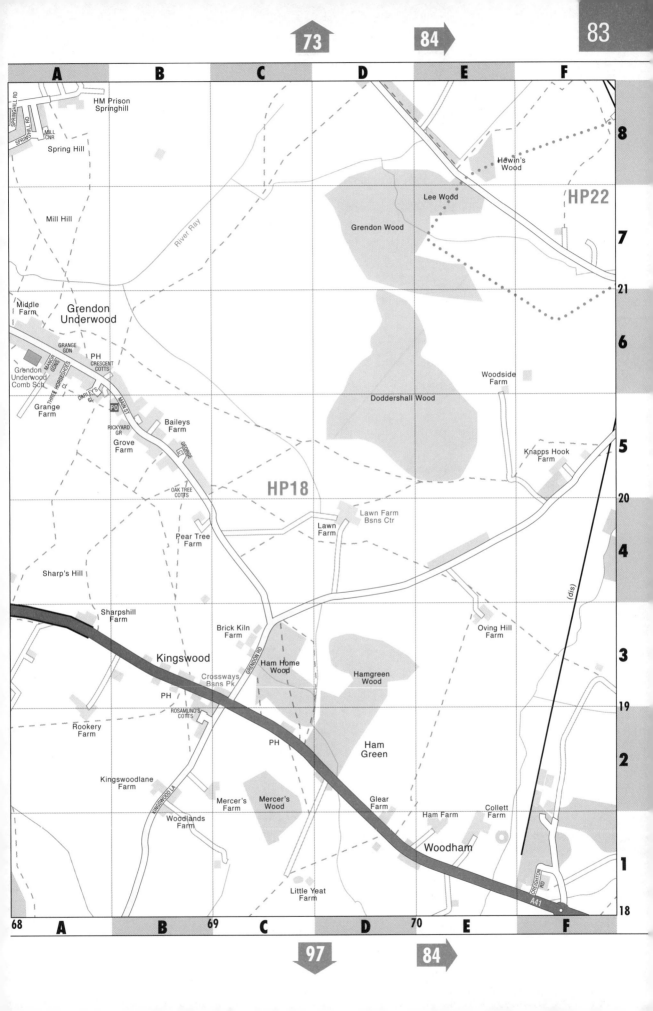

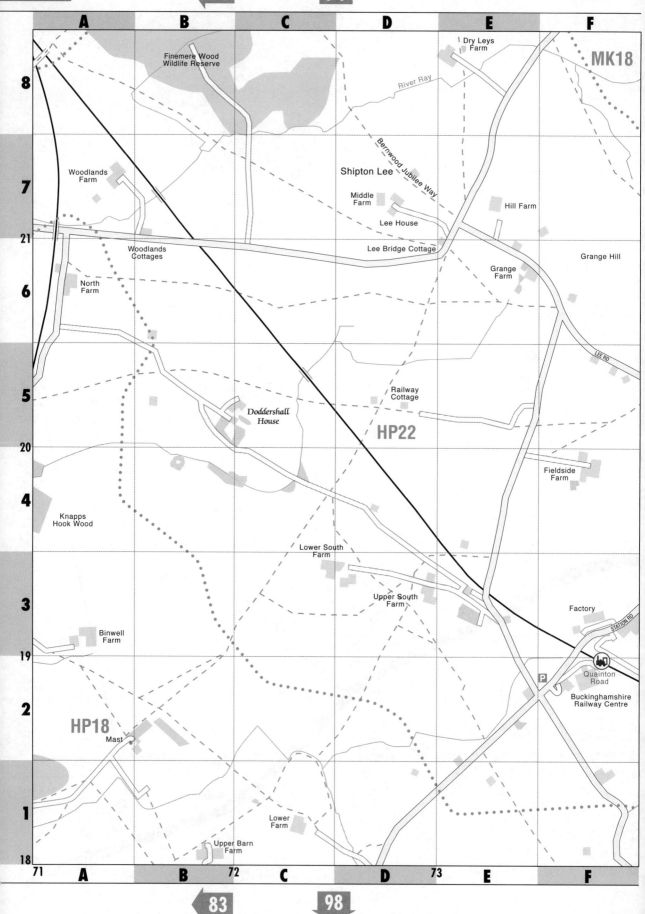

MK18

Finemere Wood
Wildlife Reserve

Dry Leys
Farm

River Ray

Woodlands
Farm

Shipton Lee

Middle
Farm

Hill Farm

Lee House

21

Woodlands
Cottages

Lee Bridge Cottage

Grange Hill

North
Farm

Grange
Farm

LEE RD

Railway
Cottage

Doddershall
House

HP22

20

Fieldside
Farm

Knapps
Hook Wood

Lower South
Farm

Binwell
Farm

Upper South
Farm

Factory

STATION RD

19

P

Quainton
Road

HP18

Buckinghamshire
Railway Centre

Mast

Lower
Farm

Upper Barn
Farm

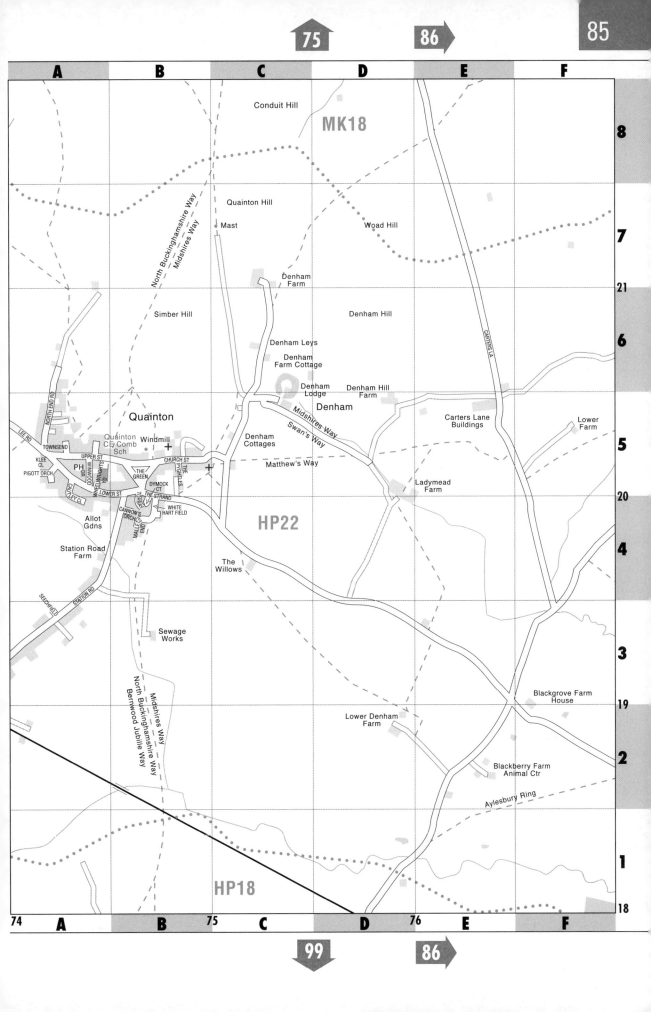

85
76

A **B** **C** **D** **E** **F**

8

MK18

MARSTON HILL

Bushy Farm

Home Farm

Crossroads Farm

Oving

WHITCHURCH LA

A413

7

PH

Church Farm

CHURCH LA

STONE VIEW

THE PIGHTLE

BOWLING ALLEY

PULPIT LA

MEADWAY

Recn Gd

Whitchurch Comb Sch

NORTH MARSTON LA

NEWMANS CL

ASHGROVE GDNS

ASHGROVE GDNS

THE MEADOWS

MANOR RD

DARK LA

Oving House

GREEN ACRES CL

OVING RD

ASHGROVE GDNS

CRABS GR

MT PLEASANT

RICKYARD BE

21

PITCHCOTT RD

Bunshill

MARKET HILL

CASTLE LA

6

Pitchcott Hill

Pitchcott Hill Farm

WEIR LA

Holbornhill Farm

Scotshill Farm

5

Pitchcott

Manor Farm

Dunn Mill

20

HP22

4

3

19

Aylesbury Ring

Folly Farm

2

Upper Blackgrove Farm

Cow Ground Buildings

Middle Blackgrove Farm

Whitesfield Farm

1

18

Whitesfield Farm Cottages

85
100

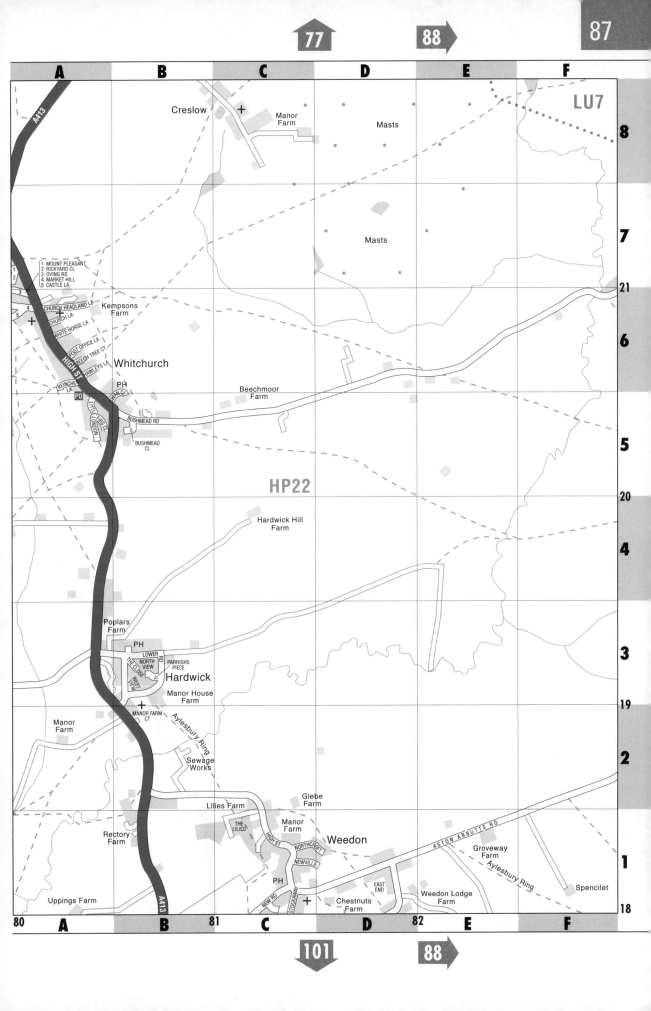

LU7

A B C D E F

8
7
21
6
20
5
4
3
19
2
18

Creslow
Manor Farm
Masts
Masts

1 MOUNT PLEASANT
2 RICKYARD CL
3 OVING RD
4 MARKET HILL
5 CASTLE LA

Kempsons Farm
CHURCH HEADLAND LA
CHURCH LA
WHITE HORSE LA
POST OFFICE LA
BEECH TREE CT
Whitchurch
HAWLEYS LA
HIGH ST
PH
KEINCHES LA
SWAN C
PO
LITTLE LONDON
BUSHMEAD RD
Beechmoor Farm
BUSHMEAD CL

HP22

Hardwick Hill Farm

Poplars Farm
PH
LOWER NORTH RD
THE CLOSE
WEST VIEW
NORTH VIEW
PARRISHS PIECE
Hardwick
Manor House Farm
MANOR FARM CT
Aylesbury Ring

Manor Farm

Sewage Works

Glebe Farm
Lilies Farm
THE LILIES
HIGH ST
Manor Farm
NORTHCROFT
NEWVILLA
Weedon
ASTON ABBOTTS RD
Groveway Farm
Aylesbury Ring
Spencilet

Rectory Farm
PH
NEW RD
STOCKAWAY
EAST END
Chestnuts Farm
Weedon Lodge Farm

Uppings Farm

A413

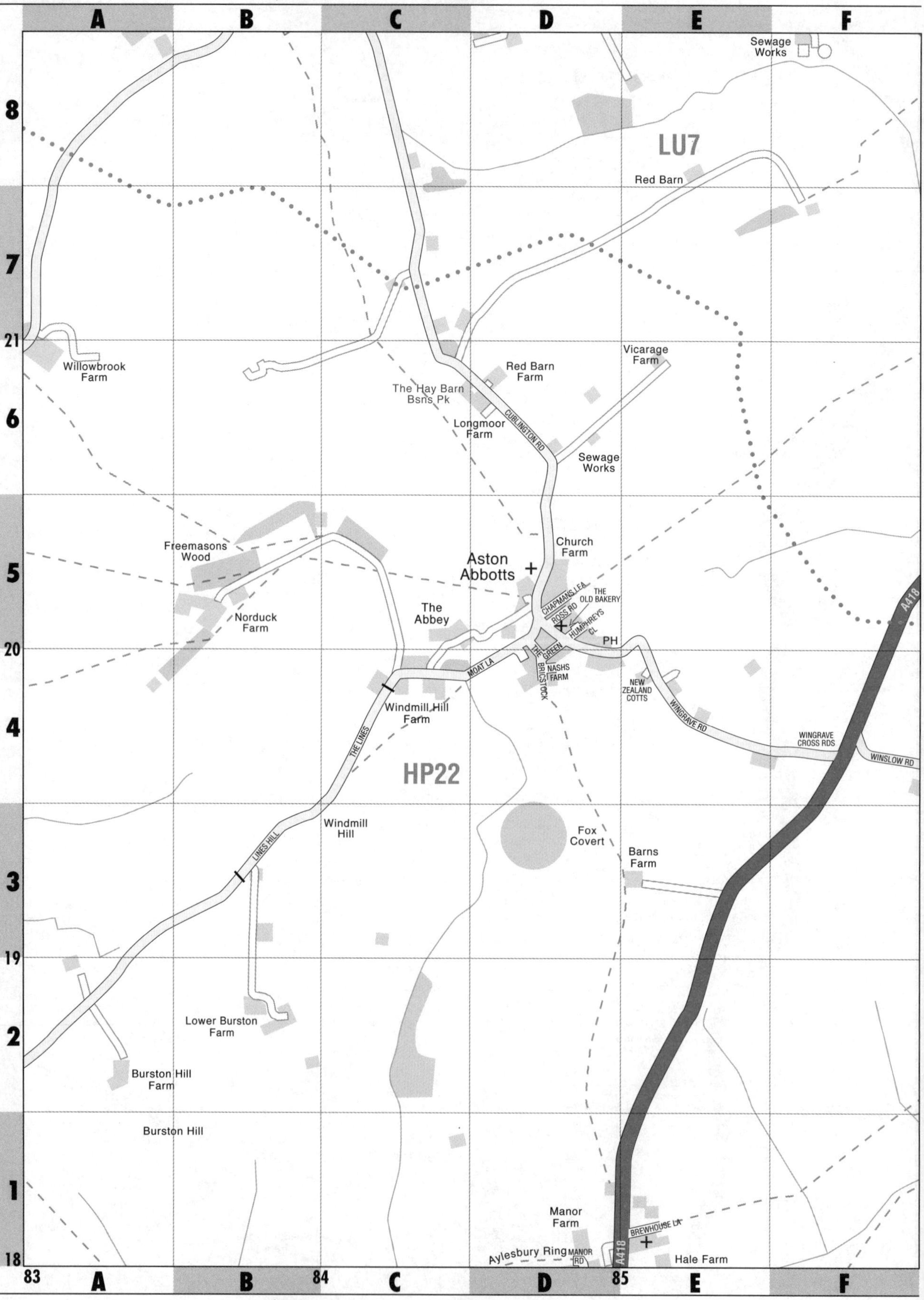

← 87
78

	A	B	C	D	E	F

Sewage Works

LU7

Red Barn

8

7

21

Willowbrook Farm

Vicarage Farm

Red Barn Farm

The Hay Barn Bsns Pk

6

Longmoor Farm

CURLINGTON RD

Sewage Works

Freemasons Wood

Church Farm

5

Aston Abbotts

Norduck Farm

CHAPMANS LEA

THE OLD BAKERY

The Abbey

ROSS RD

HUMPHREYS CL

PH

20

THE GREEN

NASHS FARM

THE BRICSTOCK

MOAT LA

NEW ZEALAND COTTS

WINGRAVE RD

WINGRAVE CROSS RDS

WINSLOW RD

A418

Windmill Hill Farm

4

THE LINES

HP22

Fox Covert

Barns Farm

Windmill Hill

LINES HILL

3

19

Lower Burston Farm

2

Burston Hill Farm

Burston Hill

1

Manor Farm

BREWHOUSE LA

18

Aylesbury Ring

MANOR RD

A418

Hale Farm

← 87
102 ↓

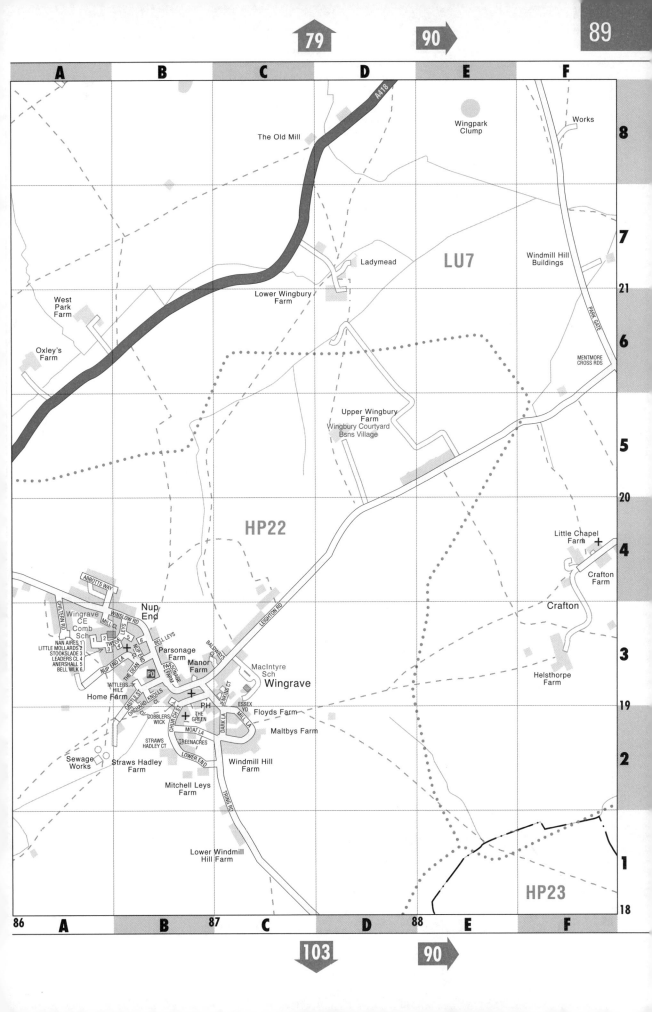

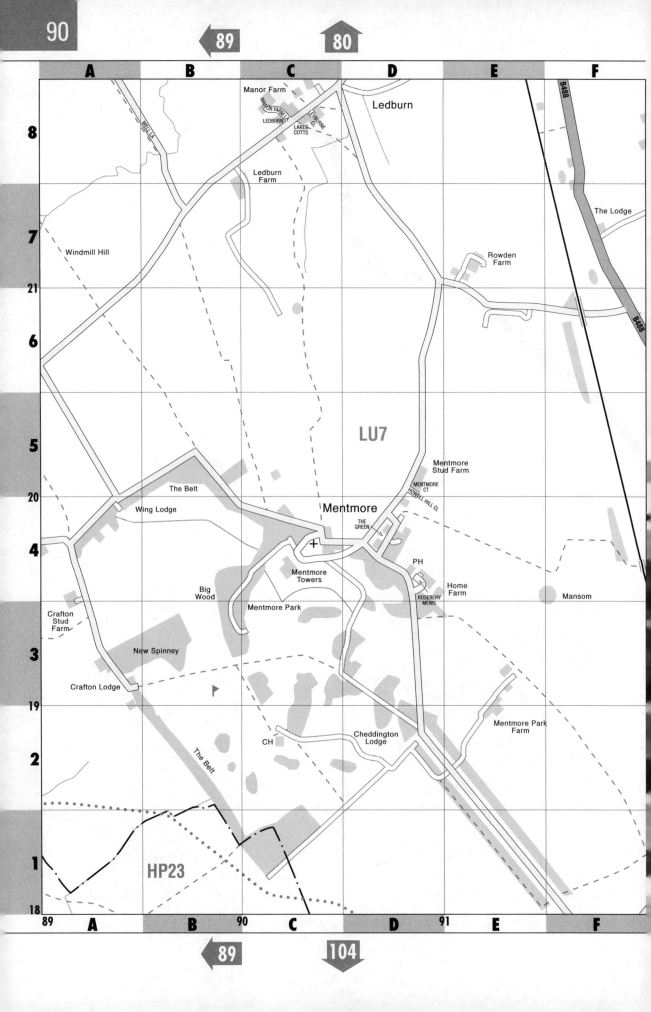

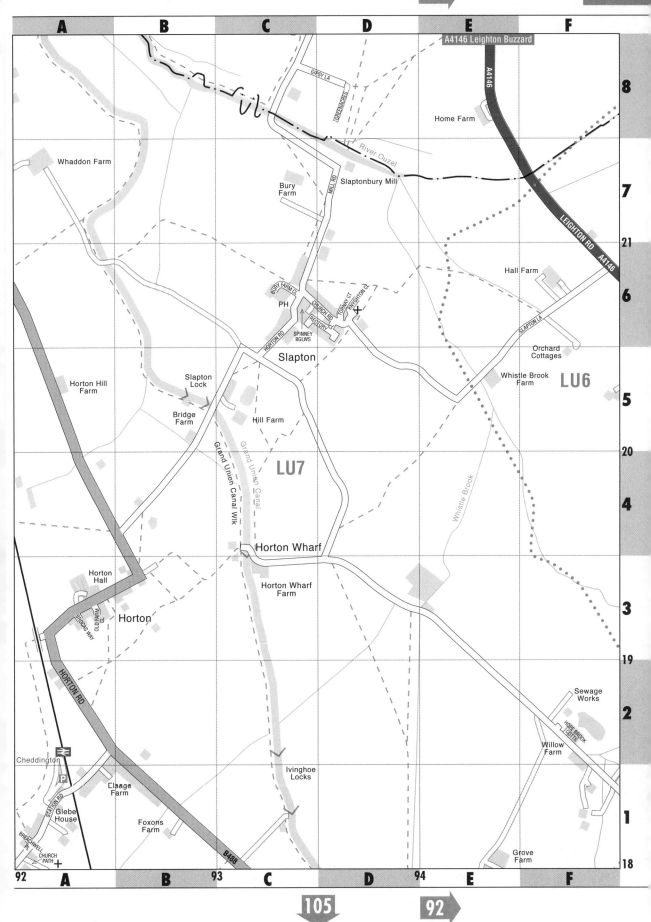

A4146 Leighton Buzzard

A
B
C
D
E
F

8
7
21
6
5
20
4
3
19
2
1
18

GIRSY LA

GREENACRES

Home Farm

River Ouzel

A4146

Whaddon Farm

Bury Farm

MILL RD

Slaptonbury Mill

LEIGHTON RD   A4146

Hall Farm

BURY FARM CL

PH

CHURCH RD

TORNAY CT

KNYGHTON CL

RECTORY

SPINNEY BGLWS

HORTON RD

Slapton

SLAPTON LA

Orchard Cottages

Whistle Brook Farm

LU6

Horton Hill Farm

Slapton Lock

Bridge Farm

Hill Farm

Grand Union Canal Wlk

Grand Union Canal

LU7

Whistle Brook

Horton Wharf

Horton Hall

Horton

BRIGGAS WAY

OLD FARM CL

Horton Wharf Farm

Sewage Works

HODB BROOK COTTS

Willow Farm

HORTON RD

Cheddington

P

STATION RD

Clsage Farm

Glebe House

BREACHWELL PL

CHURCH PATH

Foxons Farm

B488

Ivinghoe Locks

Grove Farm

91

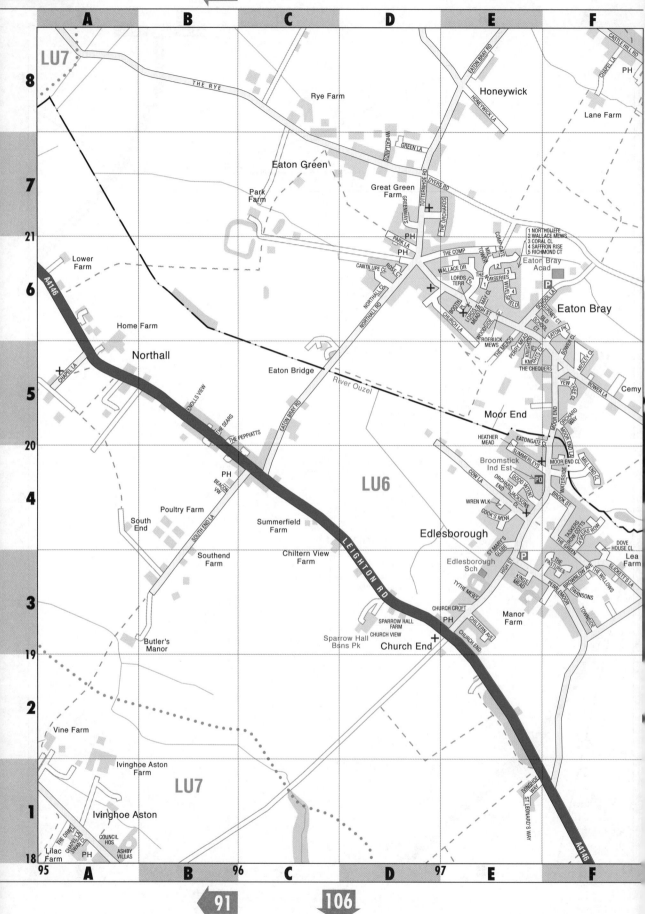

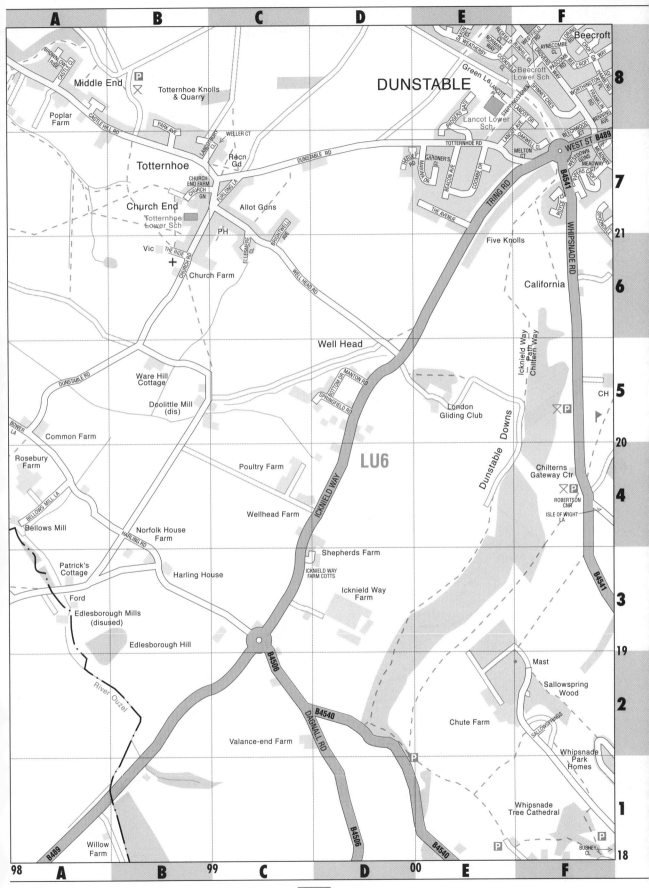

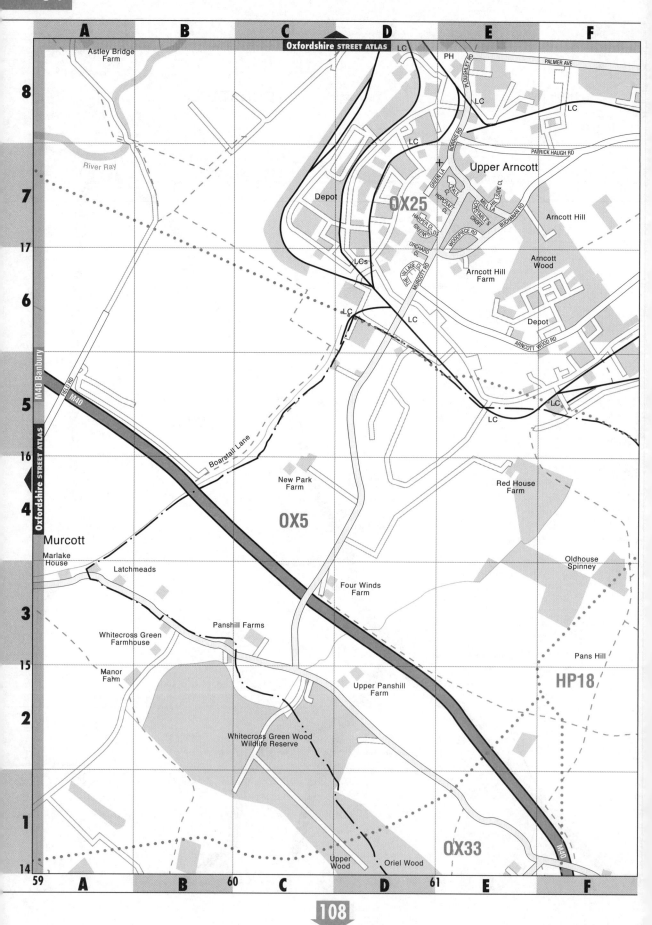

LC
PH
PALMER AVE
PLOUGHLEY RD
LC
LC
PATRICK HAUGH RD
Upper Arncott
Depot
OX25
NORRIS RD
GREEN LA
TEALE CL
HOPCRAFT CL
CONSTABLE'S CROFT
MILL HILLSIDE CL
BUCHANAN RD
Arncott Hill
HARPER CL
GREENFIELDS
WOODPIECE RD
Arncott Wood
LCs
ORCHARD CL
THE VILLAGE
MURCOTT RD
Arncott Hill Farm
Depot
LC
LC
ARNCOTT WOOD RD
LC
LC
LC

River Ray

Astley Bridge Farm

M40 Banbury
M40
FIELD RD

Boarstall Lane

New Park Farm

Red House Farm

OX5

Oldhouse Spinney

Murcott
Marlake House
Latchmeads
Four Winds Farm

Whitecross Green Farmhouse
Panshill Farms

Pans Hill

Manor Farm

HP18

Upper Panshill Farm

Whitecross Green Wood Wildlife Reserve

M40

Upper Wood
Oriel Wood
OX33

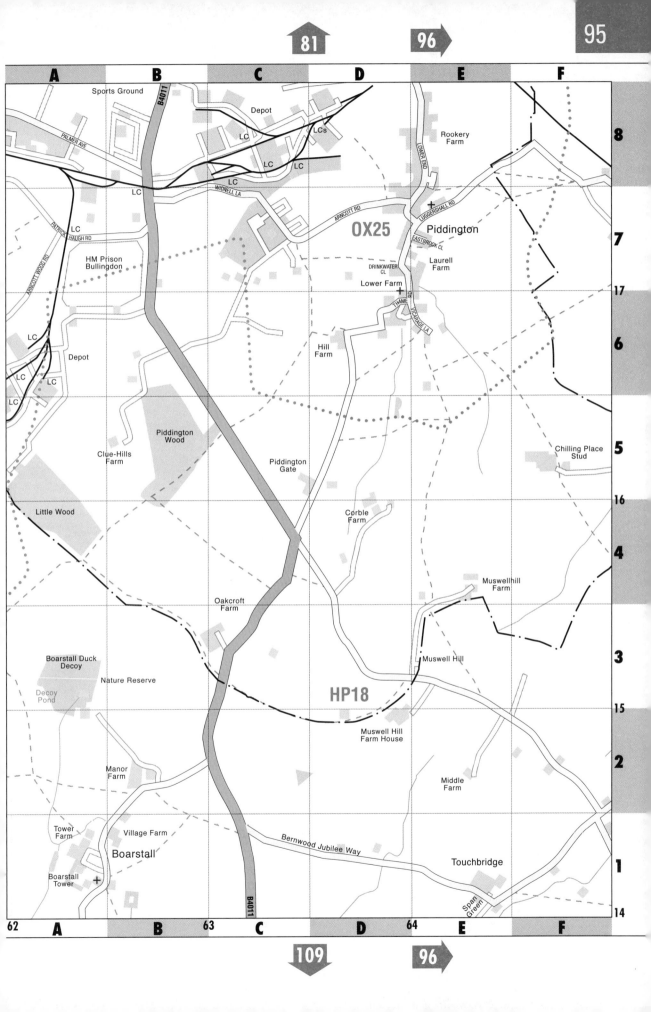

A   B   C   D   E   F

8

Sports Ground

B4011

PALMER AVE

Depot

LC

LCs

LC

LC

LC

Rookery
Farm

LOWER END

LUGGERSHALL RD

+

Piddington

7

PATRICK HAUGH RD

ARNCOTT WOOD RD

LC

HM Prison
Bullingdon

WIDNELL LA

ARNCOTT RD

OX25

EASTBROOK CL

DRINKWATER
CL

Laurell
Farm

17

LC

Depot

LC

LC

LC

Lower Farm

+

THAME RD

VICARAGE LA

6

Hill
Farm

Piddington
Wood

Clue-Hills
Farm

Piddington
Gate

Chilling Place
Stud

5

16

Little Wood

Corble
Farm

4

Oakcroft
Farm

Muswellhill
Farm

Boarstall Duck
Decoy

Nature Reserve

Decoy
Pond

Muswell Hill

3

HP18

Muswell Hill
Farm House

15

Manor
Farm

Middle
Farm

2

Tower
Farm

Village Farm

Bernwood Jubilee Way

Boarstall

Touchbridge

1

Boarstall
Tower

+

Span
Green

14

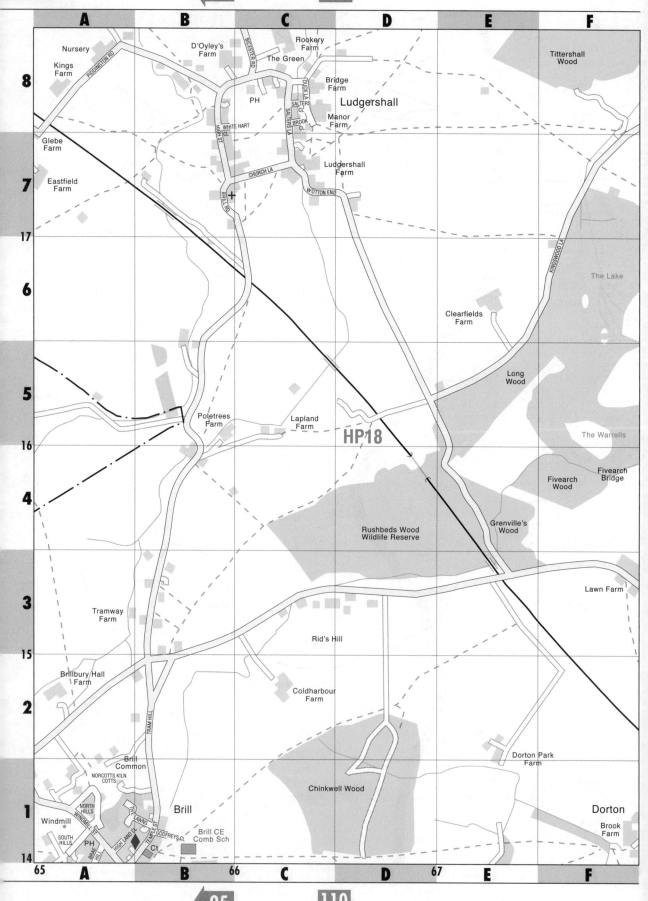

A   B   C   D   E   F

8 Nursery
   Kings Farm
   D'Oyley's Farm
   Rookery Farm
   The Green
   Bridge Farm
   Ludgershall
   Tittershall Wood
   PH
   PIDDINGTON RD
   BICESTER RD
   DUCK LA
   SALTERS CL
   Manor Farm

7 Glebe Farm
   Eastfield Farm
   WHITE HART CL
   HIGH ST
   SALTERS LA
   BROOK CL
   Ludgershall Farm
   CHURCH LA
   BRILL RD
   WOTTON END

17

6 The Lake
   KINGSWOOD LA
   Clearfields Farm

5 Poletrees Farm
   Lapland Farm
   Long Wood
   HP18
   The Warrells

16 Fivearch Bridge
   Fivearch Wood

4 Rushbeds Wood Wildlife Reserve
   Grenville's Wood

3 Tramway Farm
   Rid's Hill
   Lawn Farm

15 Brillbury Hall Farm
   Coldharbour Farm

2 TRAM HILL
   Brill Common
   NORCOTTS KILN COTTS
   Dorton Park Farm

1 Windmill
   NORTH HILLS
   WINDMILL ST
   THE LAWNS
   TEMPLE ST
   GODFREYS CL
   Brill
   Brill CE Comb Sch
   Chinkwell Wood
   Dorton
   Brook Farm
   SOUTH HILLS
   PH
   BRAE HILL
   HIGH LAND CL
   Ct

14
   65   66   67
   A   B   C   D   E   F

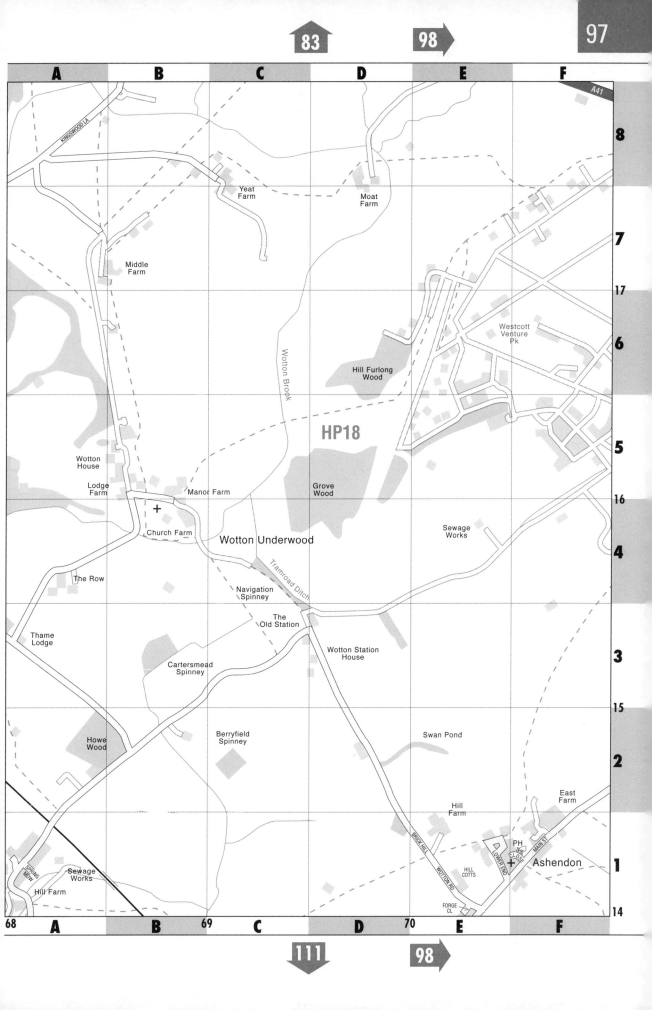

83
98

A   B   C   D   E   F

A41

8

7

17

6

5

16

4

15

3

2

1

14

Kingswood La

Yeat Farm

Moat Farm

Middle Farm

Wotton Brook

Westcott Venture Pk

Hill Furlong Wood

HP18

Wotton House

Lodge Farm

Manor Farm

Grove Wood

Church Farm

Wotton Underwood

Sewage Works

The Row

Tramroad Ditch

Navigation Spinney

The Old Station

Thame Lodge

Wotton Station House

Cartersmead Spinney

Berryfield Spinney

Howe Wood

Swan Pond

East Farm

Hill Farm

PH

THE CLOSE

MAIN ST

Brick Hill

Wotton Rd

Lower End

Hill Cotts

Ashendon

Spring Mdw

Sewage Works

Hill Farm

Forge Cl

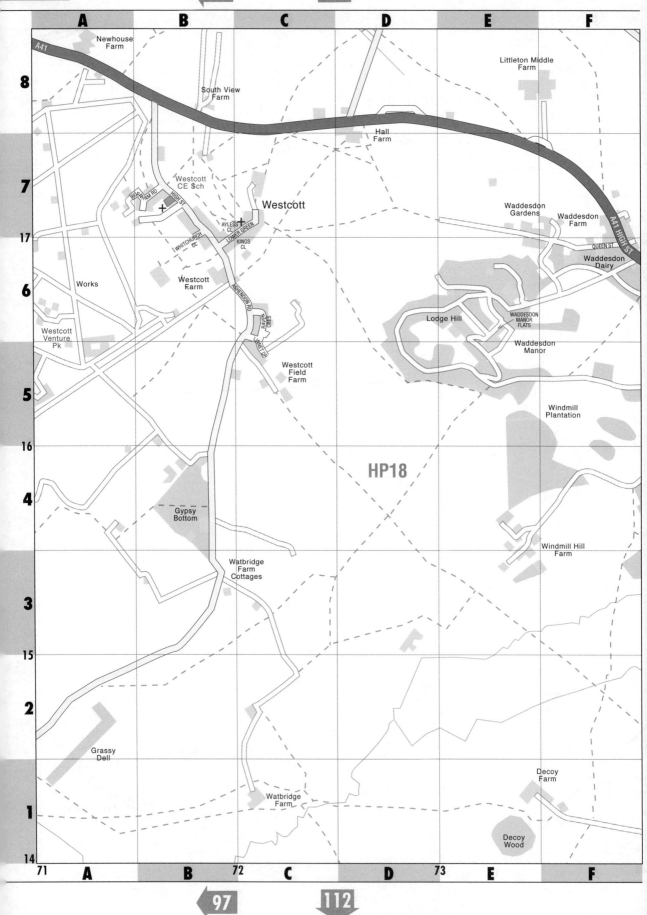

A B C D E F

8

7

17

6

5

16

4

3

15

2

1

14

Newhouse Farm

A41

South View Farm

Littleton Middle Farm

Hall Farm

Westcott CE Sch

BUCKINGHAM RD

HIGH ST

WHITCHURCH CL

AYLES CL
LOWER GREEN
KINGS CL

Westcott

Waddesdon Gardens

Waddesdon Farm

QUEEN ST

A41 HIGH ST

Waddesdon Dairy

Works

Westcott Farm

ASHENDON RD

RAINS CRES

JANET DR

Lodge Hill

WADDESDON MANOR FLATS

Waddesdon Manor

Westcott Venture Pk

Westcott Field Farm

Windmill Plantation

HP18

Gypsy Bottom

Windmill Hill Farm

Watbridge Farm Cottages

Grassy Dell

Decoy Farm

Watbridge Farm

Decoy Wood

71 A B 72 C D 73 E F

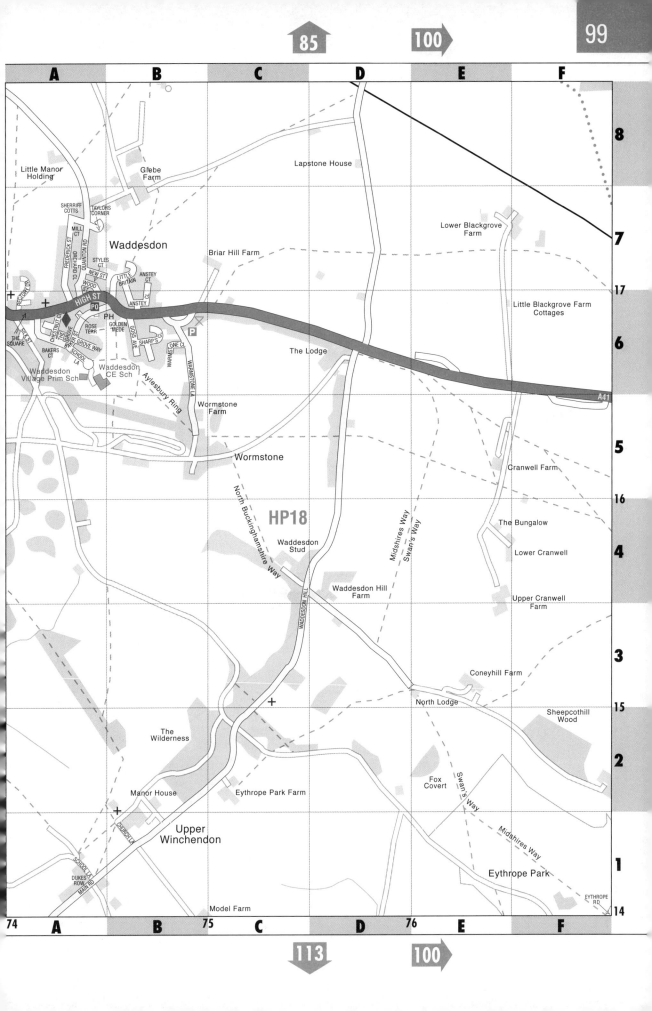

A B C D E F

8

Little Manor
Holding

Glebe
Farm

Lapstone House

Lower Blackgrove
Farm

7

SHERRIFF
COTTS
TAYLORS
CORNER
MILL
CT
FREDERICK ST
ORD QUAINTON RD
STYLES
CT
NEW ST
WOOD
ST
LITTLE
BRITAIN
ANSTEY
CT

Waddesdon

Briar Hill Farm

17

Little Blackgrove Farm
Cottages

RECTORY RD
HIGH ST
PO
PH
ROSE
TERR
ANSTEY
THE GROVE
GOLDEN
MEDE
GOSS AVE
SHARP'S
CT
GROVE WAY
THE
SQUARE
SILK ST
CHESTNUT CT
BAKERS
CT
PARKER ST
SCHOOL
LA
GROVE WAY
WARMSTONE CL
P

The Lodge

A41

6

Waddesdon
Village Prim Sch

Waddesdon
CE Sch

Aylesbury Ring

WARMSTONE LA

Wormstone
Farm

Cranwell Farm

5

Wormstone

North Buckinghamshire Way

HP18

16

Waddesdon
Stud

Midshires Way

Swan's Way

The Bungalow

Lower Cranwell

4

WADDESDON HILL

Waddesdon Hill
Farm

Upper Cranwell
Farm

Coneyhill Farm

3

The
Wilderness

North Lodge

Sheepcothill
Wood

15

Manor House

Eythrope Park Farm

Fox
Covert

Swan's Way

2

Upper
Winchendon

Midshires Way

SCHOOL LA
DUKES
ROW
MAIT RD
CHURCH LA

Eythrope Park

1

Model Farm

EYTHROPE
RD

14

← 99   ⬆ 86

A   B   C   D   E   F

8

HP22

Lower Farm

Lower Fleetmarston Farm

7

17

6

Fleet Marston Cottages

A41

Fleet Marston Farm
Hunters Farm
Ind Est

Berryfields Farm

5

Berryfield

Fleet Marston

16

HP18

+

MORELLO CL 1
LAMBERT RD 2
COLNEY RD 3
BENTON MEWS 4
LITTLE GROUND 5
OXYARD 6
THE WARREN 7
PONDECROFT 8
BROKEND 9
BANKS YARD 10
COW GROUND 11
GEORGE HAMMOND LA 12

ASHMEAD ST
BRAEBURN RD
LIMELIGHT AVE
MONAR

NEWTON AVE
GRIEVSON RD
BRAMLEY RD

NORTHCLIFFE WY 1
BEELEY ST 2
FREYBERG DR 3

PIXIE RD
DOMINO WY

10 WINSTON MEWS
11 GILLIFLOWER ST
12 DERBY PL
13 DISCOVERY ST
14 FIESTA END
15 BREEDON DR
16 GALA RD
17 FORTUNE ST
18 KESWICK ST

REDCURRANT AVE

ELDERBERRY RD
MORGAN DR

MENDIP ST
MERTON CL

PIPPIN RD
AMBER CL

SIDDINGTON DR
PRIMA DR
ARCH GR
CALVILLE GDNS

HOWGATE ST

Berryfields CE Prim Sch

MARTIN DALBY WY

1 POMEROY CT
2 AVERDAL DR
3 AURALIA CL
4 AMOROSA GDNS
5 ALDERMAN DR
6 PERRINE CL
7 ELIZE CL
8 CARDINAL DR
9 ELMORE ST

NOBLE CRES
WYATT WY

HEYFORD LA
JOHN FITZJOHN AVE

OX GROUND

PARADISE ORCHARD
OXPEN

NICHOLAS CHARLES CRES

Aylesbury Vale Acad

4

WESTERN LINK RD
MOORCROFT LA
SIERRA RD

1 CRAWFORD RD
2 OLDFIELD ST
3 BRANDY ST
4 SPARTLET MEWS
5 LAWSON WY
6 THORNLEY CL
7 BARLAND WY

Putlowes Cottages

PUTLOWES DR

SIR HENRY LEE CRES

P&R

Billingsfield Cottages

SIR HENRY LEE CRES

1 OPAL MEWS
2 EXCALIBUR RD

READING RD 1
NAPPIN CL 2
ROBINSON CL 3

HAYWOOD WAY
LANCER RD
GRIMMER CL
FLETCHER CL
DICKS WAY
BELGRAVE RD

3

Aylesbury Vale Parkway

VALOR DR
AVALON ST
PERSIMORE WY

GAINSBOROUGH PL

BICESTER RD

EELES RD
JACKSON RD
ADKINS CL

Fleet Marston Spinney

Putlowes

15

Haydon Hill

A41

BADRICK RD

2

River Thame

Sewage Works

MULLINS WAY 1
CONSTABLE PL 2

REMBRANDT END
MONET
HIGH RD
LOWTHER WY
PICASSO RD
DICKENS WAY
DRAKE WY
HANES CL
SCOTT SMITH

MEREDITH DR
BARRIE CL
AUSTEN PL
PRIORY RD

BURNS
SEWELL SILVER
ELIOT WY
BRONTE CL
DEFOE CL

HP19

Bear Brook

Sheepcote Hill Farm

RABANS CL
RABANS LA
COMPTON RD

Rabans Lane Ind Est

EDISON RD
BESSEMER CRES

BRUNEL RD
TELFORD GATE
SMEATON CL

Bell Bsns Pk

1

Eythrope

EYTHROPE RD

CHELSEA RD

Haydon Mill Farm

HUDSON MS
GROSVENOR WY
NAPIER RD

ARNCOTT WAY
BRAMMERS WAY
FIRCREST
COOMBE CL

14

← 99   ⬇ 114

F1
1 SPRUCE RD
2 HIGHGATE MEWS
3 KENSINGTON PATH
4 CRAFTON PL
5 PINE ST
6 COLDHARBOUR WAY
7 HAMPSTEAD CL
8 PADDOCK CL
9 CAVENDISH WY

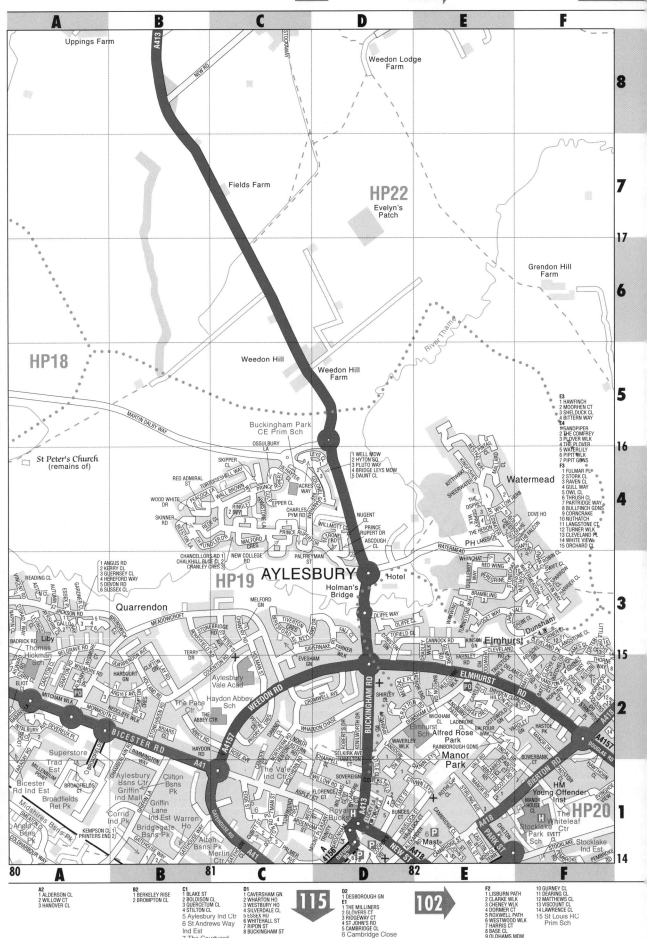

101
88

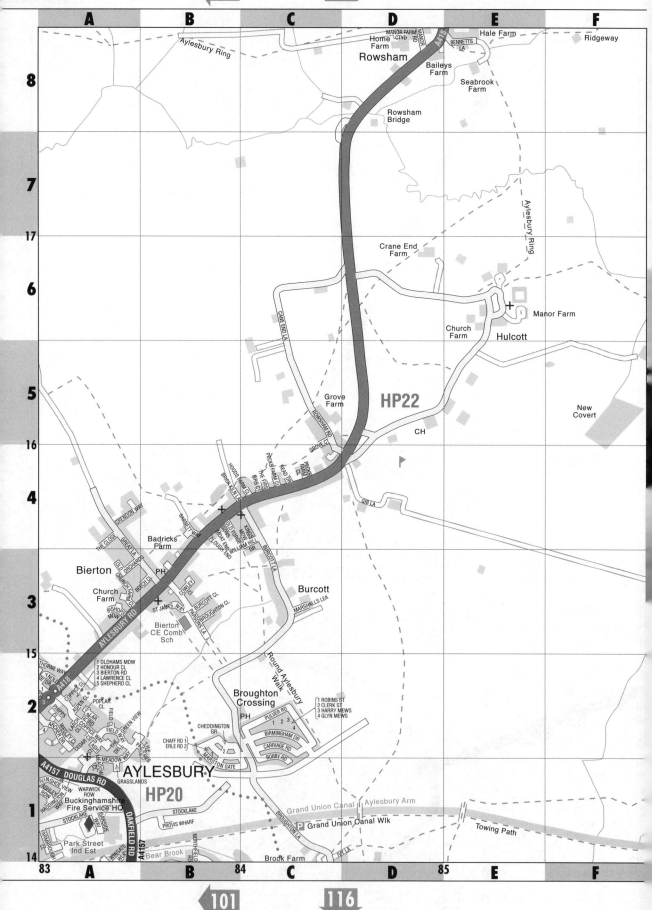

101
116

A | B | C | D | E | F

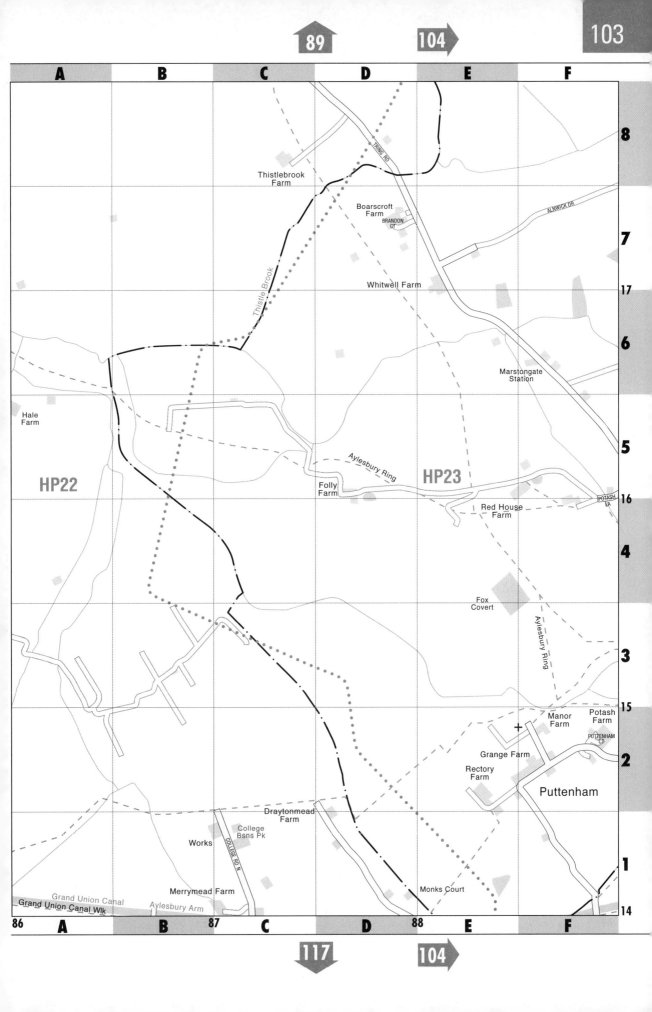

8

Thistlebrook
Farm

Boarscroft
Farm
BRANDON
CT

ALNWICK DR

7

Whitwell Farm

17

Thistle Brook

6

Marstongate
Station

Hale
Farm

HP22

5

Aylesbury Ring

Folly
Farm

HP23

Red House
Farm

POTASH
LA

16

Fox
Covert

Aylesbury Ring

4

Manor
Farm

Potash
Farm

15

Grange Farm

PUTTENHAM
CT

2

Rectory
Farm

Puttenham

Draytonmead
Farm

College
Bsns Pk

Works

COLLEGE RD N

1

Grand Union Canal

Grand Union Canal Wlk

Merrymead Farm

Aylesbury Arm

Monks Court

14

← 103
90

A **B** **C** **D** **E** **F**

8

Broadmead Farm

Cheddington

BLENHEIM CL

STATION RD

MENTMORE RD

CHURCH HILL

Alnwick Farm

ALNWICK DR

LU7

PARTRIDGE CL

Manor House

WEST END RD

BARWAM CL

MANOR RD

NEW ST

7

West End Farm

THE BAULK

BERRYFIELD

SUNNY BANK

GOOSE ACRE

HILL SIDE

Betlow Farm

17

Westend Hill

Mast

6

Old Airfield Ind Est

Southend Hill

CHEDDINGTON LA

LONG MARSTON RD

5

Long Leys Farm

POTASH LA

16

Old Toms Farm

Central Farm

BROMLEY

CHURCH VIEW

STATION RD

4

PH

HP23

1 RAVENS CT
2 THE OLD FORGE

CHAPEL LA

MARSTON

Long Marston CE Prim Sch

Old Church Farm

2
1

Long Marston

Great Farm

TRING RD

Church Farm

Sewage Works

CHURCH FARM LA

3

Astrope

ASTROPE LA

Millfield

LENDON GR

LUKES LA

Gubblecote

Lower End

15

GREGORYS FIELD

Astrope Farm

Gubblecote Farm

Moat Farm

Grand Union Canal

VICARAGE RD

PH

2

Dover Castle

College Farm

Gurney's Farm

CHURCH LA

AYLESBURY RING

DIXON'S WHARF

WINGRAVE RD

Locks

Dixon's Gap Bridge

WATERY LA

MARSWORTH WHARF

Aylesbury Arm

Locks

1

Grand Union Canal

Grand Union Canal Wlk

Wilstone Bridge

Locks

Wilstone

Startop's End

PH

TRING RD

GRANGE RD

SANDBROOK LA

THE WICK

ROSEBARN LA

PH

Startop Farm

LOWER ICKNIELD WAY

B489

P

14

89 **A** **B** 90 **C** **D** 91 **E** **F**

← 103
118

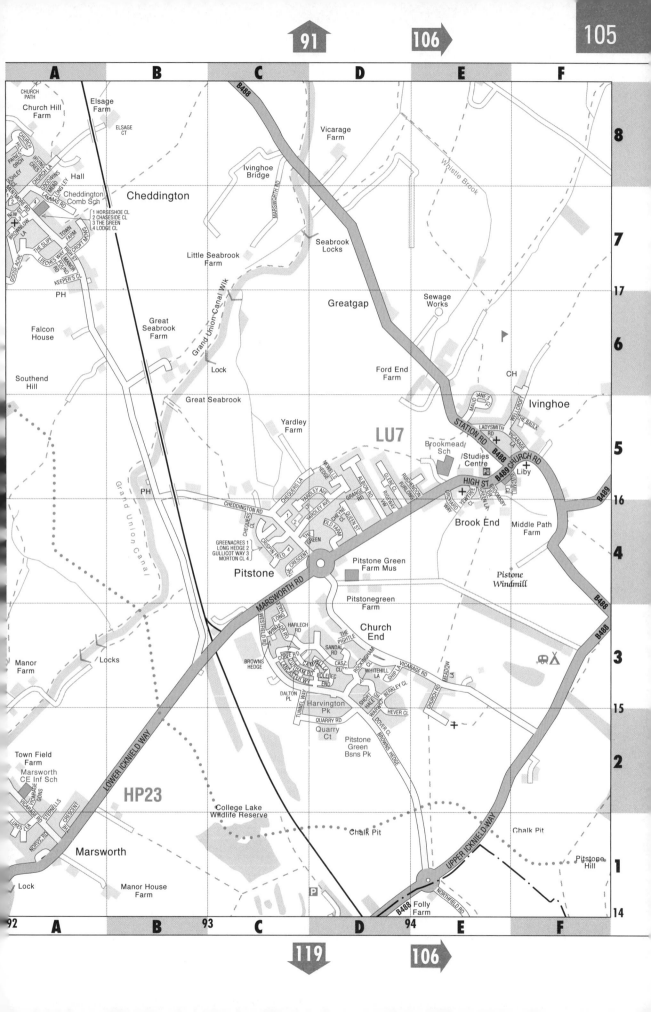

A B C D E F

8

7

17

6

5

16

4

15

2

1

14

CHURCH PATH
Church Hill Farm
Elsage Farm
ELSAGE CT

Vicarage Farm

Whistle Brook

Ivinghoe Bridge

Hall
Cheddington Comb Sch
1 HORSESHOE CL
2 CHASESIDE CL
3 THE GREEN
4 LODGE CL

Cheddington

B488

MARSWORTH RD

Seabrook Locks

Little Seabrook Farm

Greatgap

Sewage Works

PH

Falcon House

Great Seabrook Farm

Grand Union Canal Wlk

Lock

CH

Ivinghoe

Southend Hill

Great Seabrook

Yardley Farm

Ford End Farm

STATION RD
MAUD JANE'S
LADYSMITH RD
JANE S
NICARAGE LA
WELLCROFT
THE BAULK

LU7

Brookmead Sch
Studies Centre

PH

Grand Union Canal

CHEDDINGTON RD

CHEQUERS LA
NEW WELLS HEDGE
YARDLEY AVE
YARDLEY AVE
ALBION RD
RIDGEWAY
GLEBE CL
RUSHENDON FURLONG
HIGH ST
B489
CHURCH RD
B489
Liby
PO

CHEQUERS CL

GREENACRES 1
LONG HEDGE 2
GULLICOT WAY 3
MORTON CL 4

CRISPIN FIELD

CHEYNE CL
QUEEN ST
OLD FARM
THE GREEN
ORCHARD WAY
KEMP CL
GREEN LA
CROSSWAY

B489

Pitstone

THE CRESCENT

Brook End

Middle Path Farm

Pitstone Green Farm Mus

Pistone Windmill

B488

MARSWORTH RD

Pitstonegreen Farm

WESTFIELD RD
WING RD
LONG RD

HARLECH RD

Church End

THE PIGHTLE

VICARAGE RD

MEADOW LA

B488

Manor Farm

Locks

BROWNS HEDGE

CUBBE RD
DUNSTAN RD
LANCASTER WY
DALTON PL

SANDAL RD
CASW CL
BOLEBEC END
SHORT ST
WATLING ST

ROCKINGHAM CL
WHITEHILL LA
SHIP LA
BERKLEY CL

CHURCH RD

LOWER ICKNIELD WAY

TUNNEL WAY
Harvington Pk
QUARRY RD
Quarry Ct

DOVER CL
HEVER CL
BROWNS HEDGE

15

Pitstone Green Bsns Pk

Town Field Farm

Marsworth CE Inf Sch

HP23

College Lake Wildlife Reserve

Chalk Pit

UPPER ICKNIELD WAY

Chalk Pit

VICARAGE GDNS
STEPNELLS
CRESCENT
VICARAGE RD
LUKES CT
NORTHFIELD

Marsworth

Manor House Farm

P

P

B488

NORTHFIELD RD

Folly Farm

Pitstone Hill

Lock

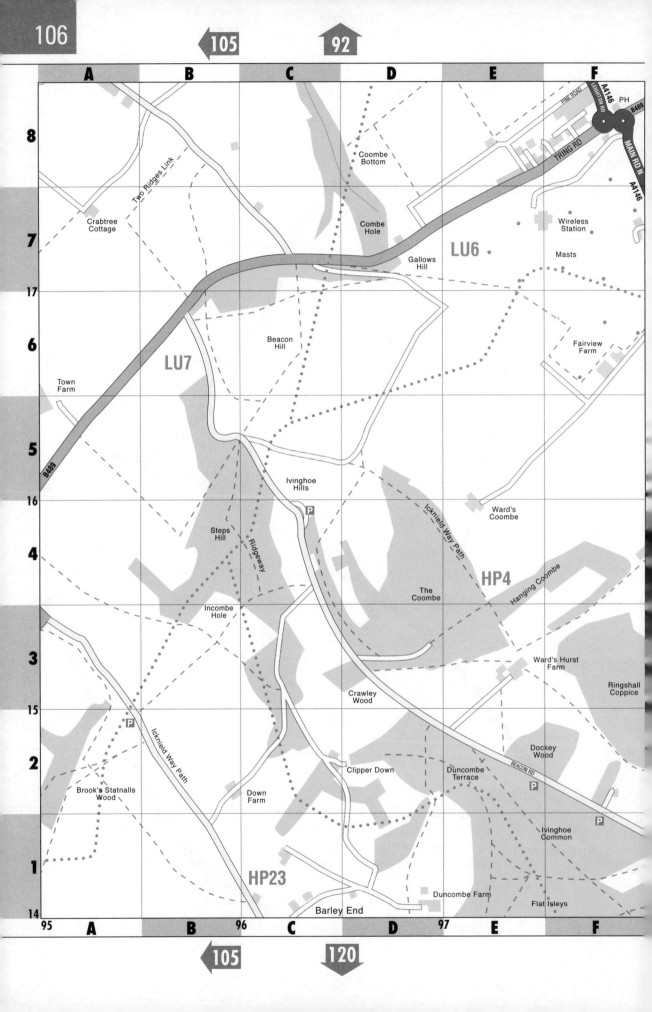

A   B   C   D   E   F

8

Crabtree
Cottage

7

17

6

LU7

5

16

4

3

15

2

1

14

95   96   97

A   B   C   D   E   F

Two Ridges Link

PINE ROAD
LEIGHTON RD
A4146
B489
PH
TRING RD
MAIN RD N
A4146

Coombe
Bottom

Combe
Hole

Gallows
Hill

LU6

Wireless
Station

Masts

Fairview
Farm

Beacon
Hill

Ward's
Coombe

Ivinghoe
Hills

Icknield Way Path

HP4

Steps
Hill

Ridgeway

The
Coombe

Hanging Coombe

Town
Farm

B489

Incombe
Hole

Ward's Hurst
Farm

Ringshall
Coppice

Crawley
Wood

Dockey
Wood

BEACON RD

Brook's Statnalls
Wood

Icknield Way Path

Clipper Down

Duncombe
Terrace

Ivinghoe
Common

Down
Farm

HP23

Duncombe Farm

Flat Isleys

Barley End

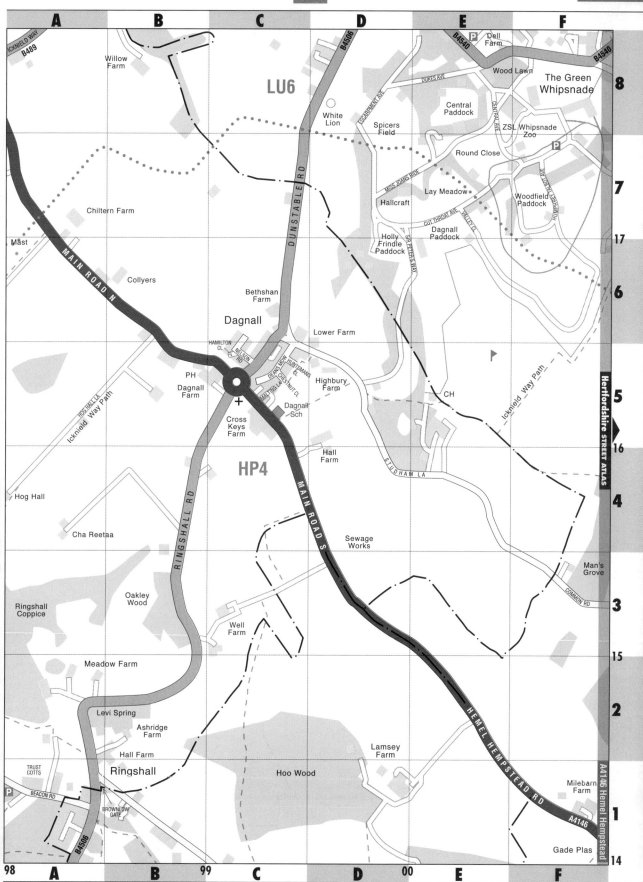

A | B | C | D | E | F

LU6

ICKNIELD WAY
B489

Willow Farm

White Lion

DUNSTABLE RD
B4506

B4540

Dell Farm

DUKES AVE

Wood Lawn

The Green
Whipsnade

Central Paddock

ZSL Whipsnade Zoo

CENTRAL AVE

8

ESCARBRACHT AVE

Spicers Field

Round Close

7

MISS JOANS RIDE

Lay Meadow

Woodfield Paddock

HUMBERSHOE RD

17

Chiltern Farm

Hallcraft

CUT THROAT AVE

VALLEY CL

Dagnall Paddock

Mast

Collyers

Bethshan Farm

SIR PETERS WAY

Holly Frindle Paddock

6

Dagnall

Lower Farm

Ickfield Way Path

5

HAMILTON CL

NELSON RD

MAIN ROAD N

PH
Dagnall Farm

DEANS MDW

HUNTSMANS CL

CHESTNUT CL

MALTING LA

Highbury Farm

CH

Ickfield Way Path

16

HOE HALL LA

Ickfield Way Path

Cross Keys Farm

Dagnall Sch

Hall Farm

STUDHAM LA

HP4

Hog Hall

RINGSHALL RD

MAIN ROAD S

Sewage Works

Man's Grove

4

COMMON RD

3

Cha Reetaa

Oakley Wood

Well Farm

15

Ringshall Coppice

Meadow Farm

HEMEL HEMPSTEAD RD

Lamsey Farm

2

Levi Spring

Ashridge Farm

Hoo Wood

A4146 Hemel Hempstead

Milebarn Farm

Hall Farm

Ringshall

TRUST COTTS

1

BEACON RD

BROWNLOW GATE

B4506

Gade Plas

14

98 | A | B | 99 | C | D | 00 | E | F

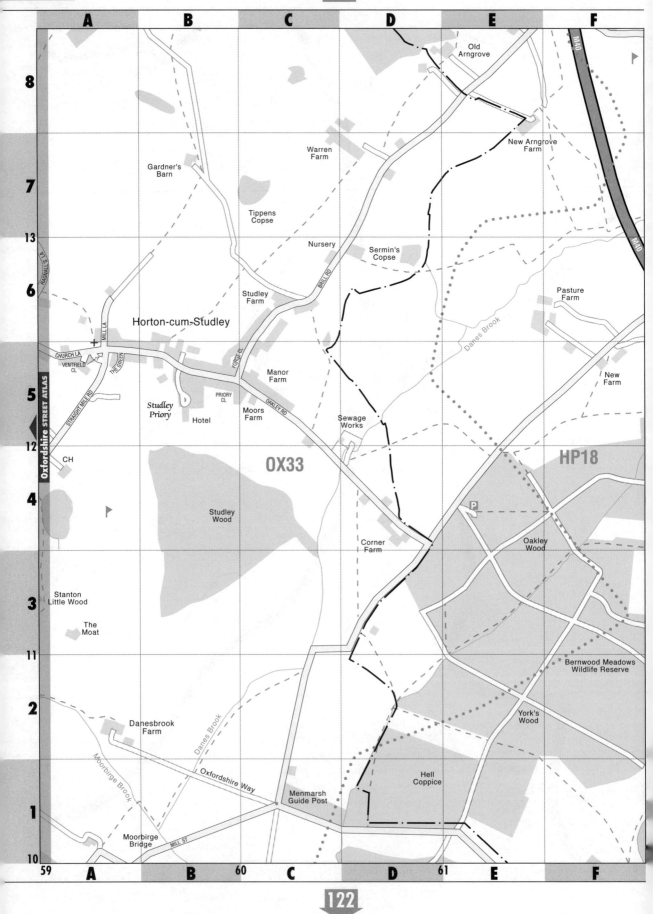

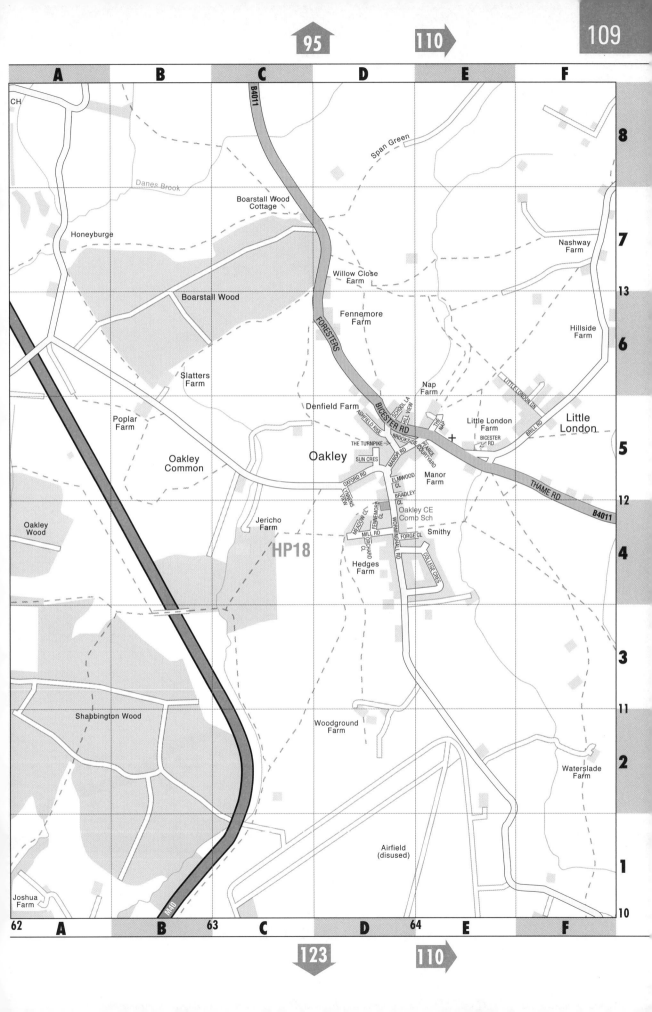

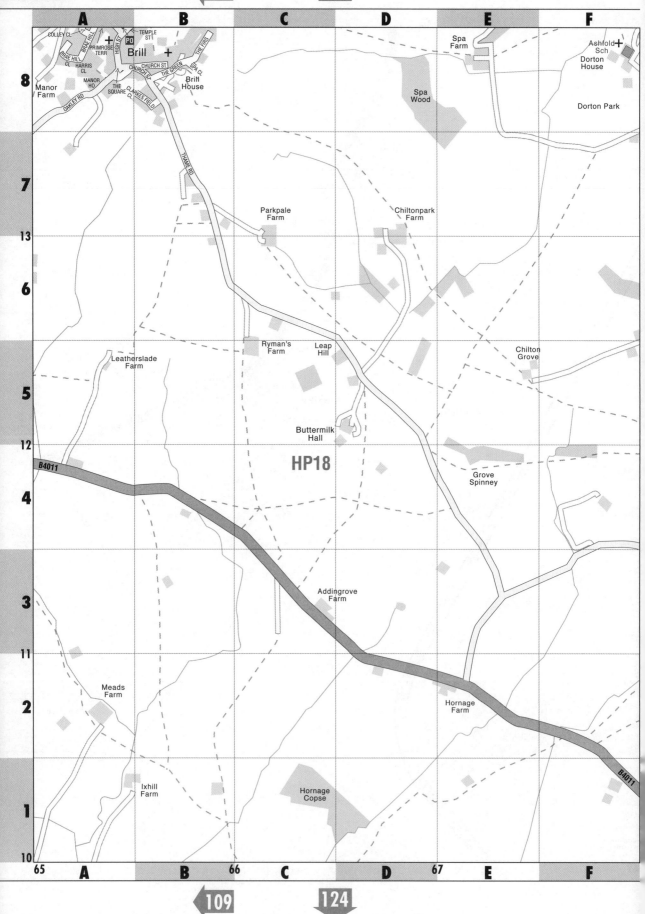

109

96

A   B   C   D   E   F

COLLEY CL·

BRAE HILL

PRIMROSE TERR

TEMPLE ST

PO

Brill

HIGH ST

THE FIRS

BRAE HILL CL·

HARRIS CL

Manor Farm

MANOR HO

CHURCH ST

THE GREEN

CHURCH ST

Brill House

Spa Farm

Ashfold Sch

Dorton House

8

OAKLEY RD

THE SQUARE

CLARKES CL

CLARKES FIELD

SPA CL

Spa Wood

Dorton Park

THAME RD

7

Parkpale Farm

Chiltonpark Farm

13

6

Ryman's Farm

Leap Hill

Chilton Grove

Leatherslade Farm

5

Buttermilk Hall

12

HP18

Grove Spinney

B4011

4

Addingrove Farm

3

11

Meads Farm

Hornage Farm

2

Ixhill Farm

Hornage Copse

B4011

1

10

65   A   B   66   C   D   67   E   F

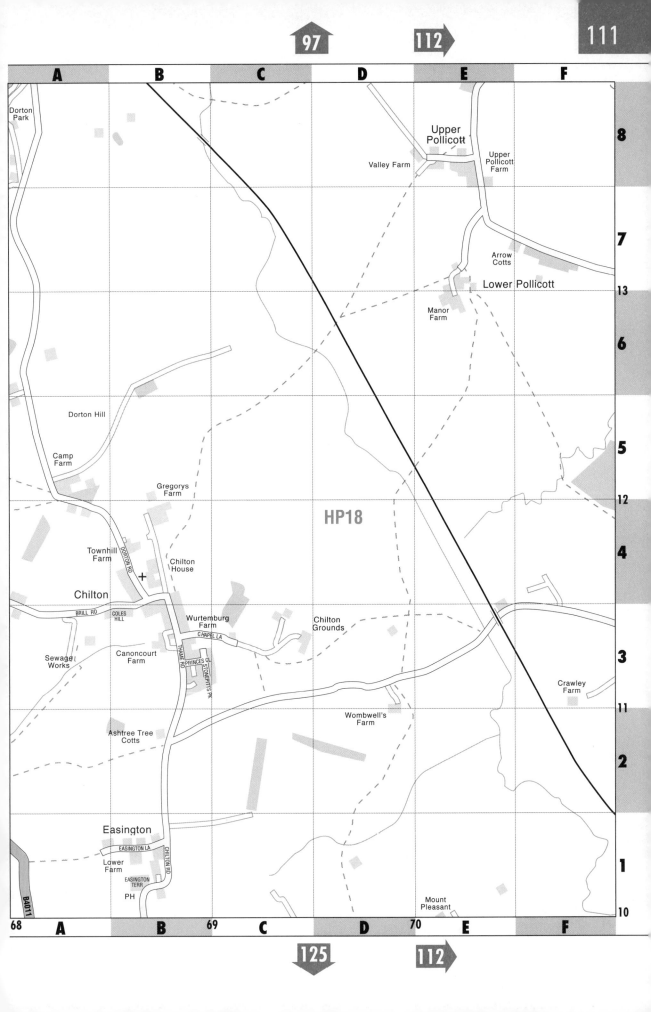

111 98

A B C D E F

8

7

13

6

5

12

4

3

11

2

1

10

Marsh Farm

Musk Hill Farm

Cedarwood Bungalow

Obsy

Winchendon Hill Farm

Brackwell Farm

BARRACK HILL

Hall

Nether Winchendon
or
Lower Winchendon

Chearsley Furze

WINCHENDON RD

CANNON'S HILL

Manor Farm

The Old Mill

HP18

Nether Winchendon House

Whaddonfield Farm

The Villas

Sewage Works

River Thame

Holyman's Farm

Cuddington Bridges

FROG LA
KETTS
SPURT CL
LOWER GN

1 COUSINS PIECE
2 EVANS CL
3 CHURCH PIECE

Cuddington Mill Farm

CUDDINGTON HILL

Cuddington & Dinton CE Sch (Inf)

GREAT STONE
SWAN

BBS LA
LOWER CHURCH LA
UPPER CHURCH LA
PO
PH

THE GREEN
SWAN LA
COTTS

CHILTON RD

Furze Farm

WILLOW GATE
AYLESBURY RD
LAMMAS LA

LAMMAS PATH

BRIDGEWAY

WELFORD WAY

BERNARD CL
DADBROOK

Chearsley Hill House

STONEY FURLONG

OLD PLOUGH LA
TURNIP CL

SCHOOL LA

Bernwood Jubilee Way
Thame Valley Walk

HILLSIDE COTTS

DADBROOK CL 1
DADFIELD CL 2

1
2

WINCHENDON RD

THE BERNARD CL

PH

THE GREEN

DARK LA
LOWER GREEN LA

WATTS GN
SHUPP'S LA
ELM BROOK CL

Lower Green Farm

Dadbrook House

Chearsley

CRENDON RD

Manor Farm

CHURCH LA

BOTTOM ORCH

Dad Brook

HP17

Grove Farm

CHEARSLEY RD

Hawks Bridge

Bettymoor Plantation

A418
AYLESBURY RD

71 A 72 B C 72 D 73 E F

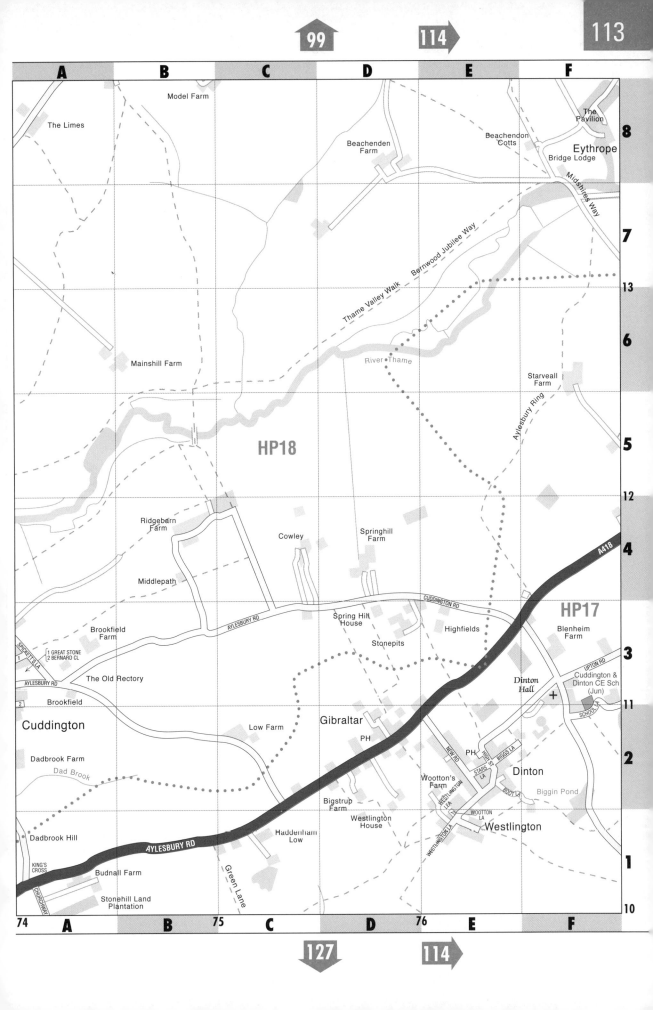

A   B   C   D   E   F

8
7
13
6
5
12
4
3
11
2
1
10

The Limes
Model Farm
Beachenden Farm
Beachendon Cotts
The Pavilion
Eythrope
Bridge Lodge
Midshires Way

Thame Valley Walk
Bernwood Jubilee Way

River Thame

Mainshill Farm

Starveall Farm

Aylesbury Ring

HP18

Ridgebarn Farm
Cowley
Springhill Farm

Middlepath

CUDDINGTON RD

A418

HP17

Blenheim Farm

Brookfield Farm
AYLESBURY RD
Spring Hill House
Highfields
Stonepits

SACKETT'S LA
1 GREAT STONE
2 BERNARD CL
1
The Old Rectory
AYLESBURY RD
2
Brookfield

Dinton Hall

Cuddington & Dinton CE Sch (Jun)
SCHOOL LA

Cuddington
Low Farm
Gibraltar
PH

Dadbrook Farm
Dad Brook

NEW RD
PH
STAIRS LA
HIGH ST
BIGGS LA
Dinton
BOOT LA
Biggin Pond

Bigstrup Farm
Wootton's Farm
Westlington House
WESTLINGTON LEA
WOOTTON LA
Westlington
WESTLINGTON LA

Dadbrook Hill
AYLESBURY RD
Haddenham Low

KING'S CROSS
CHURCHWAY
Budnall Farm
Stonehill Land Plantation
Green Lane

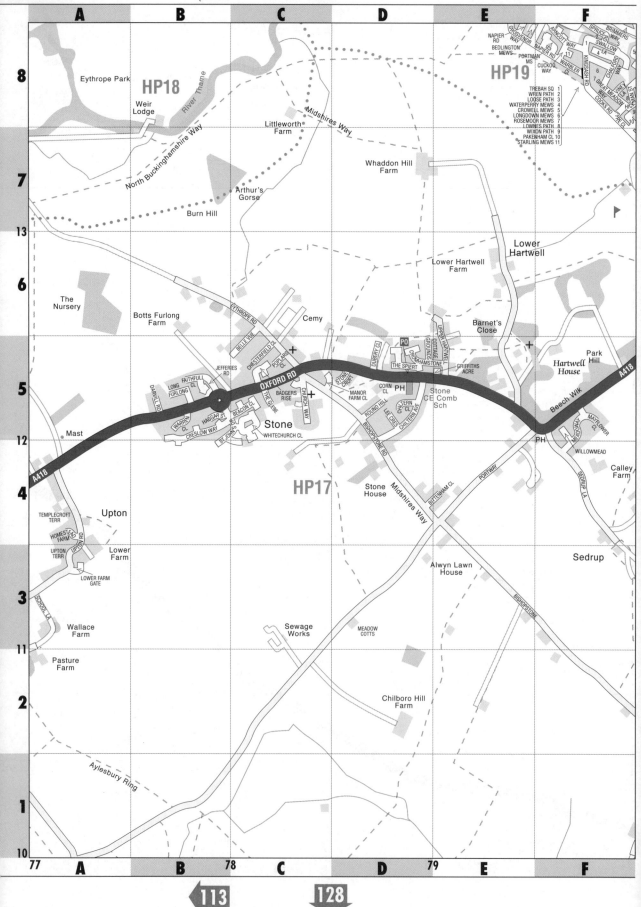

A   B   C   D   E   F

8

Eythrope Park

HP18

Weir Lodge

River Thame

North Buckinghamshire Way

Littleworth Farm

Midshires Way

Whaddon Hill Farm

HP19

NAPIER RD
BEDLINGTON MEWS
PORTMAN MS
CUCKOO WAY

GROSVENOR WAY
NAPIER RD
ABINGTON WAY
SPRUCE RD
SWALLOW LA
BRIMMERS WAY

WARBLER CL
KINGSASH RD
GREAT MEADOW
COOKS RD

TREBAH SQ   1
WREN PATH   2
LOOSE PATH   3
WATERPERRY MEWS 4
CROWELL MEWS 5
LONGDOWN MEWS 6
ROSEMOOR MEWS 7
LOWNES PATH   8
WIXON PATH   9
PAKENHAM CL 10
STARLING MEWS 11

7

Arthur's Gorse

Burn Hill

13

Lower Hartwell Farm

Lower Hartwell

6

The Nursery

Botts Furlong Farm

EYTHROPE RD

Cemy

Barnet's Close

Park Hill

Hartwell House

BEECH WLK

A418

5

DARVILL RD
LONG FURLONG
FAITHFULL CL
BELLE VUE
CHESTERFIELD CL
POPLARS CL
THE GLEBE
JEFFERIES RD
OXFORD RD
BADGERS RISE
CHURCH WAY

DUBERY CL
UPPER HARTWELL
CROMHAMSTONE
COTTAGE GROUNDS
PO
THE SPIERT
GRIFFITHS ACRE

STONE CROFT
MANOR FARM CL
CORN CL
ROUND HILL
PH
CHILTERN AVE
STERN CL
Stone CE Comb Sch
PH

12

Mast

WARREN CL
HAGGAR ST
ST JOHN'S
BEACON CL
CRESLOW WAY

Stone

WHITCHURCH CL

BISHOPSTONE RD
LEE CRES

Stone House

Midshires Way

PORTWAY

WILLOWMEAD

MAYFLOWER CL

Calley Farm

4

A418

TEMPLECROFT TERR
HOMESTEAD FARM

Upton

HP17

BITTENHAM CL

SEDRUP LA

Sedrup

3

UPTON TERR
UPTON RD

Lower Farm

LOWER FARM GATE

Alwyn Lawn House

BISHOPSTONE

BISHOPSTONE LA

Wallace Farm

Sewage Works

MEADOW COTTS

11

Pasture Farm

2

Chilboro Hill Farm

1

Aylesbury Ring

10

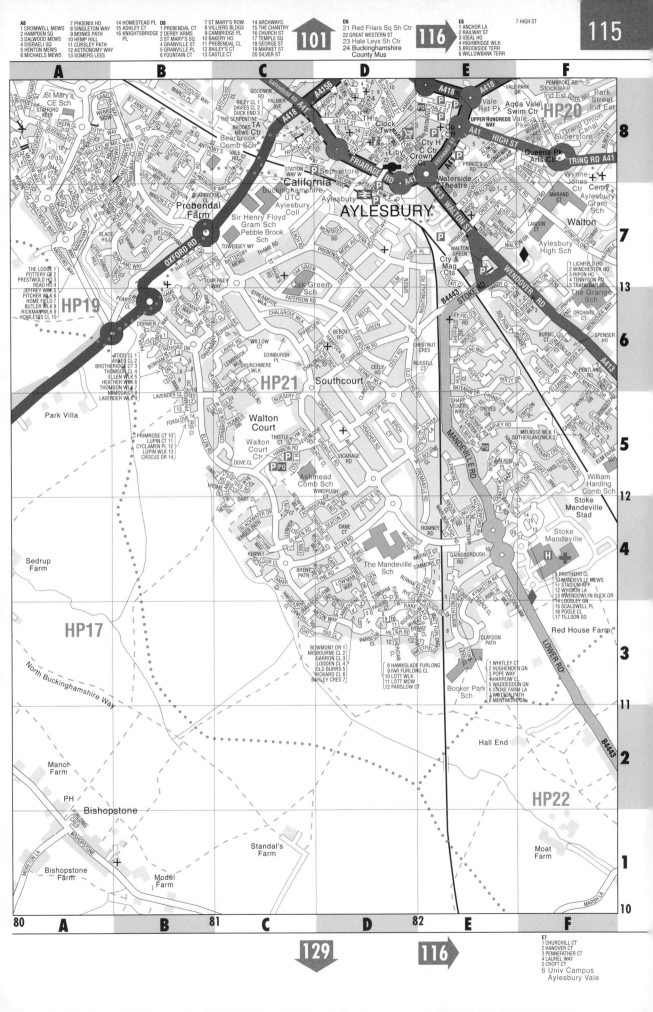

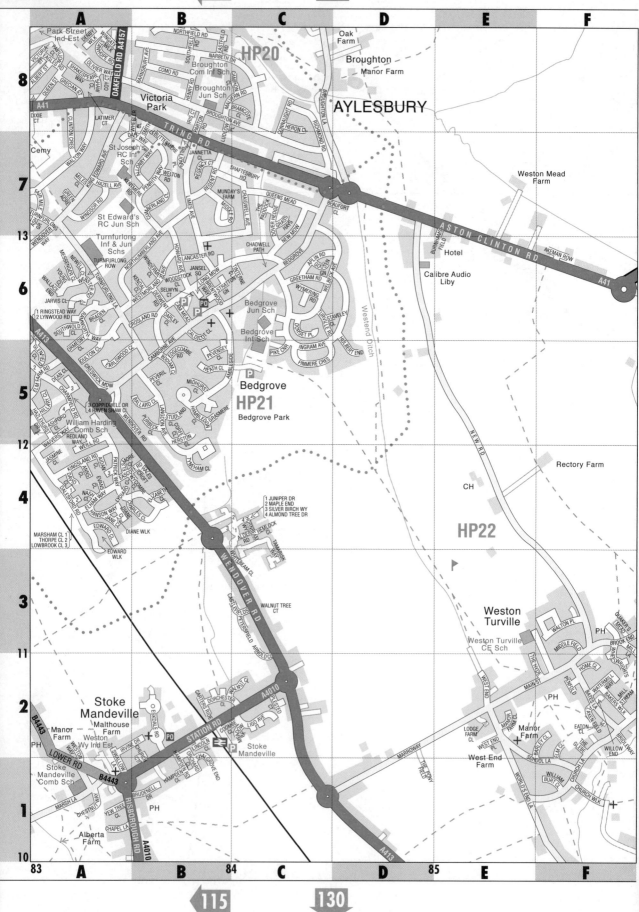

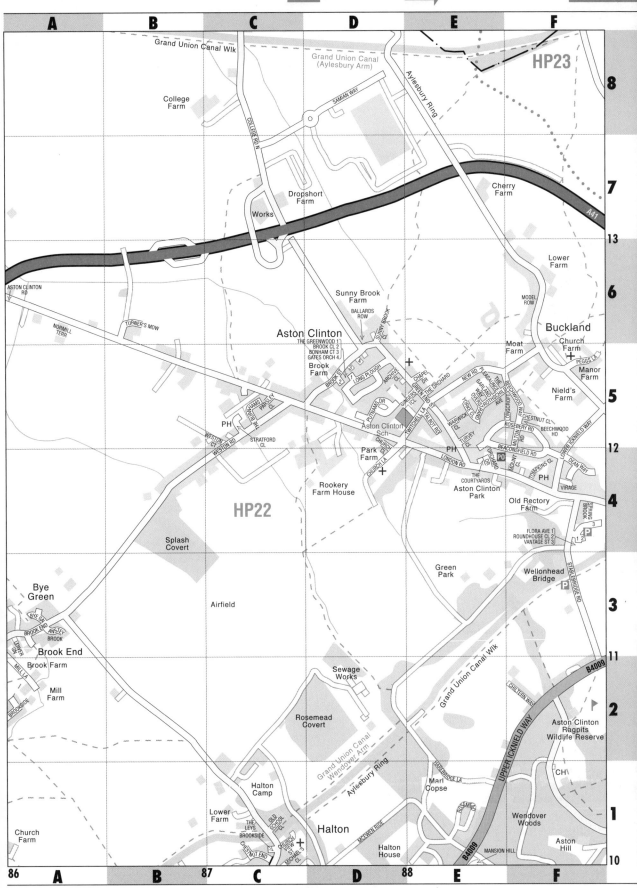

HP23

8

Grand Union Canal Wlk

Grand Union Canal (Aylesbury Arm)

College Farm

SAMIAN WAY

COLLEGE RD N

Aylesbury Ring

7

Dropshort Farm

Cherry Farm

A41

13

Works

Lower Farm

ASTON CLINTON RD

Sunny Brook Farm

MODEL ROW

6

NORMILL TERR

TURNER'S MDW

BALLARDS ROW

SUNNY BROOK CL

Buckland

Aston Clinton

Church Farm

PEGGS LA

THE GREENWOOD 1
BROOK CL 2
BONHAM CT 3
GATES ORCH 4

Moat Farm

Manor Farm

Brook Farm

BROOK'S CL

LONG PLOUGH

ARCHIVE CL

CHAPEL DR

GREEN END ST

THE ORCHARD

NEW RD

PLEASAUNCE WAY

GARLAND CT

OVERSTROTTSCHILD

LONGCROFT

BEECHWOOD WAY

Nield's Farm

5

GINGERS CL

PITMANS DR

TWITCHELL LA

TALBOT RD

WARWICK CL

YORKE CL

ROTHSCHILD

CHESTNUT CL

BEECHWOOD HO

SHAMS CL

PARSLEY CL

THE

PH

Aston Clinton Sch

ROSEBERY RD

MILTON RD

WESTON CT

WESTON RD

STRATFORD CL

Park Farm

CHURCH CL

PH

LONDON RD

TURVEY CL

BEACONSFIELD RD

PO

MOUNT CL

TOMPKINS CL

PH

LOWER ICKNIELD WAY

DEAN WAY

12

Rookery Farm House

THE COURTYARDS

Aston Clinton Park

VIRAGE

Old Rectory Farm

SPRING BROOK

4

HP22

FLORA AVE 1
ROUNDHOUSE CL 2
VANTAGE ST 3

P

Splash Covert

Green Park

Wellonhead Bridge

P

STABLEBRIDGE RD

Bye Green

BYE GN

Airfield

3

BROOK END

ANSLEY BROOK

LOWER GN

Brook End

MILL LA

Brook Farm

BROOKSIDE

Grand Union Canal Wlk

B4009

11

Mill Farm

Sewage Works

CHILTERN WAY

2

Rosemead Covert

Aston Clinton Ragpits Wildlife Reserve

CH

UPPER ICKNIELD WAY

Grand Union Canal Wendover Arm

Aylesbury Ring

Marl Copse

BIERIBRIDGE LA

Wendover Woods

1

Halton Camp

Lower Farm

THE LEYS

OLD SCHOOL CL

Halton

McEWEN RIDGE

ROSEMED CL

B4009

Aston Hill

BROOKSIDE

CHURCH VIEW

ST MICHAEL'S CL

Halton House

MANSION HILL

CHESTNUT END

Church Farm

Halton

10

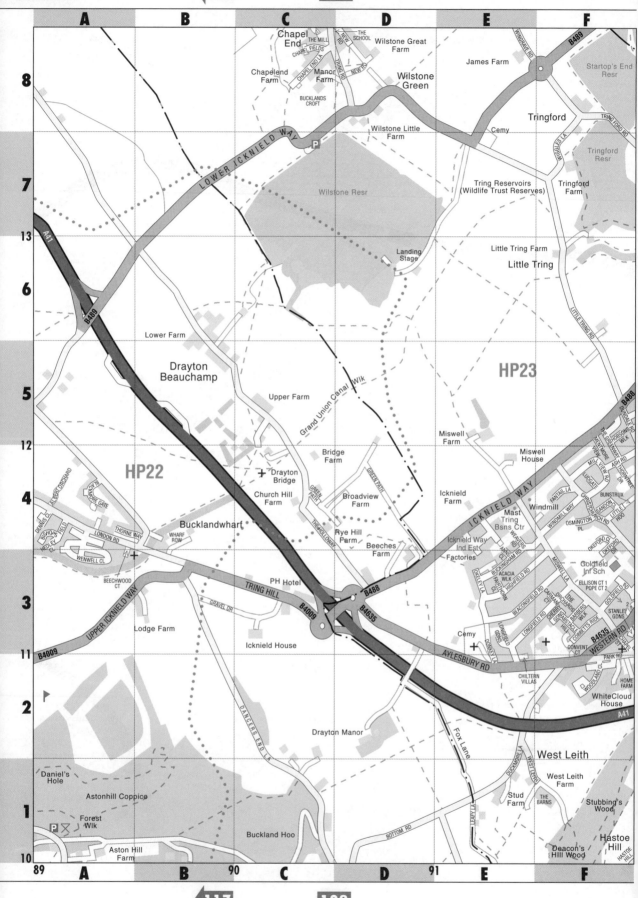

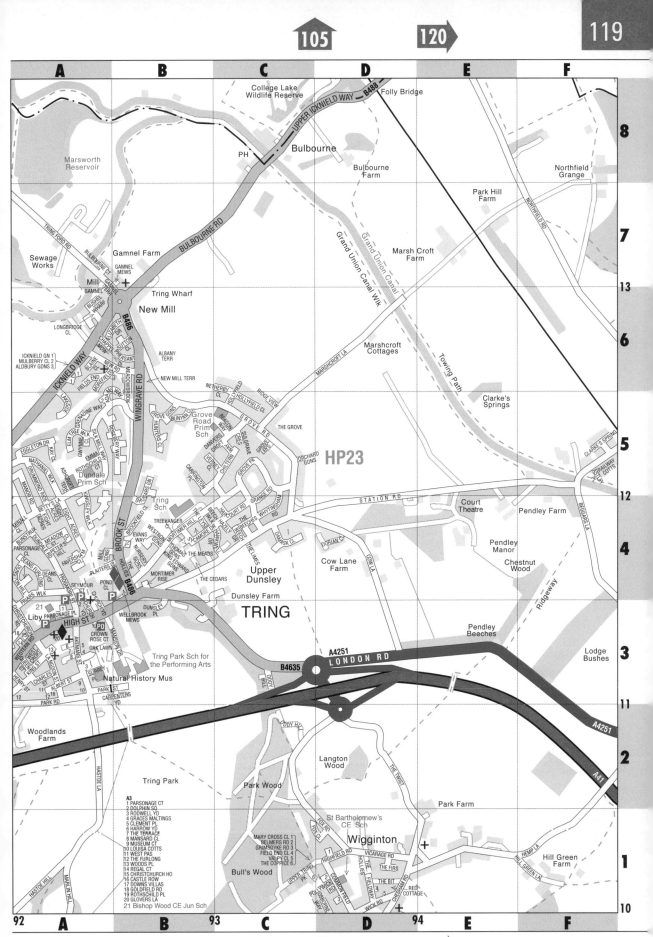

A   B   C   D   E   F

College Lake
Wildlife Reserve
UPPER ICKNIELD WAY   B488
Folly Bridge

8

Bulbourne
PH   Bulbourne
Farm
Marsworth
Reservoir   Park Hill
Farm   Northfield
Grange

7

Sewage
Works   Gamnel Farm
BULBOURNE RD   Marsh Croft
Farm
NORTHFIELD RD

13

GAMNEL MEWS
Mill   Tring Wharf   Grand Union Canal   Grand Union Canal Wlk   Marshcroft
Cottages

6

New Mill
LONGBRIDGE CL
ICKNIELD GN 1
MULBERRY CL 2
ALDBURY GDNS 3
B486   ALBANY TERR
NEW MILL TERR   MARSHCROFT LA   Towing
Path   Clarke's
Springs   Clarke's Spring

5

ICKNIELD WAY
WINGRAVE RD   Grove
Road
Prim
Sch   THE GROVE   HP23

12

EGGLETON DR   Dundale
Prim Sch   Tring
Sch   ORCHARD
GDNS   STATION RD   Court
Theatre   Pendley Farm

4

BROOK ST   Upper
Dunsley   Cow Lane
Farm   Pendley
Manor   Chestnut
Wood

Liby
HIGH ST
Tring Park Sch for
the Performing Arts   THE CEDARS
Dunsley Farm   TRING   Pendley
Beeches   Ridgeway   Lodge
Bushes

3

Natural History Mus   OAK LAWN
A4251 LONDON RD
B4635

11

PARK RD
Woodlands
Farm   ODY HL   A4251   A41

2

Tring Park   Park Wood   Langton
Wood   THE TWIST   Park Farm

A3
1 PARSONAGE CT
2 DOLPHIN SQ
3 RODWELL YD
4 GRACES MALTINGS
5 CLEMENT PL
6 HARROW YD
7 THE TERRACE
8 MANSARD CL
9 MUSEUM CT
10 LOUISA COTTS
11 WEST PAS
12 THE FURLONG
13 WOODS PL
14 REGAL CT
15 CHRISTCHURCH HO
16 CASTLE ROW
17 DOWNS VILLAS
18 GOLDFIELD RD
19 ROTHSCHILD PL
20 GLOVERS LA
21 Bishop Wood CE Jun Sch   St Bartholomew's
CE Sch
MARY CROSS CL 1
BELMERS RD 2
GRIMSDYKE RD 3
FIELD END CL 4
VALPY CL 5
THE COPPICE 6.   Wigginton
VICARAGE RD
THE FIRS   Hill Green
Farm

1

Bull's Wood   RED
COTTAGE

10

92   A   93   B   C   94   D   E   F

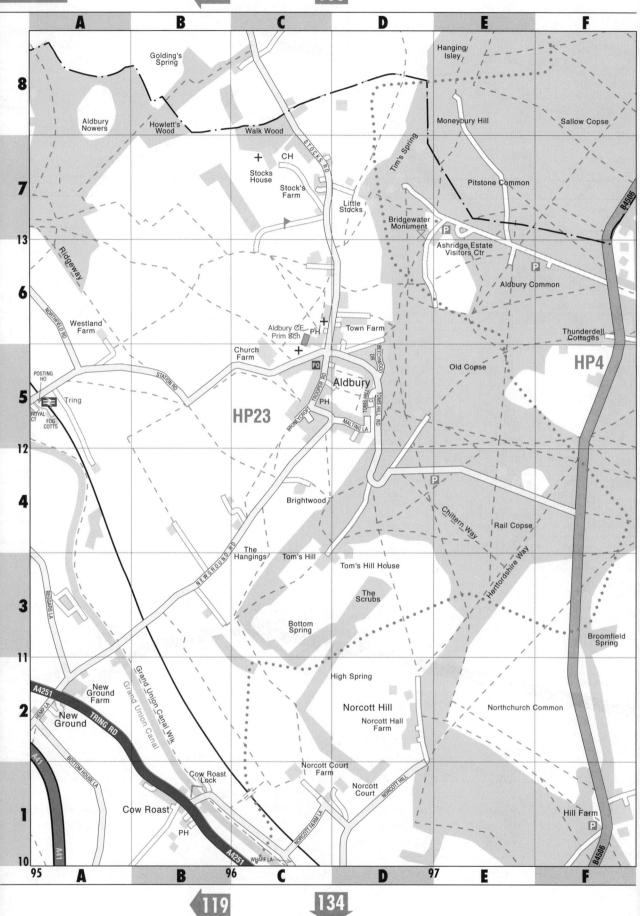

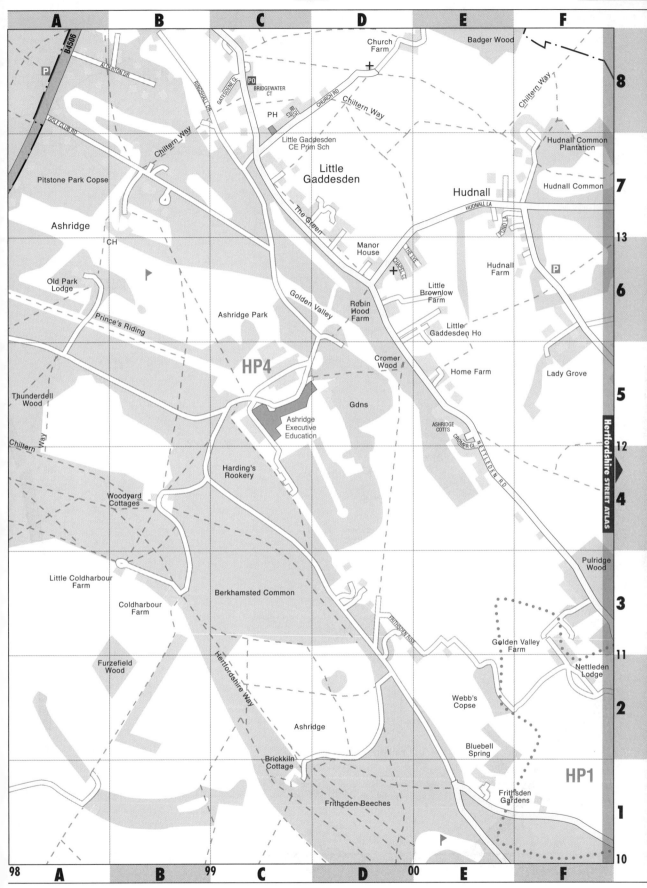

Oxfordshire STREET ATLAS

MILL ST

Moorbirge Brook

Clearsale

Hursthill

HP18

Wood Farm

Waterperry Common

SMITH'S LA

Bernwood Forest

Commonleys Farm

Waterperry Wood

Park Farm

Polecat End

Drunkard's Corner

Park Farm House

Oxfordshire Way

Parson's Farm

Polecat End Hollows

Marsh Copse

Ledall Cottage

Holton Wood

OX33

M40

Buryhook Barn

Holton Brook

B4027

Keeper's Cottage

Warren Farm

Pond Farm

WHEATLEY RD

Warren Wood

Old Park Farm

Cottage Copse

A40 Oxford

Lyehill Quarries (dis)

BURYHOOK CNR

B4027

Warwick Close Farm

A40

Recn Gd

Wheatley Park Sch

Holton

The Rectory

Holton Place

Liby

Park Sports Ctr

BARNS CL

Wheatley

John Watson Sch

Church Farm

Moat

WESTFIELD RD

WESTFIELD RD

LONDON RD

PARK HILL

A40

Garden Copse

Brookes Univ (Wheatley Campus)

COLLEGE CL

M40

Oxfordshire STREET ATLAS

A40 High Wycombe (M40)

M40 High Wycombe, London

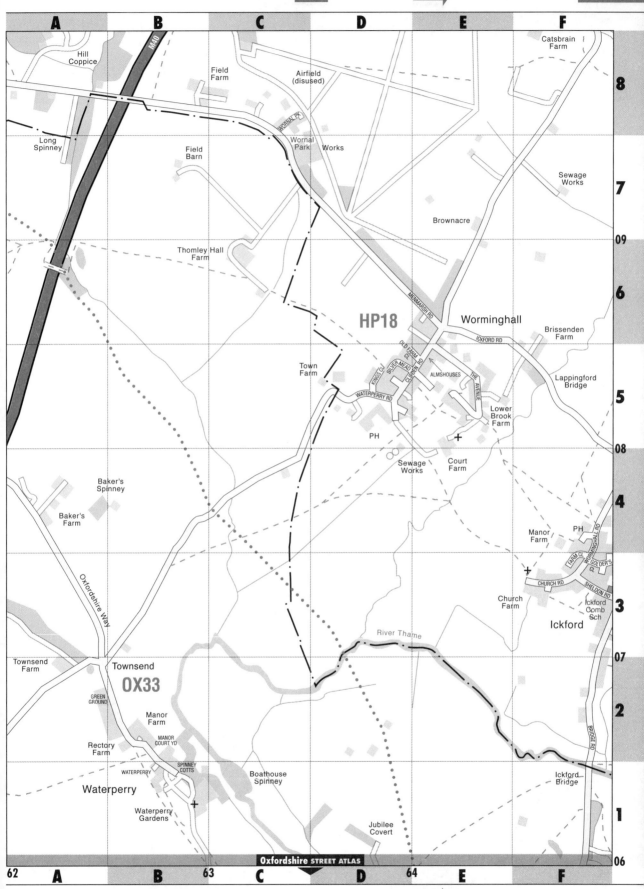

123 110

A B C D E F

8

7

09

6

Woodway
Woodway Farm Farm
Ind Est

Westfield Farm

Lower
Peppershill Farm

Peppershill

Peppershill Farm

Crendon
House

Hill
Farm

5

HP18

Bernwood Jubilee Way

Marsh
Farm

08

Peacehaven
Farm

4

Upper
Farm

Ickford

GOLDER'S CL

PO

SCHOOL CL

FIELD CL

TURNFIELDS

SHELDON RD

Ickford
Comb Sch

BULLS LA

BRIDGE
RD

Little
Ickford

Marsh
Farm

Sewage
Works

Rookery
Farm

THE BURNHAMS

MARSH RD

LOWER
FARM
CL

Lower
Farm

MORTON CL

KING CL

LONG CRENDON RD

HOME CL

Shabbington

THE VINE

Village
Farm

SCHOOL LA

3

07

LIMES WAY

DUKES CL

ICKFORD RD

KIMBELLS CL

River Thame

2

Franklins
Farm

PH

MILL RD

OX9

1

River Thame

Manor Farm

North
Weston

06

65 A B 66 C D 67 E F

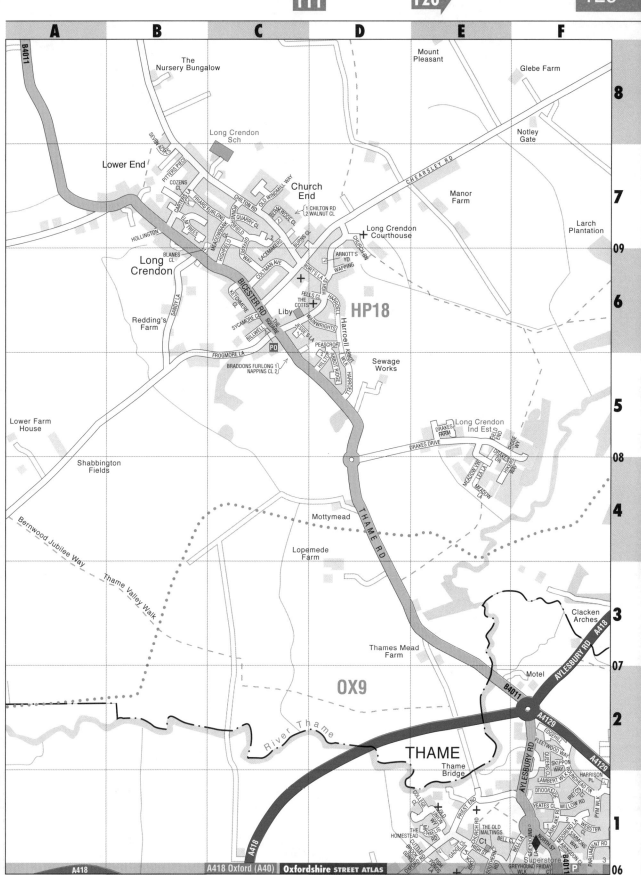

A   B   C   D   E   F

The Nursery Bungalow

Mount Pleasant

Glebe Farm

Long Crendon Sch

Notley Gate

8

Lower End

Chearsley Rd

Church End

Manor Farm

7

1 CHILTON RD
2 WALNUT CL

Long Crendon Courthouse

Larch Plantation

09

Arnott's Yd

Long Crendon

Wapping

HP18

6

Redding's Farm

Liby

The Cotts

Harroell Abbot

Sewage Works

5

Lower Farm House

Long Crendon Ind Est

Drakes Farm

Shabbington Fields

Drakes Drive

08

4

Mottymead

Thame Valley Walk

Bernwood Jubilee Way

Lopemede Farm

Clacken Arches

3

Thames Mead Farm

07

Motel

OX9

2

River Thame

THAME

Thame Bridge

1

F1
1 MEADOW WAY
2 GREENWAY
3 Barley Hill Prim Sch

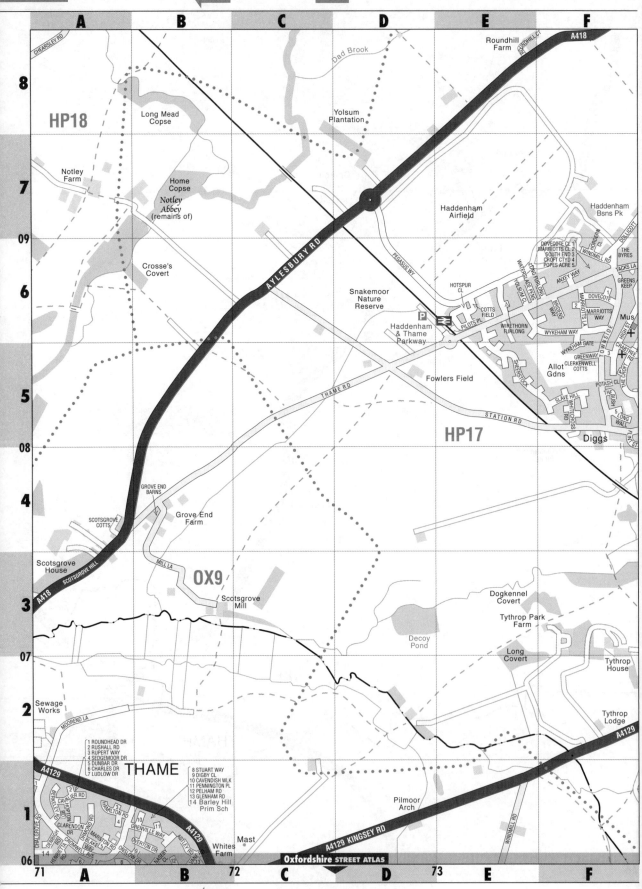

8

HP18

Long Mead
Copse

Dad Brook

Yolsum
Plantation

Roundhill
Farm

A418

7

Notley
Farm

Home
Copse

*Notley
Abbey*
(remains of)

Haddenham
Airfield

Haddenham
Bsns Pk

09

DOVECOTE CL 1
MARRIOTTS CL 2
SOUTH END 3
CROFT CTYD 4
POPES ACRE 5.

THE
BYRES

TACKS LA

Crosse's
Covert

AYLESBURY RD

PEGASUS WY

HOTSPUR
CL

WINDMILL RD

ANXEY WAY

GREENS
KEEP

DOVECOTE

6

Snakemoor
Nature
Reserve

COTTS
FIELD

MARRIOTTS
WAY

Mus

P

Haddenham
& Thame
Parkway

PILOTS PL

WIRETHORN
FURLONG

WYKEHAM WAY

CRABTREE
RD

WYKEHAM GATE

5

THAME RD

Fowlers Field

GREENWAY
CLERKENWELL
COTTS

Allot
Gdns

STATION RD

SLAVE HILL

HP17

THE
BUSH

LONG
WALL

08

Diggs

4

GROVE END
BARNS

Grove End
Farm

SCOTSGROVE
COTTS

Dogkennel
Covert

Tythrop Park
Farm

3

A418   SCOTSGROVE HILL

Scotsgrove
House

MILL LA

OX9

Scotsgrove
Mill

Decoy
Pond

Long
Covert

Tythrop
House

07

2

Sewage
Works

MOOREND LA

Tythrop
Lodge

A4129

1 ROUNDHEAD DR
2 RUSHALL RD
3 RUPERT WAY
4 SEDGEMOOR DR
5 DUNBAR DR
6 CHARLES DR
7 LUDLOW DR

THAME

8 STUART WAY
9 DIGBY CL
10 CAVENDISH WLK
11 PENNINGTON PL
12 PELHAM RD
13 GLENHAM RD
14 Barley Hill
   Prim Sch

A4129

A4129

Pilmoor
Arch

WINDMILL RD

A4129

1

A4129   KINGSEY RD

Mast

Whites
Farm

06

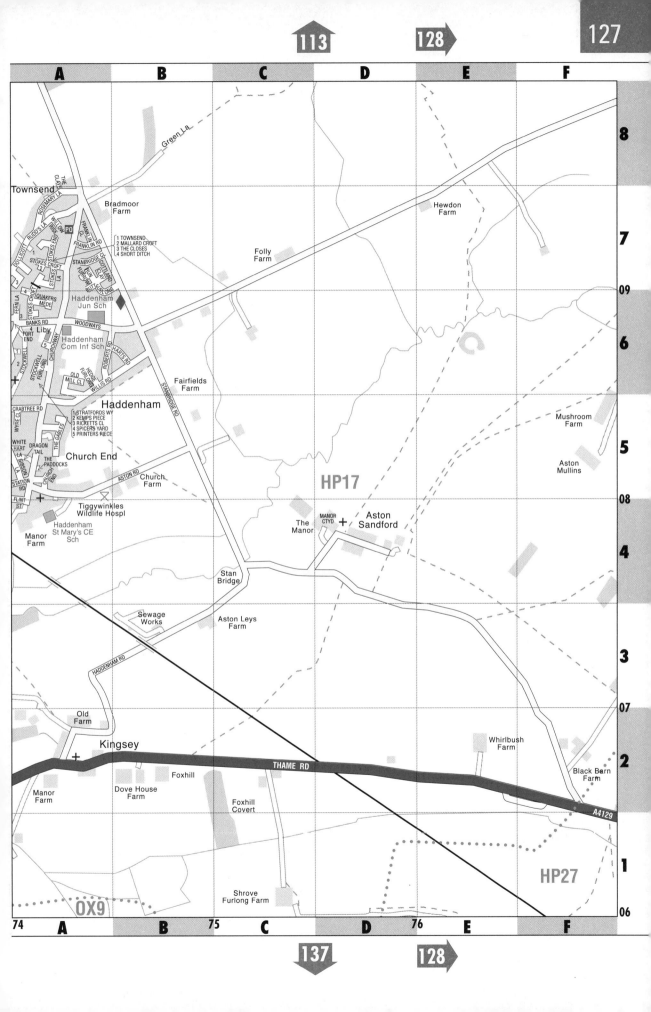

127
114

A **B** **C** **D** **E** **F**

8

BRIDGE FARM BLDGS

Moat Farm

Moreton Village

PH

WATER LA

Ford

Moreton Farm

7

Manor Farm

FRANCIP CL

BURGESS LA

CHAPEL RD

LINDEN WAY

Ford Farm

09

North Buckinghamshire Way

Midshires Way

6

Aylesbury Ring

HP17

5

Lower Waldridge Farm

Fox Covert

Pollard Farm

08

Poplar Farm

4

Waldridge Manor

3

Black Barn

Waldridge Village

07

Swan's Way

Midshires Way

Pasture Farm

2

Stockwell Lane Farm

Hill Ground Farm

HP27

Owlswick Farm

A4129

STOCKWELL LA

Midshires Way

Green Lane Farm

GREEN LA

Owlswick

THAME RD

Little Acre Farm

Manor Farm

+

1

A4129

Ray Farm

06

77 **A** **78** **B** **C** **79** **D** **E** **F**

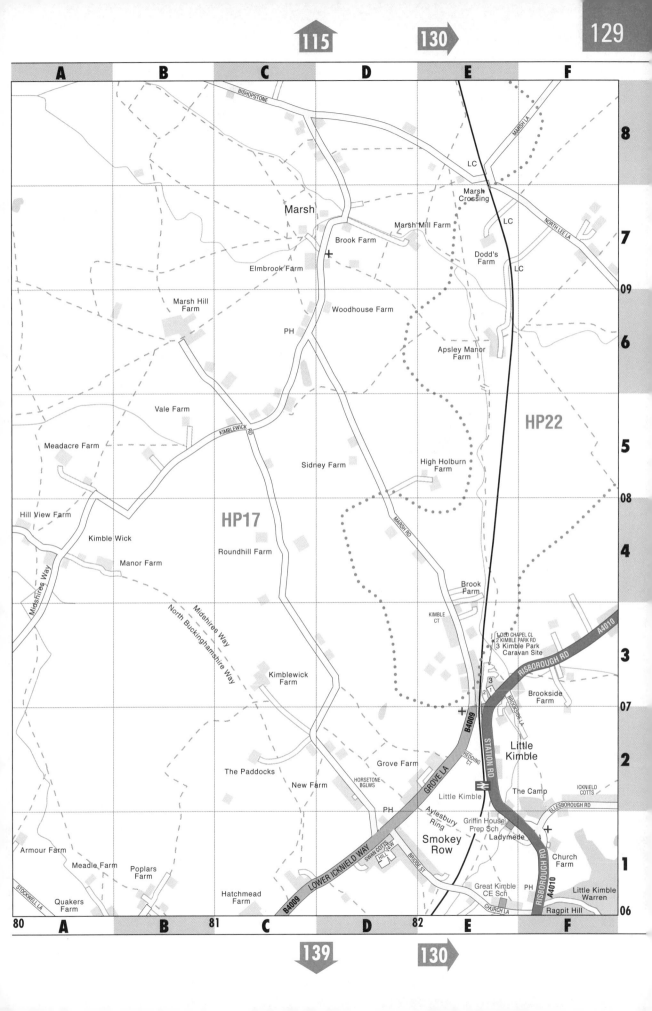

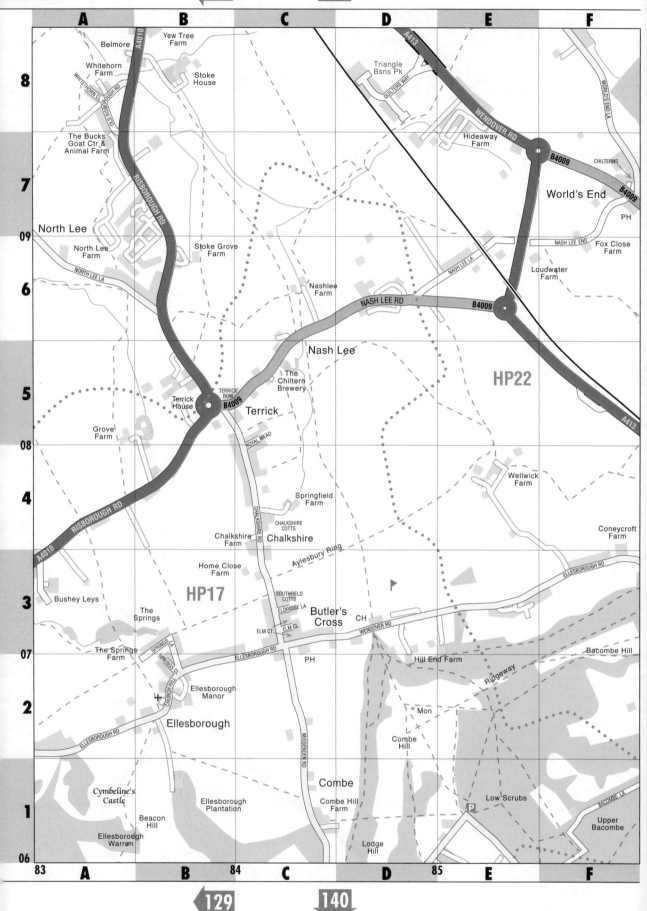

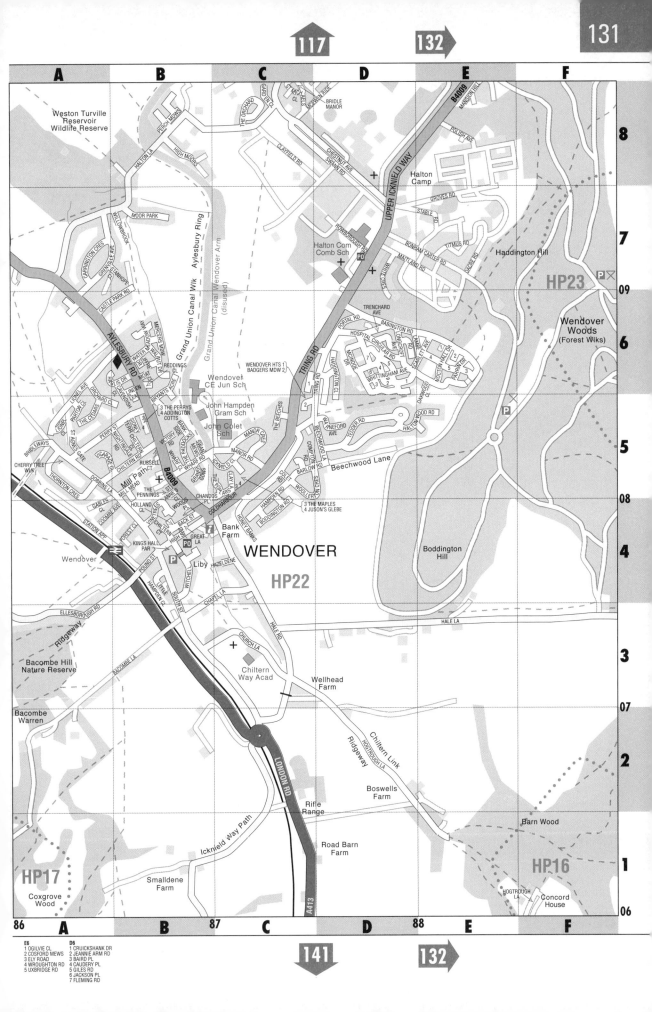

A B C D E F

8
7
09
6
5
08
4
3
07
2
1
06

Weston Turville
Reservoir
Wildlife Reserve

MOOR PARK

Grand Union Canal Wlk Aylesbury Ring

Grand Union Canal Wendover Arm
(disused)

HALTON LA

HIGH MOORS

PERCH MDWS

CARRINGTON CRES

GREVILLE AVE

WILLOWBROOK

STANHOPE

CASTLE PARK RD

AYLESBURY RD

MERCERS MDW

WALNUT DR

WATER LA

ORCHARD CL

THE CEDARS

REDDINGS CL

BRYANTS ACRE

LINDEN LEA

MOAT LA

PARTON

PERRY ST

LIONEL AVE

ST AGNES GATE

VICARAGE LA

CHILTERN RD

NIGHTINGALE

DOBBINS LA

RUSSELL CT

MILL MEAD

THE PENNINGS

COOMBE AVE

GABLES

HOLLAND CL

VINCHELTERN

VICTORY RD

WHARF RD

SWAN LA

THE PADDOCKS

BANK RISE

CHANDOS PL

COLDHARBOUR

CLAY LA

MANOR CRES

MANOR RD

ICKNIELD CL

BARLOW RD

COMPTON LA

WOOLLERS

HAMPDEN RD

BODDINGTON RD

HONEY BANKS

GREAT LA

BACK ST

HIGH ST

WITCHEL

POUND ST

LITTLE HAMPDEN CL

STATION APP

FOREST CH

KINGS HALL PAR

HAZELDENE

CHAPEL LA

SOUTH ST

HALE RD

CHURCH LA

ELLESBOROUGH RD

BACOMBE LA

Ridgeway

THORNTON CRES

BRIDLE WAYS

Cherry Tree Wlk

Bacombe Hill
Nature Reserve

Bacombe
Warren

HP17

Coxgrove
Wood

Smalldene
Farm

Icknield Way Path

LONDON RD

A413

Rifle
Range

Road Barn
Farm

Chiltern
Way Acad

Wellhead
Farm

HALE LA

Chiltern Link
Ridgeway

HOGTROUGH LA

Boswells
Farm

Barn Wood

HP16

HOGTROUGH LA

Concord
House

Boddington
Hill

Beechwood Lane

HALTON WOOD RD

OAKWOOD CL

NOCTON HALL DR

PARHAM RD

SCARLETT AVE

WHITTINGHAM AVE

DARE RD

TITMUS RD

GROVES RD

STABLE RD

BONHAM CARTER RD

MAITLAND RD

POLISH AVE

MANSION HILL

B4009

Haddington Hill

Wendover
Woods
(Forest Wlks)

HP23

Halton
Camp

Halton Com
Comb Sch

UPPER ICKNIELD WAY

WHITE CRES

ROWBOROUGH RD

CHESTNUT AVE

SWANK RD

CLAYFIELD RD

THE ORCHARD

GARDEN LA

ST MICHAELS CL

MCEWEN THDE

BRIDLE
MANOR

TRING RD

TRENCHARD
AVE

BABINGTON RD

PORTAL RD

HOSPITAL CIRCULAR RD

MCINDOE DR

HADDINGTON CL

LONGCROFT

TARGE

TEDDER RD

NEFELD AVE

WA

WENDOVER HTS 1
BADGERS MDW 2

Wendover
CE Jun Sch

John Hampden
Gram Sch

John Colet
Sch

THE BEECHES

BEECHWOOD LA

3 THE PERRYS
4 ADDINGTON
COTTS

B4009

Mill Path

3 THE MAPLES
4 JUSON'S GLEBE

Bank
Farm

WENDOVER

HP22

Wendover

Liby

P

PO

86 87 88

A B C D E F

E6
1 OGILVIE CL
2 COSFORD MEWS
3 ELY ROAD
4 WROUGHTON RD
5 UXBRIDGE RD

D6
1 CRUICKSHANK DR
2 JEANNIE ARM RD
3 BAIRD PL
4 CAUDERY PL
5 GILES RD
6 JACKSON PL
7 FLEMING RD

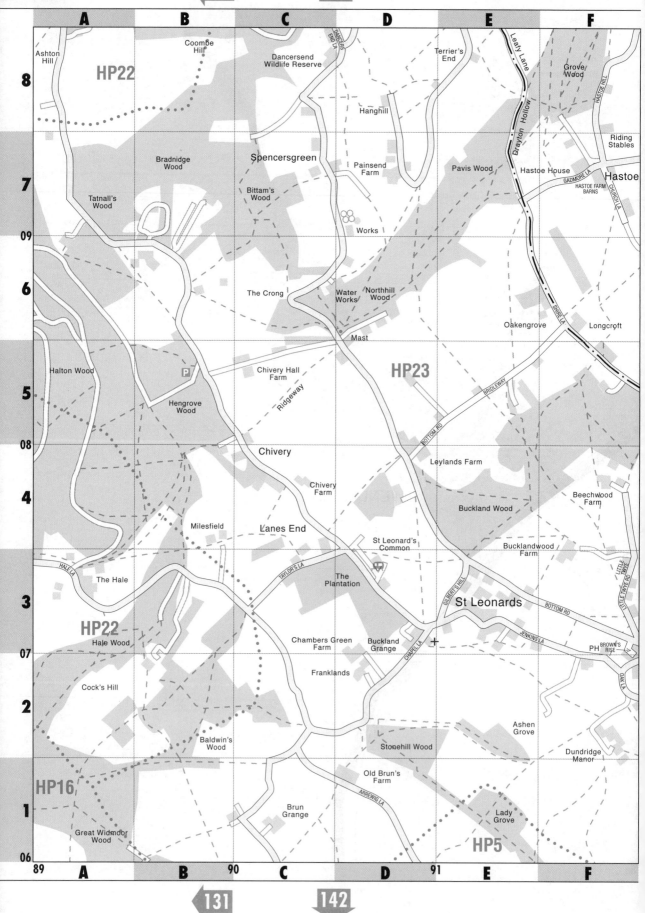

A B C D E F

8 Ashton Hill

HP22

Coombe Hill

Dancersend Wildlife Reserve

Terrier's End

Grove Wood

Hanghill

Riding Stables

Spencersgreen

Bradnidge Wood

Painsend Farm

Pavis Wood

Hastoe House

Hastoe

7 Tatnall's Wood

Bittam's Wood

HASTOE FARM BARNS

09 Works

6 The Crong

Water Works

Northhill Wood

Oakengrove

Longcroft

Mast

Halton Wood

HP23

5 Chivery Hall Farm

BRIDLEWAY

Hengrove Wood

Ridgeway

08 Chivery

Leylands Farm

4 Chivery Farm

Buckland Wood

Beechwood Farm

Milesfield

Lanes End

St Leonard's Common

Bucklandwood Farm

The Hale

The Plantation

St Leonards

BOTTOM RD

3 HP22

TAYLOR'S LA

GILBERT'S HILL

JENKINS LA

PH BROWN'S RISE

07 Hale Wood

Chambers Green Farm

Buckland Grange

CHAPEL LA

OAK LA

Franklands

2 Cock's Hill

Ashen Grove

Dundridge Manor

Baldwin's Wood

Stonehill Wood

HP16

Old Brun's Farm

ARREWIG LA

1 Great Widmoor Wood

Brun Grange

Lady Grove

HP5

06

89 A B 90 C D 91 E F

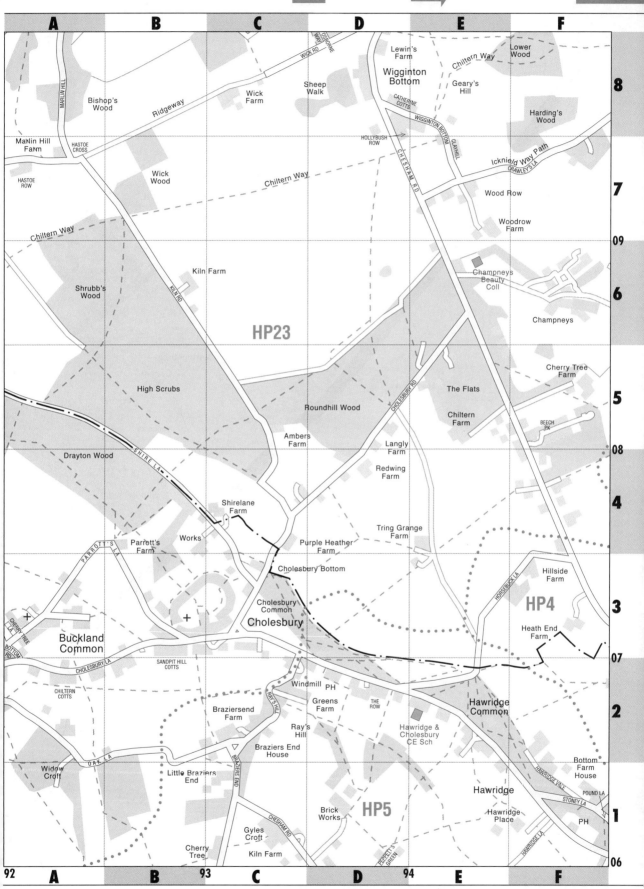

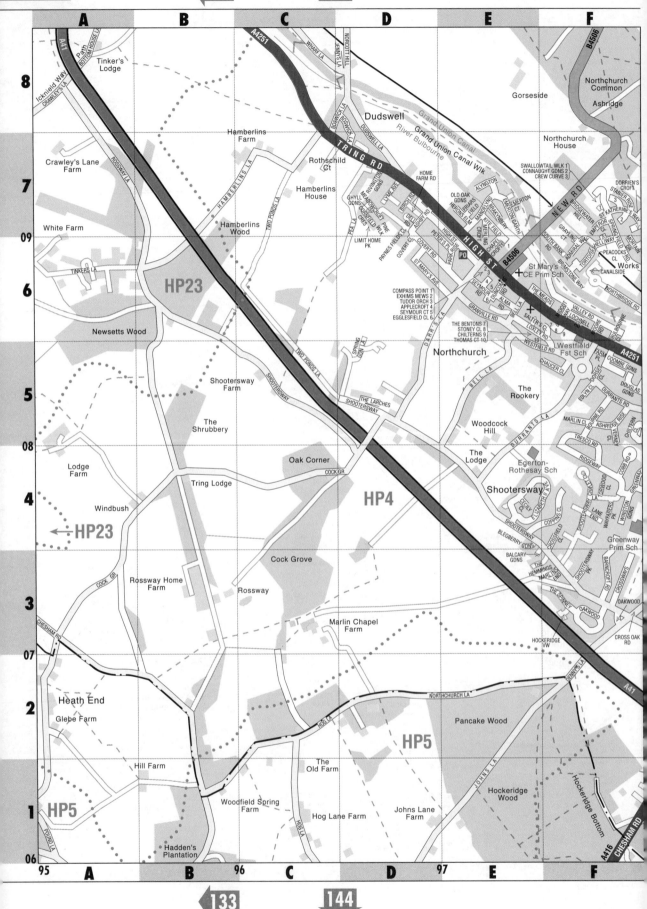

133
120

A B C D E F

8

Icknield Way
CRAWLEY'S LA
BOTTOM HOUSE LA
Path
Tinker's Lodge
A4251
WHARF LA
NORCOTT HILL
BOSWICK LA
BOSWICK LA
DUDSWELL LA
DUDSWELL LA

Gorseside
Northchurch Common
Ashridge

Dudswell
Grand Union Canal
River Bulbourne
Grand Union Canal Wlk
Northchurch House

B4506

7

Crawley's Lane Farm
ROSSWAY LA
HAMBERLINS LA
Hamberlins Farm
Rothschild Ct
TRING RD
Hamberlins House
TWO PONDS LA

HOME FARM RD
LYME AVE
BIRCH RD
DELL RD
ASHBY RD
OLD OAK GDNS
HERONS EL
KING'S RD
ALYNGTON
EMERTON CT
SWALLOWTAIL WLK 1
CONNAUGHT GDNS 2
CREW CURVE 3
NEW RD
BRIDGEWATER HILL
GRAYLING CT
ST KATHERINE'S WAY
SPRINGFIELD RD
EXMOOR CT
MORGAN CL
DORRIEN'S CROFT
STONIER REC
SOUTH BANK RD
ADMIRAL WAY
TORTOISESHELL RD
BRIMSTONE WAY
PEACOCKS CL
Works

09

White Farm
TINKERS LA
Hamberlins Wood
GHYLL GDNS
PEN LA
MEADOWCROFT PINE
OAKFIELD WLK
ORS
LIMIT HOME PK
PAYNES FIELDS CL
ST MARY'S AVE
COVERT RD
COVERT RD
HIGH ST
PARK ST
PETER'S PL
KING'S RD
PO
HEADS LYNS
CAPEL'S LYNS
KYE FIELD
BRAKYNBERY
HIGH ST
B4506
St Mary's CE Prim Sch
CANALSIDE
NORTHBRIDGE RD

6

HP23
Newsetts Wood
COMPASS POINT 1
EXHIMS MEWS 2
TUDOR ORCH 3
APPLECROFT 4
SEYMOUR CT 5
EGGLESFIELD CL 6
SEYMOUR RD
GRANVILLE RD
JUNCTION RD
ALMA RD
BELL LA
SALTER'S CL
THE MEADS
CROFT
LOCHNELL
VALLEY RD
BULBOURNE RD
A4251

Northchurch
THE BENTONS 7
STONEY CL 8
CHILTERNS 9
THOMAS CT 10
DARR'S LA
LOXLEY RD
WESTFIELD RD
Westfield Fst Sch
FARM PL
COOMBE GDNS

5

Shootersway Farm
SHOOTERSWAY
TWO PONDS LA
SPRING GDN LA
THE LARCHES
SHOOTERSWAY
BELL LA
The Rookery
CHAUCER CL
EDLYN CL
DURRANTS RD
DOUGLAS GDNS
TRESCO CL
CHILTERN RD

The Shrubbery
Woodcock Hill
BURRANTS LA
MARLIN CL
BOURNE RD
ASHRIDGE RISE
FERNEY
RIDGEWAY

08

Oak Corner
COCK GR
The Lodge
Egerton-Rothesay Sch
COBB RD

4

Lodge Farm
Tring Lodge
HP4
Shootersway
SHOOTERSWAY
CICELY LA
ELIZABETH CL
COPPINS CL
CROSSFIELD
SHOOTERSWAY PK
WAYFARERS PK
LANE END
WINSTON CL
GREENWAY PRIM SCH

HP23
Windbush
BLEGBERRY GDNS
BALCARY GDNS
THE HEMMINGS
MARLINS RD

3

COCK GR
Rossway Home Farm
Cock Grove
Rossway
HOCKERIDGE VW
THE SPINNEY
OAKWOOD
CROSS OAK RD

07

CHESHAM RD
Marlin Chapel Farm
A41
HENNY'S LA
A41

2

Heath End
Glebe Farm
HOG LA
NORTHCHURCH LA
Pancake Wood
JOHNS LA

HP5

1

Hill Farm
The Old Farm
Hog Lane Farm
Johns Lane Farm
Hockeridge Wood
Hockeridge Bottom

HP5
FOUND LA
Woodfield Spring Farm
HOG LA
A416
CHESHAM RD

06

95 A B 96 C D 97 E F

Hadden's Plantation

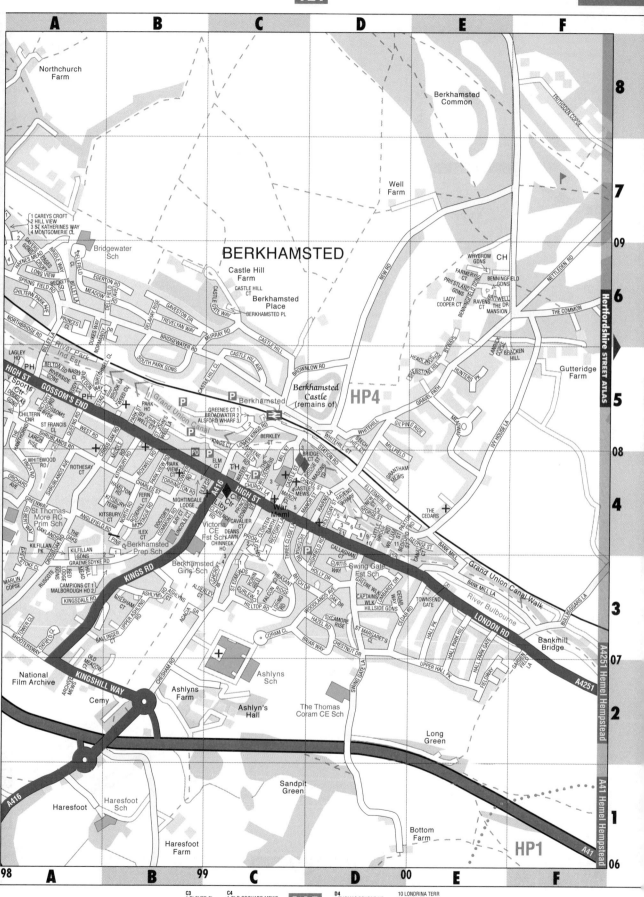

A	B	C	D	E	F

Northchurch Farm

8

Berkhamsted Common

7

Well Farm

09

1 CAREYS CROFT
2 HILL VIEW
3 ST KATHERINES WAY
4 MONTGOMERIE CL

BERKHAMSTED

Bridgewater Sch

WHYBROW GDNS
CH

FARMERYS CT
PRIESTLAND GDNS
BENNINGFIELD GDNS

6

Castle Hill Farm

CASTLE HILL CT
Berkhamsted Place
BERKHAMSTED PL

LADY COOPER CT
RAVENS CT
BATTWELL
THE DR
MANSION

Hertfordshire STREET ATLAS

NORTHBRIDGE RD

River Park Ind Est

CASTLE HILL AVE

BROWNLOW RD

HP4

HEADLANDS

HUNTERS PK

Gutteridge Farm

5

HIGH ST

GOSSOM'S END

Grand Union Canal

Berkhamsted

Berkhamsted Castle (remains of)

GILPIN'S RIDE

08

GREENES CT 1
BROADWATER 2
ALSFORD WHARF 3

STATION RD

Grantham Mews

War Meml

THE CEDARS

4

St Thomas More RC Prim Sch

Berkhamsted Prep Sch

Victoria CE Fst Sch

Berkhamsted Girls Sch

HIGH ST

Liby

Swing Gate Fst Sch

KINGS RD

Grand Union Canal Walk

3

Berkhamsted Girls Sch

CAMPIONS CT 1
MALBOROUGH HO 2
KINGSDALE RD

Townsend Gate

River Bulbourne

LONDON RD

07

Bankmill Bridge

A4251 Hemel Hempstead

National Film Archive

KINGSHILL WAY

Ashlyns Farm

Ashlyns Sch

Ashlyn's Hall

The Thomas Coram CE Sch

UPPER HALL PK

2

Cemy

A416

Haresfoot

Haresfoot Sch

Sandpit Green

Long Green

Bottom Farm

HP1

1

Haresfoot Farm

A41 Hemel Hempstead

06

A	B	C	D	E	F

99   00

C3
1 PLOVER CL
2 KESTREL CL
3 DAVIS HO
4 FROST HO

C4
1 OLD ORCHARD MEWS
2 PRIORY CT
3 CHURCHGATES
4 WILLIAM FISKE HO
5 DOWER MEWS
6 DWIGHTS YARD
7 Berkhamsted Sch

D4
1 THOMAS BOURNE HO
2 AUGUSTUS SMITH HO
3 COOPER WAY
4 GLASSMILL HO
5 NEW PROVIDENT PL
6 ROBERTSON RD
7 COSTINS WLK
8 MCDOUGALL RD
9 LONDRINA CT

10 LONDRINA TERR
11 UNION CT
12 OLD MILL GDNS
13 CAMBRIDGE TERR

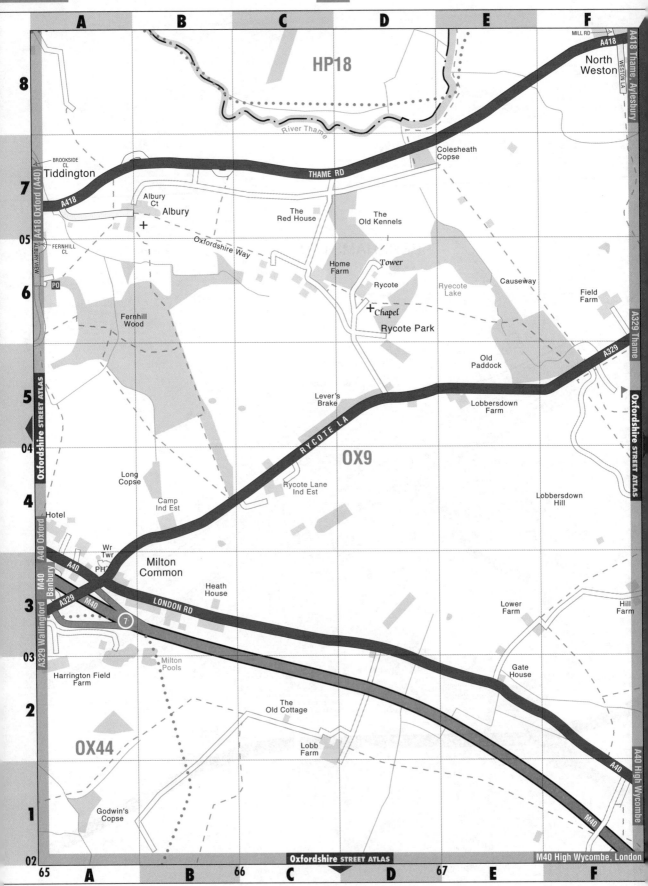

HP18

North Weston

MILL RD
A418
A418 Thame, Aylesbury

WESTON LA

Colesheath Copse

BROOKSIDE CL
Tiddington

A418 Oxford (A40)

THAME RD

Albury Ct
Albury

The Red House

The Old Kennels

Oxfordshire Way

A418

FERNHILL CL

ALBURY VIEW

PO

Home Farm

Tower

Rycote

Chapel

Rycote Park

Ryecote Lake

Causeway

Field Farm

A329 Thame

Fernhill Wood

Old Paddock

A329

Oxfordshire STREET ATLAS

Lever's Brake

Lobbersdown Farm

Oxfordshire STREET ATLAS

RYCOTE LA

OX9

Long Copse

Rycote Lane Ind Est

Lobbersdown Hill

Camp Ind Est

Hotel

A40 Oxford

Wr Twr

PH

Milton Common

Heath House

M40 Banbury

A40

M40

A329 Wallingford

LONDON RD

Lower Farm

Hill Farm

7

Milton Pools

Gate House

Harrington Field Farm

The Old Cottage

OX44

Lobb Farm

A40 High Wycombe

Godwin's Copse

M40

M40 High Wycombe, London

65 A B 66 C D 67 E F

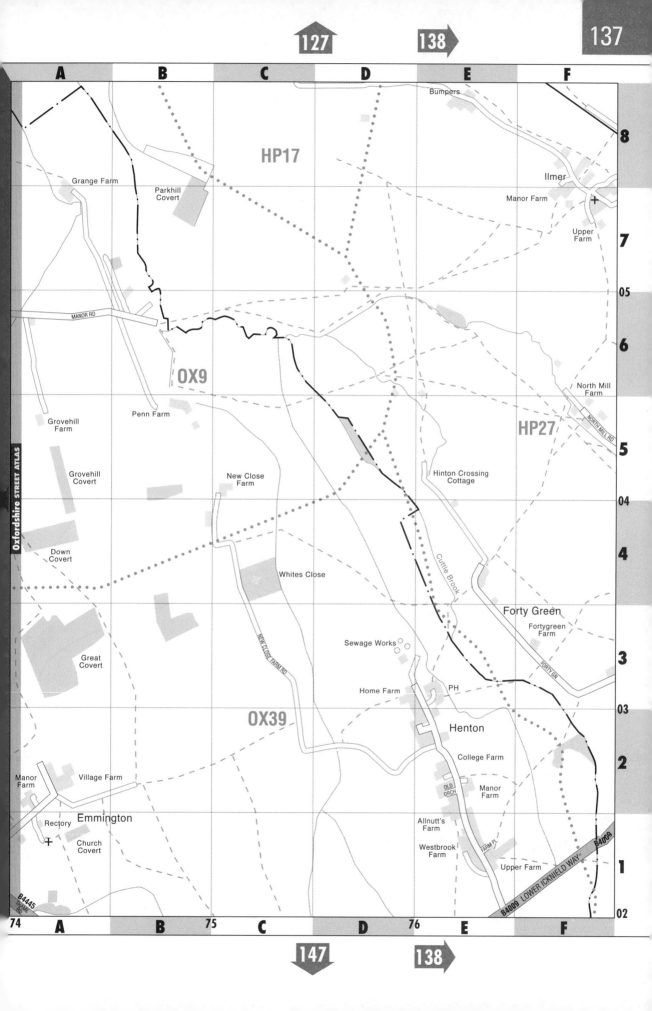

A   B   C   D   E   F

HP17

Bumpers

Grange Farm

Parkhill Covert

Ilmer

Manor Farm

Upper Farm

8

7

05

6

MANOR RD

OX9

Penn Farm

North Mill Farm

NORTH MILL RD

HP27

Grovehill Farm

Grovehill Covert

New Close Farm

Hinton Crossing Cottage

5

04

Down Covert

Whites Close

Cuttle Brook

Forty Green

Fortygreen Farm

4

Great Covert

NEW CLOSE FARM RD

Sewage Works

FORTY GN

OX39

Home Farm

PH

3

03

Henton

College Farm

2

Manor Farm

Village Farm

OLD ORCH

Manor Farm

Allnutt's Farm

Rectory

Emmington

Church Covert

Westbrook Farm

FARM PL

Upper Farm

B4009

LOWER ICKNIELD WAY

1

B4445 THAME RD

B4009

02

74 A   B   75   C   D   76   E   F

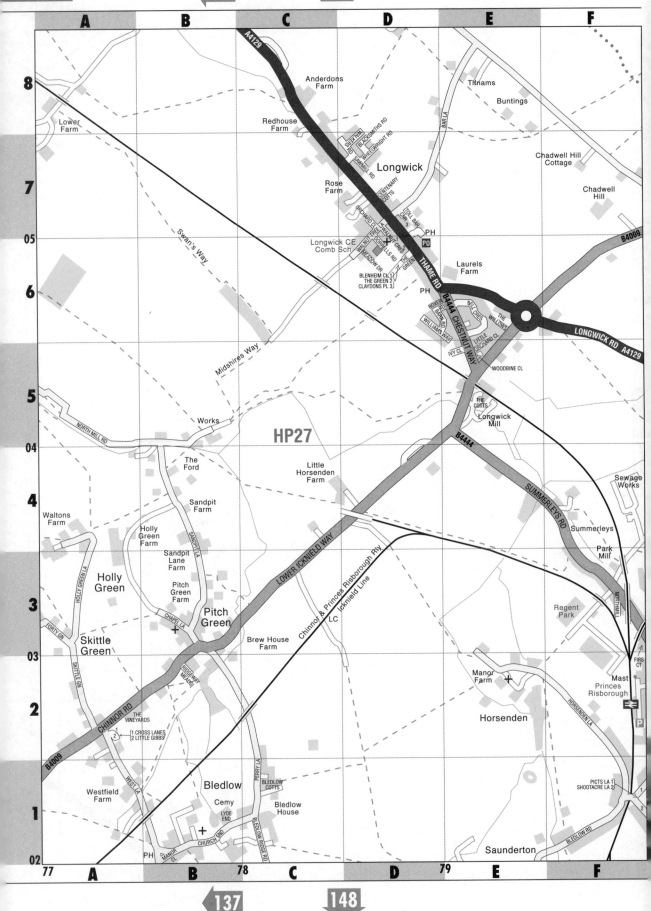

A | B | C | D | E | F

Lower Farm
Anderdons Farm
Titnams
Buntings
Redhouse Farm
Chadwell Hill Cottage
Chadwell Hill
SHED WN RD
BLACKSMITHS RD
WHEELWRIGHT RD
SAWMILL RD
BAR LA
Longwick
Rose Farm
CENTENARY COTTS
TOLL BAR
ORCHARD CL
WALNUT TREE
PURCELLS RD
WALNUT CRES
CNR 3
PH
PO
Swan's Way
Longwick CE Comb Sch
MEADOW DR
THE GREEN
Laurels Farm
BLENHEIM CL 1
THE GREEN 2
CLAYDONS PL 3
PH
BELL CRES
THE WILLOWS
B4009
THAME RD
BOXER RD
BARNARD
WILLIAMS WAY
LITTLE ORCHARD CL
IVY CL
B4444 CHESTNUT WAY
LONGWICK RD A4129
WOODBINE CL
Midshires Way
THE COTTS
Longwick Mill
Works
B4444
HP27
NORTH MILL RD
The Ford
Little Horsenden Farm
Sewage Works
Waltons Farm
Sandpit Farm
SUMMERLEYS RD
Summerleys
Holly Green Farm
Park Mill
Sandpit Lane Farm
SANDPIT LA
LOWER ICKNIELD WAY
NORTH MILL
HOLLY GREEN LA
Pitch Green Farm
Holly Green
Chinnor & Princes Risborough Rly
Icknield Line
Regent Park
CHAPEL LA
Pitch Green
FORTY GN
SKITTLE GN
Skittle Green
LC
RIDGEWAY MEADS
Brew House Farm
Manor Farm
FIRS CT
Mast
Princes Risborough
CHINNOR RD
THE VINEYARDS
1 CROSS LANES
2 LITTLE GIBBS
PERRY LA
Horsenden
HORSENDEN LA
P
B4009
WEST LA
BLEDLOW COTTS
Westfield Farm
Bledlow
Cemy
LYDE END
Bledlow House
PICTS LA 1
SHOOTACRE LA 2
BLEDLOW RIDGE RD
PH
MANOR CL
CHURCH END
BLEDLOW RD
Saunderton

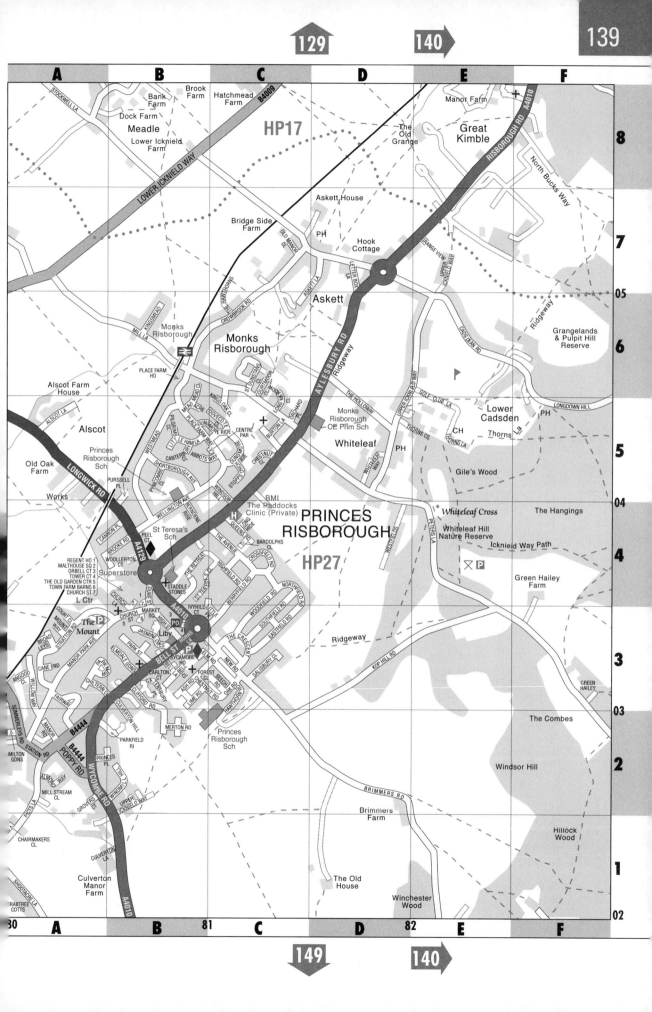

139
130

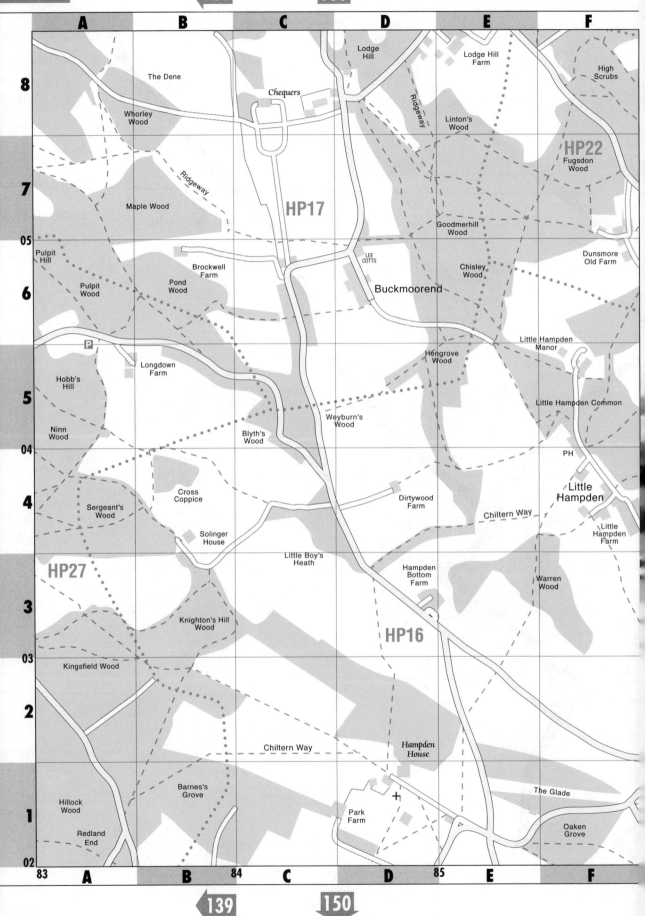

139
150

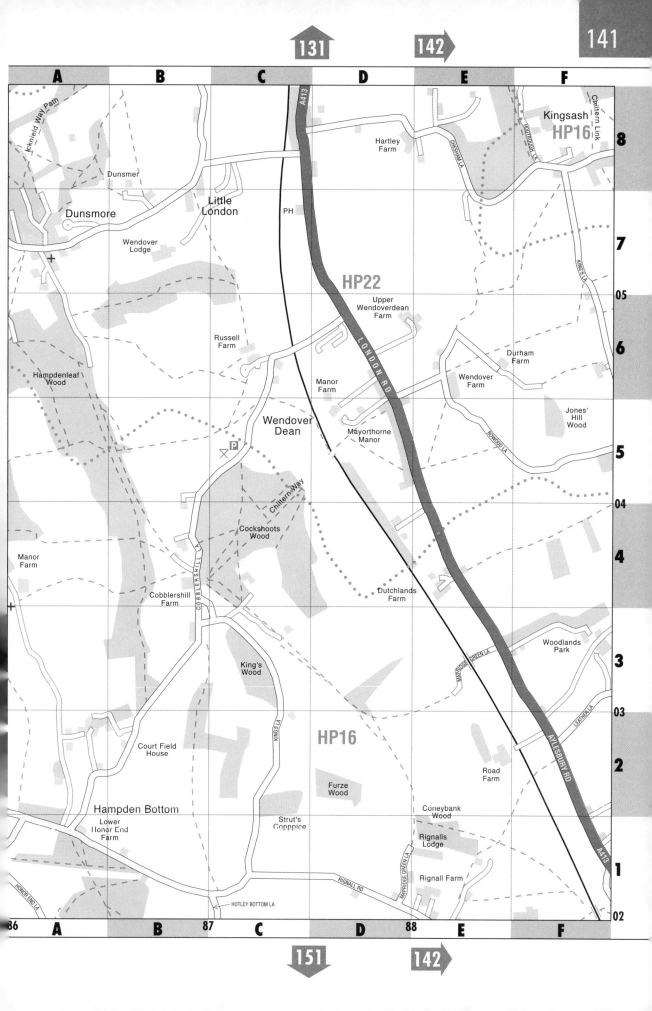

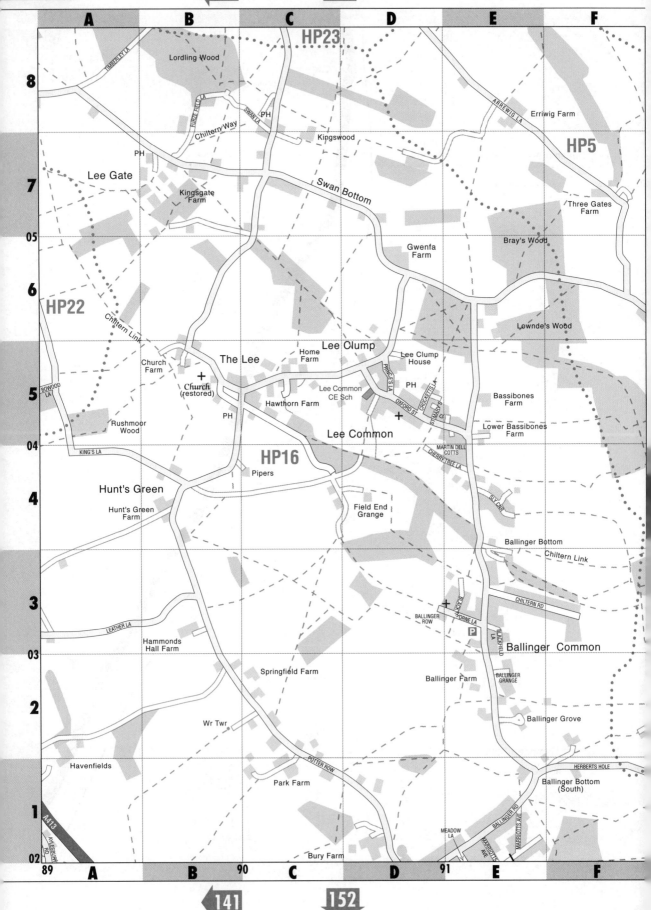

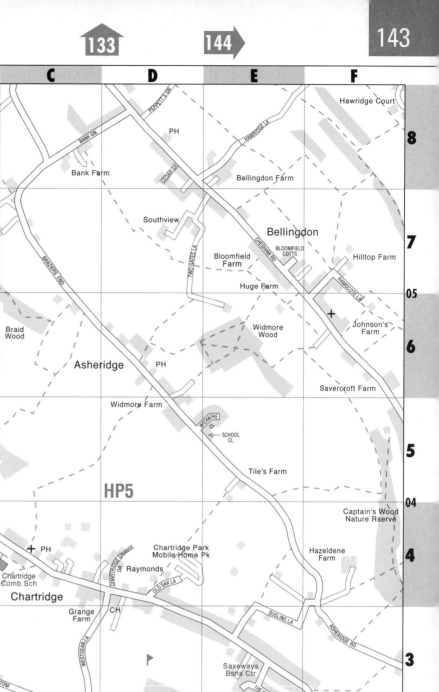

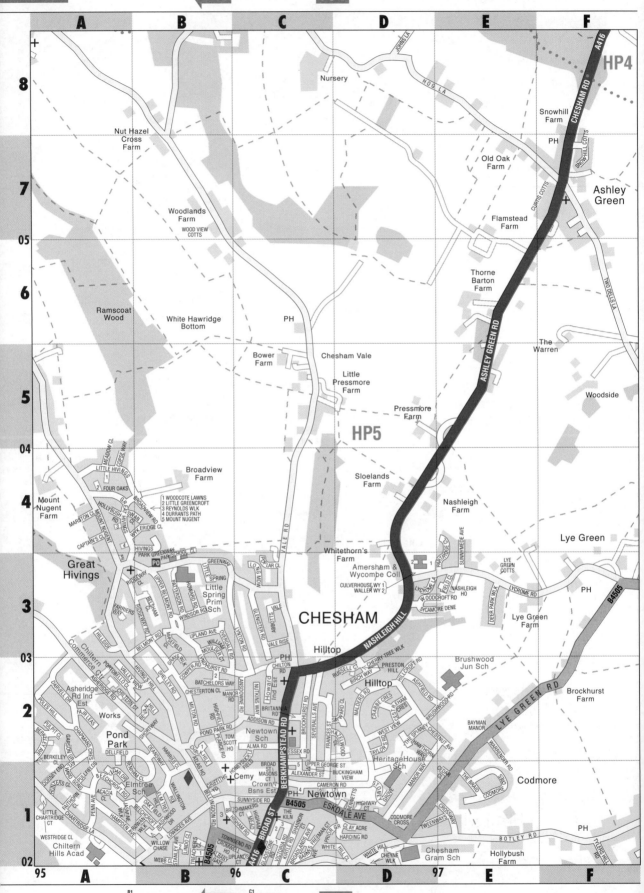

B1
1 WESLEY HILL
2 UPPER MDW
3 Phoenix Bsns Ctr
B2
1 THE CHASE
2 NIGHTINGALE RD

C1
1 QUEENS RD
2 UPPER GLADSTONE RD
3 FRANCHISE ST
4 TURNERS WLK
5 GEORGE ST
6 CAMERON RD
7 GREATACRE

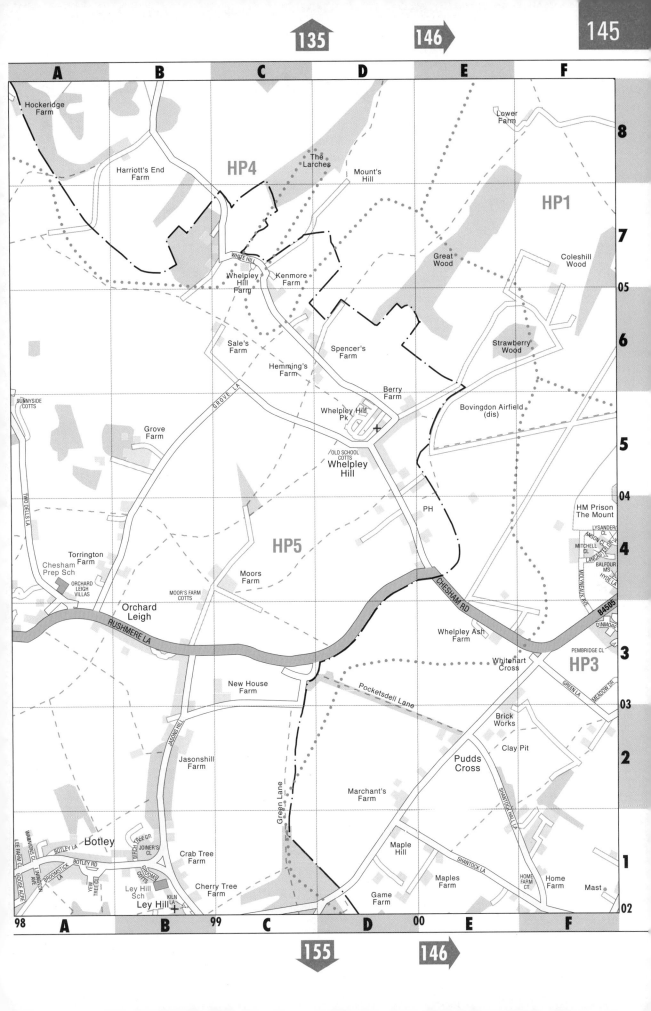

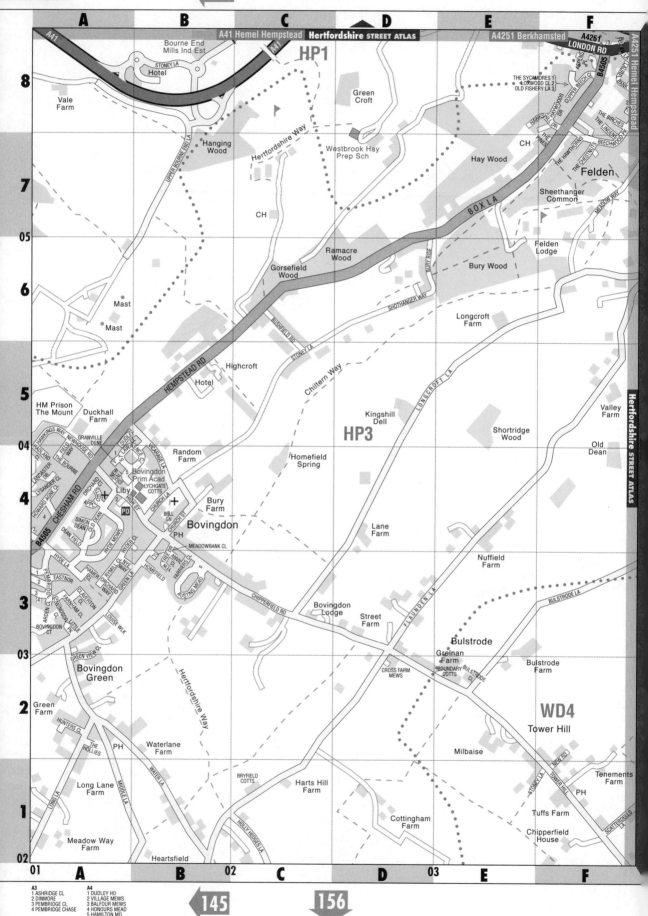

145

A B C D E F

A41
Bourne End
Mills Ind Est
A41 Hemel Hempstead **Hertfordshire** STREET ATLAS
A4251 Berkhamsted
A4251 Hemel Hempstead
A4251
LONDON RD
B4505

HP1

THE SYCAMORES 1
LOXWOOD CL 2
OLD FISHERY LA 3

8

Hotel
STONEY LA

Vale
Farm

Green
Croft

THE BIRCHES
THE LINDENS
BEECHWOOD CT

Hanging
Wood
Herttordshire Way

Westbrook Hay
Prep Sch

Hay Wood

CH

Felden

HAWKSHILL DR
HAWKWOOD DR
COPPER BEECH CL
ASPEN CL
THE HAWTHORNS
THE CHESTNUTS
THE PINES

7

CH

Sheethanger
Common

MEADOW WAY

05

Ramacre
Wood

BOX LA

Felden
Lodge

Gorsefield
Wood

BURY RISE

Bury Wood

6

Mast

SHOTHANGER WAY

Longcroft
Farm

BUSHFIELD RD

Mast

STONEY LA

HEMPSTEAD RD

Highcroft

Chiltern Way

LONGCROFT LA

Valley
Farm

5

Hotel

HM Prison
The Mount

Duckhall
Farm

Kingshill
Dell

Shortridge
Wood

Old
Dean

HAWKINGS WAY
NEWHOUSE RD
FIELD WAY
DUDLEY
LANK CL
MC CL
GRANVILLE
DENE

VICARAGE LA

04

Random
Farm

HP3

LYSANDER CL
HALL AND
THE BOURNE
LANCASTER DR

NEW
CL
ORCHARD
APPLE
Bovingdon
Prim Acad
LYCHGATE
COTTS

Homefield
Spring

4

Liby
PO

HIGH ST
CHURCH LA

Bury
Farm

CHESHAM RD

SIMON
DEAN
ED DEAN
B4505
DEAN FIELD

BELL
GN
CHURCH ST
✠

Lane
Farm

Nuffield
Farm

HOWARD AGNE CL

Bovingdon

PH
MEADOWBANK CL

BULSTRODE LA

3

HYDE LA
PEMBRIDGE
CL
EASTNOR
CLAVERTON
FARNHAM CL
WINDSOR PK
LITTLE
BOVINGDON
CT

HAMER CL
RYDAL CL
ORCHARD
WAY
NYE
TREE
CL
ANWELL
GREEN LA
FAIRBROOKS
CL
AUSTINS MEAD

CHIPPERFIELD RD

Bovingdon
Lodge

Street
Farm

FLAUNDEN LA

Bulstrode

Greinan
Farm

Bulstrode
Farm

03

LOUISE WLK

GREEN VIEW CL

CROSS FARM
MEWS

BOUNDARY
COTTS
BULSTRODE
CL

Bovingdon
Green

Herttordshire Way

WD4

Tower Hill

2

Green
Farm

HUNTERS CL

THE
ROLLIES

PH

Waterlane
Farm

WATER LA

Milbaise

SNOW RD

Tenements
Farm

STONEY LA
TOWER HILL

PH

1

Long Lane
Farm

MIDDLE LA

BRYFIELD
COTTS

HOLLY HEDGES LA

Harts Hill
Farm

Tuffs Farm

SCATTERELL

LONG LA

Cottingham
Farm

Chipperfield
House

Meadow Way
Farm

Heartsfield

02

01 A B 02 C D 03 E F

145 156

A3
1 ASHRIDGE CL
2 DINMORE
3 PEMBRIDGE CL
4 PEMBRIDGE CHASE

A4
1 DUDLEY HO
2 VILLAGE MEWS
3 BALFOUR MEWS
4 HONOURS MEAD
5 HAMILTON MD

Hertfordshire STREET ATLAS

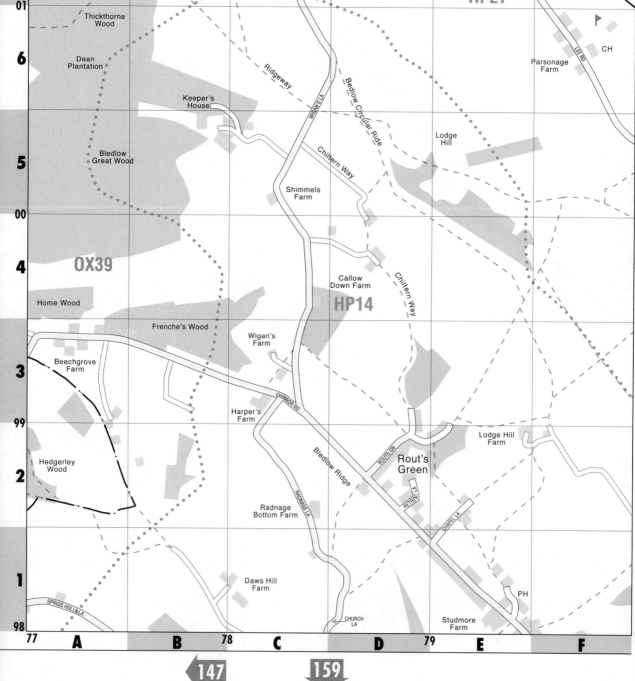

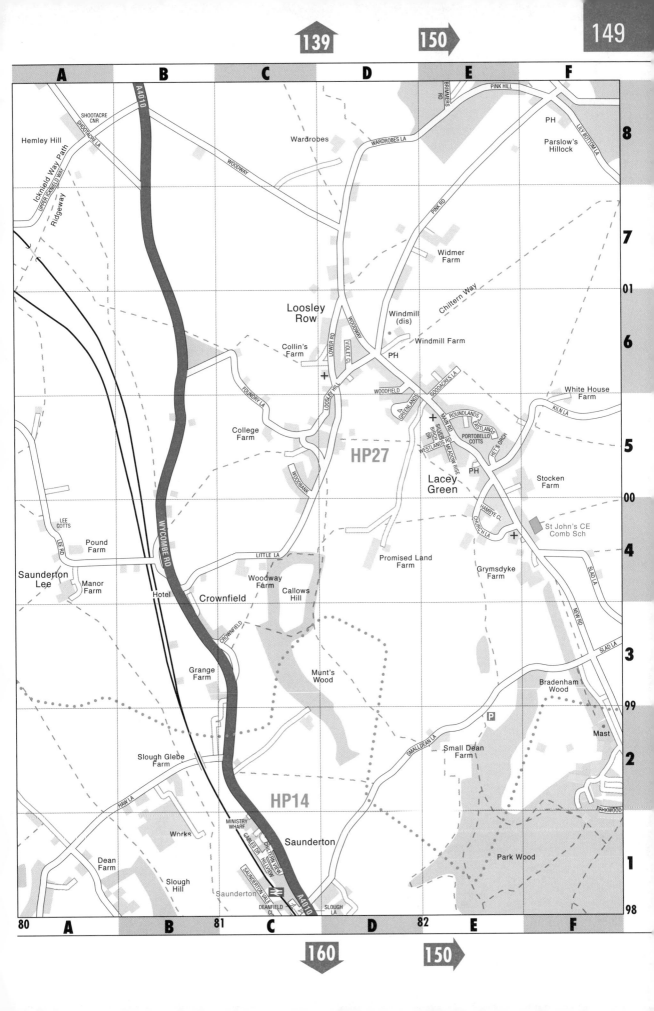

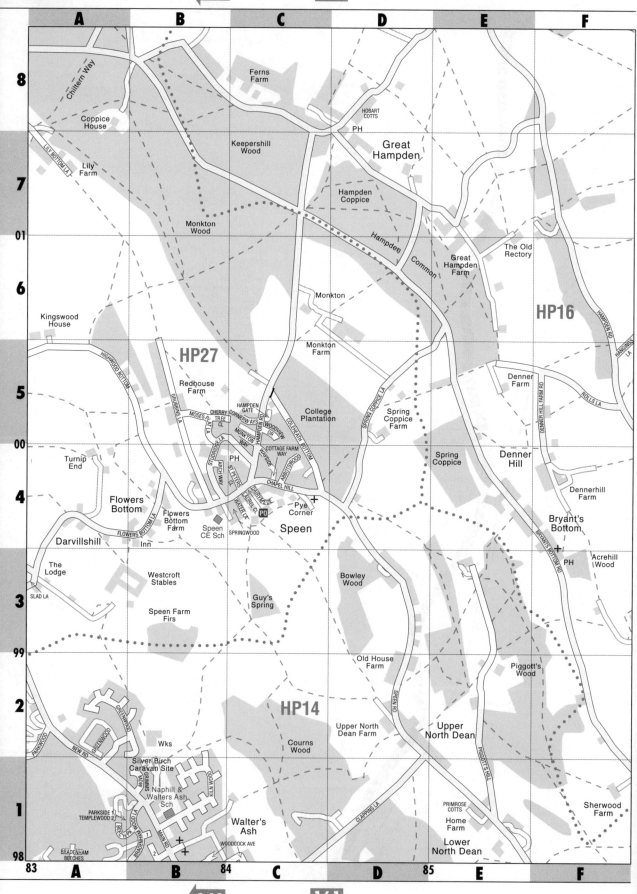

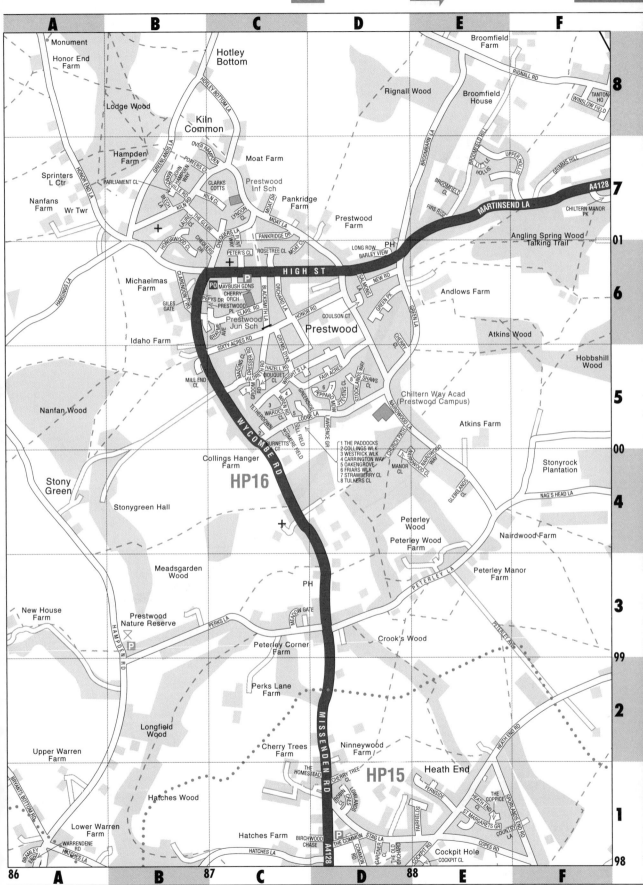

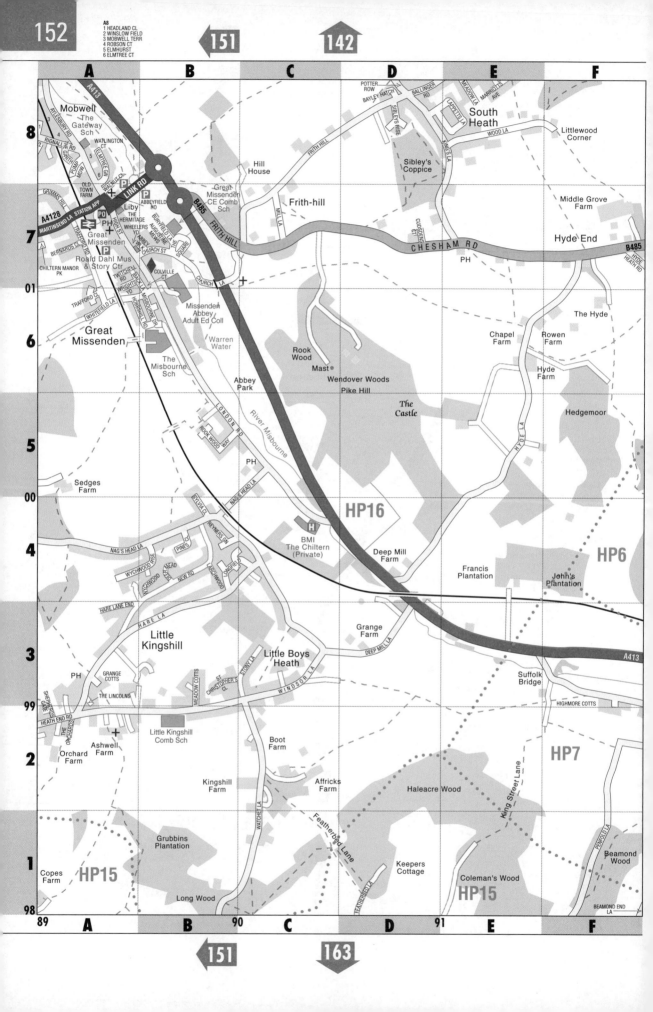

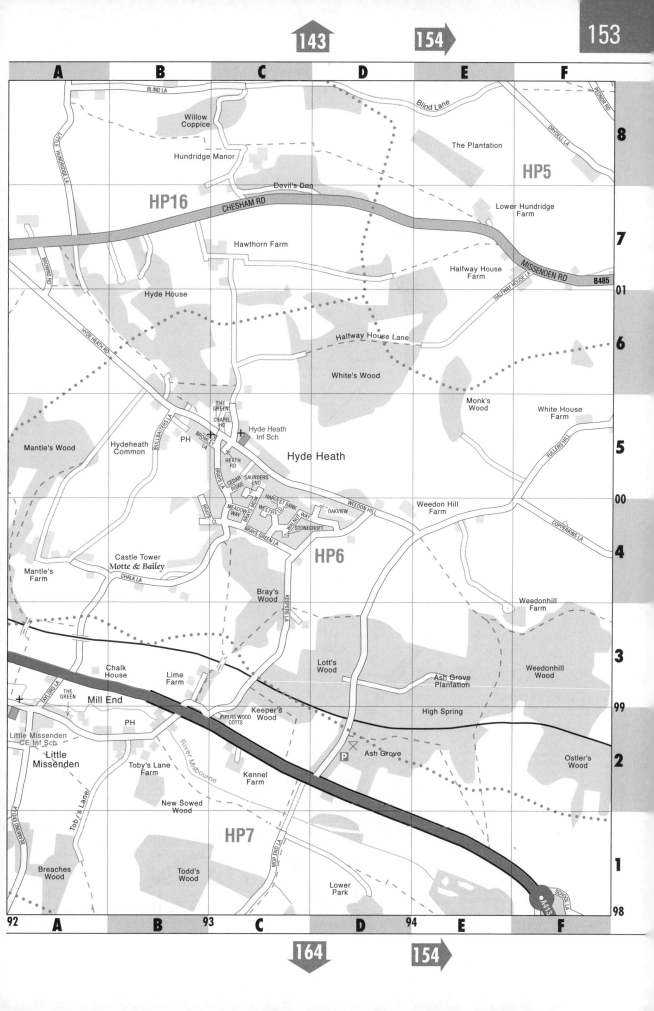

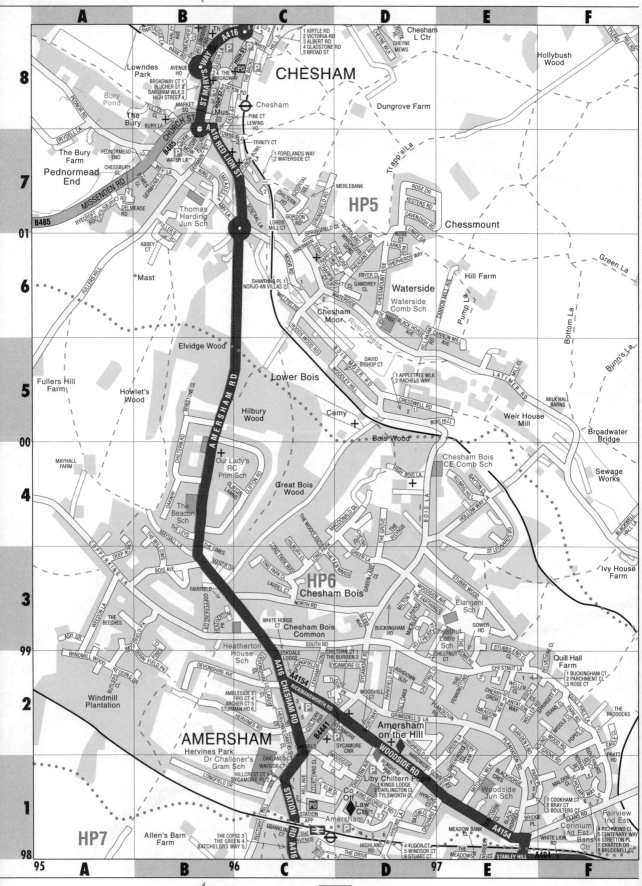

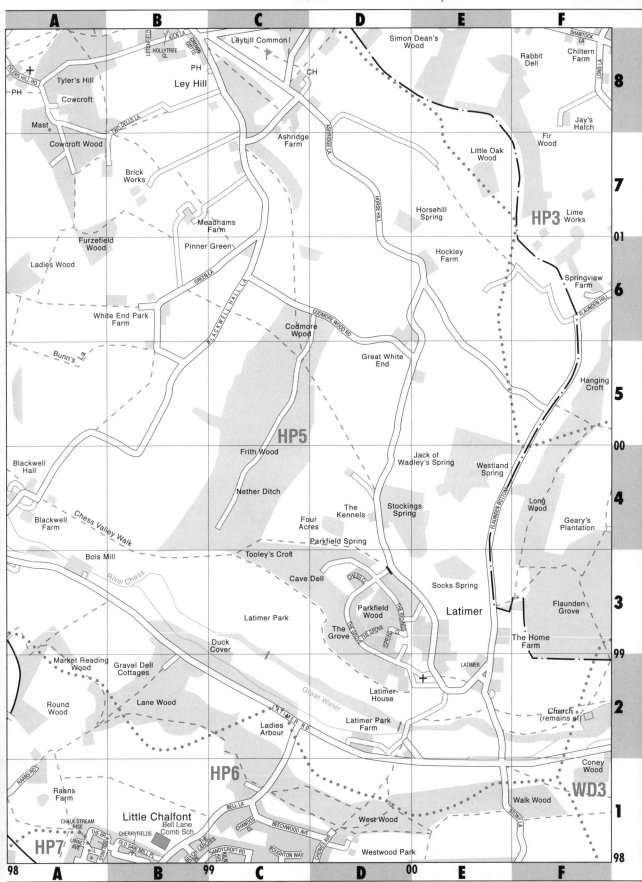

155
146

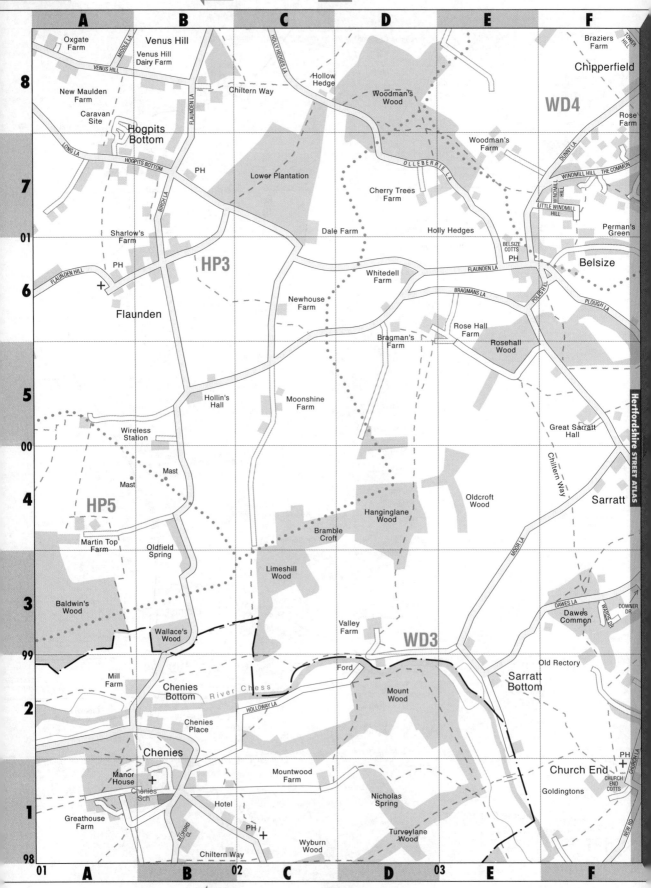

M40 Oxford (A40), Banbury

A40 Oxford

Oxfordshire STREET ATLAS

OX39

Lewknor

Manor House

Church Farm

Lewknor CE Prim Sch

THE GLEBE

BEACON VIEW

PH

6

Beacon Cottage

The White House

The Glade Warren Farm

Grove Wood

Juniper Bank

Cuckoo Pen

Beacon Hill

Aston Wood

ASTON HILL

A40

The Knapp

B4009

Hill Farm

Aston Rowant National Nature Reserve

Grants Plantation

Hailey Wood

HILL RD

P

M40

OX49

Ridgeway Swan's Way

Old Cricketground Plantation

Bald Hill

Upper Vicar's Farm

Sadler's Wood

HP14

White's Wood

Lower Vicar's Farm

Nature Reserve

P

Cowleaze Wood

Shirburn Hill

Wellground Wood

Field House

Weston Wood

Lydall's Wood

Warren Hill

Shirburn Wood

Portobello Farm

PORTOBELLO COTTS

Bell Plantation

Dean Wood

Young Wood

Wormsley

Pyrton Hill

Shirburn Lodge

Cop Grove

Copgrove Wood

Shotridge Wood

RG9

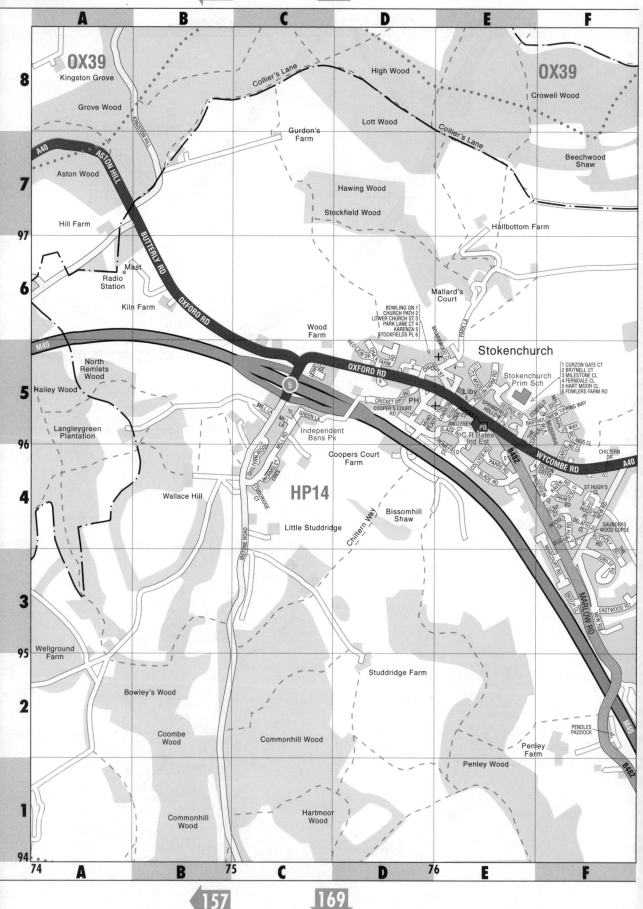

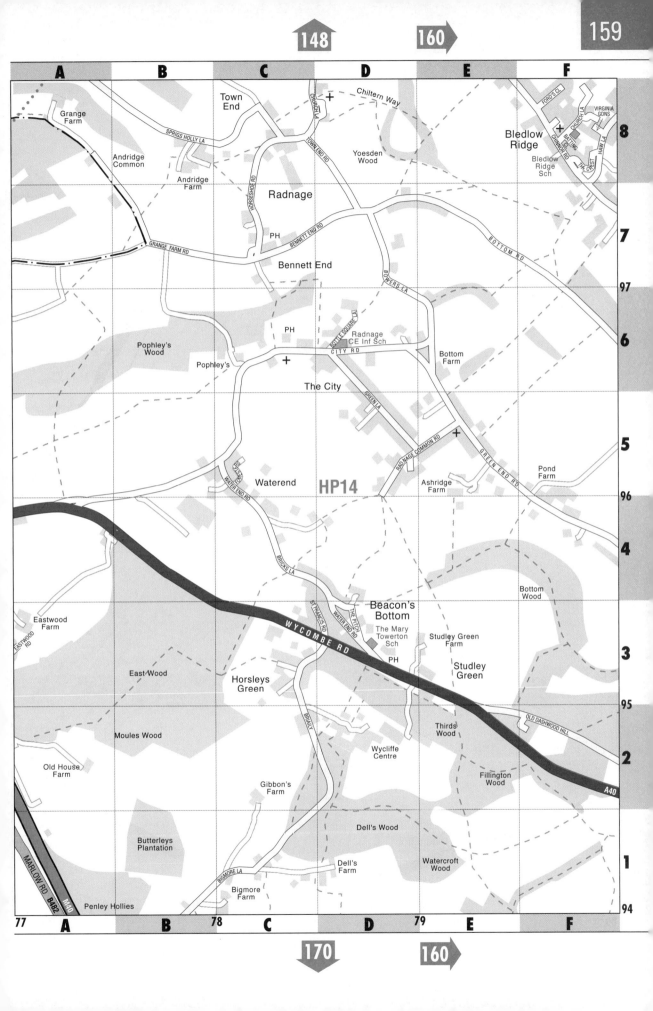

A B C D E F

148
160

Town End

Chiltern Way

Grange Farm

SPRIGS HOLLY LA

Andridge Common

Andridge Farm

Yoesden Wood

Bledlow Ridge

FORD'S CL.

VIRGINIA GDNS

CHURCH LA

BATTING

Bledlow Ridge Sch

THE CREST

HAW LA

CHINNOR RD

TOWN END RD

CHURCH LA

HORSESHOE RD

Radnage

8

PH

BENNETT END RD

GRANGE FARM RD

Bennett End

BOWERS LA

BOTTOM RD

7

97

Pophley's Wood

Pophley's

PH

BOTTLE SQUARE LA

Radnage CE Inf Sch

CITY RD

Bottom Farm

6

The City

GREEN LA

RADNAGE COMMON RD

Ashridge Farm

GREEN END RD

Pond Farm

5

Waterend

WATER END RD

BRICKS LA

HP14

96

4

Eastwood Farm

EASTWOOD RD

East Wood

Horsleys Green

ST FRANCIS RD

THE PITCH

WATER END RD

WYCOMBE RD

Beacon's Bottom

The Mary Towerton Sch

PH

Studley Green Farm

Studley Green

Bottom Wood

3

95

Moules Wood

BRIALY

Wycliffe Centre

Thirds Wood

OLD DASHWOOD HILL

2

Old House Farm

Gibbon's Farm

Fillington Wood

A40

1

Butterleys Plantation

Dell's Wood

Dell's Farm

Watercroft Wood

MARLOW RD
B482
M40

BIGMORE LA

Bigmore Farm

Penley Hollies

94

77 A B 78 C D 79 E F

170
160

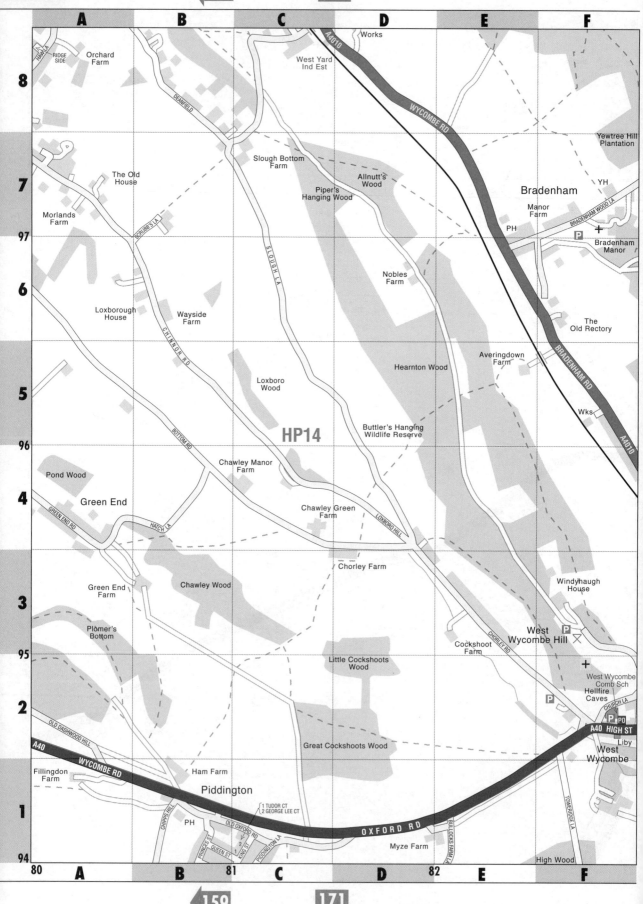

159
149

A B C D E F

8

Works

Orchard Farm

RIDGE SIDE

HAM LA

West Yard Ind Est

DEANFIELD

WYCOMBE RD

A4010

Yewtree Hill Plantation

7

The Old House

Slough Bottom Farm

Piper's Hanging Wood

Allnutt's Wood

Bradenham

YH

Manor Farm

BRADENHAM WOOD LA

Morlands Farm

SCRUBB'S LA

97

PH

P

Bradenham Manor

6

Loxborough House

Wayside Farm

CHINNOR RD

SLOUGH LA

Nobles Farm

The Old Rectory

BRADENHAM RD

Loxboro Wood

Hearnton Wood

Averingdown Farm

5

BOTTOM RD

Wks

A4010

96

HP14

Buttler's Hanging Wildlife Reserve

Chawley Manor Farm

Pond Wood

4

Green End

HATCH LA

Chawley Green Farm

Loxboro Hill

LOXBORO HILL

Windyhaugh House

Chorley Farm

3

Green End Farm

GREEN END RD

Chawley Wood

West Wycombe Hill

P

Cockshoot Farm

CHORLEY RD

Plomer's Bottom

95

Little Cockshoots Wood

West Wycombe Comb Sch

Hellfire Caves

CHURCH LA

2

OLD DASHWOOD HILL

A40

WYCOMBE RD

Ham Farm

Great Cockshoots Wood

P

P PO

A40 HIGH ST

Liby

West Wycombe

Fillingdon Farm

Piddington

CHIPPS HILL

PH

1 TUDOR CT
2 GEORGE LEE CT

OXFORD RD

BULLOCKS FARM LA

TOWERIDGE LA

1

PRINCES ST

QUEEN ST

KING ST

OLD OXFORD RD

PIDDINGTON LA

Myze Farm

94

High Wood

80 A B 81 C D 82 E F

159
171

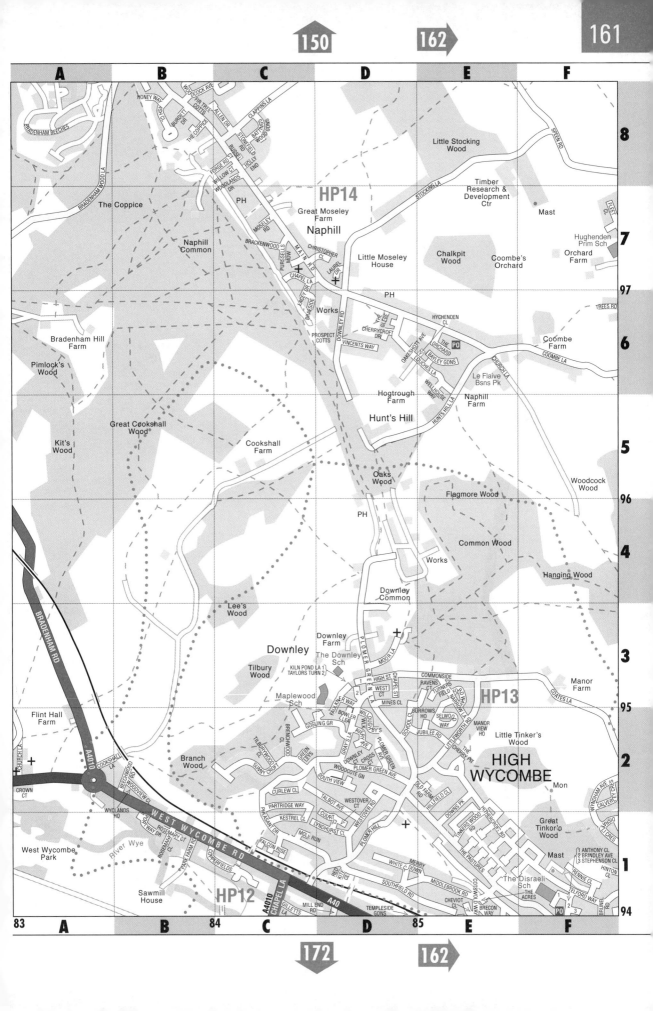

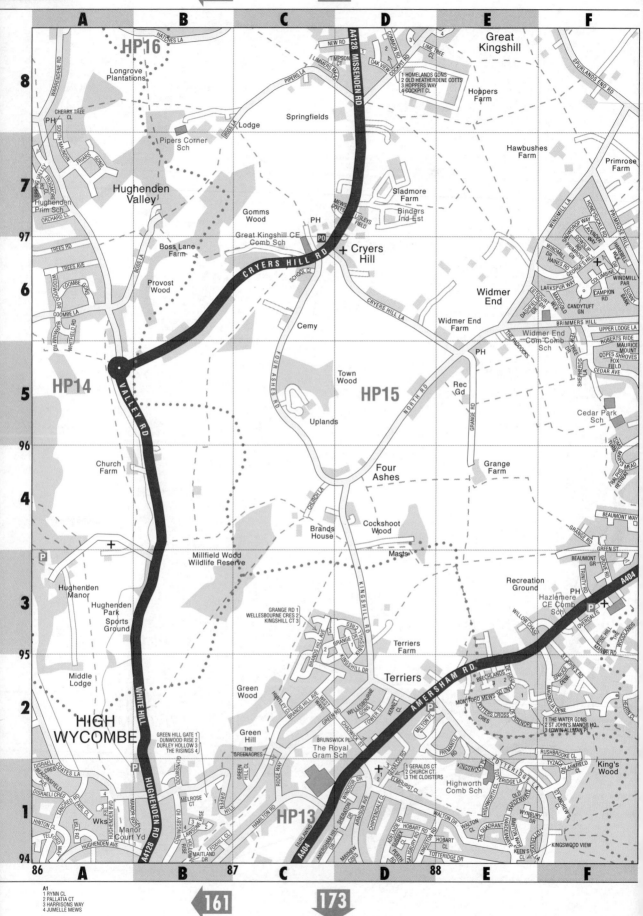

A1
1 RYNN CL
2 PALLATIA CT
3 HARRISONS WAY
4 JUMELLE MEWS

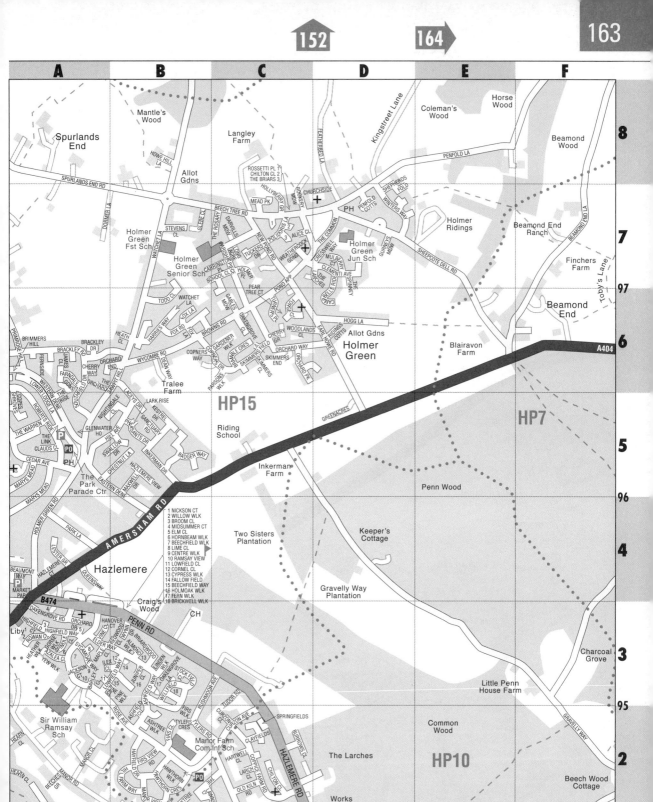

163
153

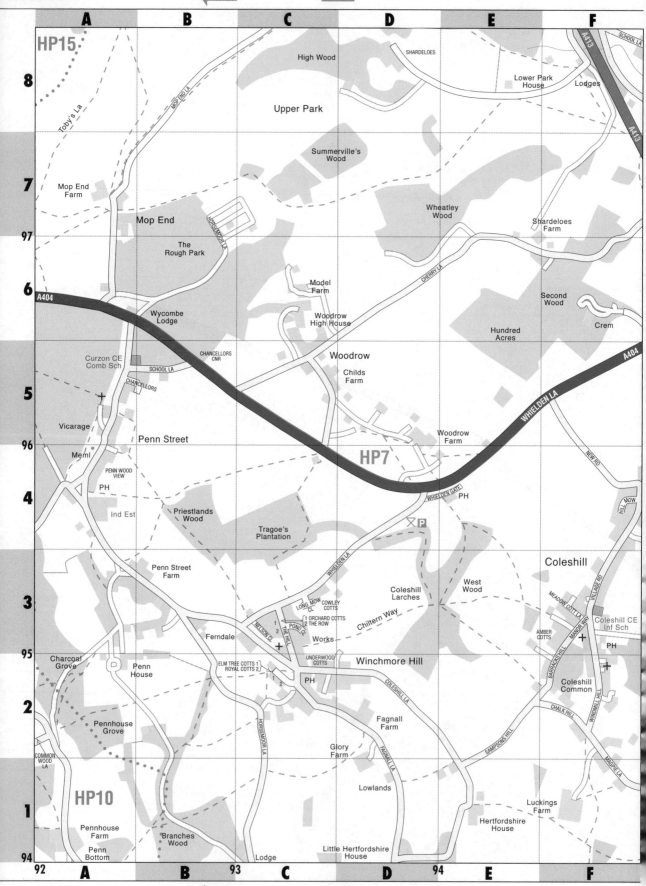

HP15

A **B** **C** **D** **E** **F**

8

Toby's La

Mop End Farm

Mop End
The Rough Park

7

HORSEMOOR LA

MOP END LA

High Wood

Upper Park

SHARDELOES

Lower Park House

Lodges

A413

SCHOOL RD

Summerville's Wood

Wheatley Wood

97

Shardeloes Farm

6

A404

Wycombe Lodge

Model Farm

Woodrow High House

CHERRY LA

Second Wood

Crem

A404

Curzon CE Comb Sch

CHANCELLORS CNR

SCHOOL LA

Woodrow

Childs Farm

Hundred Acres

WHIELDEN LA

5

CHANCELLORS

Vicarage

Penn Street

Meml

PENN WOOD VIEW

PH

Woodrow Farm

HP7

NEW RD

96

Ind Est

Priestlands Wood

Tragoe's Plantation

WHIELDEN GATE

PH

HILL MDW

4

WHIELDEN LA

P

West Wood

Coleshill

HILL

Penn Street Farm

Ferndale

LONG MDW CL

COWLEY COTTS

1 ORCHARD COTTS
2 THE ROW

Coleshill Larches

Chiltern Way

MEADOW COTT LA

VILLAGE RD

Coleshill CE Inf Sch

3

NELSON CL

THE HILL

POND CL

Works

AMBER COTTS

MANOR WAY

95

Charcoal Grove

Penn House

ELM TREE COTTS 1
ROYAL COTTS 2

1
2

UNDERWOOD COTTS

PH

Winchmore Hill

COLESHILL LA

BARRACKS HILL

PH

Coleshill Common

2

Pennhouse Grove

HORSEMOOR LA

Fagnall Farm

FAGNALL LA

SAMPSONS HILL

CHALK HILL

WINDMILL HILL

MAGPIE LA

COMMON WOOD LA

HP10

Glory Farm

Lowlands

Luckings Farm

1

Pennhouse Farm

Penn Bottom

Branches Wood

Lodge

Little Hertfordshire House

Hertfordshire House

94

92 **A** 93 **B** **C** 94 **D** **E** **F**

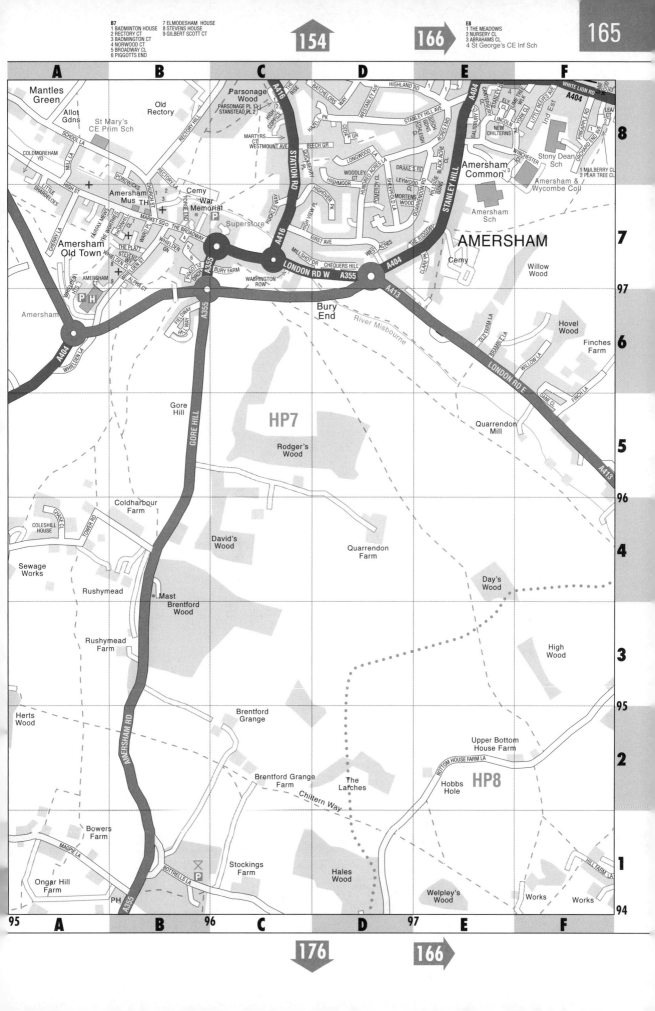

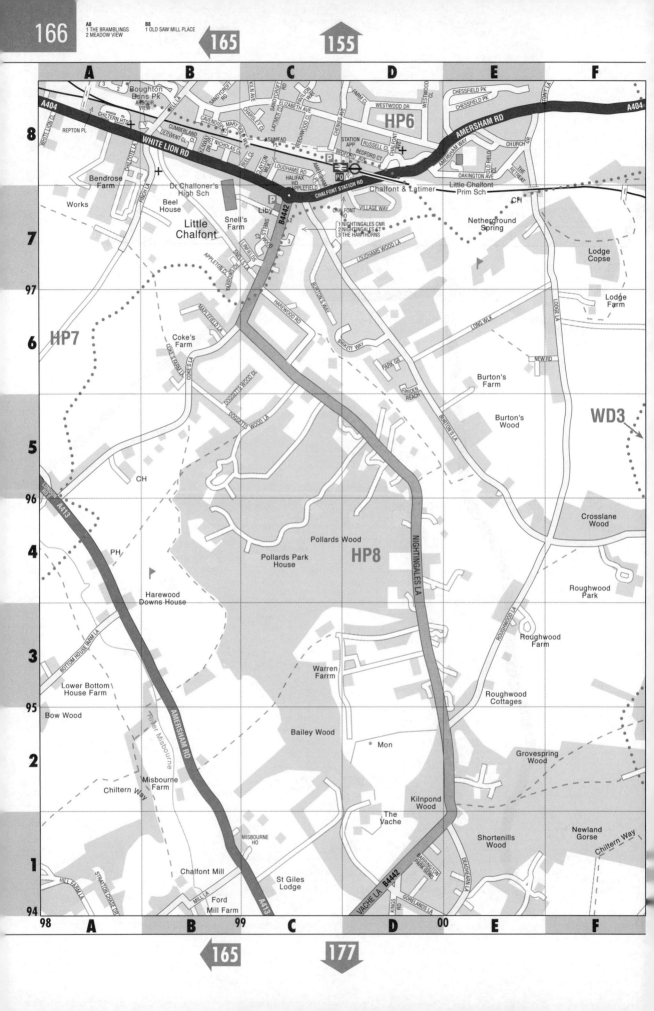

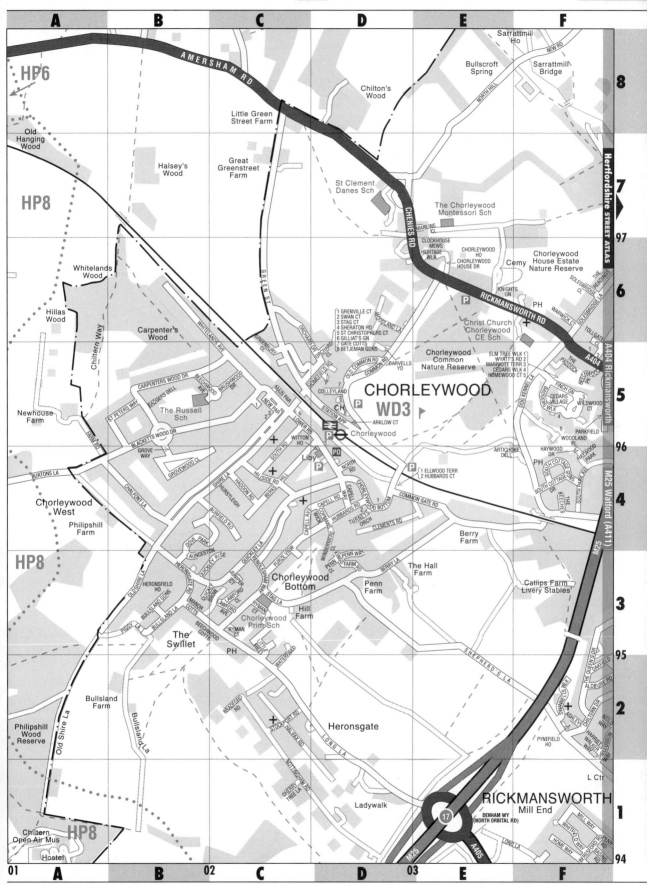

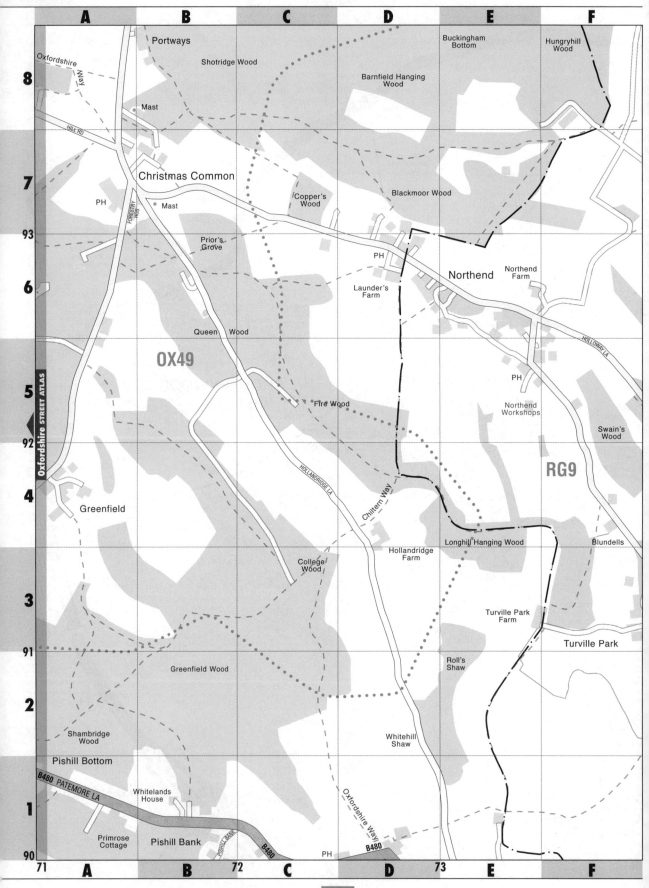

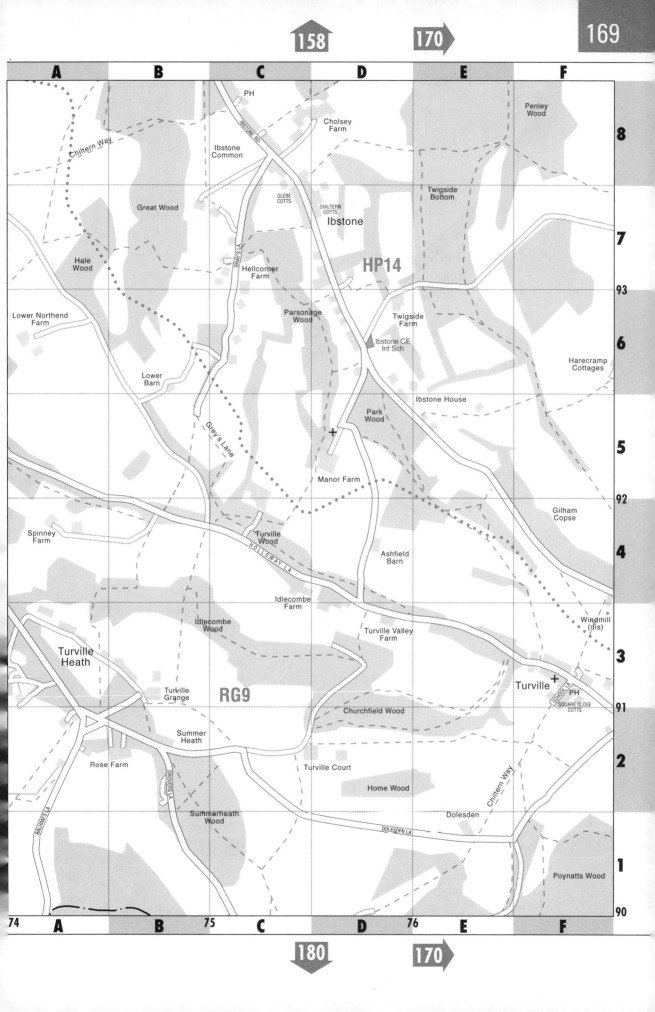

← 169   159

A   B   C   D   E   F

B482

M40

8

Barn Wood

Leygrove's Wood

Chequers Manor Farm

7

Watercroft Farm

Huckenden Farm

PH

Pound Wood

HP14

MARLOW RD

BIGMORE LA

93

Kensham Farm

Cadmore End Common

6

Pound Farm

Cadmore End CE Comb Sch

Cadmore End

PH

Bolter End

M40

NEW RD

BOLTER END LA

Hill Farm

Rackley's Farm

PH

FININGS RD   B482

CHEQUERS LA

5

Hanger Wood

Priestley's Farm

92

Gravesend

4

Manor Farm

Long Copse

Mill Hanging Wood

Hanger Farm

FINGEST LA

Hanover Hill

3

Turville Hill

Fingest

RG9

PH

91

Fingest Wood

Mousell's Wood

Dovers Farm

Murrage Farm

DOLESDEN LA

WATERY LA

Chiltern Way

Maiden House

Spurgrove

PH

2

Goddard's Wood

Adam's Wood

SPURGROVE LA

Little Frieth

PERRIN SPRINGS LA

ELLERY RISE

HORNBEAM CL

Frieth

PH

Poynatts Farm

Bottom Wood

1

PH

SHOGMOOR LA

Upper Goddards

Colliers Farm

INNINGS GATE

Maiden Farm

Frieth CE Comb Sch

Stud Farm

Lower Goddards Farm

SHOGMOOR LA

PARMOOR LA

HAYLES LEAD

90

Skirmett

← 169   181

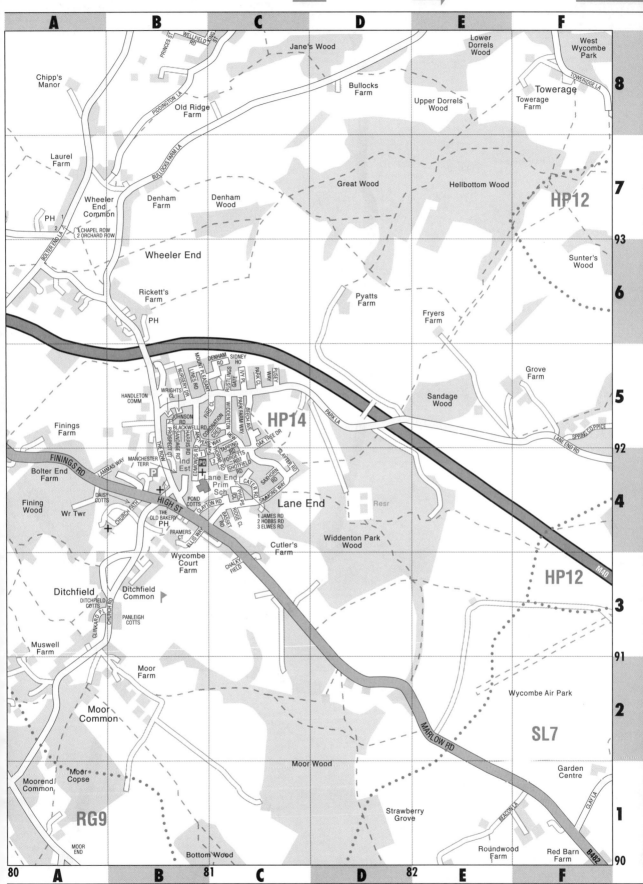

A   B   C   D   E   F

8
7
93
6
5
92
4
3
91
2
1
90

Chipp's Manor

Laurel Farm

PH
1 CHAPEL ROW
2 ORCHARD ROW

PRINCES ST
WELLFIELD RD
KING ST
PIDDINGTON LA
Old Ridge Farm
BULLOCKS FARM LA

Jane's Wood

Bullocks Farm

Upper Dorrels Wood

Lower Dorrels Wood

West Wycombe Park

TOWERIDGE LA

Towerage
Towerage Farm

HP12

Wheeler End Common

Denham Farm

Denham Wood

Great Wood

Hellbottom Wood

Sunter's Wood

BOLTER END LA

Wheeler End

Rickett's Farm

PH

Pyatts Farm

Fryers Farm

Grove Farm

Finings Farm

DENHAM RD
SIDNEY HO
NURSERY DR
MOUNT PLEASANT
LINES RD
WRIGHTS CL
PARK CL
IVY PL
FOSTERS LA
PUSEY WAY

HANDLETON COMM

JOHNSON RD
PROSPECT RD
BLACKWELL
HARRIS RD
FOS CL
CORONATION CRES
WIDDENTON
PARK FARM WAY
SANDAGE RD
AYERS WAY
BEECH AVE
OAK TREE DR

HP14

PARK LA

Sandage Wood

SPRING COPPICE
LANE END RD

Bolter End Farm

FININGS RD

LAMMAS WAY

MANCHESTER TERR

THE ROW

P

Ind Est

TAPPING RD
EDMONDS RD
FORGETTS RD
SHOTFIELD
SLATER RD
SAXHORN RD
SIMMONS WAY

Lane End Prim Sch

PO

Lane End

1 JAMES RD
2 HOBBS RD
3 ELWES RD

Resr

M40

HP12

Fining Wood

Wr Twr

DAISY COTTS

CHURCH PATH

HIGH ST

POND COTTS

CLAYTON RD

PHIL'S

CATER RD

RIDGE CL

BASSET CL

ELLES WAY

FRAMERS CT

THE OLD BAKERY PH

Cutler's Farm

Widdenton Park Wood

Wycombe Court Farm

CHALKY FIELD

Ditchfield

DITCHFIELD COTTS

CLINKARD PL

CHURCH RD

Ditchfield Common

PANLEIGH COTTS

Muswell Farm

Moor Farm

Wycombe Air Park

HP12

SL7

Moor Common

MARLOW RD

Garden Centre

Moorend Common

Moor Copse

Moor Wood

Strawberry Grove

BEACON LA

CLAY LA

RG9

MOOR END

Bottom Wood

Roundwood Farm

Red Barn Farm

B482

80   A   B   81   C   D   82   E   F

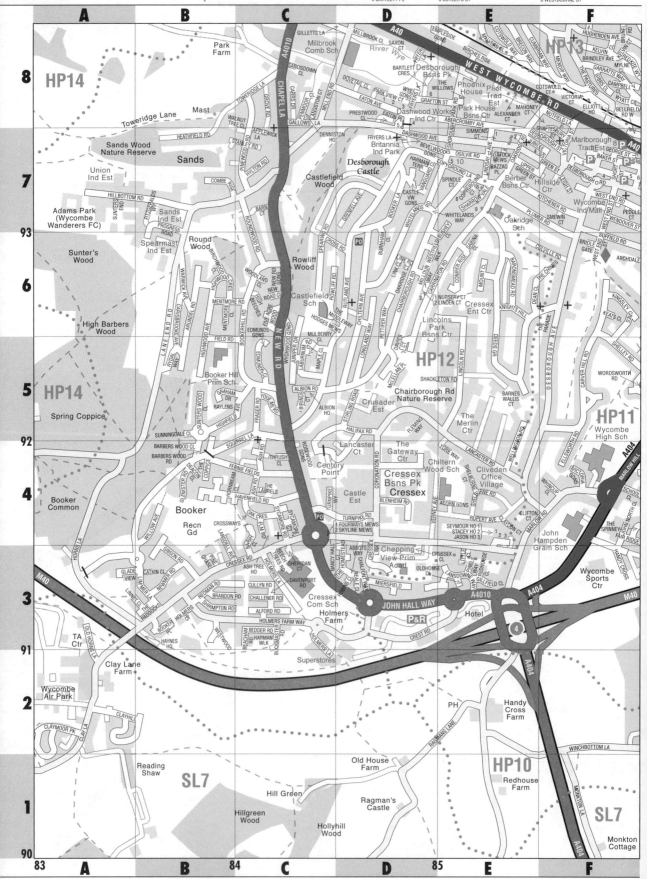

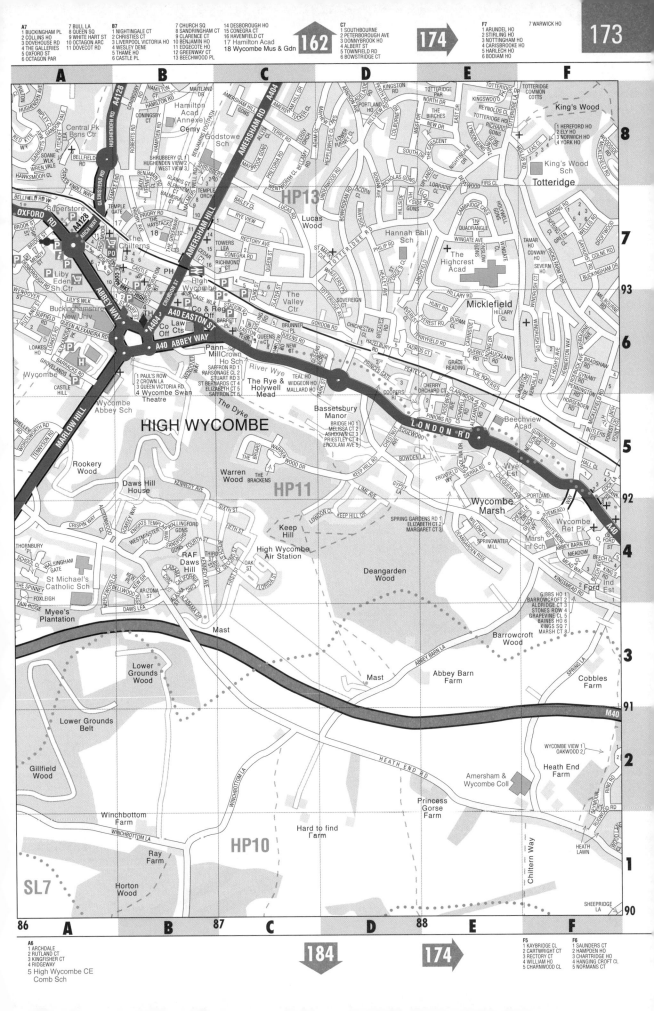

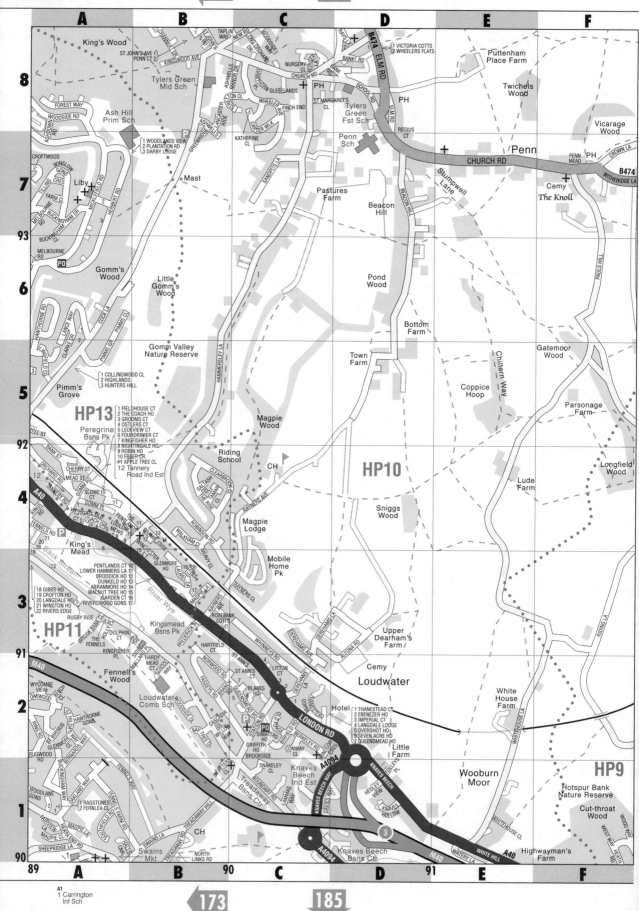

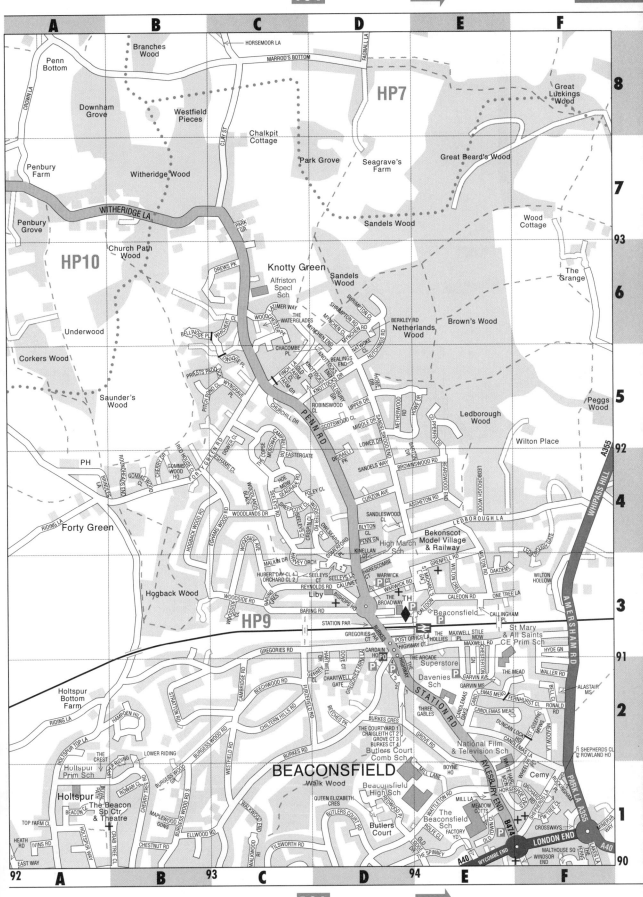

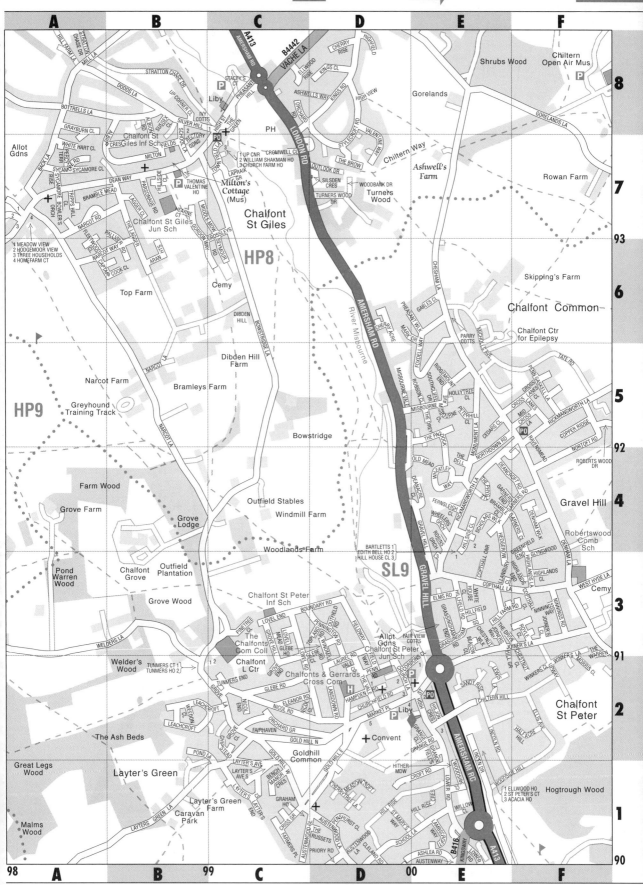

D2
1 STRINGERS COTTS
2 ADSTOCK MEWS
3 THE BROADWAY
4 BUCKINGHAM PAR
5 MARKET HO

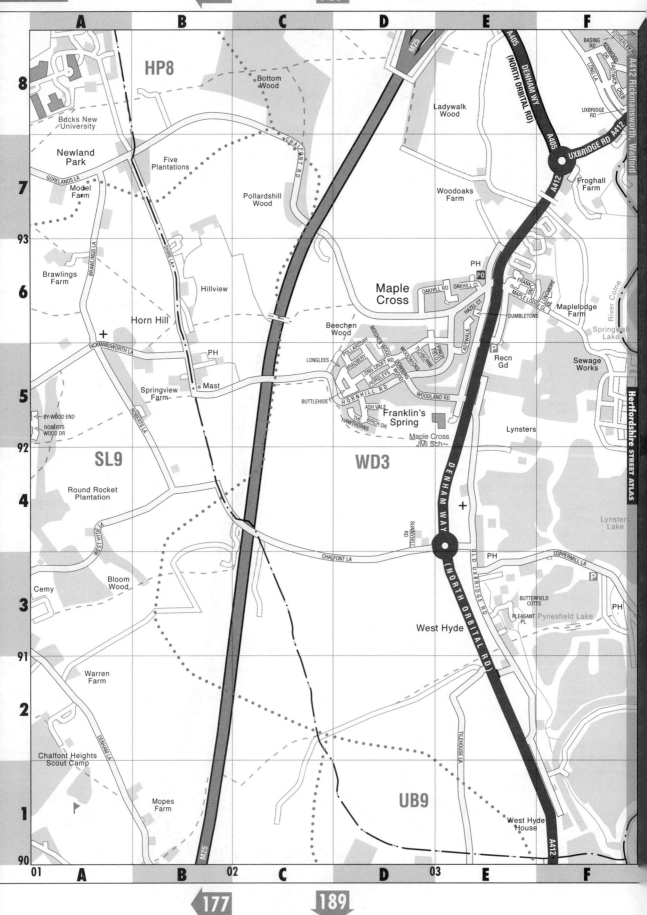

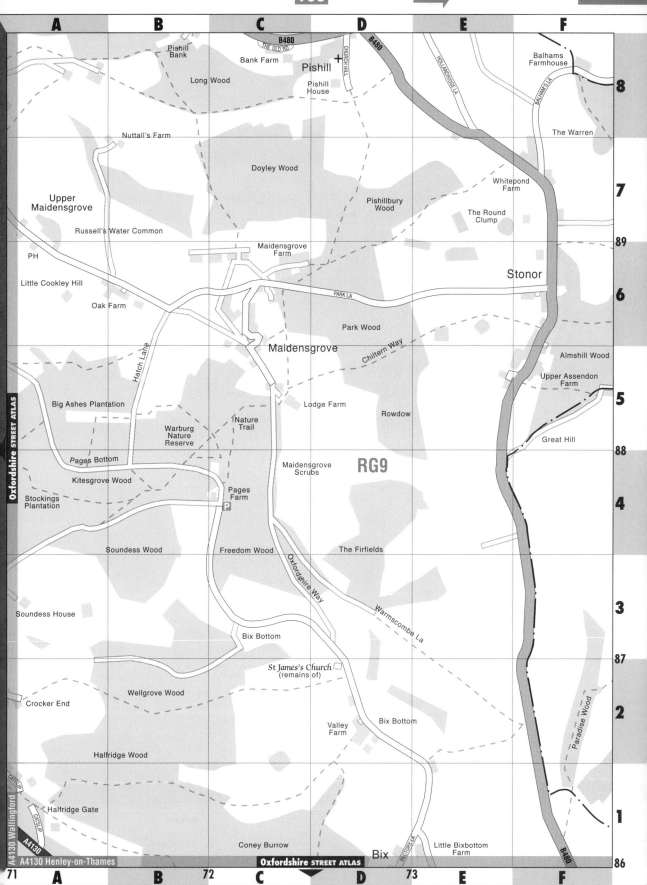

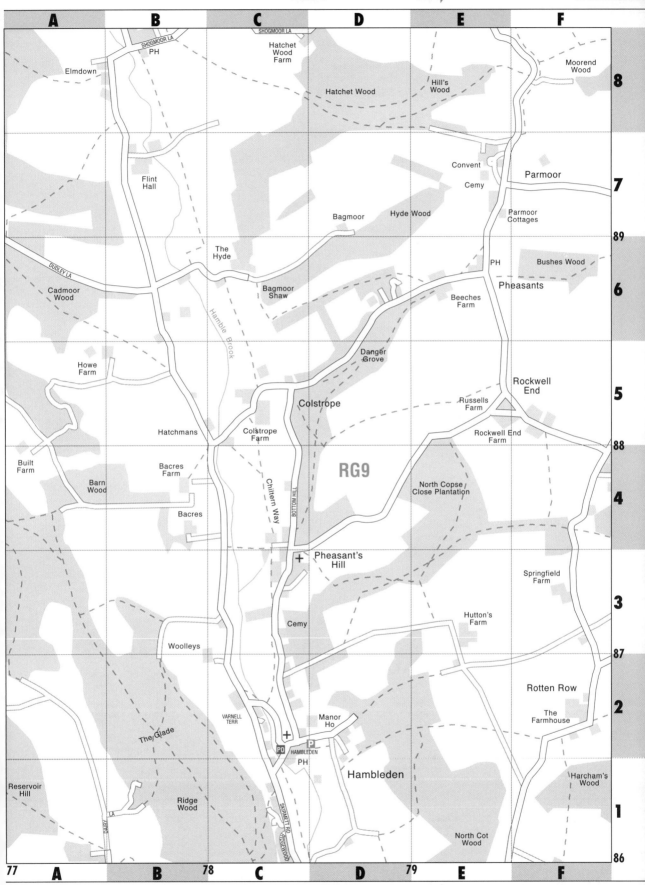

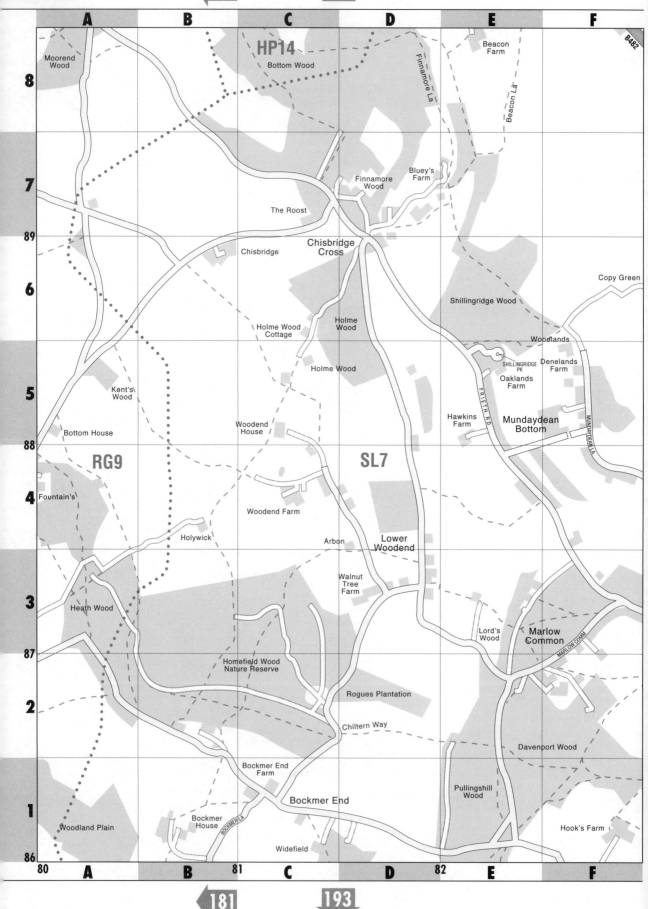

← 181
171

A B C D E F

HP14

Moorend Wood

Bottom Wood

Finnamore La

Beacon Farm

Beacon La

8

Finnamore Wood

Bluey's Farm

7

The Roost

89

Chisbridge

Chisbridge Cross

Copy Green

6

Shillingridge Wood

Woodlands

Holme Wood Cottage

Holme Wood

SHILLINGRIDGE PK

Denelands Farm

Holme Wood

Oaklands Farm

Kent's Wood

Hawkins Farm

FRIETH RD

Mundaydean Bottom

MUNDAYDEAN LA

5

Bottom House

Woodend House

88

RG9

SL7

4

Fountain's

Woodend Farm

Holywick

Arbon

Lower Woodend

Walnut Tree Farm

3

Heath Wood

Lord's Wood

Marlow Common

MARLOW COMM

87

Homefield Wood Nature Reserve

Rogues Plantation

2

Chiltern Way

Davenport Wood

Bockmer End Farm

Bockmer End

Pullingshill Wood

1

Bockmer House

BOCKMER LA

Hook's Farm

Woodland Plain

Widefield

86

80 A B 81 C D 82 E F

B482

← 181
193

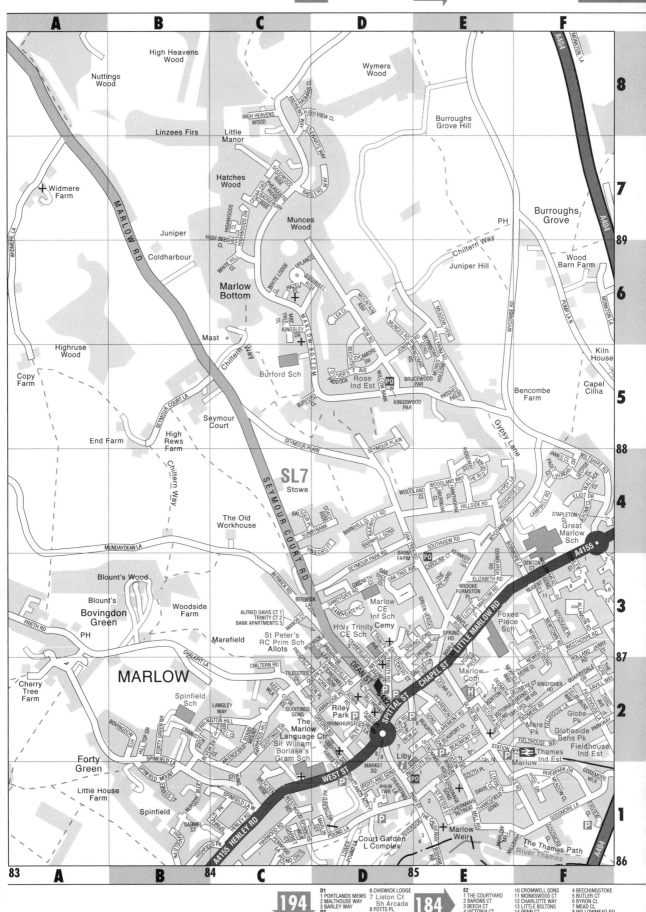

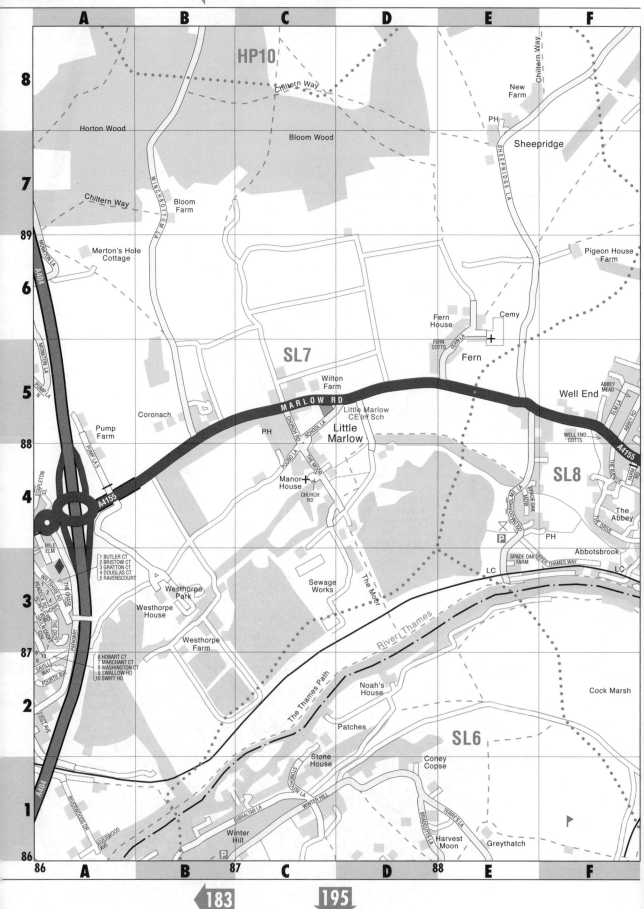

183
173

A · B · C · D · E · F

8

HP10

Chiltern Way

New Farm

Chiltern Way

PH

Sheepridge

Horton Wood

Bloom Wood

7

Chiltern Way

Bloom Farm

WINCHBOTTOM LA

SHEEPRIDGE LA

Pigeon House Farm

89

Merton's Hole Cottage

A404

MONKTON LA

6

MONKTON LA

PUMP LA N

Fern House

FERN COTTS

FERN LA

Cemy

Fern

ABBEY MEAD

SL7

Well End

ELM LA

ABBEY RD

5

Coronach

Wilton Farm

MARLOW RD

Little Marlow CE Inf Sch

Little Marlow

88

Pump Farm

PUMP LA

PH

CHURCH RD

SCHOOL LA

WELL END COTTS

A4155

STAPLETON SCL

PUMP LA S

A4155

POUND LA

THE MOOR

SL8

4

MILE ELM

Manor House

CHURCH RD

PH

The Abbey

LYTE LA

MONKTON LA

SPADE OAK MDW

THE DRIVE

THE AVENUE

FARM RD

P

Abbotsbrook

1 BUTLER CT
2 BRISTOW CT
3 GRATTON CT
4 DOUGLAS CT
5 RAVENSCOURT

SPADE OAK FARM

UPPER THAMES WAY

LC

LC

PEACOCK RD

THE CHASE

WILTSHIRE RD

Westhorpe Park

Sewage Works

The Moor

3

GUNTHORPE RD

QUOITIN CROFT

THE CROFT

THE CROFT

PARKWAY

Westhorpe House

Westhorpe Farm

River Thames

87

SAVILL WAY

FOURTH AVE

6 HOBART CT
7 MARCHANT CT
8 WASHINGTON CT
9 SWALLOW HO
10 SWIFT HO

The Thames Path

Noah's House

Cock Marsh

2

FIRST AVE

Patches

SL6

RIVERWOODS DR

RIVERWOOD AVE

A404

Stone House

Coney Copse

1

GIBRALTAR LA

STONEHOUSE LA

WINTER HILL

TERRY'S LA

BRACDUTS LA

P

Winter Hill

Harvest Moon

Greythatch

86

183
195

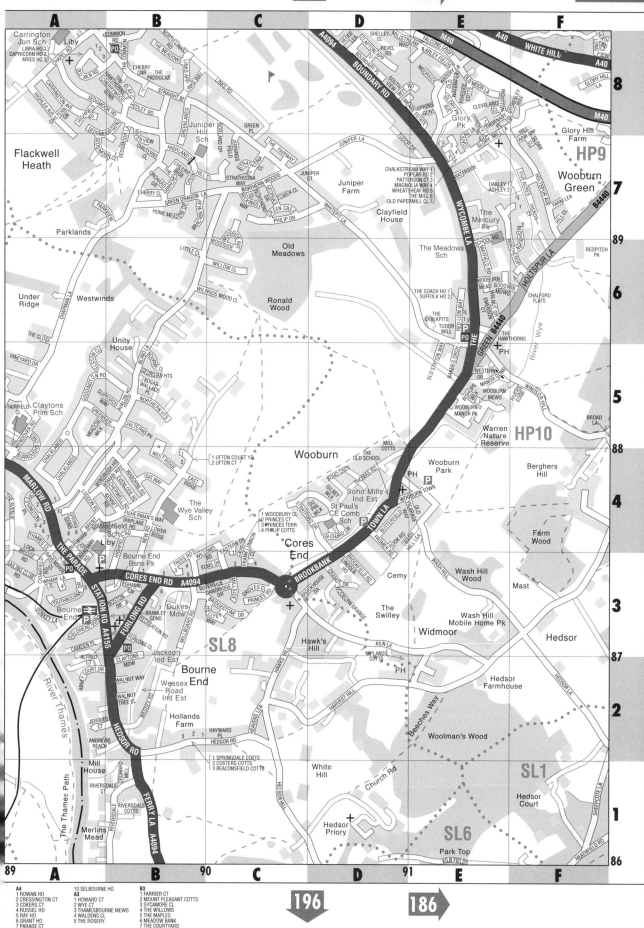

Flackwell Heath

HP9

Wooburn Green

Under Ridge

Westwinds

Parklands

Unity House

Old Meadows

Ronald Wood

Juniper Farm

Clayfield House

The Meadows Sch

Wooburn Mead

The Chalkpits

The Mercury Pk

Chalford Flats

Claytons Prim Sch

Fairfield

The Wye Valley Sch

Wooburn

The Old School

Wooburn Park

HP10

Berghers Hill

Warren Nature Reserve

Wooburn Manor Pk

Westfield Sch

Cores End

Soho Mills Ind Est

St Paul's CE Comb Sch

Farm Wood

Bourne End Bsns Pk

Brookbank

Cemy

Wash Hill Wood

Mast

Dukes Mdw

The Swilley

Wash Hill Mobile Home Pk

Widmoor

Hedsor

SL8

Jackson Ind Est

Bourne End

Hawk's Hill

Bourne End

Wessex Road Ind Est

Hollands Farm

Hedsor Farmhouse

Mill House

Riversdale

White Hill

SL1

SL6

Woolman's Wood

Hedsor Court

Merlins Mead

Hedsor Priory

Park Top

River Thames

The Thames Path

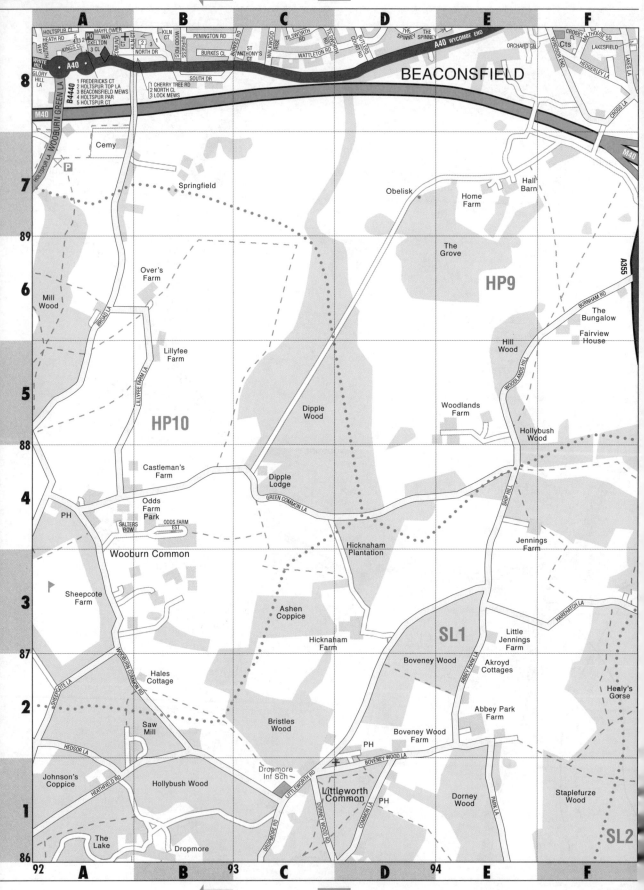

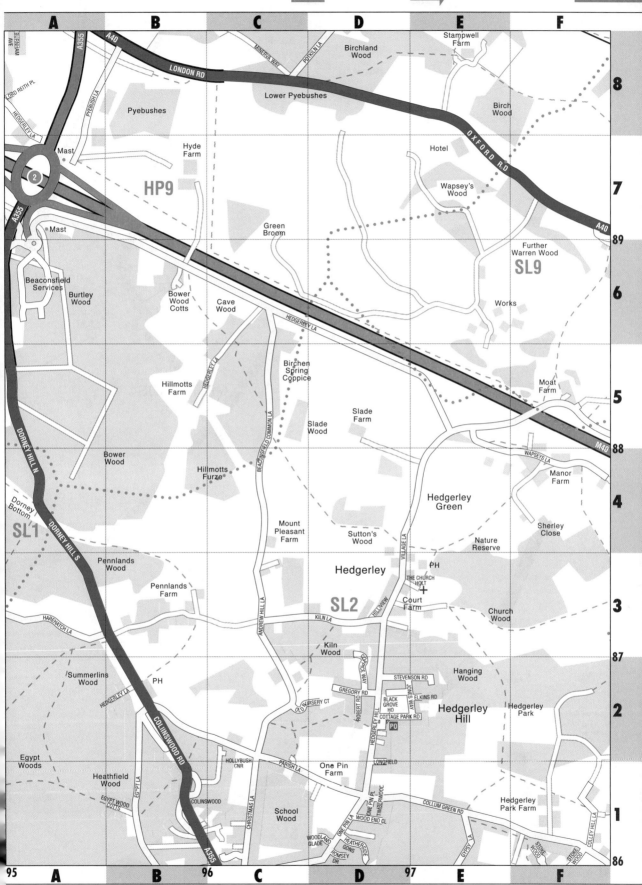

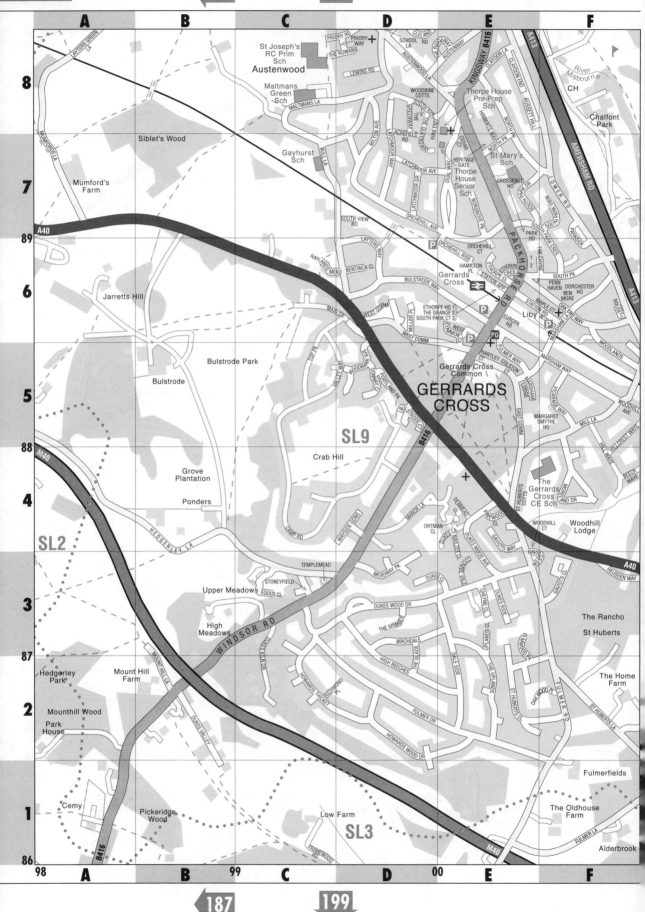

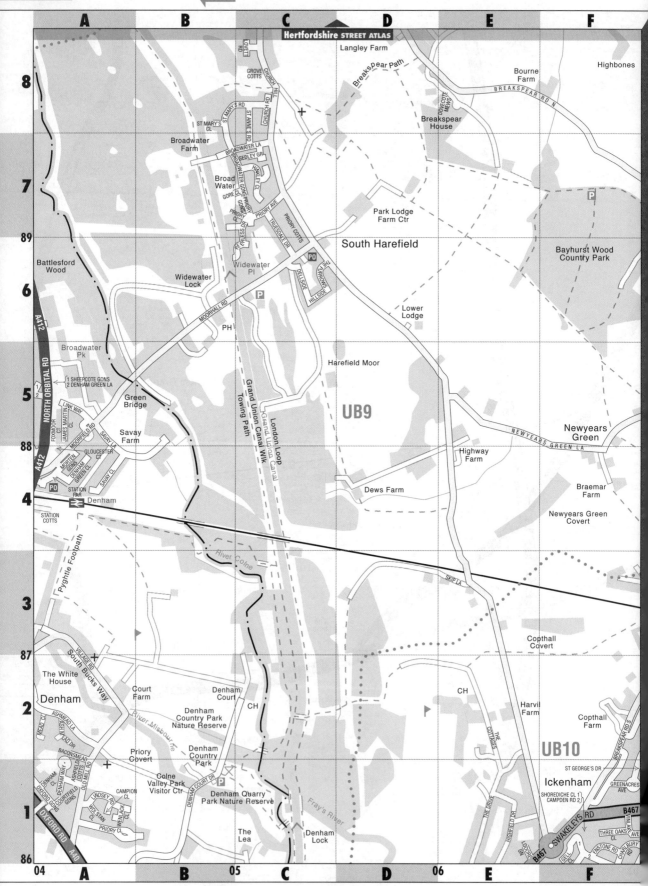

Hertfordshire STREET ATLAS

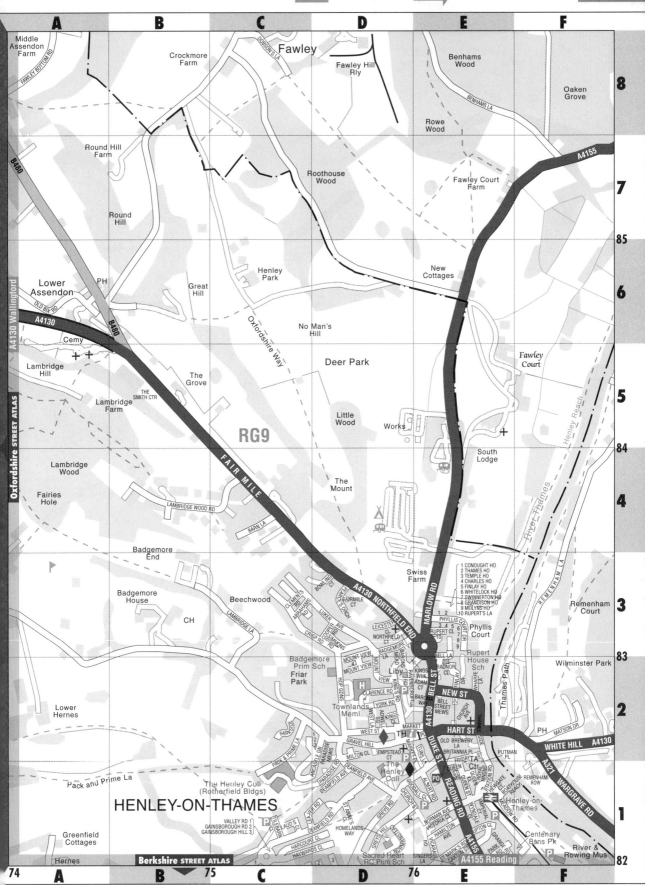

A   B   C   D   E   F

Middle Assendon Farm

Fawley

Crockmore Farm

Fawley Hill Rly

Benhams Wood

Oaken Grove

8

B480

Round Hill Farm

Roothouse Wood

A4155

Fawley Court Farm

7

Round Hill

85

Lower Assendon

PH

Great Hill

Henley Park

New Cottages

6

Oxfordshire Way

A4130 Wallingford

A4130

B480

Cemy

Lambridge Hill

No Man's Hill

Deer Park

Fawley Court

5

The Grove

THE SMITH CTR

Little Wood

Works

Henley Reach

Lambridge Farm

RG9

South Lodge

84

Oxfordshire Street Atlas

Lambridge Wood

FAIR MILE

LAMBRIDGE WOOD RD

The Mount

River Thames

4

Fairies Hole

BARN LA

Badgemore End

Swiss Farm

1 Conought Ho
2 Thames Ho
3 Temple Ho
4 Charles Ho
5 Finlay Ho
6 Whitelock Ho
7 Swinnerton Ho
8 Grandison Ho
9 Molyns Ho
10 Rupert's La

Remenham Court

REMENHAM LA

3

Badgemore House

Beechwood

CH

LAMBRIDGE LA

A4130 NORTHFIELD END

MARLOW RD

Phyllis Court

Phyllis Court Dr

Rupert House Sch

Thames Path

Wilminster Park

83

Lower Hernes

Badgemore Prim Sch
Friar Park

H

BELL ST

NEW ST

Bell Street Mews

2

Townlands Meml

WEST ST

HART ST

DUKE ST

A4130

OLD BREWERY LA
BRITANNIA PL

PUTMAN PL

PH MATSON DR

WHITE HILL A4130

Pack and Prime La

The Henley Coll (Rotherfield Bldgs)

The Henley Coll

READING RD

A321 WARGRAVE RD

HENLEY-ON-THAMES

P

Henley-on-Thames

Centenary Bsns Pk

1

Greenfield Cottages

VALLEY RD 1
GAINSBOROUGH RD 2
GAINSBOROUGH HILL 3

A4155

River & Rowing Mus

Hernes

Sacred Heart RC Prim Sch

A4155 Reading

82

74   A   B   75   C   D   76   E   F

D2
1 CEDAR
2 BEECH
3 ACACIA
4 MOUNT VIEW CT
5 MARKET PLACE MEWS

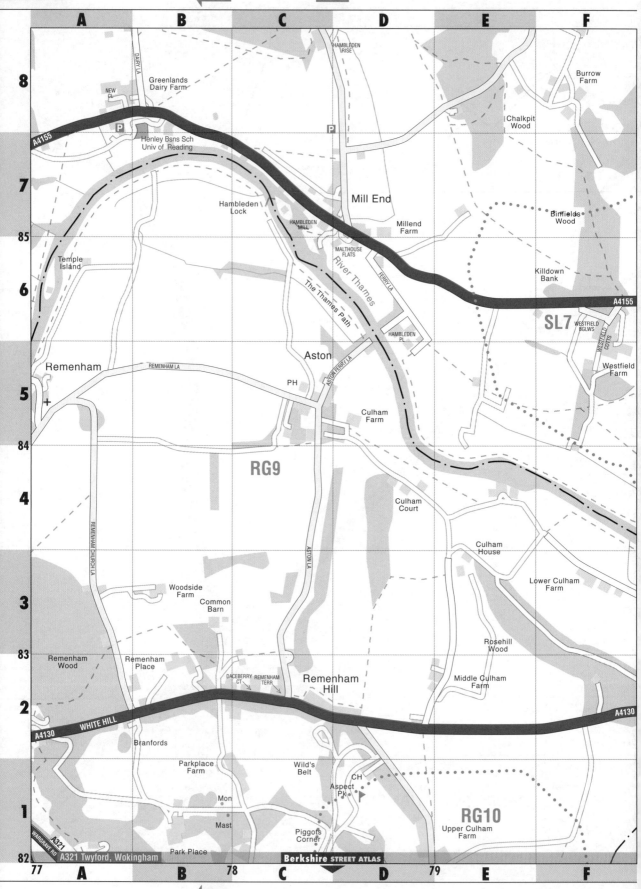

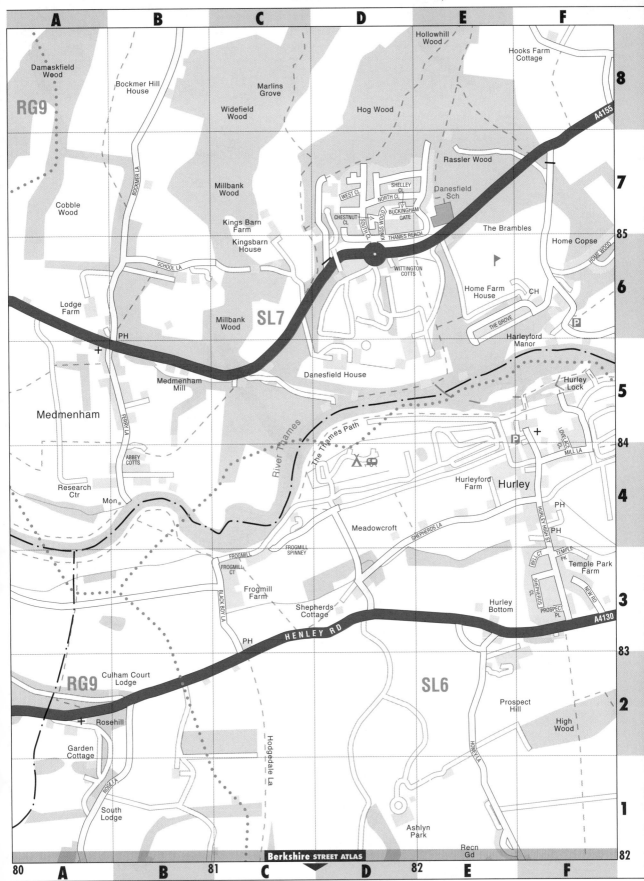

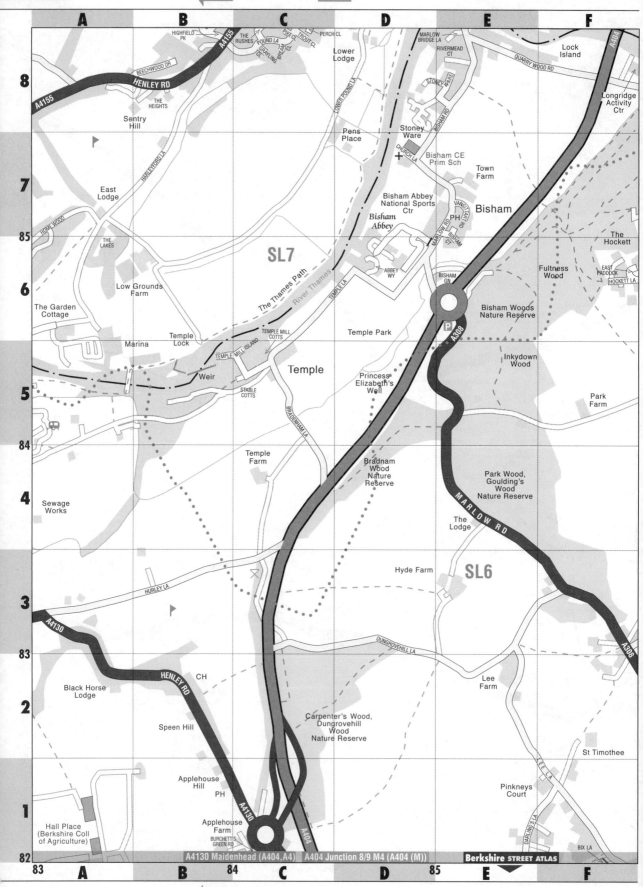

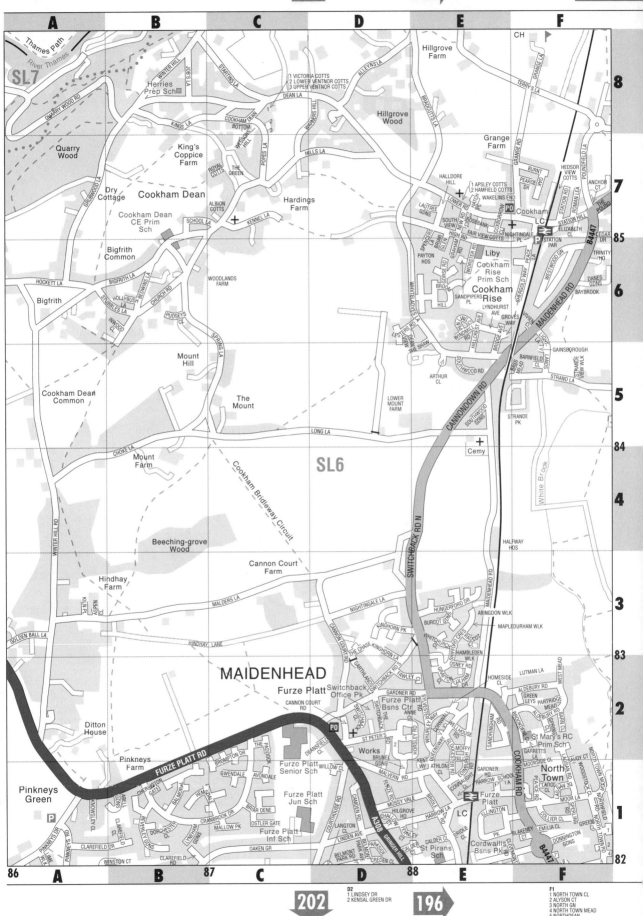

D2
1 LINDSEY DR
2 KENSAL GREEN DR

F1
1 NORTH TOWN CL
2 ALYSON CT
3 NORTH GN
4 NORTH TOWN MEAD
5 NORTHDEAN
6 COLBY GDNS
7 DALBY GDNS

195 185

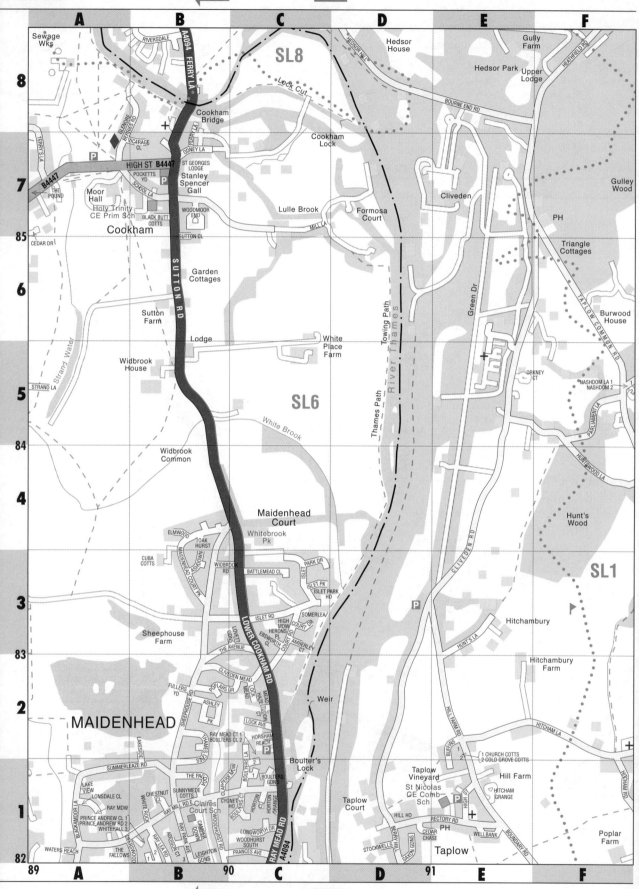

195 203

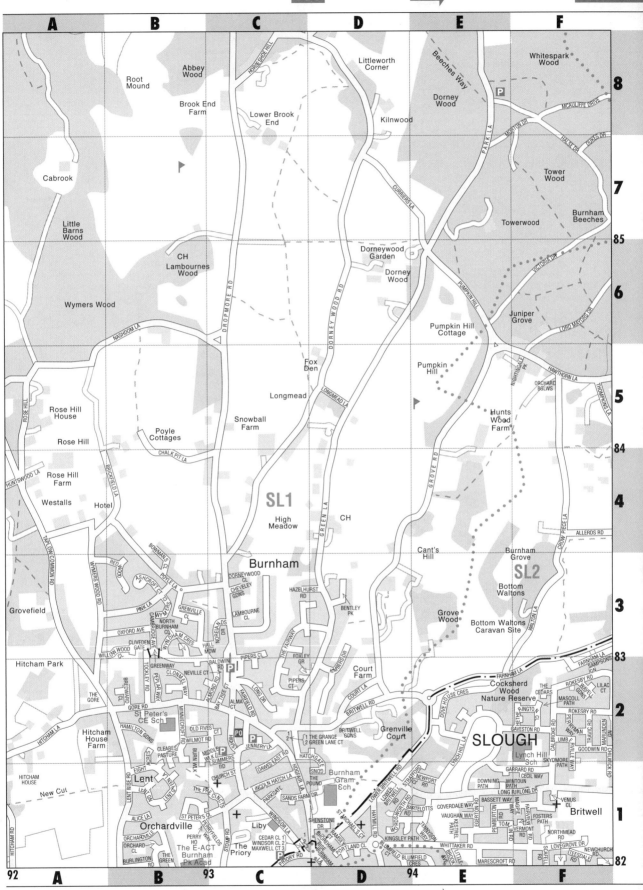

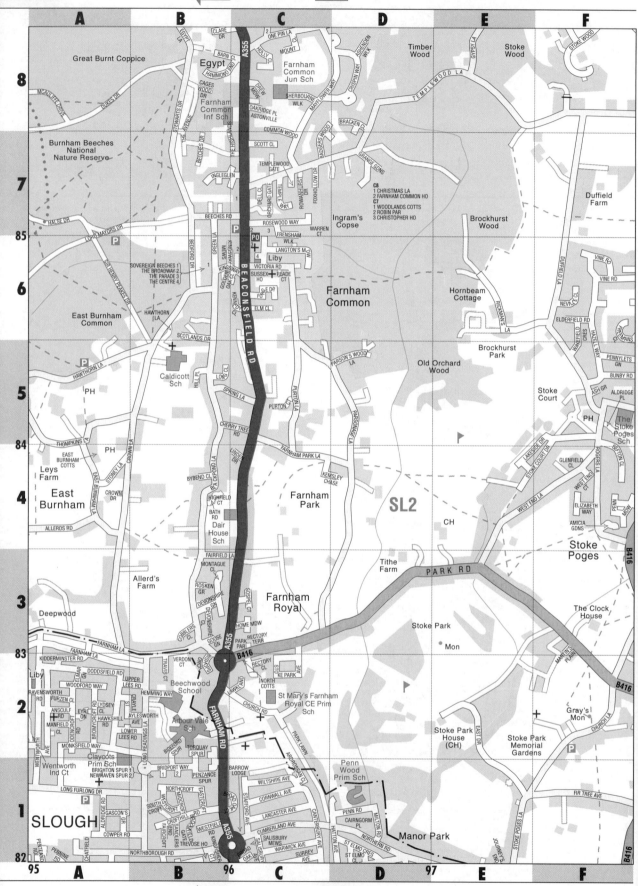

Great Burnt Coppice

Egypt

Farnham
Common Jun Sch

Timber
Wood

Stoke
Wood

Burnham Beeches
National
Nature Reserve

Farnham
Common
Inf Sch

Duffield
Farm

C8
1 CHRISTMAS LA
2 FARNHAM COMMON HO
C7
1 WOODLANDS COTTS
2 ROBIN PAR
3 CHRISTOPHER HO

Brockhurst
Wood

Ingram's
Copse

Liby

East Burnham
Common

Farnham
Common

Hornbeam
Cottage

Brockhurst
Park

SOVEREIGN BEECHES 1
THE BROADWAY 2
THE PARADE 3
THE CENTRE 4

Old Orchard
Wood

Stoke
Court

PH

Caldicott
Sch

The Stoke
Poges Sch

PH

Leys Farm

EAST
BURNHAM
COTTS

East
Burnham

Farnham Park La

Kemsley
Chase

SL2

Farnham
Park

CH

Stoke
Poges

Dair
House
Sch

Allerd's
Farm

Deepwood

Tithe
Farm

PARK RD

Stoke Park

Mon

The Clock
House

Farnham
Royal

Beechwood
School

St Mary's Farnham
Royal CE Prim
Sch

Stoke Park
House
(CH)

Gray's
Mon

Arbour Vale
Sch

Liby

Penn Wood
Prim Sch

Stoke Park
Memorial
Gardens

Claycots
Prim Sch

Wentworth
Ind Ct

Manor Park

SLOUGH

COLLUM GREEN RD
WINDSOR RD
B416
PH
JARDINE COTTS
TEMPLEWOOD LA

The Pickeridge

FRAMEWOOD RD
HAY LA
BRADBURY GDNS
CHURCH ROW
FULMER RD

M40
M40

FULMER CHASE
Fulmer Hall
PH

NORTH ROW
SOUTH ROW
Fulmer Inf Sch
ALLHUSEN GDNS

Furzeney Wood

SL9

8

Fulmer

STOKE COMMON RD

Church Farm

WINDMILL RD

Fulmer House Farm

ALDERBOURNE LA

Larchmoor Pk

GERRARDS CROSS RD

Stoke Common

Church Farm

Beeches Way

Alder Bourne

Watersplash Farm

7

VINE CT
VINE RD
FIRCROFT CT
FIRCROFT

Frame Wood

Fernacres Farm

Penn Wood

Fulmer Rise Estate

CLEVEHURST CL

FULMER COMMON RD

HAWKSWOOD GR

85

FREEMANS CL

Mill House Farm

Fulmer Common

LANGLEY CNR

CHERRY TREE LA

HAWKSWOOD LA

6

PENNYLETS GN
BELLS HILL
RUBY RD
POST OFFICE COTTS
BROOM
CHERRY ORCH

Hollybush Hill

SL2

FRAMEWOOD MANOR

FRAMEWOOD RD

WEXHAM PL

BOLD'S CT
PO
ROGERS LA

HOLLYBUSH HILL

Fairfield Lodge

Teikyo Sch UK

Upton Farm

5

WILLOW PK
P

SCHOOL LA

CHAPEL COTTS

CHAPEL LA

HOCKLEY LA

PH

Upton Wood

Upton Lake

84

DECIES WAY

Sefton Park

Focus Sch Stoke Poges Campus

SEFTON PARK COTTS

FARTHING GREEN LA

PLOUGH LA

FARM WAY
HARTLEY CL
LARKINGS LA
TUBWELL RD
DEANS CL

Twin Trees Farm

ROWLEY LA

SL3

4

HASTINGS MDW

H
Spire Thames Valley

Wexham Street

Rowley Wood

BLACK PARK RD

QUEEN'S DR

CHURCH RD

WEXHAM ST

Sports Ctr

THURLEY COTTS

CH

GALLIONS LANE

Rowley Wood

Black Park Country Park
P

Blackpark Lake

3

GRAYS PARK RD

PARK RD

Berry Farm

BUCKLAND GATE

Gallions Wood

Rowley Farm

Visitor Ctr

SAWMILL COTTS

83

HAMPDEN CL
THE MEADS

Spring Wood

PERCE RD

2

DUFFIELD PK

Bell Farm

Rowley Lake

A412

UXBRIDGE RD

A412

PH

Stoke Place

STOKE RD

STOKE GN

RED LION COTTS

H
Wexham Park

WEXHAM PARK LA

AVENUE DR

BLUE CT

1

Stoke Green

WEXHAM RD
PO

WICKEY CL

OPECKS CL

OPAL CT

CHURCH GR

VALLEY

82

1 WILLIAM HARTLEY YD
2 BENJAMIN LA

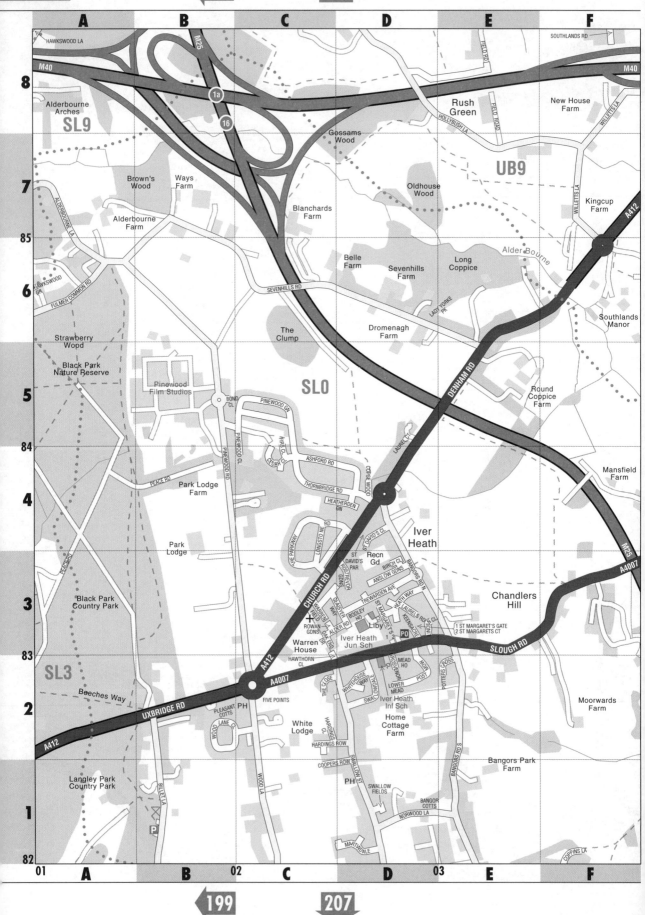

A   B   C   D   E   F

HAWKSWOOD LA

SOUTHLANDS RD

8

M40

M40

Alderbourne
Arches

SL9

Rush
Green

UB9

New House
Farm

HOLLYBUSH LA

FIELD ROAD

WILLETTS LA

Gossams
Wood

7

Brown's
Wood

Ways
Farm

M25

Oldhouse
Wood

WILLETTS LA

Kingcup
Farm

A412

Blanchards
Farm

ALDERBOURNE LA

Alderbourne
Farm

85

Alder Bourne

HAWKSWOOD
GR

Belle
Farm

Sevenhills
Farm

Long
Coppice

Southlands
Manor

6

FULMER COMMON RD

SEVENHILLS RD

LADY YORKE
PK

Dromenagh
Farm

Round
Coppice
Farm

Strawberry
Wood

The
Clump

SL0

DENHAM RD

Black Park
Nature Reserve

5

Pinewood Film Studios

BOND
CL

PINEWOOD GN

LAUREL CT

84

PINEWOOD CL

ASHFORD RD

PINEWOOD RD

CEDAR CL

FIR CL

Mansfield
Farm

Park Lodge
Farm

PEACE RD

THORNBRIDGE RD

COPSE WOOD

4

HEATHERDEN
GN

Iver
Heath

M25

Park
Lodge

BEECH RD

AVE PARKWAY

LONGSTO NE
RD

ST DAVID'S CL

A4007

RD

ST
DAVID'S
PAR

Recn
Gd

BIRCH CL

BANGORS RD N

Chandlers
Hill

3

Black Park
Country Park

CHURCH RD

ROS TREVOR
GDNS

ANSLOW GDNS

HEATH RD

LAURELS RD

KENSINGTON CL

TREWARDEN AVE

BODLEY
HO

ST MARGARETS RD

1 ST MARGARET'S GATE
2 ST MARGARETS CT

WARREN
FIELD

GLAISTER RD

Liby

PO

ROWAN
GDNS

OAK END WAY

83

SL3

Warren
House

A412

HAWTHORN CL

Iver Heath
Jun Sch

MEAD
HO

POTTERS CROSS

NOVA

SLOUGH RD

Beeches Way

A4007

Iver Heath
Inf Sch

LOWER
MEAD

POST

Moorwards
Farm

2

UXBRIDGE RD

PLEASANT
COTTS

PH

FIVE POINTS

WOOD
LANE CL

THE CLOSE

WHITEHOUSE
WAY

Home
Cottage
Farm

A412

White
Lodge

HARDINGS
CL

SWALLOW WAY

BANGORS RD S

Bangors Park
Farm

BILLET LA

WOOD LA

HARDINGS ROW

COOPERS ROW

SWALLOW ST

PH

SWALLOW
FIELDS

BANGOR
COTTS

1

Langley Park
Country Park

P

NORWOOD LA

MARTINDALE

COPPINS LA

82

01   A   B   02   C   D   03   E   F

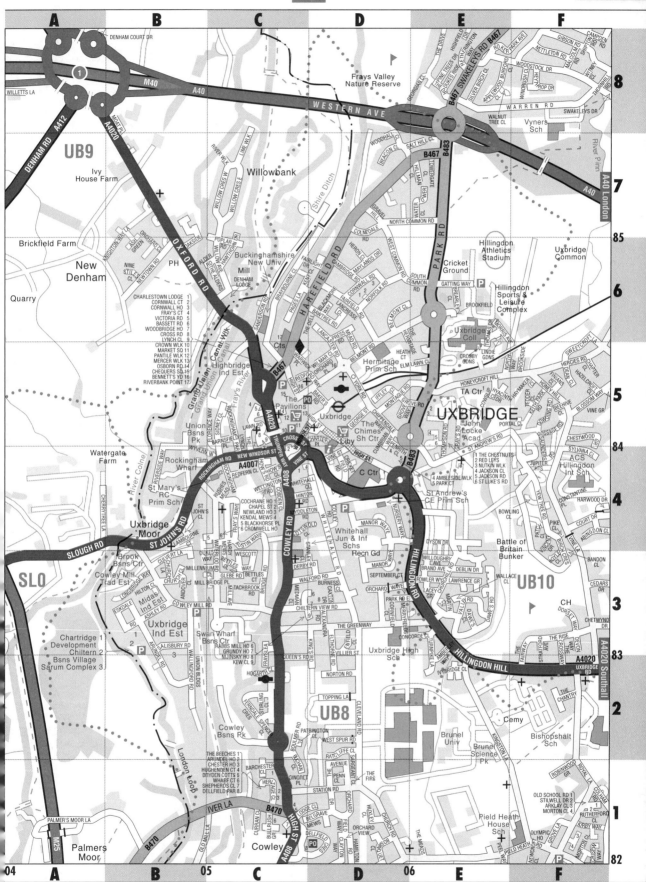

B8
1 WELLINGTON CL
2 BUSHNELL PL

D6
1 THE COURTYARD
2 VICARAGE MEWS
3 BHAMRA GDNS

195

E8
1 Gladstone
Ind Est

F7
1 WHITE HART RD
2 Nicholsons Sh Ctr
3 REGENT CT
4 FROGMORE CT
5 WHITCHURCH HO
6 KINGSWAY HO

7 WILBERFORCE MEWS
8 SYGNUS CT
9 PROVIDENCE PL
10 ST MARY'S WLK
11 OLD POST OFFICE LA
12 QUEEN'S LA
13 Heritage Ctr

14 KING ST

F8
1 COLBY GDNS
2 St Luke's
CE Prim Sch

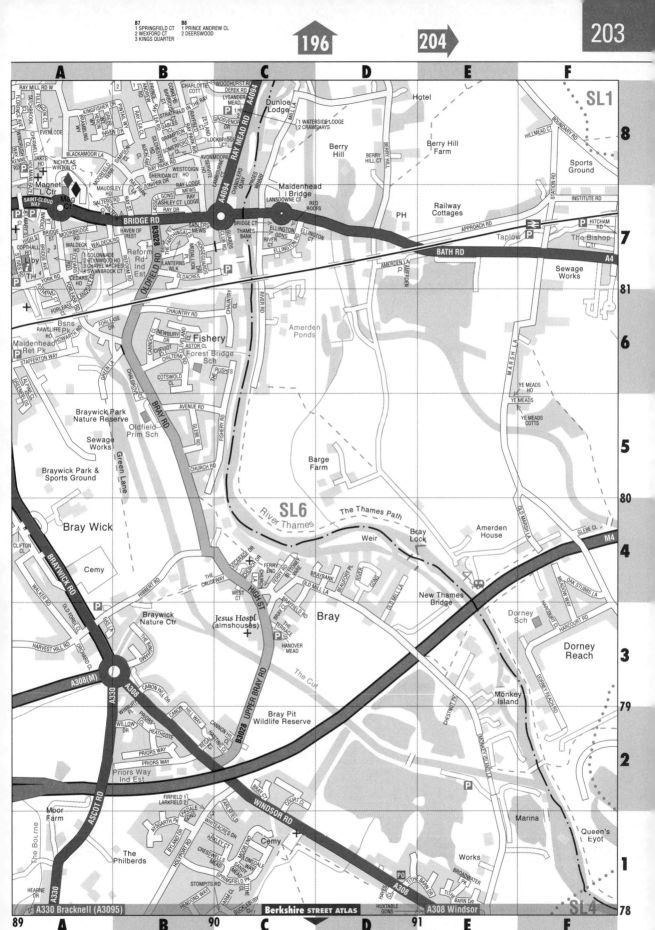

B7
1 SPRINGFIELD CT
2 WEXFORD CT
3 KINGS QUARTER

B8
1 PRINCE ANDREW CL
2 DEERSWOOD

SL1

Berkshire STREET ATLAS

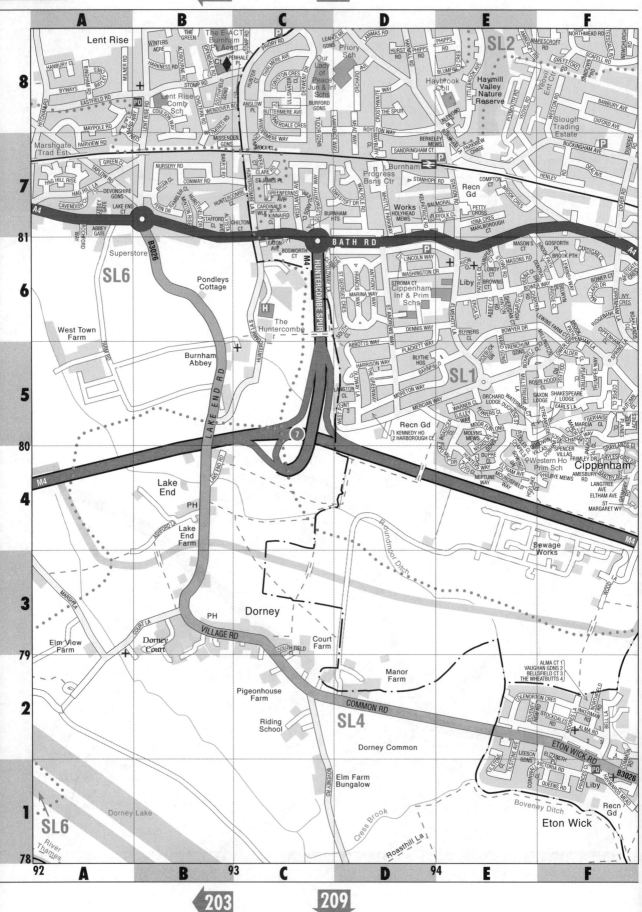

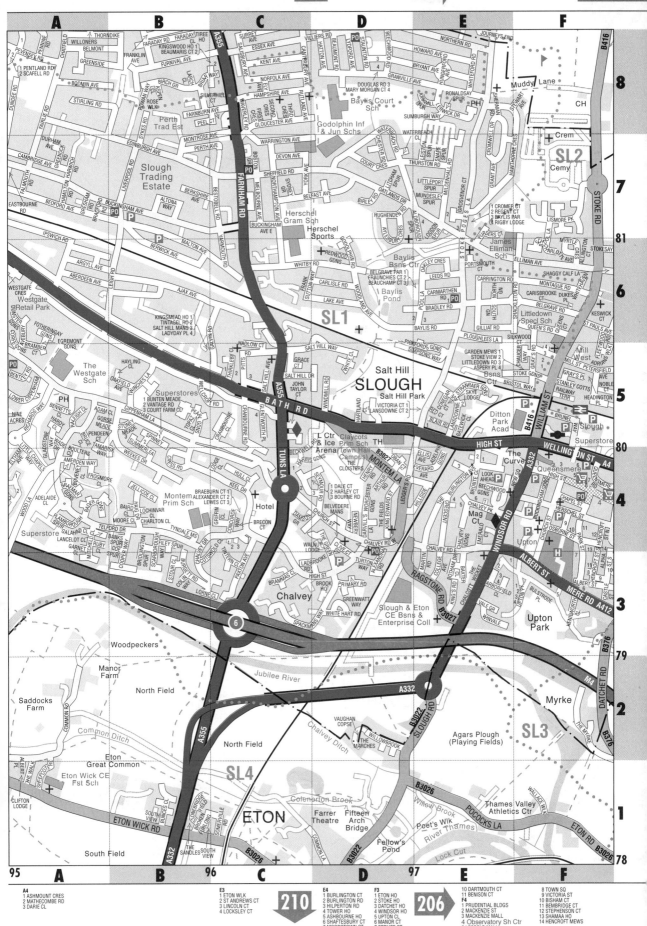

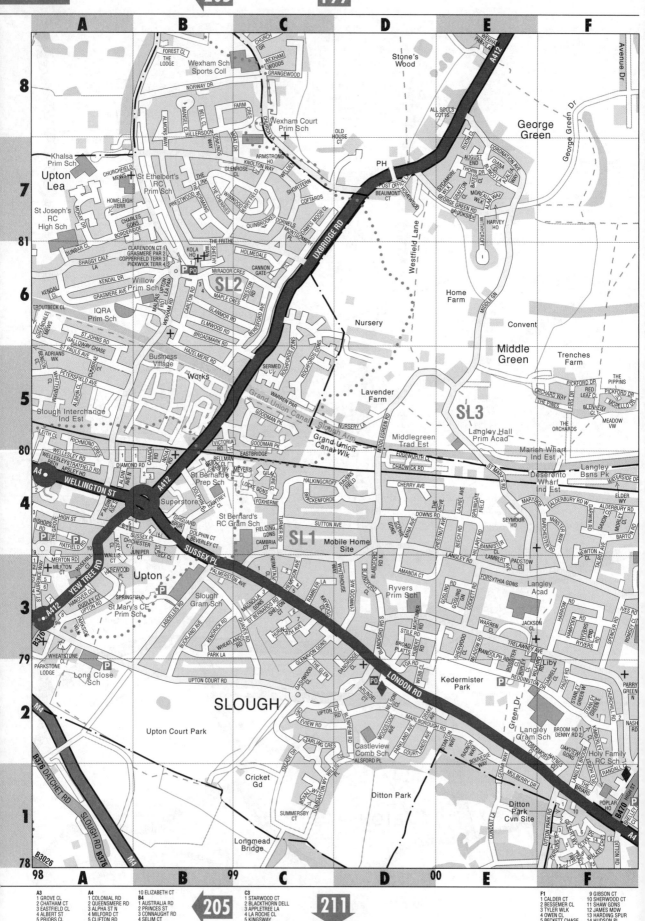

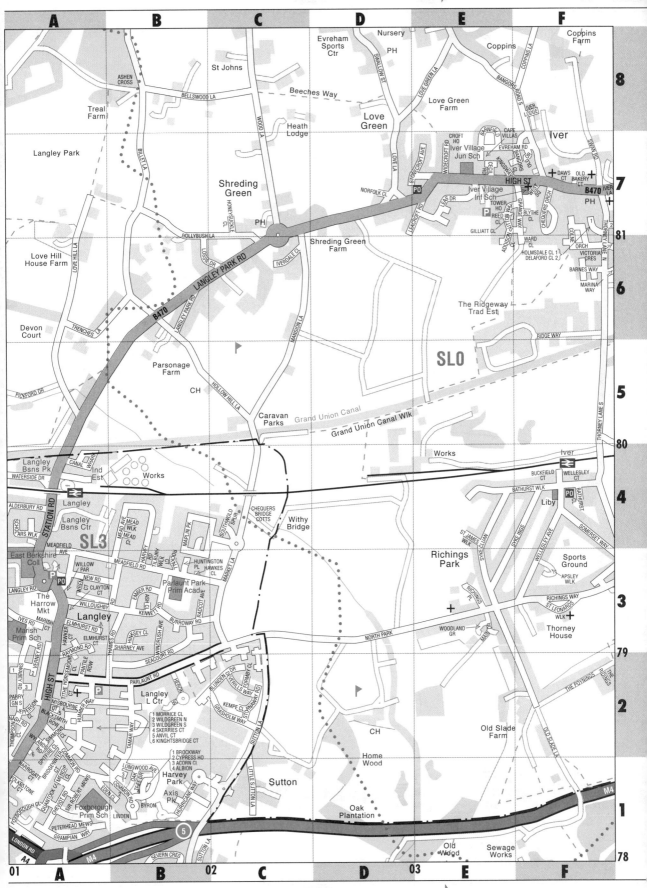

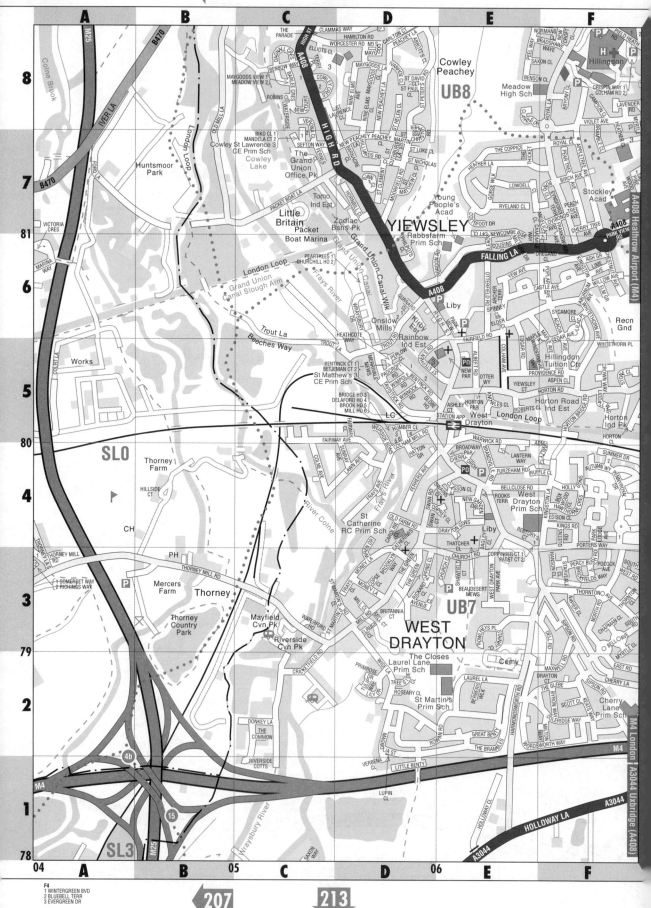

207

201

F7
1 BEECHWOOD AVE
2 EVELYNS CL
3 Moorcroft Sch

8

7

81

6

5

80

4

79

2

1

78

A   B   C   D   E   F

04   05   06

F4
1 WINTERGREEN BVD
2 BLUEBELL TERR
3 EVERGREEN DR

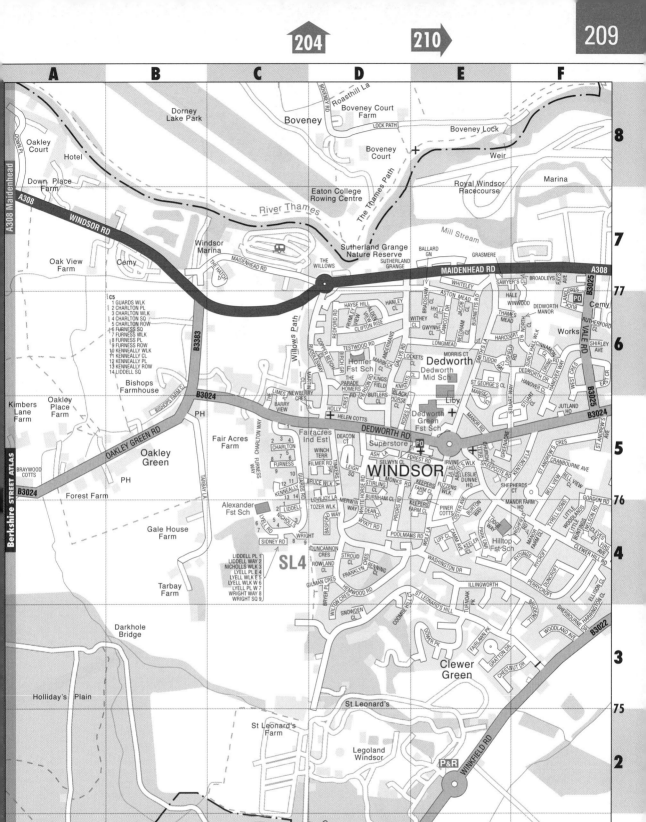

Berkshire STREET ATLAS

Berkshire STREET ATLAS

C5
1 GUARDS WLK
2 CHARLTON PL
3 CHARLTON WLK
4 CHARLTON SQ
5 CHARLTON ROW
6 FURNESS SQ
7 FURNESS WLK
8 FURNESS PL
9 FURNESS ROW
10 KENNEALLY WLK
11 KENNEALLY CL
12 KENNEALLY PL
13 KENNEALLY ROW
14 LIDDELL SQ

LIDDELL PL 1
LIDDELL WAY 2
NICHOLLS WLK 3
LYELL PL E 4
LYELL WLK E 5
LYELL WLK W 6
LYELL PL W 7
WRIGHT WAY 8
WRIGHT SQ 9

WINDSOR

Dedworth

Clewer
Green

SL4

Oakley Green

Forest Park

Forest Farm

Tarbay Farm

Gale House Farm

Darkhole Bridge

Holliday's Plain

High Standinghill Woods

Forbe's Fields

Orchard Lea

St Leonard's

St Leonard's Farm

Legoland Windsor

Flemish Farm

210

A5
1 ST ANDREWS COTTS
2 ALBION PL
3 ST CATHERINES CT
4 THE MEADS
5 BRIDGEMAN CT
6 CEDAR CT

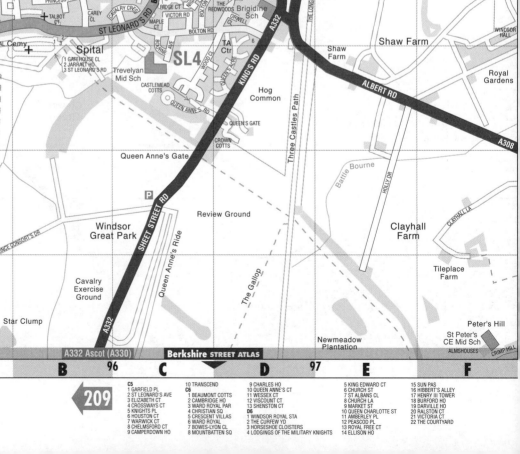

C5
1 GARFIELD PL
2 ST LEONARD'S AVE
3 ELIZABETH CT
4 CROSSWAYS CT
5 KNIGHTS PL
6 HOUSTON CT
7 WARWICK CT
8 CHELMSFORD CT
9 CAMPERDOWN HO

C6
1 BEAUMONT COTTS
2 CAMBRIDGE HO
3 WARD ROYAL PAR
4 CHRISTIAN SQ
5 CRESCENT VILLAS
6 WARD ROYAL
7 BOWES-LYON CL
8 MOUNTBATTEN SQ

10 TRANSCEND

9 CHARLES HO
10 QUEEN ANNE'S CT
11 WESSEX CT
12 VISCOUNT CT
13 SHENSTON CT

D6
1 WINDSOR ROYAL STA
2 THE CURFEW YD
3 HORSESHOE CLOISTERS
4 LODGINGS OF THE MILITARY KNIGHTS

5 KING EDWARD CT
6 CHURCH ST
7 ST ALBANS CL
8 CHURCH LA
9 MARKET ST
10 QUEEN CHARLOTTE ST
11 AMBERLEY PL
12 PEASCOD PL
13 ROYAL FREE CT
14 ELLISON HO

15 SUN PAS
16 HIBBERT'S ALLEY
17 HENRY III TOWER
18 BURFORD HO
19 DARVILLE HO
20 RALSTON CT
21 VICTORIA CT
22 THE COURTYARD

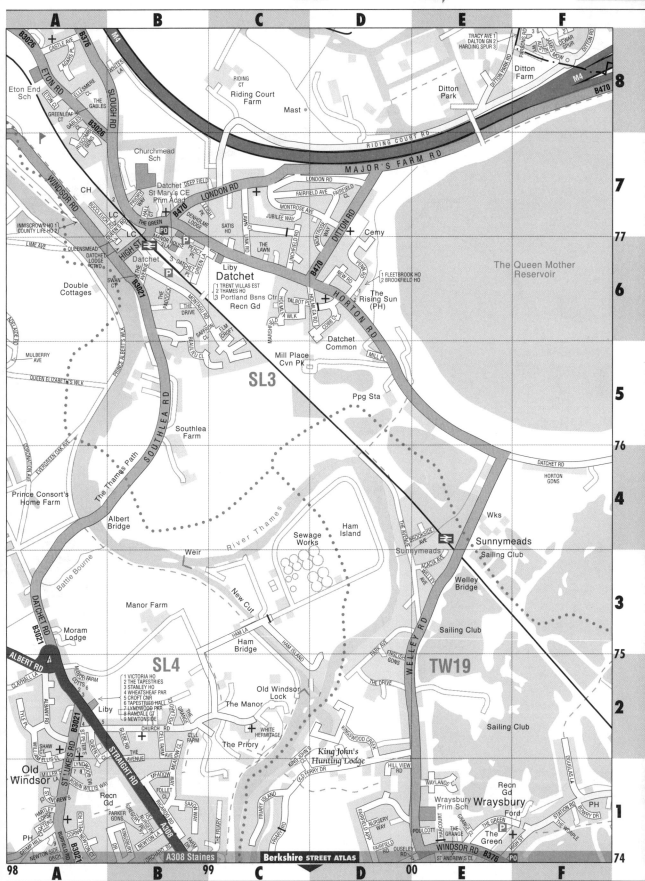

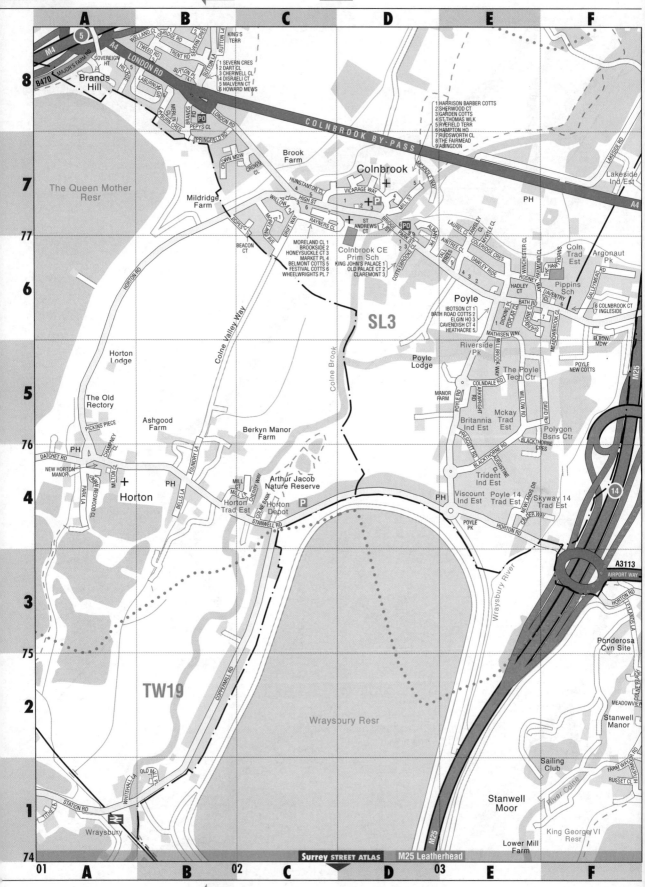

A B C D E F

8

7

77

6

5

76

4

3

75

2

1

74

The Queen Mother Resr

Brands Hill

M4
B470
A4
London Rd

Severn Cres
Dart Cl
Cherwell Cl
Disraeli Ct
Malvern Ct
Howard Mews

1 Severn Cres
2 Dart Cl
3 Cherwell Cl
4 Disraeli Ct
5 Malvern Ct
6 Howard Mews

Sovereign Ht
Welland Cl
Bridge Rd
Trent Rd
Sutton La
Tweed Rd
Severn Cres
King's Terr
Sutton Pl
Sutton La
Laburnum Gr
Hilvars
Merlins
Laburn Cres
Pepys Cl
Brands Rd
London Rd

Springfield Rd
Crown Mdw
Crown Cl

Brook Farm
Mildridge Farm

COLNBROOK BY-PASS

1 Harrison Barber Cotts
2 Sherwood Ct
3 Garden Cotts
4 St.Thomas Wlk
5 Ryefield Terr
6 Hampton Ho
7 Rudsworth Cl
8 The Fairmead
9 Abingdon

Lakeside Ind Est
Lakeside Rd
A4

Colnbrook
Vicarage Way
Monroe Dri

Hunstanton Cl
High St
Willow Cl
Moreland Ave
Drift Way
Beacon Ct
Rayners Cl
Egres Cl
St Andrews Ct

Moreland Cl 1
Brookside 2
Honeysuckle Ct 3
Market Pl 4
Belmont Cotts 5
Festival Cotts 6
Wheelwrights Pl 7

Colnbrook CE
Prim Sch
King John's Palace 1
Old Palace Ct 2
Claremont 3

Cottesbrook Cl

Bridge St
Park St
Albany Rd
Laurel Cl
Kingsley Cl
Myrtle Cl
Aintree Cl
Tait
Pines
Coleridge Cres
Dawley Ride
Rodney
Hadley Ct
Daventry Cl
Winchester Cl
Raymond Cl
The Thorns
The Hall
Coln Trad Est
Argonaut Pk
Pippins Sch
Gallymead Rd

Poyle
Ibotson Ct 1
Bath Road Cotts 2
Elgin Ho 3
Cavendish Ct 4
Heathacre 5

Dickins Cl
Poplar Cl
Shire
Meadowbrook La
Sherwood
6 Colnbrook Ct
7 Ingleside

Elbow Mdw

SL3

Colne Valley Way

Colne Brook

Horton Lodge

The Old Rectory

Pickins Piece

Ashgood Farm

Berkyn Manor Farm

Datchet Rd
PH
New Horton Manor
Champney Cl
Park La
Milton Cl
Dawn Redwood Cl

Horton
Bells La
PH
Foundry La

Riverside Pk
The Poyle Tech Ctr
Poyle Lodge

Manor Farm
Coldale Cl
Cartwright
Poyle Rd
Prescott La
Mathisen Way
Millbrook Way
Britannia Ind Est
Mckay Trad Est
Willow Rd
David Rd
Polygon Bsns Ctr
Blackthorne Cres
Blackthorne Rd
Augustine
Trident Ind Est

Poyle New Cotts

M25

Mill Ct
Mill Ct
Horton Trad Est
Cherry Way
Colne Bank
Horton Depot
P
Stanwell Rd
Arthur Jacob Nature Reserve

Viscount Ind Est
Poyle 14 Trad Est
Skyway 14 Trad Est
Newlands Dri
Laser Way
PH
Poyle Pk
Horton Rd

14

A3113
Airport Way

Horton Rd
Eylands La

Wraysbury River

Ponderosa Cvn Site

TW19

Coppermill Rd

Wraysbury Resr

Meadowview
Stanwell Manor

Colne Beach
Farm Windsor Rd

Station Rd
Little La
Whitehall La
Old Mill La

Stanwell Moor

M25

Sailing Club

River Colne

Russet Cl

Wraysbury

King George VI Resr

Lower Mill Farm

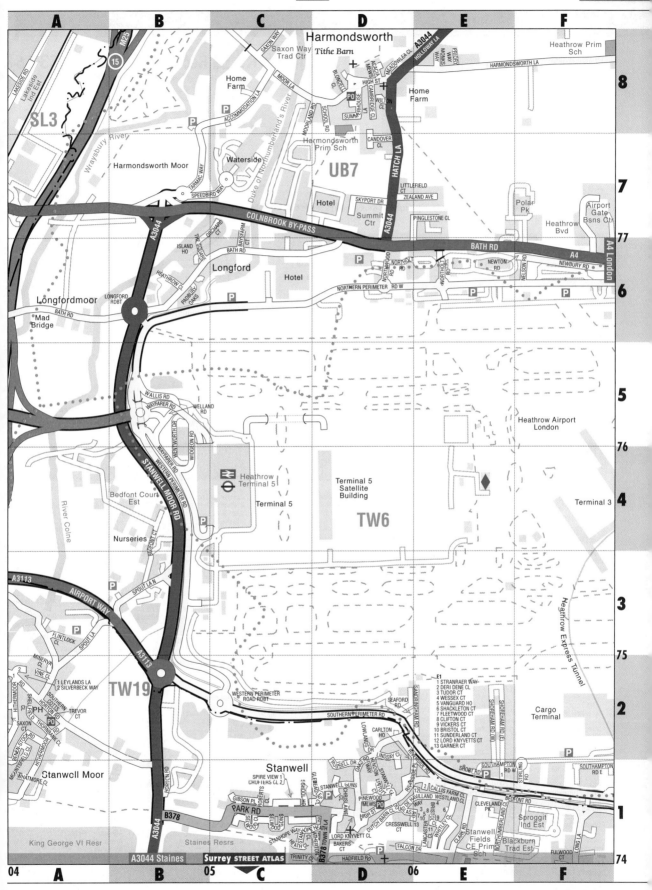

Index

Place name May be abbreviated on the map

Location number Present when a number indicates the place's position in a crowded area of mapping

Locality, town or village Shown when more than one place has the same name

Postcode district District for the indexed place

Page and grid square Page number and grid reference for the standard mapping

Church Rd **6** Beckenham BR2.........**53** C6

Cities, towns and villages are listed in CAPITAL LETTERS

Public and commercial buildings are highlighted in **magenta** **Places of interest** are highlighted in blue with a star★

Abbreviations used in the index

Acad	Academy	Comm	Common	Gd	Ground	L	Leisure	Prom	Promenade
App	Approach	Cott	Cottage	Gdn	Garden	La	Lane	Rd	Road
Arc	Arcade	Cres	Crescent	Gn	Green	Liby	Library	Recn	Recreation
Ave	Avenue	Cswy	Causeway	Gr	Grove	Mdw	Meadow	Ret	Retail
Bglw	Bungalow	Ct	Court	H	Hall	Meml	Memorial	Sh	Shopping
Bldg	Building	Ctr	Centre	Ho	House	Mkt	Market	Sq	Square
Bsns, Bus	Business	Ctry	Country	Hospl	Hospital	Mus	Museum	St	Street
Bvd	Boulevard	Cty	County	HQ	Headquarters	Orch	Orchard	Sta	Station
Cath	Cathedral	Dr	Drive	Hts	Heights	Pal	Palace	Terr	Terrace
Cir	Circus	Dro	Drove	Ind	Industrial	Par	Parade	TH	Town Hall
Cl	Close	Ed	Education	Inst	Institute	Pas	Passage	Univ	University
Cnr	Corner	Emb	Embankment	Int	International	Pk	Park	Wk, Wlk	Walk
Coll	College	Est	Estate	Intc	Interchange	Pl	Place	Wr	Water
Com	Community	Ex	Exhibition	Junc	Junction	Prec	Precinct	Yd	Yard

Index of towns, villages, streets, hospitals, industrial estates, railway stations, schools, shopping centres, universities and places of interest

Aba–Alf

A

Abacus Dr MK10 . . . . 35 E2
Abbey Barn La HP10 . . 173 E3
Abbey Barn Rd HP11 . . 173 F4
Abbey Cl SL1 . . . . 204 E6
Abbey Cotts SL7 . . . . . . 193 B4
Abbey Ct HP5 . . . . 154 B6
Abbey Ctr The HP19 . . . 101 B2
Abbeydore Gr MK10 . . . . 35 F1
Abbeyfield Ho HP16 . . . 152 A7
Abbey Gate SL6 . . . . . . 204 A7
Abbeyhill Rdbt MK12 . . . 33 E4
Abbey Mead SL8 . . . . . . 184 F5
Abbey Park La SL1 . . . . 186 E2
Abbey Rd
  Aylesbury HP19 . . . . . 101 B2
  Bourne End SL8 . . . . . 184 F5
  Milton Keynes, Bradwell
    MK13 . . . . 34 A4
  Milton Keynes, Simpson
    MK6 . . . . 47 E5
  Syresham NN13 . . . . . . 27 C7
Abbey's Prim Sch MK3 . 47 A2
Abbey Sq MK43 . . . . .8 E5
Abbey Terr MK16 . . . . . . 22 D4
Abbey Way
  High Wycombe HP13 . 173 A6
  Milton Keynes MK13 . . 34 B6
  Ravenstone MK46 . . . . . 5 E2
Abbey Wlk HP16 . . . . . . 152 B7
Abbey Wy SL7 . . . . 194 D6
Abbot Ridge HP18 . . . . 125 D5
Abbotsbury MK4 . . . . . . 45 E2
Abbots Cl MK18 . . . . . . 34 B6
Abbotsfield MK6 . . . . . . 47 B8
Abbots Way
  High Wycombe HP12 . 172 D3
  Monks Risborough HP27 139 C5
Abbot's Wlk SL4 . . . . . . 209 E5
Abbotswood HP27 . . . . 150 C4
Abbotts Cl HP20 . . . . . . 101 E1
Abbott's Cl UB8 . . . . . . 208 D8
Abbotts Rd HP20 . . . . . 101 E1
Abbotts Vale HP5 . . . . . 144 C3
Abbotts Way
  Slough SL1 . . . . 204 D5
  Wingrave HP22 . . . . . . 89 A4

Abbot Wlk HP18 . . . . . . 125 D5
Abell Gdns SL6 . . . . 195 B1
Abercromby Ave HP12 . 172 E8
Abercromby Ct **4** HP12 172 D8
Aberdeen Ave SL1 . . . . 205 A6
Aberdeen Cl MK3 . . . . . . 46 F2
Abingdon Cl
  Thame OX9 . . . . 125 F1
  Uxbridge UB10 . . . . . . 201 F4
Abingdon Wlk SL6 . . . . 195 E3
Abington SL3 . . . . 212 D7
Abney Court Dr SL8 . . . 185 A2
Abraham Cl MK15 . . . . . 35 C6
Abrahams Cl HP7 . . . . . 165 E8
Abrahams Rd RG9 . . . . 191 C3
Abstacle Hill HP23 . . . . 118 F3
Acacia **3** RG9 . . . . 191 D2
Acacia Ave
  West Drayton UB7 . . . . 208 F6
  Wraysbury TW19 . . . . . 211 E3
Acacia Cl HP5 . . . . 144 A1
Acacia Gr HP4 . . . . 135 B3
Acacia Ho SL9 . . . . 177 E2
Acacia Mews UB7 . . . . . 213 D8
Acacia Wlk HP23 . . . . . 118 E3
Accommodation La UB7. 213 C8
Ackerman Cl MK18 . . . . 52 F8
Ackroyd Pl MK5 . . . . 46 B5
Acorn Bsns Ctr LU7 . . . . 78 F3
Acorn Cl
  High Wycombe HP13 . . 173 D8
  Slough SL3 . . . . 207 B1
Acorn Gdns HP12 . . . . . 172 E4
Acorn Ho MK9 . . . . 34 D2
Acorn Wlk MK9 . . . . 34 E2
Acrefield Rd SL9 . . . . . . 188 D8
Acre Pas SL4 . . . . 210 D6
Acres End HP7 . . . . 165 E8
Acres The HP13 . . . . . . 161 E1
Acres Way HP19 . . . . . . 101 C4
Acre The SL7 . . . . 183 F2
ACS Hillingdon Int Sch
  UB10. . . . . 201 F4
Adam Cl
  High Wycombe HP13 . . 173 D8
  Slough SL1 . . . . 205 A5
Adam Ct RG9 . . . . 191 E2
Adams Cl MK18 . . . . 41 C1
Adams Ct MK6 . . . . 47 C8
Adams Park (Wycombe
  Wanderers FC) HP12 . 172 A7
Adams Way HP23 . . . . . 119 B6
Ada Wlk MK10 . . . . 35 E2

Addenbrookes MK16 . . . 22 F3
ADDINGTON 65 A6
Addington Cl SL4 . . . . . 210 A4
Addington Cotts HP22 . 131 B5
Addington Rd MK18 . . . . 41 D1
Addington Terr MK18 . . . 41 D1
Addison Cl SL0 . . . . 207 E6
Addison Ct SL6 . . . . 196 B1
Addison Rd
  Chesham HP5 . . . . 144 C2
  Steeple Claydon MK18. . 63 D2
Adelaide Cl SL1 . . . . . . 205 A4
Adelaide Rd
  High Wycombe HP13 . . 162 D1
  Windsor SL4 . . . . 210 F6
Adelaide Sq SL4 . . . . . . 210 D5
Adelphi Gdns SL1 . . . . . 205 E4
Adelphi St MK9 . . . . 34 F4
Adkins Cl HP21 . . . . 100 F3
Adkins Ct HP14 . . . . 158 E5
Admiralty Cl UB7 . . . . . . 208 F4
Admiral Way HP4 . . . . . 134 F6
Adrians Wlk SL2 . . . . . . 205 F5
ADSTOCK 53 F1
Adstock Mews **2** SL9 . . 177 D2
Adwell Sq RG9 . . . . 191 D2
Agars Pl SL3 . . . . 211 A8
Agora Ctr MK12 . . . . 33 D7
Agora Ctr (Sh Ctr) **7**
  MK2 . . . . 58 C8
Aidan Cl HP21 . . . . 116 A4
Aiken Grange MK10 . . . . 35 E2
Ailward Rd HP19 . . . . . . 101 A2
Ainsdale Cl MK3 . . . . . . 46 D1
Aintree Cl
  Milton Keynes MK3 . . . 57 C6
  Poyle SL3 . . . . 212 E6
Airport Gate Bsns Ctr
  UB7. . . . . 213 C8
Airport Way TW19 . . . . . 213 A3
Aiston Pl HP20 . . . . 101 D2
Ajax Ave SL1 . . . . 205 B6
AKELEY 41 E8
Akeley Wood Jun Sch
  MK19 . . . . 31 A1
Akeley Wood Sch
  Akeley MK18 . . . . 29 B4
  Akeley MK18 . . . . 41 C7
Akeman Row HP22 . . . . 116 F6
Akeman St HP23 . . . . . . 119 A3
Akerlea Cl MK6 . . . . 47 C6
Akerman Cl MK18 . . . . . 33 B5
Akister Cl MK18. . . . . . . 52 E8

Alabama Circ HP11 . . . . 173 B4
Alabama Dr HP11 . . . . . 173 B3
Alan Way SL3 . . . . 206 E7
Alaska St HP11 . . . . 173 B4
Alastair Mews HP9 . . . . 175 F2
Albany Ct MK14 . . . . 34 D7
Albany Gate HP5 . . . . . 144 B1
Albany Pk SL3 . . . . 212 D7
Albany Pl HP19 . . . . 101 A2
Albany Rd
  Old Windsor SL4 . . . . . 211 A2
  Windsor SL4 . . . . 210 D5
Albany Terr HP23 . . . . . 119 B6
Albert Cl **9** SL1. . . . . . 205 F3
Albert Orchard HP22 . . 118 A4
Albert Pl SL4 . . . . 205 A1
Albert Rd
  Chesham HP5 . . . . 154 C8
  Henley-on-Thames RG9. 191 E1
  West Drayton UB7. . . . . 208 E5
  Windsor SL4 . . . . 210 E3
Albert St
  Aylesbury HP20 . . . . . 116 A8
  4 High Wycombe HP13 173 C7
  Maidenhead SL6 . . . . . 202 F7
  Milton Keynes MK2 . . . . 58 C8
  Slough SL1 . . . . 205 F3
  Tring HP23 . . . . 119 A3
  Windsor SL4 . . . . 210 B6
Albion SL3 . . . . 207 B1
Albion Cl SL2 . . . . 206 A5
Albion Cotts SL6 . . . . . 195 C7
Albion Cres HP8 . . . . . . 177 B7
Albion Ho HP12 . . . . . . 172 C5
Albion Pl
  Milton Keynes MK9 . . . . 35 A3
  2 Windsor SL4 . . . . . 210 A5
Albion Row
  Chalfont St Giles HP8 . 177 B8
  High Wycombe HP12 . . 172 C5
  Pitstone LU7 . . . . 105 D5
Albion St HP20. . . . . 115 E8
ALBURY 136 B7
Albury Ct **3** MK8 . . . . . 33 F1
Albury View OX9 . . . . . . 136 A6
Aldborough Spur SL1 . . 205 E7
Aldbourne Rd SL1. . . . . 204 B8
ALDBURY. 120 D5
Aldbury CE Prim Sch
  HP23. . . . . 120 C6
Aldbury Gdns HP23 . . . 119 B6
Aldbury Rd WD3 . . . . . . 167 F2
Aldebury Rd SL6 . . . . . 195 F2

Aldene Rd MK19 . . . . 11 B3
Aldenham MK6 . . . . 47 D5
Alden View SL4 . . . . 209 D6
Alderbourne La SL3. . . . 199 E8
Alderbourne Manor SL6. 189 A1
Alderbury Rd SL3 . . . . . 207 A4
Alderbury Road W SL3 . 206 F4
Alder Cl SL1 . . . . 204 F5
Alder Ct MK14 . . . . 21 F3
Aldergill MK13. . . . . 34 C5
Alderley Ct HP4 . . . . . . 135 C3
Alderman Dr HP18 . . . . 100 E5
Aldermead MK12. . . . . . 33 E5
Alderney Ave MK3 . . . . . 58 B4
Alderney Pl MK5 . . . . . . 45 F4
Alder Rd
  Aylesbury HP22 . . . . . 116 C4
  Iver Heath SL0 . . . . . . 200 D3
  New Denham UB9 . . . . 201 C6
Alderson Cl **1** HP19 . . 101 A2
Alders The UB9 . . . . 201 C6
ALDERTON 9 A2
Alderton Dr HP4 . . . . . . 121 B8
Aldin Avenue N SL1 . . . 206 A4
Aldin Avenue S SL1 . . . 206 A4
Aldrich Dr MK15 . . . . . . 35 E7
Aldridge Ct HP11 . . . . . 173 F4
Aldridge Pl SL2 . . . . . . 198 F5
Aldridge Rd SL2 . . . . . . 198 A1
Aldwick Dr SL6 . . . . 202 C6
Aldwycks Cl MK5. . . . . . 45 F6
Alexander Ct
  High Wycombe HP12 . . 172 E8
  Slough SL1. . . . . 205 C4
Alexander Fst Sch SL4 . 209 C4
Alexander Ho **1** MK2 . . 58 C8
Alexander Rd HP20. . . . 101 D1
Alexander St HP5 . . . . . 144 C1
Alexandra Ct
  Leighton Buzzard LU7 . . 80 F8
  4 Milton Keynes MK13 34 A4
  Windsor SL4 . . . . 210 D5
Alexandra Dr MK16. . . . . 22 C2
Alexandra Pk HP11. . . . 173 A6
Alexandra Rd
  High Wycombe HP13 . . 173 E5
  Maidenhead SL6 . . . . . 202 D8
  Slough SL1 . . . . 205 D3
  Uxbridge UB8. . . . . . . 201 D3
  Windsor SL4 . . . . 210 D5
Alford Pl MK3. . . . . 47 B1
Alford Rd HP12 . . . . 172 C3
Alfred Ct SL8 . . . . 185 B3

Alfred Davis Ct SL7 . . . . 183 D3
Alfriston Specl Sch HP9 . . 175 C6
Alham Rd HP21 . . . . 115 C6
Alice Cl HP15 . . . . 163 C7
Alice La SL1 . . . . 197 B1
Alladale Pl MK12 . . . . 33 D4
Allanson Rd SL7 . . . . 183 F3
Allenby Rd SL6 . . . . 202 B7
Allen Cl MK2 . . . . 58 C5
Allen Dr HP14 . . . . 161 C8
Allerford Ct MK4 . . . . 46 C4
Alleyns La SL6 . . . . 195 D8
Allhusen Gdns SL3 . . . . 199 E8
Allington Circ MK4 . . . . 45 E1
Allington Ct SL2 . . . . 205 F6
Allison Ct MK15 . . . . 35 C1
Allkins Ct SL4 . . . . 210 D5
Allonby Way HP21 . . . . 116 B7
All Saints' Ave SL6 . . . . 202 D7
All Saints CE Jun Sch
  SL6 . . . . 202 C6
All Saints View MK5 . . . . 46 B8
All Souls Cotts SL3 . . . . 206 E8
Allyn Cl HP13 . . . . 173 C8
Alma Ct
  Burnham SL1 . . . . 197 C2
  Eton Wick SL4 . . . . 204 F2
Alma Rd
  Berkhamsted HP4 . . . . 134 E6
  Chesham HP5 . . . . 144 C2
  Eton Wick SL4 . . . . 204 F2
  Windsor SL4 . . . . 210 C6
Alma St HP18 . . . . 100 D4
Almshouses MK14 . . . . 21 E1
Almond Cl
  Newport Pagnell MK16 . . . . 22 B3
  Windsor SL4 . . . . 210 B5
Almond Rd SL1 . . . . 197 C2
Almond Tree Dr HP22 . . . . . 116 C4
Almond Way HP27 . . . . 139 A2
Almond Wlk HP15 . . . . 163 B3
Almons Way SL2 . . . . 206 B8
Almshouses
  Eton SL4 . . . . 210 D7
  Old Windsor SL4 . . . . 210 F1
  Worminghall HP18 . . . . 123 E5
Almshouses The MK46 . . . . . . 5 E2
Alnwick Dr HP23 . . . . 103 F7
Alpha Ct HP7 . . . . 165 B7
Alpha Street N ❸ SL1 . . . . . 206 A4
Alpha Street S SL1 . . . . 205 F3
Alpine Cl SL6 . . . . 203 A6
Alpine Croft MK5 . . . . 46 A3
ALSCOT 139 A5
Alscot La HP27 . . . . 139 A5
Alsford Pl SL1 . . . . 206 D2
Alsford Wharf HP4 . . . . 135 C5
Alston Dr MK13 . . . . 33 F3
Alstonefield ❶ MK4 . . . . 46 B3
Alston Gdns SL6 . . . . 202 E7
Althorpe Cres MK13 . . . . 34 B6
Altair Rd MK10 . . . . 35 E2
Altona Rd HP10 . . . . 174 D3
Altona Way SL1 . . . . 205 B7
Alton Bsns Pk HP19 . . . . . . 101 B1
Alton Gate MK4 . . . . 45 F3
Altwood Bailey SL6 . . . . 202 B5
Altwood Cl
  Maidenhead SL6 . . . . 202 B5
  Slough SL1 . . . . 204 E8
Altwood Dr SL6 . . . . 202 B5
Altwood Rd SL6 . . . . 202 B5
Alverton MK14 . . . . 34 F8
Alvista Ave SL6 . . . . 202 F8
Alvric Way ❸ MK12 . . . . 33 A6
Alwin Cl HP21 . . . . 115 C4
Alwins Field LU7 . . . . 80 D8
Alwyn Inf Sch SL6 . . . . 202 C8
Alwyn Rd SL6 . . . . 202 B8
Alyngton HP4 . . . . 134 E2
Alyson Ct ❷ SL6 . . . . 195 F1
Amanda Ct SL3 . . . . 206 D3
Amber Cl HP18 . . . . 100 E5
Amber Cotts HP7 . . . . 164 F3
Ambergate MK16 . . . . 36 B4
Amberley Ct SL6 . . . . 196 C3
Amberley Pl ❶ SL4 . . . . 210 D6
Amberley Rd SL2 . . . . 204 E8
Amberley Way UB10 . . . . . . 201 E3
Amberley Wlk MK4 . . . . 45 E1
Amblers Way MK18 . . . . 53 A1
Ambleside
  Amersham HP6 . . . . 154 C2
  Aylesbury HP21 . . . . 116 B6
Ambleside Wlk UB8 . . . . 201 D4
Ambridge Gr SL6 . . . . 35 C1
Ambrose Ct MK15 . . . . 35 C2
Amelias La MK9 . . . . 35 A3
Amerdcn Cl SL6 . . . . 203 D7
Amerden La SL6 . . . . 203 D7
Amerden Way SL1 . . . . 205 A4
AMERSHAM 154 B2
AMERSHAM COMMON 165 E8
Amersham Ct HP7 . . . . 165 A7
Amersham Hill HP13 . . . . . . 173 B7
Amersham Hill Dr HP13 . . . . 173 C8
Amersham Hill Gdns
  HP13 . . . . 173 B7
Amersham Hospl HP7 . . . . . 165 A6
Amersham Mus ⁎ HP7 . . . . . 165 B7
AMERSHAM OLD TOWN . . . 165 A7
AMERSHAM ON THE
  HILL 154 D2
Amersham Pl HP7 . . . . 166 C8
Amersham Rd
  Beaconsfield HP7 . . . . 176 A6

Amersham Rd continued
Chalfont Common HP8,
  SL9 . . . . 177 D6
Chalfont St Giles HP8 . . . . . 166 B2
Chalfont St Peter SL9 . . . . . 177 E2
Chesham HP5 . . . . 154 B5
Chorleywood WD3 . . . . 167 C8
Denham Green SL9 . . . . . . 189 A4
Gerrards Cross SL9 . . . . . . 188 F7
Hazlemere HP15 . . . . 162 E2
High Wycombe HP13 . . . . . 173 C8
Little Chalfont HP6 . . . . 166 E8
Amersham Sch HP7 . . . . . . 165 E7
Amersham Sta/U Sta
  HP6 . . . . 154 C1
Amersham Way HP6 . . . . . . 166 E8
Amersham & Wycombe Coll
  Amersham HP7 . . . . 165 E4
  Chesham HP5 . . . . 144 D3
  Flackwell Heath HP10 . . . . 173 E2
Amesbury Rd SL1 . . . . 204 F4
Ames Cl MK6 . . . . 46 F8
Amherst Ct MK15 . . . . 35 C7
Amicia Gdns SL2 . . . . 198 F4
Amorosa Gdns HP18 . . . . . . 100 E5
Amos Ct MK13 . . . . 34 A6
Amy La HP5 . . . . 154 B7
Ancastle Gr RG9 . . . . 191 D1
Ancell Rd MK11 . . . . 32 E5
Anchor Ct SL6 . . . . 195 F7
Anchor La ❶ HP20 . . . . 115 E8
Ancona Gdns ❶ MK5 . . . . . . 45 F3
Andermans SL4 . . . . 209 D6
Andersen Gate MK4 . . . . 57 A7
Anderson Cl HP14 . . . . 158 F4
Anding Cl MK46 . . . . 6 E4
Andover Cl UB8 . . . . 201 B3
Andrewes Croft MK14 . . . . . . 34 F8
Andrew Hill La SL2 . . . . 187 C3
Andrews Cl LU7 . . . . 69 E3
Andrews Reach SL8 . . . . . . 185 A2
Andrews Way
  Aylesbury HP19 . . . . 115 A7
  Marlow Bottom SL7 . . . . . . 183 C8
Anershall HP22 . . . . 89 B3
Angel Cl MK15 . . . . 35 A7
Angelica Cl UB7 . . . . 208 F7
Angelica Ct MK7 . . . . 48 A5
Angels Cl MK18 . . . . 65 F4
Anglefield Rd HP4 . . . . 135 B4
Anglesey Ct
  Milton Keynes MK8 . . . . . . 46 A8
  Stokenchurch HP14 . . . . . 158 E5
Anglesey View MK17 . . . . . . 58 D4
Angling Spring Wood Talking
  Trail ⁎ HP16 . . . . 151 F7
Anglo Bsns Pk HP19 . . . . . . 101 A1
Angood Ct HP27 . . . . 139 A3
Angora Cl MK5 . . . . 46 A3
Angstrom Cl MK5 . . . . 46 B5
Angus Dr MK3 . . . . 46 F2
Angus Rd HP19 . . . . 101 A3
Anne Cl SL6 . . . . 195 E2
Annes Gr MK14 . . . . 21 D1
Annesley Rd MK16 . . . . 22 B3
Anns Cl
  Aylesbury HP21 . . . . 116 A4
  Tring HP23 . . . . 118 E3
Ansculf Rd SL2 . . . . 198 A2
Anslow Gdns SL0 . . . . 200 D3
Anslow Pl SL1 . . . . 204 C8
Anson Cl
  Aylesbury HP21 . . . . 115 E4
  Bovingdon HP3 . . . . 145 F4
Anson Rd MK12 . . . . 33 C6
Anstey Brook HP22 . . . . 117 A3
Anstey Cl HP18 . . . . 99 B6
Anstey Ct HP18 . . . . 99 B7
Anthony Cl HP13 . . . . 161 F1
Anthony Ct MK11 . . . . 32 D5
Anthony Way SL1 . . . . 204 D6
Antigua Wy MK3 . . . . 58 C4
Antonia Wy ❷ MK16 . . . . . . 36 B5
Anton Way HP21 . . . . 115 D3
Anvil Cl HP3 . . . . 146 B3
Anvil Ct SL3 . . . . 207 A2
Anxey Way HP17 . . . . 126 F6
Aplin Rd HP21 . . . . 116 C6
Apollo Ave MK11 . . . . 32 F3
Appleacres MK17 . . . . 69 D8
Applefield HP7 . . . . 166 C7
Appleton Cl HP7 . . . . 166 B7
Appleton Mews ❹ MK4 . . . . 46 B3
Appletree Ave SL8, UB8 . . . 208 F7
Apple Tree Cl
  Leighton Buzzard LU7 . . . . 80 D6
  Loudwater HP13 . . . . 174 A4
Appletree La SL3 . . . . 206 C3
Appletree Wlk HP5 . . . . 154 D5
Applewick La HP12 . . . . 172 C8
Applewood Cl UB10 . . . . . . 201 E8
Appleyard Pl ❶ MK6 . . . . . . 34 E1
Approach Rd SL6 . . . . 203 E7
Approach The MK8 . . . . 33 E2
Apsley Cotts SL6 . . . . 195 E7
Apsley Ho SL1 . . . . 206 A4
Apsley Wlk SL0 . . . . 207 F3
Aqua Vale Swimming &
  Fitness Ctr HP20 . . . . 115 F8
Aquila Gdns MK11 . . . . 33 A3
Aran Ct MK13 . . . . 34 B8

Aran Hts HP8 . . . . 177 B6
Arborfield Cl SL1 . . . . 205 E3
Arbour Vale Sch SL2 . . . . . 198 B2
Arbour View HP7 . . . . 166 B8
Arbroath Cl MK3 . . . . 46 E3
Arbrook Ave MK13 . . . . 34 D3
Arcade The HP9 . . . . 175 E3
Archdale ❶ HP11 . . . . 173 A6
Archer Cl SL6 . . . . 202 D8
Archer Ct HP6 . . . . 154 C2
Archer Dr HP20 . . . . 102 A2
Archers Way HP14 . . . . 171 B5
Archers Wells MK3 . . . . 47 B2
Archer Terr UB7 . . . . 208 E6
Archford Croft MK4 . . . . 46 C3
Arch Gr HP18 . . . . 100 E5
Archive Cl HP22 . . . . 117 D5
Archive Mews HP4 . . . . 135 A2
Arch Way
  High Wycombe HP13 . . . . . 173 A7
  Speen HP27 . . . . 150 B4
Archways ❶❹ HP20 . . . . . . 115 D8
Arden Cl HP3 . . . . 146 A3
Ardenham La HP19 . . . . 101 D1
Ardenham St HP19 . . . . 101 C1
Arden Park MK12 . . . . 33 B7
Ardley Mews ❼ MK10 . . . . . 36 B3
Ardrossan Cl SL2 . . . . 198 C1
Ardwell La MK12 . . . . 33 B3
Ardys Ct MK5 . . . . 46 B8
Arena MK1 . . . . 47 C3
Argonaut Pk SL3 . . . . 212 C6
Argyle Ave HP19 . . . . 101 B2
Argyll Ave SL1 . . . . 205 A6
Argyll Ho MK3 . . . . 46 F1
Aries Ho HP10 . . . . 185 A8
Aris Way MK18 . . . . 52 D6
Arizona St HP11 . . . . 173 B4
Arklay Cl UB8 . . . . 201 F1
Arkley Ct SL6 . . . . 203 C1
Arklow Ct WD3 . . . . 167 D5
Ark Royal MK16 . . . . 36 B5
Arkwright Mews MK14 . . . . . 34 C8
Arkwright Rd SL3 . . . . 212 E5
Arlington Cl SL6 . . . . 202 A8
Arlington Ct MK4 . . . . 46 E3
Arlott Cres MK6 . . . . 46 F8
Armada Ave ❸ MK16 . . . . . . 36 C4
Armourer Dr MK14 . . . . 34 F6
Armstrong Cl MK8 . . . . 45 E7
Armstrong Ho SL2 . . . . 206 C7
Arncliffe Dr MK13 . . . . 34 B5
Arncott Rd MK13 . . . . 34 B5
Arncott Way MK18 . . . . 100 F1
Arncott Wood Rd OX25 . . . . 94 E6
Arne La MK7 . . . . 48 D5
Arnison Ave HP13 . . . . 162 D1
Arnold Cl HP22 . . . . 116 C2
Arnold Cott MK19 . . . . 32 C7
Arnold Ct HP21 . . . . 115 F6
Arnolds MK18 . . . . 53 A1
Arnold's Cotts HP5 . . . . 143 B4
Arnos Gr MK10 . . . . 35 F1
Arnott's Yd HP18 . . . . 125 D6
Arranmore Ho HP11 . . . . . . 174 B4
Arrewig La HP5 . . . . 142 E8
Arrow Pl MK2 . . . . 58 D4
Arthur Cl MK16 . . . . 195 E5
Arthur Jacob Nature
  Reserve ⁎ SL3 . . . . 212 C4
Arthur Rd
  Slough SL1 . . . . 205 D4
  Windsor SL4 . . . . 210 C6
Artichoke Dell WD3 . . . . . . 167 E4
Aruba Cl MK3 . . . . 58 B3
Arundel Cl SL6 . . . . 202 A8
Arundel Ct SL3 . . . . 206 D2
Arundel Gn HP20 . . . . 101 F2
Arundel Gr MK3 . . . . 57 E7
Arundel Ho
  ❶ High Wycombe HP13 . . . 173 F7
  Uxbridge UB8 . . . . 201 C1
Arundel Rd
  High Wycombe HP12 . . . . . 172 B6
  Uxbridge UB8 . . . . 201 B2
Ascension Gdns MK3 . . . . . . 58 B4
Ascot Dr LU7 . . . . 80 D6
Ascot Ho MK9 . . . . 34 C2
Ascot Pl MK3 . . . . 57 D7
Ascot Rd SL6 . . . . 203 A1
ASCOTT 80 A2
Ascott House ⁎ LU7 . . . . 80 A2
Ascott Rd HP20 . . . . 101 E1
Ascough Cl HP19 . . . . 101 D3
Ashbourne End HP21 . . . . . 115 D4
Ashbourne Gr SL6 . . . . 202 C3
Ashbourne Ho ❺ SL1 . . . . . 205 E4
Ashbrook Sch MK8 . . . . 33 F1
Ashburnham Cl ❷ MK3 . . . . 46 D1
Ashburnham Cres LU7 . . . . . 80 E6
Ashby MK6 . . . . 47 A8
Ashby Rd HP4 . . . . 134 D7
Ashby Villas LU7 . . . . 92 A1
Ash Cl
  Aylesbury HP20 . . . . 102 A2
  Slough SL3 . . . . 207 B3
  Walter's Ash HP14 . . . . . . 161 B8
Ashcroft Cl SL1 . . . . 197 B3
Ashcroft Dr UB9 . . . . 189 F4
Ashcroft Rd SL6 . . . . 202 C6
Ashcroft Terr HP23 . . . . 119 A5
Ashdown Cl MK14 . . . . 35 A8
Ashdown Ct MK14 . . . . 35 A8
Ashdown Rd HP13 . . . . 173 D6
Ashdown Way HP6 . . . . 154 D2
Ashen Cross SL3 . . . . 207 B8

Ashenden Wlk SL2 . . . . 198 D8
ASHENDON 97 C1
Ashendon Rd HP18 . . . . 98 C6
ASHERIDGE 143 C6
Asheridge Rd HP5 . . . . 144 A2
Asheridge Rd Ind Est
  HP5 . . . . 144 A2
Ashfield MK14 . . . . 34 D8
Ashfield Cl HP15 . . . . 163 B6
Ashfield Cotts UB9 . . . . 190 A1
Ashfield Gr MK2 . . . . 58 C7
Ashfield HP5 . . . . 144 A2
Ashfield Rise HP15 . . . . 109 D5
Ashfield Way HP15 . . . . 163 B3
Ashford Cl HP21 . . . . 116 A5
Ashford Cres MK8 . . . . 45 D6
Ashford La SL4 . . . . 204 B4
Ashford Rd SL0 . . . . 200 C4
Ashgrove MK18 . . . . 63 D2
Ashgrove Gdns HP22 . . . . . . 86 E7
Ash Hill Prim Sch HP13 . . . 174 A7
Ash Hill Rd MK16 . . . . 22 B4
Ash La SL4 . . . . 209 D5
Ashland Rdbt MK1 . . . . 47 C5
Ashlea MK46 . . . . 6 E3
Ashlea Rd SL9 . . . . 177 E1
Ashleigh Cl HP7 . . . . 165 E8
Ashley HP10 . . . . 185 F7
Ashley Cl LU7 . . . . 105 A8
Ashley Ct
  ❸ Aylesbury HP19 . . . . . . 115 A8
  Maidenhead SL6 . . . . 203 B7
  Tylers Green HP10 . . . . . . 163 B1
  West Drayton UB7 . . . . . . 208 E5
Ashley Dr HP10 . . . . 163 C1
Ashley Green Rd HP5 . . . . . 144 E5
Ashley Pk SL6 . . . . 196 B2
Ashley Rd UB8 . . . . 201 B3
Ashley Row HP20 . . . . 102 A1
Ashleys WD3 . . . . 167 F2
Ashlyns Ct HP4 . . . . 135 B3
Ashlyns Rd HP4 . . . . 135 B3
Ashlyns Sch HP4 . . . . 135 C2
Ashmead Comb Sch
  HP21 . . . . 115 C5
Ash Mead Dr UB9 . . . . 190 A2
Ashmead La UB9 . . . . 190 A2
Ashmead Pl HP7 . . . . 166 C8
Ashmead St HP18 . . . . 100 D6
Ashmount Cres ❶ SL1 . . . . 205 A4
Ashotts La
  Chartridge HP5 . . . . 143 A5
  Chartridge HP5 . . . . 143 B7
Ashover ❺ MK10 . . . . 36 C4
Ashpole Furlong MK5 . . . . . . 46 B7
Ash Rd
  High Wycombe HP12 . . . . . 172 C4
  Princes Risborough HP27 . . 139 B3
  Tring HP23 . . . . 118 F4
Ashridge OX39 . . . . 147 B6
Ashridge Cl
  ❶ Bovingdon HP3 . . . . 146 A3
  Milton Keynes MK3 ⁎ 57 D7
Ashridge Coll Gdns ⁎
  HP4 . . . . 121 D5
Ashridge Cotts HP4 . . . . . . 121 E5
Ashridge Est Visitor Ctr ⁎
  HP4 . . . . 120 E6
Ashridge Executive
  Education HP4 . . . . 121 C5
Ashridge La HP5 . . . . 155 D7
Ashridge Rise HP4 . . . . 134 F5
ASHTON 9 E8
Ashton Pl SL6 . . . . 202 A6
Ashton Rd NN12 . . . . 9 D8
Ash Tree Ho HP12 . . . . 172 C4
Ashtree Wlk HP15 . . . . 163 B2
Ash Vale WD3 . . . . 178 D5
Ashwells MK13 . . . . 34 A7
Ashwood Dr HP5 . . . . 144 B1
Askerton Cres MK4 . . . . 56 E8
ASKETT 139 D6
Askett La HP27 . . . . 139 D7
Aspen Cl
  Aylesbury HP20 . . . . 102 A2
  Maidenhead SL6 . . . . 195 A3
  Slough SL2 . . . . 205 B8
  West Drayton UB7 . . . . . . 208 F5
Aspens Pl HP1 . . . . 146 F8
Aspery Pl SL1 . . . . 205 F5
Asplands Cl MK17 . . . . 49 B4
Aspley Ct
  Aylesbury HP19 . . . . 101 C1
  Woburn Sands MK17 . . . . . 49 C3
APSLEY GUISE 49 F4
Aspley Guise Lower Sch
  MK17 . . . . 49 F4
Aspley Guise Sta MK17 . . . . 49 D6
APSLEY HEATH 49 A2
Aspley Hill MK17 . . . . 49 C4
Aspley La MK17 . . . . 49 E2
Aspreys MK46 . . . . 6 E4
Assetton Rd HP9 . . . . 175 E4
Astlethorpe MK8 . . . . 33 F2
Astley Pl HP23 . . . . 119 F5

Alf–Avo 215

Astley Rd OX9 . . . . 126 B1
ASTON 192 C5
ASTON ABBOTTS 88 D5
Aston Abbotts Rd
  Cublington LU7 . . . . 78 C1
  Weedon HP22 . . . . 87 E1
Aston Cl
  Aylesbury HP19 . . . . 101 A3
  Milton Keynes MK5 . . . . . . 46 B5
ASTON CLINTON 117 D6
Aston Clinton Ragpits
  Wildlife Reserve ⁎
  HP22 . . . . 117 F2
Aston Clinton Rd HP22 . . . . 116 E6
Aston Clinton Sch HP22 . . . 117 D5
Aston Ferry La RG9 . . . . . . 192 C5
Aston Hill OX49 . . . . 157 E7
Aston La RG9 . . . . 192 C3
Aston Mead SL4 . . . . 209 E6
Aston Rd HP17 . . . . 127 B5
Aston Rowant National
  Nature Reserve ⁎ HP14 . . . 157 E6
ASTON SANDFORD 127 D4
Astonville SL2 . . . . 198 C8
Astor Cl SL6 . . . . 202 B8
Astronomy Way ❶❷ HP19 . . 115 A8
ASTROPE 104 A3
Astrope La HP23 . . . . 104 B3
ASTWOOD 16 A3
Astwood Rd MK43 . . . . 25 C7
Atherstone Ct MK8 . . . . 33 C2
Atherton Cl TW19 . . . . 213 D1
Atherton Ct SL6 . . . . 210 D7
Athlone Cl SL6 . . . . 195 E1
Athlone Sq SL4 . . . . 210 C5
Atkins Cl MK13 . . . . 34 B3
Atlas Ho HP5 . . . . 144 B1
Atlas Wy MK10 . . . . 35 E2
Atterbrook MK13 . . . . 34 A4
ATTERBURY 36 A4
Attingham Hill
  ❻ Milton Keynes MK8 . . . . 33 F1
  Milton Keynes MK8 . . . . . . 34 A1
Atwell Cl MK8 . . . . 45 E7
Auckland Cl SL6 . . . . 203 B8
Auckland Pk MK1 . . . . 47 D4
Auckland Rd HP13 . . . . 173 E6
Auden Cl MK16 . . . . 22 A5
Audley Dr SL6 . . . . 202 B6
Audley Mead MK13 . . . . 34 B3
August End SL3 . . . . 206 E7
Augustine Cl SL3 . . . . 212 E4
Augustine Mews HP16 . . . . 152 B7
Augustus Rd MK11 . . . . 32 E4
Augustus Smith Ho ❷
  HP4 . . . . 135 D4
Auralia Cl HP18 . . . . 100 E5
Aurelia Cl MK11 . . . . 33 A3
Austen Ave MK46 . . . . 7 A4
Austen Pl HP19 . . . . 100 F2
Austenway SL9 . . . . 188 E8
AUSTENWOOD 188 C8
Austenwood Cl
  Chalfont St Peter SL9 . . . . 177 C1
  High Wycombe HP11 . . . . . 173 A4
Austenwood La
  Chalfont St Peter SL9 . . . . 177 D1
  Gerrards Cross SL9 . . . . . 188 D8
Austins Mead HP3 . . . . 146 B3
Austin Way SL3 . . . . 211 F8
Austin Waye UB8 . . . . 201 C4
Australia Ave SL6 . . . . 202 F8
Australia Rd ❶ SL1 . . . . . . 206 B4
Austwick La MK4 . . . . 46 B2
Autumn Cl
  Aylesbury HP19 . . . . 101 A3
  Slough SL1 . . . . 204 F5
Autumn Wlk SL6 . . . . 202 A5
Autumn Wy UB7 . . . . 208 F4
Avalon Rd SL8 . . . . 185 B5
Avalon St HP18 . . . . 100 E3
Avant Bsns Ctr MK1 . . . . . . 47 C2
Avebury SL1 . . . . 205 A6
Avebury Bvd MK9 . . . . 34 E2
Avebury Rdbt MK9 . . . . 34 D1
Aveling Rd HP13 . . . . 173 C6
Avenue Cl UB7 . . . . 208 D3
Avenue Dr
  Iver Heath SL3 . . . . 199 F1
  Slough SL3 . . . . 206 D8
Avenue Ho HP5 . . . . 154 B8
Avenue Rd
  Buckingham MK18 . . . . 41 E3
  Maidenhead SL6 . . . . 203 B5
  Winslow MK18 . . . . 65 F4
Avenue The
  Amersham HP7 . . . . 154 C1
  Bourne End SL8 . . . . 184 F4
  Chinnor OX39 . . . . 147 D6
  Datchet SL3 . . . . 211 B6
  Dunstable LU6 . . . . 93 E7
  Farnham Common SL2 . . . 198 B8
  Maidenhead SL6 . . . . 196 C3
  Old Windsor SL4 . . . . 211 B2
  Princes Risborough HP27 . . 139 C4
  Uxbridge UB8 . . . . 201 D1
  Whitfield NN13 . . . . 26 D4
  Worminghall HP18 . . . . . . 123 D8
  Wraysbury TW19 . . . . 211 D4
Averdal Dr HP18 . . . . 100 E5
Averil Ct SL6 . . . . 204 C7
Avery Ave HP13 . . . . 161 D2
Avery Ct MK16 . . . . 22 C2
Avington MK8 . . . . 33 E1
Avocet Way HP19 . . . . 101 E3

Avonbury Ct NN13 . . . . 38 A5
Avon Cl
  Newport Pagnell MK16 . . . . 22 D3
  Slough SL1. . . . . 204 E6
Avondale SL6. . . . . 195 C1
Avon Gr MK3 . . . . 57 E8
Avonmoore SL6. . . . . 203 B8
Avon Pl HP21. . . . . 115 D4
Axis Pk SL3. . . . . 207 B1
AYLESBURY 115 D7
Aylesbury Bsns Ctr HP19 101 B1
Aylesbury Coll HP21 . . . . . . 115 C7
Aylesbury Cres SL1 . . . . . . 205 D6
Aylesbury End HP9. . . . . . . 175 E1
Aylesbury Gram Sch
  HP21. . . . . 115 F7
Aylesbury High Sch
  HP21. . . . . 115 F7
Aylesbury Ind Ctr 5
  HP19. . . . . 101 C1
Aylesbury Rd
  Aston Clinton HP22 . . . . . 117 B5
  Bierton HP22. . . . . 102 B3
  Cuddington HP18. . . . . . . 113 A3
  Great Missenden HP16 . . . 141 F2
  Haddenham HP17, OX9. . . 126 C6
  Monks Risborough HP27. . 139 D6
  Thame OX9 . . . . 125 F2
  Tring HP23. . . . . 118 E2
  Wendover HP22. . . . . 131 B6
  Wing LU7. . . . . 79 E1
Aylesbury St
  Milton Keynes, Bletchley
    MK2 . . . . 58 E8
  Milton Keynes, Wolverton
    MK12 . . . . 33 D6
Aylesbury Sta HP20 . . . . . . 115 D7
Aylesbury Street W MK12. 33 C6
Aylesbury Vale Acad
  Aylesbury HP18. . . . . 100 E4
  Aylesbury HP19 . . . . 101 C2
Aylesbury Vale Parkway Sta
  HP18. . . . . 100 D3
Aylesbury Waterside Theatre
  HP20. . . . . 115 E8
Aylesford Gr MK10 . . . . 36 A1
Ayless Cl HP18. . . . . 98 B7
Ayleswater HP21. . . . . 101 E4
Aylesworth Ave SL2. . . . . . 198 B2
Aylward Gdns HP5 . . . . 144 A1
Aynho Ct MK8 . . . . 45 F8
Aynscombe Cl LU6. . . . . 93 F8
Ayres Cl HP21 . . . . 115 B6
Ayrshire Cl HP21 . . . . 101 A3
Ayrton Cl MK8 . . . . 45 D6
Ayr Way MK3 . . . . 46 E2
Aysgarth Pk SL6 . . . . 203 B1
Azalea Cl HP15 . . . . 163 A3
Azalea Way SL3. . . . . 206 E7

B

Babbage Gate MK10. . . . . . 35 E2
Babington Cl MK10. . . . . . . 36 A3
Babington Rd HP22 . . . . . . 131 D6
Babylon Gr 10 MK4. . . . . . . 45 F1
Baccara Gr MK2 . . . . 58 C7
Bacchus La
  Milton Keynes MK11 . . . . . 32 F3
  Milton Keynes MK11 . . . . . 33 A3
Bachelors Acre SL4 . . . . . . 210 D6
Back Dr MK16 . . . . 12 F3
Back La
  Chalfont St Giles HP8 . . . . 177 A7
  Great Missenden HP16 . . . 152 B7
  Tingewick MK18. . . . . 51 A6
Backleys MK7. . . . . 48 A2
Back St
  Gawcott MK18. . . . . 51 F4
  Thornborough MK18 . . . . . 54 A8
  Wendover HP22. . . . . 131 B4
Backs The HP5 . . . . 154 C8
Bacombe Hill Nature
  Reserve★ HP22. . . . . 131 A3
Bacombe La HP22 . . . . 131 B3
Bacon Hill MK46. . . . . 6 E3
Baconsmead UB9. . . . . 190 A2
Bader Gdns SL1. . . . . 205 A4
Badgebury Rise SL7. . . . . . 183 C7
Badgemore Ct MK8 . . . . . . 33 C2
Badgemore La RG9. . . . . . . 191 D3
Badgemore Prim Sch
  RG9. . . . . 191 D2
Badger Cl SL6 . . . . 202 D4
Badgers Cl MK43. . . . . 25 B2
Badgers Gate LU6. . . . . 93 E8
Badgers Holt 7 MK17. . . . . 49 A5
Badgers Mdw HP22 . . . . . . 131 C5
Badgers Oak MK7. . . . . 48 B7
Badgers Rise HP17. . . . . . . 114 C5
Badgers Way
  Buckingham MK18. . . . . . . 52 E7
  Marlow Bottom SL7. . . . . . 183 D2
Badgers Wlk WD3. . . . . 167 F5
Badgers Wood SL2. . . . . . . 198 C7
Badger Way HP15. . . . . 163 B5
Bad Godesberg Way SL6 202 F7
Badminton Ct 3 HP7. . . . . . 165 B7
Badminton Ho 1 HP7. . . . . 165 B7
Badminton Rd SL6. . . . . . . 202 B6
Badminton View MK8. . . . . 34 A1
Badrick Rd HP19. . . . . 100 F2
Bagley Cl UB7. . . . . 208 E4
Bagshot Ct MK2. . . . . 58 C7

Bailey Cl
  High Wycombe HP13 . . . . 173 C7
  Maidenhead SL6 . . . . 202 F7
  Windsor SL4. . . . . 210 A5
Bailey Ho 9 SL6. . . . . 185 A4
Bailey's Ct 12 HP20. . . . . . 115 D8
Baily Ct MK5. . . . . 46 A5
Baines Ho HP11. . . . . 173 F4
Baird Cl SL1. . . . . 205 B4
Baird Pl 3 HP22. . . . . 131 D6
Baisley Ho MK2. . . . . 58 D8
Bakers Cl
  Stoke Goldington MK16. . . 12 B5
  Turvey MK43 . . . . 8 E5
Bakers Ct
  Stanwell TW19. . . . . 213 D1
  Waddesdon HP18 . . . . 99 A6
Baker's Orch HP18 . . . . 185 E5
Baker's Piece Ho OX39. . . 147 A4
Baker's Rd UB8. . . . . 201 D5
Baker St
  High Wycombe HP11. . . . . 172 F7
  Waddesdon HP18 . . . . 99 A6
Bakers Wlk HP22 . . . . 116 F2
BAKER'S WOOD. 189 D3
Bakers Wood UB9. . . . . 189 D3
Bakery Cl MK43. . . . . 25 B1
Bakery Ho 10 HP20. . . . . . . 115 D8
Bala Cl MK2. . . . . 58 D5
Bala Lake Cres MK10. . . . . 36 B4
Bala Way MK2 . . . . 58 C5
Balcary Gdns HP4. . . . . 134 F3
Balcary Gr MK4 . . . . 56 F8
Baldways Cl HP22. . . . . 89 C3
Baldwin Cres MK16. . . . . . . 22 C3
Baldwin Pl SL6. . . . . 202 C7
Baldwin Rd
  Beaconsfield HP9. . . . . . . 176 B1
  Burnham SL1. . . . . 197 C2
Baldwin's Shore SL4 . . . . . 210 D8
Balfe Mews MK7. . . . . 48 D4
Balfour Mews 3 HP3 . . . . . 146 A4
Balfour Pl SL7 . . . . 183 D4
Balfour Way HP20. . . . . 101 E2
Balham's La RG9. . . . . 179 F8
Ballard Cl HP21 . . . . 116 B5
Ballard Gn SL4. . . . . 209 E7
Ballards Row HP22. . . . . . . 117 D6
BALLINGER COMMON 142 E3
Ballinger Ct HP4 . . . . 135 B3
Ballinger Grange HP16. . . . 142 E2
Ballinger Rd HP16 . . . . 142 E1
Ballinger Row HP16. . . . . . 142 D3
Ball Moor MK18. . . . . 52 D6
Balmer Bridge MK18 . . . . . 52 E5
Balmer Cut MK18. . . . . 52 E6
Balmerino Cl MK10. . . . . . . 36 B2
Balmoral SL6 . . . . 195 B1
Balmoral Cl SL1 . . . . 204 E7
Balmoral Ct
  High Wycombe HP13. . . . . 173 B7
  Newport Pagnell MK16 . . . 22 B3
Balmoral Gdns SL4. . . . . . . 210 D4
Balsam Cl MK7. . . . . 48 B6
Bamburgh Gate MK4 . . . . . 45 E1
Bamfords La MK43. . . . . 8 E6
Bamfords Yd MK43. . . . . 8 E5
Bampton Cl MK4. . . . . 46 E2
Banburies Cl MK3. . . . . 47 A3
Banbury Ave SL1. . . . . 204 F8
Bancroft Rdbt MK13. . . . . . 34 A5
Bandon Cl UB10. . . . . 201 F3
Bangor Cotts SL0 . . . . 200 D1
Bangors Cl SL0. . . . . 207 F7
Bangors Road N SL0. . . . . 200 D3
Bangors Road S SL0. . . . . . 207 E8
Bank Apartments HP11. . . 183 D3
Bank Court Mews MK12 . . . 33 D7
Bankfield Rdbt MK9. . . . . . . 35 A2
Bank Gn HP5 . . . . 143 C8
Bank Mill HP4 . . . . 135 E4
Bank Mill La HP4 . . . . 135 E3
Bank Rd HP10 . . . . 174 D8
Bankside HP22. . . . . 131 B5
Banks Rd HP17 . . . . 127 A6
Banks Spur SL1. . . . . 205 B4
Bank St HP13. . . . . 174 A4
Banks Yd HP18 . . . . 100 D4
Banktop Pl MK4. . . . . 46 C3
Bannard Rd SL6. . . . . 202 A5
Banner Ct 1 HP12. . . . . 172 D8
Bannister Cl SL3. . . . . 206 E4
Bantock Cl MK7 . . . . 48 C5
Bantry Rd SL1. . . . . 204 F4
Barbados Row MK3. . . . . . . 58 B4
Barbers Mews MK14 . . . . . 34 F6
Barbers Wlk HP23. . . . . 118 F3
Barbers Wood Cl HP12 . . . 172 B4
Barbers Wood Rd HP12 . . . 172 B4
Barbicus Ct SL6. . . . . 203 B8
Barbury Ct MK14. . . . . 35 A8
Barchester Cl UB8. . . . . . . 201 C1
Barchester Rd SL3. . . . . . . 206 F4
Barclay Cl OX27. . . . . 72 E6
Barclay Ct 3 HP12. . . . . . . 172 E7
Bardeen Cl MK10 . . . . 35 E2
Bardney Cl SL6 . . . . 202 D3
Bardolphs Cl HP27 . . . . . . 139 C4
Bardon Gn HP20 . . . . 101 E2
Bardsey Cl MK10. . . . . 36 A2
Barford MK11. . . . . 32 F4
Bargeman Rd SL6 . . . . 202 E5
Barham Lodge 5 MK18 . . . 52 C8
Baring Cres HP9. . . . . 175 C3
Baring Rd
  Beaconsfield HP9 . . . . 175 D3

Baring Rd continued
  High Wycombe HP13 . . . . 173 C7
Barkers Croft MK12. . . . . . . 33 C4
Barkestone Cl MK4. . . . . . . 46 C1
Barkham Cl LU7. . . . . 104 F7
Barkus Way HP14. . . . . 158 F5
Bar La HP27 . . . . 138 E7
Barland Wy HP18 . . . . 100 E3
Barlee Cres UB8. . . . . 208 C8
Barley Cl
  Hazelmere HP15 . . . . 163 A3
  Lewknor OX49. . . . . 157 A8
  Weston Turville HP22. . . . 116 F2
Barley Cres HP21. . . . . 115 D3
Barleycroft MK4 . . . . 46 E4
Barley Fields HP10. . . . . . . 185 E8
Barley Hill Prim Sch
  OX9. . . . . 126 A1
Barley Mead SL6. . . . . 202 A5
Barley View HP16. . . . . 151 D6
Barley Way 3 SL7. . . . . 183 D1
Barlow Rd HP22 . . . . 131 C5
Barnabas Rd LU7. . . . . 80 D6
Barnacre Cl UB8. . . . . 208 D7
Barnard Cres HP21. . . . . . . 115 F5
Barnards Hill SL7. . . . . 183 C2
Barn Cl
  Farnham Common SL2. . . 198 B8
  Maidenhead SL6. . . . . 195 F2
Barncroft MK43. . . . . 8 E6
Barncroft Rd HP4 . . . . 134 F3
Barn Ct HP12 . . . . 172 C7
Barn Dr SL6. . . . . 202 A4
Barnes Ave HP5. . . . . 144 C1
Barnes Pl MK6 . . . . 46 E8
Barnes Wallis Ct HP12. . . . 172 E5
Barnes Way SL0 . . . . 207 F6
Barnet Cl MK5. . . . . 45 D5
Barnett Way HP22. . . . . 102 B4
Barnfield
  Iver SL0. . . . . 207 E7
  Slough SL1. . . . . 204 D5
Barnfield Cl SL6 . . . . 195 F5
Barnfield Dr MK6 . . . . 47 C5
Barnhill Cl SL7. . . . . 183 D4
Barnhill Gdns SL7. . . . . 183 D4
Barnhill Rd SL7. . . . . 183 D4
Barn La RG9 . . . . 191 C4
Barn Rd HP27. . . . . 138 E6
Barnsbury Ave HP20 . . . . . 116 B8
Barnsbury Gdns MK16. . . . 22 C3
Barns Cl OX33 . . . . 122 B1
Barnsdale Dr MK4. . . . . 45 F2
Barnsfield Pl UB8. . . . . 201 C5
Barnstable Ct MK4 . . . . 46 D3
Barns The MK23 . . . . 118 F1
Baroma Way RG9 . . . . 191 E2
Barons Cl MK2. . . . . 58 C8
Barons Ct 2 SL7. . . . . 183 E2
Baronsmead RG9 . . . . 191 D2
Baronsmead Rd HP12 . . . . 172 E6
Barrack Hill HP18 . . . . 112 C5
Barrack La SL4. . . . . 210 D6
Barracks Hill HP7. . . . . 164 F2
Barracks Rd HP11 . . . . 173 A6
Barrards Way HP9. . . . . 176 C4
Barrett Pl
  High Wycombe HP11. . . . . 173 C6
  Milton Keynes MK5 . . . . . . 45 F6
BARRETTS END 42 F7
Barrie Cl HP19. . . . . 100 F2
Barrington Ct NN13 . . . . . . 38 A5
Barrington Mews 4 MK6. . 34 E1
Barrington Park Gdns
  HP8 . . . . 166 D1
Barrosa Wy
  Crownhill MK19. . . . . 45 D8
  Two Mile Ash MK8. . . . . . . 33 D1
Barrowcroft HP11. . . . . 173 D4
Barrow Lodge SL2 . . . . 198 C1
Barr Piece MK12 . . . . 33 C6
Barr's Rd SL6. . . . . 204 B7
Barry Ave
  Eton SL4. . . . . 210 C7
  Milton Keynes MK14 . . . . . 34 C7
Barry Cl HP12. . . . . 172 C4
Barry View SL4 . . . . 209 C5
Bartelotts Rd SL2. . . . . 197 E1
Bartholomew Cl MK7. . . . . . 48 A5
Bartholomew Tipping Way
  HP14. . . . . 158 F5
Bartlett Cres HP13. . . . . . . 172 D8
Bartlett Pl
  Buckingham MK18. . . . . . . 41 E1
  6 High Wycombe HP13 . . 172 D8
Bartletts SL9. . . . . 177 E3
Barton Dr HP9 . . . . 175 E4
BARTON HARTSHORN. 50 D2
Barton Rd
  Milton Keynes MK2 . . . . . . 58 C6
  Slough SL3 . . . . 206 F4
Bartons Rd HP10. . . . . 163 A1
Barton Way HP13. . . . . 162 E1
Bascote MK6 . . . . 47 D5
Base Cl 8 HP20 . . . . 101 F2
Basford Way SL4. . . . . 209 D4
Basildon Ct
  1 Leighton Buzzard LU7. . 80 F7
  Milton Keynes MK8 . . . . . . 45 F8
Basing Rd WD3 . . . . 167 F1
Baskerfield Gr MK6 . . . . 47 C8
Basset Rd HP14 . . . . 171 C4
Bassetsbury La HP11. . . . . 173 D5
Bassett Ct MK16 . . . . 22 C4
Bassett Rd
  Leighton Buzzard LU7 . . . . 80 F7
  Uxbridge UB8. . . . . 201 C5

Bassett Way SL2 . . . . 197 E1
Bass Mead SL6 . . . . 195 F5
Batchelor Cl HP20 . . . . 101 F2
Batchelors Way
  Amersham HP7 . . . . 165 D8
  Chesham HP5 . . . . 144 B2
Bateman Croft MK5 . . . . . . 45 F6
Bateman Dr HP21. . . . . 115 E5
Bates Cl
  Granborough MK18 . . . . . . 75 F8
  Milton Keynes MK15 . . . . . 35 D7
  Slough SL3. . . . . 206 E7
Bates Ct HP20 . . . . 101 F2
Bates Gdns MK17 . . . . 68 B6
Bates La HP22 . . . . 116 F2
Bath Cl SL6. . . . . 202 C6
Bath La MK18 . . . . 52 C8
Bath Lane Terr MK18. . . . . 52 C8
Bath Rd
  Harmondsworth UB7. . . . . 213 C6
  Maidenhead SL6. . . . . 202 C6
  Poyle SL3 . . . . 212 E6
  Slough SL1, SL6. . . . . 204 D6
  Slough SL1. . . . . 198 B4
  Taplow SL6. . . . . 203 E7
Bath Road Cotts SL3 . . . . . 212 E6
Bathurst Cl SL0 . . . . 207 F4
Bathurst Wlk SL0 . . . . 207 F4
Battersby Mews HP21. . . . 115 C7
Batt Furlong HP21 . . . . 115 E3
Batting Cl HP14. . . . . 159 F8
Battings Wood Gdns
  HP14. . . . . 161 C8
Battle Cl MK46. . . . . 13 F8
Battlemead Cl SL6 . . . . 196 C3
Battle of Britain Bunker★
  UB10. . . . . 201 F4
Battoney Vare SL6 . . . . 203 C4
Baulk The
  Cheddington LU7. . . . . . . 104 F7
  Ivinghoe LU7. . . . . 105 F5
Bawtree Rd UB8 . . . . 201 D6
Baxter Cl
  Milton Keynes MK8 . . . . . . 45 E7
  Slough SL1. . . . . 205 E3
Baybrook SL6. . . . . 195 F6
Bay Cl HP4 . . . . 135 B4
Bayhurst Wood Ctry Pk★
  UB9. . . . . 190 F6
Bay La MK46 . . . . 5 D2
Bayley Cres SL1 . . . . 204 A8
Bayley Gdns HP14. . . . . . . 161 E6
Bayley Hatch HP16. . . . . . . 152 D8
Baylis Bsns Ctr SL1 . . . . . . 205 D6
Baylis Court Sch SL1. . . . . 205 D8
Baylis Par SL1 . . . . 205 E7
Baylis Rd SL1. . . . . 205 E6
Bayman Manor HP5. . . . . . 144 E2
Bayne Hill HP9. . . . . 176 D3
Bayne Hill Cl HP9. . . . . 176 D3
Baynham Mead MK7 . . . . . . 48 B8
Bayntor Rd HP21. . . . . 115 E4
Baysfarm Ct UB7. . . . . 213 C6
Bay Tree Cl
  Loudwater HP11 . . . . 174 B2
  Newton Longville MK17. . . 57 D4
Bay Tree Ct SL1 . . . . 197 C2
BEACHAMPTON. 44 B6
Beachampton Bsns Pk
  MK19 . . . . 44 C4
Beacham Rd HP12 . . . . 172 C3
Beachborough Sch NN13. . 39 A4
Beacon Ave LU6. . . . . 93 E7
Beacon Cl
  Beaconsfield HP9 . . . . 175 A1
  Chalfont St Peter SL9 . . . . 177 E3
  Stone HP17 . . . . 114 C5
  Uxbridge UB8. . . . . 201 D7
Beacon Ct
  Colnbrook SL3 . . . . 212 C7
  Milton Keynes MK4 . . . . . . 46 D2
Beacon Hill HP10 . . . . 174 D7
Beacon La SL7. . . . . 171 E1
Beacon Rd HP4. . . . . 106 E2
BEACON'S BOTTOM. 159 D3
Beacon Sch The HP6. . . . . 154 B4
BEACONSFIELD 175 D1
Beaconsfield Ave HP13. . . 162 A1
Beaconsfield Common La
  SL2. . . . . 187 C5
Beaconsfield Cotts HP9. . . 185 B2
Beaconsfield High Sch
  HP9. . . . . 175 D1
Beaconsfield Mews HP9. . 186 A8
Beaconsfield Pl MK16 . . . . 22 C4
Beaconsfield Rd
  Aston Clinton HP22 . . . . . 117 F4
  Aylesbury HP21. . . . . 115 E8
  Farnham Common SL2. . . 198 C5
  Tring HP23. . . . . 118 E3
Beaconsfield Sch The
  HP9. . . . . 175 E1
Beaconsfield Sta HP9. . . . 175 E1
Beacon Sports Ctr & Theatre
  The HP9. . . . . 175 A1
Beacon View
  Dunstable LU6. . . . . 92 B4
  Lewknor OX49. . . . . 157 B8
Beacon Way HP23. . . . . . . 119 C5
Beadlemead MK6. . . . . 47 C6
Beales La MK7. . . . . 48 A5
Bealings End HP9. . . . . 175 D5
Beamish Way MK18. . . . . . 66 B5
BEAMOND END 163 F6
Beamond End La HP7,
  HP15. . . . . 163 F7
Beanfare MK6 . . . . 47 B4
BEANHILL. 47 B4

Bearbrook Cl HP21. . . . . . . 115 C7
Bearbrook Comb Sch
  HP19. . . . . 115 C8
Bearswood End HP9 . . . . . 175 E4
Beatrice Cl OX27. . . . . 72 E6
Beauchamp Ct MK14 . . . . . 34 E6
Beauchamp Ct SL1. . . . . . . 205 E6
Beaudesert Mews UB7 . . . 208 E4
Beaufort Cl
  Aylesbury HP21. . . . . 116 C7
  Marlow SL7. . . . . 183 E2
Beaufort Dr MK15. . . . . 35 C7
Beaufort Gdns SL7. . . . . . . 183 E2
Beaufort Pl SL6. . . . . 203 D4
Beaulieu Cl SL3. . . . . 211 B5
Beaumaris Ct SL1. . . . . . . 205 C8
Beaumaris Gr MK5. . . . . . . 46 A6
Beaumont Cl SL6 . . . . 202 A3
Beaumont Cotts 1 SL4. . . 210 C6
Beaumont Ct SL3. . . . . 206 D7
Beaumont Gr HP15. . . . . . . 162 F4
Beaumont Rd
  Slough SL2. . . . . 205 D8
  Windsor SL4. . . . . 210 C5
Beaumont Rise SL7 . . . . . . 183 E2
Beaumont Way HP15 . . . . . 162 F4
Beaverbrook Ct MK3 . . . . . 46 F1
Beaver Cl MK18. . . . . 52 E7
Beckets Sq HP4. . . . . 135 A6
Beckett Chase 5 SL3. . . . . 206 F1
Beckings Way HP10. . . . . . 185 C7
Beckinsale Gr MK8. . . . . . . 45 E7
Beckton Rise MK10. . . . . . . 35 E1
Beckwell Rd SL1. . . . . 205 C4
Bec La MK15. . . . . 35 B7
Bedder Rd HP12 . . . . 172 C3
Beddoes Croft MK5 . . . . . . 45 E4
Bede Ct HP4 . . . . 121 C8
Bedfont Court Est TW19 . . 213 B4
Bedfont Rd TW19. . . . . 213 F1
Bedford Ave
  Little Chalfont HP6 . . . . . . 166 D8
  Slough SL1. . . . . 205 A7
Bedford Cl
  Chenies WD3. . . . . 156 B1
  Maidenhead SL6. . . . . 202 A3
Bedford Ct HP6. . . . . 166 D8
Bedford Dr SL2 . . . . 198 B6
Bedford Rd
  Aspley Guise MK17. . . . . . 49 F5
  Cold Brayfield MK46. . . . . . 8 B5
  Cranfield MK43 . . . . 25 C2
  Sherington MK16. . . . . . . 14 A1
Bedford Road E NN7 . . . . . . 1 D5
Bedford Road W NN7 . . . . . 1 A6
Bedford St
  Berkhamsted HP4. . . . . . . 135 D4
  Milton Keynes, Bletchley
    MK2. . . . . 58 C8
  Milton Keynes, Wolverton
    MK12 . . . . 33 D6
  Woburn MK17. . . . . 60 F7
Bedgebury Pl MK7 . . . . 48 A8
BEDGROVE. 116 C5
Bedgrove HP21 . . . . 116 C6
Bedgrove Inf Sch HP21. . . 116 C5
Bedgrove Jun Sch HP21 . . 116 C6
BEDLAM 14 C1
Bedlam La MK16. . . . . 14 C1
Bedlam Wlk MK16. . . . . 14 C1
Bedlington Mews HP19. . . 114 E8
Bedwins La SL6. . . . . 195 B6
Bedwyn Wlk HP21. . . . . . . 115 D4
Beech 2 RG9. . . . . 191 D2
Beechams The MK17 . . . . . 67 C6
Beech Ave
  Lane End HP14 . . . . 171 C5
  Olney MK46. . . . . 6 E3
Beech Cl
  Bierton HP22. . . . . 102 B3
  Buckingham MK18. . . . . . . 41 E8
  Flackwell Heath HP10. . . . 174 A2
  High Wycombe HP11. . . . . 173 F4
  Maidenhead SL6. . . . . 202 B8
  Stokenchurch HP14. . . . . 158 F3
Beechcroft HP4. . . . . 135 C3
Beechcroft Rd
  Chesham HP5 . . . . 144 B1
  Milton Keynes MK3 . . . . . . 57 E6
Beech Ct
  Berkhamsted HP4. . . . . . . 135 D4
  3 Marlow SL7 . . . . 183 E2
Beech Dr HP4. . . . . 135 C3
Beechen Wood WD3. . . . . . 178 D5
Beeches Dr SL2. . . . . 198 B7
Beeches Gr HP10 . . . . 163 A2
Beeches Pk HP9. . . . . 175 D6
Beeches Rd SL2. . . . . 198 B7
Beeches The
  Amersham HP6 . . . . 154 A3
  Chorleywood WD3. . . . . . 167 F4
  Deanshanger MK19. . . . . . 31 A5
  Milton Keynes MK1 . . . . . . 47 E1
  Tring HP23. . . . . 119 C4
  Uxbridge UB8. . . . . 201 C1
  Wendover HP22. . . . . 131 C5
Beeches Way SL1 . . . . 197 C2
Beech Fern MK7. . . . . 48 A5
Beechfield Way HP15 . . . . 163 B3
Beechfield Wlk HP15. . . . . 163 A3
Beech Gr HP21. . . . . 115 D6
Beech Gr
  Amersham HP7 . . . . 165 D8
  Leighton Buzzard LU7 . . . . 80 E7
  Tring HP23. . . . . 119 C4
Beech Hill Ct HP4. . . . . 135 D5
Beech House Dr NN12. . . . 18 F4

Beechingstoke 4 SL7. . . 183 F3
Beech La
  Prestwood HP16 . . . . 151 B7
  Seer Green HP9. . . . . 176 E3
Beechlands HP15 . . . . 162 E2
Beech Leys MK18 . . . . 63 E3
Beech Pk
  Little Chalfont HP6 . . . . . . 155 B1
  Naphill HP14 . . . . 150 A1
  Wigginton HP23. . . . . 133 F5
Beech Rd
  Aylesbury HP21 . . . . 115 C6
  Chinnor OX39. . . . . 147 C6
  High Wycombe HP11 . . . . . 173 F4
  Newport Pagnell MK16 . . . . 22 B3
  Princes Risborough HP27 . . 139 C3
  Slough SL3. . . . . 206 C4
Beech St HP11 . . . . 173 C4
Beechtree Ave SL7. . . . . . 183 C6
Beech Tree Cl MK19. . . . . . . 20 D2
Beech Tree Ct HP22. . . . . . . 87 A6
Beech Tree Rd HP15 . . . . . 163 C7
Beech Trees Rd HP12 . . . . 172 C3
Beechview Acad HP13. . . . 173 E5
Beech Waye SL9 . . . . 189 A4
Beech Wlk HP23 . . . . 119 B4
Beechwood Ave
  Chorleywood WD3. . . . . . 167 B5
  Little Chalfont HP6 . . . . . . 155 C1
  1 Uxbridge UB8. . . . . 208 F7
Beechwood Cl HP6. . . . . . 166 C8
Beechwood Cotts WD3. . . 167 B3
Beechwood Ct
  Aston Clinton HP22 . . . . . . 118 A3
  Dunstable LU6. . . . . 93 F7
Beechwood Dr
  Aldbury HP23. . . . . 120 D5
  Maidenhead SL6 . . . . 202 A6
  Marlow SL7 . . . . 194 B8
Beechwood Gdns SL1 . . . 205 E4
Beechwood Ho HP22. . . . . 117 F5
Beechwood La HP22 . . . . . 131 D5
Beechwood Pk
  Chorleywood WD3. . . . . . 167 F5
  Felden HP3 . . . . 146 F7
Beechwood Pl 13 HP13. . 173 B7
Beechwood Rd
  Beaconsfield HP9 . . . . 175 C2
  High Wycombe HP12. . . . . 161 B2
  Slough SL2. . . . . 205 D8
Beechwood Sch SL2 . . . . 198 B2
Beechwood Way HP22 . . . 117 F5
BEECROFT. 93 F8
Beecroft Lower Sch LU6. . 93 F8
Beecroft Way LU6. . . . . 93 F8
Beehive Cl UB10 . . . . 201 F5
Beel Cl HP7. . . . . 166 C8
Beeley St HP18 . . . . 100 D5
Beeston La HP19. . . . . 101 B4
Beethoven Cl MK7. . . . . 48 E4
Beeward Cl MK12 . . . . 33 A5
Beggars La HP23. . . . . 119 F4
Bekonscot Ct MK15 . . . . . . 21 F1
Bekonscot Model Village &
  Railway ★ HP9 . . . . 175 C4
Belfast Ave SL1 . . . . 205 D7
Belgrave Mews UB8. . . . . . 201 D1
Belgrave Par SL1 . . . . 205 E6
Belgrave Pl 6 SL1 . . . . . . 206 A4
Belgrave Rd
  Aylesbury HP19 . . . . 101 A3
  Slough SL1. . . . . 205 F6
Bellamy Mews 5 MK4. . . . 45 E3
Bellamy Rd HP13. . . . . 173 C8
Bell Ave UB7. . . . . 208 F3
Bell Bsns Pk HP19 . . . . . . 100 F1
Bell Cl
  Beaconsfield HP9 . . . . 175 F2
  Cublington LU7 . . . . 78 B1
  Drayton Parslow MK17 . . . . 68 B6
  Princes Risborough HP27 . . 139 B3
  Slough SL2. . . . . 206 B8
  Thame OX9 . . . . 125 E1
Bellclose Rd UB7 . . . . 208 E4
Bell Cres HP27. . . . . 138 E6
Bell Ct SL6 . . . . 193 F3
Belle Vue HP17. . . . . 114 C5
Bellfield Rd HP13 . . . . 173 A8
Bellfield Road W HP11 . . . 172 F7
Bellfounder Ho MK13 . . . . . 34 B4
Bell Gn HP3 . . . . 146 B4
BELLINGDON. 143 E7
Bellingdon Rd HP5. . . . . . 144 B1
Bellini Cl MK7 . . . . 48 D5
Bellis Gr MK6 . . . . 47 C8
Bell La
  Berkhamsted HP4 . . . . 134 E5
  Eton Wick SL4 . . . . 204 F2
  Henley-on-Thames RG9. . . 191 E2
  Little Chalfont HP6 . . . . . . 155 C1
  Princes Risborough HP27 . . 139 B3
  Syresham NN13. . . . . 27 B8
  Thame OX9 . . . . 125 F1
Bell Lane Comb Sch
  HP6. . . . . 155 B1
Bell Leys HP22. . . . . 89 B3
Bellman Cl SL1 . . . . 206 B4
Bellows Mill La LU6. . . . . . . 93 A4
Bellridge Pl HP9. . . . . 175 B6
Bellsfield Ct SL4 . . . . 204 F2
Bells Hill Gn SL2. . . . . 199 A4
Bells Hill Gn SL2. . . . . 199 A5
Bells La SL3 . . . . 212 A4
Bells Mdw MK15 . . . . 35 B7
Bell St
  Henley-on-Thames RG9. . . 191 E2
  Maidenhead SL6 . . . . 202 F6
  Princes Risborough HP27 . . 139 B3

Bell Street Mews RG9. . . . 191 E2
Bellswood La SL0. . . . . . . 207 B8
Bell View SL4. . . . . 209 F5
Bell View Cl SL4 . . . . 209 F5
Bellway MK17. . . . . 49 A6
Bellwether
  Wingrave HP22 . . . . 89 B3
  Winslow MK18. . . . . 65 F3
Bellwood Rise HP11. . . . . 173 B4
Belmers Rd HP23 . . . . 119 D1
Belmont SL2. . . . . 205 A8
Belmont Cl UB8. . . . . 201 D6
Belmont Cotts SL3 . . . . . . 212 C7
Belmont Cres SL6. . . . . . . 202 D8
Belmont Ct MK8 . . . . 33 C2
Belmont Dr SL6. . . . . 202 D8
Belmont Park Ave SL6. . . . 202 D8
Belmont Park Rd SL6 . . . . 202 D8
Belmont Rd
  Chesham HP5 . . . . 144 B3
  Maidenhead SL6 . . . . 202 D8
  Uxbridge UB8. . . . . 201 D5
Belmont Vale SL6. . . . . . . 202 D8
BELSIZE. 156 F6
Belsize Ave MK6 . . . . 35 B1
Belsize Cotts WD3. . . . . . 156 E6
Belton Rd HP4. . . . . 135 A5
Belvedere Cl HP6. . . . . . . 154 F2
Belvedere La MK17. . . . . . . 58 F8
Belvedere Mans SL1 . . . . . 205 D4
Belvedere Rdbt MK9 . . . . . . 34 F4
Belvoir Ave MK4 . . . . 46 C1
Bembridge Ct 11 SL1. . . . 205 F4
Benbow Ct MK5. . . . . 46 A7
Benbow Way UB8. . . . . . . 208 C8
Bench Manor Cres SL9 . . . 177 C1
Bencombe Rd SL7 . . . . . . 183 E5
Benen-Stock Rd TW19 . . . 213 A2
Benham Cl HP5. . . . . 144 B1
Benhams La RG9. . . . . 180 D2
Benison Ct 1 SL1. . . . . . . 205 F3
Benjamin Ho 10 HP13. . . . 173 B7
Benjamin La SL3. . . . . 199 B1
Benjamin Rd HP13. . . . . . 173 B8
Benjamins Footpath
  HP13 . . . . 173 B8
Ben More SL9 . . . . 188 F6
Benmore Rise 2 MK4. . . . 45 E2
Bennet Cl MK11. . . . . 32 D4
Bennet's Yd UB8. . . . . 201 D5
BENNETT END 159 C7
Bennett End Rd HP14 . . . . 159 C7
Bennetts HP5. . . . . 144 D1
Bennetts Cl
  Padbury MK18. . . . . 53 B1
  Slough SL1. . . . . 205 A5
Bennett's Hill MK18. . . . . . 76 C8
Bennetts La HP22 . . . . 102 E8
Benning Ave LU6. . . . . 93 F8
Benning Cl SL4 . . . . 209 D6
Benningfield Gdns HP4. . . 135 E6
Bens Cl MK19 . . . . 19 F5
Bensheim Way HP6 . . . . . . 154 D1
Benson Cl
  Slough SL2. . . . . 206 A5
  Uxbridge UB8. . . . . 208 E8
Bentall Cl MK15. . . . . 35 C7
Bentinck Cl SL9. . . . . 188 D6
Bentinck Ct UB7 . . . . 208 D5
Bentinck Rd UB7. . . . . 208 D5
Bentley Ct SL6 . . . . 202 D5
Bentley Pk SL1 . . . . 197 D3
Bentley Rd SL1 . . . . 205 A5
Benton Dr OX39. . . . . 147 C2
Benton Mews HP18 . . . . . . 100 D4
Bentons The HP4 . . . . 134 F6
Benwell Cl MK13. . . . . 33 F5
Benwells OX39. . . . . 147 C6
Beresford Ave
  Aylesbury HP19 . . . . 101 C3
  Slough SL2. . . . . 206 C6
Beresford Ct MK4. . . . . 46 B3
Beresford Rd WD3. . . . . . . 167 F1
Beretun MK8 . . . . 33 E1
Bereville Ct MK10. . . . . 35 E3
Berevilles La MK10. . . . . . . 35 E3
Bergamot Gdns MK7. . . . . . 48 B5
Bergman Cl 1 MK4. . . . . . 45 D2
Berkeley Ave HP5. . . . . . . 143 F1
Berkeley Cl
  Chesham HP5 . . . . 144 A1
  Stoke Goldington MK16. . . . 12 B6
Berkeley Mews
  Marlow SL7 . . . . 183 F2
  Slough SL1. . . . . 204 E7
Berkeley Rd
  Loudwater HP10 . . . . 174 C2
  Thame OX9 . . . . 126 A1
Berkeley Rise 1 HP19. . . 101 B2
Berkhampstead Rd HP5. . 144 C2
BERKHAMSTED. 135 C6
Berkhamsted Castle ★
  HP4. . . . . 135 C6
Berkhamsted Girls' Sch
  HP4. . . . . 135 B4
Berkhamsted Pl HP4. . . . . 135 C5
Berkhamsted Prep Sch
  HP4. . . . . 135 B4
Berkhamsted Sch 7
  HP4. . . . . 135 C5
Berkhamsted Sta HP4. . . . 135 C5

Berkley Cl
  Maidenhead SL6 . . . . 202 A8
  Pitstone LU7. . . . . 105 D3
Berkley Ct HP4 . . . . 135 C4
Berkley Rd HP9. . . . . 175 D6
Berks Hill WD3. . . . . 167 C4
Berkshire Ave SL1 . . . . . . 205 B7
Berkshire Gn 2 MK5. . . . . 45 F3
Berkshire Lodge 1 SL6 . . 202 F6
Berling Rd MK8. . . . . 33 F2
Bernard Cl HP18 . . . . 112 F2
Bernardines Way MK18. . . . 52 E7
Bernards Hill HP16. . . . . . 152 A7
Bernards Way HP10. . . . . . 174 A2
Bernay Gdns MK15. . . . . . . 35 F3
Berndene Rise HP27 . . . . . 139 B4
Berners Cl SL1. . . . . 204 E6
Berners Rd MK7 . . . . 48 C4
Bernewode Cl HP18. . . . . . 125 C7
Bernstein Cl MK7. . . . . 48 C4
Bernwood Mdws Wildlife
  Reserve ★ HP18 . . . . 108 F2
Berrell's Ct 2 MK46. . . . . . 6 F3
Berries Rd SL6. . . . . 196 A8
Berrington Gr 4 MK4. . . . . 45 E2
BERRYFIELD. 100 D5
Berryfield LU7 . . . . 104 F7
Berry Field SL2 . . . . 206 C7
Berry Field Pk HP6. . . . . . 154 B2
Berryfield Rd
  Aylesbury HP19 . . . . 101 B3
  Princes Risborough HP27 . . 139 C4
Berryfields CE Prim Sch
  HP18. . . . . 100 E4
Berry Hill SL6. . . . . 203 B8
Berry Hill Ct SL6. . . . . 203 B8
Berry La
  Aspley Guise MK17. . . . . . . 49 F6
  Chorleywood WD3. . . . . . 167 C3
Berrystead MK7 . . . . 48 B3
Berry Way MK17 . . . . 57 D4
Bertram Cl MK13. . . . . 34 B8
Berwald Cl MK7. . . . . 48 D4
Berwick Cl
  Beaconsfield HP9 . . . . 176 B1
  Marlow SL7 . . . . 183 D3
Berwick Dr MK3 . . . . 46 F2
Berwick La SL7 . . . . 183 D3
Berwick Rd SL7. . . . . 183 C3
Bessemer Cl 2 SL3. . . . . 206 F1
Bessemer Cres HP19 . . . . 100 E1
Bessemer Ct MK14. . . . . . . 22 A1
Bestobell Rd SL1. . . . . 205 C7
Betjeman Ct UB7. . . . . 208 D5
Betjeman Gdns WD3. . . . . 167 C4
Bettina Gr MK2. . . . . 58 C7
Bettles Cl UB8 . . . . 201 C3
Bettles Cl UB8 . . . . 201 C3
Betty's Cl MK17. . . . . 57 D4
Betty's La HP23 . . . . 119 A4
Bevan Cl MK18. . . . . 65 F4
Bevan Hill HP5. . . . . 144 B2
Bevelwood Gdns HP12 . . . 172 D7
Beverley Cl SL7. . . . . 183 B2
Beverley Ct SL1. . . . . 206 B4
Beverley Gdns SL6. . . . . . 195 B5
Beverley Pl MK6. . . . . 35 B2
Bewcastle Row MK4. . . . . . 45 E1
Bewdley Dr LU7. . . . . 80 C7
Bewdley Rd MK10. . . . . 36 A4
Bexley St SL4. . . . . 210 C6
Bhamra Gdns 3 SL6. . . . . 202 D6
Bicester Rd
  Aylesbury HP19 . . . . 101 B2
  Long Crendon HP18. . . . . . 125 C6
  Ludgershall HP18 . . . . 96 C8
  Marsh Gibbon OX27. . . . . . . 71 E3
  Oakley HP18 . . . . 109 D5
  Twyford MK18 . . . . 62 C1
Bicester Road Ind Est
  HP19. . . . . 101 A1
Bickleigh Cres MK4 . . . . . . 46 D3
Biddles Cl SL1 . . . . 204 E5
BIDDLESDEN. 27 D5
Biddlesden Rd NN13 . . . . . 39 A5
Bideford Ct SL1. . . . . 80 C8
Bideford Gn LU7. . . . . 80 C8
Bideford Spur SL2 . . . . . . 198 B2
BIERTON. 102 A3
Bierton CE Comb Sch
  HP22. . . . . 102 B3
Bierton Rd HP20. . . . . 101 F1
Bigfrith La SL6. . . . . 195 B6
Biggs La HP17 . . . . 113 E2
Bigmore La
  Beacon's Bottom HP14 . . . 170 B8
  Stokenchurch HP14. . . . . . 159 C1
Bignell Croft MK5. . . . . 34 B1
Bigton Chase 2 MK10. . . . 36 B2
Biko Cl UB8. . . . . 208 C7
Bilbrook La MK4. . . . . 46 C4
Billet La
  Berkhamsted HP4 . . . . 135 A6
  Iver SL0, SL3. . . . . 207 B7
Billings Cl HP14. . . . . 158 F5
Billingwell Pl MK6. . . . . 35 B2
Billwell HP18 . . . . 125 C6
Bilton Rd MK1 . . . . 47 D2
Binders Ind Est HP15. . . . 162 D7
Bingham Cl MK4. . . . . 46 C1
Bingham Rd SL1. . . . . 204 A8
Binghams The SL6. . . . . . 203 B3
Birch Ave UB7. . . . . 208 F7
Birch Cl
  Amersham HP6 . . . . 154 C1
  Bedford MK43 . . . . 25 C3
  Iver Heath SL0 . . . . 200 D3
Birch Cres UB10. . . . . 201 F4

Birch Ct HP21. . . . . 115 D5
Birchdale SL3 . . . . 188 D3
Birch Dr WD3. . . . . 178 D5
Birchen Lee MK4. . . . . 46 C2
Birches Rise HP12 . . . . . . 172 E8
Birches The
  Felden HP3 . . . . 146 F8
  High Wycombe HP13. . . . . 173 D8
Birchfield Gr MK2. . . . . 58 C7
Birch Gdns HP7. . . . . 165 E8
Birch Gr
  Slough SL4. . . . . 205 B8
  Windsor SL4 . . . . 209 D6
Birchington Rd SL4 . . . . . 210 A5
Birch La HP3 . . . . 156 B7
Birchmoor Gn MK17. . . . . . 60 F8
Birch Rd HP4 . . . . 134 D7
Birch St HP11. . . . . 173 B3
Birch Tree Gr HP5 . . . . 145 B1
Birch Way
  Chesham HP5 . . . . 144 D2
  Tylers Green HP10. . . . . . . 163 B1
Birchwood Chase HP15. . . 151 D1
Birchwood Cl HP12 . . . . . 172 B6
Birdcage Wlk HP13 . . . . . 173 B6
Birdlip La MK7. . . . . 48 B7
Bird Mount Cotts SL4 . . . . 210 C8
Birdwood Rd SL6 . . . . 202 B7
Birfield Rd HP10 . . . . 174 C2
Birinus Ct HP12 . . . . 172 C5
Birkdale Cl MK3. . . . . 57 D7
Birkett Way HP8 . . . . 166 C6
Birley Rd SL1. . . . . 205 D7
Birmingham Rd HP22. . . . 102 C2
Birtchnell Cl HP4 . . . . 135 A5
BISHAM. 194 E7
Bisham Abbey National
  Sports Ctr SL7. . . . . 194 D7
Bisham CE Prim Sch
  SL7. . . . . 194 D7
Bisham Ct
  10 Slough SL1. . . . . 205 F4
Bisham Gn SL7. . . . . 194 E6
Bisham Rd
  Bisham SL7. . . . . 194 E8
  Marlow SL7 . . . . 183 E1
Bisham Woods Nature
  Reserve ★ SL6 . . . . 194 E6
Bishop Cl SL6. . . . . 202 D6
Bishop Ctr The SL6. . . . . . 203 F7
Bishop Parker Catholic Sch
  MK2 . . . . 58 C6
Bishops Ct MK18. . . . . 52 C7
Bishops Farm Cl SL4 . . . . 209 B6
Bishops Field HP22 . . . . . 118 A4
Bishopshalt Sch UB8. . . . . 201 F2
Bishops Ho HP9. . . . . 175 D3
Bishops Mdw HP22. . . . . . 102 A3
Bishops Orch SL2 . . . . . . 198 B2
Bishops Rd SL1. . . . . 206 A4
BISHOPSTONE 115 A1
Bishopstone
  Milton Keynes MK13 . . . . . 34 B5
  Stone HP17 . . . . 115 A1
Bishopstone Rd HP17 . . . 114 D5
Bishops Wlk
  Aylesbury HP21 . . . . 115 F6
  Woburn Sands MK17. . . . . . 49 B3
  Wooburn Green HP10. . . . . 185 E5
Bishop Wood Sch 21
  HP23. . . . . 119 A3
Bissley Dr SL6. . . . . 202 A3
Bittenham Ct HP17 . . . . . . 114 D4
Bittern Way 4 HP20. . . . . 101 E3
Bit The HP23. . . . . 119 D1
BIX. 179 D1
Bix La SL6. . . . . 194 F1
Black Acre Cl HP7. . . . . . . 165 E8
Blackamoor La SL6. . . . . . 196 A1
Blackbeard MK16 . . . . 36 B5
Blackberry La MK7. . . . . . . 48 B6
Black Boy La SL6. . . . . . . 193 C3
Blackburn Trad Est
  TW19 . . . . 213 F1
Black Butt Cotts SL6 . . . . 196 B7
Blackdown MK11 . . . . 32 F4
Blacketts Wood Dr WD3. . 168 B5
Blackfield La HP16. . . . . . 142 E3
Blackheath Cres MK13 . . . 34 B3
Black Horse Ave HP5. . . . . 154 D6
Black Horse Cl SL4. . . . . . 209 D5
Blackhorse Cres HP6. . . . . 154 E1
Blackhorse Dr MK19 . . . . . 32 B7
Black Horse Pl UB8 . . . . . 201 C4
Blackmoor Gate MK4. . . . . 46 E2
Blackmore Gate HP22. . . . 118 A4
Blackmore Way UB8. . . . . 201 D6
Black Park Ctry Pk ★ SL0,
  SL3. . . . . 199 F3
Black Park Ctry Pk Visitor
  Ctr ★ SL3. . . . . 199 F2
Black Park Nature Reserve ★
  SL0 . . . . 200 A3
Black Park Rd SL3 . . . . . . 199 E4
Blackpond La SL2 . . . . . . 198 B4
Blacksmith La HP16. . . . . 151 C6
Blacksmith Row SL3 . . . . 207 A2
Blacksmith's La UB9 . . . . 189 D2
Blacksmiths Rd HP14. . . . 159 B1
Blacksmiths Way MK17. . . . 49 B5
BLACKTHORN. 81 A4
Blackthorn Cl OX25 . . . . . 304 C3
Blackthorn Dell 2 SL3. . . 206 C3

Blackthorne Cres SL3 . . . 212 E5
Blackthorne Ind Pk SL3 . . 212 E5
Blackthorne La HP16. . . . . 142 E3
Blackthorne Rd SL3 . . . . . 212 E4
Blackthorn Gr MK17. . . . . . 49 A4
Blackwater Dr HP21. . . . . . 115 C4
Blackwell End NN12. . . . . . 18 C3
Blackwell Hall La HP5. . . . 155 C6
Blackwell Pl MK5. . . . . 46 A4
Blackwell Pl HP14. . . . . . . 171 B5
Blackwells Yd NN17. . . . . . . 1 B6
Blackwood Cres MK13. . . . 33 C6
Blaine Cl HP23. . . . . 119 A6
Blairmont St MK9 . . . . 34 F4
Blair Rd SL1 . . . . 205 E5
Blakedown Rd LU7. . . . . . . 80 C6
BLAKELANDS. 22 B1
Blakelands Hospl (Private)
  MK14. . . . . 22 A2
Blakeney Ct
  Maidenhead SL6 . . . . 195 F1
  Milton Keynes MK4. . . . . . . 57 B8
Blakes Ho HP10. . . . . 174 C2
Blake Way OX9 . . . . 126 A1
Blanchland Circ MK10. . . . . 36 A1
Blandford Cl SL3. . . . . 206 D3
Blandford Ho SL6. . . . . . . 202 A5
Blandford Road N SL3. . . . 206 D3
Blandford Road S SL3. . . . 206 D3
Blanes Cl HP18 . . . . 125 C6
Blansby Chase MK4 . . . . . . 46 C3
Blatherwick Ct MK5. . . . . . 45 F7
Blaydon Cl MK3. . . . . 57 D6
BLEAK HALL 46 F5
Bleak Hall Rdbt MK6 . . . . . 47 A5
Bleasdale MK13. . . . . 34 C5
BLEDLOW. 138 B1
Bledlow Cotts HP27 . . . . . 138 C1
Bledlow Rd HP27 . . . . 148 E8
BLEDLOW RIDGE 159 F8
Bledlow Ridge Rd HP14 . . 148 C8
Bledlow Ridge Sch HP14 . 159 F8
Blegberry Gdns HP4 . . . . . 134 E4
Blenheim Ave MK11. . . . . . 32 E4
Blenheim Cl
  Cheddington LU7. . . . . 104 F8
  Longwick HP27 . . . . 138 D6
  Slough SL3. . . . . 206 F5
Blenheim Ct HP13. . . . . . . 173 B7
Blenheim Pl
  Aylesbury HP21 . . . . 115 E5
  Syresham NN13. . . . . 27 C7
Blenheim Rd
  High Wycombe HP12. . . . . 172 D4
  Maidenhead SL6 . . . . 202 B8
  Slough SL3. . . . . 206 D2
Bletcham Rdbt MK1. . . . . . 47 E3
Bletcham Way
  Milton Keynes MK1 . . . . . . 47 C2
  Milton Keynes MK1 . . . . . . 47 E2
  Walton Park MK7. . . . . 48 B4
BLETCHLEY. 58 A7
Bletchley Bsns Campus
  MK2 . . . . 58 C6
Bletchley Com Hospl MK3 47 A1
Bletchley L Ctr MK2. . . . . . 58 C8
Bletchley Park ★ MK3 . . . . 58 A8
Bletchley Rd
  Milton Keynes MK5 . . . . . . 46 B4
  Newton Longville MK17. . . . 57 D4
  Stewkley LU7 . . . . 68 D3
Bletchley Sta MK3 . . . . 58 B8
Blinco La SL3. . . . . 206 E7
Blind La
  Bourne End HP10, SL8. . . . 185 B5
  South Heath HP16. . . . . . . 153 B8
Blind Pond Ind Est MK17. . 48 D2
Bliss Ave MK43. . . . . 25 C2
Bliss Ct MK7. . . . . 48 C4
Blisworth MK11. . . . . 47 D5
Blondell Cl UB7. . . . . 213 D8
Bloomfield Cotts HP5 . . . . 143 E7
Bloomfield Rd SL6. . . . . . 202 A5
Bloomsbury Cl MK17. . . . . 60 F6
Blossom Way UB10. . . . . . 201 F5
Blucher St HP5. . . . . 154 B8
Blue Anchor Ave 1 MK10 36 B3
Bluebell Cl MK18. . . . . 52 C7
Bluebell Croft MK7. . . . . . . 48 B6
Bluebell Gdns 11 MK10. . . 36 A4
Bluebell Terr 2 UB7 . . . . 208 F4
Blue Lagoon Nature
  Reserve ★ MK3. . . . . 58 B7
Blumfield Cres SL1. . . . . . 204 E8
Blumfield Ct SL1. . . . . 197 D1
Blundells Rd MK13 . . . . . . 34 C6
Blunden Dr SL3. . . . . 207 C2
Blyth Ct MK4. . . . . 57 A8
Blythebridge MK10. . . . . . . 36 C3
Blythe Cl
  Aylesbury HP21 . . . . 115 C5
  Iver SL0. . . . . 207 F7
  Newport Pagnell MK16. . . . 22 D3
Blythe Hos SL1 . . . . 204 D5
Blyton Cl HP9. . . . . 175 D4
Blyton La MK4. . . . . 56 F8
Boadicea Cl SL1. . . . . 204 E5
Boarlands Cl SL1. . . . . 204 F6
BOARSTALL. 95 B1
Boarstall Duck Decoy ★
  HP18. . . . . 95 A3
Boarstall Tower ★ HP18. . . 95 A1
Boathouse Reach RG9. . . . 191 E1
Bobbins Wy MK18. . . . . 52 F6

Bobby Rd HP22 . . . . 102 C2
Bobmore La SL7 . . . . 183 F3
BOCKMER END 182 C1
Bockmer La SL7 . . . . 193 B7
Boddington Rd HP22 . . . . 131 C4
Bodenham Cl MK18 . . . . . . 52 F8
Bodiam Cl
Aylesbury HP21 . . . . 116 B5
Milton Keynes MK5 . . . . 46 A5
Bodiam Ho 6 HP13 . . . . . 173 F7
Bodle Cl MK15 . . . . 35 A7
Bodley Ho SL0 . . . . 200 D3
Bodmin Ave SL2 . . . . 205 A8
Bodmin Pl MK10 . . . . 36 C3
Bodnant Ct MK4 . . . . 45 F2
Bogart Pl MK4 . . . . 45 D2
Bois Ave HP6 . . . . 154 B3
Bois Hill HP5 . . . . 154 E5
Bois La HP6 . . . . 154 D4
Bois Moor Rd HP5 . . . . . . 154 D5
Bolan Ct MK8 . . . . 45 E6
BOLBECK PK 35 A7
Boldison Cl 2 HP19 . . . . . 101 C1
Bold's Ct SL2 . . . . 199 A5
Bolebec End LU7 . . . . 105 D3
BOLTER END 170 F5
Bolter End La HP14 . . . . . 171 A6
Bolton Ave SL4 . . . . 210 D4
Bolton Cres SL4 . . . . 210 C4
Bolton Rd SL4 . . . . 210 C4
Boltwood Gr MK5 . . . . 45 E5
Bonaire Grange MK3 . . . . . 58 B3
Bond Ave MK1 . . . . 47 D3
Bond Cl
Aylesbury HP21 . . . . 115 B6
Iver Heath SL0 . . . . 200 B5
West Drayton UB7 . . . . 208 F7
Bone Hill MK18 . . . . 52 C7
Bonham Carter Rd HP22. 131 E7
Bonham Cl HP21 . . . . 115 B6
Bonham Ct HP22 . . . . 117 D5
Bonnards Rd MK17 . . . . 57 D4
Bonnersfield HP18 . . . . . . 125 C7
BOOKER 172 B4
Booker Ave MK13 . . . . 34 D4
Booker Hill Prim Sch
HP12 . . . . 172 B5
Bookerhill Rd HP12 . . . . . 172 C6
Booker La HP12 . . . . 172 D7
Booker Park Sch HP21 . . 115 E3
Booker Pl HP12 . . . . 172 B3
Booth Pl LU6 . . . . 92 E6
Boot La HP17 . . . . 113 E2
Border La MK18 . . . . 52 F6
Borderside SL2 . . . . 206 A7
Borodin Ct MK7 . . . . 48 D5
Boroma Way RG9 . . . . 191 E2
Borough Ct NN13 . . . . 38 A5
Borough Rd NN13 . . . . 38 A5
Borough Wlk MK9 . . . . 34 E3
Bosanquet Cl UB8 . . . . 201 D1
Bossiney Pl MK6 . . . . 34 F1
Bossington La LU7 . . . . 80 E7
Boss La
Great Kingshill HP15 . . . . . 162 B8
Hughenden Valley HP14 . . 162 B6
Bostock Ct MK18 . . . . 52 C8
Boston Dr SL8 . . . . 185 B3
Boston Gr SL1 . . . . 205 C7
Boswell Ct MK18 . . . . 41 E2
Boswell La MK19 . . . . 31 E4
Boswick La HP4 . . . . 134 D8
Bosworth Cl MK3 . . . . 46 E2
Bosworth Ct SL1 . . . . 204 C6
Botham Dr SL1 . . . . 205 E3
BOTLEY 145 A1
Botley La HP5 . . . . 145 A1
Botley Rd HP5 . . . . 144 E1
BOTOLPH CLAYDON 74 F6
Bottesford Cl MK3 . . . . 46 D1
Bottle Dump Rdbt MK17 . . 56 E6
Bottle Square La HP14 . . 159 D6
Bottom Dr LU6 . . . . 93 D5
Bottom Hill RG9 . . . . 181 C4
Bottom House Farm La
HP8 . . . . 165 E2
Bottom House La HP23 . . 120 A1
Bottom La HP9 . . . . 176 C5
Bottom Orch HP18 . . . . . . 112 C1
Bottom Rd
Bledlow Ridge HP14 . . . . . 160 B5
Buckland Common HP23 . . 132 F3
Bottom Waltons Caravan Site
SL2 . . . . 197 F3
Bottrells La HP8 . . . . 176 E8
Botyl Rd MK18 . . . . 74 E6
Boughton Bsns Pk HP6 . . 166 B8
Boughton Way HP6 . . . . . 155 C1
Boulevard The MK9 . . . . . . 34 E2
Boulmer Rd UB8 . . . . 201 C2
Boulters Cl
Maidenhead SL6 . . . . 196 C1
Slough SL1 . . . . 205 A4
Boulters Ct
Amersham HP6 . . . . 154 E1
Maidenhead SL6 . . . . 196 C1
Boulters Gdns SL6 . . . . . . 196 C1
Boulters La SL6 . . . . 196 C1
Boulters Lock MK14 . . . . . . 21 F2
Boundary Cotts WD4 . . . . 146 E2
Boundary Cres MK11 . . . . . 32 E6
Boundary Pl HP10 . . . . 185 D8
Boundary Rd
Brackley NN13 . . . . 38 A6
Chalfont St Peter SL9 . . . . 177 D3
Boundary Rd *continued*
Loudwater HP10 . . . . 174 C1
Taplow SL6 . . . . 203 F8
Wooburn Green HP10 . . . . 185 D8
Boundary The 1 MK6 . . . . . 34 F1
Bounds Croft MK12 . . . . . . 33 C4
Bounty St MK13 . . . . 33 F7
Bouquet Cl HP16 . . . . 151 C5
Bourbon St HP20 . . . . 115 D8
Bourne Ave SL4 . . . . 210 C3
Bourne Cl SL8 . . . . 185 B5
BOURNE END 185 B2
Bourne End MK43 . . . . 25 C6
Bourne End Bsns Pk SL8 185 B3
Bourne End Mills Ind Est
HP1 . . . . 146 B8
Bourne End Rd
Bourne End SL6, SL8 . . . . . 196 E8
Cranfield MK43 . . . . 25 C4
Bourne End Sta SL8 . . . . . 185 A3
Bourne Rd
Berkhamsted HP4 . . . . 134 F5
Slough SL1 . . . . 205 D4
Bourne The HP3 . . . . 146 A4
BOURTON 52 F8
Bourton Low MK7 . . . . 48 B5
Bourton Meadow Sch
MK18 . . . . 52 F8
Bourton Rd MK18 . . . . 52 E8
Bourtonville MK18 . . . . 52 D8
Bouverie Way SL3 . . . . 206 E2
BOVENEY 209 D8
Boveney Cl SL1 . . . . 205 A4
Boveney New Rd SL4 . . . . 204 E2
Boveney Rd SL4 . . . . 204 C1
Boveney Wood La SL1 . . . 186 D1
BOVINGDON 146 B4
Bovingdon Ct HP3 . . . . . . 146 A3
BOVINGDON GREEN 146 A2
Bovingdon Hts SL7 . . . . . . 183 B2
Bovingdon Prim Acad
HP3 . . . . 146 B4
BOW BRICKHILL 48 C1
Bow Brickhill CE Prim Sch
MK17 . . . . 48 D2
Bow Brickhill Rd MK17 . . . 48 F3
Bow Brickhill Sta MK7 . . . 48 B2
Bowden La HP11 . . . . 173 D5
Bowen Cl MK7 . . . . 48 C5
Bowerbank Ct HP20 . . . . . 101 F1
Bower Cl LU6 . . . . 92 F5
Bower Ct SL1 . . . . 204 F6
Bowerdean Rd HP13 . . . . 173 D7
Bower La LU6 . . . . 92 F5
Bowers La HP14 . . . . 159 D7
Bower Way SL1 . . . . 204 E6
Bowes Cl MK16 . . . . 22 C3
Bowes-Lyon Cl 7 SL4 . . . 210 C6
Bowland Dr MK4 . . . . 46 B1
Bowler Lea HP13 . . . . 161 D2
Bowler Rd HP21 . . . . 115 E4
Bowler's Orch HP8 . . . . . . 177 A7
Bowles Pl MK6 . . . . 47 D7
Bowling Alley HP22 . . . . . . 86 D7
Bowling Cl UB10 . . . . 201 F4
Bowling Ct RG9 . . . . 191 D3
Bowling Gn HP14 . . . . 158 D5
Bowling Green Cl 1 MK3 . 58 D8
Bowling Green Rd MK43 . . 25 C1
Bowling Leys MK10 . . . . . . 36 A2
Bowl Rdbt The MK4 . . . . . . 46 D5
Bowmans Cl SL1 . . . . 197 B3
Bowmont Dr HP21 . . . . . . 115 D4
Bowood Ct 5 MK8 . . . . 33 F1
Bowood La HP22 . . . . 141 E5
Bow Rd MK10 . . . . 36 C4
Bowry Dr TW19 . . . . 211 F1
Bowstridge Ct 6 HP13 . . 173 C7
Bowstridge La HP8 . . . . . . 177 C5
Bowyer Cres UB9 . . . . 189 F5
Bowyer Dr SL1 . . . . 204 E6
Bowyers Mews MK14 . . . . . 34 F6
Boxall Wy SL1 . . . . 206 C1
Boxberry Gdns MK7 . . . . . . 48 A6
Boxer Rd HP27 . . . . 138 E6
Boxgrove Ct MK10 . . . . 36 A1
Box La HP3 . . . . 146 E7
Box Tree Cl HP5 . . . . 154 D6
Boxwell Rd HP4 . . . . 135 B4
Boxwood Cl UB7 . . . . 208 F4
Boyce Cres MK7 . . . . 48 E5
Boycott Ave MK6 . . . . 34 E1
Boyle Cl UB10 . . . . 201 F3
Boyndon Rd SL6 . . . . 202 D7
BOYNE HILL 202 D6
Boyne Hill CE Inf Sch
SL6 . . . . 202 D6
Boyne Ho HP9 . . . . 175 E1
Boyn Hill Ave SL6 . . . . 202 D6
Boyn Hill Cl SL6 . . . . 202 D6
Boyn Hill Rd SL6 . . . . 202 D6
Boyn Valley Ind Est SL6 . . 202 E6
Boyn Valley Rd SL6 . . . . . . 202 D5
Bozenham Mill La NN7 . . . . . 9 F5
Bracken Cl SL2 . . . . 198 D8
Brackenforde SL3 . . . . 206 C4
Bracken Hill HP4 . . . . 135 E5
Bracken Rd SL6 . . . . 202 C4
Brackens The HP11 . . . . . . 173 C5
Bracken Way
Aylesbury HP21 . . . . 115 B8
Flackwell Heath HP10 . . . . 185 B7
Brackenwood HP14 . . . . . . 161 C7
BRACKLEY 38 A8
Brackley Dr HP15 . . . . 163 A6
Brackley La MK18 . . . . 73 B6
Brackley Rd
Chackmore MK18 . . . . 41 B1
Brackley Rd *continued*
Hazelmere HP15 . . . . 163 A6
Westbury NN13 . . . . 39 B5
Bradbery WD3 . . . . 178 D5
Bradbourne Dr MK7 . . . . . . 48 C3
Bradbury Cl MK13 . . . . 34 A3
Bradbury Gdns SL3 . . . . . 199 D8
Bradcutts La SL6 . . . . 195 E8
Braddenham Wlk HP21 . . 115 E4
Braddons Furlong HP18 . 125 C6
Braden Cl HP21 . . . . 116 A6
BRADENHAM 160 F7
Bradenham Beeches
HP14 . . . . 161 A8
Bradenham La SL7 . . . . . . 194 C5
Bradenham Rd HP14 . . . . 161 A3
Bradenham Wood La
Naphill HP14 . . . . 150 B1
Walter's Ash HP14 . . . . . . 161 A7
Bradfield Ave MK18 . . . . . . 41 D2
Bradford Gdns MK5 . . . . . . 46 B4
Bradford Rd
Heronsgate WD3 . . . . 167 C2
Slough SL1 . . . . 205 A7
Bradley Cl HP18 . . . . 109 D5
Bradley Gr MK4 . . . . 46 B2
Bradley Rd SL1 . . . . 205 E6
Bradnam Wood Nature Reserve★ SL6 . . . . 194 D4
Bradshaw Cl SL4 . . . . 209 E6
Bradshawe Waye UB8 . . . 208 F8
Bradshaw Rd HP13 . . . . . . 173 F6
BRADVILLE 34 B7
Bradvue Cres MK13 . . . . . . 34 B6
BRADWELL 34 A4
BRADWELL ABBEY 33 F3
BRADWELL COMMON 34 B3
Bradwell Common Bvd
MK13 . . . . 34 C3
Bradwell Pk MK8 . . . . 33 E3
Bradwell Rd
Milton Keynes, Bradville
MK13 . . . . 34 A6
Milton Keynes, Loughton
MK5 . . . . 46 B8
Milton Keynes MK5, MK8 . . . 34 A1
Bradwell Village Sch
MK13 . . . . 34 B4
Braeburn Ct SL1 . . . . 205 C4
Braeburn Rd HP18 . . . . . . 100 D6
Braeburn Wy MK43 . . . . 25 B2
Brae Hill HP18 . . . . 110 A8
Brae Hill Cl HP18 . . . . 110 A8
Braemar Ct 5 SL7 . . . . 183 D2
Braemar Gdns SL1 . . . . . . 205 A4
Braeside HP14 . . . . 161 C6
Braford Gdns MK5 . . . . 46 B4
BRAGENHAM 70 C6
Bragenham La LU7, MK17 . 70 D5
Bragenham Side MK17 . . . 69 F7
Bragmans La WD4 . . . . . . 156 E6
Brahms Cl MK7 . . . . 48 C5
Braid End MK18 . . . . 52 F6
Braid The HP5 . . . . 144 E1
Brailsford Wy 2 MK7 . . . . . 48 A5
Brakynbery HP4 . . . . 134 E7
Bramber Cl MK3 . . . . 57 E7
Bramber Ct SL1 . . . . 205 A5
Bramble Ave MK14 . . . . 34 E4
Bramble Cl
Chalfont St Peter SL9 . . . . 177 E4
Uxbridge UB8 . . . . 208 F7
Bramble Cres HP15 . . . . . 163 C6
Bramble Dr SL6 . . . . 202 A4
Bramble La HP7 . . . . 165 E6
Bramble Mead HP8 . . . . . 177 B7
Brambleside HP11 . . . . . . 174 B4
Brambles The UB7 . . . . . . 208 E2
Brambling HP19 . . . . 101 E3
Bramblings The
Little Chalfont HP6 . . . . . . 155 A1
1 Little Chalfont HP6 . . . . . 166 A8
Brambling Wy SL6 . . . . . . 203 A8
Bramcote Cl HP20 . . . . . . 116 C8
Bramley Chase SL6 . . . . . 202 C4
Bramley Cl SL6 . . . . 202 C3
Bramley Ct MK43 . . . . 3 F6
Bramley End HP14 . . . . . . 151 A1
Bramley Gdns SL8 . . . . . . 185 B3
Bramley Grange MK2 . . . . . 58 D4
Bramley Mdws MK16 . . . . . 22 B3
Bramley Rd
Aylesbury HP18 . . . . 100 E6
Milton Keynes MK1 . . . . 47 D3
Brammas Cl SL1 . . . . 205 C3
Brampton Ct
Maidenhead SL6 . . . . 203 B8
Milton Keynes MK13 . . . . . . 34 A6
Branch Rd HP10 . . . . 174 B2
Brand Ave UB10 . . . . 201 E3
Brandon Ct HP23 . . . . 103 D7
Brandon Mead HP5 . . . . . 143 F2
Brandon Rd HP12 . . . . 172 B3
BRANDS HILL 212 A8
Brands Hill Ave HP13 . . . . 162 C2
Brands Rd SL3 . . . . 212 B8
Brandville Rd UB7 . . . . . . 208 E4
Brandy St HP18 . . . . 100 E4
Bransgill Ct MK13 . . . . 34 B4
Bransworth Ave MK10 . . . . 48 C8
Brantham Cl MK7 . . . . 48 A3
Brantwood Cl 7 MK4 . . . . . 45 F1
Braunston MK6 . . . . 47 D6
Bravenfield MK18 . . . . 53 C2
Brawlings La SL9 . . . . 178 A6
BRAY 203 D3
Braybank SL6 . . . . 203 D4
Braybourne Cl UB8 . . . . . . 201 C6
Braybrooke Dr MK4 . . . . . . 46 E4
Bray Cl SL6 . . . . 203 C3
Bray Ct
Amersham HP6 . . . . 154 E1
Maidenhead SL6 . . . . 203 C2
Brayfield Ho MK46 . . . . 8 B5
Brayfield Rd SL6 . . . . 203 C4
Bray Pit Wildlife Reserve★
SL6 . . . . 203 C2
Bray Rd SL6 . . . . 203 B5
Brays Cl HP6 . . . . 153 C4
Brays Green La HP6 . . . . . 153 C4
Brays La HP6 . . . . 153 C5
Brays Mdw HP6 . . . . 153 C4
Brayton Ct MK5 . . . . 46 C6
BRAY WICK 203 A4
Braywick Nature Ctr★
SL6 . . . . 203 B3
Braywick Park Nature Reserve★ SL6 . . . . 203 A5
Braywick Park & Sports Gd
SL6 . . . . 203 A5
Braywick Rd SL6 . . . . 203 A4
Braywood Cotts SL4 . . . . 209 A5
Braziers End HP5 . . . . 133 C1
Breachwell Pl LU7 . . . . 91 A1
Breakspear Road N UB9 . 190 E8
Breakspear Road S UB10 190 F2
Bream Cl SL7 . . . . 194 C8
Breamore Ct MK8 . . . . 45 F8
Brearley Ave MK6 . . . . 46 E7
Brearley Cl UB8 . . . . 201 E6
Breckland MK14 . . . . 34 D6
Brecon Ct
Milton Keynes MK10 . . . . . . 35 F1
Slough SL1 . . . . 205 C4
Brecon Way HP13 . . . . 172 E8
Bredward Cl SL1 . . . . 197 B2
Breedon Dr HP18 . . . . 100 E5
Breezes The SL6 . . . . 202 E4
Bremen Gr MK5 . . . . 46 A4
Brenchwood Cl HP13 . . . . 161 C2
Brendon Ct MK4 . . . . 46 D2
Brent MK6 . . . . 47 D5
Brent Path HP21 . . . . 115 D4
Brent Rd SL8 . . . . 185 A4
Brentwood Way HP21 . . . 116 B6
Bretby Chase MK4 . . . . 45 F3
Breton MK11 . . . . 32 E6
Brewhouse La HP22 . . . . . . 88 E1
Brewster Cl MK5 . . . . 45 D5
Brew Twr SL7 . . . . 183 D1
Briaily HP14 . . . . 159 C2
Briar Cl SL6 . . . . 204 B7
Briar Dene SL6 . . . . 195 C1
Briar Glen SL6 . . . . 195 E6
Briar Hill MK12 . . . . 33 E4
Briar Lodge MK12 . . . . 33 D5
Briars Cl HP19 . . . . 101 B2
Briars The
High Wycombe HP11 . . . . . 173 C5
Holmer Green HP15 . . . . . 163 C7
Slough SL3 . . . . 206 F1
Briarswood HP15 . . . . 163 B3
Briarswood Cl HP14 . . . . . 158 E5
Briar Way
Berkhamsted HP4 . . . . 135 D3
Slough SL2 . . . . 205 B8
Briary Ct MK18 . . . . 74 F8
Briary View MK17 . . . . 56 C8
Brices Mdw MK5 . . . . 46 A3
Brick Cl MK11 . . . . 33 C2
Brickfield La SL1 . . . . 197 B4
Brickfields Way UB7 . . . . 208 F3
Brick Hill HP18 . . . . 97 E1
Brickhill Manor Ct MK17 . 59 D5
Brickhill St
Giffard Park MK14 . . . . 22 A1
Milton Keynes, Monkston Park
MK10 . . . . 35 E2
Milton Keynes, Willen Park
MK15 . . . . 35 C6
Walton Park MK7 . . . . 48 A4
Brickhill Way MK18 . . . . . . 73 B5
Brick Kiln La HP22 . . . . . . 102 B4
Bricks La HP14 . . . . 159 C4
Brickwell Wlk HP15 . . . . . 163 B3
Bricstock HP22 . . . . 88 D4
Bridens Way HP17 . . . . . . 126 F6
Bridge Acad Central MK6 47 A6
Bridge Ave
Cookham Rise SL6 . . . . 195 E6
Maidenhead SL6 . . . . 203 A7
Bridge Bank Cl HP11 . . . . 174 A3
Bridge Cl SL1 . . . . 204 F6
Bridge Ct
Berkhamsted HP4 . . . . 135 D4
Maidenhead SL6 . . . . 203 C7
Bridge Farm Bldgs HP17 128 B8
Bridgeford Ct MK6 . . . . 46 E8
Bridgegate Bsns Pk
HP19 . . . . 101 B1
Bridge Ho
High Wycombe HP13 . . . . . 173 D6
West Drayton UB7 . . . . 208 D5
Bridge Hook Cl 4 MK12 . . 33 A6
Bridge Leys Mdw HP19 . . 101 D4
Bridgeman Ct 5 SL4 . . . . 210 A5
Bridgeman Dr SL4 . . . . . . 210 A5
Bridge Pl HP6 . . . . 154 F1
Bridge Rd
Cosgrove MK19 . . . . 19 E2
Ickford HP18 . . . . 123 F2
Maidenhead SL6 . . . . 203 B7
Stoke Bruerne NN12 . . . . 9 A8
Uxbridge UB8 . . . . 201 C3
Bridge St
Berkhamsted HP4 . . . . 135 D4
Bridge St *continued*
Buckingham MK18 . . . . 52 D8
Colnbrook SL3 . . . . 212 D7
Great Kimble HP17 . . . . . . 129 D1
High Wycombe HP11 . . . . . 173 A7
Leighton Buzzard LU7 . . . . . 80 F7
Maidenhead SL6 . . . . 203 A7
Milton Keynes MK13 . . . . . . 33 F7
Olney MK46 . . . . 6 F2
Thornborough MK18 . . . . . . 54 B8
Turvey MK43 . . . . 8 D5
Bridgestone Dr SL8 . . . . . 185 C3
Bridgeturn Ave MK12 . . . . . 33 D8
Bridgewater Ct
Little Gaddesden HP4 . . . . 121 C8
Slough SL3 . . . . 207 A2
Bridgewater Hill HP4 . . . . 134 F7
Bridgewater Ho 6 MK18 . . 52 C8
Bridgewater Monument★
HP4 . . . . 120 E7
Bridgewater Rd HP4 . . . . 135 B5
Bridgewater Sch HP4 . . . 135 A6
Bridgewater Terr SL4 . . . 210 D6
Bridgewater Way SL4 . . . 210 D6
Bridgeway
Cuddington HP18 . . . . 112 E3
Milton Keynes MK13 . . . . . . 34 A7
Bridge Wlk MK19 . . . . 31 E4
Bridgnorth Dr MK4 . . . . 45 E1
Bridle Cl
Maidenhead SL6 . . . . 195 E1
Milton Keynes MK13 . . . . . . 34 B6
Bridle Gate HP11 . . . . 172 F6
Bridle Manor HP22 . . . . . . 131 C8
Bridle Rd SL6 . . . . 195 E1
Bridleway
Buckland Common HP22 . . 132 E5
Weston Turville HP22 . . . . 116 F2
Bridle Way HP4 . . . . 135 A6
Bridleways HP22 . . . . 131 A5
Bridlington Cres MK10 . . . 36 A1
Bridlington Spur SL1 . . . . 205 B4
Bridport Way SL2 . . . . 198 B1
Briery Way HP6 . . . . 154 E1
Brighton Spur SL2 . . . . . . 198 B1
Brightwell Ave LU6 . . . . . . 93 C7
Brigidine Sch SL4 . . . . . . 210 D4
BRILL 96 B1
Brill CE Comb Sch HP18 . . 96 B1
Brill Cl
Maidenhead SL6 . . . . 202 D3
Marlow SL7 . . . . 183 C2
Brill Ho SL6 . . . . 202 C3
Brill Pl MK13 . . . . 34 C3
Brill Rd
Chilton HP18 . . . . 111 A3
Horton-cum-S OX33 . . . . . . 108 C6
Ludgershall HP18 . . . . 96 B7
Oakley HP18 . . . . 109 F5
Brill Windmill★ HP18 . . . . 96 A1
Brimmers Hill HP15 . . . . . 162 F6
Brimmers Rd HP27 . . . . . . 139 D2
Brimmers Way HP19 . . . . 114 F8
Brimstone La HP19 . . . . . . 101 C4
Brimstone Way HP4 . . . . . 134 F6
Brindlebrook MK8 . . . . 33 E1
Brindles Cl MK18 . . . . 73 B5
Brindles La HP9 . . . . 175 A4
Brindley Ave HP13 . . . . . . 161 F1
Brinkburn Chase MK10 . . . 36 A1
Brinkhurst SL7 . . . . 183 D2
Brinklow Rdbt MK10 . . . . . 36 C1
Briskman Way HP21 . . . . . 115 B6
Bristle Hill MK18 . . . . 52 C8
Bristol Cl TW19 . . . . 213 E1
Bristol Ct 10 TW19 . . . . . . 213 E1
Bristol Way SL1 . . . . 205 F5
Bristow Cl MK2 . . . . 47 E1
Britania Ct UB7 . . . . 208 D3
Britannia Ind Est
High Wycombe HP12 . . . . . 172 D7
Poyle SL3 . . . . 212 E5
Britannia Pl RG9 . . . . 191 E1
Britannia Rd 6 HP5 . . . . . 144 C2
Britannia St HP20 . . . . 115 E8
Britnell Ct HP14 . . . . 158 E5
Britten Gr MK7 . . . . 48 D5
Brittens Ct MK46 . . . . 7 C3
Brittons La MK17 . . . . 37 C3
BRITWELL 197 F1
Britwell Dr HP4 . . . . 135 E6
Britwell Gdns SL1 . . . . 197 D2
Britwell Rd SL1 . . . . 197 D2
Broad Arrow Cl MK14 . . . . 34 E7
Broad Dean MK6 . . . . 47 A8
Broadfields HP19 . . . . 101 A1
Broadfields Ct HP19 . . . . . 101 A1
Broadfields Ret Pk HP19 101 A1
Broad Gn MK43 . . . . 25 C3
BROAD GREEN 25 B3
Broad La HP9, HP10 . . . . . 186 A6
Broadlands MK6 . . . . 47 C5
Broadlands Ave HP5 . . . . 144 C1
Broadleys SL4 . . . . 209 F7
Broad Leys HP27 . . . . 139 A3
Broadmark Rd SL2 . . . . . . 206 B6
Broad Oak SL2 . . . . 198 C1
Broad Oak Ct SL2 . . . . 198 C1
Broadpiece MK15 . . . . 35 A7
Broad Platts SL3 . . . . 206 D3
Broad Rush Gn LU7 . . . . . . 80 E8
Broad St
Chesham HP5 . . . . 144 C1
Newport Pagnell MK16 . . . . 22 C4
Syresham NN13 . . . . 27 B8
Broadview Rd HP5 . . . . . . 144 B4
Broadwater
Berkhamsted HP4 . . . . 135 C5

Bro–Cal 219

Broadwater *continued*
Milton Keynes MK6 47 D6
Broadwater Gdns UB9 190 C7
Broadwater La UB9 190 C7
Broadwater Pk UB9 190 A5
Broadwater Pk SL6 203 E1
Broadway SL6 202 F7
Broadway Ave MK14 21 F2
Broadway Cl 5 HP7 165 B7
Broadway Ct HP5 154 B8
Broadway Par UB7 208 E4
Broadway The
Amersham HP7 165 B7
Beaconsfield HP9 175 D3
3 Chalfont St Peter SL9 177 D2
Chesham HP5 154 B8
Farnham Common SL2 198 C6
Grendon Underwood HP18 82 F6
Brocas St SL4 210 D7
Brocas Terr SL4 210 D7
Brocas Way LU7 91 A3
Brockhampton MK15 35 B6
Brockhurst Rd HP5 144 C2
Brock La SL6 202 F7
Brockton Ct SL6 202 F6
Brockway SL3 207 B1
Brockwell MK16 22 C4
Broddick Ho HP11 174 B4
Brokend HP18 100 D4
Broken Furlong SL4 205 B1
Broken Gate La UB9 189 C3
Bromham Mill MK14 21 F2
Bromley HP23 104 A4
Bromley La HP6 153 C5
Brompton Cl 2 HP19 101 B2
Brompton Cres HP19 101 B2
Brompton Dr SL6 195 C2
Bromycroft Rd SL2 198 A2
Bronsdon Way UB9 189 F2
Bronte Cl
Aylesbury HP19 100 F2
Slough SL1 205 E4
Brookbank HP10 185 D3
Brook Bsns Ctr UB8 201 B3
Brook Cl
Aston Clinton HP22 117 D5
Ludgershall HP18 96 C8
Brook Cres SL1 204 E7
Brook Dene MK18 65 F4
Brookdene Cl SL6 195 F2
Brooke Cl MK3 57 F7
Brooke Furmston Pl SL7 183 E3
BROOK END
Ivinghoe 105 E4
North Crawley 23 F5
Weston Turville 117 A3
Brook End
North Crawley MK16 24 A6
Weston Turville HP22 117 A3
Brook End Sp Ctr MK5 46 A3
Brooke Rd HP27 139 B4
Brookes Univ (Wheatley Campus) OX33 122 C1
Brook Farm Cl MK18 62 C1
Brookfield UB8 201 E6
Brookfield Cl HP23 119 B4
Brookfield Ho SL3 211 D6
Brookfield La MK18 52 D7
Brookfield Rd
Haversham MK19 20 D2
Newton Longville MK17 57 D3
Wooburn HP10 185 D3
Brook Ho
Slough SL1 205 D3
West Drayton UB7 208 D5
Brookhouse Dr HP10 185 C3
Brook La
Berkhamsted HP4 135 B5
Harrold MK43 3 F7
Newton Blossomville MK43 8 B3
Thame OX9 125 E1
Brooklands Farm Prim Sch (Countess Wy Campus) MK10 36 D3
Brooklands Farm Prim Sch (Fen St Campus) MK10 36 C5
Brooklands Rd MK2 58 C7
Brooklyn Way UB7 208 D3
Brookmead Sch LU7 105 E5
Brook Path SL1 204 F6
Brooks Ct MK18 52 D8
Brookside
Colnbrook SL3 212 C7
Halton HP22 117 C1
Lillingstone Lovell MK18 30 A6
Loudwater HP10 174 C2
Milton Keynes MK12 33 D4
Oakley HP18 109 D5
Slough SL3 206 E7
Thame OX9 125 F1
Uxbridge UB10 201 F5
Weston Turville HP22 117 A2
Brookside Ave TW19 211 E4
Brookside Cl
Old Stratford MK19 32 B6
Tiddington OX9 136 A7
Brookside La HP17 129 E3
Brookside Terr 5 HP21 115 E8
Brooks Mews HP19 115 C8
Brook St
Aston Clinton HP22 117 D5
Edlesborough LU6 92 F4
High Wycombe HP11 173 A7
Tring HP23 119 B4
Windsor SL4 210 D5
Brooksward Sch MK14 34 F7
Brookway MK19 31 E4
Broombarn La HP16 151 E7
Broom Cl HP15 163 A3
Broomfield MK12 33 D4
Broomfield Cl HP16 151 E7
Broomfield Gate SL2 198 B1
Broomfield Hill HP16 151 E7
Broom Hill
Cookham Rise SL6 195 E6
Stoke Poges SL2 199 A5
Broom Ho SL3 206 F2
Broomlee MK13 34 A5
Broomstick Ind Est LU6 92 E4
Broomstick La HP5 145 A1
Brora Cl MK2 58 C5
Brotheridge Ct HP21 115 B6
Brough Cl MK5 46 A5
BROUGHTON
Aylesbury 116 D8
Milton Keynes 36 A3
Broughton Ave HP20 116 B8
Broughton Cl HP22 102 B3
Broughton Com Inf Sch HP20 116 B8
BROUGHTON CROSSING
HP22 102 C2
Broughton Fields Prim Sch MK10, MK16 36 B4
Broughton Grounds Bsns Pk MK16 37 A6
Broughton Grounds Com Woodlands★ MK16 36 E6
Broughton Grounds Rd MK16 36 B4
Broughton Jun Sch HP20 116 B8
Broughton La HP20, HP22 116 C8
Broughton Manor Bsns Pk MK16 36 B4
Broughton Manor Prep Sch MK10 36 C4
Broughton Rd
Milton Keynes MK10 36 B4
Salford MK17 37 C3
Brow Bsns Ctr 10 HP11 172 E7
Brownbaker Ct MK14 34 F6
Browne Willis Cl MK2 58 D8
Brownfield Gdns SL6 202 E5
Browning Cl MK16 22 A4
Browning Cres MK3 58 A7
Brownlow Ave LU6 92 F3
Brownlow Gate HP4 107 A1
Brownlow La LU7 105 A7
Brownlow Rd HP4 135 C5
Brownlow Rise LU6 93 A8
Browns Cl MK18 65 E4
Browns Ct SL1 204 E6
Brownset Dr MK4 45 E1
Brownsfield Rd NN12 18 E6
Browns Hedge
Leighton Buzzard LU7 105 D2
Pitstone LU7 105 C3
Browns Rd
Holmer Green HP15 163 C6
South Heath HP16 153 A7
Brown's Rise HP23 132 F3
Browns Way MK17 49 E5
BROWNS WOOD 48 C4
Brownswood Dr NN12 18 D3
Brownswood Rd HP9 175 E4
Browns Wood Rdbt MK7 48 C5
Brow The HP8 177 D7
Broxbourne Cl MK14 21 F2
Bruce Cl SL1 205 A5
Bruce Wlk SL4 209 D5
Brucewood Par SL7 183 E5
Bruckner Gdns MK7 48 D5
Brudenell SL4 209 F3
Brudenell Cl HP6 154 F1
Brudenell Dr
Milton Keynes MK10 48 C8
Stoke Mandeville HP22 116 B1
Brunel Cl SL6 202 E5
Brunel Ctr SL6 202 D5
Brunel Ctr (Sh Ctr) MK2 58 C8
Brunel Gate HP19 100 F1
Brunel Gdns SL9 195 D1
Brunel Rd
Aylesbury HP19 100 F1
High Wycombe HP13 161 F1
Maidenhead SL6 202 D5
Brunel Science Pk UB8 201 E2
Brunel Univ UB8 201 E2
Brunel Way SL1 205 F5
Brunleys MK11 33 B3
Brunner Pl HP13 173 C6
Brunswick Cl HP19 101 B3
Brunswick Pl HP13 162 D2
Brushford Cl MK4 46 D3
Brushmakers Ct HP5 144 B1
Brushwood Dr WD3 167 C5
Brushwood Jun Sch HP5 144 E2
Brushwood Rd HP5 144 E2
Bryans Cres MK16 24 A6
Bryanston Ave HP20 101 F2
Bryant Ave SL2 205 E8
Bryants Acre HP22 131 B6
BRYANT'S BOTTOM 150 F4
Bryants Bottom Rd HP16 150 F4
Bryden Cotts UB8 201 C1
Bryer Pl SL4 209 D4
Bryfield Cotts HP3 146 C1
Bryher The SL6 202 A7
Bryne La MK18 53 B2
Bryony Cl UB8 208 F8
Bryony Pl MK14 34 E5
Buccaneer MK10 36 B5
Buccleuch Rd SL3 211 B7
Buchanan Rd OX25 94 E7
Buchan Cl UB8 201 C2
Buckby MK6 47 D6
Buckfast Ave MK3 47 A2
Buckfield Ct SL0 207 F4
BUCKINGHAM 41 D2
Buckingham Ave SL1 205 B7
Buckingham Avenue E
SL1 205 C7
Buckingham Canal Wildlife Reserve★ MK18 42 D3
Buckingham Chantry Chapel MK18 41 D1
Buckingham Cl HP13 174 A7
Buckingham Com Hospl MK18 41 D1
Buckingham Ct
Amersham HP6 154 E2
Brackley NN13 38 A6
Newport Pagnell MK16 22 B3
Buckingham Ctr 8 MK18 41 D1
Buckingham Dr HP13 174 A7
Buckingham Gate
Medmenham SL7 193 D7
Milton Keynes MK6 35 B1
Buckingham Gdns SL1 205 F4
Buckingham Ho
Amersham HP6 154 D3
4 Maidenhead SL6 202 F6
Buckingham Ind Pk MK18 52 D5
Buckingham Par 4 SL9 177 D2
Buckingham Park CE Prim Sch HP19 101 C5
Buckingham Pl 1 HP13 173 A7
Buckingham Prim Sch MK18 41 E2
Buckingham Rd
Aylesbury HP19, HP20 101 D3
Brackley NN13 38 A6
Deanshanger MK19 31 E2
Edgcott HP18 72 F2
Gawcott MK18 52 A5
Milton Keynes, Church Hill MK17 56 E6
Milton Keynes MK3 57 D7
Steeple Claydon MK18 63 E3
Tring HP23 118 E3
Winslow MK18 65 F5
Buckingham Road Ind Est NN13 38 A6
Buckingham Sch MK18 52 D7
Buckinghamshire County Mus★ HP20 115 D8
Buckinghamshire New Univ
Chalfont St Peter HP8 178 A8
High Wycombe HP11 173 A6
Uxbridge UB8 201 C6
Buckinghamshire Railway Ctr★ HP22 84 F2
Buckinghamshire UTC HP21 115 C7
Buckingham Sq 1 MK9 34 C2
Buckingham St
8 Aylesbury HP20 101 D1
Milton Keynes MK12 33 D7
Tingewick MK18 51 B6
Buckingham View HP5 144 C1
Buckingham Way HP10 174 A1
BUCKLAND 117 F6
Buckland Ave SL3 206 B3
BUCKLAND COMMON 133 A3
Buckland Cres SL4 209 F6
Buckland Dr MK6 47 C6
Buckland Gate SL3 199 B2
Buckland Lodge MK6 47 B6
Buckland Rd HP22 118 A4
Bucklands Croft HP23 118 C8
BUCKLANDWHARF 118 B4
Bucklebury Cl SL6 203 C1
Buckley Ct MK11 32 F4
Buckman Cl MK12 33 B5
Buckmaster Rd HP12 172 C3
BUCKMOOREND 140 D6
Bucks Goat Ctr & Animal Farm The★ HP22 130 A7
Buckthorn MK12 33 E5
Budge Rd NN12 18 F5
Buffins SL6 196 E2
BUFFLER'S HALT 40 C3
BULBOURNE 119 C8
Bulbourne Cl HP4 134 F6
Bulbourne Ct HP23 119 A7
Bulbourne Rd HP23 119 B7
Bulkeley Ave SL4 210 B4
Bullbaiters La HP6 153 B5
Bullbeggars La HP4 135 F3
Bullfinch Gdns 8 HP19 101 F3
BULLINGTON END 20 C7
Bullington End Rd MK19 20 A6
Bull La
Gerrards Cross SL9 188 C7
7 High Wycombe HP11 173 A7
Milton Keynes MK2 58 D8
Bullocks Farm La HP14 171 B7
Bullrush Gr UB8 201 C1
Bulls La HP18 124 A3
Bullsland Gdns WD3 167 B3
Bullsland La WD3 167 B3
Bulmer Cl MK10 36 B3
BULSTRODE 146 E3
Bulstrode Cl WD4 146 E2
Bulstrode Ct SL9 188 D5
Bulstrode La WD4 146 F3
Bulstrode Pl SL1 205 F3
Bulstrode Way SL9 188 D6
Bunby Rd SL2 198 F5
Bunces Cl SL4 205 B1
Bunces Ct HP20 101 D1
Bungalows The MK18 51 A6
Bunhill Cl LU6 93 F8
Bunkers La LU7 80 D6
Bunsen Pl MK5 46 C4
Bunstrux HP23 119 A4
Bunsty Ct MK11 32 F5
Bunten Meade SL1 205 B5
Bunyan Cl HP23 119 B5
Burano Cl MK7 48 C6
Burchard Cres MK5 46 A6
Burchett's Green Rd SL6 194 C1
Burcot Gdns SL6 195 E3
BURCOTT 79 E4
Burcott Cl HP22 102 B3
Burcott La HP22 102 C3
Burdeleys La MK5 46 A4
Burdett Dr HP14 161 B8
Burdock Ct MK16 21 F4
Bure Valley 5 MK10 36 C3
Burewelle MK8 33 D1
Burfield Rd
Chorleywood WD3 167 C4
Old Windsor SL4 211 A1
Burford Cl
Ickenham UB10 201 E8
Marlow Bottom SL7 183 C5
Burford Gdns SL1 204 C8
Burford Ho 18 SL4 210 D6
Burford Sch SL7 183 C5
Burgess Gdns MK16 22 B2
Burgess La HP17 128 B7
Burgess Wood Gr HP9 175 B1
Burgess Wood Rd HP9 175 B2
Burgess Wood Road S
HP9 175 B1
Burgett Rd SL1 205 B3
Burghley Ct MK8 45 F8
Burholme MK4 46 C3
Burke Rd HP22 131 C5
Burkes Cl HP9 186 B8
Burkes Cres HP9 175 D2
Burkes Ct HP9 175 D2
Burkes Par HP9 175 D3
Burkes Rd HP9 175 C2
Burleigh Ct MK18 52 F8
Burleigh Piece MK18 41 F1
Burleys Rd MK18 65 F4
Burlington Ave SL1 205 E4
Burlington Ct 1 SL1 205 E4
Burlington Rd
Burnham SL1 197 B1
2 Slough SL1 205 E4
Burma Cl HP13 173 E6
Burners La MK11 33 B4
Burners Lane Ind Pk MK11 33 B4
Burners Lane S MK11 33 B3
Burness Cl UB8 201 D3
Burnet MK14 34 C7
Burnetts Ct HP16 151 C5
Burnetts Rd SL4 209 E6
BURNHAM 197 C3
Burnham Ave HP9 176 A1
Burnham Beeches National Nature Reserve★ SL2 198 A7
Burnham Cl
Bourne End SL8 185 A4
High Wycombe HP12 172 D6
Windsor SL4 209 D5
Burnham Ct SL6 202 F8
Burnham Dr MK13 34 C3
Burnham Gram Sch SL1 197 D1
Burnham Hts SL1 204 C7
Burnham La SL1 204 E7
Burnham Pl NN13 27 B8
Burnham Rd
Beaconsfield HP9 186 F6
Hughenden Valley HP14 162 A6
Westcott HP18 98 B7
Burnhams Field HP22 116 E7
Burnham Sta SL1 204 D7
Burnhams The
Aston Clinton HP22 117 C5
Shabbington HP18 124 D3
Burnmoor Cl MK2 58 D4
Burns Cl
Long Crendon HP18 125 D7
Newport Pagnell MK16 22 A4
Burns Ct HP21 115 F6
Burns Rd MK3 58 A7
Burnt Oak SL6 195 F7
Burn Wlk SL1 197 B1
Burrell Cl HP21 115 C6
Burren The HP6 154 D2
Burroughs Cres SL8 185 A4
Burrow Ash Cl MK19 10 F2
Burroway Rd SL3 207 B3
Burrows Cl
Tylers Green HP10 163 C2
Woburn Sands MK17 49 B5
Burrows Ho HP13 161 E2
Burton La HP27 139 C5
Burtons La WD3 167 A4
Burton's La HP8 166 E5
Burton's Way HP8 166 C7
Burton Way SL4 209 E4
Burtree Cl MK12 33 D5
Burt's La HP18 125 D6
Bury Ave MK16 22 C4
Bury Cl MK16 22 C4
BURY END 165 D6
Bury Farm HP7 165 C7
Bury Farm Cl LU7 91 C6
Buryfield La HP16 152 B7
Buryhook Cnr OX33 122 C2
Bury La HP5 154 B8
Bury Rise HP3 146 D6
Bury St MK16 22 C4
Busby Cl MK18 41 F1
Buscot Pl MK8 45 F8
Bushel Wharf HP23 119 A6
Bushes La MK18 51 C1
Bushey Bartrams MK5 46 A3
Bushey Cl
Buckingham MK18 41 F1
High Wycombe HP12 172 E7
Whipsnade LU6 93 F1
Bushfield Rd HP3 146 C6
Bushfields MK12 33 D6
Bushfield Sch MK12 33 D6
Bushmead Cl HP22 87 B5
Bushmead Rd HP22 87 B5
Bushnell Pl 2 SL6 202 B8
Bush The HP17 126 F5
Bushy Cl MK3 47 A3
Business Ctr The HP6 154 F1
Business Village SL2 206 B5
Buslins La HP5 143 E3
Butcher La 7 MK5 45 F3
Bute Brae MK3 46 E2
Butler Ct 5 SL7 183 F3
Butlers Cl
Amersham HP6 154 A2
Windsor SL4 209 D6
Butlers Court Comb Sch HP9 175 D1
Butlers Court Rd HP9 175 D1
BUTLERS CROSS 176 F6
BUTLER'S CROSS 130 C3
Butlers Ct HP13 173 F5
Butlers Gr MK14 34 D8
Butler Wlk HP19 115 A7
Butterfield HP10 185 D4
Butterfield Cl MK15 35 C2
Butterfield Cotts WD3 178 E3
Butterfly Cl MK18 52 F6
Butterfly Gate 5 MK10 36 B3
Butterly Rd
High Wycombe HP14 158 B6
Stokenchurch HP14 158 F4
Buttermere HP21 116 B7
Buttermere Ave SL1 204 C8
Buttermere Cl MK2 58 D6
Butterton Gdns MK10 36 C3
Buttfurlong HP17 127 A7
Buttlehide WD3 178 D5
Buttler's Hanging Wildlife Reserve★ HP14 160 D5
Button Gr MK6 47 A7
Buzzacott La MK4 46 C3
Bybend Cl SL2 198 B4
Bycell Rd MK18 41 C6
Bye Gn HP22 117 A3
BYE GREEN 117 A3
Byerly Ho MK14 34 F5
Byerly Pl MK14 34 F5
Byford Way MK18 65 F4
Byland Dr SL6 203 B1
Byrd Cres MK7 48 D6
Byres The HP17 126 F6
Byron SL3 207 B1
Byron Cl
6 Marlow SL7 183 F3
Milton Keynes MK3 57 F7
Byron Ct SL4 210 A4
Byron Dr MK16 22 A4
Byron Rd HP21 115 F6
Byron Way UB7 208 F2
Byward Cl MK14 34 E7
Byways
Berkhamsted HP4 135 E5
Burnham SL1 204 A8
Bywell Ct MK4 56 E8
By-Wood End SL9 178 A5

C

Cable Cres MK17 49 B5
Cable Gr MK13 34 C8
Cadeby Ct MK10 36 B3
Cadman Sq MK5 46 C5
CADMORE END 170 C6
Cadmore End CE Comb Sch HP14 170 C6
Cadsdean Rd HP27 139 E6
Cadwell Dr SL6 202 D3
Caernarvon Cres MK3 57 E7
Caesars Cl MK13 34 A5
Caesars Gate NN13 38 A6
Cages Wood Dr SL2 198 B8
Cagney Cres 1 MK4 45 E3
Cairngorm Gate MK6 46 D8
Cairngorm Pl SL2 198 D1
Cairnside HP13 173 E6
Caister Ct MK4 56 E8
Caithness Ct MK3 46 E2
Calamus Ct MK7 48 B6
Calbroke Rd SL2 197 F2
CALDECOTE 22 E1
Caldecote La MK16 22 F2
Caldecote St MK16 22 C4
CALDECOTTE 48 A2
Caldecotte La MK7 48 A3
Caldecotte Lake Dr MK7 48 A2
Caldecotte Rdbt MK7 47 F3
Calder Cl SL6 195 E1
Calder Ct
Maidenhead SL6 195 D1
1 Slough SL3 206 F1
Calder Gdns LU7 80 B7
Calder Vale MK3 46 E1
Calder Way SL3 212 E4
Caldewell MK8 33 D1

Caldicot Cl HP21 . . . . 116 B6
Caldicott Sch SL2 . . . . 198 B5
Caledon Cl HP9 . . . . 175 E3
Caledonian Rd
  Milton Keynes MK11 . . . . . 33 A3
  Milton Keynes MK13 . . . . . 33 E7
Caledon Rd HP9 . . . . 175 E3
Calewen MK8 . . . . 33 E1
CALIFORNIA
  Aylesbury 115 C7
  Dunstable 93 F6
California Circ HP11 . . . . 173 B4
Callaghan Ct HP4 . . . . . . 135 D4
Callingham Pl HP9 . . . . . . 175 E3
Callis Farm Cl TW19. . . . . 213 E1
Calluna Dr MK3 . . . . 47 A3
Calumet HP9 . . . . 175 D3
Calvards Croft MK12 . . . . 33 C4
Calverleigh Cres MK4 . . . 46 D3
Calverley Cres HP13. . . . . 161 F2
CALVERT. 73 B6
Calvert Cotts MK18. . . . . 73 D7
Calvert Jubilee Wildlife
  Reserve★ MK18, OX27 . . . 73 A7
CALVERTON 32 E3
Calverton La MK19 . . . . . . 33 B1
Calverton Lane Rdbt
  MK11 . . . . 33 B2
Calverton Rd MK11. . . . . . 32 D4
Calves Cl MK5 . . . . 46 A3
Calvie Croft MK12 . . . . . . 33 D4
Calville Gdns HP18 . . . . . 100 E5
Cambell Sq MK9 . . . . 35 A3
Camber Cl MK3 . . . . 57 E7
Camberton Rd LU7. . . . . . 80 E6
Cambian Bletchley Pk Sch 🏫
  MK3 . . . . 57 F8
Camborne Ave HP21 . . . . 116 B5
Cambria Ct SL3 . . . . 206 C4
Cambridge Ave
  Burnham SL1 . . . . 197 B3
  Slough SL1. . . . . 205 A7
Cambridge Cl
  Aylesbury HP20 . . . . 101 E1
  🄳 Aylesbury HP20 . . . . . . 101 E1
  Harmondsworth UB7. . . . . 213 D8
Cambridge Close Ret Pk 🏫
  HP20. . . . . 101 E1
Cambridge Cres HP13 . . . 173 E2
Cambridge Ho 🄴 SL4 . . . 210 C6
Cambridge Pl 🄺 HP20. . . 115 D8
Cambridge Rd
  Beaconsfield HP9 . . . . 175 C2
  Marlow SL7 . . . . 183 D2
  Uxbridge UB8. . . . . 201 D6
Cambridge St
  Aylesbury HP20 . . . . 101 E1
  Milton Keynes, Bletchley
  MK2 . . . . 58 C8
  Milton Keynes, Wolverton
  MK12 . . . . 33 C6
Cambridge Terr 🄳 HP4 . 135 D4
Cambron MK8 . . . . 33 D2
Cam Ct MK3 . . . . 57 E8
Camden Ct HP19 . . . . 101 C1
Camden Cl SL6. . . . . 195 D1
Camden Pl SL8 . . . . 185 A3
Cameron Rd 🄺 HP5. . . . . 144 C1
Camfield Ct SL6 . . . . 202 A8
Camlet Dr MK14 . . . . 34 D7
Camley Gdns SL6 . . . . . . 202 A8
Camm Ave SL4. . . . . 209 E4
Cam Mead MK16 . . . . 116 B6
Camomile Ct MK7. . . . . . . 48 C5
Camomile Way UB7 . . . . . 208 E6
Campania Cl MK10 . . . . . . 36 A2
Campbell Cl
  Buckingham MK18. . . . . . . 52 F8
  High Wycombe HP13 . . . . . 172 F8
Campbell Dr HP9 . . . . 175 C5
Campbell La LU7. . . . . 105 D3
CAMPBELL PARK 35 A3
Campbell Park Rdbt MK9. 34 F3
Campbell Rd SL7 . . . . 183 D4
Campbells Ride HP15 . . . 163 D7
Campden Rd UB10 . . . . . . 190 F1
Camperdown SL6 . . . . . . 196 B1
Camperdown Ho 🄺 SL4 . 210 C5
Camp Ind Est OX9 . . . . . . 136 B4
Campion MK14 . . . . 21 E2
Campion Cl
  Aylesbury HP20 . . . . 116 C8
  Denham UB9 . . . . 190 A1
  Uxbridge UB8. . . . . 208 F8
Campion Rd HP15. . . . . . . 162 F6
Campions Ct HP4 . . . . 135 B3
Camp Rd SL9 . . . . 188 C4
Canada Rd SL1 . . . . 206 B4
Canal Ct HP4 . . . . 135 C4
Canal La MK19 . . . . 31 F4
Canal Mus The★ NN12 . . 9 A8
Canalside
  Berkhamsted HP4 . . . . . . 134 F6
  Old Stratford MK19 . . . . . . 32 C7
  Stoke Bruerne NN12 . . . . . 9 A8
Canalside Rdbt MK9. . . . . 35 B4
Canal Wharf SL1 . . . . 207 A4
Canberra Chase 🄴 MK16 . 36 B5
Candleford Ct MK18. . . . . 52 D8
Candlemas La HP9 . . . . . . 175 E2
Candlemas Mead HP9 . . . 175 E2
Candlemas Oaks HP9 . . . 175 E2
Candlewicks MK7. . . . . . . 48 B6
Candover Cl UB7. . . . . 213 D7
Candy La MK5 . . . . 46 B4

Candytuft Gn HP15. . . . . . 162 F6
Cane End HP27 . . . . 139 A3
Cane End La HP22 . . . . . . 102 C6
Canford HP21 . . . . 115 F5
Cannock Cl SL6. . . . . 203 B6
Cannock Rd HP20. . . . . . . 101 E3
Cannon Court Rd SL6 . . . 195 D3
Cannondown Rd SL6. . . . . 195 E5
Cannon Gate SL2 . . . . . . 206 C6
Cannon Hill Cl SL6. . . . . . 203 C2
Cannon La SL6. . . . . 202 A6
Cannon Mill Ave HP5. . . . 154 E5
Cannon Pl HP27 . . . . 139 B4
Cannon's Hill HP18. . . . . . 112 C5
Cannon's Orch HP22 . . . . 85 B4
Canonbury MK10. . . . . 35 E1
Canon Harnett Ct MK12 . 32 F6
Canon Hill Dr SL6. . . . . . . 203 B3
Canon Hill Way SL6 . . . . . 203 B2
Canon Ind Pk MK12 . . . . . 33 C7
Canon's Cloisters SL4 . . . 210 D7
Canon's Ct MK16 . . . . 22 E3
Canons The MK16. . . . . . . 22 E3
Cantell Cl MK18. . . . . 41 D1
Canterbury Ave SL2. . . . . 198 C1
Canterbury Cl
  Amersham HP7 . . . . 165 E8
  Monks Risborough HP27. . 139 B5
Cantilupe Cl LU6. . . . . 92 D6
Cantle Ave MK14 . . . . 35 A5
Cantley Cl HP20. . . . . 101 E2
Cape End MK14 . . . . 21 F3
Capek Rd MK10 . . . . 35 E2
Capel Cl MK18 . . . . 41 F7
Capel Dr MK14. . . . . 34 F5
Capell Ave WD3 . . . . 167 C4
Capell Rd WD3 . . . . 167 D4
Capell Way WD3 . . . . 167 D4
Cape Villas SL0 . . . . 207 E7
Capian Wlk MK8 . . . . 33 E1
Capital Dr MK14 . . . . 34 E6
Capps La HP5. . . . . 143 A5
Capricorn Ho HP10. . . . . . 185 A8
Capron 47 B5
Capswood Bsns Ctr UB9 189 C3
Captain Cook Cl HP8 . . . . 177 B6
Captain's Cl HP5. . . . . 144 A4
Captains Wlk HP4 . . . . . . 135 D3
Captain's Wood Nature
  Reserve★ HP5. . . . . 143 F4
Caraway Cl MK7 . . . . 48 B4
Cardain Ho HP9. . . . . 175 D3
Cardigan Cl
  Milton Keynes MK3 . . . . . . 46 F1
  Slough SL1. . . . . 204 F6
Cardinal Dr HP18 . . . . . . 100 E5
Cardinals Wlk SL6 . . . . . . 204 C7
Carding Pl MK13 . . . . 34 B8
Cardwell Cl MK4 . . . . 46 C2
Carey Cl
  Aylesbury HP21 . . . . 115 D4
  Windsor SL4 . . . . 210 B4
Careys Croft HP4 . . . . . . 135 A7
Careys Rd NN12. . . . . 17 A8
Carey Way MK46 . . . . 7 A4
Carhampton Ct MK4. . . . . 46 D3
Carisbrooke Ave HP12. . . 172 B6
Carisbrooke Cl SL6. . . . . . 202 C6
Carisbrooke Ct
  Buckingham MK18. . . . . . . 41 E2
  Slough SL1. . . . . 205 F6
Carisbrooke Ho 🄴 HP13 . 173 F7
Carisbrooke Way MK4. . . 45 E1
Carleton Gate MK15. . . . . 35 E7
Carlina Pl MK14. . . . . 34 D3
Carlisle Rd SL1 . . . . 205 D6
Carlton Cl
  Aylesbury HP19 . . . . 101 A2
  Newport Pagnell MK16 . . . 22 E4
Carlton Ct HP27. . . . . 139 B3
Carlton Ho TW19. . . . . . . 213 D2
Carlton Rd
  Slough SL2. . . . . 206 B6
  Turvey MK43 . . . . 8 E7
Carlyle Ave HP21. . . . . . . 115 F7
Carlyle Cl MK16. . . . . 22 A4
Carman Ct HP23 . . . . 118 F3
Carmarthen Rd SL1 . . . . . 205 E6
Carmel Ct SL7 . . . . 183 B1
Carnation Way HP21. . . . . 115 E5
Carne The MK11 . . . . 32 E5
Carnot Cl MK5 . . . . 46 C4
Carnoustie Cl MK3 . . . . . . 57 C7
Carnweather Ct MK4 . . . . 57 B8
Carolina Dr HP11 . . . . 173 E5
Caroline Cl UB7. . . . . 208 D4
Caroline Ct SL7 . . . . 183 E3
Caroline Haslett Comb Sch 🏫
  MK5 . . . . 46 B4
Carolus Creek MK15 . . . . 35 A7
Carpenter Ct MK14. . . . . . 34 F6
Carpenters Wood Dr
  WD3. . . . . 167 B5
Carpenter's Wood, Dungrove
  Wood Nature Reserve★
  SL6. . . . . 194 C2
Carpenters Yd HP23. . . . . 119 B3
Carradine Cres MK4. . . . . 45 E3
Carr Cl HP19. . . . . 101 A2
Carriage Rd HP22 . . . . . . 102 C2
Carrick Rd MK6 . . . . 34 F1
Carrick St HP18 . . . . 100 F4
Carriers Cl MK19. . . . . 11 A2
Carrington Ave HP10. . . . . 185 A8
Carrington Cl MK18. . . . . . 77 E5
Carrington Cres HP22. . . . 131 A7
Carrington Ct 🄳 HP12. . . 172 E7
Carrington Hall Rd MK17 . 68 C6

Carrington Inf Sch 🏫
  HP10. . . . . 174 A1
Carrington Jun Sch 🏫
  HP10. . . . . 185 A8
Carrington Pl
  Holmer Green HP15 . . . . . 163 C7
  Tring HP23. . . . . 119 B5
Carrington Rd
  Aylesbury HP21 . . . . 115 D6
  High Wycombe HP12 . . . . . 172 D6
  Newport Pagnell MK16 . . . 22 B3
  Slough SL1. . . . . 205 E6
Carrington Way HP16 . . . 151 C5
Carroll Cl MK16 . . . . 22 A5
Carron Cl LU7 . . . . 80 B7
Carron Ct MK2. . . . . 58 C4
Carrs Dr HP12 . . . . 172 C8
Carter Cl SL4 . . . . 210 A5
Carteret Cl MK15. . . . . . . 35 E7
Carters Cl MK16 . . . . 13 F1
Carters La
  Long Crendon HP18. . . . . 125 B7
  Milton Keynes MK11 . . . . . 33 A3
  Quainton HP22, MK18. . . . 85 E6
Carters Mdw MK18. . . . . . 76 A2
Carters Ride HP22 . . . . . . 116 B2
Carter Wlk HP10 . . . . 174 C4
Cartington Gdns MK4 . . . 56 E8
Cartmel Cl MK3 . . . . 57 C6
Cartwright Ct 🄴 HP13. . . 173 F5
Cartwright Pl MK6 . . . . . . 46 E8
Carver Hill Rd HP11 . . . . . 172 F5
Carvers Mews MK14. . . . . 34 F6
Cascadia Cl HP11 . . . . . . 174 B2
Cashmere Cl MK5. . . . . . . 46 A4
Cassius Cl MK11 . . . . 33 A3
Casterton Cl MK13 . . . . . . 34 C4
Castle Acre MK10 . . . . . . 35 F1
Castle Ashby Rd NN7. . . . 1 B7
Castle Ave
  Datchet SL3. . . . . 211 A8
  West Drayton UB7. . . . . . . 208 F6
Castle Cl
  Marsh Gibbon OX6 . . . . . . 72 A3
  Pitstone LU7 . . . . 105 D3
  Totternhoe LU6 . . . . 93 A8
  Wing LU7. . . . . 79 E3
Castle Ct
  🄳 Aylesbury HP20 . . . . . . 115 D8
  Buckingham MK18. . . . . . . 52 D8
  Maidenhead SL6 . . . . 202 D7
Castle Dr SL6. . . . . 202 D7
Castle Est HP12. . . . . 172 A6
Castlefields HP22 . . . . . . 116 C3
Castlefield Sch HP12. . . . 172 C6
Castle Gate Way HP4. . . . 135 C6
Castle Hill
  Berkhamsted HP4 . . . . . . 135 C5
  High Wycombe HP11 . . . . . 173 A6
  Maidenhead SL6 . . . . 202 E7
  Windsor SL4 . . . . 210 D6
Castle Hill Ave HP4 . . . . . 135 C5
Castle Hill Cl HP4 . . . . . . 135 C5
Castle Hill Ct HP4 . . . . . . 135 C5
Castle Hill Rd LU6. . . . . . . 93 A8
Castle Hill Terr SL6 . . . . . 202 E7
Castle Ho 🄳 LU7. . . . . . . 80 E7
Castle La HP22. . . . . 86 F6
Castle Lodge SL6 . . . . . . 202 F7
Castlemead Cotts SL4. . . 210 C3
Castle Meadow Cl MK16. . 22 E4
Castle Mews
  Berkhamsted HP4 . . . . . . 135 C4
  Maidenhead SL6 . . . . 202 E7
Castlemilk 🄴 MK18 . . . . . 41 D3
Castle Park Rd HP22 . . . . 131 B6
Castle Pl 🄷 HP13 . . . . . . 173 B7
Castle Rd MK46 . . . . 2 F1
Castle Rose MK6 . . . . 47 D6
Castle Row 🄶 HP23 . . . . . 119 A3
Castle St
  Aylesbury HP20 . . . . 115 D8
  Berkhamsted HP4 . . . . . . 135 C4
  Buckingham MK18. . . . . . . 52 D8
  High Wycombe HP13 . . . . . 173 B7
  Marsh Gibbon OX27. . . . . . 72 A3
  Slough SL1. . . . . 205 F3
  Wingrave HP22 . . . . 89 B3
Castlesteads MK13 . . . . . 33 F5
CASTLETHORPE 19 E5
Castlethorpe Fst Sch 🏫
  MK19 . . . . 19 F5
Castlethorpe Rd MK19. . . 11 A2
Castleton Cl SL7 . . . . 183 E2
Castleview Comb Sch 🏫
  SL3 . . . . 206 D2
Castle View Gdns HP12. . 172 D7
Castleview Ho SL4 . . . . . . 210 D7
Castleview Rd SL3 . . . . . . 206 C2
Caswell La MK17. . . . . 60 F7
Catchpin St MK18 . . . . . . 52 F6
Catchpole Cl MK12. . . . . . 33 B5
Cater Rd HP14 . . . . 171 C4
Catesby Croft MK5 . . . . . . 46 C8
Cathay Cl MK3 . . . . 58 B7
Cathedral of Trees★
  MK15 . . . . 35 C5
Catherine Cotts HP23 . . . 133 E8
Catherine Ct MK18. . . . . . 41 E2
Catherines Cl UB7 . . . . . . 208 D4
Catkin Cl HP12. . . . . 172 B3
Catslip RG9. . . . . 179 A1
Caudery Pl 🄴 HP22 . . . . . 131 D6
Causeway The
  Bray SL6 . . . . 203 C4
  Marlow SL7 . . . . 183 E1
Causey Arch MK10 . . . . . . 36 C3
Cautley Cl HP22. . . . . 85 A5

Cavalier Ct HP4. . . . . 135 C4
Cavalier Rd OX9 . . . . 126 A1
Cavalry Cres SL4. . . . . . . 210 C4
Cavan Way MK10. . . . . . . 36 A4
Cavendish Cl
  Burnham SL6 . . . . 204 A7
  Little Chalfont HP6 . . . . . . 166 B8
  Wendover HP22. . . . . 131 B6
Cavendish Ct
  Milton Keynes MK5 . . . . . . 46 A7
  Poyle SL3 . . . . 212 E6
Cavendish Rd HP4 . . . . . . 135 E4
Cavendish Way 🄴 HP19 . 100 F1
Cavendish Wlk OX9 . . . . . 126 B1
Cavenham MK8 . . . . 33 F2
Caversham Gn 🏫 HP20. . 101 D1
Cawardon MK14 . . . . 34 C7
Cawcott Dr SL4. . . . . 209 E6
Cawdor Rise MK4 . . . . . . 45 E2
Cawkwell Way MK2. . . . . . 58 C8
Caxton Ct RG9 . . . . 191 E1
Caxton Dr UB8 . . . . 201 D3
Caxton Rd MK12 . . . . 33 B7
Cayman Wk MK3. . . . . . . 58 B3
Cecil Rd SL0 . . . . 207 E7
Cecils Yd 🄷 MK18 . . . . . . 41 D1
Cecil Way SL2 . . . . 197 F1
Cecily Cl HP4 . . . . 134 E4
Cecily Ct MK5. . . . . 46 A5
Cedar 🄳 RG9 . . . . 191 D2
Cedar Ave
  Hazelmere HP15 . . . . 163 A5
  West Drayton UB7. . . . . . . 208 F6
Cedar Chase SL6. . . . . . . 196 D1
Cedar Cl
  Aylesbury HP20 . . . . 102 A2
  Burnham SL1 . . . . 197 C1
  Chesham HP5 . . . . 144 E1
  Iver Heath SL0 . . . . 200 C4
  Milton Keynes MK19 . . . . . 32 B7
Cedar Ct
  Gerrards Cross SL9 . . . . . 188 E7
  High Wycombe HP13 . . . . . 173 B7
  Maidenhead SL6 . . . . 202 D7
  Marlow SL7 . . . . 183 E2
  🄶 Windsor SL4 . . . . 210 A5
Cedar Dr
  Chesham HP5 . . . . 144 A1
  Cookham Rise SL6 . . . . . . 195 F7
  Cookham SL6. . . . . 196 A4
  Marlow Bottom SL7 . . . . . 183 C7
Cedar Gr
  Amersham HP7 . . . . 165 D8
  Bellingdon HP5 . . . . 143 D8
Cedar Lodge Dr MK12 . . . 33 D7
Cedar Park Sch HP15 . . . 162 F5
Cedar Rd HP4 . . . . 135 D3
Cedar Ridge HP6 . . . . 153 C5
Cedars Cl
  Akeley MK18 . . . . 41 F8
  Chalfont St Peter SL9 . . . . 177 E5
Cedars Dr UB10. . . . . 201 F3
Cedars Ho SL6. . . . . 203 A7
Cedars Prim Sch MK16 . . 22 C4
Cedars Rd SL6 . . . . 203 A7
Cedars The
  Berkhamsted HP4 . . . . . . 135 E4
  Slough SL2. . . . . 197 F2
  Tring HP23. . . . . 119 B4
  Wendover HP22. . . . . 131 A5
Cedars Upper Sch & Com
  Coll LU7. . . . . 80 E5
Cedars Village WD3. . . . . 167 F5
Cedars Way
  Leighton Buzzard LU7 . . . . 80 E5
  Newport Pagnell MK16 . . . 22 C4
Cedars Wlk WD3. . . . . . . 167 F5
Cedar Terr 🄳 HP11 . . . . . 172 F7
Cedar Way
  Berkhamsted HP4 . . . . . . 135 D3
  Slough SL3. . . . . 206 E2
Ceely Ho HP21 . . . . 115 D6
Ceely Rd HP21. . . . . 115 D6
Celandine Ct MK7. . . . . . . 48 A5
Celina Cl MK2 . . . . 58 C7
Cell Farm SL4 . . . . 211 B2
Cell Farm Ave SL4 . . . . . . 211 B2
Centenary Bsns Pk RG9 . 191 F1
Centenary Cotts HP27. . . 138 F7
Centenary Way HP6 . . . . . 154 F1
Central Ave
  Cranfield MK43 . . . . 24 E2
  Whipsnade LU6 . . . . 107 E8
Central Dr SL1 . . . . 204 F6
Central Est SL6 . . . . 202 E7
Central Est SL6 . . . . 202 E8
CENTRAL MILTON
  KEYNES 34 D1
Central Park Bsns Ctr
  HP13. . . . . 173 A8
Centre Par HP27. . . . . . . 139 C5
Centre The SL2. . . . . 198 C6
Centre Wlk HP15. . . . . . . 163 A3
Centurion Ct MK11. . . . . . 33 C6
Centurion Rdbt MK1 . . . . 47 C2
Century Ave
  Milton Keynes MK6 . . . . . . 46 E7
  Oldbrook MK6 . . . . 46 E8
Century Point HP12. . . . . . 172 C4
Cestreham Cres HP5 . . . . 144 D2
CHACKMORE 41 B4
Chacombe Pl HP9. . . . . . . 175 D5
Chadbone Cl HP20 . . . . . 115 D8
Chadds La MK6 . . . . 47 C8
Chadwell Path HP11 . . . . 116 C6
Chadwick Dr MK6. . . . . . . 47 B7
Chadwick Rd SL1 . . . . . . 206 D4
Chadwick St HP13 . . . . . . 162 D2

Chaffinch HP19 . . . . 101 F4
Chaff Rd HP22 . . . . 102 B2
Chaffron Way
  Leadenhall MK6. . . . . 46 F7
  Milton Keynes, Oakgrove MK6,
  MK10, MK15. . . . . 35 D1
  Milton Keynes, Shenley Lodge
  MK4, MK5, MK6 . . . . 46 C5
Chairborough Rd HP12 . . 172 D6
Chairborough Rd Nature
  Reserve★ HP12. . . . . 172 D5
Chairmakers Cl HP27. . . . 139 A1
Chalcot Pl MK8 . . . . 45 F8
Chalcott SL1. . . . . 205 E3
Chalet Cl HP4. . . . . 134 F4
Chalfont Ave HP6 . . . . . . 166 D8
Chalfont Cl MK13 . . . . 34 A6
CHALFONT COMMON 177 F6
Chalfont & Gerrards Cross
  Com Hospl SL9 . . . . 177 D2
Chalfont Ho HP7 . . . . 166 D7
Chalfont La
  Chorleywood WD3. . . . . . 167 B4
  Maple Cross WD3 . . . . . . 178 D3
Chalfont & Latimer Sta/U Sta
  HP7. . . . . 166 C8
Chalfont L Ctr SL9 . . . . . . 177 C2
Chalfont Rd
  Maple Cross SL9 . . . . 178 C7
  Seer Green HP9. . . . . 176 D5
CHALFONT ST GILES 177 C7
Chalfont St Giles Inf Sch 🏫
  HP8. . . . . 177 B7
Chalfont St Giles Jun Sch 🏫
  HP8. . . . . 177 B7
CHALFONT ST PETER . . . 177 F2
Chalfont St Peter Inf Sch 🏫
  SL9 . . . . 177 C1
Chalfont St Peter Jun Sch 🏫
  SL9 . . . . 177 D2
Chalfonts Com Coll The 🏫
  SL9 . . . . 177 C3
Chalfont Station Rd HP7 166 C7
Chalfont Way HP12 . . . . . 172 D3
Chalford Flats HP10. . . . . 185 F6
Chalford Way HP19 . . . . . 114 F8
Chalgrove Cl SL6 . . . . 203 B6
Chalgrove End HP22 . . . . 116 B1
Chalgrove Rd OX9 . . . . . . 126 A1
Chalgrove Wlk HP11 . . . . 115 C6
Chalkdell Dr MK5 . . . . 45 F4
Chalk Farm Rd HP14 . . . . 158 C3
Chalk Hill
  Chesham HP5 . . . . 144 B2
  Coleshill HP7 . . . . 164 F2
  Windsor SL4 . . . . 210 F6
Chalkhill Blue Cl HP19 . . 101 C4
Chalk La HP6, HP7 . . . . . . 153 B4
Chalklands SL8 . . . . 185 A4
Chalkpit La
  Chinnor OX39. . . . . 147 C5
  Marlow SL7 . . . . 183 B3
Chalk Pit La SL1. . . . . 197 B3
Chalkpits The HP10 . . . . . 185 E6
CHALKSHIRE. 130 C4
Chalkshire Cotts HP17 . . 130 C4
Chalkshire Rd HP17. . . . . 130 C4
Chalk Stream Rise HP6. . 155 A1
Chalkstream Way HP10. . 185 E7
Chalky Field HP14. . . . . . . 171 C3
Challacombe MK4 . . . . . . 46 D2
Challener Rd HP12. . . . . . 172 C3
Challenge Ho MK3 . . . . . . 47 B1
Challow Ct SL6 . . . . 195 D1
Chalmers Ave MK19 . . . . 20 D2
Chaloner Pl HP21. . . . . . . 115 D6
Chaloner Rd HP21 . . . . . . 115 D6
Chaloners Hill MK18 . . . . 63 D3
CHALVEY 205 C4
Chalvey Gdns SL1 . . . . . . 205 E4
Chalvey Gr SL1 . . . . 205 C4
Chalvey Pk SL1 . . . . 205 E4
Chalvey Road E SL1. . . . . 205 E4
Chalvey Road W SL1 . . . . 205 D4
Chalwell Ridge MK5. . . . . 46 B4
Chamberlain Rd HP19. . . 101 B1
Champflower MK4 . . . . . . 46 D3
Champney Cl SL3 . . . . . . 212 A4
Champneys Beauty Coll
  HP23. . . . . 133 E6
Chancellors HP7. . . . . . . 164 B5
Chancellors Cnr HP7 . . . 164 B5
Chancellors Rd HP19. . . . 101 C4
Chancery Cl MK13. . . . . . . 34 A4
Chancerygate Bsns Ctr
  MK1 . . . . 47 B3
Chancery Pl SL4. . . . . 210 D7
Chandlers Ct MK6. . . . . . . 47 E5
CHANDLERS HILL. 200 E3
Chandlers Quay SL6. . . . . 203 C8
Chandos Cl
  Buckingham MK18. . . . . . . 52 D7
  Little Chalfont HP6 . . . . . . 155 C1
Chandos Ct MK18 . . . . . . 52 D7
Chandos Mall 🄷 SL1 . . . 205 F4
Chandos Pl
  Milton Keynes MK2 . . . . . . 58 B8
  Wendover HP22. . . . . 131 B4
Chandos Rd MK18. . . . . . 52 D8
Channer Dr HP10 . . . . 163 B1
Channory Cl MK4 . . . . 46 A1
Chantry Cl
  Windsor SL4 . . . . 210 A4
  Woburn Sands MK17. . . . . 49 A6
Chantry Rd HP19. . . . . . . 101 C3
Chantry Rise 🄸 MK46 . . . 6 F3
Chantry The
  🄸🄱 Aylesbury HP20 . . . . . 115 D8

Chantry The *continued*
Uxbridge UB8. . . . . 201 F2
Chapel Arches SL6. . . . . . 203 A7
Chapel Cl
Blackthorn OX25 . . . . 81 A3
Little Gaddesden HP4 . . . . 121 D6
Chapel Cotts SL2 . . . . 199 B5
Chapel Crofts HP4 . . . . . . 134 E6
Chapel Ct SL6 . . . . 202 D4
Chapel Dr HP22. . . . . 117 E5
CHAPEL END. 118 C8
Chapel End La HP23. . . . . 118 C8
Chapel Farm NN7 . . . . 10 C6
Chapel Fields HP23 . . . . . 118 C8
Chapel Hill
Soulbury LU7 . . . . 69 E3
Speen HP27 . . . . 150 C4
Windsor SL4 . . . . 210 D6
Chapel Ho HP6 . . . . 153 C5
Chapel La
Akeley MK18 . . . . 41 F8
Chilton HP18 . . . . 111 B3
Drayton Parslow MK17 . . . . 68 B5
High Wycombe HP12. . . . . . 172 C8
Ivinghoe Aston LU7 . . . . 92 A1
Long Marston HP23. . . . . . 104 B4
Northall LU6. . . . . 92 A5
Pitch Green HP27 . . . . 138 B3
Rout's Green HP14 . . . . . . 148 E2
St Leonards HP23 . . . . 132 D3
Stoke Bruerne NN12 . . . . 9 A8
Stoke Mandeville HP22 . . . 116 A1
Stoke Poges SL2 . . . . 199 B5
Thornborough MK18 . . . . . . 54 B8
Totternhoe LU6 . . . . 92 F8
Turweston NN13 . . . . 38 B7
Walter's Ash HP14 . . . . . . 161 C7
Wendover HP22. . . . . 131 B4
Whitfield NN13 . . . . 26 D3
Chapel Rd
Flackwell Heath HP10 . . . . 185 A8
Ford HP17 . . . . 128 A7
Chapel Row HP14. . . . . . . 171 A7
Chapels Cl SL1. . . . . 204 E5
Chapel Sq LU7. . . . . 68 E1
Chapel St
Berkhamsted HP4 . . . . 135 D4
High Wycombe HP13. . . . . 161 D3
Marlow SL7 . . . . 183 E2
Slough SL1. . . . . 205 F4
Tring HP23. . . . . 118 F3
Uxbridge UB8. . . . . 201 C4
Woburn Sands MK17. . . . . . 49 B4
Chaplin Gr MK8. . . . . 45 D7
Chaplin Mews 7 SL3. . . . 206 F1
Chapman Ave MK14. . . . . . 35 A6
Chapman Cl
Aylesbury HP21 . . . . 115 B6
West Drayton UB7 . . . . 208 F3
Chapman La HP8, HP10 . . 185 A6
Chapmans Cres HP5 . . . . 144 A2
Chapmans Dr MK19 . . . . . . 32 B7
Chapmans Lea HP22 . . . . . 88 D5
Chappell Cl HP19 . . . . 101 D2
Chappel Mdw HP23 . . . . . 119 B6
Chapter MK6 . . . . 47 A5
Chapter Cl UB10 . . . . 201 F5
Chapter Ho MK6 . . . . 47 A5
Chapter Mews SL4 . . . . . . 210 D7
Charbray Cres MK5 . . . . . . 46 A4
Chardacre MK8 . . . . 33 E1
Charisse Gdns MK4 . . . . . . 45 D3
Charlbury Rd UB10. . . . . . 190 F1
Charles Cl HP21. . . . . 116 B4
Charles Dr OX9 . . . . 126 A1
Charles Gdns SL2 . . . . 206 A7
Charles Ho
Henley-on-Thames RG9. . . 191 E3
9 Windsor SL4. . . . . 210 C6
Charles Pym Rd HP19 . . . 101 C4
Charles St
Berkhamsted HP4 . . . . 135 B4
Tring HP23. . . . . 119 A3
Windsor SL4 . . . . 210 C6
Charlestown Lodge UB8 201 D6
Charles Warren Acad
MK6 . . . . 47 D5
Charles Way MK16 . . . . 22 C4
Charlewood Ho MK17 . . . . 49 B3
Charlock Ct MK16. . . . . 21 F4
Charlotte Ave SL2. . . . . . . 205 F6
Charlotte Cl LU7 . . . . 79 F2
Charlotte Cott SL6 . . . . . . 203 B8
Charlotte Way 12 SL7 . . . 183 E2
Charlton SL4 . . . . 209 C5
Charlton Cl
Slough SL1. . . . . 205 B4
Swanbourne MK17 . . . . 66 F3
Charlton Pl 2 SL4 . . . . . . 209 C5
Charlton Row 5 SL4. . . . . 209 C5
Charlton Sq 4 SL4. . . . . . 209 C5
Charlton Way SL4. . . . . . . 209 C5
Charlton Wlk 3 SL4 . . . . . 209 C5
Charmfield Rd HP21 . . . . 116 A5
CHARNDON. 72 E6
Charnwood Cl 5 HP13 . . . 173 F5
Charsley Cl HP6 . . . . 166 C8
Charter Cl 8 SL1 . . . . 205 F3
Charter Dr HP6 . . . . 154 F1
Charter Pl UB8 . . . . 201 D5
Charter Rd SL1 . . . . 204 E6
Chartley Ct MK5 . . . . 46 B4
CHARTRIDGE 143 C4
Chartridge Comb Sch
HP5. . . . . 143 C4
Chartridge Development
UB8. . . . . 201 B3
Chartridge Grange Dr
HP5 . . . . 143 D4
Chartridge Ho 3 HP13 . . 173 F6
Chartridge La HP5 . . . . . . 143 F2
Chartridge Park Mobile
Home Pk HP5 . . . . 143 D4
Chartwell Gate HP9 . . . . . 175 D2
Chartwell Rd MK16. . . . . . . 22 E4
Chase Ave MK7 . . . . 48 A4
Chase Cl HP7 . . . . 165 A4
Chase Farm Barns MK17. . 56 C4
Chase Park Rd NN7 . . . . 1 A5
Chaseport Cl MK46. . . . . 5 D2
Chaseside Cl LU7 . . . . 105 A7
Chase The
1 Chesham HP5. . . . . 144 B2
Maidenhead SL6 . . . . 195 D3
Marlow SL7 . . . . 184 A3
Tylers Green HP10. . . . . . . 163 C1
Chasewater Cres MK10. . . 36 B3
Chatfield SL2 . . . . 205 A8
Chatham Ct 2 SL1. . . . . . 206 A3
Chatsworth MK8 . . . . 33 F1
Chatsworth Cl SL6 . . . . . . 202 C5
Chaucer Cl
Berkhamsted HP4 . . . . 134 F5
Newport Pagnell MK16 . . . . 22 A4
Windsor SL4 . . . . 210 D4
Chaucer Dr HP21 . . . . 115 F6
Chaucer Rd MK3. . . . . 58 A7
Chaucer Way SL1 . . . . 205 F5
Chaundler Dr HP19 . . . . . 101 B4
Chauntry Cl SL6 . . . . 203 C6
Chauntry Rd SL6. . . . . 203 B6
Chawton Cres MK8. . . . . . . 33 F1
Cheapside La UB9 . . . . . . 189 F2
CHEARSLEY 112 A2
Chearsley Rd HP18. . . . . . 125 E7
CHEDDINGTON. 105 B7
Cheddington Comb Sch
LU7. . . . . 105 A7
Cheddington Gr HP22 . . . 102 B2
Cheddington La HP23 . . . 104 C5
Cheddington Rd LU7 . . . . 105 C4
Cheddington Sta LU7 . . . . 91 A2
Chelmsford Ct 8 SL4 . . . 210 C5
Chelsea Gn LU7. . . . . 80 D6
Chelsea Ho 6 LU7 . . . . 80 E7
Chelsea Rd HP19. . . . . 100 E1
Cheltenham Gdns MK3 . . . 57 D6
Cheney Cl LU7 . . . . 78 B1
Cheneys Wlk MK3. . . . . 47 A2
Cheney Way HP20. . . . . . . 101 E1
Cheney Wlk 3 HP20 . . . . 101 F2
CHENIES 156 B2
Chenies Ave HP6. . . . . 166 D8
CHENIES BOTTOM. 156 B2
Chenies Manor Ho★
WD3 . . . . 156 A1
Chenies Par HP7. . . . . 166 C7
Chenies Rd WD3 . . . . 167 D7
Chenies Sch WD3 . . . . 156 B1
Chenille Dr HP11 . . . . 173 E4
Cheniston Gr SL6 . . . . 202 A7
Chepping Cl HP10. . . . . . . 163 A1
Chepping View Prim Acad
HP12. . . . . 172 D3
Chepstow Dr MK3. . . . . 57 D6
Chequers Ave HP11 . . . . . 173 E5
Chequers Bridge Cotts
SL0. . . . . 207 C4
Chequers Cl LU7 . . . . 105 C4
Chequers Ct HP21. . . . . . . 115 E4
Chequers Dr HP16 . . . . . . 151 C6
Chequers End MK18. . . . . . 66 A4
Chequers Hill HP7 . . . . . . 165 D7
Chequers La
Ibstone HP14, RG9 . . . . . . 170 A5
North Crawley MK16. . . . . . 24 B6
Pitstone LU7 . . . . 105 C5
Prestwood HP16 . . . . 151 C7
Chequers Orch SL0 . . . . . 207 F7
Chequers Sq UB8 . . . . 201 C5
Chequers The
Castlethorpe MK19 . . . . 19 F5
Eaton Bray LU6 . . . . 92 F5
Cherington Gate SL6. . . . 195 B1
Cheriton MK4. . . . . 46 E3
Cherleton MK8. . . . . 33 E1
Cherries The SL2 . . . . 206 B7
Cherry Acre SL9 . . . . 177 D6
Cherry Ave SL3 . . . . 206 D4
Cherry Cl
Flackwell Heath HP10 . . . . 185 B7
Prestwood HP16 . . . . 151 D6
Cherry Cnr HP10. . . . . 185 B8
Cherrycroft Dr HP14 . . . . 161 D6
Cherry Dr HP9 . . . . 175 B4
Cherryfields HP6. . . . . 155 B1
Cherry Gdns HP23 . . . . . . 118 F3
Cherry Gr HP15 . . . . 163 C6
Cherry La
Amersham HP7 . . . . 165 A7
West Drayton UB7. . . . . . . 208 F2
Woodrow HP7 . . . . 164 D6
Cherry Lane Prim Sch
UB7. . . . . 208 F2
Cherry Leys MK18. . . . . 63 E3
Cherry Orch
Amersham HP6 . . . . 154 E2
Olney MK46 . . . . 6 E4
Prestwood HP16 . . . . 151 C6
Stoke Poges SL2 . . . . 199 A5
West Drayton UB7. . . . . . . 208 E4
Cherry Orchard Ct HP13. 173 E6
Cherry Pit The HP13 . . . . 161 E2
Cherry Rd MK16. . . . . 22 B3
Cherry Rise
Chalfont St Giles HP8 . . . . 177 D8
Flackwell Heath HP10 . . . . 185 B7
Cherry St HP13 . . . . 174 A4
Cherry Tree Ave UB7. . . . 208 F7
Cherry Tree Cl
Great Kingshill HP15 . . . . . 151 D1
Hughenden Valley HP14 . . 162 A7
Speen HP27 . . . . 150 B5
Cherry Tree Ho 4 SL7 . . 183 D2
Cherrytree La
Chalfont St Peter SL9 . . . . 177 D1
Iver Heath SL0 . . . . 201 A4
Cherry Tree La
Buckland Common HP23 . . 133 A3
Fulmer SL3. . . . . 199 F6
Heronsgate WD3 . . . . 167 C1
Lee Common HP16 . . . . . . 142 E4
Cherry Tree Rd
Beaconsfield HP9 . . . . 175 B1
Chinnor OX39. . . . . 147 C6
Farnham Common SL2. . . . 198 C5
Cherry Tree Way HP10 . . 163 C1
Cherry Tree Wlk
Chesham HP5 . . . . 144 D2
Leighton Buzzard LU7 . . . . . 80 E7
Wendover HP22. . . . . 131 A5
Cherry Way
Hazelmere HP15 . . . . 163 A6
Horton SL3. . . . . 212 C4
Cherrywood Cl HP9 . . . . . 176 D5
Cherrywood Gdns HP10 . 185 B8
Chervil MK6 . . . . 47 B5
Cherwell Cl
Maidenhead SL6 . . . . 203 A8
Slough SL3. . . . . 212 B8
Cherwell Ho MK3 . . . . 57 E8
Cherwell Rd
Aylesbury HP21 . . . . 115 C6
Bourne End SL8 . . . . 185 B4
CHESHAM 154 C8
Chesham Ave MK13 . . . . . . 34 C3
CHESHAM BOIS 154 C3
Chesham Bois CE Comb Sch
HP6. . . . . 154 D4
Chesham Grammar Sch
HP5. . . . . 144 D1
Chesham La
Chalfont St Peter SL9 . . . . 177 E6
Wendover HP22, HP16 . . . 141 E8
Chesham L Ctr HP5 . . . . . 154 D8
Chesham Mus★ HP5 . . . . 154 B8
Chesham Prep Sch HP5 . 145 A4
Chesham Rd
Amersham HP6 . . . . 154 C2
Ashley Green PH4, PH5. . . 144 F8
Bellingdon HP5 . . . . 143 E7
Berkhamsted HP4 . . . . 135 B2
Bovingdon HP3, HP5 . . . . . 145 E4
Hyde Heath HP16 . . . . 153 C7
Wigginton HP23. . . . . 133 D7
Chesham U Sta HP5. . . . . 154 C8
Cheshire Cotts OX27 . . . . . 72 F6
Cheshire Ct 6 SL1. . . . . . 206 B4
Cheshire Rise MK3. . . . . . . 46 E1
Cheslyn Gdns MK14 . . . . . . 35 A8
Chesney Wold MK6 . . . . . . 46 F5
Chessbury Cl HP5 . . . . 154 A7
Chessbury Rd HP5 . . . . . . 154 A7
Chess Cl
Aylesbury HP21 . . . . 115 D3
Latimer HP5. . . . . 155 D3
Chessfield Pk HP6 . . . . . . 166 E8
CHESSMOUNT 154 E7
Chessmount Rise HP5. . . 154 D6
Chester Cl MK3 . . . . 57 D7
Chesterfield Cl HP17 . . . . 114 C5
Chesterfield Cres LU7. . . . . 79 E3
Chesterfield Pl HP19 . . . . 115 B8
Chester Ho UB8. . . . . 201 C1
Chesterholm MK13. . . . . . . 33 F5
Chester Rd SL1 . . . . 205 D7
Chesterton Cl HP5 . . . . . . 144 B2
Chesterton Gn HP9 . . . . . 175 E2
Chestnut Ave
Chesham HP5 . . . . 144 E2
Halton HP22 . . . . 131 D8
High Wycombe HP11. . . . . 173 D5
Slough SL3. . . . . 206 E4
West Drayton UB7. . . . . . . 208 F6
Chestnut Cl
Amersham HP6 . . . . 154 D2
Aston Clinton HP22 . . . . . . 117 F5
Chalfont St Peter SL9 . . . . 177 F2
Dagnall HP4. . . . . 107 C5
Maidenhead SL6 . . . . 196 B1
Medmenham SL7. . . . . 193 D7
Milton Keynes MK11 . . . . . . 32 D5
Monks Risborough HP27 . . 139 C5
Newton Longville MK17. . . . . 57 D2
Waddesdon HP18 . . . . 99 A6
Chestnut Cotts MK18. . . . . . 52 C7
Chestnut Cres
Aylesbury HP21 . . . . 115 D6
Milton Keynes MK2 . . . . 58 D7
Chestnut Ct HP6 . . . . 154 D2
Chestnut Dr
Berkhamsted HP4 . . . . 135 D3
Windsor SL4 . . . . 209 F3
Chestnut End HP22. . . . . . 117 C1
Chestnut Gn NN13 . . . . 26 E4
Chestnut Hill LU7 . . . . 80 D8
Chestnut La
Amersham HP6 . . . . 154 E2
Hazelmere HP15 . . . . 163 B5
Chestnut Lane Sch HP6 . 154 E3
Chestnut Leys MK18. . . . . . 63 E3
Chestnut Pk SL6 . . . . 203 E3
Chestnut Rd
Beaconsfield HP9 . . . . 175 B1
Princes Risborough HP27 . 139 C3
Yardley Gobion NN12. . . . . . 18 F6
Chestnut Rise LU7 . . . . 80 D8
Chestnuts Mill Farm
Courtyard The M19 . . . . . 32 B1
Chestnuts Prim Sch MK3 . 57 E7
Chestnuts The
Castlethorpe MK19 . . . . 19 F5
Felden HP3 . . . . 146 F7
Uxbridge UB10. . . . . 201 E5
Chestnut View MK18 . . . . . 74 F7
Chestnut Way
Longwick HP27 . . . . 138 E6
Stoke Mandeville HP22 . . . 116 A1
Chestnut Wlk SL9. . . . . . . 177 E3
Chestwood Gr UB10. . . . . 201 F5
Chettle Pl NN12. . . . . 18 E2
CHETWODE. 61 E8
Chetwode Ave MK10 . . . . . 36 B1
Chetwode Cl MK18. . . . . . . 41 E2
Chetwynd Dr UB10. . . . . . 201 F3
Chevalier Gr MK8 . . . . 45 D7
Cheveley Gdns SL1. . . . . . 197 C3
Cheviot Cl
High Wycombe HP13. . . . . 161 E1
Leighton Buzzard LU7 . . . . . 80 C8
Maidenhead SL6 . . . . 203 B6
Cheviot Gdns MK14 . . . . . . 21 C1
Cheviot Rd SL3 . . . . 207 A1
Cheyne Cl
Amersham HP6 . . . . 154 D3
Buckingham MK18. . . . . 41 F1
Gerrards Cross SL9. . . . . . 188 E3
Pitstone LU7 . . . . 105 D4
Cheyne Mews HP5 . . . . . . 154 D8
Cheyne Wlk HP5 . . . . 154 D8
CHICHELEY 23 C8
Chicheley Hall★ MK16. . . . 23 D8
Chicheley Hill MK16. . . . . . 23 A8
Chicheley Rd MK16. . . . . . . 23 E7
Chicheley St MK16 . . . . 22 E4
Chichester Cl HP13 . . . . . 173 D6
Chichester Ct SL1. . . . . . . 206 A4
Chicksands Ave MK10 . . . . 36 A2
Chievely Ct MK4 . . . . 46 C1
Chilcote La HP7. . . . . 166 A8
Childs Way MK4, MK5, MK6,
MK10 . . . . 46 C7
Chillery Leys MK15. . . . . . . 35 E7
Chillingham Ct MK5. . . . . . 46 A4
Chiltern Ave
Amersham HP6 . . . . 154 D1
Edlesborough LU6 . . . . 92 E3
High Wycombe HP12. . . . . 172 D6
Stone HP17 . . . . 114 D5
Chiltern Brewery The★
HP17. . . . . 130 C5
Chiltern Bsns Village
UB8. . . . . 201 B3
Chiltern Cl
Berkhamsted HP4 . . . . 134 F5
Princes Risborough HP27 . 139 A3
Stone HP17 . . . . 114 D5
Wendover HP22. . . . . 131 B5
Chiltern Cnr HP4. . . . . 135 A5
Chiltern Commerce Ctr
HP5. . . . . 144 A2
Chiltern Cotts
Buckland Common HP23 . . 133 A2
Ibstone HP14. . . . . 169 D7
Chiltern Court Mews
SL4. . . . . 210 B6
Chiltern Ct
Amersham HP6 . . . . 154 C2
Chesham HP5 . . . . 144 A2
5 High Wycombe HP12 . . . 172 E7
Wendover HP22. . . . . 131 B4
Windsor SL4 . . . . 210 B6
Winslow MK18. . . . . 65 F3
Chiltern Dr
Rickmansworth WD3 . . . . . 167 F2
Stokenchurch HP14. . . . . . 158 F4
Chiltern Gn HP10 . . . . 185 A8
Chiltern Hill SL9 . . . . 177 E2
Chiltern Hills Acad HP5 . 144 A1
Chiltern Hills Rd HP9. . . . 175 C2
Chiltern Ho HP5 . . . . 154 C7
Chiltern Hospl The (BMI)
HP16. . . . . 152 C4
Chiltern Hts HP7 . . . . 166 A8
Chiltern Manor Pk HP16. 152 A7
Chiltern Open Air Mus★
HP8. . . . . 177 F8
Chiltern Par HP6. . . . . 154 C2
Chiltern Park Ave HP4 . . 135 A6
Chiltern Pools The HP6. . 154 D1
Chiltern Rd
Amersham HP6 . . . . 154 B4
Ballinger Common HP16 . . 142 E3
Burnham SL1 . . . . 204 B8
Maidenhead SL6 . . . . 203 B6
Marlow SL7 . . . . 183 C2
Wendover HP22. . . . . 131 B5
Wingrave HP22 . . . . 89 A3
Chiltern Ridge HP14 . . . . 158 C4
Chilterns
Berkhamsted HP4 . . . . 134 F6
World's End HP22 . . . . 130 F7
Chilterns Cl HP10 . . . . 185 B7
Chilterns Gateway Ctr★
LU6. 93 F4
Chilterns Pk SL8 . . . . 185 B5
Chiltern St HP21 . . . . 115 E6
Chilterns The (Sh Ctr)
HP13. . . . . 173 A7
Chiltern Valley Winery &
Brewery★ RG9. . . . . 180 F7
Chiltern View
Chinnor OX39. . . . . 147 D5
Saunderton HP14 . . . . 149 C1
Chiltern View Rd UB8 . . . 201 D3
Chiltern Villas HP23. . . . . 118 E2
Chiltern Way
Aston Clinton HP22 . . . . . . 117 F2
Tring HP23. . . . . 119 C5
Chiltern Way Acad HP22 131 C3
Chiltern Way Acad
(Prestwood Campus)
HP16. . . . . 151 D5
Chiltern Wood Sch HP12 172 E4
CHILTON 111 A4
Chilton Cl
Holmer Green HP15 . . . . . 163 C7
Tylers Green HP10. . . . . . . 163 C2
Chilton Ct SL6 . . . . 204 C7
Chilton Pl HP20. . . . . 101 E1
Chilton Rd
Chearsley HP18. . . . . 112 A2
Chesham HP5 . . . . 144 C2
Long Crendon HP18. . . . . . 125 C7
Chilwick Rd SL2 . . . . 197 F1
Chimes Sh Ctr The UB8. . 201 D5
Chimes The HP12 . . . . 172 E6
Chimney La HP10 . . . . 185 E8
Chimney Mdws MK18. . . . . 73 B5
Chinalls Cl MK18. . . . . 50 D6
Chingle Croft MK4 . . . . 46 C2
Chinneck Ho HP4 . . . . 135 C4
CHINNOR. 147 D7
Chinnor Hill OX39. . . . . . . 147 E4
Chinnor Hill Wildlife
Reserve★ OX39. . . . . 147 F5
Chinnor & Princes
Risborough Rly★ OX39 . 147 E7
Chinnor Rd
Bledlow HP27 . . . . 138 A2
Bledlow Ridge HP14 . . . . . 148 C3
Chinnor OX39. . . . . 147 A4
Chinnor Sta★ OX39 . . . . . 147 D5
Chippendale Cl HP13. . . . 162 D1
Chippendale Waye UB8 . 201 D5
Chippenham Dr MK10 . . . . 36 C1
CHIPPERFIELD 156 F8
Chipperfield Cl MK13. . . . . 34 A7
Chipperfield Rd HP3 . . . . 146 C3
Chipping Vale MK4. . . . . . . 46 C2
Chipstead SL9 . . . . 177 C2
Chirbury Cl MK10 . . . . 35 F1
CHISBRIDGE CROSS 182 D6
Chislehampton MK15. . . . . 35 C3
Chiswick Cl MK4. . . . . 45 F2
Chiswick Lodge 6 SL7. . . 183 D2
CHIVERY 132 C4
Choke La SL6. . . . . 195 B4
CHOLESBURY 133 C3
Cholesbury La HP23. . . . . 133 A2
Cholesbury Rd HP23 . . . . 133 D5
Chorley Rd HP14. . . . . 160 E3
CHORLEYWOOD. 167 D5
CHORLEYWOOD
BOTTOM. 167 C3
Chorleywood Bottom
WD3. . . . . 167 D4
Chorleywood Comm Nature
Reserve★ WD3 . . . . 167 E5
Chorleywood Ho WD3. . . 167 E6
Chorleywood House Dr
WD3. . . . . 167 E6
Chorleywood House Est
Nature Reserve★ WD3 . 167 F6
Chorleywood Montessori Sch
The WD3 . . . . 167 E7
Chorleywood Prim Sch
WD3 . . . . 167 C3
Chorleywood Sta/U Sta
WD3 . . . . 167 D5
CHORLEYWOOD WEST . . . 167 A4
Chrislaine Cl TW19. . . . . . 213 D1
Christ Church Chorleywood
CE Sch WD3 . . . . 167 F6
Christchurch Gr MK12. . . . 33 B6
Christchurch Ho 15
HP23 . . . . 119 A3
Christchurch Rd HP23. . . 118 F4
Christian Ct MK15. . . . . 35 D7
Christian Smith Ho SL6. . 202 A1
Christian Sq 4 SL4 . . . . . . 210 C6
Christie Cl MK16 . . . . 22 A5
Christies Ct 2 HP13 . . . . 173 B7
Christine Ho 3 MK2 . . . . . 58 C8
CHRISTMAS COMMON . . . 168 B7
Christmas La 1 SL2. . . . . 198 C8
Christopher Cl HP14 . . . . 161 D7
Christopher Ho 2 SL2 . . 198 C7
Christ the Sower Ecumenical
Prim Sch MK8 . . . . 45 D6
Chrysalis Theatre The★
MK15 . . . . 35 C6
Church Ave RG9 . . . . 191 E2
Church Cl
Aston Clinton HP22 . . . . . . 117 D5
Cuddington HP18. . . . . 112 F3
Eton SL4. . . . . 210 D8
Maidenhead SL6 . . . . 202 D6
Maids Moreton MK18 . . . . . 41 F3
Uxbridge UB8. . . . . 201 B3
West Drayton UB7. . . . . . . 208 E3
Wicken MK19. . . . . 31 B3
Church Cotts SL6 . . . . 196 E2
Church Croft LU6 . . . . 92 E3

Church Ct
Aylesbury HP22 . . . . **116** B2
High Wycombe HP13 . . . . . **162** D1
Church Dr SL6 . . . . **203** C4
CHURCH END
Chorleywood **156** F1
Drayton Parslow **68** B5
Haddenham **127** A5
Hanslope **11** A2
Long Crendon **125** C7
Pitstone **105** D3
Steeple Claydon **63** E2
Totternhoe **93** B7
Church End
Adstock MK18 . . . . **53** F1
Bledlow HP27 . . . . **138** B1
Drayton Parslow MK17 . . . **68** B5
Edlesborough LU6 . . . . . . **92** E3
Haddenham HP17 . . . . . . **127** A5
Hillesden MK18 . . . . **63** B6
Leckhampstead MK18 . . . . **42** D8
Newton Longville MK17 . . . **57** D3
Potterspury NN12 . . . . **18** E3
Sherington MK16 . . . . **14** A2
Syresham NN13 . . . . **27** C8
Wavendon MK17 . . . . **48** E7
Church End Cotts WD3 . . **156** F1
Church End Farm LU6 . . . **93** B7
Church End Rd MK5 . . . . **46** A4
Church Farm Cl HP22 . . . **102** B3
Church Farm Cres MK14 . **34** E8
Church Farm Ho HP8 . . . . **177** C7
Church Farm La HP23 . . . **104** F3
Churchfield Mews SL2 . . **206** A4
Churchfield Rd SL9 . . . . . **177** D2
Churchgates 3 HP4 . . . . **135** C4
Church Gn
Long Crendon HP18 . . . . . **125** D7
Totternhoe LU6 . . . . **93** B7
Church Gr
Little Chalfont HP6 . . . . . . **166** E8
Slough SL3 . . . . **206** C8
Church Green Rd MK3 . . . **58** A8
Church Headland La
HP22 . . . . **87** A6
CHURCH HILL **56** A8
Church Hill
Akeley MK18 . . . . **41** F8
Aspley Guise MK17 . . . . . . **49** E5
Cheddington LU7 . . . . **105** A8
Ellesborough HP17 . . . . . . **130** B2
Milton Keynes MK8 . . . . . . **33** F2
Pishill RG9 . . . . **179** D8
South Harefield UB9 . . . . . **190** C8
Whaddon MK17 . . . . **45** B1
Church Holt The SL2 . . . . **187** E3
Churchill Ave HP21 . . . . . **115** D5
Churchill Cl HP10 . . . . . . **185** B7
Churchill Ct 1 HP21 . . . . **115** E7
Churchill Dr
Beaconsfield HP9 . . . . **175** C5
Marlow SL7 . . . . **183** F4
Churchill Ho UB7 . . . . . . **208** D6
Churchill Rd SL3 . . . . . . **206** F2
Church La
Alderton NN12 . . . . **9** A2
Aston Clinton HP22 . . . . . **117** D4
Berkhamsted HP4 . . . . . . **135** C4
Bisham SL7 . . . . **194** F7
Bledlow Ridge HP14 . . . . . **159** F8
Bovingdon HP3 . . . . **146** B4
Bray SL6 . . . . **203** C4
Chalfont St Peter SL9 . . . . **177** D2
Chearsley HP18 . . . . **112** B1
Cheddington LU7 . . . . **105** A8
Chinnor OX39 . . . . **147** D6
Clifton Reynes MK46 . . . . . . **7** C3
Cryers Hill HP15 . . . . **162** C4
Deanshanger MK19 . . . . . . **31** E4
Eaton Bray LU6 . . . . **92** E6
Edgcott HP18 . . . . **72** F2
Emberton MK46 . . . . **13** F7
Grafton Regis NN12 . . . . . . **9** D2
Granborough MK18 . . . . . . **75** F6
Great Horwood MK17 . . . . **55** A3
Great Kimble HP17 . . . . . . **129** E1
Great Missenden HP16 . . . **152** B7
Hastoe HP23 . . . . **132** F7
Horton-cum-S OX33 . . . . . **108** A5
Lacey Green HP27 . . . . . . **149** E4
Lillingstone Lovell MK18 . . . **30** A6
Ludgershall HP18 . . . . **96** C7
Marsworth HP23 . . . . **104** F1
Milton Keynes MK5 . . . . . . **46** B8
Mixbury NN13 . . . . **38** D1
Mursley MK17 . . . . **67** D5
Newport Pagnell MK16 . . . **22** D7
Oving HP22 . . . . **86** C7
Padbury MK18 . . . . **53** C2
Potterspury NN12 . . . . **18** E3
Princes Risborough HP27 . . **139** B4
Radnage HP14 . . . . **159** D8
Sarratt WD3 . . . . **156** F1
Slough SL2, SL3 . . . . **206** C8
Soulbury LU7 . . . . **69** E2
Stoke Bruerne NN12 . . . . . . **9** A8
Stoke Goldington MK16 . . . **12** A4
Stoke Poges SL2 . . . . **198** F2
Thornborough MK18 . . . . . **54** A8
Tingewick MK18 . . . . **51** B7
Upper Winchendon HP18 . . **99** B1
Uxbridge UB8 . . . . **201** B3
Walter's Ash HP14 . . . . . . **161** E4
Walton MK7 . . . . **47** F6
Wendover HP22 . . . . **131** C3

Church La continued
Weston Turville HP22 . . . . **116** F1
West Wycombe HP14 . . . . **161** A2
Whaddon MK17 . . . . **45** B1
Whitchurch HP22 . . . . **87** A6
Wicken MK19 . . . . **31** B3
8 Windsor SL4 . . . . **210** D6
Yardley Hastings NN7 . . . . . . **1** B7
Church Lees MK14 . . . . . . **21** D1
Churchmead Sch SL3 . . . **211** B7
Churchmere Wlk HP21 . . . **115** C6
Church Pas MK16 . . . . . . **22** D4
Church Path
Cheddington LU7 . . . . **91** A1
Cublington LU7 . . . . **78** B1
Lane End HP14 . . . . **171** B4
Prestwood HP16 . . . . **151** D5
Stokenchurch HP14 . . . . . **158** D5
Church Rd
Aspley Heath MK17 . . . . . . **49** B3
Bow Brickhill MK17 . . . . . . **48** D1
Brackley NN13 . . . . **38** A7
Chinnor OX39 . . . . **147** D6
Cookham Dean SL6 . . . . . **195** B6
Farnham Royal SL2 . . . . . **198** C2
Ickford HP18 . . . . **123** F3
Iver Heath SL0 . . . . **200** C3
Ivinghoe LU7 . . . . **105** F5
Lane End HP14 . . . . **171** B3
Leighton Buzzard LU7 . . . . **80** E6
Lewknor OX49 . . . . **157** B8
Little Gaddesden HP4 . . . . **121** D8
Little Marlow SL7 . . . . **184** C5
Maidenhead SL6 . . . . **203** B5
Old Windsor SL4 . . . . **211** B2
Penn HP10 . . . . **174** E7
Pitstone LU7 . . . . **105** E3
Seer Green HP9 . . . . **176** D4
Sherington MK16 . . . . **13** F2
Slapton LU7 . . . . **91** D6
South Harefield UB9 . . . . . **190** C8
Stoke Hammond MK17 . . . **69** D8
Stokenchurch HP14 . . . . . **158** D5
Thame OX9 . . . . **125** E1
Totternhoe LU6 . . . . **93** B6
Tylers Green HP10 . . . . . . **174** C8
Uxbridge UB8 . . . . **201** D1
West Drayton UB7 . . . . . . **208** E3
Church Row SL3 . . . . **199** D8
Churchside HP15 . . . . **163** D7
Church Sq
7 High Wycombe HP11 . . . **173** B7
Leighton Buzzard LU7 . . . . **80** F6
Church St
Amersham HP7 . . . . **165** B7
Aspley Guise MK17 . . . . . . **49** E5
16 Aylesbury HP20 . . . . . **115** D8
Bovingdon HP3 . . . . **146** B4
Brill HP18 . . . . **110** B8
Buckingham MK18 . . . . . . **52** C8
Burnham SL1 . . . . **197** C1
Chesham HP5 . . . . **154** B7
Gawcott MK18 . . . . **52** A4
Great Missenden HP16 . . . **153** A1
Henley-on-Thames RG9 . . . **191** D1
High Wycombe HP11 . . . . **173** B7
Little Horwood MK17 . . . . . **55** E2
Maids Moreton MK18 . . . . **41** F3
Marsh Gibbon OX27 . . . . . **71** F3
Milton Keynes, Fenny Stratford
MK2 . . . . **47** E1
Milton Keynes, New Bradwell
MK13 . . . . **33** F7
Milton Keynes, Stony Stratford
MK11 . . . . **32** D5
Milton Keynes, Wolverton
MK12 . . . . **33** D7
North Marston MK18 . . . . . **76** B2
6 Olney MK46 . . . . **6** F3
Olney MK46 . . . . **7** A3
Princes Risborough HP27 . **139** B3
Quainton HP22 . . . . **85** B5
Slough, Chalvey SL1 . . . . **205** D4
Slough, Upton Park SL1 . . **205** F4
Stokenchurch HP14 . . . . . **158** D5
Twyford MK18 . . . . **62** C2
6 Windsor SL4 . . . . **210** D6
Wing LU7 . . . . **79** E2
Wingrave HP22 . . . . **89** B2
Winslow MK18 . . . . **65** F4
Church Terr
Turvey MK43 . . . . **8** E5
Windsor SL4 . . . . **209** E5
Church View
Brackley NN13 . . . . **38** A7
Edlesborough LU6 . . . . . . **92** D3
Halton HP22 . . . . **117** C1
Long Marston HP23 . . . . . **104** A4
Newport Pagnell MK16 . . . **22** D4
9 Slough SL1 . . . . **206** A3
Steeple Claydon MK18 . . . **63** E2
Church View Ct LU7 . . . . . **80** E6
Church Views SL6 . . . . . . **202** F8
Churchway HP17 . . . . **127** A6
Church Way
East Claydon MK18 . . . . . . **74** F8
Stone HP17 . . . . **114** C5
Church Wlk
Milton Keynes MK3 . . . . . . **57** F7
North Crawley MK16 . . . . . **24** B6
Weston Turville HP22 . . . . **116** F1
Wing LU7 . . . . **79** E2
Winslow MK18 . . . . **65** F4
Church Yd HP23 . . . . **119** A3
Churston 1 MK10 . . . . . . **36** C3
Chyne The SL9 . . . . **188** F6
Cicero Cres MK11 . . . . . . **32** F3
Cinnamon Cl SL4 . . . . . . **209** F6

Cinnamon Gr MK7 . . . . . . **48** A5
CIPPENHAM **204** F4
Cippenham Cl SL1 . . . . . **204** F6
Cippenham Inf Sch SL1 . . **204** D6
Cippenham La SL1 . . . . . **205** B5
Cippenham Prim Sch
SL1 . . . . **204** D6
City Rd HP14 . . . . **159** D6
CITY THE **159** D6
Clailey Ct MK11 . . . . **32** F5
Claires Court Girls Schs
SL6 . . . . **202** E7
Claires Court Sch SL6 . . . **196** B1
Clammas Way UB8 . . . . . **208** D8
Clapham Pl MK13 . . . . . . **34** C2
Clappers Mdw SL6 . . . . . **196** B1
Clappins La
Naphill HP14 . . . . **150** D1
Walter's Ash HP14 . . . . . . **161** C8
Clapton App HP10 . . . . . . **185** D8
Clare Croft MK10 . . . . **36** A3
Clare Dr SL2 . . . . **198** B8
Clarefield Cl SL6 . . . . **195** A1
Clarefield Rd SL6 . . . . . . **195** A1
Claremont SL3 . . . . **212** D6
Claremont Ave MK11 . . . . **32** E4
Claremont Cl HP21 . . . . . **115** F5
Claremont Gdns SL7 . . . . **183** E2
Claremont Rd
Marlow SL7 . . . . **183** E2
Windsor SL4 . . . . **210** C5
Clarence Cres SL4 . . . . . **210** C6
Clarence Ct
9 High Wycombe HP13 . . . **173** B7
Maidenhead SL6 . . . . **202** E8
Windsor SL4 . . . . **210** B6
Clarence Ho 2 MK9 . . . . . **34** C2
Clarence Rd
Berkhamsted HP4 . . . . . . **135** C4
Henley-on-Thames RG9 . . . **191** D2
Milton Keynes MK11 . . . . . **32** E5
Windsor SL4 . . . . **210** B6
Clarendon Copse SL6 . . . **202** D6
Clarendon Ct
Slough SL2 . . . . **206** B6
Windsor SL4 . . . . **210** B6
Clarendon Dr
Milton Keynes MK8 . . . . . . **33** F2
Clarendon Ind Pk MK8 . . . **33** F2
Clarendon Rd
High Wycombe HP13 . . . . **173** E5
Prestwood HP16 . . . . **151** B6
Clare Park HP7 . . . . **165** E7
Clare Rd
Maidenhead SL6 . . . . **202** D6
Prestwood HP16 . . . . **151** C6
Slough SL3 . . . . **204** C7
Stanwell TW19 . . . . **213** E1
Claridge Dr MK10 . . . . . . **36** A2
Clarke Ct HP20 . . . . **101** F2
Clarke Dr HP13 . . . . **174** A6
Clarke Rd MK1 . . . . **47** D4
Clarkes Dr UB8 . . . . **208** E8
Clarkes Field Cl HP18 . . . **110** B8
Clarkes Orch MK16 . . . . . **12** B5
Clarke's Spring HP23 . . . **119** F5
Clarke Wlk 2 HP20 . . . . . **101** F2
Clarks Cotts HP16 . . . . . **151** C7
Classon Cl HP18 . . . . **124** A6
Claudius Wy MK11 . . . . . . **33** A3
Clauds Cl HP15 . . . . **163** A5
Claverton Cl HP3 . . . . **146** A3
Clay Acre HP5 . . . . **144** D1
Clay Cl HP10 . . . . **185** B8
Claycots Prim Sch SL2 . . **198** A1
Claycots Prim Sch (Town
Hall Campus) SL1 . . . . **205** D5
Claycutters MK18 . . . . **66** A4
Claydon Cl HP21 . . . . **115** D6
Claydon Ct HP12 . . . . **172** E4
Claydon End SL9 . . . . **188** E8
Claydon Ho* MK18 . . . . . . **74** C7
Claydon La SL9 . . . . **188** E8
Claydon Path HP21 . . . . . **115** E3
Claydons Pl HP27 . . . . . . **138** D7
Clayfield Rd HP22 . . . . . . **131** C8
Clayfields HP10 . . . . **163** C2
Clay Gdns 5 MK17 . . . . . . **49** A5
Clayhall La SL4 . . . . **210** F2
Clayhill
Marlow Bottom SL7 . . . . . **172** A2
Wigginton HP23 . . . . **133** E2
Clay Hill MK8 . . . . **33** E2
Clay La
Calvert MK18 . . . . **73** A5
Marlow Bottom SL7 . . . . . **172** A2
Wendover HP22 . . . . **131** C5
Claymoor Pk SL7 . . . . **172** A2
Clay Pit La 9 MK46 . . . . . . **6** F3
Clays La MK17 . . . . **55** E2
Clay St HP7, HP9 . . . . **175** C7
Clays The HP17 . . . . **127** A7
Clayton Ct SL3 . . . . **207** A3
Clayton Gate MK14 . . . . . **35** A8
Clayton Rd HP14 . . . . **171** B4
Claytons Mdw SL8 . . . . . **185** B2
Claytons Prim Sch SL8 . . **185** A5
Clayton Way UB8 . . . . . . **201** D1
Clayton Wlk HP7 . . . . **166** C8
Clearbrook Cl HP13 . . . . . **174** B4
Cleares Pasture SL1 . . . . **197** B2
Cleavers OX39 . . . . **147** B6
Cleavers Ave MK14 . . . . . **34** E3
Cleeve Cres MK3 . . . . **47** A2
Clegg Sq MK5 . . . . **46** B5
Cleland Rd SL9 . . . . **177** D1

Clementi Ave HP15 . . . . . **163** D7
Clement Pl 5 HP23 . . . . . **119** A3
Clements Cl 5 SL1 . . . . . . **206** B4
Clements La OX27 . . . . . . **71** C7
Clements Rd
Chorleywood WD3 . . . . . . **167** D4
Henley-on-Thames RG9 . . . **191** C3
Clerkenwell Cotts HP17 . **126** F5
Clerkenwell Pl MK6 . . . . . **35** B2
Clerk St MK12 . . . . **102** C2
Clevehurst Cl SL2 . . . . . . **199** A6
Cleveland MK13 . . . . **34** B6
Cleveland Cl
Maidenhead SL6 . . . . **203** B6
Wooburn Green HP10 . . . . **185** E8
Cleveland Dr LU7 . . . . **80** C8
Cleveland Pk
Aylesbury HP20 . . . . **101** F3
Stanwell TW19 . . . . **213** E1
Cleveland Pl 13 HP20 . . . **101** F3
Cleveland Rd
Aylesbury HP20 . . . . **101** F3
Uxbridge UB8 . . . . **201** D2
Cleves Cl SL6 . . . . **209** F4
Clewer Ave SL4 . . . . **210** A5
Clewer Court Rd SL4 . . . . **210** B7
Clewer Fields SL4 . . . . . . **210** B6
CLEWER GREEN **209** E3
Clewer Green CE Fst Sch
SL4 . . . . **210** A4
Clewer Hill Rd SL4 . . . . . . **209** F4
CLEWER NEW TOWN **210** A5
Clewer New Town SL4 . . . **210** A5
Clewer Pk SL4 . . . . **210** A7
CLEWER VILLAGE **210** A7
Clicker Yd MK46 . . . . **6** F4
Clifden Rd HP18 . . . . **123** E5
Clifford Ave MK2 . . . . **58** C7
Clifford Rd HP27 . . . . **139** B3
Cliffords Way SL8 . . . . . . **185** B5
Clifton Bsns Pk HP19 . . . **101** B1
Clifton Cl SL6 . . . . **203** B4
Clifton Ct
High Wycombe HP11 . . . . **172** E4
Olney MK46 . . . . **7** A3
8 Stanwell TW19 . . . . **213** E1
Clifton Gn HP19 . . . . **101** B2
Clifton Lawns HP6 . . . . . . **154** C4
Clifton Lodge
Eton Wick SL4 . . . . **205** A1
7 Slough SL1 . . . . **206** A4
Clifton Moor MK5 . . . . **45** D5
Clifton Rd
Amersham HP6 . . . . **154** C4
Newton Blossomville MK43 . . **8** A4
5 Slough SL1 . . . . **206** A4
CLIFTON REYNES **7** C3
Clifton Rise SL4 . . . . **209** D6
Cline Ct MK8 . . . . **45** E6
Clinkard Pl HP14 . . . . **171** A3
Clinton Cres HP21 . . . . . . **116** A8
Clipstone Brook Way 4
MK10 . . . . **36** B3
Clive Ct SL1 . . . . **205** D4
Cliveden* SL6 . . . . **196** E7
Cliveden Gate SL1 . . . . . . **197** B3
Cliveden Mead SL6 . . . . . **196** C5
Cliveden Office Village
HP12 . . . . **172** E4
Cliveden Pl MK4 . . . . **45** F2
Cliveden Rd SL6 . . . . **196** E4
Clivemont Rd SL6 . . . . . . **202** F8
Clock Ho The MK17 . . . . . **59** D6
Clockhouse Mews WD3 . . **167** E6
Cloebury Paddock MK15 . . **35** C3
Cloister Garth HP4 . . . . . **135** C4
Cloisters The
High Wycombe HP13 . . . . **162** D2
Slough SL1 . . . . **205** D4
Clonmel Way SL1 . . . . . . **197** B2
Closes The HP17 . . . . **127** A7
Close The
Akeley MK18 . . . . **42** A8
Ashendon HP18 . . . . **97** F1
Bierton HP22 . . . . **102** A4
Bourne End SL8 . . . . **185** A6
Great Horwood MK17 . . . . **55** B3
Hardmead MK16 . . . . **15** D4
Hardwick HP22 . . . . **87** B3
Iver Heath SL0 . . . . **200** C2
Lathbury MK16 . . . . **22** D7
Milton Keynes, Bradwell
MK13 . . . . **34** A4
Milton Keynes, The Green
MK6 . . . . **47** D7
Newton Blossomville MK43 . . **7** D3
Ravenstone MK46 . . . . **5** E2
Slough SL1 . . . . **204** D6
Weston Underwood MK46 . . . **6** A1
Cloudberry MK7 . . . . **48** A6
Cloutsham Cl MK4 . . . . . . **46** B8
Clover Cl MK5 . . . . **46** B8
Clover End MK18 . . . . **52** C7
Clover La HP21 . . . . **115** E5
Club Cotts MK17 . . . . **49** B4
Cluny Cl MK7 . . . . **48** D6
Clyde Pl MK3 . . . . **46** E1
Clydesdale Pl MK14 . . . . . **34** F4
Coach Ho The
Loudwater HP11 . . . . **174** A4
Wooburn Green HP10 . . . . **185** D6
Coachmaker Ct MK14 . . . . **34** F6
Coachman's Lodge SL4 . . **210** D5
Coach Ride SL7 . . . . **183** D4
Coach Yd NN12 . . . . **18** E3
Coalmans Way SL1 . . . . . **204** A8
Coaters La HP10 . . . . **185** E7
Coates La HP13 . . . . **162** A1

Coat Wicks HP9 . . . . **176** C4
Cobb Cl SL3 . . . . **211** D6
Cobbetts Mount MK18 . . . **63** D2
Cobbetts Ride HP23 . . . . **118** F3
Cobblers Cl SL2 . . . . **198** B3
Cobblershill La HP16 . . . . **141** B4
Cobblers Wick HP22 . . . . **89** B3
Cobb Rd HP4 . . . . **134** F4
Cobbs Gdn MK46 . . . . **6** F4
Cobden Cl UB8 . . . . **201** C4
Coberley Cl MK15 . . . . . . **35** B6
Cobham Cl
Buckingham MK18 . . . . . . **41** C1
Slough SL1 . . . . **204** F5
Cochran Cl MK8 . . . . **45** E7
Cochrane Ho UB8 . . . . . . **201** C4
Cockerell Gr MK5 . . . . **46** C5
Cockett Rd SL3 . . . . **206** E3
Cock Gr HP4 . . . . **134** D4
Cock La HP10 . . . . **174** A6
Cockpit Cl HP15 . . . . **151** E1
Cockpit Rd HP15 . . . . **162** D8
**Cocksherd Wood Nature
Reserve*** SL2 . . . . **197** E2
Cockton Rd HP19 . . . . **101** C1
Coddimoor La MK17 . . . . . **56** B7
CODMORE **144** E1
Codmore Cres HP5 . . . . . **144** E1
Codmore Cross HP5 . . . . **144** D1
Codmore Wood Rd HP5 . . **155** B3
Coe Spur SL1 . . . . **205** B3
COFFEE HALL **46** F7
Coffee Hall Rdbt MK6 . . . . **47** B6
Cofferidge Cl MK11 . . . . . **32** D5
Coftards SL2 . . . . **206** C7
Cogan Ct MK8 . . . . **45** E7
Cogdells Cl HP5 . . . . **143** B4
Cogdells La HP5 . . . . **143** B4
Coggeshall Gr MK7 . . . . . **48** C7
Coin Cl MK10 . . . . **35** F3
Cokers Ct 3 SL8 . . . . **185** A4
Coke's Farm La HP8 . . . . **166** B6
Coke's La HP8 . . . . **166** B6
Colborne Rd HP13 . . . . . . **173** D8
Colby Gdns 1 SL6 . . . . . **202** F8
Colchester Ct MK3 . . . . . . **57** E7
Colchester Wlk MK3 . . . . . **57** E7
COLD BRAYFIELD **8** B5
Coldeaton La MK4 . . . . . . **46** B3
Cold Grove Cotts SL6 . . . **196** E2
Coldharbour HP22 . . . . . . **131** C4
Cold Harbour CE Prim Sch
MK3 . . . . **46** F3
Coldharbour Way HP19 . . **115** A7
Coldmoorholme La SL8 . . **184** E4
Coldmoreham Yd HP7 . . . **165** A4
Coleheath Bottom HP27 . **150** C5
Coleman Rd MK17 . . . . . . **58** B2
Colenorton Cres SL4 . . . . **204** E2
Cole Rd HP21 . . . . **115** C3
Coleridge Cl
Milton Keynes MK3 . . . . . . **58** A7
Newport Pagnell MK16 . . . **21** F4
Coleridge Cres SL3 . . . . . **212** E6
Coleridge Way UB7 . . . . . **208** F2
Coles Ave MK6 . . . . **46** F6
Colesbourne Dr MK15 . . . **35** B6
COLESHILL **164** F3
Coles Hill HP18 . . . . **111** B3
Coleshill CE Inf Sch HP7 . **164** F4
Coleshill Ho HP7 . . . . **165** A4
Coleshill La HP7 . . . . **164** D2
Coleshill Pl MK13 . . . . **34** C3
Colet Rd HP22 . . . . **131** C5
Colgrain St MK9 . . . . **35** A4
Colham Ave UB7 . . . . **208** E5
Colham Mill Rd UB7 . . . . . **208** D5
Colham Rd UB8 . . . . **201** F1
Colindale St MK10 . . . . . . **35** E1
Colinswood SL2 . . . . **187** B1
Colin Way SL1 . . . . **205** B3
College Ave
Maidenhead SL6 . . . . **202** E7
Slough SL1 . . . . **205** E3
College Bsns Pk HP22 . . . **103** C1
College Cl
Holton OX33 . . . . **122** C1
Thame OX9 . . . . **125** C1
College Cres
Oakley HP18 . . . . **109** E4
Windsor SL4 . . . . **210** B5
College Glen SL6 . . . . **202** D7
**College Lake Wildlife
Reserve*** HP23 . . . . . . **105** C1
College Rd
Cranfield MK43 . . . . **24** E2
Maidenhead SL6 . . . . **202** E7
Slough SL1 . . . . **204** F5
College Rise SL6 . . . . **202** D7
College Road N HP22 . . . . **117** C6
College The OX27 . . . . . . **71** F3
Colley Cl HP18 . . . . **110** A8
Colley Hill MK13 . . . . **34** A4
Colley Hill La SL2 . . . . . . **187** F1
Colley Ho UB8 . . . . **201** D4
Colleyland WD3 . . . . **167** D5
Collier Cl SL6 . . . . **195** F1
Colliers Wood MK10 . . . . . **35** E8
Collings Walk MK16 . . . . . **151** C5
Collingwood Cl HP13 . . . . **174** A6
Collingwood Gdns 1
MK10 . . . . **36** B4
Collins Ho 2 HP11 . . . . . **173** A7
Collins Wlk MK16 . . . . **22** A4
Collinswood Rd SL2 . . . . **187** B2
Collum Green Rd SL2 . . . **187** E1
Collyer Rd HP14 . . . . **158** E4

COLNBROOK............212 D7
Colnbrook By-Pass
  Colnbrook SL3........212 D7
  Harmondsworth UB7....213 C7
Colnbrook CE Prim Sch
  SL3................212 D6
Colnbrook Ct SL3......212 F6
Coln Cl SL6...........202 F8
Colndale Rd SL3.......212 E5
Colne MK6.............47 D6
Colne Ave UB7.........208 C2
Colne Bank SL3........212 C4
Colnedale Rd UB8......201 D7
Colne Orch SL0........207 F6
Colne Park Cvn Site
  UB7...............208 C2
Colne Rd HP13.........173 F7
Colne Reach TW19......212 F2
Colne Valley Park Visitor
  Ctr★ UB9...........190 B1
Colney Rd HP18........100 D4
Coln Trad Est SL3.....212 F6
Colonel Grantham Ave
  HP19..............101 D4
Colonial Rd 1 SL1.....206 A4
Colonnade SL6.........203 A7
Colossus Way MK3......47 A1
Colsons Way MK46......6 F5
Colston Bassett MK4...46 C1
Colston Ct SL9........188 E5
COLSTROPE.............181 D5
Coltman Ave HP18......125 C6
Coltsfoot Dr UB7......208 E7
Coltsfoot Pl MK14.....34 D3
Colts Holm Rd MK12....33 C8
Columbia Pl MK9.......35 A3
Columbine Rd HP15.....162 F6
Colville Ct HP16......152 B7
Colville Rd HP11......172 F6
COMBE................130 C1
Combe Martin MK4......46 D3
Combe Rise HP12.......172 B7
Combermere Cl SL4.....210 B5
Combes Cres MK6.......46 F6
Comerford Way MK18....66 A5
Comfrey Cl MK7........48 A5
Comfrey The 2 HP19....101 E4
Commodore Cl MK16.....36 B5
Common Field HP23.....119 D1
Common Gate Rd WD3....167 E4
Common La
  Eton SL4...........205 D1
  Hedgerley SL1......186 D1
  Milton Keynes, Bradwell
    MK13.............34 A4
  Milton Keynes MK5...46 C8
Common Rd
  Chorleywood WD3.....167 D5
  Dagnall LU6........107 F3
  Dorney SL4.........204 D2
  Eton Wick SL4......205 A2
  Flackwell Heath HP10.185 B8
  Slough SL3.........207 A1
Commonside HP13.......161 E3
Common St MK46........5 D1
COMMON THE...........55 B4
Common The
  Berkhamsted HP4.....135 F6
  Chipperfield WD4....156 F7
  Flackwell Heath HP10.185 B8
  Great Kingshill HP15.151 D1
  Holmer Green HP15...163 D7
  Stokenchurch HP14...158 F5
  West Drayton UB7....208 C2
Common Wood SL2......198 C8
Common Wood La HP10...163 E1
Como Rd LU7..........116 B8
Compass Point HP4.....134 E6
Comp Gate LU6.........92 E6
Comp The LU6.........92 E6
Compton Ct
  Moulsoe MK16.......36 D8
  Slough SL1.........204 F7
Compton Dr SL6........202 A8
Compton Rd HP22......131 B4
Concorde Cl UB10......201 E3
Concorde Pk SL6.......202 C6
Concorde Rd SL6.......202 C6
Concorde Way SL1......205 C4
Concourse The 6 MK2...58 C8
Concra Pk MK17........49 C4
Concrete Cows★ MK13...33 F4
Condor Cl MK6.........47 A8
Conduit La SL3........206 E1
Conegar Ct SL1........205 E5
Conegra Ct 15 HP13....173 B7
Conegra Rd HP13.......173 C7
Coneygere MK46........7 A3
Conifer Rise HP12.....172 E6
Conifers The SL6......202 A8
Conigre OX39.........147 B6
Coningsby Cl SL3......202 D3
Coningsby Ct HP13.....173 B8
Coningsby Rd HP13.....162 B1
Coniston Cres SL1.....204 C8
Coniston Gn HP20......101 D3
Coniston Rd LU7.......80 C7
Coniston Way MK2......58 D6
Conkers SL6...........203 B8
Connaught Cl SL6......195 C1
Connaught Gdns HP4....134 F7
Connaught Rd
  Aylesbury HP20......116 C8
  3 Slough SL1.........206 B4
CONNIBURROW..........34 E4
Conniburrow Bvd MK14..34 E4

Conniston Cl SL7......183 B2
Conought Ho RG9.......191 E3
Constable Cl MK14.....34 F7
Constable Pl HP19.....100 F2
Constable's Croft MK18.52 E6
Constance St MK18.....52 E6
Constantine Pl UB10...201 F4
Constantine Way MK13..33 F5
Convent Ct HP23.......118 F3
Convent Rd SL4........210 A5
Conway Cl
  Aylesbury HP21......115 F7
  Loudwater HP10......174 C2
  Milton Keynes MK3...57 F8
Conway Cres MK3......57 E8
Conway Ct SL9.........189 B3
Conway Ho HP13........173 F7
Conway Rd SL6.........204 B7
Cook Cl MK7...........48 B4
Cookfield Cl LU6......93 E8
COOKHAM.............196 A7
Cookham Ct HP6........154 E1
COOKHAM DEAN.........195 B7
Cookham Dean Bottom
  SL6................195 C8
Cookham Dean CE Prim Sch
  SL6................195 B5
Cookham Lodge 15 SL6..202 F6
Cookham Rd SL6........195 F1
COOKHAM RISE.........195 E6
Cookham Rise Prim Sch
  SL6................195 E6
Cookham Sta SL6.......195 F7
Cooks Cl NN7..........9 F8
Cookshall La HP12.....161 A2
Cooks La MK17.........67 E6
Cook's Mdw LU6........92 E4
Cooks Rd HP19.........114 F8
Coombe Ave HP22.......131 B4
Coombe Cl HP22........116 C2
Coombe Dr LU6.........93 E7
Coombe Gdns
  Berkhamsted HP4.....134 F5
  Hughenden Valley HP14.162 A6
Coombe Hill Ct SL4....209 D4
Coombe La
  Aylesbury HP19......100 F1
  Walter's Ash NP14...161 F6
Coombes Quarry Nature
  Reserve★ MK18.......53 E6
Coombe Vale SL9.......188 E3
Cooper Rd RG9.........191 D3
Cooper's Court Rd HP14.158 D5
Coopers Cl MK16.......22 C4
Coopers Mews MK14....34 F6
Coopers Rise HP13.....173 D5
Coopers Row SL0.......200 D1
Cooper's Yd HP20......101 D1
Cooper Way
  3 Berkhamsted HP4...135 D4
  Slough SL1.........205 B3
Coots Cl MK18.........52 E7
Cope Ct SL6...........202 C7
Copeland Cl MK7.......48 C5
Copes Rd HP15.........151 E1
Copes Shroves HP15....162 F5
Copman's Wick WD3.....167 D4
Copners Dr HP15.......163 C6
Copners Way HP15......163 B6
Copper Beech Cl
  Felden HP3.........146 F8
  Windsor SL4........209 D6
Copperfields
  Beaconsfield HP9....175 E5
  High Wycombe HP12...161 B1
Copperfield Terr SL2..206 B6
Copperhouse Ct MK7....48 A2
Copperkins Gr HP6.....154 B3
Copperkins La HP6.....154 A3
Coppermill La WD3.....178 F3
Coppermill Rd TW19...212 B2
Coppice Cl MK7........102 A2
Coppice The
  Great Kingshill HP15.151 E1
  High Wycombe HP12...172 B4
  Seer Green HP9......176 D4
  Stokenchurch HP14...158 F5
  Walter's Ash NP14...161 B8
  West Drayton UB7....208 E7
  Wigginton HP23......119 C1
Coppice Way
  Aylesbury HP20......102 A2
  Hedgerley SL2......187 D2
Coppidwell Dr HP21....116 A5
Coppinger Ct SL1......208 E4
Coppin La MK13........34 A3
Coppins Cl HP4........134 F4
Coppins La SL0........207 F8
Copse Cl
  Marlow SL7.........183 C2
  Slough SL1.........204 F5
  West Drayton UB7....208 D3
Copse Gate MK18.......66 A4
Copse La HP9..........176 E3
Copse The
  Amersham HP7.......154 C1
  Beaconsfield HP9....175 C4
Copse Way HP5.........144 A4
Copse Wood SL0........200 D4
Copthall Cl SL9.......177 F3
Copthall Cnr SL9......177 E3
Copthall Ho SL6.......203 A7
Copthall La SL9.......177 E3
Copthorn Cl SL6.......202 A4
Copthorne Pl MK7......48 B8
Copyground Ct HP12....172 E7

Copyground La HP12....172 E7
Coral Cl LU6..........92 E6
Coram Cl MK4..........135 C3
Corbet Ride LU7.......80 D8
Corbet Sq LU7.........80 D8
Corbett Cl MK15.......35 D7
Cordons Cl SL9........177 D2
Cordwainer Ct MK14....34 F6
Cordwallis Bsns Pk SL6.195 E1
Cordwallis Est SL6....202 F8
Cordwallis Pk SL6.....202 F8
Cordwallis Rd SL6.....202 F8
Cordwallis St SL6.....202 E8
CORES END............185 C4
Cores End Rd SL8......185 B3
Corfe Cl HP21.........116 B5
Corfe Cres MK3.......57 F8
Corfe Gdns SL1........205 A6
Corfe Pl SL6..........202 C7
Corfe Rd LU7..........105 C3
Coriander Ct MK7......48 B5
Corin Cl MK2..........58 D5
Corinium Ind Est HP6..154 F1
Corin Way MK2.........58 D5
Cornbrook Rd HP21.....115 C5
Cornbury Cres MK15....35 A6
Corn Cl HP17..........114 D5
Corncrake 9 HP19......101 F3
Cornel Cl HP15........163 B3
Cornel Ho 1 SL4.......210 D4
Cornelia Cl MK2.......58 C6
Cornerways HP27.......150 C5
Cornfield Cl UB8......201 D3
Cornfield Cres HP4....134 D7
Cornflower Pl MK18....52 C7
Corn Hill MK8.........33 E1
Corn Mkt HP17.........173 B7
Cornwall Ave SL2......198 C1
Cornwall Cl
  Eton Wick SL4......204 E1
  Maidenhead SL6.....195 E2
Cornwall Ct SL8.......201 D6
Cornwall Gr MK3.......46 F1
Cornwall Ho UB8.......201 D6
Cornwall Lodge 11 SL6.202 F6
Cornwall Pl MK18......41 D1
Cornwall Rd UB8.......201 D6
Cornwalls Mdw 3 MK18..41 D1
Cornwell Rd SL4.......211 A1
Coronation Ave
  Slough SL3.........206 E2
  Windsor SL4........211 A4
Coronation Cotts MK18..41 F8
Coronation Cres HP14..171 C5
Coronation Mews LU7...80 F8
Coronation Pl MK18....63 D2
Coronation Rd
  Cranfield MK43......25 B1
  High Wycombe HP12...172 D4
  Milton Keynes MK11..32 E5
Coronation Villas HP21.115 E8
Corporation St HP13...173 B7
Corrid Ind Pk HP19....101 B1
Corrigan Cl MK3.......58 A8
Corsewall Pl 6 MK4....45 F1
Corsham Ct 4 MK8......33 F1
Cosford Mews 2 HP22..131 E6
COSGROVE............19 D2
Cosgrove Prim Sch MK19.19 E2
Cosgrove Rd MK19......32 C7
Costers Cotts SL8.....185 B2
Costins Wlk 7 HP4.....135 D4
Cosway Pl MK8.........45 D6
Cotes Way LU7.........79 F3
Cotman Cl MK12........33 B5
Cotswold Cl
  Maidenhead SL6.....203 B6
  Slough SL1.........205 B3
  Uxbridge UB8.......201 C4
Cotswold Ct HP12......172 E8
Cotswold Dr LU7.......80 C8
Cotswold Gn HP20......101 C2
Cotswolds Way MK18....73 B5
Cotswold Way HP13.....172 E8
Cottage Comm MK5.....46 B8
Cottage Farm Way HP27.150 C4
Cottage Grounds HP17..114 D5
Cottage Park Rd SL2...187 D2
Cottages The
  Ickenham UB10......190 E2
  Syresham NN13......27 C5
Cottesbrooke Cl SL3...212 D6
Cottesloe Cl LU7......79 E3
Cottesloe Ct MK11.....32 F5
Cottesloe Rd HP21.....115 E5
Cottesloe Sch The LU7..79 D1
Cottingham Gr MK3.....58 A7
Cottisford Cres MK14..21 F1
Cottland Clay HP17....127 A4
Cotton End MK18.......52 E6
Cotts Field HP17......126 E6
Cotts The
  Long Crendon HP18...125 C6
  Longwick HP27......138 E5
Coulson Ave MK8, MK5..45 E6
Coulson Ct HP16.......151 D6
Coulson Way SL1.......204 B8
Council Hos LU7.......92 A1
Countess Wy MK10......36 D3
Countisbury MK4.......46 D2
Country La HP15.......151 F1
Country Life Ho SL3...211 B7
County Rd NN13........38 A6
Courageous Wy 6 MK10..36 C4
Cours La Ville MK18...65 E3
Court Cl
  Aylesbury HP21......115 E7

Court Cl continued
  High Wycombe HP13...161 D1
  Maidenhead SL6.....203 C2
  Princes Risborough HP27.139 A3
Court Cnr MK46........6 E3
Court Cres SL1........205 D5
Court Dr
  Maidenhead SL6.....196 C3
  Uxbridge UB10......201 F4
Courteneys Lodge MK4..46 E3
Court Farm Cl SL1.....205 B5
Courtfield Dr SL6.....202 C6
Courtfield Gdns UB9...190 A1
Court Garden L Complex
  SL7................183 D1
Courthouse Cl MK18....65 F5
Courthouse Jun Sch SL6.202 B8
Courthouse Mews MK16..22 C4
Courthouse Rd SL6.....202 C8
Court La
  Burnham SL1........197 D2
  Dorney SL4.........204 B3
  Iver SL0...........208 A5
Courtlands
  Leighton Buzzard LU7..80 E6
  14 Maidenhead SL6....202 F6
Courtlands Ave SL3....206 D2
Court Lawns HP10......163 C1
Courtmoor Cl HP27.....139 C6
Courtneidge Cl LU7....78 E8
Courtney Ho UB9.......189 F5
Court Rd
  Cranfield MK43......25 B1
  Maidenhead SL6.....196 C3
Court The MK17........37 C3
Courtyard Cl HP6......154 C1
Courtyards The HP22...117 E4
Courtyard The 7 HP19..101 C1
Courtyard The
  Beaconsfield HP9....175 D2
  7 Bourne End SL8....185 B3
  1 Maidenhead SL6....202 D6
  9 Marlow SL7........183 D2
  1 Marlow SL7........183 E2
  22 Windsor SL4.......210 D6
Cousins Cl UB7........208 E6
Cousins Dr HP20.......101 F2
Coventon Rd HP19......101 C2
Coverack Pl MK4.......57 B8
Coverdale MK13........34 C5
Coverdale Way SL2.....197 E1
Covert Cl HP4.........134 D6
Covert Rd HP4.........134 D6
Cowdray Cl MK15......35 C3
Cow Ground HP18.......100 D4
Cow La
  Edlesborough LU6....92 E4
  Gawcott MK18.......51 F4
  Tring HP23.........119 D4
Cowleaze OX39........147 B6
COWLEY.............201 C1
Cowley Bsns Pk UB8....201 C2
Cowley Cl HP22........102 B3
Cowley Cotts HP7......164 C3
Cowley Cres UB8.......208 C8
Cowley Mill Rd UB8....201 B3
Cowley Mill Trad Est
  UB8...............201 B3
COWLEY PEACHEY......208 E8
Cowley Rd UB8.........201 C4
Cowley St Laurence CE Prim
  Sch UB8............208 D8
Cowper Cl MK46........22 A4
Cowper & Newton Mus The★
  MK46...............6 F3
Cowper Rd
  Berkhamsted HP4.....135 B4
  Chesham HP5........144 B2
  Slough SL2.........198 A1
Cowpers Orch MK46.....6 A1
Cowper St MK46........7 A5
COW ROAST...........120 B1
Cowslip Cl UB10.......201 E5
Cowslip Rd HP15.......162 F6
Coxborrow Cl SL6......195 E7
Coxfield Cl HP14......158 F5
COX GREEN...........202 C3
Cox Green La SL6......202 C3
Cox Green L Ctr SL6...202 A3
Cox Green Rd SL6......202 B3
Cox Green Sch SL6.....202 A4
Coxhill Way HP21......115 D7
Coxwell Cl MK18.......41 F1
Coy Ct HP20..........116 A8
Cozens Cl HP18........125 B7
Crabbe Cres HP5.......144 D2
Crabs Gr HP22........86 F7
Crab Tree Cl
  Beaconsfield HP9....175 B1
  Olney MK46.........6 E5
Crabtree Cotts HP27...139 A1
Crabtree La MK17......49 C8
Crabtree Rd HP17......127 A5
Craddocks Cl MK13.....34 B3
Cradley Wlk HP20......101 E3
CRAFTON.............89 F3
Crafton Pl 4 HP19.....100 F1
Craigleith Ct HP9.....175 D2
Craigmore Ave MK3.....57 F8
Craigwell Ave HP12....116 C7
Cranborne Ave MK4....45 E2
Cranbourne Ct SL1.....205 C5
Cranbourne Rd SL1.....205 B5
Cranbrook MK13........49 B5
Cranbrook Dr SL6......195 C1
CROFTS END..........14 A1

Cranes Cl MK43........8 E5
Crane Way MK43........25 C2
CRANFIELD...........25 B1
Cranfield Airport MK43..24 F1
Cranfield CE Acad (St Paul
  Site) MK43.........25 B2
Cranfield CE Acad (St Peter
  Site) MK43.........25 B2
Cranfield Innovation Ctr
  MK43...............37 D8
Cranfield Rd
  Astwood MK16, MK43..16 B2
  Cranfield MK43......25 F3
  Moulsoe MK16.......36 E8
  Salford MK17.......37 D5
  Wavendon MK17......49 B7
Cranfield Tech Pk MK43..37 E8
Cranfield Univ MK43...24 E2
Cranley Cres HP19.....101 C4
Cranmore Circ MK10....36 D3
Cranwell Cl MK5.......46 B3
Cranwell Ct SL6.......202 E8
Craufurd Rise SL6.....202 E8
Craven The MK13.......34 C4
Crawford Rd HP19......100 F4
Crawford Way 3 MK4...45 D2
Crawley Rd
  Cranfield MK43......25 B3
  Woburn MK17.......60 E8
Crawley's La HP23.....133 F7
Crawshays SL6........203 C8
Crayle St SL2.........198 B2
CR Bates Ind Est HP14..158 E5
Creden Cl SL6.........195 D1
Creed St MK12.........33 D7
Creighton Rd HP18.....83 F1
Crendon Rd HP18......112 A1
Crendon St HP13.......173 B7
Creran Wlk LU7........80 C7
Crescent Cotts HP18...83 A6
Crescent Dale SL6.....202 F6
Crescent Rd SL6.......202 E7
Crescent The
  Cranfield MK43......24 E2
  Haversham MK19.....20 E2
  High Wycombe HP13...173 E8
  Maidenhead SL6.....202 E7
  Marsworth HP23.....105 A1
  Milton Keynes, Fenny Stratford
    MK2..............47 C1
  Milton Keynes, Giffard Park
    MK14.............21 E2
  Pitstone LU7.......105 C4
  Princes Risborough HP27.139 C3
  Slough SL1.........205 E4
Crescent Villas 5 SL4..210 C6
CRESLOW.............87 B8
Creslow Ct MK11.......32 F5
Creslow Way MK17......114 B5
CRESSEX.............172 D4
Cressex Bsns Pk HP12..172 D4
Cressex Cl HP12.......172 D3
Cressex Com Sch HP12..172 C3
Cressex Ent Ctr HP12..172 E6
Cressex Link HP11.....172 D3
Cressex Rd HP12.......172 C3
Cressey Ave MK5.......46 B4
Cressington Ct 2 SL8..185 A4
Cressington Pl SL8....185 A4
Cress Rd SL1..........205 B4
Cresswell Ct TW19.....213 D1
Cresswell Rd HP5......154 D5
Cresswells Mead SL6...203 C1
Cresswell Way HP15....163 D7
Crest Rd HP11.........172 D3
Crest The
  Beaconsfield HP9....175 A1
  Bledlow Ridge HP14..159 F8
Creswell Row SL7......183 D2
Creswick Mdw HP21.....116 A5
Crew Curve HP4........134 F7
Cricketers Row MK18...66 A4
Cricketfield Rd UB7...208 C2
Cricket Field Rd UB8..201 D4
Cricket Ground HP14...158 D5
Cricklebeck MK13......34 B5
Crimp Hill SL4........211 A1
Crispin Cl HP9........175 C4
Crispin Field LU7.....105 C4
Crispin Rd MK13.......34 B7
Crispin Way
  Farnham Common SL2..198 C8
  High Wycombe HP11...173 A4
  Uxbridge UB8.......208 F8
Crisp Rd RG9.........191 C3
Criss Gr SL9..........177 C1
Crocketts La HP16.....142 D5
Crocus Dr HP21........115 B5
Croft Cnr SL4.........211 A2
Croft 5 HP21.........115 E7
Croft Ctyd HP17.......126 F6
Crofters SL4..........211 A1
Crofters Cl TW19......213 D1
Croft Gn LU6..........93 F8
Crofthill Rd SL2......198 B1
Croft Ho SL0..........207 E2
Croft Mdws LU7........105 A7
Crofton Ho HP11.......174 A4
Croft Rd
  Aylesbury HP21......115 E7
  Chalfont St Peter SL9..177 E1
CROFTS END..........14 A1
Crofts End MK16.......14 A1
Crofts La MK17........57 D3

Croft The
Haddenham HP17 . . . . 126 F5
Maidenhead SL6 . . . . 202 C5
Marlow SL7 . . . . 184 A3
Croftwood HP13 . . . . 173 F7
Cromarty Ct MK3 . . . . . . 46 E3
Cromer Cl HP4 . . . . 121 E5
Cromer Ct SL1 . . . . 205 E7
Cromhamstone HP17 . . . 114 D5
Cromwell Ave
Aylesbury HP19 . . . . 101 D2
Newport Pagnell MK16 . . 22 A3
Thame OX9 . . . . 126 A1
Cromwell Cl HP8 . . . . 177 C7
Cromwell Ct MK18 . . . . . 41 E2
Cromwell Dr SL1 . . . . . . 205 E7
Cromwell Gdns 10 SL7 . . 183 E2
Cromwell Ho
Chesham HP5 . . . . 144 B1
Uxbridge UB8 . . . . 201 C4
Cromwell Mews 1
HP19 . . . . 115 A8
Cromwell Rd
High Wycombe HP13 . . . . 173 E5
Maidenhead SL6 . . . . 202 D7
Marlow SL7 . . . . 183 E2
Cropredy Ct MK18 . . . . . 41 E2
Cropton Rise MK4 . . . . . 46 A2
Cropwell Bishop MK4 . . 46 C1
Crosby Cl HP9 . . . . 186 F8
Crosby Ct MK8 . . . . 45 E6
Crosby Gdns UB10 . . . . . 201 E5
Crosland Rd HP21 . . . . . 116 B6
Cross Ct HP13 . . . . 161 D2
Cross End MK17 . . . . 48 F7
Cross Farm Mews HP3 . . 146 D2
Crossfield Cl HP4 . . . . . 134 F4
Crossfield Ho SL9 . . . . . 188 E7
Crossfield Rd HP27 . . . . 139 C4
Crosshills MK11 . . . . 32 D4
Cross La
Beaconsfield HP9 . . . . . . 186 F8
Tingewick MK18 . . . . 51 B6
Weston Underwood MK46 . . 6 B2
Crosslands MK14 . . . . . . 34 E8
Cross Lanes
Bledlow HP27 . . . . 138 A2
Chalfont St Peter SL9 . . . 177 F5
Cross Lanes Cl SL9 . . . . 177 F5
Crossleys HP8 . . . . 177 C7
Crosslow Bank MK4 . . . . 46 C3
Cross Mdw HP5 . . . . 143 F2
Cross Oak SL4 . . . . 210 A5
Cross Oak Rd HP4 . . . . . 135 A4
Cross Rd
High Wycombe HP12 . . . . 172 C6
Uxbridge UB8 . . . . 201 C5
Cross St
Newport Pagnell MK16 . . 22 A3
Uxbridge UB8 . . . . 201 C5
Cross Tree Rd MK19 . . . . 31 B3
Crossway HP5 . . . . 144 E1
Crossways
Beaconsfield HP9 . . . . . . 175 F1
Berkhamsted HP4 . . . . . . 134 F3
High Wycombe HP12 . . . . 172 C5
Crossways Bsns Pk HP8 . . 83 C3
Crossways Ct 4 SL4 . . . . 210 C5
Crossway The UB10 . . . . 201 F3
Crosthwaite Way SL1 . . . 204 D8
Crowborough La MK7 . . . 48 A8
Crowbrook Rd HP27 . . . . 139 C6
CROWELL 147 B4
CROWELL HILL 147 D2
Crowell Mews HP19 . . . . 114 F8
Crowell Rd OX39 . . . . . . 147 B5
CROWFIELD 26 F8
Crow La MK17 . . . . 49 B8
Crown Bsns Est HP5 . . . 144 C1
Crown Cl SL3 . . . . 212 C7
Crown Cotts
Botley HP5 . . . . 155 B8
Windsor SL4 . . . . 210 D3
Crown Ct HP14 . . . . 161 A2
CROWNFIELD 149 B4
Crownfield HP27 . . . . 149 C3
CROWNHILL 45 E7
Crownhill Bsns Pk MK8. . . 45 E8
Crownhill Rdbt MK8. . . . . 45 E8
Crown House Sch HP11 . . 173 C6
Crown La
East Burnham SL2 . . . . . . 198 A4
High Wycombe HP11 . . . . 173 B6
Maidenhead SL6 . . . . 203 A7
Marlow SL7 . . . . 183 D2
Penn HP10. . . . . 174 F7
Crown Leys HP20 . . . . . . 101 E1
Crown Mdw SL3 . . . . 212 B7
Crown Rd SL7 . . . . 183 D2
Crown Rose Ct HP23 . . . 119 A3
Crown Way UB7 . . . . 208 F5
Crown Wlk
Milton Keynes MK9 . . . . . 34 E3
Uxbridge UB8. . . . . 201 C5
Crow Piece La SL2 . . . . . 197 F4
Crowther Ct MK5 . . . . . . 46 C5
Croxley Ct 3 LU7 . . . . . . 80 F8
Croxley Rise SL6 . . . . . . 202 D6
Croydon Cl MK4 . . . . 46 C3
Cruickshank Dr 1 HP22 . 131 D6
Cruickshank Gr MK8 . . . 45 E7
Crummock Cl SL1 . . . . . . 204 C7
Crummock Pl MK2 . . . . . 58 D6
Crusader Est HP12 . . . . . 172 D5

Crutches La HP9 . . . . . . 176 E4
CRYERS HILL 162 D6
Cryers Hill La HP15 . . . . 162 D6
Cryers Hill Rd HP15 . . . . 162 C6
Cuba Cotts SL6 . . . . 196 B3
Cubb Field HP19 . . . . . . 115 B7
Cubitt St HP19 . . . . 101 C1
CUBLINGTON 78 B1
Cublington Rd HP22. . . . . 88 D6
Cuckoo Hill Rise MK19 . . 10 F2
Cuckoo Way HP19 . . . . . 114 F8
CUDDINGTON 113 A2
Cuddington & Dinton CE Sch
(Inf) HP18 . . . . 112 F3
Cuddington & Dinton CE Sch
(Jun) HP17 . . . . 113 F3
Cuddington Hill HP18 . . 112 E3
Cuddington Rd HP17,
HP18 . . . . 113 E3
Cudsdens Ct HP16 . . . . . 152 D7
Cuff La MK17 . . . . 59 D1
Culbertson La MK13. . . . . 33 E6
Culham Dr SL6. . . . . 195 E2
Cullen Pl MK2 . . . . 58 D5
Cullen's Pass SL6 . . . . . 202 F6
Culley Way SL6 . . . . 202 A4
Cullyn Rd HP12 . . . . 172 C3
Culmstock Cl MK4 . . . . . 46 D2
Culpepper Cl HP19 . . . . 101 C4
Culrain Pl MK12. . . . . 33 D4
Culross Gr MK10 . . . . 36 A2
Culverhouse Wy HP5. . . 144 D3
Culvers Croft HP9 . . . . . 176 C4
Culvert La UB8. . . . . 201 B3
Culverton Hill HP27 . . . . 139 B3
Culverton La HP27 . . . . . 139 B1
Cumberland Ave SL2 . . . 198 C1
Cumberland Cl
Aylesbury HP21 . . . . 116 B7
Little Chalfont HP7 . . . . . 166 B8
Cumbrae Cl SL2 . . . . 206 A5
Cumbria Cl
Maidenhead SL6 . . . . 202 C4
Milton Keynes MK3 . . . . . 46 F1
Cumbrian Way
High Wycombe HP13 . . . . 172 F8
Uxbridge UB8. . . . . 201 D5
Curfew Yd The 2 SL4 . . . 210 D6
Curlew HP19. . . . . 101 F3
Curlew Cl
Berkhamsted HP4 . . . . . . 135 C3
High Wycombe HP13 . . . . 161 C2
Curls La SL6 . . . . 202 E4
Curls Rd SL6. . . . . 202 D4
Curran Cl UB8 . . . . 201 C1
Currier Dr MK14 . . . . 34 F6
Curriers La SL1 . . . . 197 D7
Cursley Path 11 HP19 . . . 115 A8
Curtis Cotts HP5 . . . . . . 144 F7
Curtis Croft MK5. . . . . . . 46 B3
Curtis Way HP4 . . . . 135 D3
Curve The★ SL1 . . . . 205 F4
Curzon Ave
Beaconsfield HP9 . . . . . . 175 D4
Tylers Green HP15. . . . . . 163 C2
Curzon CE Comb Sch
HP7. . . . . 164 A5
Curzon Cl HP15 . . . . 163 C2
Curzon Gate HP14 . . . . . 158 E5
Curzon Mall 6 SL1 . . . . . 205 F4
Curzon Pl MK7 . . . . 48 E4
Cushing Dr 7 MK4. . . . . . 45 E2
Cutler's Ct 6 HP12 . . . . . 172 E7
Cutlers Mews MK14 . . . . 34 F6
Cut Throat Ave HP4 . . . . 107 E7
Cuttle Brook Gdns OX9. . 125 E7
Cyber Ave MK10 . . . . 35 E2
Cyclamen Pl HP21 . . . . . 115 B5
Cygnet Ho SL6. . . . . 196 C1
Cypress MK16. . . . . 22 A3
Cypress Ho SL3 . . . . 207 B1
Cypress Wlk HP15. . . . . . 163 B3
Cyprus Wy MK3 . . . . 58 B3

D

Daceberry Ct RG9 . . . . . . 192 C2
Dacre Rd HP22 . . . . 131 E7
Dadbrook HP18 . . . . 112 F2
Dadbrook Cl HP18 . . . . . 112 F2
Dadfield Cl HP18 . . . . . . 112 F2
DADFORD 28 D1
Dadford Rd MK18 . . . . . . 28 D5
Dag La MK16 . . . . 12 A7
Dagmar Rd SL4 . . . . 210 D5
DAGNALL 107 C6
Dagnall Cres UB8 . . . . . . 208 C8
Dagnall Rd
Olney MK46 . . . . 6 E3
Whipsnade LU6 . . . . 93 D2
Dagnall Sch HP4. . . . . . . 107 C5
Dair House Sch SL2. . . . . 198 B4
Dairy La RG9 . . . . 192 B8
Dairymede HP27 . . . . 150 C4
Daisy Cotts HP14. . . . . . . 171 B4
Dalby Gdns 7 SL6 . . . . . . 195 F1
Dale Cl NN13 . . . . 38 A7
Dale Cl SL1 . . . . 205 C4
Dalegarth Way MK10 . . . . 36 C3
Dalegarth Wy MK10 . . . . . 36 C3
Dalesford Rd HP21 . . . . . 116 A4
Dale Side SL9. . . . . 188 E2
Dalgin Pl MK9 . . . . 35 A3
Dalston Cl HP20 . . . . 101 F2
Dalston End MK10 . . . . . . 35 E1
Dalton Gate MK10. . . . . . 35 F4
Dalton Gn 15 SL3 . . . . . . 206 F1

Dalton Pl LU7 . . . . 105 C3
Dalvina Pl MK12 . . . . 33 D4
Dalwood Mews 3 HP19 . . 115 A8
Daly Way HP20 . . . . 116 B7
Damask Cl HP23 . . . . 119 C4
Damson Gr SL1 . . . . 205 C4
Danbury Ct MK14 . . . . . . 34 E5
Dancers End La HP22,
HP23 . . . . 118 C2
Dancersend Wildlife
Reserve★ HP23 . . . . 132 C8
Dandridge Cl SL3 . . . . . . 206 D2
Dandridge Ct MK8 . . . . . 45 C6
Dandridge Dr SL8. . . . . . 185 C3
Dane Cl HP7 . . . . 165 F6
Dane Ct HP21 . . . . 115 D4
Dane Rd MK1 . . . . 47 E2
Danesborough Dr MK17 . . 49 A2
Danesbrook Cl MK4 . . . . . 46 D4
Danes Cl SL6 . . . . 202 F5
Danesfield Sch SL7 . . . . 193 E7
Danes Gdns SL6 . . . . 195 F6
Daneswood MK17 . . . . . . 49 A1
Daniels Welch MK6 . . . . . 47 A6
Dansteed Way
Milton Keynes, Bradwell
Common MK8, MK14,
MK15 . . . . 34 C4
Milton Keynes, Crownhill
MK8 . . . . 45 D7
Danvers Croft HP23 . . . . . 119 C5
Darby Cl
Milton Keynes MK5 . . . . . 46 B5
Milton Keynes MK13 . . . . 34 C2
Darby Lodge HP13 . . . . . 174 A7
Darie Cl 3 SL1 . . . . 205 A4
Darin Ct MK8 . . . . 45 F8
Dark La
Oving HP22 . . . . 86 C7
Wingrave HP22 . . . . 89 C2
Darley Cl HP21 . . . . 116 B6
Darley Gate MK14 . . . . . . 35 A5
Darley's Cl HP18 . . . . 83 A6
Darling's La SL6 . . . . 194 E1
Darlington Cl HP6 . . . . . . 154 D1
Darnel Cl MK6 . . . . 47 A5
Darrell Cl SL3 . . . . 206 F2
Darr's La HP4 . . . . 134 D6
Darsham Wlk HP5 . . . . . . 154 B8
Dart Cl
Aylesbury HP21 . . . . 115 C5
Newport Pagnell MK16 . . 22 D4
Slough SL3. . . . . 212 B8
Dartington Pl 2 MK4 . . . . 45 F1
Dartmouth Ct 10 SL1 . . . 205 F3
Dartmouth Rd MK46. . . . . 6 F4
Darvell Dr HP5. . . . . 144 A2
Darvells Yd WD3 . . . . 167 D5
Darville Ho 19 SL4 . . . . . 210 D6
Darvill Rd HP17 . . . . 114 D5
DARVILLSHILL 150 A4
Darvills Mdw HP15 . . . . . 163 C7
Darvill's La SL1. . . . . 205 E3
Dashfield Gr HP15 . . . . . 162 F6
Dashwood Ave HP12 . . . . 172 D7
Dashwood Cl SL3 . . . . . . 206 C2
Dashwood Works Ind Est
HP12. . . . . 172 D7
DATCHET. 211 C6
Datchet Ho 3 SL1 . . . . . . 205 F3
Datchet Lodge Ctyd SL3 . 211 B6
Datchet Pl SL3. . . . . 211 B6
Datchet Rd
Eton SL4. . . . . 205 F2
Horton SL3. . . . . 211 F4
Old Windsor SL4 . . . . 211 A3
Windsor SL4 . . . . 210 D7
Datchet St Mary's CE Prim
Acad SL3 . . . . 211 B6
Datchet Sta SL3 . . . . 211 B6
Daubeney Gate MK5 . . . . 45 F6
Daunt Cl HP19 . . . . 101 D4
Davenies Sch HP9 . . . . . . 175 E2
Davenport Lea MK7 . . . . . 48 E5
Davenport Rd HP12 . . . . . 172 C3
Daventry Cl SL3. . . . . 212 F6
David Bishop Ct HP5 . . . . 154 D5
David Cl HP21 . . . . 116 A4
Davidge Pl HP9 . . . . 175 C5
David Rd SL3. . . . . 212 F5
Davidson Rd 6 SL3 . . . . . 206 F1
Davies Cl HP20 . . . . 115 D8
Davies Ct HP12 . . . . 172 D5
Davies Way HP10 . . . . . . 174 C1
Davis Cl SL7 . . . . 183 E1
Davis Gr MK4 . . . . 45 E3
Davis Ho 8 MK8 . . . . 45 C3
Davison Cl MK8. . . . . 45 D6
Davy Ave MK5 . . . . 46 D6
Dawes Cl HP5 . . . . 154 B7
Dawe's Cl UB10. . . . . 201 E3
Dawes East Rd SL1. . . . . 197 C2
Dawes La WD3. . . . . 156 F3
Dawes Moor Cl SL2 . . . . . 206 C7
Dawe's Rd UB10 . . . . 201 E3
Dawley Ride SL3 . . . . 212 E6
Dawney Cl HP19 . . . . 101 C2
Dawn Redwood Cl SL3 . . 212 A4
Daws Ct SL0 . . . . 207 F7
Daws Hill La HP11 . . . . . . 173 A4
Daws Lea HP11 . . . . 173 B3
Dawson Cl SL4. . . . . 210 A5
Dawson Rd MK1 . . . . 47 D3
Daylesford Ct MK15 . . . . . 35 B5
Daylesford Gr SL1 . . . . . . 204 F4
Deacon Cl HP2 . . . . 172 B4

Deacon Ct SL4 . . . . 209 D5
Deacon Pl MK10 . . . . 35 F3
Deadhearn La HP8 . . . . . 166 E1
Deal Ave SL1 . . . . 204 F7
Deanacre Cl SL9 . . . . 177 E4
Dean Cl
Aylesbury HP21 . . . . 116 A5
High Wycombe HP12 . . . . 172 E6
Uxbridge UB10. . . . . 201 F5
Windsor SL4 . . . . 209 D4
Deancroft Rd SL9 . . . . . . 177 E4
Dean Farm La LU7 . . . . . . 69 E4
Deanfield HP14 . . . . 160 B8
Dean Field HP3 . . . . 146 A4
Deanfield Ave RG9 . . . . . 191 D1
Deanfield Cl
Marlow SL7 . . . . 183 D2
Saunderton HP14 . . . . . . 149 C1
Deanfield Rd RG9 . . . . . . 191 D1
Dean Forest Way MK10 . . 36 A5
Deangarden Rise HP11 . . 173 E4
De Angeli Cl 4 MK18 . . . . 41 E3
Dean La SL6. . . . . 195 C8
Dean Rd LU7 . . . . 68 B2
Deans Cl
Amersham HP6 . . . . 154 F2
Tring HP23. . . . . 119 A4
Wexham Street SL2. . . . . 199 B4
Dean's Cloisters SL4 . . . . 210 D7
Deansfield Cl SL6. . . . . . . 195 D2
Deans Furlong HP23 . . . . 119 A4
DEANSHANGER 31 D4
Deanshanger Dr 5 UB9 . . 17 F1
Deanshanger Prim Sch
MK19 . . . . 31 E3
Deanshanger Rd
Old Stratford MK19 . . . . . 32 B6
Wicken MK19 . . . . 31 B3
Deans Lawn HP4 . . . . 135 C4
Deans Mdw HP4 . . . . 107 C5
Dean's Rd MK12 . . . . 33 C7
Dean St SL7 . . . . 183 D2
Deansway HP5. . . . . 144 B2
Dean The HP22 . . . . 89 B3
Dean View SL6. . . . . 195 D6
Dean Way
Aston Clinton HP22 . . . . . 117 F4
Chalfont St Giles HP8 . . . 177 B7
Holmer Green HP15 . . . . 163 B6
Dean Wood Rd HP9 . . . . . 176 D2
Dearing Cl 11 HP20 . . . . . 101 F2
Debbs Cl MK11. . . . . 32 E5
Deben Cl MK16 . . . . 22 E3
Deblin Dr UB10 . . . . 201 E3
Decies Way SL2. . . . . 199 A4
De Clare Ct MK18 . . . . . . 41 E1
Dedmere Ct SL7 . . . . 183 F2
Dedmere Rd SL7. . . . . . . 183 F2
Dedmere Rise SL7 . . . . . 183 E2
DEDWORTH 209 E6
Dedworth Dr SL4 . . . . 209 F6
Dedworth Green Fst Sch
SL4 . . . . 209 E5
Dedworth Manor SL4 . . . . 209 E6
Dedworth Mid Sch SL4. . . 209 E6
Dedworth Rd SL4 . . . . . . 209 D5
Deeds Gr HP12. . . . . 172 E5
Deena Cl SL1 . . . . 204 E6
Deep Acres HP6 . . . . 154 A3
Deepdale MK13 . . . . 34 C5
Deep Field SL3 . . . . 211 B7
Deep Mill La HP16 . . . . . 152 D3
Deerfern Cl MK14. . . . . . . 21 E1
Deerfield Cl MK18. . . . . . . 52 E7
Deermead HP16 . . . . 152 B4
Deer Park Wlk HP5 . . . . . 144 A3
Deerswood 2 SL6 . . . . . . 203 B8
Deer Wlk MK9 . . . . 34 F3
Deethe Cl MK17. . . . . 49 B6
De Havilland Dr HP15 . . . 162 E2
De Havilland Way TW19 . 213 E1
Delafield Cl HP14 . . . . . . 158 F4
Delaford Cl SLO. 207 F7
Delaford Ho UB7. . . . . . . 208 D5
Delahay Rise HP4 . . . . . . 135 B6
Delamere Cl HP20 . . . . . . 101 F2
Delamere Gdns LU7. . . . . 80 C7
Delaware Dr
Milton Keynes MK15 . . . . 35 B8
Tongwell MK15, MK16. . . 22 B1
Delius Cl MK7 . . . . 48 C4
Dell Cl
Chesham HP5 . . . . 143 F2
Farnham Common SL2. . . 198 C2
Dellfield HP5 . . . . 144 A2
Dell Field HP16 . . . . 151 C5
Dell Field Ave HP4 . . . . . 135 B6
Dellfield Cl HP4. . . . . 135 A6
Dellfield Cres UB8 . . . . . 201 C1
Dellfield Par UB8 . . . . . . 201 C1
Dell Lees HP9 . . . . 176 C4
Dell Rd
Berkhamsted HP4 . . . . . . 134 D7
West Drayton UB7 . . . . . . 208 F3
Dells MK46. . . . . 6 F4
Dellside SL0 . . . . 190 C6
Dell The
Aylesbury HP20 . . . . 102 A2
Chalfont St Peter SL9 . . . 177 E4
Maidenhead SL6 . . . . 202 A2
Stokenchurch HP14 . . . . 158 F3
Tylers Green HP10. . . . . . 163 C1
Delmeade Rd HP5 . . . . . . 154 A7
Delorean Wy NN13 . . . . . . 26 A1
Deltic Ave MK13 . . . . 34 B2
Deltic Trade Pk MK9 . . . . 34 B2
Demoram Cl MK18 . . . . . . 65 F3

Denbigh East Ind Est
MK1 . . . . 47 D2
Denbigh Hall MK3. . . . . . . 46 F3
Denbigh Hall Dr MK3. . . . . 46 F3
Denbigh Hall Ind Est MK3 46 F3
Denbigh Rd
Milton Keynes MK1 . . . . . 47 B2
Thame OX9 . . . . 126 A1
Denbigh Rdbt MK1. . . . . . 47 C2
Denbigh Sch MK5. . . . . . . 46 A6
Denbigh Way MK2 . . . . . . 47 C1
Denbigh West Ind Est
MK1 . . . . 47 B2
Denby Walk HP20 . . . . . . 116 A8
Denchworth Ct 2 MK4. . . 46 C2
Dene Cl
Winslow MK18 . . . . 66 A3
Woburn Sands MK17 . . . . 49 C4
Dene The MK18 . . . . 63 D3
Denewood HP13 . . . . 173 E8
DENHAM
Denham Green. 190 A2
Quainton 85 D5
Denham Aerodrome
UB9. . . . . 189 E6
Denham Ave UB9 . . . . . . 189 F3
Denham Cl
Denham UB9 . . . . 190 A1
Maidenhead SL6 . . . . 202 C6
Milton Keynes MK3 . . . . . 57 D8
Denham Court Dr UB9 . . . 190 B1
Denham Ctry Park Nature
Reserve★ UB9. . . . . 190 B2
Denham Ctry Pk★ UB9 . . . 190 B2
Denham Garden Village
UB9 . . . . 189 F5
Denham Golf Club Sta
UB9. . . . . 189 D2
DENHAM GREEN 189 E5
Denham Green Cl UB9 . . . 190 A4
Denham Green La UB9. . . 189 F5
Denham La SL9 . . . . 178 A2
Denham Lodge UB9. . . . . 201 C6
Denham Quarry Park Nature
Reserve★ UB9 . . . . 190 C1
Denham Rd
Iver Heath SL0 . . . . 200 E5
Lane End HP14 . . . . 171 C5
Denham Sta UB9. . . . . . . 190 A4
Denham View MK18. . . . . . 75 F6
Denham Village Inf Sch
UB9. . . . . 189 F2
Denham Way UB9 . . . . . . 190 A1
Denham Way (North Orbital
Rd)
Denham Green UB9. . . . . 189 F7
Maple Cross WD3 . . . . . . 178 C4
Denholme Lodge SL3 . . . 211 B7
Denison Ct MK7. . . . . 48 D6
Denmark St
Maidenhead SL6 . . . . 202 E8
Milton Keynes MK2 . . . . . 58 E8
Denmead MK8 . . . . 33 E2
Denmead Cl SL9 . . . . 188 E4
DENNER HILL 150 E4
Denner Hill Farm Rd
HP16 . . . . 150 F5
Dennis Cl HP22 . . . . 118 A4
Denniston Ho HP12 . . . . . 172 C8
Dennis Way LU7 . . . . 204 D6
Denny Rd SL3. . . . . 206 F2
Denny's La HP4 . . . . 134 F2
Denton Ct SL7 . . . . 183 F3
Denton Wy SL1 . . . . 206 B4
De Pirenore HP15. . . . . . . 162 E2
Depot Rd SL6. . . . . 203 A6
Derby Arms 2 HP20 . . . . 115 D8
Derby Pl HP18 . . . . 100 C5
Derby Rd UB8 . . . . 201 D3
Derehams Ave HP10 . . . . 174 C3
Derehams La HP10. . . . . . 174 C2
Derek Rd SL6. . . . . 203 C8
Dere Pl MK2 . . . . 58 E4
Deri Dene Cl 2 TW19 . . . 213 E1
Derwent Cl
Little Chalfont HP7 . . . . . 166 B8
Newport Pagnell MK16 . . 22 D4
Derwent Dr
Maidenhead SL6 . . . . 202 D8
Milton Keynes MK3 . . . . . 57 E8
Slough SL1. . . . . 204 C8
Derwent Rd
Aylesbury HP21 . . . . 116 B6
Leighton Buzzard LU7 . . . 80 B7
Desborough Ave HP11 . . 172 E6
Desborough Bsns Pk
HP12. . . . . 172 E8
Desborough Coll SL6. . . . 202 E5
Desborough Cres SL6. . . 202 D5
Desborough Gn 1 HP20 . 101 D2
Desborough Ho 14 HP13. 173 E8
Desborough Park Rd
HP12. . . . . 172 E8
Desborough Rd HP11 . . . 172 F7
Desborough St HP11 . . . . 172 F7
Deseronto Wharf Ind Est
SL3 . . . . 206 E4
Develin Cl MK14 . . . . 34 F7
De Vere Cl HP5 . . . . 143 F2
Devereux Pl
Aylesbury HP19 . . . . 101 A2
Milton Keynes MK6 . . . . . 46 F7
Devereux Rd SL4. . . . . . . 210 D5
Deverill Rd HP21 . . . . 115 C3
Deverills Way SL3. . . . . . 207 C2
Devon Ave SL1. . . . . 205 C7
Devon Cl MK3 . . . . 46 F1

Devon Rd HP19 . . . . 101 A3
Devonshire Ave HP6 . . . . . 154 B2
Devonshire Cl
Amersham HP6 . . . . 154 C2
Farnham Royal SL2 . . . . . . 198 B3
Devonshire Gdns SL6 . . . . 204 A7
Devonshire Gn SL2 . . . . . . 198 B3
Devonshire Lodge 10
SL6 . . . . 202 F6
Devon Way UB10 . . . . 201 F3
Dewar Spur SL3 . . . . 211 F8
Dewsbury MK14 . . . . 34 C8
Dexter Ave MK6 . . . . 46 F8
Dexter Ho MK6 . . . . 46 F8
Dhoon Rise SL6 . . . . 202 F6
Diamond Rd SL1 . . . . 206 A4
Diana Cl SL3 . . . . 206 E7
Diane Cl HP21 . . . . 116 A4
Diane Wlk HP21 . . . . 116 A4
Dibden Hill HP8 . . . . 177 C6
Dickens Cl MK43 . . . . .3 F6
Dickens Dr HP16 . . . . 32 B6
Dickens La MK17 . . . . 58 B2
Dickens Pl SL3 . . . . 212 E6
Dickens Rd MK12 . . . . 33 C8
Dickens Spinney MK46 . . . .6 C4
Dickens Way HP19 . . . . . . 100 F2
Dickens Yd LU7 . . . . 80 E6
Dickins Pl SL3 . . . . 212 E6
Dicks Way HP19 . . . . 100 F3
Diddington Cl MK2 . . . . 58 C3
Digby Cl OX9 . . . . 126 B1
Digby Croft MK10 . . . . 35 E3
DIGGS 126 F5
Dilwyn Ct 1 HP12 . . . . 172 E2
Dingle Dell LU7 . . . . 70 F2
Dingleberry MK46 . . . . .6 F4
Dinmore 2 HP3 . . . . 145 F3
DINTON 113 F2
Discovery St HP18 . . . . . . 100 E5
Disraeli Cres HP13 . . . . . . 161 F1
Disraeli Ct SL3 . . . . 212 B8
Disraeli Pk HP9 . . . . 175 F4
Disraeli Sch The HP13 . . . 161 F1
Disraeli Sq 4 HP13 . . . . . . 115 A8
Diswell Brook Way MK19 . 31 E5
DITCHFIELD 171 A3
Ditchfield Cotts HP14 . . . . 171 A3
Ditchingham Cl HP19 . . . . 115 B7
Ditton Park Acad SL1 . . . . 205 E5
Ditton Park Rd SL3 . . . . . . 211 E8
Ditton Rd
Datchet SL3 . . . . 211 D7
Slough SL3 . . . . 211 F8
Dixie Ct HP20 . . . . 116 A8
Dixie La MK7 . . . . 48 C6
Dixon Cl HP21 . . . . 115 B6
Dixon's Wharf HP23 . . . . . 104 D2
Dobbins La HP22 . . . . 131 B5
Dobson's La RG9 . . . . 191 C8
Docton Mill 3 MK4 . . . . . . 45 E2
Doctor's Commons Rd
HP4 . . . . 135 B4
Doddsfield Rd SL2 . . . . . . 198 A2
Dodds La HP8 . . . . 177 B8
Dodkin MK6 . . . . 47 B5
Dodman Gn MK4 . . . . 57 B8
Doggetts Farm Rd UB9 . . 189 C4
Doggetts Wood Cl HP8 . . 166 B5
Doggetts Wood La HP8 . . 166 B5
Dog Kennel La WD3 . . . . . 167 F5
Dolben St MK15 . . . . 35 D8
Dolesden La RG9 . . . . 169 D1
Dollicot HP17 . . . . 126 F6
Dolphin Ct
Loudwater HP11 . . . . 174 A3
Slough SL1 . . . . 206 B4
Dolphin Pl HP21 . . . . 115 A4
Dolphin Rd SL1 . . . . 206 B4
Dolphin Sq 2 HP23 . . . . . 119 A3
Dominica Gr MK3 . . . . 58 B3
Domino Wy HP18 . . . . 100 E5
Donkey Dr SL8 . . . . 185 A3
Donkey La
Bourne End SL8 . . . . 185 A3
Tring HP23 . . . . 118 E2
West Drayton UB7 . . . . . . 208 C2
Donnay Cl SL9 . . . . 188 D5
Donnington MK13 . . . . 34 B6
Donnington Gdns SL6 . . . 195 F1
Donnybrook Ho 3 HP13 . 173 C7
Don The MK3 . . . . 46 D1
Doon Way MK2 . . . . 58 C5
Dorchester Ave MK3 . . . . . 47 A2
Dorchester Cl
Maidenhead SL6 . . . . 195 B1
Stoke Mandeville HP22 . . 116 B2
Dorchester Ho SL9 . . . . . . 188 F4
Doreen Cl MK2 . . . . 50 C7
Dorian Cl HP21 . . . . 119 D4
Dorking Pl MK5 . . . . 46 B4
Dormans Cl MK12 . . . . 36 A2
Dormer Ave LU7 . . . . 79 E3
Dormer Cl HP21 . . . . 115 B6
Dormer Ct 4 HP20 . . . . . . 101 F2
Dormer La HP15 . . . . 163 B7
Dornels SL2 . . . . 206 C7
DORNEY 204 C3
Dorney Court★ SL4 . . . . . 204 B3
Dorney End HP5 . . . . 144 A1
Dorney Hill N SL1, HP9 . . 187 A4
Dorney Hill S SL2 . . . . 187 A4
Dorney Lake Pk★ SL4 . . . 209 B8
Dorney Pl MK13 . . . . 34 C2
DORNEY REACH 203 F3
Dorney Reach Rd SL6 . . . 203 F3
Dorney Sch SL6 . . . . 203 F3

Dorneywood Cl SL1 . . . . . 197 C3
Dorneywood Gdn★ SL1 . 197 D6
Dorney Wood Rd
Burnham SL1 . . . . 197 D6
Littleworth Common SL1 . 186 C1
Dorrells Rd HP27 . . . . 138 D6
Dorrien's Croft HP4 . . . . . 134 F7
Dorset Cl
Berkhamsted HP4 . . . . 134 F5
Milton Keynes MK3 . . . . . . 46 F1
Dorset Lodge 9 SL6 . . . . 202 F6
Dorset Pl HP21 . . . . 116 C6
Dorset Rd SL4 . . . . 210 C6
Dorset Way MK43 . . . . 24 D2
Dorsey Cl MK8 . . . . 45 E6
DORTON 96 F1
Dorton Cl MK8 . . . . 33 F1
Dorton Rd HP18 . . . . 111 B4
Douglas Cl SL7 . . . . 184 A3
Douglas Gdns HP4 . . . . . . 135 A5
Douglas La TW19 . . . . 211 F1
Douglas Pl MK6 . . . . 46 E8
Douglas Rd
Aylesbury HP20 . . . . 102 A1
Slough SL2 . . . . 205 D8
Stanwell TW19 . . . . 213 D1
Douglas Wlk 6 MK10 . . . . 36 C3
Doune Ho MK3 . . . . 46 F2
Dove Cl
Aylesbury HP21 . . . . 115 C5
Buckingham MK18 . . . . 52 E7
Newport Pagnell MK16 . . . 22 D4
Dovecote
Haddenham HP17 . . . . . . 126 F6
Newport Pagnell MK16 . . . 22 C4
Dovecote Cft MK14 . . . . . . 21 E1
Dovecote Cl
Haddenham HP17 . . . . . . 126 F6
Monks Risborough HP27 . 139 C5
Dovecote Cotts MK5 . . . . . 46 A4
Dovecote Mews UB9 . . . . 190 E8
Dovecot Rd 11 HP13 . . . . 173 A7
Dove Ct HP9 . . . . 175 D3
Dove Ho HP19 . . . . 101 F4
Dove House Cl
Edlesborough LU6 . . . . . . 92 F4
Winslow MK18 . . . . 66 A4
Dove House Cres SL2 . . . 197 E2
Dovehouse Mews MK16 . . 12 B6
Dovehouse Rd 3 HP13 . . 173 A7
Doveleat OX39 . . . . 147 D7
Dove Pk WD3 . . . . 167 B4
Dover Cl LU7 . . . . 105 D2
Dover Gate MK3 . . . . 57 F8
Dover Rd SL1 . . . . 204 F7
Dove St LU7 . . . . 78 E8
Dovetail Cl HP12 . . . . 172 D8
Dowding Rd UB10 . . . . 201 F5
Dower Cl HP9 . . . . 175 C5
Dower Mews 5 HP4 . . . . . 135 C4
Dower Pk SL4 . . . . 209 E3
Downdean MK6 . . . . 47 A8
Downderry Croft MK4 . . . . 57 B8
Downer Cl MK18 . . . . 52 E8
Downer Dr WD3 . . . . 156 F3
Downham Rd MK17 . . . . . . 49 C4
DOWNHEAD PARK 35 B5
Downing Cl MK3 . . . . 58 B8
Downing Path SL2 . . . . . . 197 E1
Downings Wood WD3 . . . 178 D5
Downland MK8 . . . . 33 E2
DOWNLEY 161 C3
Downley Ave MK13 . . . . . . 34 C3
Downley Cl HP13 . . . . 161 D2
Downley Rd HP14 . . . . 161 D6
Downley Sch The HP13 . . 161 D3
Down Pl SL4 . . . . 209 A8
DOWNS BARN 35 A5
Downs Barn Bvd MK14 . . . 34 F5
Downs Barn Rdbt MK14 . . 34 F5
Downs Barn Sch MK14 . . 34 F5
Downs Field MK16 . . . . 22 F3
Downs Pk HP13 . . . . 161 E2
Downs Rd SL3 . . . . 206 D4
Downs View MK17 . . . . 48 C2
Downs Villas 17 HP21 . . . 49 D4
Doxford Heath 1 MK10 . . 36 C4
Dragon Tail HP17 . . . . 127 A5
Drake Ave SL3 . . . . 206 D2
Drake Cl HP21 . . . . 115 B6
Drakeloe Cl MK17 . . . . 60 F8
Drakes Dr HP18 . . . . 125 E5
Drakes Farm HP18 . . . . . . 125 E5
Drakes Mews MK8 . . . . 45 F7
Drakes Mews Bsns Ctr
MK8 . . . . 45 F7
Drake's Rd HP7 . . . . 165 E8
Drakewell Rd MK17 . . . . . . 48 D1
Drayhorse Cres MK17 . . . 49 A5
Draymans La SL7 . . . . 183 D1
DRAYTON BEAUCHAMP . . 118 B5
Drayton Ct 8 HP20 . . . . . . 101 F2
Drayton Gdns UB7 . . . . . . 208 E4
Drayton Park Sch MK2 . . . 58 D5
DRAYTON PARSLOW 68 C6
Drayton Parslow Village Sch
MK17 . . . . 68 C6
Drayton Rd
Aylesbury HP20 . . . . 101 D2
Milton Keynes MK2 . . . . . . 58 C7
Newton Longville MK17 . . 57 C2
Dr Challoner's Gram Sch
HP6 . . . . 154 C1
Dr Challoner's High Sch
HP7 . . . . 166 B7
Dresser Rd HP16 . . . . 151 C5
Drew Ct MK3 . . . . 47 A4

Drew Mdw SL2 . . . . 198 C8
Drews Pk HP9 . . . . 175 C6
Drey The SL9 . . . . 177 E5
Drift Rd SL4 . . . . 209 A1
Drift Way
Colnbrook SL3 . . . . 212 C7
Olney MK46 . . . . .6 F5
Drinkwater Cl OX25 . . . . . . 95 D7
Drive The
Amersham HP7 . . . . 154 D1
Bourne End SL8 . . . . 184 F4
Chalfont St Peter SL9 . . . 177 F3
Cranfield MK43 . . . . 24 D2
Datchet SL3 . . . . 211 B6
Ickenham UB10 . . . . 190 E1
Ivinghoe Aston LU7 . . . . . 92 A1
Slough SL3 . . . . 206 A4
Wraysbury TW19 . . . . 211 D2
Dromore Inf Sch SL1 . . . . 186 C1
Dropmore Rd
Burnham SL1 . . . . 197 C5
Littleworth Common SL1 . 186 C1
Drovers Croft MK12 . . . . . 33 B4
Drovers La RG9 . . . . 169 B2
Drovers Way
Dunstable LU6 . . . . 93 F8
Newton Longville MK17 . . 57 C2
Seer Green HP9 . . . . 176 C4
Drovers Wy MK12 . . . . 18 E2
Druce End NN12 . . . . 18 E6
Druids Wlk OX39 . . . . 147 C6
Drummond Ho 4 SL4 . . . . 210 D4
Drummond Ride HP23 . . . 119 A5
Drummound Hay MK15 . . 35 C7
Drydell La HP5 . . . . 153 F8
Dryden Cl
Aylesbury HP20 . . . . 101 E2
Newport Pagnell MK16 . . . 22 A4
Dubery Cl HP17 . . . . 114 D5
Duchess Ave SL1 . . . . 205 A7
Duchess Gr NN12 . . . . 18 D3
Duchess Gr MK7 . . . . 48 C7
Duchess St SL1 . . . . 204 E5
DUCK END
Akeley 42 A8
Swanbourne 66 F4
Duck End
Aylesbury HP20 . . . . 115 C8
Great Brickhill MK17 . . . . 59 D1
Duck La
Ludgershall HP18 . . . . 96 C8
Woburn MK17 . . . . 60 F7
Duck Lake MK18 . . . . 41 E3
Duck Lake Cl MK18 . . . . . . 41 E4
Duckmore La HP23 . . . . . . 118 E2
Duck Sq OX39 . . . . 147 C6
Duckworth Ct MK6 . . . . 46 E7
Dudley Cl HP21 . . . . 116 C7
Dudley Ct SL1 . . . . 206 A3
Dudley Hill MK5 . . . . 46 A6
Dudley Ho 1 HP3 . . . . 146 A4
Dudley La RG9 . . . . 181 A6
DUDSWELL 134 C4
Dudswell La HP4 . . . . 134 D7
Duffield Bank 8 MK10 . . . 36 B3
Duffield La SL2 . . . . 198 C2
Duffield Pk SL2 . . . . 199 A2
Dukes Ave LU6 . . . . 107 E8
Dukes Dr
Farnham Common SL2 . . 198 A8
Milton Keynes MK2 . . . . . . 47 C1
Dukes Kiln Dr SL9 . . . . . . 188 C3
Dukes La SL9 . . . . 188 E4
Dukes Mdw SL8 . . . . 185 B3
Dukes Piece MK18 . . . . . . 52 F8
Dukes Pl
Marlow SL7 . . . . 183 D2
Slough SL1 . . . . 205 F6
Dukes Ride
Gerrards Cross SL9 . . . . . 188 E3
Ickenham UB10 . . . . 201 E8
Leighton Buzzard LU7 . . . 70 F3
Dukes Row HP13 . . . . 99 A1
Duke St
Aspley Guise MK17 . . . . . . 49 D4
Eton SL4 . . . . 210 C7
Henley-on-Thames RG9 . 191 E2
High Wycombe HP13 . . . . 173 C6
Princes Risborough HP27 . 139 B4
Dukes Valley SL9 . . . . 188 B2
Dukes Way
Berkhamsted HP4 . . . . 135 A6
Uxbridge UB8 . . . . 201 C4
Dukes Wood Ave SL9 . . . 188 E3
Dukes Wood Dr SL9 . . . . 188 D3
Dulverton Ct LU7 . . . . 80 C8
Dulverton Dr MK4 . . . . 46 D3
Dulwich Cl MK16 . . . . 22 C2
Dumbarton Wy SL1 . . . . . 206 C1
Dumbletons WD3 . . . . 178 A6
Dumfries Cl MK3 . . . . 46 F3
Dunbar Cl
Milton Keynes MK3 . . . . . . 57 D8
Slough SL3 . . . . 206 A6
Dunbar Dr OX9 . . . . 126 A1
Duncan Gr MK5 . . . . 45 F6
Duncan Lock Ho HP9 . . . 175 F2
Duncannon Cres SL4 . . . . 209 D4
Duncan Rd MK43 . . . . 24 C2
Dunchurch Dale MK7 . . . . 48 B5
Duncombe Rd HP4 . . . . . . 134 E6
Duncombe St SL1 . . . . 58 C7
Duncroft SL4 . . . . 209 F4
Dundale Prim Sch HP23 . 119 A5
Dundale Rd HP23 . . . . 119 A4

Dundee Rd SL1 . . . . 205 A8
Dungeness Ct MK4 . . . . . . 46 A1
Dungrovehill La SL7 . . . . . 194 D3
Dunholme End SL6 . . . . . . 202 D3
Dunkeld Ho HP11 . . . . 174 B4
Dunkery Beacon MK4 . . . . 46 D3
Dunnet Cl MK4 . . . . 57 A8
Dunny La WD4 . . . . 156 F7
Dunsby Rd MK6 . . . . 47 A4
Dunsham La HP20 . . . . 101 E2
Dunsley Pl HP23 . . . . 119 B3
DUNSMORE 141 A7
Dunsmore Ave HP27 . . . . 139 C5
Dunsmore Ride HP27 . . . . 139 C5
DUNSTABLE 93 E8
Dunstable Downs★ LU6 . . 93 E4
Dunstable Ho 4 SL7 . . . . 183 E1
Dunstable Rd
Dagnall HP4 . . . . 107 C2
Eaton Bray LU6 . . . . 93 A5
Totternhoe LU6 . . . . 93 D7
Dunster Cl MK4 . . . . 46 E3
Dunster Gdns SL1 . . . . . . 205 A6
Dunston Hill HP23 . . . . . . 119 A4
Dunthorne Way MK8 . . . . . 45 D6
DUNTON 77 E5
Dunton Rd LU7 . . . . 78 D6
Dunvedin Pl MK12 . . . . 33 D4
Dunvegan Cl MK2 . . . . 58 D4
Dunwood Ct SL6 . . . . 202 C5
Dunwood Rise HP13 . . . . 162 B1
Duparc Cl MK7 . . . . 48 C5
Dupre Cl SL1 . . . . 204 E4
Dupre Cres HP9 . . . . 176 B1
Du Pre Wlk HP10 . . . . 185 D4
Durgate MK7 . . . . 48 A8
Durham Ave SL1 . . . . 205 A7
Durham Ho 1 MK3 . . . . 46 F1
Durham Rd SL1 . . . . 105 C3
Durley Hollow HP13 . . . . . 162 B1
Durlston End MK4 . . . . 57 A8
Durrans Ct MK2 . . . . 47 C1
Durrans Ho MK2 . . . . 47 C1
Durrans La HP4 . . . . 134 F5
Durrants Path HP5 . . . . . . 144 A4
Durrants Rd HP4 . . . . 134 F5
Durrell Cl LU7 . . . . 80 E7
Dutch Barn Cl TW19 . . . . 213 D1
Dutch Elm Ave SL4 . . . . . 210 F7
Dutton Way SL0 . . . . 207 E2
Dwights Yd 6 HP4 . . . . 135 C4
Dyersdale MK13 . . . . 34 C5
Dyers Mews MK14 . . . . 34 F6
Dyers Rd LU6 . . . . 92 D7
Dymchurch Cl 2 MK10 . . 36 B4
Dymock Cl HP22 . . . . 85 B4
Dyson Cl SL4 . . . . 210 B4
Dyson Dr UB8 . . . . 201 E4

E

E-ACT Burnham Pk Acad The
SL1 . . . . 204 B8
Eagle Cl HP6 . . . . 154 F2
Eagles Rd HP20 . . . . 116 A8
EAGLESTONE 47 B7
Eaglestone Rdbt MK6 . . . . 47 A8
Eagle Way MK43 . . . . .3 F6
Eagle Wlk MK9 . . . . 34 F3
EAKLEY LANES 4 D2
Ealing Chase MK10 . . . . . . 47 F8
Eames Cl HP20 . . . . 101 F3
Eardley Pl MK8 . . . . 45 D6
Earl Cl HP21 . . . . 162 A1
Earl Howe Rd HP15 . . . . . 163 D6
Earls Cl MK2 . . . . 58 C8
Earlsfield SL6 . . . . 203 C2
Earls La SL1 . . . . 204 F5
Earls Willow MK13 . . . . 34 A8
Earlswood Cl HP21 . . . . . . 116 A5
Easby Gr MK6 . . . . 36 A1
Eascote Rd HP21 . . . . 116 B4
EASINGTON 111 B1
Easington La HP18 . . . . . . 111 B1
Easington Terr HP18 . . . . 111 B1
Eastaff Croft 6 MK4 . . . . . 49 A5
East Berkshire Coll
Slough SL3 . . . . 207 A3
Windsor SL4 . . . . 210 C5
Eastbourne Rd SL1 . . . . . 205 A7
Eastbridge SL2 . . . . 206 B5
Eastbrook Cl OX25 . . . . . . 95 E7
EAST BURNHAM 198 A4
East Burnham Cotts SL2 . 198 A4
East Burnham La SL2 . . . 198 A4
Eastbury Ct MK4 . . . . 46 D1
East Chapel MK4 . . . . 57 B8
EAST CLAYDON 74 F3
East Claydon Rd MK18 . . . 65 D2
East Claydon Sch MK18 . . 74 F2
East Comm SL9 . . . . 180 C5
East Cres SL4 . . . . 209 F6
East Dales MK13 . . . . 34 C5
East Dr
High Wycombe HP13 . . . . 173 E8
Stoke Poges SL2 . . . . 198 E2
EAST END
Cranfield 25 C1
North Crawley 24 F6
East End HP22 . . . . 87 D1
Eastergate HP9 . . . . 175 C4
Eastern Dene HP15 . . . . . 163 B5
Eastern St HP20 . . . . 101 E1
Eastfield Cl 3 SL1 . . . . . . 206 A3
Eastfield Cres NN12 . . . . . 18 F5

Eastfield Dr MK19 . . . . 11 A3
Eastfield Rd
Aylesbury HP20 . . . . 116 B8
Burnham SL1 . . . . 204 A8
Princes Risborough HP27 . 139 C3
East Green Cl MK5 . . . . . . 45 F6
East Hills MK43 . . . . 25 B1
East La MK7 . . . . 47 F7
Eastlands HP27 . . . . 149 E5
Eastnor HP3 . . . . 146 A3
Eastoke Pl MK4 . . . . 57 A8
Easton St HP11 . . . . 173 B6
Easton Terr HP13 . . . . 173 C6
East Paddock SL6 . . . . 194 F6
East Rd
Cranfield MK43 . . . . 24 C2
Maidenhead SL6 . . . . 202 E7
West Drayton UB7 . . . . . . 208 F2
East Richardson St 5
HP11 . . . . 172 F7
East Ridge SL8 . . . . 185 B4
East Spur MK7 . . . . 47 F7
East St
Adstock MK18 . . . . 53 F1
Chesham HP5 . . . . 154 B8
Olney MK46 . . . . .7 A4
East Terr SL4 . . . . 210 E7
East View OX25 . . . . 81 A3
East Walk N MK9 . . . . 34 E2
East Walk S MK9 . . . . 34 E2
East Way HP9 . . . . 175 A1
Eastwick Cres WD3 . . . . . 178 F8
Eastwood Ct 1 SL7 . . . . . 183 F1
Eastwood Rd HP14 . . . . . 158 F3
Eaton Ave
High Wycombe HP12 . . . . 172 D8
Milton Keynes MK2 . . . . . . 58 D7
Slough SL1 . . . . 204 C6
EATON BRAY 92 F6
Eaton Bray Acad LU6 . . . . 92 F6
Eaton Bray Rd
Edlesborough LU6 . . . . . . 92 C5
Honeywick LU6 . . . . 92 E8
Eaton Cl HP21 . . . . 116 F2
Eatongate Cl LU6 . . . . 92 E5
EATON GREEN 92 C7
Eaton Green Rd LU6 . . . . . 36 C3
Eaton Pk LU6 . . . . 92 F6
Eaton Pl HP12 . . . . 172 D8
Eaton Rd HP21 . . . . 115 D7
Ebble Cl HP21 . . . . 115 C4
Ebbsgrove MK5 . . . . 34 B1
Ebenezer Ho HP10 . . . . . 174 C2
Ebsworth Cl SL6 . . . . 196 C3
Eclipse Ave MK10 . . . . 35 E2
Eddington Ct MK4 . . . . 46 D1
Eddy St HP4 . . . . 135 A5
Eden Cl
Aylesbury HP21 . . . . 115 D4
Slough SL3 . . . . 207 A1
Eden Sh Ctr HP11 . . . . . . 173 A7
Eden Wlk MK3 . . . . 46 E1
Edgar Rd UB7 . . . . 208 E5
EDGCOTT 72 F2
Edgecombe Rd HP21 . . . . 116 B5
Edgecote MK5 . . . . 46 A8
Edgecote Ho 11 HP13 . . . 173 B7
Edgecott Rd HP18 . . . . . . 82 F7
Edgehill OX9 . . . . 125 F2
Edge Hill Ct MK18 . . . . 41 E2
Edge St HP19 . . . . 101 C1
Edgewood HP11 . . . . 173 D5
Edgeworth Cl SL1 . . . . 206 D4
Edging La MK18 . . . . 52 F6
Edinburgh Ave SL1 . . . . . 205 B7
Edinburgh Gate UB9 . . . . 189 F5
Edinburgh Gdns SL4 . . . . 210 D5
Edinburgh Ho MK3 . . . . . . 57 D7
Edinburgh Pl HP21 . . . . . . 115 C6
Edinburgh Rd
Maidenhead SL6 . . . . 195 E1
Marlow SL7 . . . . 183 E3
Edison Ave UB7 . . . . 208 F4
Edison Rd HP19 . . . . 100 E1
Edison Sq MK5 . . . . 46 C5
Edith Bell Ho SL9 . . . . 177 E4
Edith Rd SL6 . . . . 202 A7
EDLESBOROUGH 92 E4
Edlesborough Sch LU6 . . 92 E3
Edlyn Cl HP4 . . . . 134 F5
Edmonds Cl MK18 . . . . 41 F1
Edmonds Rd HP14 . . . . . . 171 B4
Edmund Ct
Beaconsfield HP9 . . . . 186 A8
Milton Keynes MK5 . . . . . . 45 F7
Edmunds Cl HP12 . . . . 172 C5
Edmunds Gdns HP12 . . . . 172 C5
Edmunds Way SL2 . . . . . . 206 B7
Edrich Ave MK6 . . . . 46 F8
Edstone Pl MK4 . . . . 46 C3
Edward Cl HP21 . . . . 116 A4
Edwards Croft MK13 . . . . . 34 A7
Edwards Cft 8 SL8 . . . . . . 185 B3
Edward Wlk HP21 . . . . 116 A4
Edwin Allman Pl HP15 . . . 162 E2
Edwin Cl MK17 . . . . 48 D2
Edy Ct MK5 . . . . 34 A1
Edzell Cres MK4 . . . . 45 E2
Eelbrook Ave MK13 . . . . . 34 C2
Eeles Cl HP19 . . . . 100 F3
Egerton La HP19 . . . . 38 A7
Egerton Gate MK5 . . . . 46 B4
Egerton Rd
Berkhamsted HP4 . . . . 135 B6

Egerton Rd continued
Slough SL2 . . . . **197** E1
Egerton-Rothesay Sch
HP4 . . . . **134** E4
Egglesfield Cl HP4 . . . . . . **134** E6
Eggleton Dr HP23 . . . . . . **119** A5
Eghams Cl HP9 . . . . **175** C4
Eghams Gn SL8 . . . . **185** B3
Eghams Wood Rd HP9 . . **175** C4
Egmont Ave MK11 . . . . **32** E4
Egremont Gdns SL1 . . . . . **205** A5
EGYPT **198** B8
Egypt La SL2 . . . . **187** B1
Egypt Way HP15 . . . . **115** A8
Egypt Wood Cotts SL2 . . **187** B1
Eider Cl MK18 . . . . **52** E8
Eight Acres
Burnham SL1 . . . . **197** B1
East End MK43 . . . . **25** B2
Tring HP23 . . . . **119** A4
Elangeni Sch HP6 . . . . **154** E3
Elbow Mdw SL3 . . . . **212** F6
Elderberry Rd HP18 . . . . . **100** D5
Elder Cl
Loudwater HP11 . . . . **174** B3
West Drayton UB7 . . . . . . **208** E6
Elderdene OX39 . . . . **147** D8
Elderfield Rd SL2 . . . . **198** F6
Elder Gate
Milton Keynes, Rooksley
MK9 . . . . **34** C1
Milton Keynes, Winterhill
MK9 . . . . **46** C8
Elder Way HP15 . . . . **163** B3
Elder Wy SL3 . . . . **206** F4
Eldridge La HP17 . . . . **130** C3
Eleanor Cl MK17 . . . . **60** F7
Eleanor Gdns HP21 . . . . . **115** F6
Eleanor Rd SL9 . . . . **177** C2
Eleanor Wlk MK17 . . . . **60** F7
Elfords MK6 . . . . **47** A6
Elgar Gr MK7 . . . . **48** C4
Elgin Ho SL3 . . . . **212** E6
Elgiva La HP5 . . . . **154** B8
Elgiva Theatre ★ HP5 . . . . **154** B8
Elham Way HP21 . . . . **116** A4
Eliot Cl
Aylesbury HP19 . . . . **100** F2
Newport Pagnell MK16 . . . . **21** F5
Eliot Dr SL7 . . . . **183** F4
Elizabeth Ave HP6 . . . . . . **166** C8
Elizabeth Cl
Aylesbury HP21 . . . . **116** B4
Cookham Rise SL6 . . . . . . **195** F7
Elizabeth Ct
High Wycombe HP13 . . . . . **173** C6
High Wycombe, Wycombe Marsh
HP13 . . . . **173** E5
10 Slough SL1 . . . . **206** A4
3 Windsor SL4 . . . . **210** C5
Elizabeth Dr HP23 . . . . . . **119** B6
Elizabeth Ii Ave HP4 . . . . **134** E4
Elizabeth Rd
Marlow SL7 . . . . **183** E3
Stokenchurch HP14 . . . . . **158** F4
Elizabeth Sq MK2 . . . . **58** C8
Elizabeth Way SL2 . . . . . . **198** F4
Elizabeth Woodville Sch The
MK19 . . . . **31** F4
Elize Cl HP18 . . . . **100** E5
Elkins Rd SL2 . . . . **187** E2
Ellen Pl HP21 . . . . **115** C5
Ellen Rd HP21 . . . . **115** C5
Ellenstow MK13 . . . . **34** A4
Ellen Wlk HP21 . . . . **115** B6
Ellerburn Pl MK4 . . . . **46** B3
Ellery Rise RG9 . . . . **170** F1
ELLESBOROUGH **130** B2
Ellesborough Gr MK8 . . . . . **33** D3
Ellesborough Rd
Butler's Cross HP17 . . . . . **130** C3
Ellesborough HP17 . . . . . . **130** A2
Wendover HP22 . . . . **131** A3
Ellesmere Cl
Datchet SL3 . . . . **211** A8
Totternhoe LU6 . . . . **93** C6
Ellesmere Rd HP4 . . . . . . **135** D4
Elliman Ave SL2 . . . . **205** F6
Ellington Ct SL6 . . . . **203** C7
Ellington Gdns SL6 . . . . . **203** C7
Ellington Pk SL6 . . . . **195** E1
Ellington Rd SL6 . . . . **203** C7
Elliots Cl UB8 . . . . **208** C8
Elliott Ho HP11 . . . . **172** F4
Ellis Ave
Chalfont St Peter SL9 . . . . **177** F2
Slough SL1 . . . . **205** E4
Ellisgill Ct MK13 . . . . **34** B4
Ellison Cl SL4 . . . . **209** F4
Ellison Ct HP23 . . . . **118** F3
Ellison Ho **14** SL4 . . . . . . **210** D6
Ellis Way HP14 . . . . **171** B4
Ellsworth Rd HP11 . . . . . . **172** F4
Ellwood Ho SL9 . . . . **177** E2
Ellwood Rd HP9 . . . . **175** B1
Ellwood Rise HP8 . . . . . . **177** C8
Ellwood Terr WD3 . . . . . . **167** D4
Elmar Gn SL2 . . . . **198** A2
Elm Brook Cl HP18 . . . . . . **112** C1
Elm Cl
Amersham HP6 . . . . **154** C1
Butler's Cross HP17 . . . . . **130** C3
Chinnor OX39 . . . . **147** C5
Farnham Common SL2 . . . **198** C6
Hazelmere HP15 . . . . **163** A3

Elm Cl continued
Newton Longville MK17 . . . . **57** C2
Weston Turville HP22 . . . . **116** F2
Elm Croft SL3 . . . . **211** C6
Elm Ct
Berkhamsted HP4 . . . . . . **135** B4
Butler's Cross HP17 . . . . . **130** C3
Elmdale Gdns HP27 . . . . . **139** B3
Elm Dr
Chinnor OX39 . . . . **147** C5
Deanshanger MK19 . . . . . . **31** D5
Elmers Cl MK19 . . . . **44** A6
Elmers Mdw MK18 . . . . **76** A1
Elmers Pk MK3 . . . . **58** A8
Elm Farm Rd HP21 . . . . . . **116** A5
Elmfield NN12 . . . . **18** D3
Elmfields Gate MK18 . . . . . **66** A4
Elm Gn HP21 . . . . **115** D7
Elm Gr
Berkhamsted HP4 . . . . . . **135** C4
Maidenhead SL6 . . . . **202** E7
West Drayton UB7 . . . . . . **208** F6
Woburn Sands MK17 . . . . . **49** B4
ELMHURST **101** E3
Elmhurst **5** HP16 . . . . . . **152** A8
Elmhurst Cl
High Wycombe HP13 . . . . **162** D1
Milton Keynes MK4 . . . . . . **46** F4
Elmhurst Ct SL3 . . . . **207** A3
Elmhurst Rd
Aylesbury HP20 . . . . **101** E2
Slough SL3 . . . . **207** A3
Elmhurst Sch HP20 . . . . . **101** E2
Elm La SL8 . . . . **184** F5
Elm Lawn Cl UB8 . . . . **201** E5
Elmlea Dr MK46 . . . . **6** E3
Elmodesham Ho **7** HP7 . . **165** B7
Elmore St HP18 . . . . **100** E5
Elm Rd
High Wycombe HP12 . . . . **172** C4
Princes Risborough HP27 . . **139** C3
Tylers Green HP10 . . . . . . **174** D8
Windsor SL4 . . . . **210** B4
Elmridge Ct MK4 . . . . **46** C2
Elms Dr SL8 . . . . **185** C3
Elmshott Cl HP10 . . . . **163** A1
Elmshott La SL1 . . . . **204** E6
Elmside MK18 . . . . **66** A4
Elmslie Ct SL6 . . . . **202** E7
Elms Rd SL9 . . . . **177** E3
Elm St MK18 . . . . **52** D8
Elms The
Leighton Buzzard LU7 . . . . . **80** E7
Milton Keynes MK3 . . . . . . **57** F8
Preston Bissett MK18 . . . . . **51** B1
Elmswell Gate MK10 . . . . . **48** D8
Elm Tree Cl OX25 . . . . **81** A4
Elm Tree Cotts HP7 . . . . . **164** C2
Elmtree Ct **6** HP16 . . . . . **152** A8
Elmtree Gn HP16 . . . . **152** A8
Elmtree Hill HP5 . . . . **144** B1
Elm Trees HP18 . . . . **125** B7
Elmtree Sch HP5 . . . . **144** B1
Elm Tree Wlk
Chorleywood WD3 . . . . . . **167** F5
Tring HP23 . . . . **119** A5
Elmwood
Maidenhead SL6 . . . . **196** B4
Turvey MK43 . . . . **8** E6
Elmwood Cl HP18 . . . . . . **109** D5
Elmwood Pk SL9 . . . . **188** E3
Elmwood Rd SL2 . . . . **206** B6
Elora Rd HP13 . . . . **173** E7
Elruge Cl UB7 . . . . **208** D3
Elsage Ct LU7 . . . . **105** B8
Elsmore Cl HP21 . . . . **116** A4
Eltham Ave SL1 . . . . **204** E4
Elthorne Rd UB8 . . . . **201** D3
Elthorne Way MK16 . . . . . . **22** C2
Elton MK6 . . . . **47** D7
Elton Dr SL6 . . . . **202** D8
Elwes Rd HP14 . . . . **171** C4
Ely Ave SL1 . . . . **205** C8
Ely Cl HP7 . . . . **165** E8
Ely Ho HP13 . . . . **173** F8
Ely Rd **3** HP22 . . . . **131** E6
Ember Path HP21 . . . . . . **115** C4
Ember Rd SL3 . . . . **207** B3
EMBERTON **6** E1
Emberton Ctry Pk ★ MK46 . . **6** E1
Emberton Sch MK46 . . . . . **13** F8
Embleton Way MK18 . . . . . **52** C7
Emerald Cl MK15 . . . . **74** F8
Emerald Ct SL1 . . . . **205** E4
Emerald Gate MK15 . . . . . **35** E5
Emerson Ct HP10 . . . . **185** E6
EMERSON VALLEY **46** B2
Emerson Valley Sch MK4 . . **46** C2
Emerson Ct HP4 . . . . **134** E7
Emerton Garth HP4 . . . . . **134** E7
Emerton Gdns MK11 . . . . . **32** E5
Emilia Cl SL6 . . . . **195** F1
Emlyns Bldgs SL4 . . . . . . **210** D7
Emma Rothschild Ct
HP23 . . . . **119** A5
Emmett Cl MK4 . . . . **46** C1
Emmett Dr HP21 . . . . **115** E5
EMMINGTON **137** A1
Emperor Cl HP4 . . . . **134** F7
Empingham Cl MK2 . . . . . . **58** D4
Empstead Ct RG9 . . . . . . **191** D2
Enborne Cl HP21 . . . . **115** D4
Enders Ct MK5 . . . . **45** E5
Endfield Pl SL6 . . . . **202** B6
Enfield Chase MK14 . . . . . **34** D5
Enfield Cl UB8 . . . . **201** D3
Engaine Dr MK5 . . . . **45** F7
English Gdns TW19 . . . . . **211** D2

Enigma Ctr The MK1 . . . . . **47** E2
Enmore Gate MK9 . . . . **35** A3
Enmore Rdbt MK9 . . . . **35** A3
Ennell Gr MK2 . . . . **58** C5
Ennerdale Cl MK2 . . . . **58** D6
Ennerdale Cres SL1 . . . . . **204** C8
Ensbury Path HP20 . . . . . **101** E2
Enstone Rd UB10 . . . . **190** F1
Enterprise La MK9 . . . . **35** A3
Epsom Cl LU7 . . . . **80** D6
Epsom Gr MK3 . . . . **57** D6
Equus Cl SL9 . . . . **188** C3
Ercolani Ave HP13 . . . . . . **173** C6
Eriboll Cl LU7 . . . . **80** B6
Erica Cl SL1 . . . . **204** E6
Erica Rd MK12 . . . . **33** E4
Eridge Gn MK7 . . . . **48** A8
Erle Rd HP22 . . . . **102** B2
Errington Dr SL4 . . . . **210** A6
Escarpment Ave HP15 . . . **162** F6
Eskan Ct MK9 . . . . **35** B4
Eskdale Ave HP5 . . . . **144** D1
Eskdale Gdns SL6 . . . . . . **203** B2
Eskdale Lodge HP6 . . . . . **154** C2
Eskdale Rd
Stoke Mandeville HP22 . . . **116** B2
Uxbridge UB8 . . . . **201** B3
Eskdale Way MK10 . . . . . . **36** B3
Esk Way MK3 . . . . **46** E1
Essenden Ct MK11 . . . . **32** F5
Essex Ave SL2 . . . . **205** C8
Essex Cl MK3 . . . . **46** F1
Essex Ho **5** HP20 . . . . . . **101** D1
Essex Pl HP19 . . . . **101** A3
Essex Rd HP5 . . . . **144** C2
Essex Yd HP22 . . . . **89** C2
Estcourt Dr HP15 . . . . **162** F6
Esther Cl MK13 . . . . **34** A6
Eston Ct MK13 . . . . **34** A5
Estover Way OX39 . . . . . . **147** B6
Etheridge Ave MK10 . . . . . **48** C8
Ethorpe MK8 . . . . **33** E1
Ethorpe Cl SL9 . . . . **188** E6
Ethorpe Cres SL9 . . . . . . **188** E6
Ethorpe Ho SL9 . . . . **188** E6
ETON **210** C8
Eton Cl SL3 . . . . **211** A8
Eton Coll SL4 . . . . **210** D8
Eton Cres MK12 . . . . **33** C6
Eton Ct SL4 . . . . **210** D7
Eton End Sch SL3 . . . . . . **211** A8
Eton Ho **1** SL1 . . . . **205** F3
Eton Pl SL7 . . . . **183** D2
Eton Porny CE Fst Sch
SL4 . . . . **210** D8
Eton Rd SL3 . . . . **211** A8
Eton Riverside SL4 . . . . . . **210** D7
Eton Sq SL4 . . . . **210** D7
ETON WICK **204** F1
Eton Wick CE Fst Sch
SL4 . . . . **205** A1
Eton Wick Rd SL4 . . . . . . **205** B1
Eton Wlk **1** SL1 . . . . **205** E3
Eunice Gr HP5 . . . . **154** D7
Europa Bsns Pk MK10 . . . . **36** C2
Europa Ho SL9 . . . . **188** E6
Evans Cl HP21 . . . . **116** A4
Evans Gate MK6 . . . . **46** E8
Evans Way HP23 . . . . **119** B4
Evelyn Cl LU7 . . . . **79** E1
Evelyn Pl MK13 . . . . **34** A7
Evelyns Cl **2** UB8 . . . . . . **208** F7
Evenley Rd NN13 . . . . **38** D1
Evenlode SL6 . . . . **202** F8
Evenlode Cl HP21 . . . . . . **115** C5
Evenlode Rd SL8 . . . . **185** B4
Everard Ave SL1 . . . . **205** E4
Everest Cl HP13 . . . . **173** D6
Everest Rd HP13 . . . . **173** E6
Everglade MK6 . . . . **47** A8
Evergreen Dr **3** UB7 . . . . **208** F4
Evergreen Oak Ave SL4 . . **211** A4
Everley Cl MK4 . . . . **46** C3
Evesham Gn HP19 . . . . . . **101** C3
Evesham Way MK5 . . . . . . **45** D5
Evreham Rd SL0 . . . . **207** E7
Evreham Sp Ctr SL0 . . . . **207** D8
Exbury La MK4 . . . . **45** F1
Excalibur Rd HP18 . . . . . . **100** E3
Exchange Ho MK9 . . . . **34** E2
Exchange St HP20 . . . . . . **115** C8
Exebridge MK4 . . . . **46** C3
Exhims Mews HP4 . . . . . . **134** C6
Exmoor Gate MK4 . . . . **46** E2
Eynsford Terr UB7 . . . . . . **208** F7
Eynsham Ct MK15 . . . . **35** C2
Eyre Cl HP19 . . . . **114** F8
Eyre Gn SL2 . . . . **198** A2
EYTHROPE **113** F8
Eythrope Rd
Eythrope HP18 . . . . **100** A1
Stone HP17 . . . . **114** C6

F

Factory Yd HP9 . . . . **175** E1
Fadmoor Pl **3** MK4 . . . . . . **46** B3
Fagnall La HP7 . . . . **164** D2
Fairacre SL6 . . . . **202** C6
Fair Acres HP16 . . . . **151** D5
Fairacres Ind Est SL4 . . . . **209** D5
Faircroft SL2 . . . . **198** B1
Fairface Wy **4** MK17 . . . . . **49** A5
Fairfax MK13 . . . . **34** C6
Fairfax Cres HP20 . . . . . . **101** E2

Fairfax Mews HP7 . . . . . . **165** A7
Fairfield HP6 . . . . **154** B3
Fairfield App TW19 . . . . . . **211** D1
Fairfield Ave SL3 . . . . **211** D7
Fairfield Cl
Bourne End SL8 . . . . **185** A5
Datchet SL3 . . . . **211** D7
Olney MK46 . . . . **7** A3
Fairfield La SL2 . . . . **198** B3
Fairfield Rd
Burnham SL1 . . . . **197** C2
Paulerspury NN12 . . . . **17** B7
Uxbridge UB8 . . . . **201** D6
West Drayton UB7 . . . . . . **208** E6
Wraysbury TW19 . . . . **211** D1
Fairfields HP15 . . . . **151** E1
Fairford Cres MK15 . . . . . . **35** B6
Fairford Leys Way HP19 . . **115** A7
Fairford Rd SL6 . . . . **202** F8
Fairhaven SL9 . . . . **177** C2
Fair Isle Vw MK14 . . . . **21** B1
Fairlawn Pk SL4 . . . . **209** E3
Fairlawns HP13 . . . . **162** C1
Fairlea SL6 . . . . **202** B3
Fair Leas HP5 . . . . **144** A2
Fairlie Rd SL1 . . . . **205** A8
Fairlight Ave SL4 . . . . **210** D5
Fairlight Dr UB8 . . . . **201** D6
Fair Mdw MK18 . . . . **66** A4
Fairmead The SL3 . . . . . . **212** D7
Fair Mile
Aylesbury HP21 . . . . **116** A7
Henley-on-Thames RG9 . . . **191** C4
Fairmile Ct RG9 . . . . **191** D3
Fair Ridge HP11 . . . . **172** F4
Fairthorn Cl HP23 . . . . . . **118** E3
Fair View Cotts
Chalfont St Peter SL9 . . . . **177** E3
Cookham Rise SL6 . . . . . . **195** E7
Fairview Ind Est
Amersham HP6 . . . . **154** F1
High Wycombe HP11 . . . . **173** F4
Fairview Rd
Burnham SL6 . . . . **204** A7
Slough SL2 . . . . **197** F1
Fairway HP27 . . . . **139** A3
Fairway Ave UB7 . . . . **208** D5
Fairway Cl UB7 . . . . **208** D5
Fairways Rdbt MK8 . . . . . . **33** C2
Fairway The
Burnham SL1 . . . . **197** C3
Flackwell Heath HP10 . . . . **185** C7
Maidenhead SL6 . . . . **202** B3
Uxbridge UB10 . . . . **201** F3
Faithfull Cl HP17 . . . . **114** B5
Faithorn Cl HP5 . . . . **144** A1
Faith Terr MK19 . . . . **11** A2
Falaise MK15 . . . . **35** B7
Falcon Ave MK6 . . . . **35** B2
Falcon Dr
Milton Keynes MK19 . . . . . **32** B7
Stanwell TW19 . . . . **213** E1
Falconhurst Sch MK6 . . . . **47** B8
Falcon Ridge HP4 . . . . . . **135** C3
Falcon Rise HP13 . . . . . . **161** C1
Falcons Croft HP10 . . . . . **185** E8
Falcon The HP19 . . . . **101** F4
Falkland Ho SL6 . . . . **202** F8
Falklands Cl MK18 . . . . **63** D2
Fall Cl HP19 . . . . **101** D3
Falling La UB7 . . . . **208** E6
Fallow Field HP15 . . . . . . **163** B3
Fallows The SL6 . . . . **196** A1
Falmouth Pl MK6 . . . . **34** F1
Falmouth Rd SL1 . . . . **205** A7
Fane Way SL6 . . . . **202** D5
Fantail La HP23 . . . . **118** F4
Faraday Cl SL2 . . . . **205** B8
Faraday Dr MK5 . . . . **46** C5
Faraday Rd
Aylesbury HP19 . . . . **101** A1
Slough SL2 . . . . **205** B8
FAR BLETCHLEY **57** D7
Far Furlong Cl HP21 . . . . . **115** D3
Farinton MK8 . . . . **33** F2
Farjeon Ct MK7 . . . . **48** D4
Farmborough MK6 . . . . **47** C6
Farmbrough Cl HP20 . . . . **102** A1
Farm Cl
High Wycombe HP13 . . . . **174** A7
Ickford HP18 . . . . **123** F3
Little Chalfont HP6 . . . . . . **166** D8
Maidenhead, Highway SL6 . **202** A7
Maidenhead SL6 . . . . **203** C1
Stewkley LU7 . . . . **78** E7
Farm Cres SL2 . . . . **206** C8
Farm Dr SL4 . . . . **211** B1
Farmers Cl SL6 . . . . **202** A4
Farmers Pl SL9 . . . . **177** C1
Farmers Way
Maidenhead SL6 . . . . **202** A4
Seer Green HP9 . . . . **176** C4
Farmery Ct HP4 . . . . **135** E6
Farm Gr HP4 . . . . **175** C5
Farm La HP9 . . . . **176** D3
Farm Lea HP10 . . . . **185** F7
Farm Pl
Berkhamsted HP4 . . . . . . **134** F5
Henton OX39 . . . . **137** D1
Farm Rd
Bourne End SL8 . . . . **184** F4
Brackley NN13 . . . . **38** A6
Burnham SL6 . . . . **204** A5
Chorleywood WD3 . . . . . . **167** A5
Maidenhead SL6 . . . . **202** A7
Farm Way TW19 . . . . **212** F1

Farm Yd SL4 . . . . **210** D7
Farnburn Ave SL1 . . . . . . **205** B8
Farndale Gdns HP15 . . . . **163** A6
Farnell Ct MK5 . . . . **46** C8
Farnham Cl HP3 . . . . **146** A3
FARNHAM COMMON **198** D6
Farnham Common Ho **2**
SL2 . . . . **198** C8
Farnham Common Inf Sch
SL2 . . . . **198** B8
Farnham Common Jun Sch
SL2 . . . . **198** C8
Farnham Ct MK8 . . . . **33** F1
Farnham La SL2 . . . . **198** A2
FARNHAM PARK **198** C4
Farnham Park La SL2 . . . . **198** C4
Farnham Rd SL1, SL2 . . . . **205** C7
FARNHAM ROYAL **198** C3
Farnley Rd HP20 . . . . **101** E2
Farrer Cl NN13 . . . . **26** D4
Farrer Theatre Eton ★
SL4 . . . . **205** C1
Farrier Ct **1** SL8 . . . . **185** B3
Farrier Pl MK14 . . . . **35** A5
Farriers Cl HP3 . . . . **146** A3
Farriers Way HP5 . . . . **144** A3
Farringdon St MK10 . . . . . **35** F1
Farthingales The SL6 . . . . **203** B7
Farthing Ent Ctr The MK6 . **47** C6
Farthing Gr MK6 . . . . **47** C6
Farthing Green La SL2 . . . **199** B4
Farthings The HP6 . . . . . . **154** A3
Fassets Rd HP10 . . . . **174** B2
Faulkner Dr MK3 . . . . **47** B1
Faulkner's Way LU7 . . . . . . **80** E7
Faulkner Way HP13 . . . . . **161** D3
Favell Dr MK4 . . . . **46** F4
Faversham Ct HP23 . . . . . **119** A4
Fawcett Rd SL4 . . . . **210** B6
FAWLEY **191** C8
FAWLEY BOTTOM **180** B2
Fawley Bottom La RG9 . . . **180** B1
Fawley Cl SL6 . . . . **195** D2
Fawley Court ★ RG9 . . . . . **191** E5
Fawley Gn RG9 . . . . **180** D2
Fawley Hill Rly ★ RG9 . . . . **191** D8
Fawsley Cl SL3 . . . . **212** E7
Featherbed Cl MK18 . . . . . **65** E4
Featherbed La HP15 . . . . **163** D8
Featherstone Rd MK12 . . . **33** A5
Fedden Ho MK43 . . . . **24** D3
Fegans Ct MK11 . . . . **32** D6
Felbridge MK7 . . . . **48** A7
FELDEN **146** F7
Felden La HP3 . . . . **146** F8
Fells Cl HP18 . . . . **125** D6
Fellstead Ct SL6 . . . . **202** C6
Felstar Wlk MK6 . . . . **47** C4
Felsted MK7 . . . . **48** A3
Fences MK16 . . . . **13** A2
Fennel Dr MK14 . . . . **34** E4
Fennels Farm Rd HP10 . . . **174** A1
Fennels Rd HP11 . . . . **174** A4
Fennels The HP11 . . . . . . **174** A3
Fennels Way HP10 . . . . . . **174** A1
Fennemore Ct HP18 . . . . . **109** D4
Fennings The HP6 . . . . . . **154** D3
FENNY LOCK **47** E2
Fennymere MK8 . . . . **33** D1
Fenny Rd MK17 . . . . **69** E8
FENNY STRATFORD **47** D1
Fenny Stratford Sta MK1 . **47** E1
Fen St
Atterbury MK10 . . . . **36** B5
Milton Keynes MK17 . . . . . **36** F1
Fenton Ct MK8 . . . . **45** F8
FERN **184** E5
Fernan Dell MK8 . . . . **45** D7
Fernborough Haven **4**
MK4 . . . . **46** C2
Fern Cotts SL7 . . . . **184** E5
Fern Ct HP4 . . . . **135** B4
Ferndale MK6 . . . . **35** B1
Ferndale Cl HP14 . . . . **158** F4
Ferndale Cres UB8 . . . . . . **201** C2
Fern Dr SL6 . . . . **204** B7
Ferne Furlong MK46 . . . . . . **6** F5
Fernes Cl UB8 . . . . **208** C7
Fernfield MK17 . . . . **56** A5
Fern Gr MK2 . . . . **58** D5
Fernhill Cl OX9 . . . . **136** A6
Fernhurst Cl HP9 . . . . **175** F2
Fernie Fields HP12 . . . . . **172** C4
Fern La
Fern SL7 . . . . **184** E5
Haddenham HP17 . . . . . . **127** A6
Fernlea Cl HP10 . . . . **174** A1
Fernley Ct SL6 . . . . **195** D1
Fernside
Great Kingshill HP15 . . . . . **151** E1
Hazelmere HP15 . . . . **163** A6
Fernsleigh Cl SL9 . . . . . . **177** E4
Ferns The HP9 . . . . **175** F1
Fern Wlk HP15 . . . . **163** B3
Fernwood Sch MK17 . . . . . **49** B2
Ferranti Pl MK10 . . . . **35** E2
Ferrers Ave UB7 . . . . **208** D4
Ferrers Cl SL1 . . . . **204** E5
Ferry End SL6 . . . . **203** C4
Ferry La
Bourne End SL8 . . . . **196** B8
Medmenham SL7 . . . . **193** C3
Mill End RG9 . . . . **192** D6
Ferry Mdws Cl MK10 . . . . . **36** A4
Ferry Rd SL6 . . . . **203** C4
Festival Cotts SL3 . . . . . . **212** C7
Fetty Pl SL6 . . . . **202** D4

Field Cl
Aylesbury HP20 . . . . 102 A2
Buckingham MK18 . . . . 51 B6
Chesham HP5 . . . . 144 E3
Ickford HP18 . . . . 124 A3
Sherington MK16 . . . . 14 A2
Field Ct MK5 . . . . 46 B8
Field End HP18 . . . . 125 F5
Field End Cl HP23 . . . . . . 119 D1
Fieldfare HP19 . . . . 101 E4
Field Farm Bsns Ctr OX26 71 C3
Fieldhead Gdns SL8 . . . . 185 A3
Fieldhouse Ct HP13 . . . . 174 A4
Fieldhouse Ind Est SL7 . 183 F2
Fieldhouse La SL7 . . . . . 183 F2
Fieldhouse Way SL7 . . . 183 F2
Field Hurst SL3 . . . . 206 F1
Fielding Gdns SL3 . . . . . 206 C4
Fielding Rd SL6 . . . . 202 B8
Field La MK12 . . . . 33 B5
Field Rd
Denham, Rush Green
  UB9 . . . . 200 E8
Denham UB9 . . . . 189 E1
High Wycombe HP12 . . . 172 B5
Murcott OX5 . . . . 94 A5
Fields End HP23 . . . . . . 119 A6
Fields The SL1 . . . . 205 D4
Fieldway
Amersham HP7 . . . . 165 B6
Berkhamsted HP4 . . . . . . 135 E2
Chalfont St Peter SL9 . . . 177 D3
Wigginton HP23 . . . . 119 D1
Field Way
Aylesbury HP20 . . . . 102 A2
Bovingdon HP3 . . . . 146 A4
Chalfont St Peter SL9 . . . 177 D2
Uxbridge UB8 . . . . 201 D1
Field Wlk MK9 . . . . 34 F3
Fiesta End HP18 . . . . . . 100 E5
Fife Ct MK4 . . . . 57 A8
Fife Ho MK3 . . . . 46 F1
Fifth St HP11 . . . . 173 C4
Filey Spur SL1 . . . . 205 B4
FILGRAVE 13 C5
Filgrave Sch MK16 . . . . . 13 C5
Filmer Rd SL4 . . . . 209 D5
Finch Cl MK10 . . . . 35 F3
Finch Cres LU7 . . . . 80 E5
Finch Ct SL6 . . . . 202 D5
Finch End HP10 . . . . . . 174 C8
Finch Gn WD3 . . . . 167 F5
Finch La
Amersham HP7 . . . . 165 F5
Beaconsfield HP9 . . . . . . 175 C5
Little Chalfont HP7 . . . . . 166 B7
Finch Rd HP4 . . . . 135 A4
Findlay Way MK2 . . . . . . 58 C8
Finemere Wood Wildlife
  Reserve★ HP22 . . . . 84 B8
Fingest La RG9 . . . . 170 D4
Fingle Dr MK13 . . . . 33 E7
Finians Cl UB10 . . . . . . 201 F5
Finings Rd HP14 . . . . . . 171 A4
Finlay Dr RG9 . . . . 191 E2
Finlay Ho RG9 . . . . 191 E3
FINMERE 50 D7
Finmere CE Prim Sch
  MK18 . . . . 50 D6
Finmere Cres HP21 . . . 116 C5
Finsbury Chase MK10 . . 47 F8
Fircroft Cl SL2 . . . . 199 A6
Fircroft Ct SL2 . . . . 199 A6
Firecrest Way HP19 . . . 100 F1
Fire La MK17 . . . . 57 D4
Firemans Run MK17 . . . . 49 B5
Firfield SL6 . . . . 203 B1
Firs Ave SL4 . . . . 209 F4
Firs Cl
Hazelmere HP15 . . . . 163 B2
High Wycombe HP13 . . . 173 E8
Iver Heath SL0 . . . . 200 C4
Lane End HP14 . . . . 171 C5
Whitchurch HP22 . . . . 87 A5
Firs Ct
Amersham HP6 . . . . 154 C2
Bierton HP22 . . . . 102 C4
Princes Risborough HP27 138 C3
Firs Dr SL3 . . . . 206 F5
Firs End SL9 . . . . 188 D8
Firs Rise HP16 . . . . 151 E7
First Ave
Amersham HP7 . . . . 165 D7
Marlow SL7 . . . . 184 A2
Milton Keynes MK1 . . . . . . 47 C1
First Cres SL1 . . . . 205 C8
Firs The
Bierton HP22 . . . . 102 C4
Brill HP18 . . . . 110 B8
Maidenhead SL6 . . . . . . 202 E7
Uxbridge UB8 . . . . 201 D1
Wigginton HP23 . . . . 119 D1
First St HP11 . . . . 173 C3
Firs View Rd HP15 . . . . 163 B2
Firs Wlk HP15 . . . . 163 B2
Fir Tree Ave SL2 . . . . . . 198 F1
Fir Tree Cotts HP14 . . . 161 B8
Firview Cl SL7 . . . . 183 F1
Fishermans Cl MK46 . . . . 6 E4
Fishermans Retreat SL7 183 E1
Fisherman's Way SL8 . . 185 B4
FISHERMEAD 35 A1
Fishermead Bvd MK6 . . . 34 F1
Fishermead Rdbt MK1 . . 47 B2
Fishers Field MK18 . . . . . 52 C8
Fishery Rd SL6 . . . . 203 C5
Fishguard Spur SL1 . . . 206 B4
Fish Ponds La OX9 . . . . 125 E1

Fishweir LU7 . . . . 68 D1
Fitzgerald Gr MK4 . . . . . 56 E8
Fitzgeralds Way HP12 . . 172 B7
Fitzhamon Ct MK12 . . . . 33 A5
Fitzwilliam St MK3 . . . . . 58 B8
Five Acres
Chesham HP5 . . . . .154 D6
Wooburn Green HP10 . . . 185 F7
Five Acre Wood HP12 . . 172 C6
Five Points SL0 . . . . 200 C2
FLACKWELL HEATH . . . 185 A7
Flaggs Mdw MK46 . . . . . . 6 E4
Flambard Cl MK15 . . . . . 35 A7
Flamborough Spur SL1 . 205 A4
Flamstead Gate MK5 . . . 45 E5
FLAUNDEN 156 A6
Flaunden Bottom HP5 . . 155 F4
Flaunden Hill HP3 . . . . . 156 A6
Flaunden La
Bovingdon HP3 . . . . 146 D3
Chipperfield WD3 . . . . . . 156 E6
Flavius Gate NN13 . . . . . 38 A7
Flaxbourne Ct MK7 . . . . . 48 C7
Flaxen Field HP22 . . . . . 116 F2
Flaxley Gate MK10 . . . . . 36 A2
Fledgelings Wlk MK18 . . . 66 E4
Fleetbrook Ho SL3 . . . . . 211 D6
Fleet Cl
Buckingham MK18 . . . . . . 41 F2
Walter's Ash HP14 . . . . . 161 F7
FLEET MARSTON 100 B4
Fleet St MK18 . . . . 101 D1
Fleet The MK6 . . . . 35 B2
Fleetwood Cl HP8 . . . . . 177 A6
Fleetwood Ct ⑦ TW19 . . 213 E1
Fleetwood Rd SL2 . . . . . 205 F6
Fleetwood Way OX9 . . . 125 F2
Fleming Ct ⑦ SL3 . . . . . 206 C3
Fleming Dr MK6 . . . . 47 B6
Fleming Rd ⑦ HP22 . . . 131 D6
Fleming Way HP12 . . . . 172 D5
Fletcher Cl HP19 . . . . . . 100 F3
Fletchers Mews MK14 . . . 34 F6
Fletton Dell MK17 . . . . . . 49 A5
Fletton End MK18 . . . . . . 73 B5
Flexerne Cres MK6 . . . . . 47 D5
Flintergill Ct MK13 . . . . . 34 B4
Flint Ho ⑦ MK3 . . . . 46 F1
Flint Hollow OX39 . . . . . 147 B6
Flintlock Cl TW19 . . . . . 213 A3
Flint St HP17 . . . . 127 A5
Flint Way HP16 . . . . 151 C7
Flitcroft Lea HP13 . . . . . 173 A8
Flitt Leys Cl MK43 . . . . . 25 B2
Flitton Ct MK11 . . . . 32 F5
Flora Ave HP22 . . . . 117 F4
Flora Thompson Dr MK16 21 F6
Florence Ave SL6 . . . . . 203 A8
Florence Ct HP19 . . . . . 101 D1
Florence Way UB8 . . . . 201 C5
Florey Gdns HP20 . . . . . 115 F8
Florida St HP11 . . . . 173 C4
Florin Cl MK15 . . . . 35 A7
FLOWERS BOTTOM . . . 149 A4
Flowers Bottom La HP27 150 B4
Flynn Croft MK4 . . . . 45 D1
Focus St Stoke Poges
  Campus SL2 . . . . 199 B5
Fog Cotts HP23 . . . . 120 A8
Folding Cl LU7 . . . . 78 E8
Foley Cl HP9 . . . . 175 C4
Foliejohn Way SL6 . . . . 202 A1
Folkestone Ct SL3 . . . . 207 A1
Follet Cl SL4 . . . . 211 B1
Folleys Pl HP10 . . . . . . 174 D1
Folly La
Hartwell NN7 . . . . 10 C8
North Crawley MK16 . . . . 24 B5
Folly Rd MK19 . . . . 31 D4
Fonda Mdws MK4 . . . . . . 45 D3
Fontwell Cl SL6 . . . . 202 A8
Fontwell Dr MK3 . . . . . . 57 C6
Forbes Pl MK5 . . . . 45 E4
Forches Cl MK4 . . . . 46 D2
FORD 128 B7
Fordcombe Lea MK7 . . . . 48 B8
Ford End UB9 . . . . 189 F2
Ford La SL0 . . . . 208 A7
Ford St
Buckingham MK18 . . . . . . 52 D8
High Wycombe HP11 . . . 173 F4
Ford Way HP13 . . . . 161 E3
Forelands Way HP5 . . . 154 A4
Foresters
Beacon's Bottom HP14 . . 159 C5
Chinnor OX39 . . . . 147 B6
Oakley HP18 . . . . 109 D6
Forest Pk SL4 . . . . 209 E1
Forest Point HP13 . . . . 173 F5
Forest Rd
Hanslope MK19 . . . . 10 F5
Piddington (Northants) NN7 . 4 A8
Windsor SL4 . . . . 209 E5
Forest Rise MK6 . . . . 47 B8
Forestry Hos OX49 . . . . 168 A7
Forfar Dr MK3 . . . . 46 F2
Forge Cl
Ashendon HP18 . . . . 97 E1
Holmer Green HP15 . . . . 163 C6
Horton-cum-S OX33 . . . . 108 B5

Forge Cl *continued*
Marsh Gibbon OX27 . . . . . 71 F3
Oakley HP18 . . . . 109 D4
Steeple Claydon MK18 . . . 63 D2
Forge Dr SL2 . . . . 198 C6
Forge End HP7 . . . . 165 B7
Forge Rd HP14 . . . . 161 C8
Forge The MK46 . . . . 13 F8
Forgetts Rd HP14 . . . . . 171 C4
Forlease Cl SL6 . . . . . . 203 A6
Forlease Dr SL6 . . . . . . 203 A6
Forlease Rd SL6 . . . . . . 203 A6
Formby Cl
Milton Keynes MK3 . . . . . 57 C7
Slough SL3 . . . . 207 C2
Forrabury Ave MK13 . . . . 34 C3
Forrester Wlk MK10 . . . . 35 E2
Forsythia Gdns SL3 . . . 206 E3
Fort End HP17 . . . . 127 A6
Fortescue Dr MK5 . . . . . 46 B6
Forthill Pl MK5 . . . . 45 F7
Fortuna Ct MK7 . . . . 48 C6
Fortune St HP18 . . . . . . 100 E5
Forty Gn HP27 . . . . 137 F3
FORTY GREEN
Beaconsfield 175 A4
Princes Risborough 137 F3
Forty Green Dr SL7 . . . . 183 B2
Forty Green Rd HP9 . . . 175 C4
Forum The MK14 . . . . 34 E5
FOSCOTE 42 B4
Foscote Cotts MK18 . . . . 42 B4
Foscote Rd MK18 . . . . . . 41 F3
Foscot Way MK18 . . . . . . 41 E2
Foskett Way HP21 . . . . . 115 E5
Fossey Cl MK5 . . . . 45 F3
Foster Ave SL4 . . . . 209 E4
Foster Cl HP20 . . . . 101 F3
Fosters La MK13 . . . . 34 A3
Fosters Path SL2 . . . . . . 197 F1
Fotherby Ct SL6 . . . . . . 203 A6
Fotheringay Gdns SL1 . 205 A6
Fotherley Rd WD3 . . . . . 178 F8
Founders Mews MK14 . . . 34 F6
Foundry Dr MK18 . . . . . . 52 C8
Foundry La
Horton SL3 . . . . 212 B4
Lacey Green HP27 . . . . . 149 C5
Fountain Ct
  ⑥ Aylesbury HP20 . . . . 115 D8
  ① Olney MK46 . . . . 6 F3
Fountaine Cl MK14 . . . . . 34 E7
Fountain Gdns SL4 . . . . 210 D4
FOUR ASHES 162 D4
Four Ashes Rd HP15 . . . 162 C5
Fourdrinier Ct HP11 . . . 174 A4
Four Oaks HP5 . . . . 144 A4
Fourth Ave SL7 . . . . 184 A2
Fourth St HP11 . . . . 173 B4
Fourways Mews HP12 . . 172 C4
Fowler MK14 . . . . 34 C7
Fowler Rd HP19 . . . . . . 115 B8
Fowlers Farm Rd HP14 . 158 E4
Fowler Wy UB10 . . . . . . 201 E3
Foxborough Cl SL3 . . . . 207 A1
Foxborough Ct SL6 . . . . 202 E4
Foxborough Prim Sch
  SL3 . . . . 207 A1
Fox Cl
Wigginton HP23 . . . . 119 D1
Woburn ML17 . . . . 60 F7
Fox Cover OX39 . . . . . . 147 C6
Fox Covert La MK19 . . . . 20 A5
Foxcovert Rd MK5 . . . . . 45 F4
Foxdell Way SL9 . . . . . . 177 E5
Foxes Piece SL7 . . . . . . 183 E2
Foxes Piece Sch SL7 . . . 183 E3
Fox Farm Rd MK17 . . . . . 59 D6
Foxfield MK10 . . . . 36 B3
Fox Field HP15 . . . . 162 F5
Foxgate MK16 . . . . 22 B4
Foxglove HP21 . . . . 115 B5
Foxglove Cl MK12 . . . . . . 52 C7
Foxglove Ct MK16 . . . . . . 21 F4
Foxgoles Cl MK19 . . . . . . 31 F5
Foxherne SL3 . . . . 206 C4
Foxhill MK46 . . . . 6 E5
Foxhill Cl HP13 . . . . 162 B1
Foxhollow Dr SL2 . . . . . 198 C7
Foxhunter Dr MK14 . . . . 34 E6
Fox La
Drayton Parslow MK17 . . . 68 C6
Holmer Green HP15 . . . . 163 B6
Slough SL3 . . . . 206 D2
Wigginton HP23 . . . . 119 C2
Foxton MK6 . . . . 47 D6
Fox Way MK18 . . . . 52 E7
Fraderica Cotts MK16 . . . 22 C3
Framers Ct HP14 . . . . . . 171 B4
Framewood Manor SL2 . 199 C6
Framewood Rd
Slough SL3 . . . . 188 C1
Wexham Street SL2, SL3 . 199 C5
Framlingham Ct MK5 . . . . 46 A5
Frampton Gr ⑪ MK4 . . . . 45 F1
France Furlong MK14 . . . 34 F8
Frances Ave SL6 . . . . . . 196 C1
Frances Ct LU7 . . . . 80 E7
Frances Rd SL4 . . . . . . 210 D5
Frances St HP5 . . . . 144 C2

Franchise St ③ HP5 . . . . 144 C1
Francis Ct MK5 . . . . 46 B6
Francis Way SL1 . . . . . . 204 B6
Frank Atter Croft MK12 . . 33 C5
Frank Howe Cl MK6 . . . . 35 A1
Franklin Ave SL2 . . . . . . 205 B6
Franklin Cl HP17 . . . . . . 127 A7
Franklin Ct HP7 . . . . 154 C1
Franklin Rd
Dunstable LU6 . . . . 93 F8
Haddenham HP17 . . . . . . 127 A7
Franklins Croft MK12 . . . . 33 C5
FRANKLIN'S SPRING . . . 178 D5
Frank Lunnon Cl SL8 . . . 185 C3
Franklyn Cres SL4 . . . . . 209 A4
Frankston Ave MK11 . . . . 32 E5
Frank Sutton Way SL1 . . 205 D6
Frankswood Ave UB7 . . . 208 F3
Frantons The SL6 . . . . . 202 A7
Frascati Way SL6 . . . . . 202 F7
Fraser Rd HP12 . . . . 172 C5
Fraucup Cl HP17 . . . . . . 128 B7
Fraunchies Ct SL1 . . . . . 205 E6
Frays Ave UB7 . . . . 208 D4
Frays Cl UB7 . . . . 208 D3
Fray's Ct SL8 . . . . 201 C5
Frayslea UB8 . . . . 201 C3
Frays Valley Nature
  Reserve★ UB10 . . . . . . 201 D8
Fray's Waye UB8 . . . . . . 201 C4
Frederick Pl HP11 . . . . . 174 B3
Fredericks Ct HP9 . . . . . 186 A8
Frederick Smith Ct MK12 33 D4
Frederick St HP18 . . . . . . 99 A7
Freeman Cl MK12 . . . . . . 33 B5
Freeman Ct HP5 . . . . . . 144 C1
Freemans Cl SL2 . . . . . . 199 A6
Freemans Gdns MK46 . . . 7 A3
Freer Cres HP13 . . . . . . 174 A4
Fremantle Rd
Aylesbury HP21 . . . . 115 C5
High Wycombe HP13 . . . 162 E2
Frenchum Gdns SL1 . . . 204 E5
Frensham Dr MK2 . . . . . . 58 C7
Frensham Wlk SL2 . . . . 198 C6
Freshfield Ave ① MK10 . . 36 A3
Freyberg Dr HP18 . . . . . 100 D5
Friarage Rd HP20 . . . . . 115 D8
Friarscroft Way HP20 . . 115 C8
Friars Field HP4 . . . . 134 E7
Friars Furlong HP18 . . . 125 B7
Friars Gdns HP14 . . . . . 162 A2
Friars Walk HP16 . . . . . 151 E5
Friars Wlk HP13 . . . . . . 119 A4
Friary Gdns MK16 . . . . . . 22 C2
Friary Island TW19 . . . . 211 C1
Friary Rd TW19 . . . . . . 211 C1
Friary The SL4 . . . . 211 C1
Friday Ct OX9 . . . . 125 F1
Friday St
Henley-on-Thames RG9 . . 191 E2
Leighton Buzzard LU7 . . . . 80 F7
FRIETH 170 F1
Frieth CE Comb Sch RG9 170 F1
Frieth Rd SL7 . . . . 182 E5
Frimley Dr SL1 . . . . 204 F4
Fripp Gdns MK8 . . . . 45 D6
Frithe The SL2 . . . . 206 B7
FRITH-HILL 152 C7
Frith Hill
Great Missenden HP16 . . 152 B6
South Heath HP16 . . . . . 152 C8
Frithsden Copse HP4 . . . 135 F8
Frithsden Rise HP4 . . . . 121 D3
Frithwood Cres MK7 . . . . 48 B7
Frobisher Gate MK15 . . . 35 C4
Froggy La UB9 . . . . 189 D1
Frog La HP18 . . . . 112 F3
Frogmill SL6 . . . . 193 C3
Frogmill Cl SL6 . . . . 193 C3
Frogmill Spinney SL6 . . 193 C3
Frogmoor HP13 . . . . 173 A7
Frogmore Cl
Hughenden Valley HP14 . 162 A4
Slough SL1 . . . . 205 A4
Frogmore Cotts SL4 . . . 210 E5
Frogmore Ct ④ SL6 . . . . 202 F7
Frogmore Dr SL4 . . . . . 210 F5
Frogmore Flats SL4 . . . 210 F5
Frogmore La HP18 . . . . 125 C5
Frogmore St HP23 . . . . 119 A3
Frome Cl HP21 . . . . 115 C5
Fromer Rd HP10 . . . . . . 185 D4
Frost Ho ④ HP4 . . . . . . 135 C3
Froxfield Cl MK4 . . . . 46 C1
Froxfield Wy HP11 . . . . 173 E5
Fryday St MK6 . . . . 46 F1
Fryer Cl HP5 . . . . 154 D6
Fryers Ct ③ HP12 . . . . . 172 D6
Fryers La HP12 . . . . 172 C8
Frymley View SL4 . . . . . 209 D6
Fuggle Dr HP21 . . . . . . 115 E5
Fulbrook Mid Sch MK17 . 49 B5
Fullbrook Cl SL6 . . . . . . 203 A8
Fuller's Cl HP5 . . . . 154 B6
Fuller's Hill HP5, HP6 . . 154 B6
FULLERS SLADE 33 A4
Fullers Yd SL6 . . . . 196 B2
Fulmar Pl ① HP19 . . . . . 101 F3
FULMER 198 E3
Fulmer Chase SL3 . . . . 199 C8
Fulmer Common Rd SL3,
  SL0 . . . . 199 E6
Fulmer Dr SL9 . . . . 188 D2
Fulmer Inf Sch SL3 . . . . 199 E8
Fulmer La SL9 . . . . 189 A2
Fulmer Rd SL3 . . . . 188 F2

Fulmer St
Milton Keynes, Emerson Valley
  MK4 . . . . 46 C3
Milton Keynes, Medbourne MK8,
  MK5 . . . . 45 E6
Fulmer Way SL9 . . . . . . 188 E5
Fulton Cl HP13 . . . . 173 A8
FULWELL 39 A2
Fulwell Ct MK14 . . . . 34 E8
Fulwell Rd
Finmere MK18 . . . . 50 C7
Westbury NN13 . . . . 39 A4
Fulwood Ct TW19 . . . . . 213 F1
Fulwoods Dr MK6 . . . . . . 47 A8
Furlong Cl SL8 . . . . 185 B3
Furlong Cres HP17 . . . . 115 A1
Furlong La LU6 . . . . 93 C7
Furlong Rd SL8 . . . . 185 B3
Furlong The ⑫ HP23 . . . 119 A3
Furness SL4 . . . . 209 C5
Furness Cres MK5 . . . . . 47 A1
Furness Pl ⑧ SL4 . . . . . 209 C5
Furness Row ⑨ SL4 . . . 209 C5
Furness Sq ⑥ SL4 . . . . 209 C5
Furness Way SL4 . . . . . 209 C5
Furness Wlk ⑦ SL4 . . . . 209 C5
Furnival Ave SL2 . . . . . 205 B8
Furrow Cl HP21 . . . . . . 115 D4
Furrows The UB9 . . . . . 190 C6
Furrow Way SL6 . . . . . . 202 A4
FURTHO 19 A3
Furtho Ct MK19 . . . . 32 B7
Furtho La NN12 . . . . 18 E3
Fury Ct MK8 . . . . 45 F7
Furze Down Sch MK18 . . 65 E4
Furze Field La HP16 . . . 142 B8
Furzefield Rd HP9 . . . . . 175 C2
Furzeham Rd UB7 . . . . . 208 E4
Furze La MK18 . . . . 65 E5
Furzen Cl SL2 . . . . 198 A2
FURZE PLATT 195 C2
Furze Platt Bsns Ctr SL6 195 D2
Furze Platt Inf Sch SL6 . 195 C1
Furze Platt Jun Sch SL6 195 C1
Furze Platt Rd SL6 . . . . 195 B1
Furze Platt Senior Sch
  SL6 . . . . 195 C2
Furze Platt Sta SL6 . . . . 195 E1
Furze Rd SL6 . . . . 195 D1
Furze View WD3 . . . . . . 167 C4
Furze Way MK12 . . . . 33 C6
FURZTON 46 D4
Furzton Rdbt MK4 . . . . . . 46 C4
Fuzzens Wlk SL4 . . . . . 209 E5
Fyfield Barrow MK7 . . . . 48 C6
Fyne Dr LU7 . . . . 80 C8**

G

Gables Cl
Chalfont St Peter SL9 . . . 177 E6
Datchet SL3 . . . . 211 A8
Maidenhead SL6 . . . . . . 203 B8
Wendover HP22 . . . . 131 A4
Gables Dr HP14 . . . . 149 C1
Gables Mdw HP15 . . . . . 163 C6
Gables The
Datchet SL3 . . . . 211 A8
Haddenham HP17 . . . . . . 127 A5
Leighton Buzzard LU7 . . . . 80 E6
Gable Thorne MK7 . . . . . 48 D6
Gabriel Cl MK7 . . . . 48 C5
Gaddesden Cres MK7 . . . 48 C6
Gadge Cl OX9 . . . . 125 E1
Gadmore La HP23 . . . . . 132 F7
Gadsden Cl MK43 . . . . . . 25 D3
Gadsden Ct MK17 . . . . . . 69 E8
Gage Cl SL6 . . . . 202 E4
Gainsborough SL6 . . . . . 195 F5
Gainsborough Cl MK8 . . . 45 D6
Gainsborough Dr SL6 . . 202 D3
Gainsborough Hill RG9 . 191 D1
Gainsborough Pl HP19 . . 100 F3
Gainsborough Rd
Aylesbury HP21 . . . . 115 E4
Henley-on-Thames RG9 . . 191 D1
Gairloch Ave MK2 . . . . . . 58 D5
Galahad Cl SL1 . . . . 205 A4
Gala Rd HP18 . . . . 100 E5
Gallagher Cl MK8 . . . . . . 45 E8
Galleries The ④ HP13 . . 173 A7
Galley Hill MK11 . . . . 32 F5
Galley La MK17 . . . . 59 A4
Galleymead Rd SL3 . . . . 212 F6
Galloway HP19 . . . . 101 A3
Galloway Chase SL2 . . . 206 A6
Galloway Cl MK3 . . . . 46 E2
Gallows La HP12 . . . . . . 172 C8
Gallys Rd SL4 . . . . 209 D6
Galsworthy Pl HP19 . . . . 100 F2
Galvin Rd SL1 . . . . 205 C6
Gamnel HP23 . . . . 119 A6
Gamnel Mews HP23 . . . 119 B7
Gamnel Terr HP23 . . . . . 119 A6
Gandon Vale HP13 . . . . 173 A8
Ganton Cl MK3 . . . . 46 D1
Garamonde Dr MK8 . . . . 33 F2
Garbo Cl MK8 . . . . 45 D7
Garden Cl
Halton HP22 . . . . 131 C8
Maidenhead SL6 . . . . . . 202 A5
Garden Cotts SL3 . . . . . 212 D7
Garden Ct HP11 . . . . . . 174 B3
Garden End HP6 . . . . . . 154 E2

Gardener Wlk HP15 . . . . . 163 C6
Garden Field La HP4 . . . . 135 F2
Garden Mews SL1. . . . . . . 205 F5
Garden Reach HP8. . . . . . 166 D6
Gardens Cl HP14. . . . . 158 F4
Gardens The MK18. . . . . . . 53 F1
Gardiner Ct MK13. . . . . . . 33 E6
Gardner Cl
  Aylesbury HP19. . . . . . . 101 A3
  Great Kingshill HP15 . . . 151 D1
Gardner Ho SL6. . . . . 195 E1
Gardner Rd SL6. . . . . 195 D2
Gardner's Cl LU6. . . . . 93 E7
Garfield Pl **1** SL4. . . . . . 210 C5
Garland Ct MK8. . . . . 45 E8
Garland Way HP22 . . . . . . 117 E5
Garner Ct **13** TW19. . . . . 213 E1
Garners Cl SL9. . . . . 177 F4
Garners End SL9. . . . . . . 177 E4
Garners Rd SL9. . . . . 177 E4
Garnet Cl SL1. . . . . 205 A4
Garnet Ct SL7. . . . . 183 C1
Garnett Wy MK14. . . . . 21 C1
Garrard Rd SL2. . . . . 197 F1
Garraways MK6. . . . . 47 A6
Garrett Cl HP5. . . . . 154 D6
Garretts La SL6. . . . . 195 F2
Garrick Wlk MK9. . . . . 34 F3
Garron Cl HP21. . . . . 115 D3
Garrowmore Gr MK2 . . . . 58 D5
Garry Cl MK2. . . . . 58 C5
Garside Way HP20. . . . . . 102 A1
Garson Gr HP5. . . . . 144 A2
Garston MK8. . . . . 33 F1
Garthlands SL6. . . . . 195 D2
Garth The HP16. . . . . 152 A8
Garthwaite Cres MK5. . . . 46 A4
Garvin Ave HP9. . . . . 175 E2
Garvin Mews HP9 . . . . . . 175 E2
Garwood Cres MK8 . . . . . . 45 C6
Gascon's Gr SL2. . . . . . . 198 A1
Gaskin Ct MK14. . . . . 35 A5
Gas La SL6. . . . . 203 A3
Gatcombe MK8. . . . . 33 F1
Gate Cotts WD3. . . . . 167 D5
Gatehouse Cl
  Aylesbury HP19. . . . . . . 115 C8
  Windsor SL4 . . . . 210 B4
Gatehouse Way HP19 . . . 101 B1
Gatensbury Pl HP27. . . . . 139 B3
Gatesdene Cl HP4. . . . . . 121 C8
Gates Orch HP22. . . . . . . 117 D5
Gateway Ctr The HP12. . . 172 D4
Gateway Sch The HP16 . . 152 A8
Gatewick Cl SL1. . . . . . . 205 E5
Gatewick La MK7 . . . . 48 A3
Gatting Way UB8. . . . . . . 201 E6
Gatward Ave SL6. . . . . . . 202 A3
Gaveston Dr HP4. . . . . . . 135 B6
Gaveston Rd SL2. . . . . . . 197 F2
Gaviots Cl SL9. . . . . 188 F3
Gaviots Gn SL9. . . . . 188 F3
Gaviots Way SL9 . . . . 188 E4
GAWCOTT. 51 F4
Gawcott Fields MK18. . . . . 52 B7
Gawcott Rd MK18. . . . . . . 52 B6
Gawcott Road Ind Pk
  MK18. . . . . 52 B7
Gawdrey Cl HP5. . . . . 154 D6
Gayal Croft MK5 . . . . 46 B4
GAYHURST. 12 D2
Gayhurst Ho MK16 . . . . . . 12 D1
Gayhurst Rd HP13. . . . . . 173 F7
Gayhurst Sch SL9. . . . . . 188 C7
Gayton Cl HP6. . . . . 154 E4
Geary Mews MK17. . . . . . . 58 B2
Gees Farm Cl NN7 . . . . 1 A5
Gell Cl UB10. . . . . 190 F1
Genoa Wy HP11. . . . . 173 F4
George Cl SL7. . . . . 183 F4
George Ct HP18. . . . . 83 B5
GEORGE GREEN. 206 E8
George Green Dr SL3. . . . 206 F7
George Green Rd SL3 . . . 206 E7
George Hammond La
  HP18. . . . . 100 D4
George Inn Pl MK16. . . . . . 12 B6
George Lee Ct HP14. . . . . 160 C1
George Rd HP14. . . . . 158 E5
Georges Dr HP10. . . . . . . 185 C7
George's Hill HP15. . . . . . 162 F6
George St
  18 Aylesbury HP20. . . . 115 D8
  Berkhamsted HP4 . . . . . 135 D4
  5 Chesham HP5. . . . . 144 C1
  High Wycombe HP11. . . . 172 F7
  Milton Keynes MK2 . . . . . 47 E1
  Uxbridge UB8. . . . . 201 D5
  Wing LU7. . . . . 79 E2
  Woburn MK17 . . . . 60 F7
George V Pl SL4. . . . . . . 210 D7
George Yd MK11. . . . . 32 D5
Georgian Cl UB10. . . . . . 201 E8
Georgian Hts SL8. . . . . . 185 B5
Geralds Ct HP13 . . . . 162 D1
Geralds Rd HP13. . . . . . . 162 D2
Gerard Cl MK13. . . . . 34 A7
Germains Cl HP5. . . . . . . 154 B7
Germain St HP5. . . . . 154 B7
Germander Park First Sch
  MK14. . . . . 34 D4
Germander Pl MK14. . . . . . 34 D4
GERRARDS CROSS. 188 E5
Gerrards Cross CE Sch The
  SL9. . . . . 188 F4

Gerrards Cross Rd SL2 . . 199 A6
Gerrards Cross Sta SL9. . 188 E6
Gershwin Ct MK7 . . . . 48 C4
Gervaise Cl SL1. . . . . . . 204 F5
Ghyll Gdns HP4. . . . . 134 D7
Gibbings Cl MK18. . . . . . . 76 A3
Gibbs Cl HP13. . . . . 172 F8
Gibbs Ho HP11. . . . . 173 F4
Gibbwin MK14. . . . . 34 E8
Gib La HP22 . . . . 102 D4
GIBRALTAR. 113 D2
Gibraltar La SL6. . . . . . . 184 C1
Gibson Ct **9** SL3. . . . . . 206 F1
Gibson La HP17. . . . . 127 A5
Gibson Pl TW19. . . . . 213 C1
Gibson Rd
  High Wycombe HP12. . . . 172 B3
  Ickenham UB10. . . . . . . 201 F8
Gibsons Gn MK13. . . . . . . 34 C4
Gibsons Green MK13. . . . . 34 C4
GIFFARD PARK. 22 A2
Giffard Park Prim Sch
  MK14 . . . . 22 A2
Giffard Park Rdbt MK14 . . 21 F3
Giffard Rd MK2. . . . . 58 C6
Giffard Way HP18. . . . . . 125 C7
Gifford Gate MK14. . . . . . . 34 E7
Gifford Pl MK18. . . . . 41 E1
Gilbert Cl MK3. . . . . 58 B7
Gilbert Ho **4** HP11. . . . . 172 F4
Gilbert Scott Ct **9** HP7. . 165 B7
Gilbert Scott Gdns MK18. 52 A4
Gilbert Scott Rd MK18. . . . 41 D2
Gilbert's Hill HP23. . . . . . 132 E3
Gilbert Way
  Berkhamsted HP4. . . . . . 135 A4
  Slough SL3. . . . . 206 F1
Gilbey Wlk HP10 . . . . 185 D4
Gilders Mews MK14. . . . . . 34 F6
Giles Brook Prim Sch
  MK4 . . . . 57 A7
Giles Gate HP16. . . . . . . 151 B6
Giles Rd **5** HP22. . . . . . 131 D6
Gilletts La HP12. . . . . 161 C1
Gillfield Cl HP11. . . . . . . 172 E3
Gilliat Rd SL1. . . . . 205 E6
Gilliat's Gn WD3. . . . . . . 167 D5
Gilliatt Cl SL0. . . . . 207 E7
Gilliflower St HP18. . . . . . 100 E5
Gillions Pl HP21. . . . . 116 B7
Gillott Ct SL6. . . . . 202 F8
Gilman Cres SL4. . . . . . . 209 D4
Gilmore Cl SL3. . . . . 206 C4
Gilmore Rd HP20. . . . . . . 101 E3
Gilpin's Ride HP4 . . . . . . 135 D5
Gilpin Way MK46. . . . . 7 A4
Gingers Cl HP22. . . . . . . 117 E5
Ginsberg Cres MK10. . . . . 35 E2
Gipsy La LU7. . . . . 91 D8
Girton Way MK3 . . . . 58 B8
Gisburn Cl MK13. . . . . 34 B5
Glade Ho **5** SL7. . . . . . 183 E2
Glade Rd SL7. . . . . 183 E2
Glade The
  Gerrards Cross SL9. . . . 188 D2
  Tylers Green HP10. . . . . 163 C1
Glade View HP14. . . . . . . 172 A3
Gladstone Cl MK16. . . . . . 22 D3
Gladstone Ind Est **1**
  SL6. . . . . 202 E8
Gladstone Rd HP5. . . . . . 144 C1
Gladstone Rise HP13 . . . 173 F6
Gladstone Way SL1. . . . . 205 A5
Glaisyer Way SL0 . . . . . . 200 D3
Glamis Ct HP13. . . . . 173 B8
Glamis Ho MK3 . . . . 57 E7
Glamorgan Cl MK3. . . . . . 46 F1
Glanmor Rd SL2. . . . . . . 206 B6
Glassmill Ho **4** HP4. . . 135 D4
Glastonbury Cl MK3. . . . . 47 A2
Glastonbury Thorn Fst Sch
  MK5. . . . . 46 B6
Glaven Rd HP21. . . . . . . 115 C4
Glazier Dr MK14. . . . . 34 F6
Glebe Cl
  Chalfont St Peter SL9 . . 177 D3
  Dorney SL6 . . . . 203 F4
  Holmer Green HP15 . . . 163 B7
  Maids Moreton MK18. . . 41 F3
  Milton Keynes MK5 . . . . 46 A8
  Pitstone LU7. . . . . 105 D5
Glebe Cotts HP14. . . . . . 169 C7
Glebe Dr NN13. . . . . 38 A7
Glebe Ho SL9. . . . . 177 D3
Glebe House Dr MK18. . . . 39 E6
Glebe La MK19. . . . . 10 E5
Glebelands HP10. . . . . . . 174 C8
Glebelands Cl HP16. . . . . 151 E4
Glebe Rd
  Chalfont St Peter SL9 . . 177 C2
  Deanshanger MK19. . . . . 31 E5
  Maidenhead SL6. . . . . . 203 B5
  Old Windsor SL4. . . . . . 211 B2
  Uxbridge UB8. . . . . 201 C3
Glebe Rdbt MK9. . . . . 35 B4
Glebe Terr MK18. . . . . 41 F3
Glebe The
  Lavendon MK46. . . . . 7 F8
  Lewknor OX49. . . . . 157 B8
  Prestwood HP16. . . . . . 151 C7
  Stone HP17. . . . . 114 C5
  Walter's Ash HP14. . . . . 161 D6
  West Drayton UB7. . . . . 208 F2
  Weston Turville HP22. . . 116 F2
Glebe Way HP6. . . . . 154 D3
Gledfield Pl MK12. . . . . . . 33 D4
Gleeman Cl MK12. . . . . . . 33 A5

Glenavon Gdns SL3 . . . . 206 C3
Glenduragan Ct **9** MK4 . . 45 F1
Gleneagles Cl
  Milton Keynes MK3 . . . . . 57 D7
  Stanwell TW19. . . . . . . 213 D1
Glenfield MK16 . . . . 22 D1
Glenfield Cl
  Aylesbury HP21. . . . . . . 116 A5
  Stoke Poges SL2. . . . . . 198 F4
Glenham Rd OX9. . . . . . . 126 B1
Glenister Rd
  Chesham HP5. . . . . 144 C3
  High Wycombe HP12. . . 172 B4
Glenisters Rd HP13. . . . . 173 A8
Glenmore Cl HP10. . . . . . 174 A2
Glenmore Ho HP11. . . . . 174 B3
Glenore SL6 . . . . 196 A8
Glenrose Cl SL2. . . . . . . 206 C7
Glenstal Pl MK9. . . . . 35 A3
Glen The SL3. . . . . 206 C2
Glentworth Pl SL1. . . . . . 205 C5
Glenwater Ho HP15. . . . . 163 A5
Glenwoods MK16 . . . . 22 C3
Glimbers Gr OX39. . . . . . 147 C5
Globe Ho UB7. . . . . 208 D5
Globe La LU7. . . . . 70 E1
Globe Pk (Bsns Ctr) SL7. 183 F2
Globeside Bsns Pk SL7. . 183 F2
Glory Cl HP10. . . . . 185 F7
Glory Hill La HP9. . . . . . . 185 F8
Glory Mill La HP10 . . . . . 185 E7
Glory Pk HP10 . . . . 185 E8
Glory Pk Ave HP10 . . . . . 185 E8
Gloucester Ave SL1. . . . . 205 C8
Gloucester Ct UB9. . . . . . 190 A4
Gloucester Pl SL4. . . . . . 210 D5
Gloucester Rd
  Maidenhead SL6. . . . . . 195 E2
  Milton Keynes MK12 . . . . 33 D5
Glovers Ct **2** HP20. . . . 101 E1
Glovers La
  Milton Keynes MK13 . . . . 34 B4
  2 Tring HP23. . . . . . . 119 A3
Glyn Mews HP22. . . . . . . 102 C2
Glyn Sq MK12. . . . . 33 D7
Glyn St MK13. . . . . 34 A7
Glynswood
  Chalfont St Peter SL9 . . 177 F3
  Chinnor OX39. . . . . 147 C6
  High Wycombe HP13. . . 162 B1
Glynswood Ho OX39. . . . 147 C6
Glynswood Rd MK18 . . . . . 41 C1
Glyn Valley Pl **4** MK10. . 36 C3
Glynwood Ho SL6. . . . . . 203 A7
Goathland Croft **2** MK4. 46 B2
Goddards Croft MK12 . . . . 33 C5
Goddington Rd SL8 . . . . 185 A5
Godfreys Cl HP18. . . . . . . 96 B1
GODLINGTON. 61 E3
Godolphin Inf Sch SL1 . . 205 C7
Godolphin Jun Sch SL1 . 205 D7
Godolphin Rd
  Seer Green HP9. . . . . . 176 C4
  Slough SL1. . . . . 205 D6
Godrevy Gr MK4 . . . . 57 B8
Godstowe Sch HP13. . . . 173 B8
Godwin Cl MK7 . . . . 48 C7
Gogh Rd HP19 . . . . 100 F2
Gold Crest HP19 . . . . 101 F2
Golden Ball La SL6. . . . . 195 A3
Golden Dr MK6 . . . . 47 B8
Golden Hills OX39. . . . . . 147 D6
Golden Mede HP18. . . . . . 99 B6
Golden Miller Ct LU7. . . . . 79 E2
Golden Oak Cl SL2. . . . . 198 C6
Golden Riddy LU7. . . . . . . 80 E8
Golder's Cl HP18. . . . . . . 123 F3
Goldfield Inf Sch HP23 . . 118 F3
Goldfield Rd HP23. . . . . . 118 F3
Goldhawk Rd MK10 . . . . . . 47 E8
Gold Hill E SL9. . . . . 177 D1
Gold Hill N SL9 . . . . 177 C2
Gold Hill W SL9. . . . . 177 C1
Goldilocks MK7. . . . . 48 B6
Goldmark Cl MK7. . . . . . . 48 D5
Gold Oak Wlk MK9 . . . . . . 34 F3
Goldsmith Dr MK16 . . . . . . 21 F4
Gold St MK19 . . . . 11 A2
Goldsworthy Way SL1. . . 204 C7
Golf Club La HP27. . . . . . 139 E5
Golf Club Rd HP4 . . . . . . 121 A8
Golspie Croft MK12 . . . . . 33 C4
Gomez Cl MK4. . . . . 45 D3
Gomm Pl HP13. . . . . 174 A4
Gomm Rd HP13. . . . . 174 A4
Gomms Wood Cl HP9 . . . 175 B4
Gomms Wood Ho HP9. . . 175 B4
Gomm Valley Nature
  Reserve* HP13. . . . . . . 173 B5
Goodacres La HP27. . . . . 149 E6
Goodall Cl HP22. . . . . . . 116 F2
Good Intent LU6. . . . . 92 E4
Goodlake Ct UB9. . . . . . . 189 F4
Goodman Gdns MK6 . . . . . 47 D8
Goodman Pk SL2. . . . . . . 206 C5
Goodrich Gn MK4. . . . . 56 E8
Goodrington Pl **2** MK10. 36 A4
Goodwick Gr MK4. . . . . . . 57 B8
Goodwin Mdws HP10. . . . 185 E6
Goodwin Rd
  Aylesbury HP19. . . . . . . 115 C8
  Slough SL2. . . . . 197 F2
Goodwins Mead LU7. . . . 105 A7
Goodwin Villas SL1. . . . . 204 F5
Goodwood MK8 . . . . 45 F8
Goodwood Rise SL7. . . . 183 C7
Goose Acre
  Botley HP5. . . . . 145 A1

Goose Acre continued
  Cheddington LU7. . . . . . 105 A7
Goose Gn SL2. . . . . 198 B3
Goosemere MK19. . . . . . . 31 E4
Goosen Gn HP21. . . . . . . 116 C6
Goran Ave MK11. . . . . 32 E4
Gordale MK13. . . . . 34 C5
Gordon Rd
  Chesham HP5. . . . . 154 C7
  High Wycombe HP13. . . 173 D6
  Maidenhead SL6. . . . . . 202 D7
  West Drayton UB7. . . . . 208 E6
  Windsor SL4 . . . . 209 F5
Gordon Way HP8. . . . . . . 177 B7
Gore Cl UB9. . . . . 190 C7
Gore Hill HP7. . . . . 165 B5
Gorelands La HP8. . . . . . 177 F8
Gorell Rd HP9. . . . . 176 B1
Gore Rd SL1. . . . . 197 B2
Gore The SL1. . . . . 197 A2
Goring MK14. . . . . 34 C7
Gorman Pl MK2. . . . . 58 E4
Gorrell Cl MK18. . . . . 51 B6
Gorrell La MK18. . . . . 51 B6
Gorricks MK11. . . . . 32 D4
Gorse Meade SL1. . . . . . 205 B5
Gorse Rd SL6. . . . . 195 E6
Gorse Wlk
  Hazlemere HP15. . . . . . 163 A3
  West Drayton UB7. . . . . 208 E7
Gosforth Pl SL1. . . . . 204 F6
Goslar Way SL4. . . . . . . 210 B5
Gosling Gn SL3. . . . . 206 E3
Gosling Gr HP13. . . . . . . 161 D2
Gosling Rd SL3. . . . . 206 F3
Gossage Rd UB10. . . . . . 201 F5
GOSSARD'S GREEN. 25 C4
Goss Ave HP18. . . . . 99 B6
Gossmore Cl SL7. . . . . . . 183 F1
Gossmore La SL7. . . . . . 183 F1
Gossmore Wlk SL7. . . . . 183 F1
Gossom's End HP4. . . . . 135 A5
Gossoms Ryde HP4 . . . . 135 A5
Goswell Hill SL4 . . . . 210 D6
Goswell Rd SL4. . . . . 210 D6
Goudhurst Ct MK7. . . . . . 48 B7
Governors Cl HP6. . . . . . 154 F1
Gower Ho HP6. . . . . 154 F1
Gowers Field HP19, HP20 101 D1
Gowers The HP6. . . . . . . 154 E2
Gowings Gn SL1. . . . . . . 204 E4
Goya Pl HP19 . . . . 100 F2
Grable Ave MK4. . . . . 45 E3
Grace Ave MK6. . . . . 46 E8
Grace Ct SL1. . . . . 205 C5
Grace Reading HP13 . . . 173 E6
Grace Reading Cl HP13. . 173 E6
Graces Cl MK43. . . . . 25 C3
Graces Maltings **4**
  HP23 . . . . 119 A3
Graeme Ave HP16. . . . . . 151 C6
Grafham Cl MK14. . . . . . . 35 A8
Grafton Cl
  Maidenhead SL6. . . . . . 195 E2
  Pottersbury NN12. . . . . . 18 E3
  Slough SL3. . . . . 206 E7
Grafton Ct NN7. . . . . 4 A8
Grafton Gate MK9. . . . . . . 34 C1
Grafton Ho OX39. . . . . . . 147 D7
Grafton Orch OX39. . . . . 147 D7
Grafton Park MK9. . . . . . . 34 D1
Grafton Rd
  Aylesbury HP19. . . . . . . 101 A4
  Yardley Gobion NN12. . . 18 F6
GRAFTON REGIS. 9 D2
Grafton St
  High Wycombe HP12. . . 172 D8
  Milton Keynes HP13, Bradwell
    MK13 . . . . 34 B4
  Milton Keynes, Granby MK1 47 B3
  Milton Keynes, New Bradwell
    MK12, MK13, MK19 . . . 33 E8
  Milton Keynes, Winterhill
    MK6 . . . . 46 E7
Graham Cl SL6. . . . . 202 C5
Graham Dr HP12. . . . . . . 172 B5
Graham Ho SL9. . . . . 177 C1
Graham Rd SL6. . . . . 195 E6
Grainge Chase MK17. . . . 55 A3
Grainge Cl NN13. . . . . . . 39 A5
Grampian Gate MK6. . . . . 46 E7
Grampian Way SL3. . . . . 207 A1
Gramwell MK5. . . . . 45 F7
Granary Cl MK19. . . . . 21 A3
GRANBOROUGH. 75 E7
Granborough Rd
  North Marston MK18. . . . 76 A2
  Winslow MK18. . . . . 65 D2
GRANBY. 47 B3
Granby Ct MK1. . . . . 47 A3
Granby Ind Est MK1. . . . . 47 A3
Granby Rdbt MK1. . . . . . . 47 C3
Grandison Ho RG9 . . . . . 191 E3
Grand Union Office Pk The
  UB8. . . . . 208 C7
Granes End MK14. . . . . . . 34 E8
Grange Chase MK17. . . . . 55 A3
Grange Cl
  Chalfont St Peter SL9 . . 177 E2
  Leighton Buzzard LU7. . . 80 D6
  Maids Moreton MK18. . . 41 E3
  Twyford MK18. . . . . 62 D2
  Wraysbury TW19. . . . . . 211 E1
Grange Cotts HP16. . . . . 152 A3
Grange Dr
  Terriers HP13 . . . . 162 D3
  Wooburn HP10 . . . . 185 D3
Grange Farm Rd HP14. . 159 B7

Grange Farm Rdbt MK8 . . 45 D7
Grange Fields SL9 . . . . . 177 E2
Grange Gdn HP18. . . . . . . 83 A6
Grange Gdns
  Farnham Common SL2. . 198 D7
  Wendover HP22. . . . . . . 131 B5
Grange La SL6. . . . . 195 F8
Grangelands & Pulpit Hill
  Reserve* HP27. . . . . . . 139 F6
Grange Rd
  Chalfont St Peter SL9 . . 177 E2
  Cookham Rise SL6. . . . . 195 F7
  Hazlemere HP15. . . . . . 162 F4
  Hazlemere, Widmer End
    HP15. . . . . 162 E5
  Henley-on-Thames RG9. 191 E1
  Milton Keynes MK3 . . . . . 57 F7
  Pitstone LU7. . . . . 105 D5
  Terriers HP13 . . . . 162 D3
  Tring HP23. . . . . 119 C4
  Wilstone HP23. . . . . . . 104 D1
Grangers Croft MK12. . . . 33 C4
Grange Sch The HP21 . . 115 F6
Grange The
  Burnham SL1. . . . . 197 C2
  Gerrards Cross SL9. . . . 188 E6
  Old Windsor SL4. . . . . . 211 B2
  Wraysbury TW19. . . . . . 211 E1
Grange View HP27 . . . . . 139 C7
Grange Way SL0. . . . . . . 207 F7
Grangewood SL3 . . . . . . 206 C8
Grant Ave SL1. . . . . 205 C7
Grant Gdns MK4. . . . . 45 D3
Grantham Ct MK5. . . . . . . 46 C5
Grantham Mews HP4. . . . 135 D4
Grant Ho **6** SL8. . . . . . 185 A4
Granville Ave SL2. . . . . . 205 D8
Granville Dene HP3 . . . . 146 A4
Granville Pl **5** HP20. . . 115 D8
Granville Rd HP4. . . . . . . 134 E6
Granville Sq MK15 . . . . . . 35 C7
Granville St **4** HP20. . . 115 D8
Grapevine Cl HP11. . . . . 173 F4
Grasholm Way SL3. . . . . 207 C2
Grasmere
  Aylesbury HP21. . . . . . . 116 B5
  Windsor SL4 . . . . 209 E7
Grasmere Ave SL2 . . . . . 206 A6
Grasmere Par SL2. . . . . . 206 B6
Grasmere Way
  Leighton Buzzard LU7 . . . 80 D7
  Milton Keynes MK2 . . . . . 58 D6
Grasscroft MK4 . . . . 46 E4
Grass Hays HP21. . . . . . 116 C7
Grassingham End SL9. . . 177 E3
Grassingham Rd SL9. . . . 177 E3
Grassington MK13. . . . . . 34 A5
Grasslands HP20. . . . . . . 102 A1
Grassy La SL6. . . . . 202 E7
Grattan Ct SL7. . . . . 184 A3
Gratton Ct MK4. . . . . 46 C3
Gratton Dr SL4. . . . . 209 E3
Gravel Dr HP23. . . . . 118 B3
GRAVEL HILL. 177 F4
Gravel Hill
  Chalfont St Peter SL9 . . 177 E3
  Henley-on-Thames RG9 . 191 D7
  Uxbridge UB8. . . . . 201 D7
Gravelly Way HP10. . . . . 163 C2
Gravel Path HP4 . . . . 135 E5
Gravel Wlk MK46. . . . . 13 F7
Graveney Pl MK6. . . . . 35 B2
Grayburn Cl HP8. . . . . . . 177 A8
Graylands Cl SL1. . . . . . 204 F5
Grayling Cl SL7 . . . . 194 C8
Grayling Ct HP4. . . . . 134 F6
Grays Cl NN12. . . . . 17 D8
Grays La
  Paulerspury NN12. . . . . . 17 D8
  Yardley Gobion NN12. . . 18 E6
Gray's La
  High Wycombe HP13. . . 161 D2
  Ibstone HP14. . . . . 169 C7
Gray's Mon* SL2. . . . . . . 198 F2
Grays Park Rd SL2. . . . . 199 A3
Gray's Pl SL2. . . . . 205 F5
Gray's Rd
  Slough SL1. . . . . 205 F5
  Uxbridge UB10. . . . . . . 201 E5
Grays Wlk HP5. . . . . 144 B2
Gr Corner MK14. . . . . 21 F3
Greamesdyke Rd HP4 . . 135 A3
Greatacre **7** HP5. . . . . 144 C1
Great Benty UB7. . . . . . . 208 E2
GREAT BRICKHILL. 59 D2
Great Brickhill La MK17. . 59 D5
Greatchesters MK13. . . . . 33 F5
Great Denson MK6. . . . . . 47 A8
GREATGAP. 105 D6
Great Ground MK14. . . . . 34 D7
GREAT HAMPDEN. 150 D7
Greatheed Dell MK7. . . . . 48 C5
Great Hill Cres SL6. . . . . 202 C6
GREAT HIVINGS. 144 A3
Great Hivings HP5. . . . . . 144 A4
GREAT HOLM. 45 E8
GREAT HORWOOD. 55 A1
Great Horwood CE Comb Sch
  MK17. . . . . 55 A3
Great Horwood Rd MK18 . 65 F7
GREAT KIMBLE. 139 E8
Great Kimble CE Sch
  HP17. . . . . 129 C1
GREAT KINGSHILL. 162 E8
Great Kingshill CE Comb Sch
  HP15. . . . . 162 C6
Great La
  Bierton HP22. . . . . 102 A4

Great La *continued*
Wendover HP22. . . . .**131** B4
Great Linch MK10. . . . . .**36** A2
GREAT LINFORD. **34** E8
Great Linford Comb Sch
MK14. . . . .**34** E8
Great Linford Lakes★
MK14. . . . .**21** D3
Great Marlow Sch SL7 . .**183** F4
Great Meadow Way
HP19. . . . .**114** F8
GREAT MISSENDEN. **152** A6
**Great Missenden CE Comb
Sch** HP16. . . . .**152** B7
Great Missenden Sta
HP16. . . . .**152** A7
Great Monks St
Milton Keynes, Wolverton
MK12. . . . .**33** C5
Milton Keynes, Wymbush
MK8. . . . .**33** E2
Great Ormes MK4. . . . . . .**56** F8
Great Pasture MK10. . . . . .**35** F3
Great Slade MK18. . . . .**52** D6
Great Stone HP18. . . . . . .**112** F3
Great Western St 22
HP20. . . . .**115** D8
Greaves Rd HP13. . . . . . .**173** D6
Grebe Cl
Aylesbury HP19. . . . .**101** F3
Calvert MK18. . . . .**73** B5
Grebe Wy SL6. . . . .**203** A8
Grecian St HP20. . . . .**116** A8
Greenacre SL4. . . . .**209** E5
Green Acre HP21. . . . .**116** A7
Greenacres
Aylesbury HP22. . . . .**89** B2
Holmer Green HP15 . . . . .**163** D5
Pitstone LU7. . . . .**105** C4
Slapton LU7. . . . .**91** D8
Greenacres Ave UB10 . . . .**190** F1
Greenacres La HP10 . . . . .**163** A1
Greenacres The HP13 . . . .**162** A1
Greenbury Cl WD3 . . . . . .**167** C5
Green Cl
Burnham SL6. . . . .**204** A7
High Wycombe HP13 . . . . .**173** F4
Maidenhead SL6 . . . .**195** F1
Green Common La HP10, HP9,
SL1. . . . .**186** C4
Green Cres HP10. . . . .**185** C7
Greendale Mews SL2. . . . .**206** A6
Green Dragon La HP10 . . .**185** B7
Green East Rd HP9. . . . . .**176** E3
Greene Field Rd HP4. . . . .**135** C4
Greenell Cl MK19. . . . .**31** F4
GREEN END
Granborough **76** A7
High Wycombe. **160** A4
Green End
Aylesbury HP20. . . . .**115** D8
Granborough MK18. . . . . . .**76** A7
Great Brickhill MK17 . . . . .**59** D2
Green End La MK19. . . . . . .**11** A3
Green End Rd HP14 . . . . . .**159** E5
Green End St HP22. . . . . . .**117** E5
Greenes Ct HP4. . . . .**135** C5
Greene Wlk HP4. . . . .**135** D3
Green Farm Rd MK16. . . . . .**22** C4
Greenfern Ave SL1. . . . . . .**204** C7
GREENFIELD. **168** A4
Greenfield End SL9 . . . . . .**177** F3
Greenfield Rd MK16. . . . . . .**22** A4
Greenfields
Adstock MK18. . . . .**53** F1
Maidenhead SL6 . . . .**203** A5
Upper Arncott OX6 . . . . . .**94** D7
Green Ground OX33. . . . . .**123** A2
Green Hailey HP27 . . . . . .**139** F3
Green Hill HP13. . . . .**162** B1
Greenhill Cl MK5. . . . .**46** A8
Green Hill Cl HP13. . . . . . .**162** C1
Green Hill Gate HP13. . . . .**162** B1
Green La
Amersham HP6 . . . .**154** E2
Aspley Guise MK17 . . . . . .**49** E4
Botley HP5. . . . .**155** B6
Bovingdon HP3 . . . .**146** A3
Burnham SL1. . . . .**197** D4
Chesham Bois HP6 . . . . . .**154** D3
Datchet SL3. . . . .**211** B6
Eaton Bray LU6 . . . .**92** D7
Farnham Common SL2. . . .**198** B6
Ivinghoe LU7. . . . .**105** E5
Maidenhead SL6 . . . .**203** A6
Milton Keynes MK12 . . . . . .**33** D6
Owlswick HP27 . . . .**128** B1
Prestwood HP16. . . . .**151** E6
Radnage HP14. . . . .**159** D5
Stokenchurch HP14 . . . . . .**158** C5
Upper Arncott OX6 . . . .**94** E7
Windsor SL4 . . . .**210** B5
Greenlands
Flackwell Heath HP10 . . . .**185** B8
Lacey Green HP27. . . . . . .**149** D5
Greenlands Cl MK16. . . . . .**22** A3
Greenlands Ct SL6 . . . . . .**202** B8
Greenlands La HP16. . . . . .**151** B7
Green Lane HP4. . . . .**154** D3
Green Lane Ct SL1. . . . . . .**197** C2
Green Lane Rdbt MK9. . . . . .**35** B5
Green Leas MK3. . . . .**47** A3
Greenleaf Cl SL3. . . . .**211** A8
Greenleas Lower Sch LU7 .**80** C7
GREENLEYS. **33** B5
Green Leys
High Wycombe HP13. . . . .**161** C2

Green Leys *continued*
Maidenhead SL6 . . . .**195** F2
Greenleys Fst Sch MK12. . .**33** C5
Greenleys Jun Sch MK12 . .**33** C5
Greenleys La MK12. . . . . . .**33** C4
Greenleys Rdbt MK12 . . . . .**33** B6
Green North Rd HP9 . . . .**176** E4
Greenock Rd SL1 . . . .**205** A7
Green Park Dr MK16. . . . . .**22** C3
Green Park Sch MK16. . . . .**22** B3
Green Path HP22, HP23. . .**118** D4
Green Pk HP16 . . . .**151** D6
Green Pl HP10. . . . .**185** C8
Green Rd HP13 . . . .**162** C2
Greenridge HP10 . . . .**174** B8
Greensand View MK17. . . . .**49** B5
Greenside
Bourne End SL8. . . . .**185** A5
Prestwood HP16. . . . .**151** C5
Slough SL2. . . . .**205** A8
Greenside Hill MK4 . . . . . .**46** B1
Greens Keep HP17 . . . . . .**126** F6
Green St
Chorleywood WD3. . . . . .**167** C6
Hazlemere HP15 . . . .**162** F4
High Wycombe HP11. . . . .**172** F7
GREEN THE
Milton Keynes **47** D8
Newport Pagnell **22** C3
Whipsnade. **107** F8
Green The
Amersham HP7 . . . .**154** C1
Aston Abbotts HP22 . . . . . .**88** D4
Brill HP18 . . . .**110** B8
Burnham SL1. . . . .**197** B1
Chalfont St Giles HP8 . . . .**177** C8
Cheddington LU7. . . . . . .**105** A7
Cosgrove MK19 . . . .**19** F2
Cranfield MK43 . . . .**24** E2
Cuddington HP18 . . . .**112** F3
Deanshanger MK19 . . . . . .**31** E4
Edlesborough LU6 . . . .**92** F4
Great Horwood MK17 . . . . .**55** A3
Hanslope MK19 . . . .**11** A2
Horton-cum-S OX33. . . . .**108** A5
Hyde Heath HP6 . . . .**153** C5
Little Missenden HP7 . . . .**153** A2
Longwick HP27 . . . .**138** D6
Maidenhead SL6 . . . .**195** C7
Mentmore LU7. . . . .**90** D4
Milton Keynes, Loughton
MK5. . . . .**46** A8
Milton Keynes, The Green
MK6 . . . .**47** C8
Newport Pagnell MK16 . . . .**22** C3
Paulerspury NN12 . . . .**17** B7
Pitstone LU7. . . . .**105** D4
Quainton HP22. . . . .**85** B5
Slough SL1. . . . .**205** D4
Soulbury LU7. . . . .**69** E3
Steeple Claydon MK18. . . .**63** D3
Stoke Hammond MK17 . . . .**69** E7
Thornborough MK18 . . . . . .**54** A8
Turvey MK43 . . . .**8** E5
West Drayton UB7. . . . . . .**208** D3
Wingrave HP22 . . . .**89** B2
Wooburn Green HP10 . . . .**185** E5
Wraysbury TW19 . . . .**211** E1
Green Tiles UB9 . . . .**189** F4
Green Tiles La UB9. . . . . .**189** F5
Green Verges SL7. . . . . . .**183** E3
Green View HP20 . . . .**102** A2
Green View Cl HP3. . . . . . .**146** A2
Greenwatt Wy SL1. . . . . .**205** D3
Greenway
Berkhamsted HP4. . . . . . .**135** A4
Burnham SL1. . . . .**197** B3
Chesham HP5 . . . .**144** B3
Great Horwood MK17 . . . . .**55** A2
Haddenham HP17 . . . .**126** F5
Milton Keynes MK10 . . . . . .**36** C3
2 Thame OX9 . . . .**125** F1
Green Way MK17. . . . .**57** D4
Greenway Bsns Pk MK17 . .**55** A1
Greenway Ct 12 HP13 . . . .**173** B7
Greenway Par HP5. . . . . . .**144** B4
Greenway Prim Sch HP4 . .**134** F4
Greenways
Bow Brickhill MK17 . . . . . .**48** C2
Eaton Bray LU6 . . . .**92** D7
Greenways Dr SL6 . . . . . .**202** A8
Greenway The
Gerrards Cross SL9. . . . . .**188** D8
High Wycombe HP13. . . . .**173** B7
Slough SL1. . . . .**204** D5
Tring HP23. . . . .**118** F5
Tylers Green HP10. . . . . .**163** B1
Uxbridge UB8. . . . .**201** D3
Greenway Wlk MK18 . . . . . .**41** F1
Green West Rd HP9. . . . . .**176** E3
Greenwich Gdns MK16 . . . . .**22** C2
Greenwood HP14 . . . .**150** A2
Greenwood Ave OX39 . . . .**147** C5
Greenwood Cl
Amersham HP6 . . . .**154** E1
Seer Green HP9 . . . .**176** E4
Greenwood Mdw OX39 . . .**147** D6
Greenwood Pl MK18 . . . . . .**63** D3
Greenwood The HP22 . . . .**117** D5
Greenyard The NN7 . . . .**1** B7
Greetham Rd HP21. . . . . . .**116** C6
Gregories Ct HP9 . . . .**175** D3
Gregories Dr MK7. . . . .**48** D6
Gregories Farm La HP9 . . .**175** D2
Gregories Rd HP9. . . . . . .**175** D3
Gregory Dr SL4. . . . .**211** B1
Gregory Rd SL2. . . . .**187** D2
Gregorys Field HP23 . . . . .**104** A3

Grenada Cres MK3. . . . . . .**58** B3
Grenadine Way HP23. . . . .**119** A5
Grendon Rd
Edgcott HP18. . . . .**72** F1
Kingswood HP18 . . . .**83** C3
GRENDON UNDERWOOD. . .**83** A6
**Grendon Underwood Comb
Sch** HP18. . . . .**83** A6
Grendon Way HP22 . . . . . .**102** A4
Grenfell Ave
High Wycombe HP12 . . . . .**172** D7
Maidenhead SL6 . . . .**202** F6
Grenfell Pl SL6 . . . .**202** F6
Grenfell Rd
Beaconsfield HP9 . . . .**175** E3
Maidenhead SL6 . . . .**202** E6
Tring HP23. . . . .**119** C5
Waddesdon HP18 . . . .**99** A6
Grenville Ave HP22. . . . . .**131** A7
Grenville Cl SL1. . . . .**197** B3
Grenville Comb Sch
MK18. . . . .**52** D7
Grenville Ct WD3 . . . .**167** C5
Grenville Gn HP21 . . . . . .**115** D4
Grenville Rd
Aylesbury HP21 . . . .**115** D5
Buckingham MK18. . . . . . .**41** C1
Grenville Way OX9 . . . . . .**126** B1
Gresham Ct HP4. . . . .**135** B3
Gresham Rd SL1. . . . .**205** A7
Greyfriars Ct MK10. . . . . . .**36** B2
Greyhound Ct MK18. . . . . .**66** A4
Greyhound La
Thame OX9 . . . .**125** F1
Winslow MK18. . . . .**66** A4
Greyhound Wlk OX9 . . . . .**125** F1
Greys Hill RG9 . . . .**191** D1
Greys Rd RG9. . . . .**191** D1
Greys The MK6 . . . .**47** C8
Greystoke Cl HP4 . . . .**135** A3
Greystoke Rd SL2. . . . . . .**204** F8
Greystonley 1 MK4 . . . . . .**46** C2
Griffin Cl
Maidenhead SL6 . . . .**202** E5
Slough SL1. . . . .**205** C4
Griffin Field LU7 . . . .**78** E8
Griffin House Prep Sch
HP17. . . . .**129** E1
Griffin Ind Mall HP19. . . . .**101** B1
Griffin La HP19 . . . .**101** B1
Griffin Lane Ind Est
HP19. . . . .**101** B1
Griffith Gate MK10. . . . . . .**36** A3
Griffith Gate Rdbt MK10. . .**36** A2
Griffith Ho HP10 . . . .**174** C2
Griffiths Acre HP17 . . . . . .**114** E5
Griffiths Yd HP5 . . . .**144** B1
Grigby Rise MK6 . . . .**47** A7
Griggs Orch MK16. . . . .**14** A2
Grimbold Ct MK15 . . . .**35** C7
Grimmer Cl HP19 . . . .**100** F3
Grimms Hill HP16. . . . . . .**151** F7
Grimms Mdw HP14. . . . . .**150** B1
Grimsby Rd SL1. . . . .**204** F4
Grimsdell's La HP6. . . . . .**154** D2
Grimsdyke Rd HP23. . . . . .**119** D5
Gringer Hill SL6 . . . .**202** E8
Grizedale MK13. . . . .**34** B5
Groombridge MK7 . . . .**48** A7
Groom Rd HP16. . . . .**151** C6
Groomsby Dr LU7 . . . .**105** E5
Grooms Cotts HP5 . . . . . .**145** B1
Grooms Ct HP11 . . . .**174** A4
Grosmont Cl 1 MK4 . . . . . .**46** B2
Grosvenor Cl SL0 . . . .**200** D2
Grosvenor Ct SL1 . . . .**205** E7
Grosvenor Dr SL6. . . . . . .**203** C8
Grosvenor Way HP19. . . . .**114** E8
Groundsel Cl MK7. . . . .**48** B6
Grove Ash MK1 . . . .**47** D3
Grovebury Rd LU7 . . . .**80** F4
Grove Cl
Chalfont St Peter SL9 . . . .**177** C2
1 Slough SL1 . . . .**206** A3
Grove Cotts UB9 . . . .**190** C8
Grove Ct
Beaconsfield HP9 . . . .**175** D4
Bierton HP22. . . . .**102** C5
Maidenhead SL6 . . . .**202** D7
Turvey MK43 . . . .**8** E6
Grove End SL9 . . . .**177** C2
Grove End Barns OX9 . . . .**126** B4
Grove Gdns HP23 . . . .**119** B5
Grove Ind Sch The MK5. . .**46** C7
Grove La
Ashley Green HP5 . . . .**145** C5
Chalfont St Peter SL9 . . . .**177** C2
Little Kimble HP17 . . . . . .**129** E2
Uxbridge UB8 . . . .**201** F1
Grovelands HP11 . . . .**173** A6
Grove Leys HP23 . . . .**119** C5
Grove Pk HP23. . . . .**119** C5
Grove Rd
Amersham HP6 . . . .**154** F1
Beaconsfield HP9 . . . .**175** E2
Burnham SL1. . . . .**197** E4
Hazlemere HP15 . . . .**162** F3
High Wycombe HP12 . . . . .**172** C8
Maidenhead SL6 . . . .**202** F7
Tring HP23. . . . .**119** C5
Turvey MK43 . . . .**8** E6
Uxbridge UB8. . . . .**201** D5
Windsor SL4 . . . .**210** D5
Grove Road Prim Sch
HP23. . . . .**119** C5
Grovers Ct HP27 . . . .**139** D3
Grovesbrook MK17. . . . . . .**48** D2
Groves Cl SL8. . . . .**185** C3

Groves Rd HP22. . . . .**131** E7
Groves Way
Chesham HP5 . . . .**143** F2
Cookham Rise SL6 . . . . . .**195** E6
Grove The
Amersham HP6 . . . .**154** D4
Latimer HP5. . . . .**155** D3
Medmenham SL7 . . . .**193** E6
Milton Keynes, Bradwell
MK13. . . . .**34** A4
Milton Keynes, Rickley Park
MK3 . . . .**58** A8
Newport Pagnell MK16 . . . .**22** B3
Slough SL1. . . . .**206** A4
Waddesdon HP18 . . . .**99** A6
Groveway
Bow Brickhill MK7 . . . .**48** B7
Milton Keynes, Redmoor
MK3 . . . .**47** A3
Milton Keynes, Simpson
MK6 . . . .**47** D5
Grove Way
Chorleywood WD3 . . . . . .**167** B4
Uxbridge UB8. . . . .**201** D5
Waddesdon HP18 . . . .**99** A6
Grovewood Cl WD3 . . . . . .**167** B4
Grubbins La HP27. . . . . . .**150** B5
Grubbs Ct LU7. . . . .**68** D2
Grubwood La SL6. . . . . . .**195** A7
Grundy Rd SL2. . . . .**201** D3
Gryms Dyke HP16. . . . . . .**151** D6
Guards Club Rd SL6. . . . . .**203** C7
Guards Rd SL4. . . . .**209** C5
Guards View SL4. . . . .**210** D6
Guards Wlk 1 SL4 . . . . . .**209** C5
GUBBLECOTE. **104** D3
Guernsey Cl HP19. . . . . . .**101** A3
Guest Gdns MK13. . . . .**34** B8
Guildford Ave MK4. . . . . . .**45** E1
Guildford Cl MK18. . . . .**52** A4
Guillemot Way HP19. . . . .**101** E3
Guinea Orch MK46 . . . .**6** E4
Guinions Rd HP13. . . . . . .**173** F5
Guise Ct MK17. . . . .**49** F4
Gullet Nature Reserve The★
SL6. . . . .**202** E5
Gullicot Way LU7 . . . .**105** C4
Gulliver's SL4. . . . .**210** D8
Gulliver's Land★ MK15 . . . .**35** C4
Gull Way 4 HP19 . . . .**101** F3
Gundale Ct MK4 . . . .**46** B2
Gun La MK16. . . . .**14** A2
Gunmaker Ct MK14 . . . .**34** F6
Gunthorpe Rd SL7. . . . . . .**184** A3
Gunver La MK4 . . . .**57** B8
Gurnard Cl UB7. . . . .**208** D6
Gurnards Ave MK6 . . . .**35** A2
Gurnells Rd HP9 . . . .**176** C5
Gurney Cl
10 Aylesbury HP20 . . . . . .**101** F2
Beaconsfield HP9 . . . .**175** D2
Milton Keynes MK5 . . . . . .**46** A7
Gurney Ct LU6. . . . .**92** F6
Gurneys Mdw HP15 . . . . . .**163** D7
Guttmann Rd HP21. . . . . .**115** F5
Guyana La MK17 . . . .**58** A3
Gwendale SL6 . . . .**195** C1
Gwendolyn Buck Dr
HP21. . . . .**115** F4
Gweneth Ct SL7. . . . .**183** D3
Gwent Cl SL6. . . . .**202** B4
Gwynant Ct MK2. . . . .**58** C3
Gwynne Cl
Tring HP23. . . . .**119** A5
Windsor SL4 . . . .**209** E6
Gyles Cl MK18 . . . .**65** F4
Gynant Rd HP13 . . . .**173** F6
Gyosei Gdns MK15 . . . .**35** B5
Gypsy La
Aspley Guise MK17 . . . . . .**49** F3
High Wycombe HP11 . . . . .**173** D5
Marlow SL7 . . . .**183** E4
Stoke Poges SL2 . . . .**187** E1

Hadrians Dr MK13. . . . . . .**34** A5
Hadrian's Gate NN13 . . . . .**38** A7
Haggar St HP17. . . . .**114** B5
Hag Hill La SL6 . . . .**204** A7
Hag Hill Rise SL6 . . . .**204** A7
Haglis Dr HP22 . . . .**131** B6
Haig Dr SL1 . . . .**205** B4
Haileybury Ct SL4. . . . . . .**210** A4
Hailey Croft OX39 . . . .**147** B6
Hailey Cl SL6 . . . .**202** F5
Hainan Dr MK3. . . . .**58** B3
Hainault Ave MK14. . . . . . .**22** A1
Haines Cl HP19 . . . .**100** F2
Haines Rd HP15. . . . .**162** F6
Haithewaite MK8. . . . .**33** D1
Haldene MK8. . . . .**33** E2
Hale SL4. . . . .**209** F6
Hale Ave MK11. . . . .**32** E5
Hale La HP22 . . . .**131** E3
Hale Leys Sh Ctr 23
HP20. . . . .**115** D8
Hale Rd HP22. . . . .**131** D3
Hales Croft HP21. . . . .**116** B4
Hale St HP20 . . . .**115** E8
Halfacre Hill SL9. . . . .**177** F2
Halfway Hos
Hanslope MK19 . . . .**10** F4
Maidenhead SL6 . . . .**195** E4
Halfway House La HP5 . . . .**153** F7
Halifax SL6. . . . .**202** A8
Halifax Ho HP7 . . . .**166** C8
Halifax Rd
Heronsgate WD3 . . . .**167** C2
High Wycombe HP12 . . . . .**172** D5
Maidenhead SL6 . . . .**202** A8
Halifax Way SL6 . . . .**202** A8
Halings La UB9 . . . .**189** E7
Halkingcroft SL3. . . . .**206** C4
Hall Cl
High Wycombe HP13. . . . .**173** F5
Maids Moreton MK18 . . . . .**41** F3
Old Stratford MK19. . . . . . .**32** B6
Hall Cotts HP18. . . . .**82** F7
Hall Ct SL3 . . . .**211** B7
Halldore Hill SL6. . . . .**195** E7
Hall Green MK17. . . . .**58** B2
Hall La MK16 . . . .**23** C8
Hall Park Gate HP4 . . . . . .**135** E3
Hall Park Hill HP4. . . . . . .**135** E3
Hall Pk HP4 . . . .**135** E3
**Hall Place (Berkshire Coll of
Agriculture)** SL6 . . . . . .**194** A1
Halls Cnr HP10. . . . .**174** A1
Halse Dr SL1. . . . .**197** F7
Halswell Pl MK10 . . . .**36** A3
HALTON. **117** D1
Haltonchesters MK13 . . . . .**33** F6
Halton Com Comb Sch
HP22. . . . .**131** D7
Halton Wood Forest Wlks★
HP23. . . . .**132** A3
Halton Wood Rd HP22. . . .**131** D5
Haly Cl MK13 . . . .**34** B4
Hamberlins La HP4, HP23 .**134** B7
HAMBLEDEN. **181** D1
Hambleden RG9. . . . .**181** C2
Hambleden Mill RG9 . . . . .**192** C7
Hambleden Pl RG9. . . . . . .**192** D6
Hambleden Rise RG9. . . . .**192** D8
Hambleden Wlk SL6 . . . . .**195** E3
Hambledines MK14 . . . .**21** E3
Hambledon Cl HP21. . . . . .**116** B5
Hamble Dr HP21. . . . .**115** C6
Hambleton Gr MK4. . . . . . .**46** B2
Hambling Pl LU6. . . . .**93** F8
Hamburg Croft MK5. . . . . .**46** B3
Hambye Cl HP27. . . . .**149** E4
Hamer Cl HP3 . . . .**146** A3
Hamfield Cotts SL6 . . . . . .**195** E7
HAM GREEN. **83** D2
**Hamilton Acad
(annexe)** HP13. . . . .**173** B8
**Hamilton Acad
(main site)** 17 HP13 . . . .**173** B7
Hamilton Ave RG9. . . . . . .**191** E1
Hamilton Cl HP4 . . . .**107** C5
Hamilton Ct
Aylesbury HP19. . . . .**101** D1
High Wycombe HP13. . . . .**173** B8
Hamilton Gdns SL1. . . . . .**197** B2
Hamilton La MK3. . . . .**57** C6
Hamilton Mead 5 HP3 . . . .**146** A4
Hamilton Pk SL6 . . . .**202** A8
Hamilton Pl SL9 . . . .**188** E4
Hamilton Rd
Berkhamsted HP4 . . . .**135** B4
High Wycombe HP13 . . . . .**162** C1
Slough SL1. . . . .**205** A4
Thame OX9 . . . .**126** A1
Uxbridge UB8. . . . .**201** D1
Ham Island SL4 . . . .**211** C3
Ham La SL4. . . . .**211** C3
Hamlins MK6 . . . .**47** A6
Hammersley La HP10,
HP11. . . . .**174** B5
Hammerwood Gate MK7. . . .**48** A7
Hammond Cres MK15 . . . . .**35** B6
Hammond End SL2. . . . . . .**198** B8
Hamon Way 2 MK12. . . . . .**33** A6
Hampden Ave HP5. . . . . . .**144** A1
HAMPDEN BOTTOM. **141** B2
Hampden Cl
Aylesbury HP21 . . . .**115** D6

Hampden Cl *continued*
Stoke Mandeville HP22 . . 116 B1
Stoke Poges SL2 . . . . 199 A2
Hampden Gate HP27 . . . 150 C5
Hampden Gdns HP21. . . . 115 D6
Hampden Hill
Beaconsfield HP9 . . . . 175 B2
Charndon OX27 . . . . 72 E6
Hampden Ho 1 HP13 . . . 173 F6
Hampden Rd
Aylesbury HP21 . . . . 115 D6
Chalfont St Peter SL9 . . . . 177 D2
High Wycombe HP13 . . . . . 173 B8
Hughenden Valley HP16 . . 151 B3
Maidenhead SL6 . . . . 202 B8
Slough SL3 . . . . 206 F3
Speen HP27 . . . . 150 C5
Stoke Mandeville HP22 . . 116 B1
Wendover HP22 . . . . 131 C5
Hampden Sq 2 HP19 . . . 115 A8
Hampden Villas OX27 . . . 71 F7
Hampshire Ave SL1 . . . . 205 C8
Hampshire Ct MK3 . . . . . . 46 F2
Hampshire Lodge 8 SL6 202 F6
Hampson Cl MK13 . . . . . . 34 A3
Hampstead Cl 7 HP19 . . 100 F1
Hampstead Gate MK13 . . 34 C3
Hampton 7 MK8 . . . . 45 F8
Hampton Ho SL3 . . . . . . 212 D7
Hanbury Cl SL1 . . . . 204 A8
Hancock Cl HP21 . . . . . . 115 E5
Handel Mead MK7 . . . . . . 48 E5
Handleton Comm HP14 . 171 B5
Handley Page Cl MK43 . . 24 E2
Handy Cross HP11 . . . . . 172 F3
Hangar Rd UB9 . . . . 189 E7
Hanging Croft Cl 4
HP13 . . . . 173 F6
Hangings HP16 . . . . 151 A6
Hanley Cl SL4 . . . . 209 D6
Hanmer Rd MK6 . . . . 47 E5
Hannah Ball Sch HP13 . . 173 D7
Hannon Rd HP21 . . . . . . 115 C5
Hanover Cl
3 Aylesbury HP19 . . . . . 101 A2
Slough SL1 . . . . 206 A3
Windsor SL4 . . . . 209 F6
Hanover Ct
2 Aylesbury HP21 . . . . . 115 E7
Hazelmere HP15 . . . . 163 B3
Leighton Buzzard LU7 . . . . 80 D7
Milton Keynes MK14 . . . . . 34 D7
Hanover Mead SL6 . . . . . 203 C3
Hanover Way SL4 . . . . . . 209 F6
Hanscomb Cl MK15 . . . . . 35 C2
Hansen Croft MK5 . . . . . . 46 B5
HANSLOPE 11 B3
Hanslope Prim Sch MK19. 11 A4
Hanslope Rd MK19 . . . . . . 19 F6
Hanson Ave MK10 . . . . . . 35 E2
Hanson Cl UB7 . . . . 208 F3
Hanson Way HP21 . . . . . 116 A4
Harborne Ct MK8 . . . . 33 C2
Harborough Cl SL1 . . . . . 204 D5
Harbourne Ct HP21 . . . . 115 C3
Harby Cl MK4 . . . . 46 C1
Harcourt
Milton Keynes MK13 . . . . . 34 A3
Wraysbury TW19 . . . . 211 E1
Harcourt Cl
Dorney SL6 . . . . 203 F3
Henley-on-Thames RG9 . . 191 C1
Leighton Buzzard LU7 . . . . 80 E7
Harcourt Gn HP19 . . . . . 101 B2
Harcourt Rd
Dorney SL4 . . . . 203 F3
Tring HP23 . . . . 119 C4
Windsor SL4 . . . . 209 F6
Har Ct MK43 . . . . 25 B2
Hardenwaye HP13 . . . . . 162 E1
Harding Cl
Chesham HP5 . . . . 144 D1
Milton Keynes MK10 . . . . . 48 C8
Hardings Cl SL0 . . . . 200 C2
Harding Spur 13 SL3 . . . 206 F1
Hardings Row SL0 . . . . . 200 D2
HARDMEAD 15 D3
Hardmead Rd MK43 . . . . . 8 A3
HARDWICK 87 B3
Hardwick Cl SL6 . . . . 202 A8
Hardwicke Gdns HP6 . . 154 E1
Hardwick Mews MK17 . . 49 B3
Hardwick Pl MK17 . . . . . . 49 B4
Hardwick Rd MK17 . . . . . 49 B4
Hardy Cl
Aylesbury HP21 . . . . 115 E7
Slough SL1 . . . . 205 A5
Hardy Mead Ct HP11 . . . 174 B2
Hardy Mews UB8 . . . . . . 201 C3
Harebell Cl MK7 . . . . 48 B5
Harebell Wlk HP15 . . . . . 162 F6
Harebridge La HP22 . . . . 117 E1
Hare Cl MK18 . . . . 52 E7
Hareden Croft MK4 . . . . . 46 B2
Harefield Rd
Maidenhead SL6 . . . . 202 A7
Uxbridge UB8 . . . . 201 D6
Harehatch La SL1 . . . . . . 186 F3
Hare La HP16 . . . . 152 B3
Hare Lane End HP16 . . . . 152 A3
Harescombe Ct HP9 . . . . 175 D3
Haresfoot Sch HP4 . . . . . 135 B1
Hare Shoots SL6 . . . . 202 E5
Harewood Pl SL1 . . . . . . 206 A3
Harewood Rd HP8 . . . . . 166 C6

Hargrave Rd SL6 . . . . . . 202 D8
Hargreaves Nook MK14. . 22 B2
Harkness Cl MK2 . . . . 58 D6
Harkness Rd SL1 . . . . . . 204 B8
Harlans Cl MK6 . . . . 47 B8
Harlech Ho 5 HP13 . . . . 173 F7
Harlech Pl MK3 . . . . 57 E7
Harlech Rd LU7 . . . . 105 C3
Harlesden Cl MK10 . . . . . 35 E1
Harle Stone Ct MK14 . . . . 22 A1
Harley Ct SL1 . . . . 205 C4
Harley Dr MK7 . . . . 48 A5
Harleyford La SL7 . . . . . 194 B7
Harling Rd LU6 . . . . 93 B4
Harlow Cres 6 MK4 . . . . 45 E2
Harlow Rd HP13 . . . . 173 C6
Harmans Cross MK10 . . . 36 B3
Harman Terr HP12 . . . . . 172 D7
Harman Wlk HP12 . . . . . 172 C3
HARMONDSWORTH 213 D8
Harmondsworth La UB7. 213 E8
Harmondsworth Prim Sch
UB7 . . . . 213 D8
Harmondsworth Rd UB7 208 D4
Harnett Dr MK12 . . . . 32 F6
Harper Cl OX25 . . . . 94 D7
Harpers La MK14 . . . . . . 34 F8
Harrier Cl HP20 . . . . 101 C4
Harrier Ct MK6 . . . . 47 A8
Harrier Dr MK6 . . . . 47 A8
Harries Cl HP5 . . . . 144 B1
Harries Way HP15 . . . . . 163 B6
Harriet Walker Way
WD3 . . . . 167 F2
Harrington Cl SL4 . . . . . . 209 F3
Harris Cl
Brill HP18 . . . . 110 A8
Milton Keynes MK17 . . . . . 58 B2
Harris Ct 7 HP20 . . . . . . 101 F2
Harris Gdns SL1 . . . . 205 C4
Harrison Barber Cotts
SL3 . . . . 212 D7
Harrison Cl MK5 . . . . 46 D6
Harrison Pl OX9 . . . . 125 F1
Harrisons Wy 3 HP13 . . 162 A1
Harrison Way SL1 . . . . . . 204 D5
Harris Rd HP14 . . . . 171 B5
Harroell
Long Crendon, Church End
HP18 . . . . 125 D6
Long Crendon HP18 . . . . . 125 D5
Harrogate Ct SL3 . . . . . . 207 A1
HARROLD 3 F6
Harrold Lower Sch MK43. 3 F6
Harrold Priory Mid Sch
MK43 . . . . 3 F6
Harrold Rd MK46 . . . . 3 B1
Harrow Cl
Aylesbury HP21 . . . . 115 E4
Maidenhead SL6 . . . . 195 E1
Harrowden MK13 . . . . 34 B7
Harrow La SL6 . . . . 195 E1
Harrow Mkt The SL3 . . . 207 A3
Harrow Rd SL3 . . . . 206 F3
Harrow Yd 6 HP23 . . . . 119 A3
Hartdames MK5 . . . . 46 A3
Hartfield Cl MK7 . . . . 48 A7
Hartington Gr 5 MK4 . . . 46 B3
Hartland Ave MK4 . . . . . . 57 B8
Hartland Cl SL1 . . . . 205 D5
Hartley MK14 . . . . 34 E8
Hartley Cl SL3 . . . . 199 C4
Hartley Copse SL4 . . . . . 211 A1
Hartley Ct SL9 . . . . 188 E5
Hart Moor Cl HP14 . . . . . 158 E4
Harts Rd HP17 . . . . 127 B6
Hart St RG9 . . . . 191 E2
HARTWELL 10 D8
Hartwell Cl HP10 . . . . . . 163 C2
Hartwell Dr HP9 . . . . 175 D3
Hartwell End HP21 . . . . . 115 B7
Hartwell Rd
Ashton NN7 . . . . 9 F8
Hanslope MK19 . . . . 10 E5
Hartwort Cl MK7 . . . . 48 B5
Harvard Cl MK14 . . . . 21 F2
Harvest Bank MK6 . . . . . 153 C4
Harvester Cl MK12 . . . . . 33 B5
Harvest Hill HP10 . . . . . . 185 D2
Harvest Hill Rd SL6 . . . . 202 F3
Harvey Dr MK46 . . . . 6 F1
Harvey Ho SL3 . . . . 206 E7
Harvey Orch HP9 . . . . . . 175 C3
Harvey Rd
Aylesbury HP21 . . . . 115 E5
Dunstable LU6 . . . . 93 D7
Slough SL3 . . . . 207 B4
Harvil Rd UB9, UB10 . . . . 190 E4
Harvington Pk LU7 . . . . . 105 D3
Harwich Rd SL1 . . . . 205 A4
Harwood Dr UB10 . . . . . 201 F4
Harwood Rd SL7 . . . . . . 183 C1
Harwood St MK13 . . . . . . 34 A7
Hasgill Ct MK13 . . . . 34 B4
Haslemere Rd SL4 . . . . . 210 A6
Haslerig Ct HP21 . . . . . . 115 F5
Haslow Ct MK8 . . . . 33 B4
Hasting Cl SL6 . . . . 203 C2
Hastings MK11 . . . . 32 E5
Hastings Mdw SL2 . . . . . 199 A4
HASTOE 132 F7
Hastoe Cross HP23 . . . . 133 A7
Hastoe Farm Barns
HP23 . . . . 132 F7
Hastoe Hill HP23 . . . . . . 132 F8
Hastoe La HP23 . . . . 119 A2

Hastoe Pk HP20 . . . . 101 F2
Hastoe Row HP23 . . . . . 133 A7
Hatches La
Great Kingshill HP15 . . . . 151 C1
Hughenden Valley HP15 . . 162 B8
Hatchet Leys La MK18 . . . 53 F8
Hatchgate Gdns SL1 . . . 197 D1
Hatch La
Harmondsworth UB7 . . . . 213 D7
Radnage HP14 . . . . 160 B4
Windsor SL4 . . . . 210 A5
Hatchlands MK8 . . . . 33 F1
Hatch Pl SL6 . . . . 195 E7
Hatch The SL4 . . . . 209 C7
Hatfield Cl SL6 . . . . 202 C6
Hatfield Rd SL1 . . . . 206 A4
Hathaway Ct MK8 . . . . . . 45 E8
Hatter's La HP13 . . . . . . 173 F6
Hatton MK6 . . . . 47 D6
Hatton Ave SL2 . . . . 198 D1
Hatton Ct SL4 . . . . 210 C5
Hatton Gr UB7 . . . . 208 D4
Hauksbee Gdns MK5 . . . 46 D5
Havelock Bsns Pk SL6. . 202 C7
Havelock Cres SL6 . . . . . 202 B7
Havelock Ct HP20 . . . . . 101 D1
Havelock Rd SL6 . . . . . . 202 B7
Havelock St HP20 . . . . . 101 D1
Havenfield Ct 16 HP13 . 173 B7
Havenfield Rd HP12 . . . . 172 C4
Haven of Rest SL6 . . . . . 203 B7
Haven Shaw Cl HP21 . . . 116 A5
Haven St MK10 . . . . 36 C3
HAVERSHAM 20 D2
Haversham Rd MK19 . . . . 20 D1
Haversham Village Sch
MK19 . . . . 20 E2
Haverthwaite View MK10 36 C3
Hawfinch 1 HP19 . . . . . . 101 C4
Hawker Ct SL3 . . . . 207 A3
Hawkes Cl SL3 . . . . 207 B3
Hawkhurst Gate MK7 . . . 47 F7
Hawkings Way HP3 . . . . 146 A5
Hawkins Cl MK11 . . . . . . 32 D5
Hawkmoor Cl MK6 . . . . . 47 B8
Hawkshead Dr MK4 . . . . 46 C3
Hawks Hill SL8 . . . . 185 C3
Hawkshill Dr HP3 . . . . . 146 F8
Hawkshill Rd SL2 . . . . . 198 A2
Hawkslade Furlong
HP21 . . . . 115 D3
Hawksmoor Cl HP13 . . . 173 A8
Hawkswood MK6 . . . . 6 F5
Hawkswood Gr SL3 . . . . 199 F6
Hawkswood La SL3, SL9. 199 F8
Hawkwell Dr HP23 . . . . . 119 C4
Hawkwell Est MK19 . . . . . 32 B7
Hawleys La HP22 . . . . 87 A6
Haworth Croft 2 MK10. . 36 B3
HAWRIDGE 133 E1
Hawridge & Cholesbury CE
Sch HP5 . . . . 133 E2
HAWRIDGE COMMON . . . 133 E2
Hawridge La HP5 . . . . . . 143 E8
Hawridge Vale HP5 . . . . 133 F1
Hawthorn Ave MK2 . . . . . 58 E8
Hawthorn Cl
Aylesbury HP20 . . . . 101 F2
Iver Heath SL0 . . . . 200 C2
Turvey MK43 . . . . 8 E6
Hawthorn Cres HP15 . . . 163 B2
Hawthorn Dr UB9 . . . . . . 201 C6
Hawthorne Cl
Leighton Buzzard LU7 . . . . 80 E8
Marlow SL7 . . . . 183 E4
Hawthorne Cres
Slough SL1 . . . . 205 F7
West Drayton UB7 . . . . . . 208 F4
Hawthorne Gdns HP10 . 174 A2
Hawthorne Rd HP13 . . . . 174 A6
Hawthorn Gdns SL6 . . . 202 E5
Hawthorn Gr 6 MK16 . . . 36 B5
Hawthorn La SL2 . . . . . . 198 A5
Hawthorn Pl HP10 . . . . . 174 C8
Hawthorn Rd HP27 . . . . 139 C3
Hawthorns The
Berkhamsted HP4 . . . . . . 135 A5
Cranfield MK43 . . . . 25 B1
Felden HP3 . . . . 146 F7
Little Chalfont HP8 . . . . . 166 C7
Maple Cross WD3 . . . . . . 178 D5
Monks Risborough HP27. . 139 C6
Poyle SL3 . . . . 212 F6
Wooburn Green HP10 . . . 185 E6
Hawthorn Way
Chesham HP5 . . . . 144 D2
Wing LU7 . . . . 79 E3
Hawthorn Wlk HP15 . . . 163 B2
Hawtrey Cl SL1 . . . . 206 B4
Hawtrey Rd SL4 . . . . 210 C5
Hay Barn Bsns Pk The
HP22 . . . . 88 C6
Haybrook Coll SL1 . . . . . 204 E8
Hayden Ho 3 HP11 . . . . 172 F7
Haydock Cl MK3 . . . . 57 C6
Haydon Abbey Sch HP19 101 C2
Haydon Ct SL6 . . . . 202 E6
HAYDON HILL 100 E2
Haydon Rd HP19 . . . . . . 101 C2
Hayes Cl SL6 . . . . 203 D1
Hayes Pl SL7 . . . . 183 D1
Hayes Rd MK19 . . . . 31 F5
Hayfield Dr HP15 . . . . . . 163 B2
Hay La SL3 . . . . 199 D8
Hayles Field RG9 . . . . . . 170 E1
Hayling Cl SL1 . . . . 205 B5

Haymaker Cl UB10 . . . . . 201 F5
Hayman Rise MK8 . . . . . . 45 D6
Haymill Rd SL1, SL2. . . . 197 D1
Haymill Valley Nature
Reserve ★ SL2 . . . . . . 204 E8
Haynes Cl
Bow Brickhill MK17 . . . . . . 48 D2
Slough SL3 . . . . 206 F1
Haynes Ho HP12 . . . . . . 172 B3
Haynes Mead HP4 . . . . . 135 A6
Hayse Hill SL4 . . . . 209 D6
Haystacks The HP13 . . . 173 B7
Hayter Cl HP19 . . . . 101 C4
Haythrop Cl MK15 . . . . . . 35 B6
Hayward Pl SL8 . . . . 185 C2
Haywards Cl RG9 . . . . . . 191 C1
Haywards Croft MK12 . . . 33 B5
Haywards Mead SL4 . . . . 204 F1
Haywood Dr WD3 . . . . . . 167 F4
Haywood Pk
Chorleywood WD3 . . . . . . 167 F4
Stewkley LU7 . . . . 68 C3
Haywoods Dr HP3 . . . . . 146 F8
Haywood Way HP19 . . . . 100 F3
Hayworth Pl 2 MK4 . . . . 45 D2
Hazelbury Rd HP13 . . . . 173 D6
Hazel Cl SL7 . . . . 183 C6
Hazelcroft Cl UB10 . . . . 201 F5
Hazel Ct WD3 . . . . 178 E5
Hazeldene HP22 . . . . 131 C4
HAZELEY 45 D5
Hazeley Acad The MK8 . . 45 D5
Hazel Gr MK2 . . . . 58 D7
Hazelhurst 7 MK4 . . . . . . 46 B2
Hazelhurst Rd SL1 . . . . . 197 D3
Hazell Ave HP21 . . . . 116 A7
Hazell Cl SL6 . . . . 202 F8
Hazell Pk HP7 . . . . 165 D8
Hazell Rd HP16 . . . . 151 C5
Hazell Way SL2 . . . . 198 F6
HAZELMERE 163 B4
Hazel Rd HP4 . . . . 135 D3
Hazelwood MK14 . . . . 34 F8
Hazelwood Cl HP5 . . . . . 144 D2
Hazely HP23 . . . . 119 C4
Hazlehurst Dr HP21 . . . . 116 A5
Hazlemere CE Comb Sch
HP15 . . . . 162 F3
Hazlemere Ct HP15 . . . . 163 A4
Hazlemere Rd
Slough SL2 . . . . 206 B5
Tylers Green HP10. . . . . . 163 C2
Hazlemere View HP15. . . 163 B5
Hazley Wlk HP15 . . . . 41 F1
Headington Cl SL6 . . . . . 202 A5
Headington Pl SL2 . . . . . 205 F5
Headington Rd SL6 . . . . 202 A5
Headland Cl 1 HP16 . . . 152 A8
Headlands Dr HP4 . . . . . 135 E5
Healey Ave HP13 . . . . . . 173 D7
Heaney Cl MK16 . . . . 22 A5
Hearn Cl HP10 . . . . 162 F2
Hearne Ct HP8 . . . . 177 B7
Hearne Dr SL6 . . . . 203 A1
Hearne Pl MK6 . . . . 46 F8
Hearnes Cl HP15 . . . . . . 176 D5
Hearne's Mdw HP9 . . . . 176 D5
Heathacre SL3 . . . . 212 E6
Heath Cl
Aylesbury HP20 . . . . 116 B5
Holmer Green HP15 . . . . . 163 B6
Stanwell TW19 . . . . 213 C1
Woburn Sands MK17 . . . . 49 C3
Heathcote SL6 . . . . 203 B2
Heathcote Ct 3 SL4 . . . . 210 D4
Heathcote Way UB7 . . . . 208 D5
Heath Ct
Leighton Buzzard LU7 . . . . 70 E3
Uxbridge UB8 . . . . 201 D5
HEATH END
Cholesbury 134 A2
Prestwood 151 E1
Heath End Cl HP15 . . . . . 151 E1
Heath End Rd
Flackwell Heath HP10 . . . 174 A1
Great Kingshill HP15,
HP16 . . . . 151 E2
Little Marlow HP10 . . . . . 173 D2
Heather Cl
Buckingham MK18 . . . . . . 52 C7
Uxbridge UB8 . . . . 208 F8
Heathercroft MK14 . . . . . 34 E7
Heatherden Gn SL0 . . . . 200 D4
Heather La UB7 . . . . 208 E2
Heather Mead LU6 . . . . . 92 E5
Heathers Cl MK18 . . . . . . 73 B5
Heatherside Gdns SL2. . 187 D1
Heatherton House Sch
HP6 . . . . 154 C3
Heatherton Pk HP6 . . . . 154 B3
Heather Wlk
Aylesbury HP21 . . . . 115 B6
Hazelmere HP15 . . . . 163 A3
Heathfield MK12 . . . . 33 C4
Heathfield Ind Est MK12. 33 B4
Heathfield Rd
High Wycombe HP12 . . . . 172 B7
Taplow SL6 . . . . 186 A1
Heath La MK17 . . . . 49 A2
Heathlands Dr SL6 . . . . . 202 A6
Heath Lawn HP10 . . . . . . 173 F1
Heath Rd
Beaconsfield HP9 . . . . 186 A8
Great Brickhill MK17, LU7. . 59 E1
Hyde Heath HP6 . . . . 153 C5
Heathrow Bvd UB7 . . . . . 213 F5
Heathrow Cl UB7 . . . . . . 213 B6
Heathrow Prim Sch UB7 213 F8

Heathrow T5 Sta/U Sta
TW6 . . . . 213 C4
Heath The LU7 . . . . 70 E4
Heath Way SL0 . . . . 200 D3
Heavens Lea SL8 . . . . . . 185 C2
Hebridean 2 MK18 . . . . . 41 D2
Hebrides Gate MK3 . . . . . 58 C3
Hedge Furlong HP17 . . . 127 A6
Hedge Lea HP10 . . . . 185 C6
HEDGERLEY 187 D3
Hedgerley OX39 . . . . 147 B6
HEDGERLEY GREEN 187 E4
HEDGERLEY HILL 187 E2
Hedgerley Hill SL2 . . . . . 187 D2
Hedgerley La
Beaconsfield HP9 . . . . 186 F8
Gerrards Cross SL9 . . . . . 188 B4
Hedgerley SL2 . . . . 187 D6
Hedgerow SL9 . . . . 177 E4
Hedgerows The MK4 . . . . 46 E4
Hedges Ct MK5 . . . . 46 B6
Hedingham Ct MK5 . . . . . 46 A5
Hedingham Mews SL6. . . 202 D7
Hedley Ct HP22 . . . . 118 A4
Hedley Rd HP10 . . . . 185 B8
Hedley View HP10 . . . . . 174 D1
HEDSOR 185 F3
Hedsor Hill SL8 . . . . 185 C1
Hedsor La
Hedsor HP10 . . . . 185 F2
Taplow SL1 . . . . 186 A2
Hedsor Rd SL8 . . . . 185 B2
Hedsor View Cotts SL6 . . 195 F7
HEELANDS 34 C4
Heelands Sch MK13 . . . . . 34 B4
Heights The SL7 . . . . 194 B8
Hele Ct MK7 . . . . 48 B3
Helena Rd SL4 . . . . 210 D5
Helen Cotts SL4 . . . . 209 D5
Helford Cl HP21 . . . . 115 D4
Helford Pl MK6 . . . . 35 A1
Heligan Pl MK4 . . . . 45 F1
Hellfire Caves ★ HP14 . 160 F2
Hellyer Way SL8 . . . . . . 185 C3
Helmsley Rise MK4 . . . . . 45 E1
Helston La SL4 . . . . 210 B6
Helston Pl 3 MK6 . . . . . . 34 F1
Hemel Hempstead Rd
HP4 . . . . 107 F1
Hemingway Cl MK16 . . . . 21 F3
Hemingway Rd HP19 . . . 100 F3
Hemlock Cl HP22 . . . . . . 116 C4
Hemmings The HP4 . . . . 134 F3
Hemming Way SL2 . . . . . 198 B2
Hemp Hill 10 HP19 . . . . 115 A8
Hemp La HP23 . . . . 119 F1
Hempson Ave SL3 . . . . . 206 C3
Hempstead Rd HP3 . . . . 146 B5
HEMPTON WAINHILL . . . 147 F7
Hemsdale SL6 . . . . 195 B1
Hemwood Rd SL4 . . . . . . 209 D4
Hencroft Mews 14 SL1 . 205 F4
Hencroft Street N SL1 . . 205 F4
Hencroft Street S SL1 . . 205 F3
Henden Mews SL6 . . . . . 202 A6
Henders MK11 . . . . 32 E5
Hendon Ct 5 MK10 . . . . . 35 F1
Hendons Way SL6 . . . . . 203 B1
Hendon Way TW19 . . . . . 213 D1
Hendrix Dr MK8 . . . . 45 D7
Hengistbury La MK4 . . . . 46 A1
Henley Business Sch Univ of
Reading RG9 . . . . 192 B7
Henley Coll The RG9 . . . 191 D1
Henley Coll The (Rotherham
Bldgs) RG9 . . . . 191 C1
Henley Lodge 12 SL6 . . . 202 F6
HENLEY-ON-THAMES . . . 191 B1
Henley-on-Thames Sta
RG9 . . . . 191 E1
Henley Rd
Hurley SL6 . . . . 193 D3
Maidenhead SL6, SL7 . . . 194 B2
Marlow SL7 . . . . 194 B8
Slough SL1 . . . . 204 F7
Hennerton Way HP13 . . . 173 F6
Henrietta Rd OX9 . . . . . . 126 A1
Henry III Tower 17 SL4 . 210 D6
Henry Rd
Aylesbury HP20 . . . . 116 B8
Slough SL1 . . . . 205 D4
Henry St HP23 . . . . 119 A3
Hensman Gate MK10 . . . . 35 F4
Henson Cl MK43 . . . . 24 E3
HENTON 137 E2
Henton Mews 5 HP19 . . 115 A8
Hepburn Cres MK4 . . . . . 45 E3
Hepleswell MK8 . . . . 33 E1
Hepplewhite Cl HP13 . . . 173 D8
Herbert Rd HP13 . . . . . . 174 A7
Herberts Hole
Chesham HP5 . . . . 143 C1
South Heath HP5, HP16. . 142 F1
Hercies Rd UB10 . . . . . . 201 F5
Herdman Ct MK12 . . . . . . 33 B5
Herd's Hill MK18 . . . . 64 A4
Hereford Ho HP13 . . . . . 173 F8
Hereford Way HP19 . . . . 101 A3
Hereford Wy MK8 . . . . . . 45 D8
Heren La MK19 . . . . 45 C8
Heritage Cl UB8 . . . . 201 C1
Heritage Gate SL9 . . . . . 188 E7
Heritage House Sch
HP5 . . . . 144 D1
Heritage Wlk WD3 . . . . . 167 E6
Hermitage Cl SL3 . . . . . . 206 C3
Hermitage La SL4 . . . . . . 210 A4

Hermitage Prim Sch
UB8 . . . 201 D5
Hermitage The
Great Missenden HP16 . . . 152 A7
Uxbridge UB8 . . . 201 D6
Hernes Oak OX39 . . . 147 D8
Heron Cl
Aylesbury HP20 . . . 116 C8
Uxbridge UB8 . . . 201 D6
Heron Dr SL3 . . . 207 B2
Heron Lodge MK14 . . . 34 C6
Herons Elm HP4 . . . 134 E7
Heronsfield Ho WD3 . . . 167 B3
HERONSGATE . . . 167 D2
Heronsgate Rd WD3 . . . 167 B3
Heronsgate Sch MK7 . . . 48 B5
Heronshaw Sch MK7 . . . 48 B5
Herons Pl
Maidenhead SL6 . . . 196 C3
Marlow SL7 . . . 183 E3
Heron The HP19 . . . 101 E4
Heron Wy SL6 . . . 203 A8
Herries Prep Sch SL6 . . . 195 B8
Herriot Cl MK16 . . . 22 A5
Herschel Gram Sch SL1 . 205 C7
Herschel Sports SL1 . . . 205 C7
Herschel St SL1 . . . 205 F4
Herston Cl HP21 . . . 116 B5
Hertford La HP18 . . . 100 D4
Hertford Pl MK3 . . . 46 F2
Hervines Ct HP6 . . . 154 C2
Hervines Rd HP6 . . . 154 C2
Hesketh Rd NN12 . . . 18 E6
Heston Wk MK4 . . . 45 D3
Hetherington Cl SL2 . . . 197 F2
Hetherington Way UB10 . 201 E8
Het's Orch HP27 . . . 149 E5
Hetton Cl MK13 . . . 34 C4
Heusden Way SL9 . . . 188 F3
Hever Cl
Maidenhead SL6 . . . 202 C6
Pitstone LU7 . . . 105 D2
Hewgate Ct RG9 . . . 191 E1
Hexham Gdns MK3 . . . 57 D6
Heybridge Cres MK7 . . . 48 B3
Heydon Ct MK13 . . . 34 A7
Heynes Gn SL6 . . . 202 B3
Heythrop Dr UB10 . . . 201 F8
Heyward Gate MK6 . . . 47 C5
Heywood Ave SL6 . . . 202 A1
Heywood Court Cl SL6 . 202 A2
Heywood Gdns SL6 . . . 202 A1
Hibbert Rd SL6 . . . 203 B4
Hibbert's Alley 16 SL4 . . . 210 D6
Hibberts Way SL9 . . . 188 E8
Hickmans Cl MK18 . . . 51 B6
Hickman St HP19 . . . 114 F8
Hickox Ct HP10 . . . 185 F7
Hicks Farm Rise HP13 . . . 173 F7
Hidcote Dr MK4 . . . 45 F1
Hide The MK6 . . . 47 C6
Higgs Ct MK5 . . . 46 A8
HIGHAM CROSS . . . 10 D3
Higham Cross Rd MK19 . . . 10 E4
Higham Mead HP5 . . . 144 C1
Higham Rd HP5 . . . 144 C1
High Ash CE Prim Sch
MK17 . . . 59 D2
High Beeches
Gerrards Cross SL9 . . . 188 D2
High Wycombe HP12 . . . 172 C6
High Beeches Cl SL7 . . . 183 C7
High Bois La HP6 . . . 154 D4
Highbridge Ind Est UB8 . 201 C5
Highbridge Rd HP21 . . . 115 E8
Highbridge Wlk 4 HP21. 115 E8
Highbury La MK9 . . . 35 B3
High Coppice HP7 . . . 165 C8
Highcrest Acad The
HP13 . . . 173 E7
Highcroft Cl NN12 . . . 18 E6
HIGHER DENHAM . . . 189 C4
Highfield
Chalfont St Giles HP8 . . . 177 D8
Long Crendon HP18 . . . 125 C7
Highfield Ave HP12 . . . 172 B5
Highfield Cl
Amersham HP6 . . . 154 D2
Milton Keynes MK3 . . . 47 B2
Newport Pagnell MK16 . . . 22 E4
Highfield Ct
Farnham Royal SL2 . . . 198 B4
Hazelmere HP15 . . . 163 A3
Highfield Dr UB10 . . . 190 E1
Highfield La SL6 . . . 202 A4
Highfield Pk SL7 . . . 183 B1
Highfield Rd
Berkhamsted HP4 . . . 135 D4
Bourne End SL8 . . . 185 B4
Chesham HP5 . . . 144 B2
Flackwell Heath HP10 . . . 185 A8
Maidenhead SL6 . . . 202 B8
Princes Risborough HP27 . 139 C4
Tring HP23 . . . 118 E3
Wigginton HP23 . . . 119 D1
Windsor SL4 . . . 209 F4
Winslow MK18 . . . 65 F5
Highfield Sch SL6 . . . 202 E7
Highfield Way
Hazelmere HP15 . . . 163 A3
Yardley Hastings NN7 . . . 1 B6
Highgate Mews 2 HP19. 100 F1
Highgate Over MK7 . . . 48 B6
Highgrove Hill MK8 . . . 45 F8
Highgrove Pk SL6 . . . 202 E8
High Halden MK7 . . . 48 B8
High Heavens Wood SL7 183 C8
Highland Cl MK3 . . . 46 F3
High Land Cl HP18 . . . 96 A1
Highland Dr MK10 . . . 36 C3
Highland Rd HP7 . . . 165 D8
Highlands
Flackwell Heath HP10 . . . 185 B7
High Wycombe HP13 . . . 174 A5
Highlands Cl SL9 . . . 177 F3
Highlands End SL9 . . . 177 F3
Highlands La SL9 . . . 177 F3
Highlands Rd
Buckingham MK18 . . . 41 E2
Seer Green HP9 . . . 176 C5
Highlands The SL2 . . . 198 C7
Highlea Ave HP10 . . . 185 A8
Highley Gr MK10 . . . 36 B3
High March Sch HP9 . . . 175 D4
High Mdw SL6 . . . 196 C3
Highmoor HP7 . . . 165 D8
High Moors HP22 . . . 131 B8
Highmore Cotts HP7 . . . 152 F3
Highmore Croft MK8 . . . 45 D6
Highover Pk HP7 . . . 165 D7
High Park Dr MK12 . . . 33 A6
High Rd
Cookham Rise SL6 . . . 195 E7
Soulbury LU7 . . . 69 E2
Uxbridge UB8 . . . 208 C7
High St The MK8 . . . 33 E1
High St
Amersham HP7 . . . 165 A7
Aylesbury HP20 . . . 115 E8
Berkhamsted HP4 . . . 135 C4
Berkhamsted, Northchurch
HP4 . . . 134 E6
Bovingdon HP3 . . . 146 A4
Bray SL6 . . . 203 C4
Brill HP18 . . . 110 A8
Buckingham MK18 . . . 28 D1
Buckingham MK18 . . . 41 D1
Burcott LU7 . . . 79 D4
Burnham SL1 . . . 197 C2
Chalfont St Giles HP8 . . . 177 C8
Chalfont St Peter SL9 . . . 177 E2
Chalvey SL1 . . . 205 D3
Cheddington LU7 . . . 105 A7
Chesham HP5 . . . 154 B8
Chinnor, Kingston Blount
OX39 . . . 147 A4
Chinnor OX39 . . . 147 D7
Colnbrook SL3 . . . 212 C7
Cookham SL6 . . . 196 B7
Cranfield MK43 . . . 25 B1
Cublington LU7 . . . 78 B1
Datchet SL3 . . . 211 B6
Deanshanger MK19 . . . 31 E4
Dinton HP17 . . . 113 E2
Downley HP13 . . . 161 D3
Eaton Bray LU6 . . . 92 E6
Edlesborough LU6 . . . 92 E3
Emberton MK46 . . . 13 F7
Eton SL4 . . . 210 D8
Great Horwood MK17 . . . 55 A3
Great Missenden HP16 . . . 152 A7
Haddenham HP17 . . . 126 F6
Hanslope MK19 . . . 11 A2
Harmondsworth UB7 . . . 213 D8
Harrold MK43 . . . 3 F6
Haversham MK19 . . . 21 A3
High Wycombe HP11 . . . 173 B6
Iver SL0 . . . 207 F7
Ivinghoe LU7 . . . 105 E5
Lane End HP14 . . . 171 B4
Lavendon MK46 . . . 7 F8
Leighton Buzzard LU7 . . . 80 F6
Lewknor OX49 . . . 157 B8
Long Crendon HP18 . . . 125 D6
Ludgershall HP18 . . . 96 B8
14 Maidenhead SL6 . . . 202 F7
Marlow SL7 . . . 183 E1
Milton Keynes, Great Linford
MK14 . . . 21 E1
Milton Keynes MK2 . . . 47 E1
Milton Keynes, New Bradwell
MK13 . . . 34 A7
Milton Keynes, Stony Stratford
MK11 . . . 32 D6
Nash MK17 . . . 44 C1
Newport Pagnell MK16 . . . 22 D4
North Crawley MK16 . . . 24 B6
North Marston MK18 . . . 76 A2
Olney MK46 . . . 6 F3
Paulerspury NN12 . . . 17 C8
Potterspury NN12 . . . 18 D3
Prestwood HP16 . . . 151 D6
Princes Risborough HP27 . 139 B3
Sherington MK16 . . . 13 F2
Slough SL3 . . . 207 A2
Slough, Upton SL1 . . . 205 F4
Stanwell TW19 . . . 213 D1
Stoke Goldington MK16 . . . 12 B6
Syresham NN13 . . . 27 D7
Taplow SL6 . . . 196 E1
Thame OX9 . . . 125 E1
Thornborough MK18 . . . 54 A8
Tring HP23 . . . 119 A3
Turvey MK43 . . . 8 E5
Uxbridge, Cowley UB8 . . . 201 C1
Uxbridge UB8 . . . 201 D5
Waddesdon HP18 . . . 99 A6
Weedon HP22 . . . 87 C1
Wendover HP22 . . . 131 B4
Westcott HP18 . . . 98 B7
West Drayton UB7 . . . 208 E6
Weston Underwood MK46 . . . 6 B2
West Wycombe HP14 . . . 160 F2
Whaddon MK17 . . . 45 B1
Whitchurch HP22 . . . 87 A6
Windsor SL4 . . . 210 D6
High St *continued*
Wing LU7 . . . 79 E2
Winslow MK18 . . . 65 F4
Woburn Sands MK17 . . . 49 B4
Wraysbury TW19 . . . 211 F1
Yardley Gobion NN12 . . . 18 F6
Yardley Hastings NN7 . . . 1 B6
High Street N LU7 . . . 68 D2
High Street S
Olney MK46 . . . 6 F3
Stewkley LU7 . . . 78 E8
High Thorn Piece MK14 . . 21 F3
High Town Rd SL6 . . . 202 F7
High Trees MK6 . . . 47 B8
Highveer Croft MK4 . . . 46 B1
High View
Chalfont St Giles HP8 . . . 177 D8
Deanshanger MK19 . . . 31 E5
High View Cl SL7 . . . 183 C8
High View Pl HP7 . . . 165 C7
HIGHWAY . . . 202 B7
Highway MK17 . . . 68 C6
Highway Ave SL6 . . . 202 A6
Highway Ct
Beaconsfield HP9 . . . 175 D3
Chesham HP5 . . . 144 D1
Highway Rd SL6 . . . 202 B6
Highway The HP9 . . . 175 D2
Highwood Ave HP12 . . . 172 B5
Highwood Bottom HP27 . 150 A5
Highwood Cres HP12 . . . 172 B6
Highwoods Cl SL7 . . . 183 C7
Highwoods Dr SL7 . . . 183 C7
Highworth Cl HP13 . . . 162 E1
Highworth Comb Sch
HP13 . . . 162 E1
HIGH WYCOMBE . . . 173 B5
High Wycombe CE Comb Sch
5 HP11 . . . 173 A6
High Wycombe Sta
HP13 . . . 173 B7
Hikers Way HP18 . . . 125 F4
Hilbre Ct 5 MK4 . . . 45 F1
Hilbury Cl HP6 . . . 154 C3
Hilda Wharf HP20 . . . 115 F8
Hildreth Rd HP16 . . . 151 C5
Hilgrove Ho SL6 . . . 195 D1
Hiljon Cres SL9 . . . 177 E2
Hillary Cl
Aylesbury HP21 . . . 116 A5
High Wycombe HP13 . . . 173 E6
Hillary Rd
High Wycombe HP13 . . . 173 E6
Slough SL3 . . . 206 E4
Hill Ave
Amersham HP6 . . . 154 C1
Hazelmere HP15 . . . 163 B5
Hillbeck Gr MK10 . . . 35 E3
Hillbottom Rd HP12 . . . 172 B7
Hill Cl HP10 . . . 185 F7
Hill Cotts HP18 . . . 97 E1
Hillcrest MK43 . . . 25 C2
Hillcrest Ave SL6 . . . 195 E6
Hillcrest Cl MK5 . . . 46 B6
Hillcrest Ct HP6 . . . 154 C1
Hillcrest Rise MK18 . . . 52 E6
Hillcrest Way MK18 . . . 52 E5
Hillcrest Waye SL9 . . . 188 F5
Hillcroft Rd
Chesham HP5 . . . 144 D2
Tylers Green HP10 . . . 163 C1
Hillersdon SL2 . . . 206 B8
Hillersdon Chase MK17 . . . 69 D8
HILLESDEN . . . 63 A6
Hillesden Hamlet MK18 . . . 51 F1
Hillesden Way MK18 . . . 41 E1
Hill Farm MK18 . . . 76 A2
Hill Farm App HP10 . . . 185 F7
Hill Farm Ct OX39 . . . 147 D6
Hill Farm La
Chalfont St Giles HP8 . . . 166 A1
Little Horwood MK17 . . . 55 E2
Hill Farm Rd
Chalfont St Peter SL9 . . . 177 E3
Chesham HP5 . . . 154 D5
Marlow Bottom SL7 . . . 183 E5
Taplow SL6 . . . 196 E2
Hill Farm Way HP15 . . . 163 B2
Hillfield Cl HP13 . . . 161 E2
Hillfield Rd SL9 . . . 177 E3
Hillfield Sq SL9 . . . 177 E3
Hill Gr SL9 . . . 177 E3
Hill Green La HP23 . . . 119 F1
Hill Ho SL6 . . . 196 D1
Hill House Cl SL9 . . . 177 E3
Hilliard Dr MK13 . . . 34 A3
Hilliards Rd UB8 . . . 208 D7
Hillier Rd HP21 . . . 115 D3
Hillingdon Athletics Stadium
UB10 . . . 201 E6
Hillingdon Hill UB10 . . . 201 E2
Hillingdon Hospl UB8 . . . 208 F8
Hillingdon Rd UB10 . . . 201 F3
Hillingdon Sports & Leisure
Complex UB10 . . . 201 E6
Hillingdon Tuition Ctr
UB7 . . . 208 E5
Hillington Cl HP19 . . . 115 B7
Hillman Cl UB8 . . . 201 E7
Hill Mdw HP7 . . . 164 F4
Hill Mead HP4 . . . 135 A3
Hillmead Ct SL6 . . . 203 F8
Hill Pastures MK14 . . . 21 F3
Hill Pl SL2 . . . 198 B5
Hill Radnor 1 MK18 . . . 41 D2
Hill Rd
Chinnor OX39 . . . 147 D5
Christmas Common OX49 . 168 A8
Hill Rd *continued*
Lewknor OX49 . . . 157 C6
Hillrise SL3 . . . 212 A8
Hill Rise SL9 . . . 177 D1
Hill Rise Cres SL9 . . . 177 E1
Hills Cl MK14 . . . 34 E7
Hillside
Chesham HP5 . . . 144 A3
Gawcott MK18 . . . 51 F4
High Wycombe HP13 . . . 173 D7
Maidenhead SL6 . . . 202 D5
Slough SL1 . . . 205 E4
South Harefield UB9 . . . 190 C6
Tingewick MK18 . . . 51 B6
Hill Side LU7 . . . 104 F7
Hillside Cl
Chalfont St Giles HP8 . . . 177 B7
Chalfont St Peter SL9 . . . 177 E4
Upper Arncott OX25 . . . 94 E7
Hillside Cotts HP18 . . . 112 F2
Hillside Ct SL0 . . . 208 B4
Hillside Ctr HP11 . . . 172 F7
Hillside Gdns
Amersham HP7 . . . 165 E7
Berkhamsted HP4 . . . 135 D3
High Wycombe HP13 . . . 173 D7
Hillside Rd
Chorleywood WD3 . . . 167 C4
Marlow SL7 . . . 183 E4
Tylers Green HP10 . . . 163 A2
Hillside View OX39 . . . 147 D5
Hills La SL6 . . . 195 D7
Hill St HP13 . . . 174 A5
Hill The
Syresham NN13 . . . 27 B8
Winchmore Hill HP7 . . . 164 C3
HILLTOP . . . 144 D2
Hilltop HP18 . . . 125 D5
Hilltop Ave MK18 . . . 41 E2
Hill Top Dr SL7 . . . 183 B2
Hilltop Fst Sch SL4 . . . 209 E4
Hill Top La OX39 . . . 147 F4
Hilltop Rd HP4 . . . 135 C3
Hillview
Saunderton HP14 . . . 149 C1
Sherington MK16 . . . 14 A1
Hill View
Berkhamsted HP4 . . . 135 A6
Great Kimble HP17 . . . 129 D1
Hedgerley SL2 . . . 187 D3
Newport Pagnell MK16 . . . 22 A3
Oakley HP18 . . . 109 D5
Hillview Rd HP13 . . . 173 D8
Hill View Rd TW19 . . . 211 D1
Hillway MK17 . . . 49 A6
Hill Way HP7 . . . 165 B6
Hill Waye SL9 . . . 188 F4
Hillwerke OX39 . . . 147 C6
Hillyer Ct MK6 . . . 35 C1
Hilperton Rd 3 SL1 . . . 205 E4
Hilton Ave HP20 . . . 101 E2
Hilton Cl UB8 . . . 201 B3
Himley Gn LU7 . . . 80 D6
Hindemith Gdns MK7 . . . 48 D5
Hindhay La SL6 . . . 195 B3
Hindhead Knoll MK7 . . . 48 B6
Hinds Way HP21 . . . 115 B6
Hinkley Cl UB9 . . . 190 C7
Hinksey Cl SL3 . . . 207 B3
Hinton Cl HP13 . . . 162 A1
Hinton Ct MK3 . . . 46 F1
Hinton Rd
Slough SL1 . . . 204 E6
Uxbridge UB8 . . . 201 C4
Hipwell Ct MK46 . . . 6 F3
Hitcham Grange SL6 . . . 196 E1
Hitcham House SL1 . . . 197 A1
Hitcham La SL6, SL1 . . . 196 F2
Hitcham Rd SL1, SL6 . . . 204 A8
Hithercroft Rd HP13 . . . 161 E1
Hither Mdw SL9 . . . 177 E1
Hithermoor Rd TW19 . . . 213 A2
Hiving's Hill HP5 . . . 144 A2
Hivings Pk HP5 . . . 144 B4
Hoathly Mews MK7 . . . 48 B8
Hobart Cl HP13 . . . 162 E1
Hobart Cotts HP16 . . . 150 D8
Hobart Cres MK15 . . . 35 B7
Hobart Ct SL7 . . . 184 A3
Hobart Rd HP13 . . . 162 D1
Hobbis Dr SL6 . . . 202 A6
Hobbshill Rd HP16 . . . 152 B6
Hobbs Rd HP14 . . . 171 C4
Hobsons Wlk HP23 . . . 118 F5
Hockeridge View HP4 . . . 134 F3
Hockett La SL6 . . . 195 A6
Hockley La SL2 . . . 199 B4
Hockliffe Brae MK7 . . . 48 C5
Hodder La MK4 . . . 46 C2
Hodds Wood Rd HP5 . . . 154 C6
Hodge Lea La MK12 . . . 33 D4
Hodgemoor View HP8 . . . 177 A7
Hodgemore Ct MK14 . . . 21 F2
Hodges Cl HP14 . . . 158 F4
Hodges Mews HP12 . . . 172 C6
Hoe Mdw HP9 . . . 175 C4
Hogarth Cl
Slough SL1 . . . 204 E6
Uxbridge UB8 . . . 201 C2
Hogarths Ct 9 MK8 . . . 33 F1
Hogback Wood Rd HP9 . . 175 B4
Hogfair La SL1 . . . 197 C1
Hogg La HP15 . . . 163 D6
Hog Hall La HP4 . . . 107 A5
Hog La
Ashley Green HP5 . . . 144 D8
Berkhamsted HP5 . . . 134 C2
HOGPITS BOTTOM . . . 156 B7
Hogpits Bottom HP3 . . . 156 B7
Hogshaw Rd MK18 . . . 75 E6
Hogtrough La
Great Missenden HP16 . . . 141 F8
Wendover HP22 . . . 131 D2
Holborn Cres MK4 . . . 57 A8
Holden Ave MK4 . . . 45 E3
Holdom Ave MK1 . . . 47 D2
Holes La MK46 . . . 6 F4
Holiday La MK19 . . . 10 F4
Holland Cl
Chinnor OX39 . . . 147 D7
Wendover HP22 . . . 131 B4
Holland Rd
Aylesbury HP19 . . . 101 B2
Marlow SL7 . . . 183 F3
Hollandridge La OX49,
RG9 . . . 168 D4
Holland Way MK16 . . . 22 C3
Holland Wy 1 MK7 . . . 48 A5
Holliday Cl MK8 . . . 45 E7
Holliday St HP4 . . . 135 D4
Hollies Ct LU7 . . . 80 E7
Hollies The
Beaconsfield HP9 . . . 175 E3
Bovingdon HP3 . . . 146 A2
Tring HP23 . . . 119 D1
HOLLINGDON . . . 69 C3
Hollingdon Depot LU7 . . . 69 D3
Hollingdon Rd LU7 . . . 69 C3
Hollington HP18 . . . 125 B7
Hollin La MK12 . . . 33 E4
Hollinwell Cl 3 MK4 . . . 46 D1
Hollis Rd HP13 . . . 173 F8
Hollister Chase MK5 . . . 46 B4
Holloway Cl UB7 . . . 208 E1
Holloway Dr MK18 . . . 41 E2
Holloway La
Chenies WD3 . . . 156 C2
Turville Heath RG9 . . . 169 C4
West Drayton UB7 . . . 208 F1
Holloway The
Monks Risborough HP27 . 139 D5
Tring HP22, HP23 . . . 118 C4
Hollow Hill End MK18 . . . 75 F7
Hollow Hill La SL0 . . . 207 C5
Hollow Rise HP13 . . . 162 B1
Hollow Way HP5 . . . 143 E1
Hollow Way La HP5, HP6 . 154 E4
Hollow Wood MK46 . . . 6 E3
Hollyberry Gr HP15 . . . 163 C7
Hollybush Cnr SL2 . . . 187 C2
Hollybush Hill SL2 . . . 199 B5
Hollybush La
Amersham HP6 . . . 154 D3
Cookham Dean SL6 . . . 195 B6
Denham UB9 . . . 200 E8
Iver SL0, SL3 . . . 207 B7
Hollybush Rd HP5 . . . 144 A4
Hollybush Row HP23 . . . 133 D8
Holly Cl
Farnham Common SL2 . . . 198 C8
Milton Keynes MK8 . . . 45 E6
Holly Cres SL4 . . . 209 D5
Holly Dr
Aylesbury HP21 . . . 115 E6
Berkhamsted HP4 . . . 135 D3
Maidenhead SL6 . . . 202 F8
Windsor SL4 . . . 210 E2
Holly End HP14 . . . 161 C8
Hollyfield HP23 . . . 119 C5
Hollyfield Cl HP23 . . . 119 C5
Holly Gdns UB7 . . . 208 F4
HOLLY GREEN . . . 138 A3
Holly Green La HP27 . . . 138 A3
Holly Hedges La HP3 . . . 156 C8
Holly Pl HP11 . . . 174 A3
Hollytree Cl
Botley HP5 . . . 155 B8
Chalfont St Peter SL9 . . . 177 E5
Holly Tree La HP18 . . . 112 F3
Holly Wlk MK17 . . . 49 B2
Holmanleaze SL6 . . . 203 A8
Holman St HP19 . . . 101 C2
Holmedale SL2 . . . 206 C6
HOLMER GREEN . . . 163 D6
Holmer Green Fst Sch
HP15 . . . 163 B7
Holmer Green Jun Sch
HP15 . . . 163 D7
Holmer Green Rd HP15 . 163 A4
Holmer Green Senior Sch
HP15 . . . 163 B7
Holmer Pl HP15 . . . 163 C7
Holmers Ct HP12 . . . 172 B3
Holmers Farm Way
HP12 . . . 172 C3
Holmers La HP12 . . . 172 C3
Holmes Mdw MK14 . . . 21 F3
Holmewood MK4 . . . 46 E4
Holmfield Cl MK6 . . . 47 D5
Holm Gate MK5 . . . 46 A8
Holmlea Rd SL3 . . . 211 D6
Holmlea Wlk SL3 . . . 211 C6
Holmoak Wlk HP15 . . . 163 B3
Holmsdale Cl SL0 . . . 207 F7
Holmwood Cl SL6 . . . 202 B5
Holmwood Sch 10 MK8 . . . 33 F1
Holne Chase Prim Sch
MK3 . . . 58 A7
Holst Cres MK7 . . . 48 D4
Holt Ave MK10 . . . 36 C4
Holt Gr MK5 . . . 46 A8
HOLTON . . . 122 C2
Holton Hill MK4 . . . 46 C2

Holton Rd MK18 . . . . 41 D2
Holts Gn MK17 . . . . 59 C1
HOLTSPUR 175 A1
Holtspur Ave HP10 . . . . 185 F7
Holtspur Cl HP9 . . . . 186 A8
Holtspur La HP10 . . . . 185 F6
Holtspur Ct HP9 . . . . 186 A8
Holtspur Par HP9 . . . . 186 A8
Holtspur Prim Sch HP9 . 175 A1
Holtspur Top La HP9 . . . . . 175 A2
Holtspur Way HP9 . . . . 175 A1
Holt The MK18 . . . . 52 E7
Holy Family RC Sch SL3 . 206 F1
Holyhead Cres MK3 . . . . . . 57 C8
Holyhead Mews SL1 . . . . . 204 D7
Holyport Rd SL6 . . . . 203 B1
Holyrood MK8 . . . . 45 E8
Holy Thorn La MK5 . . . . . . 46 A5
Holy Trinity CE Prim Sch
    SL6 . . . . 196 B7
Holy Trinity CE Sch SL7 . 183 D3
Holywell Gdns HP13 . . . . . 173 E7
Holywell Pl MK6 . . . . 35 C2
Holywell Rd MK43 . . . . 25 C1
Holywell Sch MK43 . . . . . . 25 B1
Home Cl
    Milton Keynes MK3 . . . . 47 B2
    Shabbington HP18 . . . . 124 D3
    Weston Turville HP22 . . . . . 116 F2
Home Ct MK10 . . . . 36 A3
Home Farm
    Newton Longville MK17 . . . 57 D4
    Tring HP23 . . . . 118 F2
Home Farm Cl MK19 . . . . . 31 E4
Homefarm Ct HP8 . . . . 177 A7
Home Farm Ct
    Bovingdon HP3 . . . . 145 F1
    Emberton MK46 . . . . 13 E8
Home Farm La MK17 . . . . . 59 D2
Home Farm Rd HP4 . . . . . . 134 D7
Home Farm Way SL3 . . . . . 199 C4
Homefield HP3 . . . . 146 B3
Home Field
    Aylesbury HP19 . . . . 115 A7
    Bow Brickhill MK7 . . . . 48 B3
Homefield Cl HP14 . . . . 158 E4
Homefield Rd WD3 . . . . . . 167 D5
Homefield Wood Nature
    Reserve★ SL7 . . . . 182 C2
Homeground MK18 . . . . . . 52 E6
Homelands Gdns HP15 . . 162 D8
Homelands Way RG9 . . . . . 191 D1
Homeleigh Terr SL2 . . . . . . 206 A7
Home Mdw SL2 . . . . 198 C3
Home Meadow Dr HP10 . 185 B7
Homer Fst Sch SL4 . . . . . . 209 D6
Homeridings Ho MK13 . . . 34 B4
Homers Rd SL4 . . . . 209 D6
Homeside Cl SL6 . . . . 195 E2
Homestall MK8 . . . . 52 D6
Homestall Cl MK5 . . . . 46 A7
Homestead Cl HP17 . . . . . 114 A4
Homestead Pl 14 HP19 . 115 A8
Homestead Rd SL6 . . . . . . 202 D4
Homestead The
    Great Kingshill HP15 . . . . 151 D1
    High Wycombe HP12 . . . . . 172 D3
    Milton Keynes MK5 . . . . . . 46 A6
    Thame OX9 . . . . 125 E1
Homestead Way NN12 . . . 18 E3
Homeward Ct MK5 . . . . 46 B7
Home Way WD3 . . . . 167 F1
Homewood SL3 . . . . 206 D7
Home Wood SL7 . . . . 193 F6
Homewood Ct WD3 . . . . . 167 F5
Honduras Gdns MK3 . . . . . 58 B3
Honey Banks HP22 . . . . . . 131 C4
Honeycomb Wy MK18 . . . 52 F6
Honeycroft Hill UB10 . . . . 201 E5
Honey Hill
    Emberton MK46 . . . . 13 F7
    Uxbridge UB10 . . . . 201 F5
Honey Hill Dr MK19 . . . . . 31 E5
Honey La SL6 . . . . 193 E2
Honeypot Cl MK13 . . . . . . 34 B4
Honeysuckle Cl SL0 . . . . . 207 C7
Honeysuckle Ct SL3 . . . . . 212 C7
Honeysuckle Field HP5 . 144 C2
Honeysuckle Rd HP15 . . . 162 F7
Honey Way HP14 . . . . 161 B8
HONEYWICK 92 E8
Honeywick La LU6 . . . . 92 E8
Honiton Ct MK7 . . . . 48 C7
Honor End La HP16 . . . . . . 151 A7
Honor Rd HP16 . . . . 151 D6
Honorwood Cl HP16 . . . . . 151 B6
Honour Cl HP20 . . . . 102 A2
Honours Mead 4 HP3 . . 146 A4
Hoods Farm HP22 . . . . 102 C4
Hookes Mdw MK43 . . . . . . 25 B2
Hooke The MK15 . . . . 35 D7
Hooper Gate MK15 . . . . . . 35 C7
Hopcraft Cl OX25 . . . . 94 E7
Hopcrofts Mdw MK14 . . . 21 F3
Hope Brook Cotts LU7 . . . 91 F2
Hop Gdns RG9 . . . . 191 D2
Hopkins Cl MK10 . . . . 36 A2
Hopkins Ct HP20 . . . . 101 F2
Hopkins Rd MK17 . . . . 58 B2
Hoppers Hill MK46 . . . . 6 F5
Hoppers Mdw MK5 . . . . . . 46 A8
Hoppers Way HP15 . . . . . 162 D8
Hopton Gr MK16 . . . . 22 F3
Hopton Rd OX9 . . . . 126 A1
Hordern Cl HP17 . . . . 126 F6

Hornbeam MK16 . . . . 22 A3
Hornbeam Cl
    Frieth RG9 . . . . 170 F1
    High Wycombe HP12 . . . . . 172 B4
Hornbeam Gdns 8 SL1 . 206 A3
Hornbeam Way HP22 . . . . 116 C4
Hornbeam Wlk HP15 . . . . 163 A3
Hornbill Cl UB8 . . . . 208 D7
Hornby Chase MK4 . . . . . . 46 B2
Horners Croft MK12 . . . . . 33 C5
HORN HILL 178 B6
Hornhill Rd WD3 . . . . 178 D5
Horn La MK11 . . . . 32 D5
Horns La
    High Wycombe HP12 . . . . . 172 A3
    Princes Risborough HP27 . 139 B3
Horn St MK18 . . . . 65 F4
Horsebuck La HP23 . . . . . 133 E3
Horsefair Gn MK11 . . . . . . 32 D5
Horseguards Dr SL6 . . . . . 203 B7
Horse Hill HP5 . . . . 155 D7
Horsemead Piece MK18 . . 65 F4
Horsemoor Cl SL3 . . . . 207 A2
Horsemoor La HP7 . . . . . . 164 C2
HORSENDEN 138 E2
Horsenden La HP27 . . . . . 138 F2
Horsenden Rd HP13 . . . . . 173 F5
Horsepond MK17 . . . . 59 C2
Horsepool La MK17 . . . . . . 49 F4
Horseshoe Cl LU7 . . . . 105 A7
Horseshoe Cloisters 3
    SL4 . . . . 210 D6
Horseshoe Cres HP9 . . . . 175 F1
Horseshoe Hill SL1 . . . . . . 197 C8
Horseshoe Rd HP14 . . . . . 159 C7
Horsetone Bglws HP17 . . 129 D3
Horsham Reach SL6 . . . . . 196 C2
Horsley Rd SL6 . . . . 195 E2
Horsleys WD3 . . . . 178 D5
HORSLEYS GREEN 159 C3
HORTON
    Cheddington 91 B3
    Wraysbury 212 A4
Horton Bridge Rd UB7 . . 208 F5
Horton Cl
    Aylesbury HP19 . . . . 115 A7
    Maidenhead SL6 . . . . 196 C1
    West Drayton UB7 . . . . 208 F5
HORTON-CUM-
    STUDLEY 108 B6
Horton Depot SL3 . . . . 212 C4
Horton Gate MK14 . . . . . . 21 F2
Horton Gdns SL3 . . . . 211 F4
Horton Grange SL4 . . . . . 196 C1
Horton Ind Pk UB7 . . . . . . 208 F5
Horton Par UB7 . . . . 208 F5
Horton Rd
    Datchet SL3 . . . . 211 D6
    Horton SL3 . . . . 212 A6
    Ivinghoe LU7 . . . . 91 A2
    Poyle SL3 . . . . 212 E4
    Slapton LU7 . . . . 91 C6
    Stanwell TW19 . . . . 213 A2
    West Drayton UB7 . . . . . . 208 F5
Horton Road Ind Est
    UB7 . . . . 208 F5
Hortonsfield Rd NN12 . . . 18 F5
Horton Trad Est SL3 . . . . 212 B4
HORTON WHARF 91 C4
Horwood Cl MK1 . . . . 47 D2
Hospital Circular Rd
    HP22 . . . . 131 D6
Hospital Hill HP5 . . . . 154 C7
Hospital Rdbt MK6 . . . . . . 47 B6
Hotch Croft MK43 . . . . 25 C3
HOTLEY BOTTOM 151 C8
Hotley Bottom La HP16 . 151 C8
Hotspur Bank Nature
    Reserve★ HP9 . . . . 174 F1
Hotspur Cl HP17 . . . . 126 E6
Houghton Ct 4 MK8 . . . . 45 F8
Housman Cl MK16 . . . . 22 A5
Houston Ct 6 SL4 . . . . . . 210 C5
Howard Agne Cl HP3 . . . 146 A4
Howard Ave
    Aylesbury HP21 . . . . 116 B6
    Slough SL2 . . . . 205 E8
Howard Cres HP9 . . . . 176 D5
Howard Ct 1 SL8 . . . . . . 185 A3
Howard Ind Est HP5 . . . . 144 C2
Howard Mews SL3 . . . . . . 212 B8
Howard Rd
    Chesham HP5 . . . . 144 B3
    Seer Green HP9 . . . . 176 D5
Howards Thicket SL9 . . . . 188 C2
Howards Wood Dr SL9 . 188 D2
Howard Way MK16 . . . . . . 23 A3
Howarth Rd SL6 . . . . 203 A6
Howe Ct MK10 . . . . 36 A3
Howe Dr HP9 . . . . 175 E5
Howe Hill La HP15 . . . . . . 163 B8
Howell Hill Cl LU7 . . . . 90 D5
Howe Mews MK17 . . . . 58 B2
Howe Park Sch MK4 . . . . . 46 B1
Howe Rock Pl MK4 . . . . . . 46 B1
Howgate St MK18 . . . . 100 E4
Howitt Dr MK13 . . . . 34 B8
Howland Pl MK17 . . . . 60 F7
Howletts Cl HP19 . . . . 115 A7
How's Cl UB8 . . . . 201 C4
How's Rd UB8 . . . . 201 C4
Hoylake Cl
    Milton Keynes MK3 . . . . . . 57 D7
    Slough SL1 . . . . 204 E4
Hoyton Gate MK1 . . . . 45 D6
Hubbard Cl MK18 . . . . 41 F1
Hubbards Ct WD3 . . . . . . 167 D4
Hubbards Rd WD3 . . . . . . 167 D4

Hubert Day Cl HP9 . . . . . 175 D3
Hubert Rd SL3 . . . . 206 D3
Huckleberry Cl MK7 . . . . . 48 B6
Hudnall La HP4 . . . . 121 C7
Hudson La MK8 . . . . 45 D7
Hudson Mews HP19 . . . . . 100 E1
Hudson Pl 14 SL3 . . . . . . 206 F1
Hughenden Ave HP13 . . . 173 A4
Hughenden Cl SL6 . . . . . . 202 C6
Hughenden Gn HP21 . . . 115 E4
Hughenden Manor★
    HP14 . . . . 162 A3
Hughenden Prim Sch
    HP14 . . . . 162 A7
Hughenden Rd
    High Wycombe HP13 . . . . . 162 B1
    Slough SL1 . . . . 205 D7
HUGHENDEN VALLEY 162 B2
Hughenden View HP13 . . 173 B8
Hughes Croft 3 MK3 . . . . 57 F7
Hugh Park Cl MK5 . . . . 46 C8
Hulbert End HP21 . . . . 116 D5
Hulcombe Wlk HP20 . . . . 101 E2
HULCOTE 37 E2
HULCOTT 102 E6
Hull Cl
    Aylesbury HP21 . . . . 115 E6
    Slough SL1 . . . . 205 C4
Hullwell Gate MK7 . . . . . . 48 A5
Hulme End 3 MK10 . . . . . 36 C3
Hulton Dr MK46 . . . . 13 F8
Humber Cl UB7 . . . . 208 D5
Humber Dr HP21 . . . . 115 C5
Humber Way
    Milton Keynes MK3 . . . . . . 46 E1
    Slough SL3 . . . . 207 A2
Hume Cl MK13 . . . . 34 B7
Humphreys Cl HP22 . . . . . 88 D5
Humphrey Talbot Ave
    LU6 . . . . 107 F7
Hundred Acres La HP7 . . 165 D8
Hungerford Ave SL2 . . . . . 205 E8
Hungerford Dr SL6 . . . . . . 195 E3
Hungerford Ho 1 MK4 . . 46 D1
Hunsbury Chase MK10 . . 36 A3
Hunsdon Cl MK14 . . . . 34 D6
Hunsford Lodge SL4 . . . . 210 A4
Hunstanton Cl SL3 . . . . . . 212 C7
Hunstanton Way MK3 . . . 57 D8
Hunt Ct HP14 . . . . 158 F4
Huntercombe Cl SL1 . . . . 204 C7
Huntercombe Hospl The
    SL6 . . . . 204 C6
Huntercombe Lane N
    SL6 . . . . 204 C7
Huntercombe Lane S
    SL6 . . . . 204 C6
Huntercombe Spur SL6 . 204 C7
Hunter Cl SL1 . . . . 204 C8
Hunter Dr MK2 . . . . 58 C6
Hunters Cl
    Bovingdon HP3 . . . . 146 A2
    Chesham HP5 . . . . 144 A1
    Tring HP23 . . . . 119 B5
Hunters Farm Ind Est
    HP18 . . . . 100 B5
Hunters Hill HP13 . . . . 173 F5
Hunters Mews SL4 . . . . . . 210 C6
Hunters Pk HP4 . . . . 135 E5
Hunters Point OX39 . . . . . 147 C6
Hunters Reach MK13 . . . . 34 A3
Hunter St MK18 . . . . 52 C8
Hunters Way SL1 . . . . 204 E4
HUNTGATE END 10 D2
Huntingbrooke 6 MK3 . . 45 F8
Huntingdon Cres 57 D6
Huntington Pl SL3 . . . . . . 207 B3
Huntley Cl MK13 . . . . 162 C2
Huntley Cres MK9 . . . . 35 A3
Hunt Rd HP13 . . . . 173 E6
HUNT'S HILL 161 D1
Hunts Hill La HP14 . . . . . . 161 E5
Hunt's La SL6 . . . . 196 E3
Huntsman Gr MK14 . . . . . 22 A2
Huntsmans Cl HP4 . . . . . . 107 C5
Huntswood La SL6, SL1 . 196 F4
HURLEY 193 E4
Hurley Croft MK10 . . . . . . 36 B1
Hurley High St SL6 . . . . . 193 F4
Hurley La SL7 . . . . 194 B3
Hurlstone Gr MK4 . . . . 46 D3
Hurricane Way SL3 . . . . . 207 B1
HURST END 24 A3
Hurstfield Dr SL6 . . . . 204 B7
Hurstleigh WD3 . . . . 167 C4
Hurst Rd SL1 . . . . 204 D8
Hurworth Ave SL3 . . . . . . 206 C3
Hutchings Cl MK5 . . . . 46 A8
Hutchings Rd HP9 . . . . . . 175 D5
Hutton Ave MK6 . . . . 34 F1
Hutton Ct MK17 . . . . 49 B5
Hutton Way MK17 . . . . 49 B5
Huxley Cl
    Newport Pagnell MK16 . . . 21 F4
    Slough SL3 . . . . 199 B1
    Uxbridge UB8 . . . . 201 D1
Huxtable Gdns SL6 . . . . . 203 E1
Hyacinth Dr UB10 . . . . 201 E5
Hychendon Cl HP14 . . . . . 161 B6
Hyde Cl MK16 . . . . 22 C2
HYDE END 152 F7
Hyde Gn
    Beaconsfield HP9 . . . . 175 F3
    Marlow SL7 . . . . 183 F1
HYDE HEATH 153 C5
Hyde Heath Inf Sch HP6 153 C5

Hyde Heath Rd HP6,
    HP10 . . . . 153 A6
Hyde La
    Bovingdon HP3 . . . . 146 A3
    South Heath HP16 . . . . . . 152 E5
Hyde Mdws HP3 . . . . 146 A4
Hyde The HP22 . . . . 116 F2
Hyland Ho 9 SL8 . . . . . . 185 B3
Hylle Cl SL4 . . . . 209 E6
Hylton Rd HP12 . . . . 172 C7
Hyrons Cl HP6 . . . . 154 E1
Hyrons Gn HP6 . . . . 154 E1
Hyrons La HP6 . . . . 154 D1
Hythe The MK8 . . . . 33 E3
Hythe Wy 7 MK10 . . . . . . 36 C3
Hyton Sq HP19 . . . . 101 D4

I

Ibotson Ct SL3 . . . . 212 C6
IBSTONE 169 D7
Ibstone Ave MK13 . . . . 34 D4
Ibstone CE Inf Sch HP14 169 D6
Ibstone Rd HP14 . . . . 158 C3
ICKENHAM 190 F1
ICKFORD 124 A3
Ickford Comb Sch HP18 . 124 A3
Ickford Rd
    Shabbington HP18 . . . . . . 124 C2
    Worminghall HP18 . . . . 123 E6
Icknield Cl
    Chinnor OX39 . . . . 147 A4
    Wendover HP22 . . . . 131 C5
Icknield Cotts HP17 . . . . . 129 F2
Icknield Gn HP23 . . . . 119 A6
Icknield Way
    Dunstable LU6 . . . . 93 D4
    Tring HP23 . . . . 118 E4
Icknield Way Farm Cotts
    LU6 . . . . 93 C3
Icknield Way Ind Est
    HP23 . . . . 118 E4
Ideal Ho 3 HP20 . . . . 115 E8
Iffley Cl UB8 . . . . 201 D5
Ilchester Cl SL6 . . . . 202 C5
Ilex Cl HP15 . . . . 163 B3
Ilex Ct HP4 . . . . 135 B4
Illingworth SL4 . . . . 209 E4
Illingworth Pl MK6 . . . . . . 46 F8
Illustrious MK10 . . . . 36 B5
ILMER 137 F8
Imperial Ct
    Henley-on-Thames RG9 . . 191 E1
    Loudwater HP10 . . . . 174 C2
    Windsor SL4 . . . . 210 A4
Imperial Rd SL4 . . . . 210 A5
Independent Bsns Pk
    HP14 . . . . 158 C5
India Rd SL1 . . . . 206 B4
Ingleglen SL2 . . . . 198 B7
Ingleside SL3 . . . . 212 F6
Ingleton Cl MK13 . . . . 34 C4
Ingram Ave HP21 . . . . 116 C5
Inkerman Dr HP15 . . . . . . 163 B5
Inkerman Rd SL4 . . . . 204 F2
Inkerman Terr HP5 . . . . . . 154 C6
Innes Ct MK8 . . . . 45 D6
Inn Farm Ct MK16 . . . . . . 22 D7
Innholder Ct MK14 . . . . . . 34 F6
Innings Gate RG9 . . . . 170 E1
Inniscrown Ho SL3 . . . . . 211 B7
Institute Rd
    Marlow SL7 . . . . 183 E1
    Taplow SL6 . . . . 203 F7
Intalbury Ave HP19 . . . . . 101 A2
Interchange Pk MK16 . . . 22 F3
In the Ray SL6 . . . . 203 B8
Inverewe Pl 1 MK4 . . . . . 45 E2
Inverness Cl MK3 . . . . 46 F2
Inwood Cl SL6 . . . . 195 B6
Iona Cres SL1 . . . . 204 E7
Ipswich Rd SL1 . . . . 205 A7
IQRA Prim Sch SL2 . . . . . 206 B6
Ireland Cl MK7 . . . . 48 D4
Ireton Ct OX9 . . . . 125 F1
Iris Cl HP21 . . . . 115 B5
Iris Ct HP20 . . . . 116 B8
Ironmonger Ct MK14 . . . . 34 F6
Irvine Dr HP22 . . . . 116 A2
Irvine Ho SL4 . . . . 209 E5
Irving Cres LU7 . . . . 105 A8
Irving Dale MK7 . . . . 48 E5
Isaacson Dr MK7 . . . . 48 C7
Isis Cl HP21 . . . . 115 D3
Isis Way SL8 . . . . 185 B4
Isis Wlk MK3 . . . . 46 E1
Island Ho UB7 . . . . 213 B6
Island The MK18 . . . . 63 D2
Isle of Wight La LU6 . . . . 93 F4
Islet Park Dr SL6 . . . . 196 C3
Islet Park Ho SL6 . . . . . . 196 C3
Islet Pk SL6 . . . . 196 C3
Islet Rd SL6 . . . . 196 C3
Isling Brook MK5 . . . . 46 B3
Islington Gr 6 MK10 . . . . 35 F1
Itter La MK18 . . . . 73 B5
Ivanhoe Cl UB8 . . . . 208 D8
IVER 207 F7
Iver Ct MK18 . . . . 52 C7
Iverdale Cl SL0 . . . . 207 C6
IVER HEATH 200 D2
Iver Heath Inf Sch SL0 . 200 D2
Iver Heath Jun Sch SL0 200 D3
Iver La SL0 . . . . 208 A8
Iver Lodge SL0 . . . . 207 F8
Iver Sta SL0 . . . . 207 F4
Iver Village Inf Sch SL0 . 207 F7

Iver Village Jun Sch SL0. 207 E7
Ives Rd SL3 . . . . 207 A3
Ivester Ct LU7 . . . . 80 E6
IVINGHOE 105 F5
IVINGHOE ASTON 92 A1
Ivinghoe View HP20 . . . . 101 F1
Ivinghoe Way LU6 . . . . . . 92 E1
Ivins Rd HP9 . . . . 175 A1
Ivybridge Cl UB8 . . . . 201 E6
Ivy Cl
    Buckingham MK18 . . . . 41 F8
    Longwick HP27 . . . . 138 C5
    Newport Pagnell MK16 . . . 22 E4
Ivy Cotts HP8 . . . . 177 B8
Ivy Cres SL1 . . . . 204 F6
Ivyhill Ct HP27 . . . . 139 B3
Ivy House La HP4 . . . . 135 E5
Ivy La
    Bierton HP22 . . . . 102 C1
    Burcott LU7 . . . . 79 D4
    Great Brickhill MK17 . . . . . 70 C8
    Newton Longville MK17 . . . 57 C3
    Stewkley LU7 . . . . 68 E1
Ivy Pl HP14 . . . . 171 C5

J

Jacks Cl MK46 . . . . 7 E7
Jack's La MK43 . . . . 8 E5
Jackson Cl
    Slough SL3 . . . . 206 E3
    Uxbridge UB10 . . . . 201 E5
Jackson Ct HP15 . . . . 163 A3
Jackson Ind Est SL8 . . . . 185 B2
Jackson Pl 6 HP22 . . . . . 131 D6
Jackson Rd
    Aylesbury HP19 . . . . 101 A3
    Uxbridge UB10 . . . . 201 E5
Jacksons Cl LU6 . . . . 92 E4
Jacob Cl SL4 . . . . 209 E6
Jacobs Cl MK14 . . . . 34 D7
Jakeman Way HP21 . . . . . 115 B6
Jakes Ho SL6 . . . . 203 A3
Jamaica MK6 . . . . 47 A6
James Cl
    Hazelmere HP15 . . . . 163 A6
    Marlow SL7 . . . . 183 F4
James Elliman Sch SL2 . 205 E6
James Martin Cl UB9 . . . 190 A5
James Mdw SL3 . . . . 211 B8
James Rd HP14 . . . . 171 B4
James St SL4 . . . . 210 D6
James Way MK1 . . . . 47 B1
Jane Cl HP21 . . . . 116 A4
Jannetta Cl HP20 . . . . 116 B7
Jansel Sq HP21 . . . . 116 B6
Japonica La MK15 . . . . . . 35 C6
Jardine Cotts SL2 . . . . . . 199 A8
Jarman Cl MK18 . . . . 52 F8
Jarratt Ho SL4 . . . . 210 B4
Jarry Ct SL7 . . . . 183 F3
Jarvis Cl HP21 . . . . 116 A6
Jasmine Cl HP21 . . . . 116 A4
Jasmine Cres HP27 . . . . . 139 B3
Jasmine Wlk HP5 . . . . 144 A1
Jason Ho HP12 . . . . 172 E4
Jasons Hill HP5 . . . . 145 B2
Jeannie Arm Rd 2
    HP22 . . . . 131 D6
Jeeves Cl MK6 . . . . 47 C7
Jefferies Rd HP17 . . . . . . 114 B5
Jefferson Cl SL3 . . . . 207 A2
Jeffrey Wlk HP19 . . . . 115 A7
Jeffries Ct SL8 . . . . 185 B2
Jell Cl 5 MK18 . . . . 41 E3
Jellicoe Cl SL1 . . . . 205 B4
Jenkins Ct MK5 . . . . 45 F5
Jenkins Ct HP22 . . . . 89 C3
Jenkins La HP23 . . . . 132 E3
Jenna Way MK16 . . . . 23 A3
Jenner Rd HP21 . . . . 115 E5
Jennery La SL1 . . . . 197 C2
Jennings MK14 . . . . 34 C7
Jennings Field HP10 . . . . 185 C7
Jennings Wharf SL4 . . . . 210 D7
Jennys La HP4 . . . . 134 D8
Jerome Cl SL7 . . . . 183 F4
Jersey Rd MK12 . . . . 33 C6
Jesse's La HP18 . . . . 125 D6
Job's La SL6 . . . . 195 B8
John Colet Sch HP22 . . . 131 C5
John Fitzjohn Ave HP18 . 100 D4
John Hall Way HP11 . . . . 172 D3
John Hampden Grammar Sch
    The HP22 . . . . 131 B5
John Hampden Gram Sch
    HP11 . . . . 172 F4
John Hampden Way
    HP16 . . . . 151 B7
John Hellins Prim Sch
    NN12 . . . . 18 D3
John Locke Acad UB10 . 201 E5
John North Cl HP11 . . . . 172 F4
Johns La HP5 . . . . 134 C1
Johnson Rd HP14 . . . . . . 171 B5
Johnsons Field MK46 . . . . 6 E4
Johnston Pl MK6 . . . . 46 E8
John Taylor Ct SL1 . . . . . 205 C7
John Watson Sch OX33 . 122 B1
Joiner's Cl
    Botley HP5 . . . . 145 B1
    Chalfont St Peter SL9 . . . . 177 F3
Joiners La SL9 . . . . 177 F3
Joiner's La SL9 . . . . 177 E3
Joiners Way
    Chalfont St Peter SL9 . . . . 177 F3
    Lavendon MK46 . . . . 7 F8

Jonathan Ct SL6 . . . . 202 E7
Jonathans MK6 . . . . 47 A6
Jonathans Ct MK6 . . . . . . 47 A6
Jones Way SL2 . . . . 187 E2
Joplin Ct MK8 . . . . 45 F7
JORDANS 176 F3
Jordans La HP9 . . . . 176 E3
Jordans Sch HP9 . . . . 176 F4
Jordans Way HP9 . . . . . . 176 F4
Joules Ct MK5 . . . . 46 C5
Jourdelay's Pas SL4 . . . . 210 D8
Journeys End SL2 . . . . . . 205 E8
Jubilee Cotts MK18 . . . . . 64 F3
Jubilee Rd
  High Wycombe, Downley
   HP13 . . . . 161 E2
  High Wycombe HP11 . . . . 172 E2
  Stokenchurch HP14 . . . . . 158 F3
Jubilee Terr MK11 . . . . . 32 E5
Jubilee Way SL3 . . . . . . 211 D2
Jubilee Wood Prim Sch
  MK6 . . . . 34 F1
Judge's La LU7 . . . . 80 F6
Jumelle Mews **4** HP13 . 162 A1
Juniper Cl HP15 . . . . 163 B3
Juniper Ct
  Flackwell Heath HP10 . . . 185 C7
  Rickmansworth WD3 . . . . 167 C3
  Slough SL1 . . . . 204 E6
  Slough SL1 . . . . 206 B4
Juniper Dr
  Aylesbury HP22 . . . . 116 C4
  High Wycombe HP12 . . . . 172 C5
  Maidenhead SL6 . . . . 203 B8
Juniper Gdns MK7 . . . . . 48 B7
Juniper Hill Sch HP10 . . 185 B7
Juniper La HP10 . . . . 185 D7
Juniper Rd SL7 . . . . 183 D5
Jupiter Hts UB10 . . . . . . 201 F4
Juson's Glebe HP22 . . . . 131 C5
Jutland Ho SL4 . . . . 209 F5

K

Kalman Gdns MK7 . . . . . 48 D5
Kaplan Cl MK5 . . . . 46 B5
Karenza HP14 . . . . 158 E5
Katherine Cl
  Tylers Green HP10 . . . . . 174 C8
  Walton MK7 . . . . 48 A4
Katrine Pl MK2 . . . . 58 D5
Kaybridge Cl **1** HP13 . . 173 F5
Kay Cl HP23 . . . . 119 A5
Kay Gr MK14 . . . . 34 C8
Kaywood Cl SL3 . . . . . . 206 C3
Keach Cl MK18 . . . . 66 A5
Keasden Ct MK4 . . . . 46 B2
Keaton Cl MK8 . . . . 45 D7
Keats Cl
  Aylesbury HP21 . . . . 115 F6
  High Wycombe HP11 . . . . 172 F6
  Newport Pagnell MK16 . . . 22 A4
Keats La SL4 . . . . 210 C8
Keats Way
  2 Milton Keynes MK3 . . 57 F7
  West Drayton UB7 . . . . . . 208 F2
Keble Cl HP19 . . . . 115 B8
Keble Rd SL6 . . . . 202 E8
Keel Dr SL1 . . . . 205 C4
Keeler Cl SL4 . . . . 209 E4
Keel Way MK4 . . . . 45 D3
Keen Cl HP19 . . . . 115 A8
Keensacre SL0 . . . . 200 D3
Keen's Cl HP13 . . . . 162 E1
Keens La OX39 . . . . 147 D6
Keepers Cl LU7 . . . . 105 A7
Keepers Farm Cl SL4 . . 209 E5
Keepers La HP6, HP7 . . 153 C3
Keep Hill Dr HP11 . . . . . 173 D4
Keep Hill Rd HP11 . . . . 173 D5
Keinches La HP22 . . . . . 87 A6
Keith Park Rd UB10 . . . 201 F5
Kellan Dr MK6 . . . . 35 A1
Keller Cl MK11 . . . . 33 B2
Kelling Way **3** MK10 . . 36 A4
Kelly Gdns MK4 . . . . 45 E3
Kelmarsh Ct **11** MK8 . . 33 F1
Kelpatrick Rd SL1 . . . . . 204 D7
Kelsey Cl
  Maidenhead SL6 . . . . 202 D3
  Milton Keynes MK4 . . . . . 56 F8
Kelso Cl MK3 . . . . 57 D6
Kelvin Cl HP13 . . . . 172 F8
Kelvin Ct HP13 . . . . 172 F8
Kelvin Dr MK5 . . . . 46 D6
Kemble Ct MK15 . . . . . . 35 B6
Kempe Cl SL3 . . . . 207 C2
Kempson Cl HP19 . . . . . 101 B1
Kemps Piece HP17 . . . . 127 A6
Kempton Gdns MK3 . . . 57 D6
Kemsley Chase SL2 . . . 198 D4
Kemsley Cres MK10 . . . 36 A4
Kenchester MK13 . . . . . 33 F5
Kendal Cl
  Aylesbury HP21 . . . . 116 B6
  Slough SL2 . . . . 206 A6
Kendal Dr SL2 . . . . 206 A6
Kendal Gdns LU7 . . . . . . 80 C7
Kendal Green Dr **2** SL9 . 195 D2
Kendall Pl
  Maidenhead SL6 . . . . 202 C4
  Milton Keynes MK5 . . . . . 45 E5
Kendalls Cl HP13 . . . . . . 172 F8
Kendal Mews UB8 . . . . 201 C4
Kendrick Rd SL3 . . . . . . 206 B3
Kenilworth Cl SL1 . . . . . 205 F3

Kenilworth Dr
  Aylesbury HP19 . . . . 101 D2
  Milton Keynes MK3 . . . . . 57 E8
Kenneally SL4 . . . . 209 C5
Kenneally Cl **11** SL4 . . 209 C5
Kenneally Pl **12** SL4 . . 209 C5
Kenneally Row **13** SL4 . 209 C5
Kenneally Wlk **10** SL4 . 209 C5
Kennedy Ave
  High Wycombe HP11 . . . . 173 B4
  High Wycombe HP11 . . . . 173 B5
Kennedy Cl
  Farnham Common SL2 . . 198 C6
  Maidenhead SL6 . . . . 202 C6
  Marlow SL7 . . . . 183 E3
Kennedy Ho SL1 . . . . . . 204 D5
Kennel La SL6 . . . . 195 C7
Kennels Dr NN12 . . . . . . 17 D3
Kennet Cl
  Aylesbury HP21 . . . . 115 C4
  High Wycombe HP13 . . . . 162 D2
Kennet Dr MK3 . . . . 57 E8
Kennet Pl MK3 . . . . 57 F8
Kennet Rd
  Bourne End SL8 . . . . 185 B4
  Maidenhead SL6 . . . . 202 F8
Kennett Rd SL3 . . . . 207 B3
Kennington Cl MK16 . . . 22 C3
Kennish Cl MK18 . . . . . . 65 F4
Kensal Gn MK10 . . . . . . 35 C1
Kensington Dr
  Great Holm MK8 . . . . 46 A8
  Milton Keynes MK8 . . . . . 33 F1
Kensington Path **3**
  HP19 . . . . 100 F1
Kensington Pl MK46 . . . . 6 F5
Kent Ave SL1 . . . . 205 C8
Kent Cl UB8 . . . . 201 C6
Kent Ho MK3 . . . . 46 F2
Kent Lodge **6** SL6 . . . . 202 F6
Kentmere Rd HP21 . . . . 116 B7
Kenton Cl SL7 . . . . 183 E2
Kenton Ct HP19 . . . . . . 101 C2
Kenton's La SL4 . . . . . . 209 F5
KENTS HILL 48 A7
Kents Hill Park Rdbt
  MK10 . . . . 47 E8
Kents Hill Rdbt MK10 . . 47 F8
Kents Hill Sch MK7 . . . . 48 A7
Kents Rd MK14 . . . . 34 D8
Kent Way SL6 . . . . 195 E1
Kenway Dr HP7 . . . . 166 B8
Kenwell Ct MK15 . . . . . . 35 C3
Kenwood Cl SL6 . . . . . . 202 A7
Kenwood Dr WD3 . . . . . 178 F3
Kenwood Gate MK6 . . . . 35 B2
Keppel Ave MK19 . . . . . . 20 D2
Keppel St SL4 . . . . 210 D5
Kepwick MK8 . . . . 33 E1
Kernal Cl MK10 . . . . 35 E2
Kercroft MK8 . . . . 33 E2
Kernow Cres MK6 . . . . . 35 A1
Kerria Pl MK3 . . . . 47 A3
Kerr Pl HP21 . . . . 115 E7
Kerry Cl HP19 . . . . 101 A3
Kerry Hill MK14 . . . . 21 C1
Kersey MK14 . . . . 34 C8
Kesters Rd HP5 . . . . 154 D7
Kestrel Cl
  2 Berkhamsted HP4 . . 135 C3
  High Wycombe HP13 . . . . 161 C1
Kestrel Dr HP15 . . . . . . 163 B5
Kestrel Path SL2 . . . . . . 197 E1
Kestrel Way
  Aylesbury HP19 . . . . 101 E4
  Buckingham MK18 . . . . . 52 F7
Keswick Ct SL2 . . . . 205 F6
Keswick Rd MK19 . . . . . 11 B2
Keswick St HP18 . . . . . . 100 E5
Ketchmere Cl HP18 . . . . 125 C6
Ketelbey Nook MK7 . . . . 48 E5
Ketton Cl MK15 . . . . 35 D7
Kew Cl UB8 . . . . 201 D3
Kew Ct MK8 . . . . 33 F1
Kew Gr HP11 . . . . 173 B4
Kew Pl HP11 . . . . 173 B4
Keyes Way MK18 . . . . . . 41 E2
Keynes Cl MK16 . . . . . . 22 E4
Keys Pl SL6 . . . . 202 F6
Khalsa Prim Sch SL2 . . 206 A7
Khasiaberry MK7 . . . . . . 48 B5
Kidd Cl MK8 . . . . 45 E6
Kidderminster Rd SL2 . . 198 A2
Kidderminster Wlk **3**
  MK10 . . . . 36 B2
Kidwells Cl SL6 . . . . 202 F8
Kidwells Park Dr SL6 . . 202 F7
Kildonan Pl MK12 . . . . . 33 D4
Kilfillan Gdns HP4 . . . . . 135 A4
Kilfillan Pk HP4 . . . . 135 A3
Kilgour Ct **2** LU7 . . . . . 80 F7
Kilkenny Ho MK4 . . . . . . 45 E2
Killarney Dr SL6 . . . . . . 202 E7
Killerton Cl MK4 . . . . . . 45 E2
Kiln Ave
  Chinnor OX39 . . . . 147 D5
  Little Chalfont HP6 . . . . . 155 C1
Kiln Cl
  Calvert MK18 . . . . 73 B5
  Prestwood HP16 . . . . 151 C7
KILN COMMON 151 B8
Kiln Croft Cl SL7 . . . . . . 184 A3
Kiln Ct HP9 . . . . 186 B8
Kiln Dr MK17 . . . . 49 A5
Kilner Rd HP21 . . . . 115 E5
KILN FARM 33 B3
Kiln Farm Ind Est MK11 . 33 B3
Kiln Farm Rdbt MK11 . . . 33 A3

Kiln Fields SL6 . . . . 185 E1
Kiln La
  Botley HP5 . . . . 155 B8
  Cores End SL8, HP10 . . . 185 D3
  Hedgerley SL2 . . . . 187 D3
  Lacey Green HP27 . . . . . 149 F5
Kiln Pl SL6 . . . . 195 A3
Kiln Pond La HP13 . . . . 161 D2
Kiln Rd
  Hastoe HP23 . . . . 133 B6
  Prestwood HP16 . . . . 151 B7
Kiln The HP5 . . . . 144 C1
Kilnwood HP14 . . . . 150 B1
Kilpin Gn MK16 . . . . 24 B6
Kilwinning Dr MK10 . . . 35 F1
Kimbells Cl HP18 . . . . . . 124 D2
Kimber Cl SL4 . . . . 210 A4
Kimberley Cl SL3 . . . . . . 206 F2
Kimbers Dr SL1 . . . . 197 D2
Kimber's La SL6 . . . . . . 202 C3
Kimble Ct HP22 . . . . 129 E3
Kimble Park Rd HP17 . . 129 C3
Kimblewick Rd HP17 . . 129 C5
Kimbolton Ct MK14 . . . 35 A8
Kincardine Dr MK3 . . . . 46 F3
Kindermann Ct MK5 . . . 46 B5
Kindleton MK14 . . . . 34 F8
Kinellan Ct HP9 . . . . 175 D3
King Charles Cl MK18 . . 41 E2
King Cl MK17 . . . . 58 B2
King Edward Ave HP21 . 116 A7
King Edward Ct **5** SL4 . 210 D6
King Edward Gdns HP23 . 119 B4
King Edward St
  Milton Keynes MK13 . . . . 33 F7
  Slough SL1 . . . . 205 D4
King Edward VII Ave SL4 210 E8
King Edward VII Hospl
  SL4 . . . . 210 C4
Kingfisher HP19 . . . . . . 101 E4
Kingfisher Ct
  3 High Wycombe HP11 . 173 A6
  Slough SL2 . . . . 198 B1
Kingfisher Ctr The MK16 . 22 C3
Kingfisher Dr SL6 . . . . . 203 A8
Kingfisher Ho
  Loudwater HP11 . . . . 174 A4
  Marlow SL7 . . . . 183 F2
Kingfisher Pl HP11 . . . . 174 B3
Kingfisher Rd MK18 . . . . 52 F7
King George Cres MK11 . 32 E6
King George V Rd HP6 . 154 D1
Kinghorn La SL6 . . . . . . 195 D3
Kinghorn Pk SL6 . . . . . . 195 D3
King John's Cl TW19 . . . 211 C2
King Johns Palace SL3 . 212 D6
Kingsash Rd HP19 . . . . 114 F8
Kingsbridge MK4 . . . . . . 46 D2
Kingsbury HP20 . . . . . . 115 D8
Kingsbury Dr SL4 . . . . . 211 B1
Kings Chase SL6 . . . . . . 202 F6
Kings Cl
  Beaconsfield HP9 . . . . . . 186 A8
  Chalfont St Giles HP8 . . . 177 C8
  Henley-on-Thames RG9 . . 191 D2
  Westcott HP18 . . . . 98 C6
  Worminghall HP18 . . . . . 123 D5
King's Cross HP18 . . . . 113 A1
Kings Ct HP4 . . . . 135 C5
Kingsdale Rd HP4 . . . . . 135 A3
KINGSEY 127 B2
Kingsey Rd OX9 . . . . . . 126 D1
Kings Farm Rd WD3 . . . 167 D3
Kingsfield SL4 . . . . 209 D6
Kingsfold SL4 . . . . 34 B7
Kingsgate HP19 . . . . . . 115 B8
King's Gr SL6 . . . . 202 E6
King's Grove Ind Est SL6 202 E6
Kings Hall Par HP22 . . . 131 B4
Kingshill HP13 . . . . 162 C3
Kingshill Dr
  Deanshanger MK19 . . . . 31 E5
  Terriers HP13 . . . . 162 D3
Kingshill Rd HP13, HP15 . 162 D3
Kingshill Way HP4 . . . . . 135 C2
Kings La SL6 . . . . 195 B8
King's La
  Great Missenden HP16 . . 141 C2
  Lee Common HP16, HP22 . 141 F7
  South Heath HP16 . . . . . 152 B5
Kingsland Rd HP21 . . . . 116 A4
Kingsley Cl MK16 . . . . . 21 F4
Kingsley Cres HP11 . . . 172 F6
Kingsley Dr SL7 . . . . . . 183 C6
Kingsley Path SL2 . . . . . 197 D1
Kingsley Wlk HP23 . . . . 119 A4
Kings Lodge
  Amersham HP6 . . . . 154 D1
  Finmere MK18 . . . . 50 D6
Kings Mdw HP22 . . . . . . 102 C4
Kingsmead HP27 . . . . . . 139 B6
Kings Mead LU6 . . . . . . 92 E3
Kingsmead Bsns Pk
  HP11 . . . . 174 B3
Kingsmead Rd SL1 . . . . 205 C5
Kingsmead Rd HP11 . . . 174 B3
Kingsmead Rdbt MK4 . . 56 F8
Kings Oak Cl HP27 . . . . 139 C5
Kingsoe Leys MK10 . . . . 36 A2
Kings Quarter **3** SL6 . . 203 B7
Kings Rd
  Berkhamsted HP4 . . . . . . 135 B3
  Chalfont St Giles HP8 . . . 177 D8
  Henley-on-Thames RG9 . . 191 D2
  West Drayton UB7 . . . . . . 208 F4
King's Rd
  Aylesbury HP21 . . . . 115 F8
  Henley-on-Thames RG9 . . 191 D2

King's Rd continued
  High Wycombe HP11 . . . . 173 F4
  Loudwater HP11 . . . . 174 A4
  Slough SL1 . . . . 205 E3
  Uxbridge UB8 . . . . 201 D3
  Windsor SL4 . . . . 210 D3
  Windsor SL4 . . . . 210 D5
Kings Ride HP10 . . . . . . 163 B1
Kings Road Ho SL4 . . . . 210 D5
Kings Sq HP11 . . . . 173 F4
Kings St LU7 . . . . 78 E7
King St
  Chesham HP5 . . . . 154 B7
  Maidenhead SL6 . . . . 202 F6
  Maidenhead SL6 . . . . 202 F7
  Milton Keynes MK11 . . . . 32 E6
  Piddington HP14 . . . . 160 C1
  Tring HP23 . . . . 119 A3
King Stable St SL4 . . . . 210 D7
King's Terr SL3 . . . . 212 B8
KINGSTON 36 C2
Kingston Ave
  Milton Keynes MK11 . . . . 32 E5
  West Drayton UB7 . . . . . . 208 F6
KINGSTON BLOUNT 147 A3
Kingston Bsns Pk MK10 . 36 D2
Kingston Gymnastics &
  Fitness Ctr MK10 . . . . . 36 C1
Kingston Hill OX39, HP14 . 158 B8
Kingston La
  Uxbridge UB8 . . . . 201 E2
  West Drayton UB7 . . . . . . 208 F4
Kingston Rd MK10 . . . . . 36 D1
Kingston Rdbt MK10 . . . 36 D1
Kingstons Yd NN12 . . . . 17 B7
Kingsway
  Farnham Common SL2 . . 198 C6
  Gerrards Cross SL9 . . . . . 188 E8
  Iver SL0 . . . . 207 E7
  5 Slough SL3 . . . . 206 C3
Kingsway Ho **6** SL6 . . . 202 F7
Kingsway Mews SL2 . . . 198 C6
Kingswear Dr MK10 . . . . 36 B4
Kings Wlk RG9 . . . . 191 D2
Kings Wood SL7 . . . . . . 193 D7
KINGSWOOD 83 B3
Kingswood Creek TW19 . 211 D2
Kingswood Ct SL6 . . . . . 202 F5
Kingswood Ho SL2 . . . . 205 C8
Kingswood La
  Kingswood HP18 . . . . . . 83 B2
  Ludgershall HP18 . . . . . . 96 F6
*Kings Wood National Nature
Reserve* ★ MK17 . . . . . . 60 D1
Kingswood Par SL7 . . . . 183 D5
Kingswood Park HP13 . . 173 E8
Kingswood Pl HP13 . . . . 162 E1
Kingswood Rd HP10 . . . 163 A1
Kingswood Way HP13 . . 162 E1
King's Wood Sch HP13 . 173 F8
Kinloch Pl MK2 . . . . 58 E5
Kinnaird Cl SL1 . . . . 204 C7
Kinnear Cl MK8 . . . . 45 E7
Kinross Dr MK3 . . . . 46 E2
Kinson Gn HP20 . . . . . . 101 E3
Kipling Ct SL4 . . . . 210 B5
Kipling Dr MK16 . . . . . . 21 F4
Kipling Rd MK3 . . . . 58 A7
Kippell Hill MK46 . . . . . . 6 F5
Kirby Est UB7 . . . . 208 D6
Kirby Way UB8 . . . . 201 F1
Kirkeby Cl MK14 . . . . . . 34 D6
Kirke Cl MK5 . . . . 46 A5
Kirkham Ct MK5 . . . . . . 46 C8
Kirkstall Pl MK6 . . . . . . 46 D8
Kirkwall Spur SL1, SL2 . 205 E8
Kirkwood Gr MK5 . . . . . 45 D5
Kirtle Rd HP5 . . . . 144 C1
Kirtlington MK15 . . . . . . 35 B5
Kitchener Cl MK46 . . . . . 7 A3
Kitchener Rd HP11 . . . . 172 E7
Kite Field HP4 . . . . 134 E7
Kite Hill MK6 . . . . 47 B8
Kitelee Cl MK10 . . . . 11 A3
Kite Wood Rd HP10 . . . . 163 B1
Kitsbury Ct HP4 . . . . . . 135 B4
Kitsbury Rd HP4 . . . . . . 135 B4
Kitsbury Terr HP4 . . . . . 135 B4
Kittiwake HP19 . . . . 101 E4
Klee Cl HP22 . . . . 85 A5
Klondyke SL7 . . . . 183 D2
Knapp Gate MK5 . . . . . . 45 F7
Knaresborough Ct MK3 . 57 D7
Knaves Beech HP10 . . . 174 D1
Knaves Beech Bsns Ctr
  HP10 . . . . 174 D1
Knaves Beech Ind Est
  HP10 . . . . 174 C1
Knaves Beech Way HP10 174 C1
Knaves Hill LU7 . . . . 80 D8
Knaves Hollow HP10 . . . 174 D1
Knebworth Gate MK14 . . 22 A1
Knighton-Way La UB9 . . 201 B6
Knightsbridge Ct SL3 . . 207 A2
Knightsbridge Pl **16**
  HP19 . . . . 115 A8
Knights Cl
  Eaton Bray LU6 . . . . 92 E5
  Great Brickhill MK17 . . . . 59 D1
  Windsor SL4 . . . . 209 D6
Knights Cres LU6 . . . . . . 92 E5
Knights Cl **2** MK3 . . . . 58 D8
Knights Gn WD3 . . . . . . 167 E6
Knights Hill HP12 . . . . . 172 C5
Knights Pl **5** SL4 . . . . . 210 C5
Knights Templar Way
  HP11 . . . . 173 B4

Knoll Cl MK16 . . . . 13 F2
Knolls Cl HP22 . . . . 89 B3
Knolls View LU6 . . . . . . 92 B5
Knoll The
  Aspley Heath MK17 . . . . 49 A1
  Sherington MK16 . . . . . . 13 F2
Knolton Way SL2 . . . . . . 206 C7
Knottocks Cl HP9 . . . . . 175 D5
Knottocks Dr HP9 . . . . . 175 D5
Knottocks End HP9 . . . . 175 D5
KNOTTY GREEN 175 C6
Knowles Cl UB7 . . . . . . 208 E5
Knowles Gn MK2 . . . . . . 58 C8
Knowles Prim Sch MK2 . 58 D8
Knowl Gate MK5 . . . . . . 46 C7
KNOWLHILL 46 D6
Knowlhill Rdbt MK5 . . . . 46 C6
Knowsley Cl SL6 . . . . . . 195 A1
Knox Bridge MK7 . . . . . . 48 B8
Knyghton Cl LU7 . . . . . . 91 D6
Kola Ho SL2 . . . . 206 B6
Kop Hill Rd HP27 . . . . . 139 D3
Kramer Ct MK8 . . . . 45 D6
Krohn Cl MK18 . . . . 52 F8
Krypton Cl MK5 . . . . 46 C6
Kynaston Ave HP21 . . . 115 E4

L

Laburnham Cotts LU7 . . 69 E3
Laburnham Rd SL6 . . . . 202 E6
Laburnum Ave UB7 . . . . 208 E6
Laburnum Cl SL7 . . . . . . 183 E4
Laburnum Gr
  Milton Keynes MK2 . . . . . 58 E7
  Slough SL3 . . . . 212 B8
Laburnum Rd HP12 . . . . 172 C5
Lace Hill Acad MK18 . . . 52 F6
Lace La MK18 . . . . 52 F6
Lacemakers
  Chinnor OX39 . . . . 147 C6
  Long Crendon HP18 . . . . 125 C7
Lace Mews MK46 . . . . . . 7 A4
Lacey Dr HP14 . . . . 161 C7
Lacey Gr UB10 . . . . 201 E3
LACEY GREEN 149 E5
Laceys Dr HP15 . . . . . . 163 B5
Ladbroke Cl HP20 . . . . . 101 E2
Ladbroke Gr MK10 . . . . 47 F8
Ladbroke Rd SL3 . . . . . 205 D3
Ladybridge Terr MK43 . . 8 E5
Lady Cooper Ct HP4 . . . 135 E6
Ladyday Pl SL1 . . . . 205 C6
Lady Dr MK15 . . . . 35 A8
Ladymead Cl MK17 . . . . 56 B8
Ladysmith Rd LU7 . . . . . 105 E5
Lady Verney Cl HP13 . . 173 B8
Ladywalk WD3 . . . . 178 E6
Lady Yorke Pk SL0 . . . . 200 D6
Laggan Ct MK2 . . . . 58 D4
Laggan Rd SL6 . . . . 195 F1
Laggan Sq SL6 . . . . 195 F1
Lagger Cl HP8 . . . . 177 B7
Lagger The HP8 . . . . . . 177 B7
Lagley Ho HP4 . . . . 135 A5
Lagonda Cl MK16 . . . . . 22 A4
Laidon Cl MK2 . . . . 58 D4
Lake Ave SL1 . . . . 205 D6
Lake Cl MK18 . . . . 66 B6
LAKE END 204 B4
Lake End Ct SL6 . . . . . . 204 A7
Lake End Rd SL4, SL6 . . 204 B5
Laker Ct MK6 . . . . 46 E7
Lakes Cotts LU7 . . . . . . 90 C8
Lakesfield MK6 . . . . 186 F8
Lakeside
  Aylesbury HP19 . . . . 101 E4
  Maidenhead SL6 . . . . 196 B1
  Tring HP23 . . . . 119 A5
Lakeside Dr SL2 . . . . . . 198 F4
Lakeside Est SL3 . . . . . . 212 F7
Lakeside Rd
  Chinnor OX39 . . . . 147 D5
  Poyle SL3 . . . . 212 F7
Lakes La
  Beaconsfield HP9 . . . . . . 186 F8
  Newport Pagnell MK16 . . 22 B5
Lakes The SL7 . . . . 194 A6
Lake View SL6 . . . . 196 A1
Lamb Cl MK16 . . . . 22 A4
Lambe Rd HP22 . . . . . . 131 C5
Lamberhurst Gr MK7 . . . 48 A8
Lambert Ave SL3 . . . . . . 206 E3
Lambert Rd HP18 . . . . . 100 D4
Lamberts Croft MK12 . . 33 C5
Lambert Wlk OX9 . . . . . 125 F1
Lamb La MK7 . . . . 48 C7
Lambourn Ct MK4 . . . . . 46 D2
Lambourne Ave HP21 . . 115 D3
Lambourne Cl SL1 . . . . . 197 C3
Lambourne Ct
  Maidenhead SL6 . . . . 203 C8
  Uxbridge UB8 . . . . 201 B4
Lambourne Dr SL6 . . . . 202 C3
Lambridge La RG9 . . . . . 191 C3
Lambridge Wood Rd
  RG9 . . . . 191 B4
Lambscroft Way SL9 . . . 177 E1
Lambton Ho SL3 . . . . . . 210 A4
Lambtons Way MK18 . . . 66 B5
Lamesley Ho SL6 . . . . . 202 E6
Lammas MK6 . . . . 47 A5
Lammas Ave SL4 . . . . . . 210 D5

Lammas Ct SL4 . . . . **210** C5
Lammas Rd
  Cheddington LU7 . . . . **105** A7
  Slough SL1 . . . . **204** D8
Lammas Way
  Lane End HP14 . . . . . **171** A4
  Loudwater HP10 . . . . **174** C1
Lamour La MK4 . . . . **45** E3
Lampitts Cross MK6 . . . . **47** B6
Lamport Ct MK8 . . . . . . **46** A8
Lamva Ct MK11 . . . . . . **32** F5
Lanark Ho MK3 . . . . **46** F1
Lancaster Ave SL2 . . . . **198** C1
Lancaster Cl TW19 . . . . **213** E1
Lancaster Ct HP12 . . . . **172** D4
Lancaster Dr HP3 . . . . . **145** F4
Lancaster Gate MK3 . . . . **57** E7
Lancaster Rd
  Aylesbury HP21 . . . . **116** B6
  High Wycombe HP12 . . **172** E4
  Maidenhead SL6 . . . . **202** B8
  Uxbridge UB8 . . . . . . **201** D5
Lancaster Ride HP10 . . . **174** B8
Lancaster Wy LU7 . . . . **105** C3
Lancastria La 2 MK16 . . **36** C4
Lancastria Mews **202** D7
Lancelot Cl SL1 . . . . . . **205** A4
Lance Way HP13 . . . . . **174** A6
Lanchester Rd MK43 . . . . **24** D2
Lancot Ave LU6 . . . . . . **93** F8
Lancotbury Cl LU6 . . . . **93** C7
Lancot Dr LU6 . . . . **93** E8
Lancot Lower Sch LU6 . . **93** E8
Lancot Pl LU6 . . . . **93** E8
Lancresse Cl UB8 . . . . **201** D6
Lander Rd HP19 . . . . . **100** F3
Landon Ct HP21 . . . . . **115** F7
Landrace Ct 6 MK5 . . . . **45** F3
Landsborough Gate MK15 **35** C7
Lands End Gr MK4 . . . . . **56** F8
Lands The LU7 . . . . **79** F3
LANE END **171** C4
Lane End HP4 . . . . **134** F4
Lane End Ind Est HP14 . . **171** B4
Lane End Prim Sch
  HP14 . . . . **171** B4
Lane End Rd HP12 . . . . **172** B6
Lanercost Cres MK10 . . . **36** B1
LANES END **132** C4
Lane The
  Grafton Regis NN12 . . . . **9** D2
  Mursley MK17 . . . . . . **67** D6
Lane Wood Cl HP7 . . . . **165** F8
Lanfranc Gdns MK15 . . . **35** B7
Langcliffe Dr MK13 . . . . **34** C5
Langdale Cl
  Maidenhead SL6 . . . . **203** A6
  Milton Keynes MK2 . . . **58** D4
Langdale Ho MK11 . . . . **174** A4
Langdale Lodge HP10 . . **174** C2
Langdon Ave HP21 . . . . **116** B5
Langdon St HP19 . . . . . **119** A3
Langdown Way SL6 . . . . **202** D5
Langerstone La MK4 . . . . **46** B1
Langford Pl MK7 . . . . . . **48** A3
Langham Way MK6 . . . . **47** C4
Langkawi La MK17 . . . . **58** A3
Langland Com Sch MK6 . . **47** C6
Langland Ho MK6 . . . . . **47** C6
Langland Rd MK6 . . . . . **47** C6
Langlands MK46 . . . . **7** E7
LANGLEY **207** A3
Langley Acad SL3 . . . . . **206** E3
Langley Broom SL3 . . . . **206** E1
Langley Bsns Ctr SL3 . . **207** A4
Langley Bsns Pk SL3 . . . **207** A4
Langley Cl MK18 . . . . . . **65** E4
Langley Cnr SL3 . . . . . **199** F6
Langley Gram Sch SL3 . . **206** F2
Langley Hall Prim Acad
  SL3 . . . . **206** E5
Langley L Ctr SL3 . . . . **207** B2
Langley Park Ctry Pk★ SL0,
  SL3 . . . . **200** A1
Langley Park Rd SL3 . . . **207** B6
Langley Rd SL3 . . . . . . **206** E3
Langley Sta SL3 . . . . . **207** A4
Langley Way SL7 . . . . . **183** C2
Langmuir Ct MK5 . . . . . **46** C4
Langney Gn MK4 . . . . . . **57** A8
Langport Cres MK5 . . . . **45** D5
Langston Ct HP12 . . . . **172** C8
Langstone Cl HP20 . . . . **101** F3
Langstone Ct 11 HP20 . . **101** F3
Langton Cl
  Maidenhead SL6 . . . . **202** D8
  Slough SL1 . . . . **204** D5
Langton Dr MK8 . . . . . . **33** E3
Langton's Mdw SL2 . . . **198** C6
Langtree Ave SL1 . . . . . **204** F4
Lanner Wlk MK6 . . . . . . **47** B8
Lanolin Cl MK14 . . . . . . **21** C1
Lanrick Copse HP4 . . . . **135** C5
Lansbury Rd MK17 . . . . **58** B2
Lansdell Ave HP12 . . . . **172** B3
Lansdowne Ave SL1 . . . **205** E5
Lansdowne Ct
  Maidenhead SL6 . . . . **203** C7
  Slough SL1 . . . . **205** E5
Lansdowne Rd
  Aylesbury HP20 . . . . **101** D2
  Chesham HP5 . . . . . **144** C2
Lansdowne Way HP11 . . **172** E3
Lansdown Rd SL9 . . . . . **177** D2
Lanterns Wlk SL6 . . . . **203** B7

Lantern Way UB7 . . . . **208** E4
Lanthorn Cl MK14 . . . . . **34** E6
Lappetts La HP16 . . . . **152** E8
Laputa Wy MK17 . . . . . . **58** A3
Larch Cl
  Aylesbury HP20 . . . . **102** A2
  Slough SL2 . . . . **205** B8
  Tylers Green HP10 . . . **163** C2
Larches The
  Berkhamsted HP4 . . . **134** D5
  Holmer Green HP15 . . **163** D7
  Little Chalfont HP8 . . **155** B1
Larchfield Prim Sch SL6 . **202** E4
Larchfield Rd SL6 . . . . **202** E5
Larch Gr MK2 . . . . **58** E7
Larchlands The HP10 . . . **163** D1
Larchmoor Pk SL2 . . . . **199** A7
Larch Rise HP4 . . . . . . **135** A5
Larchwood HP16 . . . . . **152** B4
Lark Cl MK18 . . . . **52** E7
Larkfield SL6 . . . . **203** B1
Larkfield Cl HP13 . . . . **162** F1
Larkin Cl MK16 . . . . . . **22** A5
Larkings La SL2 . . . . . **199** B4
Lark Rise HP15 . . . . . . **163** B5
Larkspur Ave MK14 . . . . **34** E5
Larkspur Way MK15 . . . **162** F6
Larks Rise HP5 . . . . . . **154** D6
Lark Vale HP19 . . . . . . **101** E3
Larner Cl MK17 . . . . . . **58** B2
La Roche Cl 4 SL3 . . . . **206** C3
Larson Cl MK10 . . . . . . **35** E2
Larwood Pl MK6 . . . . . . **34** F1
Lasborough Rd MK10 . . . **36** C1
Lascelles Cl MK15 . . . . . **35** B7
Lascelles Ho 8 SL1 . . . **206** A4
Lascelles Rd SL3 . . . . **206** B3
Laser Cl MK5 . . . . **46** C6
Lashlake Rd OX9 . . . . . **125** F1
Lassell Gdns SL6 . . . . **203** B7
Lastingham Gr MK4 . . . . **46** B2
Latchmoor Ave SL9 . . . **188** D7
Latchmoor Gr SL9 . . . . **188** D7
Latchmoor Way SL9 . . . **188** D7
LATHBURY **22** C7
LATIMER **155** E3
Latimer
  Latimer HP5 . . . . . . **155** E2
  Milton Keynes MK11 . . **32** E4
Latimer Cl HP6 . . . . . . **166** C8
Latimer Ct HP20 . . . . . **116** A8
Latimer Rd
  Chesham HP5 . . . . . **154** E5
  Little Chalfont HP5 . . **155** C2
Latimer Way HP9 . . . . . **175** C6
Laud's Cl RG9 . . . . **191** C1
Launceston Cl MK5 . . . . **46** B6
Launceston Ct MK5 . . . . **46** B6
Launceston Dr MK10 . . . . **36** C3
Launde 1 MK10 . . . . . . **36** B1
Laurance Ct 2 SL7 . . . . **183** D2
Laurel Ave SL3 . . . . . . **206** E4
Laurel Bank HP3 . . . . . **146** F8
Laurel Cl
  Milton Keynes MK8 . . . **45** D7
  Poyle SL3 . . . . **212** E7
  Prestwood HP16 . . . . **151** B7
  Speen HP27 . . . . . . **150** C4
Laurel Ct
  Amersham HP6 . . . . **154** C3
  Iver Heath SL0 . . . . **200** D5
Laurel Dr
  Loudwater HP11 . . . . **174** A4
  Walter's Ash HP14 . . . **161** D7
Laurel La UB7 . . . . . . **208** E2
Laurel Lane Prim Sch
  UB7 . . . . **208** D2
Laurel Rd SL9 . . . . . . **177** D2
Laurels Rd SL0 . . . . . . **200** D3
Laurels The
  High Wycombe HP12 . . **172** C4
  Milton Keynes MK1 . . . **47** D1
Laurel Way 4 HP21 . . . **115** E7
Lautrec Way HP19 . . . . **100** F2
Lautree Gdns SL6 . . . . **195** E7
Lavender Cl HP21 . . . . **115** B5
Lavender Gr MK7 . . . . . **48** A5
Lavender Hill MK10 . . . . **36** C4
Lavender Rd UB8 . . . . . **208** F8
Lavender Way HP15 . . . **162** F7
Lavender Wlk HP21 . . . **115** B6
LAVENDON **7** F7
Lavendon Rd MK46 . . . . . **7** A5
Lavendon Sch MK46 . . . . **7** F8
Laverde Wlk MK10 . . . . . **35** E2
Lavric Rd HP21 . . . . . . **115** C6
Lawford Ave WD3 . . . . **167** C3
Lawford Cl WD3 . . . . . **167** C3
Lawkland SL2 . . . . **198** C2
Lawn Ave UB7 . . . . . . **208** D4
Lawn Cl SL3 . . . . **211** C7
Lawn Farm Bsns Ctr
  HP18 . . . . **83** D4
Lawn Hill HP18 . . . . . . **73** A2
Lawn House La HP18 . . . **72** F1
Lawn Rd UB8 . . . . **201** C5
Lawnsmead Gdns MK16 . . **22** D5
Lawns The
  Brill HP18 . . . . **96** B1
  Tylers Green HP10 . . . **163** B2
Lawn The SL3 . . . . . . **211** C6
Lawrence Cl
  14 Aylesbury HP20 . . **101** F2
  Aylesbury HP20 . . . . **102** A2
Lawrence Ct SL4 . . . . . **210** C5
Lawrence Gr
  Prestwood HP16 . . . . **151** D5
  Uxbridge UB10 . . . . **201** E3

Lawrence Way SL1 . . . . **204** D8
Lawrence Wlk MK16 . . . . **21** F5
Laws Cl MK43 . . . . **8** E4
Lawsone Rise HP13 . . . **162** B1
Lawson Pl MK5 . . . . . . **46** B5
Lawson Wy HP18 . . . . . **100** E4
Laxfield Dr MK10 . . . . . **36** A4
Laxton Gn SL6 . . . . . . **202** C3
Layburn Cres SL3 . . . . **212** B8
Lay Rd HP19 . . . . **101** B2
Layer's Ave SL9 . . . . . **177** C1
Layter's Avenue S SL9 . . **177** C1
Layter's Cl SL9 . . . . . . **177** C1
Layter's End SL9 . . . . . **177** C1
LAYTER'S GREEN **177** B1
Layters Green La SL9 . . . **177** B1
Layters Way SL9 . . . . . **188** D6
Leaberry MK13 . . . . **34** A8
Leachcroft SL9 . . . . . . **177** B2
Leaches Farm Bsns Ctr
  HP18 . . . . **81** F4
Leach Rd HP21 . . . . . . **115** C7
Lea Cl SL7 . . . . **183** D6
Leacroft Cl UB7 . . . . . **208** E6
Leacroft Rd SL0 . . . . . **207** E7
LEADENHALL **47** A8
Leadenhall Rdbt MK6 . . . **46** E7
Leaders Cl HP22 . . . . . . **89** B3
Leafield Rise MK8 . . . . . **33** D2
Leafy La HP23 . . . . **118** E1
Leaholme Gdns SL1 . . . **204** D8
Lea La HP18 . . . . **125** F4
Leander Wy SL6 . . . . . **202** D8
Leapingwell La MK18 . . . **66** B5
Leary Cres MK16 . . . . . **22** E4
Leas Cl HP13 . . . . **173** F8
Leas Dr SL0 . . . . **207** E7
Leaside MK16 . . . . **12** B6
Leasowe Pl MK13 . . . . . **34** C3
Leather La HP16 . . . . . **142** A3
Leaver Rd RG9 . . . . . . **191** C1
LECKHAMPSTEAD **42** E7
Leckhampstead Rd MK18 . **42** A8
Leckhamstead Rd MK19 . . **31** A3
Ledborough Gate HP9 . . **175** F4
Ledborough La HP9 . . . . **175** E4
Ledborough Wood HP9 . . **175** E4
LEDBURN **90** D8
Ledburn LU7 . . . . **90** D8
Ledburn Gr LU7 . . . . . . **80** E6
Ledbury MK14 . . . . **21** E1
Ledeview Ct HP11 . . . . **174** A4
Ledger's Rd SL1 . . . . . **205** D4
Leeches Way LU7 . . . . **105** A7
LEE COMMON **142** D5
Lee Common CE Sch
  HP16 . . . . **142** D5
Lee Cotts
  Buckmoorend HP17 . . . **140** D6
  Lacey Green HP27 . . . **149** A4
Lee Cres HP17 . . . . . . **114** D5
Lee Ct 7 HP12 . . . . . . **172** E7
Leeds Rd SL1 . . . . **205** E6
Lee Farm Cl HP5 . . . . . **145** A1
LEE GATE **142** A1
Lee Ho 2 MK2 . . . . **58** C8
Lee La SL6 . . . . **194** F1
Lee Rd
  Aylesbury HP21 . . . . **115** D6
  Quainton HP22 . . . . . **84** F5
  Saunderton HP27 . . . **148** F6
Lees Cl SL6 . . . . **202** B5
Lees Gdns SL6 . . . . . . **202** B5
Leeson Gdns SL4 . . . . **204** E2
Lees Wlk SL7 . . . . **183** C2
Le Flaive Bsns Pk HP14 . **161** E6
Legoland Windsor★ SL4 **209** D2
Leicester Ct RG9 . . . . . **191** D3
Leigh Hill MK4 . . . . **46** D2
Leigh Pk SL3 . . . . **211** B7
Leigh Rd SL1 . . . . **205** B6
Leigh Sq SL4 . . . . **209** D5
Leigh St HP11 . . . . . . **172** F7
LEIGHTON BUZZARD **80** F6
Leighton Buzzard Sta LU7 **80** E7
Leighton Gdns SL6 . . . . **196** B1
Leighton Ho 7 SL7 . . . . **183** E2
Leighton Mid Sch LU7 . . . **80** F6
Leighton Rd
  Edlesborough LU6 . . . . **92** D4
  Leighton Buzzard LU7 . . **80** F7
  Soulbury LU7 . . . . . . **70** B1
  Stoke Hammond MK17 . . **69** E7
  Wing LU7 . . . . **80** A3
  Wingrave HP22 . . . . . **89** A5
Leighton St MK17 . . . . . **60** E6
Leiston Spur SL1 . . . . . **205** E7
Leith Cl SL1 . . . . **206** A5
Leith Rd HP19 . . . . . . **115** A8
Lembrook Wlk HP21 . . . **115** C6
Lemmon Wlk 5 MK4 . . . . **45** E2
LENBOROUGH **52** D3
Lenborough Cl MK18 . . . **52** C7
Lenborough Pk MK15 . . . **35** C2
Lenborough Rd MK18 . . . **52** C7
Lendon Gr HP23 . . . . . **104** D3
Lennon Dr MK8 . . . . . . **45** E7
Lennox Rd MK2 . . . . . . **58** D7
LENT **197** B1
Lent Gn SL1 . . . . **197** B1
Lent Green La SL1 . . . . **197** B1
Lenthall Ct MK13 . . . . . **34** A5
LENT RISE **204** A8
Lent Rise Comb Sch SL1 **204** B8
Lent Rise Rd SL1 . . . . **204** B8
Leominster Gate 4 MK10 . **36** A1

Leonards Cl HP18 . . . . . **72** F2
Leonardslee MK4 . . . . . **45** F2
Leon Ave MK2 . . . . **58** D8
Leon L Ctr MK2 . . . . . . **58** C4
Leopard Dr MK15 . . . . . **35** A7
Leopold Mall 6 SL1 . . . **205** F4
Leopold Rd LU7 . . . . . . **80** D7
Lerwick Dr SL1 . . . . . . **205** E8
Leslie Dunne Ho SL4 . . **209** E5
Lester Gr HP15 . . . . . . **163** A4
Lesters Rd SL6 . . . . . . **195** D6
Letchfield HP5 . . . . . . **155** B8
Letter Box La HP27 . . . **139** D7
Leven Cl
  Leighton Buzzard LU7 . . **80** B7
  Milton Keynes MK2 . . . **58** D5
Levens Hall Dr MK4 . . . . **45** F1
Leverkus Ct OX39 . . . . **147** C6
Leverkus Ho OX39 . . . . **147** C6
Levings Cl HP19 . . . . . **101** A3
Lewens Croft MK16 . . . . **16** A3
Lewes Ct SL1 . . . . **205** C4
Lewes Ho MK3 . . . . **57** D7
Lewins Farm Ct SL1 . . . **204** F6
Lewins Rd SL9 . . . . . . **188** D8
Lewins Way SL1 . . . . . **204** F6
Lewins Yd HP5 . . . . . . **154** B8
Lewis Cl MK16 . . . . **21** F5
Lewis La SL9 . . . . **177** C2
LEWKNOR **157** B8
Lewknor CE Prim Sch
  OX49 . . . . **157** B8
Lewknor Cl OX49 . . . . . **157** A7
Lexham Gdns HP6 . . . . **154** C2
Lexham Rd MK6 . . . . . . **47** C4
Lexington Ave SL6 . . . . **202** D5
Leybourne Gdns OX39 . . **147** C7
Leyburn Ct MK13 . . . . . **34** C5
Leyburne Cl LU7 . . . . . . **90** C8
Ley Field Rd HP21 . . . . **115** E6
LEY HILL **145** B1
Ley Hill Sch HP5 . . . . . **145** B1
Leyland Cl MK18 . . . . . **51** F4
Leyland Pl 3 MK6 . . . . . **34** E1
Leylands La TW19 . . . . **213** A2
Leys Cl HP19 . . . . **101** C4
Leys Ct MK5 . . . . **46** B8
Leys La MK18 . . . . **62** B8
Leys Rd MK5 . . . . **46** B8
Leys The
  Amersham HP6 . . . . **154** B4
  Buckingham MK18 . . . **41** F3
  Halton HP22 . . . . . . **117** C1
  Tring HP23 . . . . **119** B4
  Woburn Sands MK17 . . **49** B4
  Yardley Hastings NN7 . . **1** A6
Leys View MK16 . . . . . . **13** F1
Leywood Cl HP7 . . . . . **165** E7
Libra Ho HP10 . . . . . . **185** A8
Lichfield Down MK7 . . . . **48** B5
Lichfield Ho HP21 . . . . **115** F6
Lidcote LU7 . . . . **78** A5
Liddall Way UB7 . . . . . **208** F5
Liddell SL4 . . . . **209** C4
Liddell Pl SL4 . . . . **209** C4
Liddell Sq 14 SL4 . . . . **209** C5
Liddell Way SL4 . . . . . **209** C4
Liffre Dr HP22 . . . . . . **131** B6
Lightfoot Ct MK7 . . . . . **47** F5
Lightlands La SL6 . . . . **195** F5
Ligo Ave HP22 . . . . . . **116** C2
Lilac Cl MK17 . . . . **57** C3
Lilac Pl UB7 . . . . **208** F6
Lilies The HP22 . . . . . . **87** C1
Lilleshall Ave MK10 . . . . **35** F1
Lilley Way SL1 . . . . . . **204** E5
Lillibrooke Cres SL6 . . . **202** A3
LILLINGSTONE DAYRELL . . **29** F4
LILLINGSTONE LOVELL . . . **30** B5
Lillyfee Farm La HP10 . . **186** B5
Lilly Hill MK46 . . . . **6** F5
Lily Bottom La HP27 . . . **149** F8
Lily Dr UB7 . . . . **208** D2
Lily's Wlk HP11 . . . . . **173** A6
Limbaud Cl MK7 . . . . . . **48** A5
Lime Ave
  Buckingham MK18 . . . **52** F7
  High Wycombe HP11 . . **173** D5
  West Drayton UB7 . . . **208** F6
  Windsor SL4 . . . . . . **210** F7
Lime Cl
  Hazelmere HP15 . . . . **163** A3
  Newport Pagnell MK16 . . **22** B3
Lime Gr
  Chinnor OX39 . . . . . **147** D6
  Leighton Buzzard LU7 . . **80** E8
  Woburn Sands MK17 . . **49** B4
Limelight Ave HP18 . . . **100** E6
Lime Rd
  Princes Risborough
    HP27 . . . . **139** B3
  Yardley Gobion NN12 . . **18** E6
Limerick La MK9 . . . . . . **35** D3
Limes Ave HP21 . . . . . **116** B7
Lime St MK46 . . . . **6** F3
Limes The
  Amersham HP6 . . . . **154** B3
  Milton Keynes, Fenny Stratford
    MK2 . . . . **58** E8
  Milton Keynes MK11 . . **32** E5
  Tring HP23 . . . . **119** C4
  Windsor SL4 . . . . . . **209** C6
Limes Way HP18 . . . . . **124** D2
Lime Tree Cl HP15 . . . . **162** D8
Lime Tree Wlk HP7 . . . . **165** F8
Lime Wlk
  Maidenhead SL6 . . . . **202** A8

Lime Wlk continued
  New Denham UB9 . . . **201** C7
Limit Home Pk HP4 . . . . **134** D7
Limmer La HP12 . . . . . **172** B3
Limmers Mead HP15 . . . **162** D8
Limousin Ave MK8 . . . . . **45** D8
Linceslade Gr MK5 . . . . **34** B1
Linchfield HP13 . . . . . . **173** E7
Linchfield Rd SL3 . . . . **211** C6
Lincoln
  Buckingham MK18 . . . **41** D2
  Milton Keynes MK14 . . **34** C8
Lincoln Cl HP22 . . . . . **116** B2
Lincoln Ct
  Berkhamsted HP4 . . . **135** B4
  3 Slough SL1 . . . . . **205** E3
Lincoln Hatch La SL1 . . . **197** C1
Lincoln Ho HP10 . . . . . **185** D3
Lincoln Park Bsns Ctr
  HP12 . . . . **172** D6
Lincoln Pk
  Amersham HP7 . . . . **165** E8
  Brackley NN13 . . . . . **38** A5
Lincoln Rd
  Chalfont St Peter SL9 . **177** E2
  High Wycombe HP12 . . **172** E5
  Maidenhead SL6 . . . . **202** B8
Lincolnshire Cl MK3 . . . . **46** E1
Lincolns The HP16 . . . . **152** A3
Lincoln Way SL1 . . . . . **204** D6
Lincombe Slade LU7 . . . . **80** E8
Lincroft MK43 . . . . **25** B1
Linden SL3 . . . . **207** B1
Linden Ave SL6 . . . . . . **195** D1
Linden Cl SL0 . . . . **200** D3
Linden Ct HP12 . . . . . . **172** D6
Linden Dr
  Chalfont St Peter SL9 . **177** E1
  Farnham Royal SL2 . . **198** C4
Linden End HP21 . . . . . **115** F6
Linden Gr MK14 . . . . . . **34** E6
Linden Lea HP22 . . . . . **131** B6
Lindens The HP3 . . . . . **146** F8
Linden Way HP17 . . . . . **128** B7
Linden Wlk HP15 . . . . . **163** B3
Lindie Gdns UB10 . . . . **201** E6
Lindisfarne Dr MK10 . . . . **36** A1
Lindo Cl HP5 . . . . **144** B1
Lindores Croft MK10 . . . . **36** B1
Lindsay Ave HP12 . . . . **172** E7
Lindsay Cl TW19 . . . . . **213** D2
Lindsey Dr 1 SL9 . . . . **195** D2
Lindsey Rd UB9 . . . . . **190** A1
Linen La MK18 . . . . **52** F6
Lines Hill HP22 . . . . . . **88** B3
Lines Rd HP14 . . . . . . **171** B5
Lines The HP22 . . . . . . **88** C4
Linfields HP7 . . . . **166** C7
Linford Ave MK16 . . . . . **22** A4
Linford La
  Milton Keynes, Willen
    MK15 . . . . **35** D7
  Milton Keynes, Woolstone
    MK15 . . . . **35** C3
Linford Lakes Nature
  Reserve★ MK14 . . . . **21** C2
Lingfield MK12 . . . . **33** E4
Lingfield Cl HP13 . . . . **174** A5
Lingholm Cl SL6 . . . . . **202** C6
Linington Ave HP5 . . . . **145** A1
Link Cl HP12 . . . . **172** D6
Link Rd
  Datchet SL3 . . . . . . **211** C6
  Great Missenden HP16 . **152** A2
  High Wycombe HP12 . . **172** D6
Links App HP10 . . . . . . **185** B8
Links Rd HP10 . . . . . . **185** C8
Links Way HP10 . . . . . **185** B8
Linkswood Rd SL1 . . . . **197** C3
Link The
  Hazelmere HP15 . . . . **163** A5
  Slough SL2 . . . . **206** B7
Link Way UB9 . . . . . . **190** A5
Linnet Ave HP7 . . . . . . **155** A1
Linnet Cl HP12 . . . . . . **172** B3
Linnet Dr HP18 . . . . . . **98** C5
Linney Ct MK4 . . . . . . **46** A1
LINSLADE **80** D7
Linslade Lower Sch LU7 . . **80** D7
Linslade Mid Sch LU7 . . . **80** E5
Linslade Rd LU7 . . . . . . **70** F4
Lintlaw Pl MK3 . . . . . . **47** A3
Linton Cl MK13 . . . . . . **34** C4
Lintott Ct TW19 . . . . . **213** E1
Linx The MK3 . . . . **47** A2
Lionel Ave HP22 . . . . . **131** A6
Lionel Cl HP22 . . . . . . **131** A5
Lipscombe Dr MK18 . . . . **41** E1
Lipscomb La MK5 . . . . . **46** A7
Lisburn Path 1 HP20 . . . **101** F2
Liscombe Park LU7 . . . . **79** F8
Lisle Rd HP13 . . . . **162** A1
Lisleys Field HP15 . . . . **162** D7
Lismore Pk SL2 . . . . . **205** F7
Lissel Rd MK6 . . . . **47** E5
Lisset Rd SL6 . . . . **203** A6
Lister Cl MK6 . . . . **47** B6
Lister Gn HP21 . . . . . . **115** E5
Liston Ct (Sh Arcade) 7
  SL7 . . . . **183** D2
Liston Ho 9 SL7 . . . . . **183** E2
Liston Rd SL7 . . . . **183** D2
Litcham Spur SL1 . . . . **205** D2
Little Balmer MK18 . . . . . **52** E6
Little Benty UB7 . . . . . **208** C1
Little Boltons 13 SL7 . . . **183** E2
LITTLE BOYS HEATH **152** C5
LITTLE BRICKHILL **59** E5

Little Bridge Rd HP4 . . . . . 135 D4
LITTLE BRITAIN 208 C7
Little Britain HP18 . . . . 99 B7
Littlebrook Ave SL2 . . . . . 204 C6
Little Buntings SL4 . . . . . . 209 F4
LITTLE CHALFONT 155 B1
Little Chalfont Prim Sch
HP6 . . . . 166 E8
Little Chapels Way SL1 . . . 205 A4
Little Chartridge Ct HP5 . . 144 A1
Little CI
Aylesbury HP20 . . . . 101 D1
Flackwell Heath HP10 . . . . . 185 B6
High Wycombe HP12 . . . . . 172 E3
LITTLECOTE 78 A5
Littlecote MK8 . . . . 34 A1
Littledown Rd SL1 . . . . 205 F5
Littledown Specl Sch
SL1 . . . . 205 F6
Little Dunmow MK10 . . . . . . 36 A4
LITTLE END 23 B8
Littlefield Ct UB7 . . . . 213 D7
LITTLE FRIETH 170 E2
LITTLE GADDESDEN 121 D7
Little Gaddesden CE Prim
Sch HP4 . . . . 121 C8
Little Gaddesden Ho
HP4 . . . . 121 E5
Little Gibbs HP27 . . . . 138 A2
Little Greencroft HP5 . . . . 144 A4
Little Ground HP6 . . . . 100 D4
Little Habton 3 MK4 . . . . . . 46 B3
Little Hame MK10 . . . . 35 F3
Little Ham La HP27 . . . . . . 139 B5
LITTLE HAMPDEN 131 A7
Little Hampden CI HP22 . . 131 B4
Little Hill WD3 . . . . 167 C3
Little Hivings HP5 . . . . 144 A4
Little Hollis HP16 . . . . 151 E7
Little Hoo HP23 . . . . 118 F4
LITTLE HORWOOD 55 F2
Little Horwood Manor
MK17 . . . . 55 E4
Little Horwood Rd MK17 . . 55 C3
Little Hundridge La
HP16 . . . . 153 A8
LITTLE KIMBLE 129 E2
Little Kimble Sta HP17 . . . 129 E2
LITTLE KINGSHILL 152 B3
Little Kingshill Comb Sch
HP16 . . . . 152 B2
Little La
Lacey Green HP27 . . . . 149 C4
Yardley Hastings NN7 . . . . . . 1 A7
LITTLE LINFORD 21 C5
Little Linford La MK16,
MK19 . . . . 21 E4
Little Linford Wood Wildlife
Reserve★ MK16 . . . . 21 B8
LITTLE LONDON
Oakley 109 F5
Wendover 141 C7
Little London
Deanshanger MK19 . . . . 31 E4
Whitchurch HP22 . . . . 87 A5
Little London Gn HP18 . . . 109 F5
LITTLE MARLOW 184 D5
Little Marlow CE Inf Sch
SL7 . . . . 184 C5
Little Marlow Rd SL7 . . . . 183 E3
LITTLE MARSH 72 A3
Littlemarsh MK7 . . . . 48 A5
Little Marsh Rd OX27 . . . . . 72 A3
Little Mdw MK5 . . . . 46 C7
Littlemere MK8 . . . . 33 D1
LITTLE MISSENDEN 153 D3
Little Missenden CE Inf Sch
HP7 . . . . 153 B3
Little Mollards HP22 . . . . . . 89 A3
Little Orchard CI HP27 . . . 138 E5
Little Orchs HP20 . . . . 101 F3
Little Pk
Bovingdon HP3 . . . . 146 A3
Princes Risborough HP27 . 139 C3
Littleport Spur SL1 . . . . . . 205 E7
Little Reeves Ave HP7 . . . 165 F8
LITTLE ROW 202 A5
Little Shardeloes HP7 . . . . 165 A8
Little Spinney MK43 . . . . . . 25 C3
Little Spring HP5 . . . . 144 B3
Little Spring Prim Sch
HP5 . . . . 144 B3
Little St NN7 . . . . 1 B6
Little Stanton MK14 . . . . . . 34 D8
Littlestone Gate MK10 . . . . 36 B3
Little Stocking MK5 . . . . . . 46 A3
Little Sutton La SL3 . . . . . 207 C1
LITTLE TINGEWICK 50 E6
LITTLE TRING 118 F6
Little Tring Rd HP23 . . . . . 118 F6
Little Twye HP23 . . . . 132 F3
Little Twye Rd HP23 . . . . . 132 F3
Little Windmill Hill WD4 . 156 F7
Little Wood HP14 . . . . 158 E5
Little Woodlands SL4 . . . . 209 F4
Littleworth LU7 . . . . 79 E3
LITTLEWORTH
COMMON 186 D1
Littleworth Rd
Hedgerley SL1 . . . . 186 C1
High Wycombe HP13 . . . . . 161 E2
Litton Ct HP10 . . . . 174 C2
Liverpool Rd SL1 . . . . 205 B7
Liverpool Victoria Ho 3
HP13 . . . . 173 B7
Livesey Hill MK5 . . . . 46 B5
Living Furniture Making
Mus★ HP11 . . . . 172 F7

Livingstone Dr MK15 . . . . . 35 C5
Llanbury CI SL9 . . . . 177 E3
Lloyds MK6 . . . . 47 A7
Loakes Ho HP11 . . . . 173 A6
Loakes Rd HP11 . . . . 173 A6
Lochinvar CI SL1 . . . . 205 B4
Lochnell Rd HP4 . . . . 134 F6
Lochy Dr LU7 . . . . 80 C7
Lock Ave SL6 . . . . 196 C2
Lockbridge Ct SL6 . . . . . . 203 C8
Lock Bridge Rd SL8 . . . . . 185 A3
Locke CI HP19 . . . . 101 A2
Locke Gdns SL3 . . . . 206 C4
Locke Rd MK2 . . . . 58 C8
Lockets CI SL4 . . . . 209 D6
Lock La
Cosgrove MK19 . . . . 19 B3
Maidenhead SL6 . . . . 202 C4
Lock Mead SL6 . . . . 196 C6
Lock Mews HP9 . . . . 186 B8
Lock Path SL4 . . . . 209 D8
Lock Rd SL7 . . . . 183 F1
Locksley Ct 4 SL1 . . . . . . 205 E3
Lockton Ct MK4 . . . . 46 B3
Lockview Cotts MK1 . . . . . 47 E1
Lock View La MK1 . . . . 47 E1
Lockwood Chase MK4 . . . . 45 D2
Lodden CI HP21 . . . . 115 D3
Loddon Dr SL6 . . . . 202 D8
Loddon Rd SL8 . . . . 185 A4
Loddon Spur SL1 . . . . 205 E7
Lodge CI
Cheddington LU7 . . . . 105 A7
Marlow SL7 . . . . 183 E1
Padbury MK18 . . . . 53 C2
Slough SL1 . . . . 205 C4
Uxbridge UB8 . . . . 201 C1
Lodge Farm Bsns Ctr
MK19 . . . . 20 C3
Lodge Farm CI HP22 . . . . 116 E2
Lodge Farm Ct MK19 . . . . . 19 F6
Lodge Gate MK14 . . . . 34 E7
Lodge La
Little Chalfont HP8 . . . . . . 166 F6
Prestwood HP16 . . . . 151 D5
Stoke Hammond MK17 . . . . 69 E7
Lodge Park The MK16 . . . . 22 C4
Lodge Rd MK43 . . . . 37 F8
Lodge The
Aylesbury HP19 . . . . 115 A4
Slough SL1 . . . . 206 B8
Lodge Way SL4 . . . . 209 E4
Lodgings of the Military
Knights 4 SL4 . . . . 210 D6
Lodore Gn UB10 . . . . 190 E1
Logan Rock MK4 . . . . 57 B8
Lollards CI HP6 . . . . 154 C2
Lombardy Dr HP4 . . . . 135 D3
Lomond Dr
Leighton Buzzard LU7 . . . . 80 C7
Milton Keynes MK2 . . . . . . 58 D4
London End
Beaconsfield HP9 . . . . 175 F1
Newton Longville MK17 . . . 57 D4
Woburn MK17 . . . . 60 F6
London End La MK17 . . . . 48 D1
London Ho MK11 . . . . 32 D5
London Rd
Aston Clinton HP22 . . . . . 117 E4
Beaconsfield HP9 . . . . 187 B8
Berkhamsted HP4 . . . . 135 E3
Buckingham MK18 . . . . 52 E6
Chalfont St Giles HP8 . . . . 177 C7
Datchet SL3 . . . . 211 C7
Felden HP3 . . . . 146 F8
High Wycombe HP11 . . . . . 173 E5
Little Kingshill HP16 . . . . . 152 B5
Loughton MK5 . . . . 46 B7
Milton Common OX9 . . . . . 136 B3
Milton Keynes MK16 . . . . . 36 B5
Milton Keynes, Stony Stratford
MK11 . . . . 32 E4
Newport Pagnell MK16 . . . . 22 F3
Old Stratford MK19 . . . . . . 32 C7
Slough, Brands Hill SL3 . . . 212 B8
Slough, Langley SL3 . . . . . 206 D2
Tring HP23 . . . . 119 C3
Wendover HP22 . . . . 141 D6
Wheatley OX33 . . . . 122 B1
London Road E HP7 . . . . . 165 E6
London Road W HP7 . . . . . 165 C6
Londrina Ct 9 HP4 . . . . . . 135 D4
Londrina Terr 10 HP4 . . . . 135 D4
Long Acre HP15 . . . . 163 C7
Long Ayres MK7 . . . . 48 A3
Longbarn MK43 . . . . 25 C2
Longbottom La HP9 . . . . . . 176 C3
Longbourn SL4 . . . . 210 A4
Longbridge CI HP23 . . . . . 119 A6
Longbridge Way UB8 . . . . 201 B3
Long CI SL7 . . . . 198 B5
Long Close Sch SL3 . . . . . 206 A2
LONG CRENDON 125 B6
Long Crendon Courthouse★
HP18 . . . . 125 B7
Long Crendon Ind Est
HP18 . . . . 125 E5
Long Crendon Rd HP18 . . 124 D3
Long Crendon Sch HP18 . 125 C7
Longcroft HP22 . . . . 117 F5
Longcroft Ave HP22 . . . . . 131 D6
Longcroft La
Bovingdon HP3 . . . . 146 D5
Paulerspury NN12 . . . . 17 C8
Long Croft Rd WD3 . . . . . . 178 D5
Longcross MK15 . . . . 35 A6
Longdown Hill HP27 . . . . . 139 F5

Longdown Mews HP19 . . . 114 F8
Long Dr SL1 . . . . 197 C2
Longfellow Dr MK16 . . . . . 22 A4
Longfield
Hedgerley SL2 . . . . 187 D1
Little Kingshill HP16 . . . . . 152 B4
Longfield Dr HP6 . . . . 154 B1
Longfield Gdns HP23 . . . . 118 E3
Longfield Rd
Chesham HP5 . . . . 143 F2
Tring HP23 . . . . 118 F3
LONGFORD 213 C6
LONGFORDMOOR 213 A6
Longford Rdbt UB7 . . . . . . 213 B6
Long Furlong
Haddenham HP17 . . . . 126 F6
Stone HP17 . . . . 114 B5
Long Furlong Dr SL2 . . . . 197 E1
Long Gr HP9 . . . . 176 C4
Long Hale LU7 . . . . 105 C3
Longhedge MK7 . . . . 48 A2
Long Hedge LU7 . . . . 105 C4
Long Hide HP27 . . . . 139 C4
Longhorn Dr MK8 . . . . 45 D7
Long La
Bovingdon HP3 . . . . 155 F8
Cookham Rise SL6 . . . . . . 195 D5
Heronsgate WD3 . . . . 167 D2
Olney MK46 . . . . 6 F4
Rickmansworth WD3 . . . . . 167 F1
Stanwell TW19 . . . . 213 F1
Longland Rd 3 MK18 . . . . 41 E3
Longlands Ct MK18 . . . . . . 66 A5
Longlands Wlk MK18 . . . . . 66 A5
Longland Way HP12 . . . . . 172 D5
Longleat Ct 7 MK8 . . . . . . 33 F1
Longleat Gdns SL6 . . . . . . 202 D6
Longlees WD3 . . . . 178 D5
Long Ley LU7 . . . . 105 A7
Long Leys HP15 . . . . 148 A8
Long Lional HP20 . . . . 115 D8
LONG MARSTON 104 B3
Long Marston CE Prim Sch
HP23 . . . . 104 B4
Long Marston Rd
Cheddington LU7 . . . . 104 E7
Marsworth LU7 . . . . 104 F2
Long Massey MK46 . . . . 6 C5
Long Mdw
Aylesbury HP21 . . . . 116 B6
Chesham HP5 . . . . 144 C3
Long Meadow CI
Amersham HP7 . . . . 164 C3
Monks Risborough HP27 . . 139 C5
Long Meadow Sch MK5 . . 45 F3
Longmead SL4 . . . . 209 E6
Longmead La SL1 . . . . 197 D5
Long Orchard HP10 . . . . . 174 C8
Long Park CI HP6 . . . . 154 C3
Long Park Way HP6 . . . . . 154 C3
Longpeak CI MK4 . . . . 46 B1
Long Pk HP6 . . . . 154 C3
Long Plough HP22 . . . . . . 117 D5
Long Readings La SL2 . . . 198 B2
Long Ride HP27 . . . . 139 C3
Longridge (Activity Ctr)★
SL7 . . . . 194 F8
Long Row
Leckhampstead MK18 . . . . 30 E1
Prestwood HP16 . . . . 151 D6
Longstone Rd SL0 . . . . . . 200 C4
LONG STREET 10 F4
Longview HP9 . . . . 185 F8
Long View HP4 . . . . 135 A6
Longville MK12 . . . . 33 B7
Long Walk The★ SL4 . . . . 210 D4
Long Wall HP17 . . . . 126 F5
LONGWICK 138 D7
Longwick CE Comb Sch
HP27 . . . . 138 D6
Longwick Rd
Longwick HP27 . . . . 138 F6
Monks Risborough HP27 . . 139 A5
Long Wlk HP8 . . . . 166 E6
Longwood Ave SL3 . . . . . . 207 B1
Long Wood Dr HP9 . . . . . . 176 F4
Longwood La HP7 . . . . 165 D8
Longworth Dr SL6 . . . . 196 C1
Lonsdale MK12 . . . . 33 D7
Lonsdale CI SL6 . . . . 196 A1
Lonsdale Way SL6 . . . . . . 203 C1
Look Ahead SL1 . . . . 205 E4
Loosen Dr SL6 . . . . 202 A3
Loose Path HP19 . . . . 114 F8
Loosley Green HP21 . . . . . 115 F4
Loosley Hill HP27 . . . . 149 D6
LOOSLEY ROW 149 C6
Lord Grey Sch MK3 . . . . . 46 F1
Lord Knyvett CI TW19 . . . 213 D1
Lord Knyvetts Ct 12
TW19 . . . . 213 E1
Lord Mayors Dr SL2 . . . . . 198 A7
Lord Raglan Ho SL4 . . . . . 210 C4
Lord Reith PI HP9 . . . . 187 A8
Lords CI MK2 . . . . 47 C1
Lordsmead MK43 . . . . 25 C2
Lords Mead LU6 . . . . 92 E6
Lords Mill Ct HP5 . . . . 154 C7
Lords Terr LU6 . . . . 92 E6
Loriner PI MK14 . . . . 35 A6
Loring Rd
Berkhamsted HP4 . . . . 135 C3
Dunstable LU6 . . . . 93 F8
Windsor SL4 . . . . 209 F6

Lormay PI NN13 . . . . 39 A4
Lorne CI SL1 . . . . 205 C3
Lorraine CI HP13 . . . . 173 E8
Lorre Mews MK4 . . . . 45 E3
Loseley CI MK8 . . . . 33 F1
Losfield Rd SL4 . . . . 209 E6
Lossie Dr SL3 . . . . 207 B6
Lothersdale MK13 . . . . 34 B5
Lothian CI MK3 . . . . 46 E2
Lott Mdw HP21 . . . . 115 D3
Lott Wlk HP21 . . . . 115 D3
Louches La HP14 . . . . 161 E6
Loudhams Rd HP7 . . . . . . 166 C8
Loudhams Wood La HP8 . 166 D7
LOUDWATER 174 D2
Loudwater Comb Sch
HP11 . . . . 174 B2
Loughborough Dr 4
MK10 . . . . 36 C4
LOUGHTON 46 A8
Loughton Manor First Sch
MK5 . . . . 46 A8
Loughton Rd MK13 . . . . . . 34 A3
Loughton Rdbt MK8 . . . . . 45 F8
Loughton Sch MK5 . . . . . . 46 A7
Loughton Valley Pk★
MK5 . . . . 46 D7
Louisa Cotts 10 HP23 . . . 119 A3
Louise Wlk HP3 . . . . 146 A3
Lovat Fields Village MK15 35 C5
Lovat Meadow CI MK16 . . 22 E3
Lovat St MK16 . . . . 22 D4
Lovatt Dr MK3 . . . . 57 E8
LOVE GREEN 207 D8
Love Green La SL0 . . . . . . 207 E8
Lovegrove Dr SL2 . . . . 197 F1
Love Hill La SL3 . . . . 207 A6
Lovejoy La SL4 . . . . 209 D5
Love La SL0 . . . . 207 D7
Lovelace CI SL6 . . . . 193 F4
Lovel End SL9 . . . . 177 C1
Lovel Mead SL9 . . . . 177 C3
Lovel Rd SL9 . . . . 177 C2
Love Row MK17 . . . . 68 D6
Lovett Gdns SL6 . . . . 196 C3
Lovett Rd UB9 . . . . 190 C8
Lovetts End LU7 . . . . 78 E8
Lovibonds Ave UB7 . . . . . 208 F7
Lowbrook Acad SL6 . . . . . 202 A3
Lowbrook CI HP21 . . . . . . 116 A4
Lowbrook Dr SL6 . . . . 202 A3
Lowdell CI UB7 . . . . 208 E7
Lowdon Dr HP11 . . . . 173 D4
LOWER ASCOTT 79 F1
Lower Ash Yard MK17 . . . . 67 F8
LOWER ASSENDON 191 A6
Lower Boynton Rd SL6 . . 202 E6
Lower Britwell Rd SL2 . . . 197 D1
LOWER CADSDEN 139 E5
Lower Church St
Cuddington HP18 . . . . 112 F3
Stokenchurch HP14 . . . . . 158 E5
Lower Cippenham La
SL1 . . . . 204 F6
Lower CI HP19 . . . . 115 B7
Lower Cookham Rd SL6 . 196 C3
Lower Dr HP9 . . . . 175 D5
Lower Eighth St MK9 . . . . 34 E2
LOWER END
Long Crendon 125 B7
Marsworth 104 F3
Thornborough 53 F8
Woburn Sands 49 C8
Lower End
Ashendon HP18 . . . . 97 E1
Lower End MK18 . . . . 53 F8
Newton Longville MK17 . . . 57 C3
Piddington OX25 . . . . 95 E8
Wingrave HP22 . . . . 89 B2
Lower End Rd MK17 . . . . . 49 A8
Lower Farm CI HP18 . . . . 124 D3
Lower Farm Gate HP17 . . 114 A3
Lower Fourth St MK9 . . . . 34 D1
Lower Furney CI HP13 . . . 173 D8
Lower Gn
Cuddington HP18 . . . . 112 F3
Westcott HP18 . . . . 98 C7
Weston Turville HP22 . . . . 117 A3
Lower Green La HP18 . . . 112 C2
Lower Hammersley La
HP13 . . . . 174 B4
LOWER HARTWELL 114 E6
Lower Icknield Way
Chinnor OX39 . . . . 147 D8
Great Kimble HP17 . . . . . . 129 C1
Marsworth HP23 . . . . 105 B1
Monks Risborough HP17 . . 139 B8
Pitch Green HP27 . . . . 138 C3
Wilstone HP22, HP23 . . . . 118 C2
Lower Kings Rd HP4 . . . . . 135 C5
Lower Lees Rd SL2 . . . . . 198 B2
Lower Lodge La HP15 . . . 163 A5
Lower Mead SL0 . . . . 200 D2
Lower Mount Farm SL6 . . 195 D5
Lower Ninth St MK9 . . . . . 34 E2
LOWER NORTH DEAN . . . 150 E1
LOWER POLLICOTT 111 F7
Lower Pound La SL7 . . . . 194 D8
Lower Rd
Aylesbury HP21, HP22 . . . 115 F3
Blackthorn OX25 . . . . 81 A4
Chinnor OX39 . . . . 147 C7
Chorleywood WD3 . . . . . . 167 D5
Cookham Rise SL6 . . . . . . 195 E7
Denham UB9 . . . . 189 D4
Gerrards Cross SL9 . . . . . 188 F7
Hardwick HP22 . . . . 87 B3

Lit-Lyn 235

Lower Rd continued
Lacey Green HP27 . . . . . . 149 D6
Lower Ridge SL8 . . . . 185 B4
Lower Riding HP9 . . . . 175 D2
Lower Second St MK9 . . . 34 D1
Lower St
Pury End NN12 . . . . 17 A7
Quainton HP22 . . . . 85 A5
Lower Stonehayes MK14 . 34 F7
Lower Tenth St MK9 . . . . . 34 D1
Lower Third St MK9 . . . . . 34 D1
Lower Twelfth St MK9 . . . 34 F3
Lower Ventnor Cotts
SL6 . . . . 195 C8
LOWER WAINHILL 147 E7
Lower Ward SL4 . . . . 210 D7
Lower Way
Great Brickhill MK17 . . . . . 59 C1
Padbury MK18 . . . . 53 C2
LOWER WEALD 32 E2
Lower Weald MK19 . . . . . . 32 E2
Lower Wharf MK18 . . . . . . 41 E1
LOWER WOODEND 182 D4
Lowes CI HP14 . . . . 158 C5
Lowestoft Dr SL1 . . . . 204 D7
Lowfield CI HP15 . . . . 163 B3
Lowfield Way HP15 . . . . . 163 B3
Lowick PI 4 MK4 . . . . 46 B2
Lowland Rd MK3 . . . . 57 C8
Lowlands Cres HP15 . . . . 151 D1
Lowlands Dr TW19 . . . . . . 213 D2
Lowlands Rd TW19 . . . . . . 213 D2
Lowman Way HP21 . . . . . 115 D4
Lowndes Ave HP5 . . . . . . 144 B1
Lowndes Gr MK5 . . . . 45 F7
Lowndes Way MK18 . . . . . 66 A5
Lownes Path HP19 . . . . . . 114 F8
Loxbere Dr MK4 . . . . 46 C4
Loxboro Hill HP14 . . . . . . 160 D4
Loxley Rd HP4 . . . . 134 F6
Loxwood CI HP3 . . . . 146 F8
Loyne CI LU7 . . . . 80 C8
Lucas PI MK6 . . . . 47 D8
Lucas Rd HP13 . . . . 173 C7
Luccombe MK4 . . . . 46 D3
Lucius La MK11 . . . . 33 A3
Lucky La or Cock La
HP20 . . . . 101 D1
Lucy La MK5 . . . . 46 B8
Ludgate
Milton Keynes MK6 . . . . . . 46 E7
Tring HP23 . . . . 118 F4
LUDGERSHALL 96 D8
Ludlow CI MK3 . . . . 57 F7
Ludlow Dr OX9 . . . . 126 A1
Ludlow Ho SL6 . . . . 202 E6
Ludlow Mews HP11 . . . . . 174 A4
Ludlow PI HP20 . . . . 115 B8
Ludlow Rd SL6 . . . . 202 E6
Luff CI SL4 . . . . 209 E4
Lufford Pk MK14 . . . . 34 F8
Luggershall Rd OX25 . . . . 95 E7
Luke PI MK10 . . . . 35 F3
Luker Ave RG9 . . . . 191 D3
Lukes La HP23 . . . . 104 D3
Lukes Lea HP23 . . . . 105 A1
Lullingstone Dr MK13 . . . 33 F5
Lumber La NN12 . . . . 17 B7
Lundholme MK13 . . . . 34 B5
Lundy Ct SL1 . . . . 204 E6
Lundy Wk MK13 . . . . 58 C3
Lupin CI UB7 . . . . 208 D1
Lupin Ct HP21 . . . . 115 B5
Lupin Wlk HP21 . . . . 115 B5
Lutman La SL6 . . . . 195 F2
Lutyens Gr MK7 . . . . 48 D5
Luxborough Gr MK4 . . . . . 46 C4
Lychgate Cotts HP3 . . . . . 146 B4
Lycrome La HP5 . . . . 144 D3
Lycrome Rd HP5 . . . . 144 E3
Lydbrook La MK17 . . . . . . 49 B5
Lyde End HP27 . . . . 138 B1
Lydford Ave SL2 . . . . 205 D8
Lydiard MK8 . . . . 33 E1
Lydiard CI HP21 . . . . 116 A4
Lydsey CI SL2 . . . . 198 A2
LYE GREEN 144 E4
Lye Green Cotts HP5 . . . . 144 E3
Lye Green Rd HP5 . . . . . . 144 E2
Lyell Place E SL4 . . . . 209 C4
Lyell Place W SL4 . . . . . . 209 C4
Lyell Rd SL4 . . . . 209 C4
Lyell Walk E SL4 . . . . 209 C4
Lyell Walk W SL4 . . . . 209 C4
Lye The HP4 . . . . 121 D6
Lyme Ave HP4 . . . . 134 C7
Lynch CI UB8 . . . . 201 C5
Lynch Hill La SL2 . . . . 197 E2
Lynch Hill Sch SL2 . . . . . 197 F2
Lynch The SL1 . . . . 201 C5
Lyndhurst Ave SL6 . . . . . 195 D6
Lyndhurst CI HP13 . . . . . . 161 D1
Lyndhurst Rd HP5 . . . . . . 144 B2
Lyndon CI HP16 . . . . 151 C7
Lyndon Gdns HP15 . . . . . 173 E8
Lyndwood Dr SL4 . . . . 211 A1
Lyndwood Par SL4 . . . . . . 211 A2
Lyneham Gdns SL6 . . . . . 195 B1
Lynher CI HP21 . . . . 115 C4
Lynmouth Cres MK4 . . . . 46 D4
Lynnens View HP18 . . . . . 109 D5
Lynton Gn SL6 . . . . 202 E6
Lynton Rd HP5 . . . . 144 C3
Lynwood Ave SL3 . . . . 206 D3

Lynwood Rd HP21 . . . . . . 116 A5
Lyon Rd MK1 . . . . 47 B2
Lysander Cl HP3 . . . . . . 146 A4
Lysander Mead SL6 . . . . 203 C8

M

McArdle Way SL3 . . . . 212 D7
McAuliffe Dr SL1, SL2 . . . 197 F8
McConnell Dr MK12 . . . . 33 E6
McCorquordale Rd MK12 . 33 C7
Macdonald Cl HP6 . . . . . 154 D4
McDougall Rd **8** HP4 . . 135 D4
McEwen Ride HP22 . . . . . 117 D1
Mcindoe Dr HP22 . . . . . . 131 D6
MacIntyre Sch HP22 . . . . 89 C3
McKay Trad Est SL3 . . . . 212 E5
McKenzie Cl MK18 . . . . . 52 D8
Mackenzie Mall **8** SL1 . . 205 F4
Mackenzie St **2** SL1 . . . 205 F4
McLellan Pl HP12 . . . . . . 172 D5
McLernon Way MK18 . . . . 66 A5
Maconi Croft MK5 . . . . . . 46 C5
Madeira Mdws MK3 . . . . . 58 B4
Madeira Wlk SL4 . . . . . . 210 D6
Madeley Cl HP6 . . . . 154 D3
Madeley Rd HP21 . . . . . . 115 E6
Magdalen Cl
  Milton Keynes MK11 . . . . 32 D6
  Syresham NN13 . . . . 27 C8
Magdalen Ho MK11 . . . . . 32 D6
Magenta Cl MK2 . . . . 58 D6
Magna Pk MK17 . . . . 36 F1
Magnet L Ctr SL6 . . . . . . 203 A8
Magnolia Dene HP15 . . . . 162 F2
Magnolia Gdns SL3 . . . . . 206 C3
Magnolia St UB7 . . . . 208 D2
Magnolia Way HP10 . . . . 185 E7
Magpie Cl
  Flackwell Heath HP10 . . 174 A1
  Milton Keynes MK5 . . . . . 46 B3
Magpie La
  Coleshill HP7 . . . . 165 A1
  Flackwell Heath HP10 . . 174 A1
  Loudwater HP13 . . . . . . 174 B3
Magpie Way
  Slough SL2 . . . . 197 F1
  Winslow MK18 . . . . 66 B6
Mahler Cl MK7 . . . . 48 C5
Mahoney Ct
  High Wycombe HP11 . . . 172 F8
  Milton Keynes MK8 . . . . . 45 D6
Maida Vale **8** MK10 . . . 35 F1
MAIDENHEAD 202 F4
Maidenhead Ave MK13 . . 34 C3
MAIDENHEAD COURT . . . 196 C4
Maidenhead Court Pk
  SL6 . . . . 196 B3
Maidenhead Heritage Ctr★
  13 SL6 . . . . 202 F7
Maidenhead Rd
  Cookham Rise SL6 . . . . . 195 F6
  Windsor SL4 . . . . 209 E2
Maidenhead Ret Pk SL6 203 A6
Maidenhead Sta SL6 . . . . 202 F6
MAIDENSGROVE 179 C5
MAIDS MORETON 41 E4
Maids Moreton CE Sch
  MK18 . . . . 41 E3
Maidstone Rd MK10 . . . . 36 C2
Maigno Way **1** MK12 . . 33 A6
Main Dr
  Gerrards Cross SL9 . . . . 188 C6
  Iver SL0 . . . . 207 E3
  Potterspury NN12 . . . . . . 18 B2
Main Par WD3 . . . . 167 C5
Main Rd
  Astwood MK16 . . . . 16 B3
  Drayton Parslow MK17 . . 68 B5
  Lacey Green HP27 . . . . 149 E5
  Syresham NN13 . . . . 27 C7
  Upper Winchendon HP18 . 99 A1
  Walter's Ash HP14 . . . . 161 C7
Main Road N HP4 . . . . . . 107 A6
Main Road S HP4 . . . . . . 107 D4
Main St
  Adstock MK18 . . . . 53 F1
  Akeley MK18 . . . . 41 F8
  Ashendon HP18 . . . . 97 F1
  Beachampton MK19 . . . . 44 A6
  Buckingham MK18 . . . . . 41 F3
  Chackmore MK18 . . . . . . 41 B4
  Charndon OX27 . . . . 72 E5
  Cosgrove MK19 . . . . 19 E2
  Gawcott MK18 . . . . 51 F4
  Grendon Underwood HP18 . 83 B5
  Mursley MK17 . . . . 67 D6
  Padbury MK18 . . . . 53 B1
  Poundon OX27 . . . . 71 F7
  Preston Bissett MK18 . . . 62 B8
  Shalstone MK18 . . . . 39 E6
  Tingewick MK18 . . . . 51 B6
  Turweston NN13 . . . . 38 C8
  Twyford MK18 . . . . 62 C1
  Westbury NN13 . . . . 39 A4
  Weston Turville HP22 . . . 116 E2
Maitland Dr HP13 . . . . . . 173 B8
Maitland Rd HP22 . . . . . . 131 D7
Major's Farm Rd
  Datchet SL3 . . . . 211 E8
  Slough SL3 . . . . 212 A8
Malbons Ct MK6 . . . . 46 E7
Malborough Ho HP4 . . . . 135 A3
Malborough Way NN12 . . 18 F5

Malcolm Rd UB10 . . . . . . 201 F8
Malden Cl HP6 . . . . 154 F1
Malders La SL6 . . . . 195 C3
Maldives Terr MK3 . . . . . 58 B4
Malet Cl HP14 . . . . 158 F5
Malins Gate MK14 . . . . . . 34 E8
Malkin Dr HP9 . . . . 175 C3
Mallard Cl HP11 . . . . 101 E4
Mallard Croft HP17 . . . . 127 A7
Mallard Dr
  Buckingham MK18 . . . . . 52 E8
  Slough SL1 . . . . 204 F6
Mallard Ho HP11 . . . . . . 173 C6
Mallard Pl HP11 . . . . 174 B3
Mallets End HP22 . . . . . . 85 B4
Malletts Cl MK11 . . . . . . 32 E5
Mallow Gate MK14 . . . . . 34 E4
Mallow Pk SL6 . . . . 195 C1
Malmers Well Rd HP13 . . 173 B7
Malpas Rd SL2 . . . . 206 B6
Malthouse Flats RG9 . . 192 D6
Malthouse Sq
  Beaconsfield HP9 . . . . . 186 F8
  Princes Risborough HP27 . 139 B4
Malthouse Way **2** SL7 . 183 D1
Malting Cl MK16 . . . . 12 B6
Malting La
  Aldbury HP23 . . . . 120 D5
  Dagnall HP4 . . . . 107 C5
Maltings Cl
  Cranfield MK43 . . . . 25 A1
  Stewkley LU7 . . . . 78 E8
Maltings Field MK19 . . . . 19 F5
Maltings Row MK18 . . . . . 31 E4
Maltings The
  Chackmore MK18 . . . . . . 41 B4
  Olney MK46 . . . . 7 A3
  Tingewick MK18 . . . . 51 B6
Malt La NN13 . . . . 27 C8
Maltmans Green Sch
  SL9 . . . . 188 C8
Maltmans La SL9 . . . . . . 188 C8
Malton Ave SL1 . . . . 205 B6
Malton Cl MK10 . . . . 35 F1
Malvern Cl HP13 . . . . 172 E8
Malvern Ct SL3 . . . . 212 A7
Malvern Dr
  Leighton Buzzard LU7 . . 80 C8
  Milton Keynes MK11 . . . . 33 A4
Malvern Rd
  Aylesbury HP20 . . . . . . 116 C8
  Maidenhead SL6 . . . . . 195 D1
Malyns Cl OX39 . . . . 147 C7
Manchester Terr HP14 . . 171 B4
Mandela Ct UB8 . . . . 208 C7
Mandelyns HP4 . . . . 134 E7
Mandeville Dr MK10 . . . . 36 C2
Mandeville Mews HP21 . 115 E4
Mandeville Rd
  Aylesbury HP21 . . . . . . 115 E5
  Prestwood HP16 . . . . . . 151 B7
Mandeville Sch The
  HP21 . . . . 115 D4
Manfield Cl SL2 . . . . 198 A2
Manifold La MK4, MK5 . . . 46 B3
Manor Cl
  Berkhamsted HP4 . . . . . 135 C4
  Bledlow HP27 . . . . 138 B1
  Buckingham MK18 . . . . . 53 C2
  Cosgrove MK19 . . . . 19 E2
  Hanslope MK19 . . . . 11 A2
  Milton Keynes MK10 . . . . 35 F3
  Milton Keynes MK17 . . . . 67 D6
  Prestwood HP16 . . . . . . 151 D4
  Salford MK17 . . . . 37 D3
  Stoke Hammond MK17 . . . 69 E7
  Tylers Green HP10 . . . . 163 A2
Manor Cotts
  Chorleywood WD3 . . . . . 167 B3
  Milton Keynes MK17 . . . . 67 D6
Manor Court Yd HP13 . . . 162 A1
Manor Court Yd OX33 . . . 123 B2
Manor Cres
  Seer Green HP9 . . . . . . 176 D5
  Wendover HP22 . . . . . . 131 C5
Manor Ct
  Emberton MK46 . . . . 13 F8
  Leighton Buzzard LU7 . . 70 E2
  Marlow SL7 . . . . 183 C3
  Slough, Cippenham SL1 . 204 F5
  6 Slough, Upton Park SL1 205 F3
  Twyford MK18 . . . . 62 C1
Manor Ctyd
  Haddenham HP17 . . . . . 127 D4
  Sherington MK16 . . . . . . 13 F1
Manor Dr
  Amersham HP6 . . . . 154 B3
  Aylesbury HP20 . . . . . . 101 F2
  Haversham MK19 . . . . . . 20 E2
  Stewkley LU7 . . . . 78 E8
Manor Farm SL3 . . . . 212 E5
Manor Farm Cl
  Soulbury LU7 . . . . 69 E2
  Stone HP17 . . . . 114 C5
  Weston Turville HP22 . . . 116 E2
  Windsor SL4 . . . . 209 F4
Manor Farm Com Inf Sch
  HP15 . . . . 163 B2
Manor Farm Cotts SL4 . . 211 A2
Manor Farm Ct HP22 . . . . 87 B2
Manor Farm Ctyd HP22 . 102 D8
Manor Farm Ho SL4 . . . . 209 F4
Manor Farm La LU7 . . . . . 90 C8
Manor Farm Way HP9 . . 176 D4
Manorfields Rd MK19 . . . 32 B6
Manor Gdns
  Grendon Underwood
    HP18 . . . . 83 A6

Manor Gdns continued
  High Wycombe HP13 . . . 162 A1
  Maids Moreton MK18 . . . 41 E2
  Wooburn Green HP10 . . 185 E5
Manor Green Sch SL6 . . 202 A3
Manor Ho
  Brill HP18 . . . . 110 A8
  Hambleden RG9 . . . . . . 181 D2
Manor House Cl HP20 . . 101 F1
Manor House La SL3 . . . 211 B6
Manor La
  Gerrards Cross SL9 . . . 188 D4
  Maidenhead SL6 . . . . . 202 E4
MANOR PARK
  Aylesbury 101 E2
  Slough 198 D1
Manor Park Ave MK27 . . 139 A3
Manor Pk MK18 . . . . 41 F4
Manor Pound Rd LU7 . . . 105 A7
Manor Rd
  Akeley MK18 . . . . 41 F7
  Aylesbury HP20 . . . . . . 101 E1
  Cheddington LU7 . . . . . 104 F7
  Chesham HP5 . . . . 144 C2
  Emmington OX9 . . . . . . 137 B6
  Maidenhead SL6 . . . . . 202 E4
  Milton Keynes, Bletchley
    MK2 . . . . 58 E8
  Milton Keynes, Wolverton
    MK12 . . . . 33 B7
  Newport Pagnell MK16 . . 22 A4
  Newton Longville MK17 . 57 D3
  Oakley HP18 . . . . 109 D5
  Oving HP22 . . . . 86 C7
  Princes Risborough HP27 139 A2
  Rowsham HP22 . . . . . . 102 D8
  Seer Green HP9 . . . . . . 176 D5
  Tring HP23 . . . . 119 A5
  Tylers Green HP10 . . . . 163 A2
  Wendover HP22 . . . . . . 131 C5
  Windsor SL4 . . . . 209 E5
Manor St
  Berkhamsted HP4 . . . . . 135 D4
  Buckingham MK18 . . . . . 52 C8
Manor View HP15 . . . . . . 163 B2
Manor View Ho HP13 . . . 161 E2
Manor Way
  Chesham HP5 . . . . 144 D1
  Coleshill HP7 . . . . 164 F3
  Yardley Gobion NN12 . . . 18 E6
Manor Waye UB8 . . . . . . 201 D4
Mansard Cl **8** HP23 . . . 119 A3
Manse Cl MK11 . . . . . . 32 D6
Mansel Cl
  Cosgrove MK19 . . . . 19 E2
  Slough SL2 . . . . 206 B8
Mansell Cl
  Milton Keynes MK5 . . . . . 46 A6
  Windsor SL4 . . . . 209 E6
Manshead Ct MK11 . . . . . 32 F5
Mansion Dr HP23 . . . . . . 119 B3
Mansion Hill HP22 . . . . . 131 E8
Mansion La
  Harrold MK43 . . . . 3 F6
  Iver SL0 . . . . 207 C6
Mansion The HP4 . . . . . . 135 E6
MANTLES GN 165 A8
Manton Rd SL3 . . . . 207 A3
Maple Ave UB7 . . . . 208 F5
Maple Cl
  Hazelmere HP15 . . . . . . 163 A3
  High Wycombe HP12 . . . 172 C5
  Maidenhead SL6 . . . . . 202 C5
Maple Cres SL2 . . . . 206 B6
MAPLE CROSS 178 D6
Maple Cross JMI Sch
  WD3 . . . . 178 E5
Maple Ct
  Gerrards Cross SL9 . . . 188 F6
  Marlow SL7 . . . . 183 E3
  Windsor SL4 . . . . 210 C4
Mapledean MK3 . . . . 33 E4
Mapledurham MK7 . . . . . 48 B3
Mapledurham Wlk SL6 . . 195 E3
Maple End HP22 . . . . 116 C4
Maplefield La HP8 . . . . . 166 B6
Maple Gr
  Milton Keynes MK2 . . . . . 58 E8
  Wooburn Sands MK17 . . . 49 B4
Maple Leys MK18 . . . . . . 63 E3
Maple Lodge Cl WD3 . . . 178 E6
Maple Pl UB7 . . . . 208 F5
Maple Rise SL7 . . . . 183 E3
Maples The
  5 Bourne End SL8 . . . 185 B3
  Wendover HP22 . . . . . . 131 C5
Maplewood Gdns HP9 . . 175 B1
Maplewood Sch HP13 . . . 161 D3
Maplin Pk SL3 . . . . 207 B4
Mapperton Cl **3** MK4 . . 45 F1
Mapridge Green La
  HP16 . . . . 141 D1
Marand Ct HP21 . . . . 115 F8
Mara Pl MK9 . . . . 35 A3
Marbeck Cl SL4 . . . . 209 D6
Marcellus Wy MK11 . . . . 33 A3
Marchant Ct SL7 . . . . . . 184 A3
March Edge MK18 . . . . . . 41 E1
Marches The SL4 . . . . . . 205 D2
March Mdw MK7 . . . . 48 D7
March Pl HP19 . . . . 115 B8
Marcia Ct SL1 . . . . 204 F5
Marcourt Rd HP14 . . . . . 158 F3
Mardle Rd LU7 . . . . 80 E6
Maree Cl
  Leighton Buzzard LU7 . . 80 C7
  Milton Keynes MK2 . . . . . 58 C5
Marefield Rd SL7 . . . . . . 183 D2

Mare Leys MK18 . . . . 52 F8
Marescroft Rd SL2 . . . . . 197 E1
Margam Cres MK16 . . . . . 36 A1
Margaret Ct HP13 . . . . . 173 E5
Margaret Powell Sq MK9 . 34 F3
Margaret Smythe Ho
  SL9 . . . . 188 F5
Margarita Gdns MK17 . . . 58 B2
Marie Cl OX27 . . . . 71 F7
Marigold Pl MK14 . . . . . . 34 E4
Marigold Wlk HP15 . . . . . 162 F6
Marina Dr
  Dunstable LU6 . . . . 93 E7
  Milton Keynes MK12 . . . . 33 D6
Marina Rdbt MK6 . . . . . . 47 C7
Marina Way
  Iver SL0 . . . . 208 A6
  Slough SL1 . . . . 204 D6
Marine Ct MK6 . . . . 46 F6
Marish Ct SL3 . . . . 207 A3
Marish La UB9 . . . . 189 D7
Marish Prim Sch SL3 . . . 207 A3
Marish Wharf Ind Est
  SL3 . . . . 206 E4
Maritime Wy MK16 . . . . . 36 B5
Marjoram Pl MK14 . . . . . 34 E4
Mark Dr SL9 . . . . 177 E6
Markenfield Pl MK4 . . . . 45 E1
Market Hill
  Buckingham MK18 . . . . . 41 D1
  Milton Keynes MK6 . . . . . 47 B8
  Whitchurch HP22 . . . . . . 86 F6
Market Ho **5** SL9 . . . . . 177 D2
Market La SL3 . . . . 207 C3
Market Par HP15 . . . . . . 163 A4
Market Pl
  Chalfont St Peter SL9 . . 177 D2
  Colnbrook SL3 . . . . 212 C7
  Henley-on-Thames RG9 . 191 D2
  4 Olney MK46 . . . . 6 F3
  Woburn MK17 . . . . 60 F7
Market Place Mews **5**
  RG9 . . . . 191 D2
Market Sq
  Amersham HP7 . . . . 165 B7
  Aylesbury HP20 . . . . . . 115 D8
  5 Buckingham MK18 . . 41 D1
  Chesham HP5 . . . . 154 B8
  Hanslope MK19 . . . . 11 A2
  Marlow SL7 . . . . 183 D2
  Milton Keynes MK11 . . . . 32 D5
  Princes Risborough HP27 139 B3
  Uxbridge UB8 . . . . 201 C5
  Winslow MK18 . . . . 65 F4
Market St
  19 Aylesbury HP20 . . . 115 D8
  Maidenhead SL6 . . . . . 202 F7
  9 Windsor SL4 . . . . . 210 D6
Markham Cl HP19 . . . . . . 115 A7
Markhams Cl MK18 . . . . . 52 D8
Marks Orch MK18 . . . . . . 75 F7
Marlborough Cl SL6 . . . . 202 A6
Marlborough Ct SL1 . . . . 204 E7
Marlborough Gate MK9 . . 34 F3
Marlborough Ho 5 SL6 . 202 F6
Marlborough Rd
  Aylesbury HP21 . . . . . . 115 E4
  Maidenhead SL6 . . . . . 202 A6
  Slough SL3 . . . . 206 D2
Marlborough St
  Milton Keynes, Neath Hill
    MK14 . . . . 34 E6
  Milton Keynes, Tinkers Bridge
    MK6 . . . . 47 D6
Marlborough Trad Est
  HP11 . . . . 172 F7
Marley Dr MK8 . . . . 45 E7
Marlin Cl HP4 . . . . 134 F5
Marlin Copse HP4 . . . . . 135 A3
Marlin Ct SL7 . . . . 183 D1
Marlin Hill HP23 . . . . . . 133 A8
Marlins Cl WD3 . . . . 167 E7
Marlins End HP4 . . . . . . 134 F3
MARLOW 183 B2
MARLOW BOTTOM 183 C6
Marlow Bottom SL7 . . . . 183 D6
Marlow Bridge La SL7 . . 194 E8
Marlow CE Inf Sch SL7 . . 183 D3
Marlow Com Hospl SL7 . 183 E2
Marlow Comm SL7 . . . . . 182 F3
MARLOW COMMON 182 F3
Marlow Dr MK16 . . . . 22 A4
Marlow Hill HP11 . . . . . . 173 A5
Marlow Ho **1** SL7 . . . . . 183 E1
Marlow Language Ctr The
  SL7 . . . . 183 D2
Marlow Lodge **18** SL6 . . 202 F6
Marlow Mill SL7 . . . . 183 E1
Marlow Rd
  Bisham SL7 . . . . 194 E7
  Henley-on-Thames RG9 . 191 E3
  High Wycombe HP11 . . . 172 E4
  Lane End HP14, SL7 . . . 171 E2
  Little Marlow SL7 . . . . . 184 C5
  Maidenhead, Furze Platt
    SL6 . . . . 194 E4
  Maidenhead SL6 . . . . . 202 F7
  Stokenchurch HP14 . . . . 170 B6
Marlow Sta SL7 . . . . 183 F2
Marquess Dr **3** MK3 . . . 58 D8
Marquis Ct SL1 . . . . 204 F5
Marram Cl MK6 . . . . 47 A5
Marriotts Ave HP16 . . . . 142 E1
Marriott's Cl HP17 . . . . . 126 F6
Marriott's Way HP17 . . . 126 F6
Marriott Terr WD3 . . . . . 167 F5
Marrod's Bottom HP7 . . . 175 C8

Marron La MK12 . . . . 33 C5
Marroway HP22 . . . . 116 D2
MARSH 129 C7
Marshall Court Ind Pk
  MK1 . . . . 47 B1
Marshalls La MK15 . . . . . 35 C2
Marshalls Lea HP22 . . . . 102 C3
Marsham Cl HP21 . . . . . . 116 A4
Marsham La SL9 . . . . . . 188 F6
Marsham Lodge SL9 . . . 188 E5
Marsham Way SL9 . . . . . 188 F5
Marshaw Pl **3** MK4 . . . . 46 C2
Marshcroft La HP23 . . . . 119 D6
Marsh Ct HP11 . . . . 173 F4
Marsh Dr MK14 . . . . 21 E1
Marsh End Rd MK16 . . . . 22 D3
Marshfield SL3 . . . . 211 C6
Marshgate Trad Est SL6 . 204 A7
MARSH GIBBON 71 F3
Marsh Gibbon CE Sch
  OX27 . . . . 71 F3
Marsh Gibbon Rd HP18 . 82 E8
Marsh Inf Sch HP11 . . . . 173 F4
Marsh La
  Stoke Mandeville HP22 . 129 F8
  Taplow SL6 . . . . 203 E6
Marshment Cl HP22 . . . . 117 D5
Marsh Rd
  Great Kimble HP22 . . . . 129 D4
  Shabbington HP18 . . . . 124 D3
Marshworth MK6 . . . . . . 47 D6
Marston Cl HP5 . . . . 144 A4
Marston Ct HP23 . . . . . . 104 B4
Marstonfields Rd MK18 . 76 B2
Marston Gate HP22 . . . . 102 B1
Marston Hill
  Cranfield MK43 . . . . 25 F2
  Oving HP22 . . . . 86 C8
Marston Rd
  Granborough MK18 . . . . 75 F6
  Thame OX9 . . . . 126 A1
MARSWORTH 105 A4
Marsworth CE Inf Sch
  HP23 . . . . 105 A2
Marsworth Rd LU7 . . . . . 105 D4
Marsworth Reservoir★
  HP23 . . . . 119 A8
Marsworth Wharf HP23 . 104 F1
Martell Cl MK7 . . . . 48 C3
Martin Cl
  Buckingham MK18 . . . . . 52 F7
  Milton Keynes MK14 . . . . 34 E6
  Uxbridge UB10 . . . . 201 E3
  Windsor SL4 . . . . 209 D6
Martin Dalby Wy
  Aylesbury HP18 . . . . . . 100 F5
  Aylesbury HP19 . . . . . . 101 B5
Martindale SL0 . . . . 200 D1
Martin Dell Cotts HP16 . 142 E4
Martingale Pl MK14 . . . . 34 F5
Martinique Mdws MK17 . 58 B2
Martin Rd
  Maidenhead SL6 . . . . . 202 F8
  Slough SL1 . . . . 205 E3
Martins Dr The LU7 . . . . 80 F8
Martinsend La HP16 . . . . 151 E7
Martin's Plain SL2 . . . . . 198 F3
Martlet The MK6 . . . . 47 C4
Marunden Gn SL2 . . . . . 197 F2
Marwood Cl MK4 . . . . . . 46 D3
Mary Bassett Lower Sch The
  LU7 . . . . 80 F7
Mary Cross Cl HP23 . . . . 119 D1
Marygold Wlk HP6 . . . . . 166 C8
Maryland ML17 . . . . 60 E6
Maryland Rd MK15 . . . . . 35 B8
Mary MacManus Dr MK18 41 D1
Mary Morgan Ct SL2 . . . 205 D8
Maryot Cl MK16 . . . . 13 F2
Mary Rose MK16 . . . . 36 B5
Maryside SL3 . . . . 206 E4
Marys Mead HP15 . . . . . 163 A5
Mary Towerton Sch The
  HP14 . . . . 159 D3
Mascoll Path SL2 . . . . . . 197 F2
Masefield Cl
  Chesham HP5 . . . . 144 B3
  Newport Pagnell MK16 . . 22 A4
Masefield Gr MK3 . . . . . . 58 A7
Maslin Dr MK6 . . . . 47 B5
Mason MK14 . . . . 34 C8
Masons Cl
  Milton Keynes MK16 . . . 151 C5
  Milton Keynes HP5 . . . . 144 C1
Mason's Ct
  Aylesbury HP19 . . . . . . 115 B7
  Slough SL1 . . . . 204 E6
Masons Rd SL1 . . . . 204 E6
Masons Yd HP4 . . . . 135 D4
Massie Cl MK15 . . . . 35 B6
Mathecombe Rd **2** SL1 . 205 A4
Mathesen Rd MK13 . . . . 34 A6
Mathisen Way SL3 . . . . . 212 E6
Matilda Gdns MK5 . . . . . 46 B5
Matlock Rd HP20 . . . . . . 101 F2
Matson Dr RG9 . . . . 191 F2
Matthau La MK4 . . . . 45 D3
Matthew Ct MK5 . . . . 46 B6
Matthews Cl **12** HP20 . . 101 F2
Maude Cl HP9 . . . . 176 A1
Maude Rd HP9 . . . . 176 A1
Maud Jane's Cl LU7 . . . . 105 E5
Maudslay Cl MK5 . . . . . . 46 C6
Maudsley Ho SL6 . . . . . . 203 A7
Mauduit Cl MK19 . . . . . . 11 A3
Maulden Gdns MK14 . . . 35 A8
Maulden Cl MK19 . . . . . . 11 A3
Mauretania Wy MK10 . . . 36 D3
Maurice Mount HP15 . . . 162 F5

Mavoncliff Dr MK4 . . . . . . 57 A8
Maxham MK5 . . . . 46 A3
Maxwell Ct SL1 . . . . 197 C1
Maxwell Dr HP15 . . . . 163 B5
Maxwell Pl HP9 . . . . 175 E3
Maxwell Rd
  Beaconsfield HP9 . . . . . . 175 E3
  West Drayton UB7 . . . . . 208 F2
Maybach Ct MK5 . . . . 46 B5
Maybrook Gdns HP13 . . . 173 C8
Maybury Cl SL1 . . . . 204 D7
Maybush Gdns HP16 . . . . 151 C6
Maybush Wlk MK46 . . . . 6 E5
May Cl LU6 . . . . 92 E6
Mayditch Pl MK13 . . . . 34 C3
Mayer Gdns MK5 . . . . 46 C5
Mayfield Dr SL4 . . . . 210 A4
Mayfield Rd HP10 . . . . . . 185 E6
Mayflower Cl HP17 . . . . . 114 F5
Mayflower St MK18 . . . . . . 52 F6
Mayflower Way
  Beaconsfield HP9 . . . . . . 186 A8
  Farnham Common SL2 . . 198 C8
Maygoods Cl UB8 . . . . . . 208 D8
Maygoods Gn UB8 . . . . . . 208 D8
Maygoods La UB8 . . . . . . 208 D8
Maygoods View UB8 . . . . 208 C8
Mayhall Farm HP6 . . . . . . 154 A4
Mayhall La HP6 . . . . 154 E4
Mayhew Cres HP13 . . . . . 173 D8
Maylands Dr UB8 . . . . 201 D6
Maynard Cl MK13 . . . . 34 A3
Maynard Ct SL1 . . . . 210 A6
Mayorfield Ho 1 SL7 . . . 183 D2
Maypole Rd SL6 . . . . 204 A8
Maypool Way 1 MK10 . . . 36 B2
May Rd MK43 . . . . .8 E6
Mays Way NN12 . . . . 18 D3
May Tree Cl SL7 . . . . 183 C6
Mdw Dr HP3 . . . . 145 F3
Mead Acre HP27 . . . . 139 B5
Mead Ave SL3 . . . . 207 B4
Mead Cl
  Denham UB9 . . . . 190 A2
  7 Marlow SL7 . . . . 183 F3
  Monks Risborough HP27 . 139 B6
  Slough SL3 . . . . 207 B4
Mead Cres MK14 . . . . 21 F3
Meades La HP5 . . . . 154 B7
Meadfield Ave SL3 . . . . . 207 A3
Meadfield Rd SL3 . . . . . . 207 B3
Mead Haze SL6 . . . . 196 C2
Mead Ho SL0 . . . . 200 D2
MEADLE 139 B8
Meadoway
  Steeple Claydon MK18 . . . 63 E3
  Stone HP17 . . . . 114 F5
Meadow Bank 6 SL8 . . . 185 B3
Meadowbank Cl
  Bovingdon HP3 . . . . 146 B3
  Long Crendon HP18 . . . . 125 C2
Meadow Bank Cl HP7 . . . 154 E1
Meadowbrook HP3 . . . . . 119 B6
Meadowbrook Cl SL3 . . . 212 E5
Meadow Cl
  Aylesbury HP20 . . . . 102 A1
  Chesham HP5 . . . . 144 A4
  Cublington LU7 . . . . 78 C1
  High Wycombe HP11 . . . 173 F4
  Marlow SL7 . . . . 183 F1
  Oakley HP18 . . . . 109 A4
  Old Windsor SL4 . . . . . . 211 B2
  Tring HP23 . . . . 119 A4
Meadowcott La HP7 . . . . 164 F3
Meadow Cotts
  Beaconsfield HP9 . . . . . . 175 E1
  Little Kingshill HP16 . . . 152 B3
  Stone HP17 . . . . 114 D3
Meadowcroft
  Aylesbury HP19 . . . . 101 B3
  Berkhamsted HP4 . . . . . 134 D7
  Chalfont St Peter SL9 . . 177 D1
Meadow Ct MK46 . . . . 5 D2
Meadow Dr
  Amersham HP6 . . . . 154 E2
  Longwick HP27 . . . . 138 D6
Meadow Farm Rd MK43 . . 16 F1
Meadow Gate
  Padbury MK18 . . . . 53 B2
  Prestwood HP16 . . . . . . 151 C1
Meadow Gdns MK18 . . . . . 52 E6
Meadow High Sch UB8 . . 208 E8
Meadow La
  Beaconsfield HP9 . . . . . . 175 F2
  Eton SL4 . . . . 210 C7
  Long Crendon HP18 . . . . 125 E4
  Milton Keynes MK10 . . . . 36 A3
  Pitstone LU7 . . . . 105 E3
  South Heath HP16 . . . . . 152 E8
Meadowlea Cl UB7 . . . . . 213 D8
Meadow Pk HP22 . . . . . . 116 C2
Meadow Rd
  Berkhamsted HP4 . . . . . 135 B6
  Chinnor OX39 . . . . 147 D6
  Henley-on-Thames RG9 . 191 E4
  Slough SL3 . . . . 206 F3
Meadow Rise HP27 . . . . . 149 E5
Meadow Row MK18 . . . . . . 41 D1
Meadow Sh Ctr 4 MK18 . 41 D1
Meadowside HP7 . . . . . . 176 F4
Meadows Sch The HP10 . 185 B8
Meadows The
  1 Amersham HP7 . . . . . 154 E1
  Flackwell Heath HP10 . . 185 B8
  Old Stratford MK19 . . . . . 32 B6
  Whitchurch HP22 . . . . . . 86 F7
Meadowsweet MK7 . . . . . . 48 B5
Meadowview TW19 . . . . . 212 A2

Meadow View
  Aspley Guise MK17 . . . . . 49 D6
  Chalfont St Giles HP8 . . 177 A7
  2 Little Chalfont HP6 . . 166 A8
  Long Crendon HP18 . . . . 125 E4
  Marlow Bottom SL7 . . . . 183 E6
  Potterspury NN12 . . . . . . 18 D3
  Slough SL3 . . . . 206 F5
  Stanwell TW19 . . . . 213 A2
  Uxbridge UB8 . . . . 208 C8
Meadow Way
  Aylesbury HP20 . . . . 102 A1
  Dorney SL6 . . . . 203 F4
  Felden HP3 . . . . 146 F7
  Hyde Heath HP6 . . . . . . 153 C4
  Old Windsor SL4 . . . . . . 211 B1
  1 Thame OX9 . . . . 125 F1
  Wing LU7 . . . . 79 E3
Meadow Wlk
  Bourne End SL8 . . . . . . 185 A5
  Buckingham MK18 . . . . . 41 D1
  Tylers Green HP10 . . . . . 163 C1
Mead Pk HP15 . . . . 163 C7
Mead Platt HP14 . . . . 158 D5
Mead Rd UB8 . . . . 201 D5
Meads Cl MK13 . . . . 34 B8
Mead St HP13 . . . . 174 A4
Meads The
  Berkhamsted HP4 . . . . . 134 F6
  Eaton Bray LU6 . . . . 92 E5
  Stoke Poges SL2 . . . . . . 199 A2
  Tring HP23 . . . . 119 B4
  Uxbridge UB8 . . . . 201 E1
  4 Windsor SL4 . . . . 210 A5
Mead The
  Beaconsfield HP9 . . . . . . 175 E2
  Soulbury LU7 . . . . 69 C2
Meadway
  Berkhamsted HP4 . . . . . 135 E5
  Buckingham MK18 . . . . . 52 D6
  Dunstable LU6 . . . . 93 F7
  Oving HP22 . . . . 76 E1
Mead Way
  High Wycombe HP11 . . . 173 F4
  Slough SL1 . . . . 204 D8
Meadway Ct LU6 . . . . 93 F7
Meadway Pk SL9 . . . . 188 D3
Meadway The MK5 . . . . . . 46 A7
Mead Wlk SL3 . . . . 207 B4
Meare Estate HP10 . . . . . 185 E8
Meavy Cl HP13 . . . . 174 B3
Medale Rd MK4 . . . . 47 B5
Medallion Pl SL6 . . . . 203 B7
MEDBOURNE 45 E5
Medbourne Rdbt MK8 . . . . 45 E6
Medeswell MK4 . . . . 46 E3
Medhurst MK8 . . . . 33 E2
Medland MK6 . . . . 47 D7
Medley Cl HP14 . . . . 92 F5
Medman Cl UB8 . . . . 201 C3
MEDMENHAM 193 A5
Medway Cl MK16 . . . . 22 E3
Medway St MK43 . . . . 37 D8
Meeting Oak La MK18 . . . . 66 B5
Megdale Pl HP20 . . . . 101 D2
Melbourne Ave SL1 . . . . . 205 C7
Melbourne Cl HP21 . . . . . 115 E5
Melbourne Rd HP13 . . . . 173 F6
Melbourne Terr MK13 . . . . 34 A7
Melford Dr HP19 . . . . 101 C3
Melfort Dr
  Leighton Buzzard LU7 . . . 80 B6
  Milton Keynes MK2 . . . . . 58 D4
Melick Rd MK6 . . . . 47 B4
Melissa Ct HP13 . . . . 173 D6
Mellish Ct MK3 . . . . 47 A2
Mellstock Rd HP21 . . . . . 115 F5
Melrose Ave MK3 . . . . 47 A3
Melrose Ct HP13 . . . . 162 B1
Melrose Wlk HP21 . . . . . . 115 F5
Melton MK14 . . . . 34 C8
Melton Ct
  Dunstable LU6 . . . . 93 F7
  Maidenhead SL6 . . . . . . 202 F6
Mendelssohn Gr MK7 . . . . 48 C4
Mendip Cl SL3 . . . . 207 A1
Mendip St HP18 . . . . 100 D5
Mendip Way HP13 . . . . . . 172 F8
Mendy St HP11 . . . . 173 A7
Menmarsh Rd HP18 . . . . . 123 E6
Menteith Cl MK2 . . . . 58 C5
MENTMORE 90 D4
Mentmore Cl HP12 . . . . . 172 B6
Mentmore Cross Rds LU7 . 89 F6
Mentmore Ct
  Mentmore LU7 . . . . 90 D5
  2 Milton Keynes MK8 . . . 45 F8
Mentmore Gdns LU7 . . . . 80 E5
Mentmore Gn HP21 . . . . . 115 E3
Mentmore Rd
  Cheddington LU7 . . . . . 104 F8
  High Wycombe HP12 . . . 172 B6
  Leighton Buzzard LU7 . . . 80 E5
Mentmore Towers ★ LU7 . 90 C4
Mentmore View HP23 . . . 118 F5
Mentone Ave MK17 . . . . . . 49 D4
Menzies Ct MK5 . . . . 46 B4
Mercia Rd SL6 . . . . 202 C4
Mercury Gr MK8 . . . . 45 E7

Mercury Pk The HP10 . . . 185 E7
Merebrook Inf Sch MK4 . . 46 C3
Mere Cl SL7 . . . . 183 F2
Meredith Dr HP19 . . . . . . 100 F2
Mere La MK18 . . . . 50 E6
Mere Pk SL7 . . . . 183 F2
Mere Rd
  Finmere MK18 . . . . 50 D6
  Slough SL1 . . . . 205 F3
Meriland Ct MK2 . . . . 58 E4
Merino Green MK14 . . . . . 34 C8
Merlebank MK5 . . . . 154 C7
Merlewood Cl HP11 . . . . 173 A4
Merlewood Dr MK5 . . . . . . 45 F4
Merlin Cl SL3 . . . . 212 B8
Merlin Cl SL6 . . . . 202 B8
Merlin Ctr HP19 . . . . 101 C1
Merlin Ctr The HP12 . . . . 172 E5
Merling Croft HP4 . . . . . . 134 E7
Merlin Wlk MK6 . . . . 47 B8
Merman Rd MK4 . . . . 45 D2
Merrivale Mews UB7 . . . . 208 D5
Merrydown HP13 . . . . 161 D1
Merryfields UB8 . . . . 201 D3
Mersey Cl MK3 . . . . 46 E1
Mersey Way MK3 . . . . 46 E1
Merthen Gr MK4 . . . . 57 B8
Merton Cl
  Aylesbury HP18 . . . . . . 100 D5
  Maidenhead SL6 . . . . . . 202 C3
Merton Ct SL1 . . . . 206 A3
Merton Dr MK6 . . . . 47 A4
Merton Rd
  Princes Risborough
    HP27 . . . . 139 B2
  Slough SL1 . . . . 206 A3
Merwin Way SL4 . . . . 209 D4
Meryton Ho SL4 . . . . 210 A4
Messenger Cl HP21 . . . . . 116 A6
Metcalfe Gr MK14 . . . . 22 B2
Mews Cotts HP15 . . . . . . 162 D7
Mews Gamnel HP23 . . . . 119 B6
Mews The HP6 . . . . 154 D3
Meyers Cl SL1 . . . . 206 C4
Michael Cl SL6 . . . . 202 C5
Michaelis Rd OX9 . . . . . . 125 E1
Michaels Mews 6 HP19 . 115 A8
Michigan Dr
  Milton Keynes MK15 . . . . 35 C8
  Newport Pagnell MK15 . . 22 C1
Micholls Ave SL9 . . . . 177 E5
MICKLEFIELD 173 E6
Micklefield Rd HP13 . . . . 174 A7
Mickleton SL5 . . . . 35 A6
Midas Ind Est UB8 . . . . . 201 B3
Midbrook Cl MK14 . . . . . . 22 A2
Midcot Way HP4 . . . . 134 F6
Midcroft SL2 . . . . 198 B1
Mid Cross La SL9 . . . . . . 177 E5
Middlebrook Rd HP13 . . . 161 E1
Middle Cl HP6 . . . . 154 F2
MIDDLE CLAYDON 74 C8
Middle Cres UB9 . . . . 189 D4
Middle Dr HP9 . . . . 175 D5
MIDDLE END
  Leckhampstead 42 D8
  Totternhoe 93 A8
Middle Farm Cl OX39 . . . 147 C5
Middle Field HP22 . . . . . . 116 F3
Middlefield Ct MK18 . . . . . 41 F1
Middle Gn SL3 . . . . 206 E6
MIDDLE GREEN 206 E5
Middlegreen Rd SL3 . . . . 206 D5
Middlegreen Trad Est
  SL3 . . . . 206 D4
Middle La HP3 . . . . 146 A1
Middle Mdw HP8 . . . . 177 C7
Middle Rd
  Aylesbury HP21 . . . . 116 B7
  Berkhamsted HP4 . . . . . 135 B4
  Denham UB9 . . . . 189 D4
Middlesex Dr MK3 . . . . 46 F1
Middle Slade MK18 . . . . . . 52 D6
MIDDLETON 35 E3
Middleton MK14 . . . . 34 E7
Middleton Prim Sch
  MK10 . . . . 35 E3
Middleton Swimming Pool
  MK6 . . . . 22 E3
Middle Way OX39 . . . . . . 147 B6
Middleway The HP12 . . . . 172 C6
MIDDLE WEALD 32 E1
Middle Weald MK19 . . . . . 32 E2
Middle Wlk SL1 . . . . 197 C2
Midhurst Cl HP21 . . . . . . 116 B5
Midland Dr MK10 . . . . 36 C3
Midland Rd MK46 . . . . 7 A5
Midshires Bsns Pk HP19 . 101 A1
Midsumer Ct HP15 . . . . . 163 A3
Midsummer Arc MK9 . . . . 34 E3
Midsummer Bvd MK9 . . . . 34 E2
Midsummer Dr HP18 . . . . . 82 F6
Midsummer Pl (Sh Ctr)
  MK9 . . . . 34 E2
Midsummer Rdbt MK9 . . . 34 C1
Miersfield HP11 . . . . 172 D3
Mikern Cl MK2 . . . . 58 C8
Milburn Ave MK6 . . . . 46 E8
Milburn Dr UB7 . . . . 208 E6
Mildenhall Rd SL1 . . . . . . 205 E7
Milebush LU7 . . . . 80 C3
Milecastle MK13 . . . . 34 A5
Mile Elm SL7 . . . . 184 A3
Miles Cl
  Aylesbury HP21 . . . . 116 A7
  Milton Keynes MK14 . . . . 22 A3
Miles Ct HP22 . . . . 102 B3
Miles End HP21 . . . . 115 B6

Milesmere MK8 . . . . 33 D1
Milestone Cl HP14 . . . . . 158 E5
Milfoil Ave MK14 . . . . 34 E4
Milford Ave MK11 . . . . 32 E4
Milford Ct 4 SL1 . . . . 206 A4
Milk Hall Barns HP5 . . . . 154 F5
Milland Way MK4 . . . . 45 D3
Millards Cl MK43 . . . . 25 C2
Millards Pl MK43 . . . . 25 C2
Mill Ave UB8 . . . . 201 C3
Millbank
  Leighton Buzzard LU7 . . . 80 F8
  Marlow SL7 . . . . 183 F1
Millbank Pl HP4 . . . . 48 B8
Millboard Rd SL8 . . . . . . 185 B3
Mill Bridge Pl UB8 . . . . . 201 C3
Millbrook Cl HP12 . . . . . . 172 D8
Millbrook Comb Sch
  HP12 . . . . 172 D8
Millbrook Way SL3 . . . . . 212 E5
Mill Cl
  Buckingham MK18 . . . . . 65 F5
  Chesham HP5 . . . . 154 E5
  West Drayton UB7 . . . . . 208 D3
  Wingrave HP22 . . . . 89 A3
Mill Cnr HP18 . . . . 83 A8
Mill Cotts HP10 . . . . 185 D4
Mill Ct
  Horton SL3 . . . . 212 C3
  Milton Keynes MK12 . . . . 33 A5
  Waddesdon HP18 . . . . . . 99 A7
  West Drayton UB7 . . . . . 208 D3
Milldun Way HP12 . . . . . . 172 D6
MILL END
  Henley-on-Thames 192 D7
  Little Missenden 153 A3
  Rickmansworth 167 F1
Mill End Cl
  Edlesborough LU6 . . . . . 92 F4
  Prestwood HP16 . . . . . . 151 B5
Mill End Rd HP12 . . . . . . 172 C8
Millennium Cl UB8 . . . . . . 201 C3
Millennium Point HP19 . . 101 A1
Miller Pl SL1 . . . . 188 D6
Millers Cl HP18 . . . . 82 F6
Miller's La SL4 . . . . 211 A1
Millers Turn OX39 . . . . . . 147 B6
Millers Way
  Aylesbury HP19 . . . . 115 A9
  Milton Keynes MK12 . . . . 33 D5
Millfield HP4 . . . . 135 C5
Millfield Ave OX27 . . . . . . 71 F3
Millfield Cl
  Cranfield MK43 . . . . 25 B2
  Marsh Gibbon OX27 . . . . 71 F3
Millfield Gdns MK14 . . . . . 21 F3
Millfields HP5 . . . . 154 C6
Millfield Wood Wildlife
  Reserve ★ HP14 . . . . . . 162 B3
Mill Gdns HP23 . . . . 119 B4
Millground Field MK18 . . . 65 E4
Millhayes MK14 . . . . 34 F8
Mill Ho
  4 Buckingham MK18 . . . 52 C8
  West Drayton UB7 . . . . . 208 D5
Millholm Rise MK6 . . . . . . 47 E5
Milliners The 1 HP20 . . . 101 E1
Millington Gate MK15 . . . 35 D7
Mill La
  Amersham HP7 . . . . 165 A8
  Aspley Guise MK17 . . . . . 49 C5
  Beaconsfield HP9 . . . . . . 175 D5
  Brackley NN13 . . . . 38 A6
  Buckingham MK18 . . . . . 52 C8
  Chalfont St Giles HP8 . . 166 B1
  Chinnor OX39 . . . . 147 B7
  Cookham SL6 . . . . 196 C7
  Gerrards Cross SL9 . . . . 188 F5
  Great Brickhill MK17 . . . . 58 F2
  Horton-cum-S OX33 . . . 108 A6
  Horton SL3 . . . . 212 C4
  Hulcote MK17 . . . . 37 C3
  Hurley SL6 . . . . 193 F4
  Milton Keynes, Bradville
    MK13 . . . . 34 A7
  Milton Keynes, Stony Stratford
    MK11 . . . . 32 C5
  Milton Keynes, Woolstone
    MK15 . . . . 35 C3
  Monks Risborough HP27 . 139 B6
  Salford MK17 . . . . 37 C3
  South Heath HP16 . . . . . 152 C7
  Stokenchurch HP14 . . . . 158 C5
  Taplow SL6 . . . . 203 C8
  Thame OX9 . . . . 126 B3
  Turvey MK43 . . . . 8 D5
  Twyford MK18 . . . . 62 C1
  Upper Arncott OX25 . . . . 94 E7
  Westbury NN13 . . . . 39 A4
  Weston Turville HP22 . . . 117 A2
  Windsor SL4 . . . . 210 A7
  Wingrave HP22 . . . . 89 C2
Mill Lane Com Prim Sch
  OX39 . . . . 147 B7
Mill Mdw HP19 . . . . 115 B8
Mill Mead HP22 . . . . 131 B5
Mill Pl SL3 . . . . 211 D5
Mill Rd
  Cranfield MK43 . . . . 25 C2
  2 Leighton Buzzard LU7 . 80 D7
  Marlow SL7 . . . . 183 E1
  Milton Keynes MK2 . . . . . 58 E4
  Milton Keynes MK19 . . . . 21 B4
  Oakley HP18 . . . . 109 D4
  Slapton LU7 . . . . 91 D7
  Stokenchurch HP14 . . . . 158 C5
  Thame OX9 . . . . 124 E1

Mav–Mis 237

Mill Rd continued
  West Drayton UB7 . . . . . 208 D3
  Whitfield NN13 . . . . 26 E3
Millshot Dr HP7 . . . . 165 D7
Millside SL8 . . . . 185 C3
Mill Sq MK12 . . . . 33 A5
Mill St
  Aylesbury HP20 . . . . 101 E1
  Berkhamsted HP4 . . . . . 135 C4
  Colnbrook SL3 . . . . 212 D7
  High Wycombe HP11 . . . 172 F7
  Newport Pagnell MK16 . . 22 D5
  Oxford OX33 . . . . 108 B1
  Slough SL2 . . . . 205 F5
Millstream HP22 . . . . 116 F2
Mill Stream HP27 . . . . . . 139 A2
Millstream La SL1 . . . . . . 204 E5
Millstream Way
  Leighton Buzzard LU7 . . . 80 F7
  Wooburn Green HP10 . . 185 E8
Mill Terr MK12 . . . . 33 A6
Mill The
  Milton Keynes MK12 . . . . 32 E7
  Tring HP23 . . . . 104 C1
  Wooburn Green HP10 . . 185 E8
Mill Tower LU6 . . . . 92 E6
Mill View Rd HP23 . . . . . 118 F4
Mill Way
  Aspley Guise MK17 . . . . . 49 D5
  Aylesbury HP20 . . . . 115 C8
  Rickmansworth WD3 . . . 167 F1
Mill West SL2 . . . . 205 F5
Milner Rd SL1 . . . . 204 A8
Milton Ave SL9 . . . . 188 D5
Milton Cl
  Henley-on-Thames RG9 . 191 D2
  Horton SL3 . . . . 212 A4
MILTON COMMON 136 B3
Milton Dr MK16 . . . . 22 E4
Milton Fields HP8 . . . . . . 177 B7
Milton Gdns HP27 . . . . . . 139 A2
Milton Gr MK3 . . . . 57 F7
MILTON KEYNES 34 D5
Milton Keynes Acad MK6 . 47 A7
Milton Keynes Arts Ctr ★
  MK14 . . . . 21 E1
Milton Keynes Central Sta
  MK9 . . . . 34 D2
Milton Keynes Coll MK6 . . 46 F7
Milton Keynes Coll
  (Bletchley Ctr) MK3 . . . 58 B8
Milton Keynes Materials
  Recycling Factory ★
  . . . . 33 C8
Milton Keynes Mus ★
  MK12 . . . . 33 D5
Milton Keynes Prep Sch
  MK3 . . . . 57 D8
Milton Keynes Theatre ★
  MK9 . . . . 34 F3
Milton Keynes Univ Hospl
  MK6 . . . . 47 B7
MILTON KEYNES
  VILLAGE 35 E2
Milton Lawns HP6 . . . . . . 154 D3
Milton Pl HP13 . . . . 162 D2
Milton Rd
  Aston Clinton HP22 . . . . 117 F5
  Aylesbury HP21 . . . . 115 F6
  Chesham HP5 . . . . 144 B2
  Milton Keynes, Broughton
    MK10 . . . . 36 B3
  Milton Keynes, Willen MK15 35 D7
  Slough SL2 . . . . 198 D1
  Walton MK7 . . . . 47 F6
Milton's Cottage (Mus) ★
  HP8 . . . . 177 B7
Milton Way UB7 . . . . 208 F2
Milverton Cl SL6 . . . . 202 B3
Milward Dr MK2 . . . . 47 E1
Mimosa Cl HP21 . . . . 115 B6
Mina Ave SL3 . . . . 206 D4
Minall Cl HP21 . . . . 119 A4
Mineral La HP5 . . . . 154 C7
Minerva Cl TW19 . . . . 213 A2
Minerva Gdns MK7 . . . . . . 48 C7
Minerva Way HP9 . . . . . . 176 A1
Mines Cl HP3 . . . . 161 D3
Ministry Wharf HP14 . . . . 149 C1
Minniecroft Rd SL1 . . . . . 197 B2
Minorca Gr MK5 . . . . 46 A4
Minshull Cl MK18 . . . . 41 D1
Minster Way SL3 . . . . 206 F4
Minstrel Ct MK13 . . . . 34 B7
Minton Cl MK14 . . . . 22 A1
Minton Rise SL6 . . . . 204 B7
Mirador Cres SL2 . . . . . . 206 B6
Mirrie La UB9 . . . . 189 C6
Misbourne Ave
  Chalfont St Peter SL9 . . 177 E5
  High Wycombe HP13 . . . 173 F6
Misbourne Cl
  Aylesbury HP21 . . . . 115 D3
  Chalfont St Peter SL9 . . 177 E5
Misbourne Ct SL3 . . . . . . 207 A2
Misbourne Dr HP16 . . . . . 152 B6
Misbourne Ho HP16 . . . . 166 C1
Misbourne Mdws UB9 . . . 189 D3
Misbourne Sch The
  HP16 . . . . 152 B6
Misbourne Vale SL9 . . . . 177 D5
Miserden Cres MK4 . . . . . 45 F1
Missenden Abbey Adult Ed
  Coll HP16 . . . . 152 B6
Missenden Cl MK18 . . . . . 65 F4

Missenden Gdns SL1 . . . . 204 B7
Missenden Rd
  Chesham HP5 . . . . 154 A7
  Ellesborough HP17 . . . . 130 C2
  Great Kingshill HP15 . . . 151 D2
  Winslow MK18 . . . . 65 F4
Miss Joans Ride HP4 . . . . 107 D7
Miswell La HP23 . . . . 118 F3
Mitcham La MK13 . . . . 34 D3
Mitcham Wlk HP19 . . . . . . 101 A2
Mitchell Cl
  Bovingdon HP3 . . . . 145 F4
  Slough SL1 . . . . 205 A4
Mitchell Rd MK43 . . . . 24 C2
Mitchell Wlk HP6 . . . . . . 154 E1
Mithras Gdns MK7 . . . . . . 48 C6
Mitre Ct MK18 . . . . 52 C7
Mitre St MK18 . . . . 52 C7
MIXBURY 38 D1
MK1 Shopping & Leisure Pk
  MK1 . . . . 47 B3
Moat Cl
  Prestwood HP16 . . . . . . 151 C6
  Wendover HP22 . . . . . . 131 B6
Moat Dr
  Prestwood HP16 . . . . . . 151 C7
  Slough SL2 . . . . 206 C8
Moat End HP22 . . . . 102 B4
Moat House The MK18 . . . 52 D8
Moat La
  Aston Abbotts HP22 . . . . 88 D4
  Marsh Gibbon OX27 . . . . 71 F2
  Prestwood HP16 . . . . . . 151 C7
  Wingrave HP22 . . . . 89 B2
Moat Pl UB9 . . . . 201 B8
Moat View HP18 . . . . 82 F8
MOBWELL 152 A8
Mobwell Terr **3** HP16 . . 152 A8
Model Row HP14 . . . . 117 F6
Moeran Cl MK7 . . . . 48 C5
Moffy Hill SL6 . . . . 195 E2
Mole Run HP13 . . . . 161 C1
Molyneaux Ave HP3 . . . . . 145 F4
Molyns Ho RG9 . . . . 191 E3
Molyns Mews SL1 . . . . . . 204 E5
Monarch St HP18 . . . . . . 100 E6
Monarch Wy **4** LU7 . . . . 80 F8
Monellan Cres MK7 . . . . . 48 A3
Monellan Gr MK7 . . . . 48 A2
Monet Pl HP19 . . . . 100 E2
Money La UB7 . . . . 208 D3
Monkey Island La SL6 . . . 203 E2
Monksfield Way SL2 . . . . 198 A2
Monks Hollow SL7 . . . . . . 183 E5
Monks Path **9** HP15 . . . 115 A8
Monks Rd SL4 . . . . 209 D5
MONKS RISBOROUGH 139 C6
Monks Risborough CE Prim
  Sch HP27 . . . . 139 D5
Monks Risborough Sta
  HP27 . . . . 139 B6
MONKSTON 36 A1
MONKSTON PARK 35 E1
Monkston Prim Sch MK10 36 B1
Monkston Rdbt MK10 . . . . 36 B2
Monks Way
  Harmondsworth UB7 . . . 213 E8
  Milton Keynes MK12, MK13,
  MK14, MK15 . . . . 34 C6
Monkswood Ct **11** SL7 . . 183 E2
Monkton La SL7 . . . . 172 F1
Monkton Way HP7 . . . . . . 150 C5
Monmouth Cl HP19 . . . . . 101 A2
Monmouth Gr MK4 . . . . . . 45 E1
Monro Ave MK8 . . . . 45 E7
Montabaur Rd NN13 . . . . . 38 A7
Montagu Dr MK6 . . . . 47 B8
Montague Cl SL2 . . . . . . 198 B3
Montague Rd
  Aylesbury HP21 . . . . . . 115 D7
  Berkhamsted HP4 . . . . . 135 B4
  Slough SL1 . . . . 205 F6
  Uxbridge UB8 . . . . 201 D5
Montagu Rd SL3 . . . . 211 B6
Montem La SL1 . . . . 205 D4
Montem L Ctr SL1 . . . . . . 205 D4
Montem Prim Sch SL1 . . . 205 B4
Montford Mews HP15 . . . 162 E2
Montgomerie Cl HP4 . . . . 135 A6
Montgomery Cres MK15 . . 35 B7
Montgomery Pl SL2 . . . . 206 C7
Montpellier Ct SL4 . . . . . 210 C5
Montrose Ave
  Datchet SL3 . . . . 211 C7
  Slough SL1 . . . . 205 B7
Montrose Dr SL6 . . . . . . 202 A6
Montrose Way SL3 . . . . . 211 C7
Montserrat Rd MK3 . . . . . 58 A3
Monument La SL9 . . . . . . 177 E5
Monycrower Dr SL6 . . . . 202 E7
Moon St MK12 . . . . 33 D6
Moonstone Ct **5** HP12 . 172 D8
Moorbridge Rd SL6 . . . . . 203 A7
MOOR COMMON 171 A2
Moorcroft La HP18 . . . . . 100 E4
Moorcroft Sch **3** UB8 . . 208 F7
Moore Cl SL1 . . . . 205 B4
MOOR END
  Eaton Bray 92 E5
  Yardley Gobion 18 D6
Moor End
  Eaton Bray LU6 . . . . 92 F5
  Frieth RG9 . . . . 171 A1
  Maidenhead SL6 . . . . . . 203 C1
Moor End Cl LU6 . . . . 92 F4

Moorend La OX9 . . . . 125 F1
Moor End La LU6 . . . . 92 F5
Moorend Rd NN12 . . . . . . 18 E6
Moore Rd HP4 . . . . 134 F6
Moores Hill MK46 . . . . 6 F5
Moores La SL4 . . . . 204 F2
Moorfield MK17 . . . . 57 D3
Moorfield Rd
  Denham Green UB9 . . . 190 A5
  Uxbridge UB8 . . . . 208 D7
Moorfield Terr SL6 . . . . . 203 B8
Moorfoot MK11 . . . . 33 A4
Moorgate 46 F7
Moorhall Rd UB9 . . . . . . 190 B6
Moorhen Ct **2** HP20 . . . 101 E3
Moorhen Way MK18 . . . . . 52 E8
Moorhills Cres LU7 . . . . . 79 F3
Moorhills Rd LU7 . . . . 79 F3
Moorings The
  2 Buckingham MK18 . . 52 C8
  Windsor SL4 . . . . 210 A7
Moor La
  Harmondsworth UB7 . . . 213 C8
  High Wycombe HP13 . . . 161 D3
  Maidenhead SL6 . . . . . 195 F1
  Sarratt WD3 . . . . 156 C3
Moorland Prim Sch MK6 . 47 B5
Moorland Rd UB7 . . . . . . 213 C8
Moorlands LU7 . . . . 79 E3
Moorlands Rd LU7 . . . . . . 79 F3
Moor Pk
  Milton Keynes MK3 . . . . 57 D8
  Wendover HP22 . . . . . . 131 B7
Moor Rd HP5 . . . . 154 C6
Moors Cl MK19 . . . . 31 E5
Moorside HP10 . . . . 185 E8
Moorside Cl SL6 . . . . 195 F1
Moorstown Ct **7** SL1 . . . 205 E4
Moor The SL7 . . . . 184 C4
MOP END 164 B7
Mop End La HP7 . . . . 164 B7
Morar Cl LU7 . . . . 80 C7
Moray Dr SL2 . . . . 206 A7
Moray Pl MK3 . . . . 46 F2
Mordaunt Cl MK43 . . . . . . 8 C6
Mordaunts Ct MK15 . . . . . 35 C2
Moreau Wlk SL3 . . . . 206 E7
More Ave HP21 . . . . 115 D7
Morebath Gr MK4 . . . . . . 46 C4
Morefields HP23 . . . . . . 119 A6
Moreland Ave SL3 . . . . . 212 C7
Moreland Cl SL3 . . . . . . 212 C7
Moreland Dr SL9 . . . . . . 188 F4
Morello Cl HP18 . . . . 100 D4
Morello Dr SL3 . . . . 206 F5
Moreton Dr MK18 . . . . . . 41 E2
Moreton La HP17 . . . . . . 115 A1
Moreton Rd MK18 . . . . . . 41 D2
Moreton Way SL1 . . . . . . 204 D5
Morgan Dr HP18 . . . . . . 100 E5
Morland Dr MK8 . . . . 45 D6
Morley Cl SL3 . . . . 206 F4
Morley Cres MK7 . . . . . . 48 D4
Morrell Cl MK5 . . . . 46 B5
Morrice Cl SL3 . . . . 207 A2
Morris Ave UB10 . . . . . . 201 E6
Morris Cl SL9 . . . . 177 F2
Morris Ct
  Aylesbury HP21 . . . . . . 115 A8
  Windsor SL4 . . . . 209 E6
Morrison Ct MK8 . . . . 45 E6
Morris Wlk MK16 . . . . 22 A4
Mortain Cl MK7 . . . . 48 B3
Mortain Dr HP4 . . . . 134 F6
Morten Gdns UB9 . . . . . 190 A4
Mortens Wood HP7 . . . . . 165 E7
Mortimer Hill HP23 . . . . 119 B4
Mortimer Rd SL3 . . . . . . 206 D3
Mortimer Rise HP23 . . . . 119 B4
Morton Cl
  North Marston MK18 . . . 76 B2
  Pitstone LU7 . . . . 105 C4
  Uxbridge UB8 . . . . 201 F1
Morton Dr SL1 . . . . 197 E8
Morton King Ct HP18 . . . 124 D3
Mortons Fork MK13 . . . . . 33 F6
Moseley Rd HP14 . . . . . . 161 C7
Moses Plat La HP27 . . . . 150 B5
Moss Ct HP9 . . . . 176 D4
Mossdale MK13 . . . . 34 B5
Mossmans Cl MK2 . . . . . . 58 D7
Mossway HP9 . . . . 175 C5
Mossy Vale SL6 . . . . 195 D1
MOULSOE 36 D8
Moundsfield Way SL1 . . . 204 E4
Mountain Ash SL7 . . . . . 183 D6
Mount Ave MK1 . . . . 47 E3
Mount Cl
  Aston Clinton HP22 . . . . 117 F4
  Farnham Common SL2 . . 198 C8
  High Wycombe HP12 . . . 172 E6
Mount Farm Ind Est MK1 . 47 D4
Mount Farm Rdbt MK1 . . . 47 D4
Mounthill Ave MK19 . . . . . 32 B7
Mount Hill La SL9 . . . . . . 188 B2
Mount La UB9 . . . . 189 D2
Mount Nugent HP5 . . . . . 144 A4
MOUNT PLEASANT
  Buckingham 52 D7
  Stoke Goldington 12 B7
Mount Pleasant
  Aspley Guise MK17 . . . . 49 F4
  Aylesbury HP19 . . . . . . 101 D1
  Lane End HP14 . . . . . . 171 B5

Mount Pleasant continued
  Milton Keynes MK6 . . . . 47 E4
  Soulbury LU7 . . . . 69 E3
  Steeple Claydon MK18 . . 63 F2
  Stoke Goldington MK16 . . 12 B7
  Stoke Hammond MK17 . . 69 E7
  Whitchurch HP22 . . . . . . 86 F7
  Yardley Gobion NN12 . . . 18 F6
Mount Pleasant Cl MK18 . 52 C7
Mount Pleasant Cotts 2
  SL8 . . . . 185 B3
Mountsfield Cl
  Newport Pagnell MK16 . . 22 C3
  Stanwell TW19 . . . . 213 A2
Mount St HP20 . . . . 115 D8
Mount The
  Aspley Guise MK17 . . . . 49 D4
  Milton Keynes MK6 . . . . 47 E4
Mount View RG9 . . . . 191 D2
Mount View Ct **4** RG9 . . 191 D2
Mount Way HP27 . . . . . . 139 A3
Mowbray Dr LU7 . . . . 80 D7
Mowbray Rd HP20 . . . . . 101 D2
Mowhills MK43 . . . . 3 F6
Mow Mead MK46 . . . . 6 F5
Moyleen Rise SL7 . . . . . . 183 C1
Mozart Cl MK7 . . . . 48 C4
Muddiford La MK4 . . . . . . 46 D4
Muirfield Dr MK3 . . . . 46 D1
Mulberry Ave SL4 . . . . . . 210 C5
Mulberry Cl
  Amersham HP7 . . . . . . 165 F8
  High Wycombe HP12 . . . 172 C5
  Tring HP23 . . . . 119 A5
Mulberry Ct HP15 . . . . . . 163 D7
Mulberry Dr SL3 . . . . . . 206 E1
Mulberry Wlk SL6 . . . . . . 202 C8
Mullen Ave MK14 . . . . . . 34 F4
Mullins Way HP19 . . . . . 100 E2
Mullion Pl MK6 . . . . 35 A1
Mull La MK17 . . . . 58 A3
Mumfords La SL9 . . . . . . 188 A7
Munces Rd SL7 . . . . 183 D6
MUNDAYDEAN
  BOTTOM 182 E5
Mundaydean La SL7 . . . . 183 B4
Munday's Farm HP21 . . . 116 B7
Mundesley Spur SL1 . . . 205 E7
MURCOTT 94 A4
Murcott Rd OX6 . . . . 94 A6
Murray Rd HP4 . . . . 135 C6
Murrey Cl MK5 . . . . 46 C5
Murrin Rd SL6 . . . . 202 C8
MURSLEY 67 D6
Mursley CE Sch MK17 . . . 67 D6
Mursley Ct MK11 . . . . 32 F5
Mursley Rd
  Little Horwood MK17 . . . . 55 E2
  Swanbourne MK17 . . . . . 67 B3
Museum Ct **6** HP23 . . . 119 A3
Musgrave Rd OX39 . . . . . 147 D7
Musgrave Wlk HP14 . . . . 158 F5
Musgrove Pl MK5 . . . . 45 F6
Mus of Eton Life The *
  SL4 . . . . 210 D8
Myddleton Ho UB8 . . . . . 201 C4
Mylne Cl HP13 . . . . 172 F1
Mynchen Cl HP9 . . . . . . 175 D6
Mynchen End HP9 . . . . . 175 D6
Mynchen Rd HP9 . . . . . . 175 D6
MYRKE 205 F2
Myrke The SL3 . . . . 205 F2
Myrtle Bank MK12 . . . . . . 33 E5
Myrtle Cl
  Poyle SL3 . . . . 212 E6
  Uxbridge UB8 . . . . 208 F3
  West Drayton UB7 . . . . 208 F3
Myrtle Cres SL2 . . . . 205 F4

N

Nag's Head La HP16 . . . . 152 A4
Nailzee Cl SL9 . . . . 188 E4
Nairdwood Cl HP16 . . . . . 151 E4
Nairdwood La HP16 . . . . . 151 D5
Nairdwood Way HP16 . . . 151 E4
Nairn Ct MK3 . . . . 46 E2
Naisby Dr MK7 . . . . 59 C1
Nalders Rd HP5 . . . . 144 D2
Nan Aires HP22 . . . . 89 A3
Nancy Hall Ct HP12 . . . . 172 D3
Nans Gdn MK17 . . . . 57 C4
NAPHILL 161 D7
Naphill Pl MK13 . . . . 34 C3
Naphill & Walters Ash Sch
  HP14 . . . . 150 B1
Napier Cl UB7 . . . . 208 F3
Napier Rd
  Aylesbury HP19 . . . . . . 114 F8
  Harmondsworth TW6 . . . 213 D6
  Maidenhead SL6 . . . . . 202 B6
Napier St MK2 . . . . 58 D8
Nappin Cl HP19 . . . . 101 A3
Nappins Cl HP18 . . . . . . 125 D5
Nap The HP18 . . . . 109 E5
Narbeth Dr HP20 . . . . . . 116 B8
Narcot La HP8 . . . . 177 B5
Narcot Rd HP8 . . . . 177 A7
Narcot Way HP8 . . . . 177 B6
Narrow La HP13 . . . . 161 E3
Narrow Path MK17 . . . . . . 49 B3
Naseby Cl
  Newport Pagnell MK16 . . 22 A3
  Thame OX9 . . . . 126 B1
Naseby Ct
  Buckingham MK18 . . . . . 41 E2
  Milton Keynes MK13 . . . . 34 B6

NASH 44 C1
Nash Cl
  Aylesbury HP21 . . . . . . 116 A4
  Berkhamsted HP4 . . . . . 135 A5
Nash Croft MK4 . . . . 57 B8
Nashdom SL1 . . . . 196 F5
Nashdom La SL1 . . . . . . 197 B6
NASH LEE 130 C5
Nash Lee End HP22 . . . . 130 F6
Nash Lee La HP22 . . . . . 130 E6
Nash Lee Rd
  Nash Lee HP17 . . . . . . 130 D6
  World's End HP22 . . . . . 130 F7
Nashleigh Hill HP5 . . . . . 144 D3
Nashleigh Ho HP5 . . . . . 144 E3
Nash Pl HP10 . . . . 163 B1
Nash Rd
  Great Horwood MK17 . . . 55 A4
  Slough SL3 . . . . 207 A2
  Thornborough MK18 . . . . 54 B8
  Whaddon MK17 . . . . 45 A1
Nashs Farm HP22 . . . . . . 88 D4
Nathanial Cl MK5 . . . . 46 B5
Nathaniel Wlk HP23 . . . . 119 A5
National Badminton Ctr
  MK8 . . . . 46 E1
National Bowl ★ MK6 . . . 46 E5
National Film & Television
  Sch HP9 . . . . 175 E1
National Mus of Computing ★
  MK3 . . . . 47 A1
Natural History Mus at
  Tring ★ HP23 . . . . 119 A3
Natwoke Cl HP9 . . . . 175 D5
Neal Cl SL9 . . . . 189 B3
Neale Ct HP12 . . . . 172 D3
Neapland MK6 . . . . 47 B5
NEARTON END 67 A3
Nearton End MK17 . . . . . . 67 A3
Near Town MK46 . . . . 7 A3
Near Town Gdns MK46 . . . 7 A3
Neath Cres MK3 . . . . 47 A2
NEATH HILL 34 F6
Neath Hill Rdbt MK15 . . . 35 A6
Needham Ct SL4 . . . . . . 209 E6
Needham Ct **4** HP11 . . 172 F7
Needlepin Wy MK18 . . . . 52 F6
Neild Way WD3 . . . . 167 F2
Neilson Cl MK7 . . . . 48 C5
Nelson Cl
  High Wycombe HP13 . . . 173 F5
  Milton Keynes MK8 . . . . 45 E6
  Slough SL3 . . . . 206 D2
  Winchmore Hill HP7 . . . 164 C3
Nelson Ct SL6 . . . . 52 C8
Nelson Rd
  Dagnall HP4 . . . . 107 C5
  Harmondsworth TW6 . . . 213 F6
  Windsor SL4 . . . . 209 F4
Nelson St MK18 . . . . 52 C8
Nelson Terr HP20 . . . . . 115 D8
Nene Cl
  Aylesbury HP21 . . . . . . 115 C4
  Newport Pagnell MK16 . . 22 D3
Nene Dr MK3 . . . . 57 E8
Neptune Way SL1 . . . . . 204 E4
Ness Way MK2 . . . . 58 D5
Netherby Cl HP23 . . . . . 119 C6
Nether Cl HP13 . . . . 173 F5
Nethercote La OX49 . . . . 157 A8
NETHERFIELD 47 C6
Netherfield Rdbt MK6 . . . 47 C7
Nether Gr MK5 . . . . 46 B3
Nether Winchendon Ho ★
  HP18 . . . . 112 C5
Netherwood Rd HP9 . . . . 175 D5
Netley Cl MK10 . . . . 36 A1
Nettlecombe MK4 . . . . . . 46 C3
Nettleden Rd
  Berkhamsted HP4 . . . . . 135 F6
  Little Gaddesden HP4 . . 121 E4
Nettleton Rd UB10 . . . . . 201 F8
Neve Ho SL6 . . . . 202 F8
Nevill Cl MK19 . . . . 11 B2
Neville Ct SL2 . . . . 198 F6
Neville Ct SL1 . . . . 197 C2
Nevis Cl LU7 . . . . 80 C7
Nevis Gr MK2 . . . . 58 E4
Newark Ct MK7 . . . . 48 A3
Newbarn La HP9 . . . . . . 176 E6
Newberry Cres SL4 . . . . 209 D5
Newbery Way SL1 . . . . . 205 D4
Newbolt Cl
  Newport Pagnell MK16 . . 21 F5
  Paulerspury NN12 . . . . . 17 B8
NEW BRADWELL 33 F8
New Bradwell Sch MK13 . 33 F7
Newbridge Oval MK4 . . . . 46 B3
Newbury Ct MK3 . . . . 57 D6
Newbury Dr SL6 . . . . 203 B6
Newbury Rd UB7 . . . . . . 213 F6
Newby Pl MK4 . . . . 46 B2
New Chapter Prim sch
  MK6 . . . . 47 A5
New Chilterns HP7 . . . . . 165 E8
Newchurch Rd SL2 . . . . 204 F6
New Cl RG9 . . . . 192 A8
New Cl Farm Rd OX39 . . 137 C3
New College MK18 . . . . . . 51 F8
New College Ct MK18 . . . . 41 B4
New Coll Rd HP19 . . . . . 101 C4
Newcombe Rise UB7 . . . 208 E7
New Cotts RG9 . . . . 180 C1
Newcourt UB8 . . . . 208 C8
Newcroft Cl UB8 . . . . . . 208 D7
New Ct
  High Wycombe HP13 . . . 173 C6
  Marlow SL7 . . . . 183 D2

NEW DENHAM 201 A6
New Dr HP13 . . . . 173 E8
Newell Cl HP21 . . . . 116 A6
Newells Hedge LU7 . . . . 105 D5
Newfield Gdns SL7 . . . . . 183 F3
Newfield Rd SL7 . . . . . . 183 F3
Newfield Way SL7 . . . . . 183 F2
New Garden Dr UB7 . . . . 208 E4
NEW GROUND 120 A2
Newground Rd HP23 . . . 120 B3
New Hall Cl HP3 . . . . 146 A4
Newhaven Spur SL2 . . . . 198 B1
New Horton Manor SL3 . . 212 A4
Newhouse Rd HP3 . . . . . 146 A4
Newington Gate MK6 . . . . 47 D5
New Inn La
  MK18 . . . . 51 F4
New Inn Stowe, Visitor Ctr ★
  MK18 . . . . 41 A6
Newland Ho UB8 . . . . . . 201 C4
NEWLAND PARK 178 A7
Newlands Dr
  Maidenhead SL6 . . . . . 202 A7
  Poyle SL3 . . . . 212 E4
Newlands Girls Sch SL6 202 A7
Newlyn Pl MK6 . . . . 35 A2
Newmans Cl MK14 . . . . . . 21 E1
Newmans Ctyd MK17 . . . . 68 C6
Newmarket Ct MK10 . . . . 36 C2
New Mdw HP21 . . . . 116 C7
Newmer Rd HP12 . . . . . . 172 B3
NEW MILL 119 B6
New Mill Terr HP23 . . . . 119 B6
New Par
  Chorleywood WD3 . . . . 167 C5
  West Drayton UB7 . . . . 208 E5
New Peachey La UB8 . . . 208 D8
New Pond Rd HP15 . . . . 163 C7
NEWPORT PAGNELL . . . 22 B5
Newport Pagnell Rd
  MK43 . . . . 16 C4
Newport Rd
  Astwood MK16 . . . . 15 C2
  Emberton MK46 . . . . . . 13 F6
  Hanslope MK19 . . . . . . 11 B2
  Milton Keynes MK10 . . . . 36 D1
  Milton Keynes, New Bradwell
  MK13 . . . . 34 A4
  Milton Keynes, Oakgrove
  MK15 . . . . 35 C2
  Milton Keynes, Willen MK15 35 D7
  Milton Keynes, Woughton on the
  Green MK6 . . . . 35 D1
  Moulsoe MK16 . . . . 36 C3
  Slough SL2 . . . . 197 E1
  Wavendon MK17 . . . . . . 48 E3
  Woburn MK17 . . . . 60 F8
  Woughton on the Green
  MK6 . . . . 47 D8
  Woughton Park MK6 . . . . 47 D6
Newport Way MK19 . . . . . 11 C3
New Providant Pl 5
  HP4 . . . . 135 D4
Newquay Cl **4** MK4 . . . . 45 F1
New Rd
  Amersham HP6 . . . . . . 154 E2
  Aston Clinton HP22 . . . . 117 E5
  Berkhamsted HP4 . . . . . 135 D6
  Berkhamsted, Northchurch
  HP4 . . . . 134 F7
  Bolter End HP14 . . . . . 170 F6
  Bourne End SL8 . . . . . 185 B4
  Castlethorpe MK19 . . . . 19 F5
  Chipperfield WD4 . . . . . 146 F1
  Coleshill HP7 . . . . 164 F4
  Cookham Rise SL6 . . . . 195 E7
  Datchet SL3 . . . . 211 D6
  Dinton HP17 . . . . 113 E2
  Drayton Parslow MK17 . . 68 C5
  Great Kingshill HP15 . . . 162 D3
  Harrold MK43 . . . . 3 E6
  High Wycombe HP12 . . . 172 C5
  Hurley SL6 . . . . 193 F3
  Leighton Buzzard LU7 . . . 80 E7
  Little Chalfont HP8 . . . . 166 F6
  Little Kingshill HP16 . . . 152 B4
  Marlow Bottom SL7 . . . . 183 D6
  Naphill HP14 . . . . 150 A2
  Prestwood HP16 . . . . . 151 D6
  Princes Risborough HP27 . 139 C3
  Sarratt HP8 . . . . 156 F1
  Slough SL3 . . . . 207 A3
  Stokenchurch HP14 . . . . 158 F4
  Tring HP23 . . . . 119 B6
  Tylers Green HP10 . . . . 163 C1
  Weedon HP22 . . . . 101 B8
  Weston Turville HP22 . . . 116 E5
  Wilstone HP23 . . . . 118 D3
New Road Cl HP12 . . . . . 172 C6
New Road Gdns HP12 . . . 172 C6
New Row MK46 . . . . 7 E8
New Sq SL1 . . . . 205 F4
New St
  Aylesbury HP20 . . . . . . 101 D1
  Berkhamsted HP4 . . . . . 135 D4
  Cheddington LU7 . . . . . 104 F7
  Henley-on-Thames RG9 . 191 E2
  Milton Keynes MK11 . . . . 32 D5
  Tingewick MK18 . . . . . . 51 B6
  Waddesdon HP18 . . . . . 99 A1
NEWTON 144 C1
NEWTON BLOSSOMVILLE . . 8 A4
Newton Blossomville CE Sch
  MK43 . . . . 8 A4
Newton Cl SL3 . . . . 206 F4
Newton Ct SL4 . . . . 211 A1
Newton La SL4 . . . . 211 B3
NEWTON LONGVILLE 57 D3

Newton Longville CE Comb Sch MK17 57 D3
NEWTON PURCELL 50 B2
Newton Rd
Drayton Parslow MK17 68 D8
Milton Keynes MK3 57 E6
Stoke Hammond MK17 69 D8
Turvey MK43 8 E5
West Drayton UB7 213 F6
Newtonside SL4 211 A1
Newton Side Orch SL4 211 A1
Newton St MK46 7 A4
Newtown Rd
Marlow SL7 183 F3
New Denham UB9 201 B6
Newtown Sch HP5 144 C2
Newville HP22 87 C1
New Windsor St UB8 201 C4
NEWYEARS GREEN 190 F5
Newyears Green La UB9 190 F5
New Zealand Cotts HP22 88 E4
New Zealand Gdns LU7 79 E2
Neyland Dr HP19 101 D3
Nicholas Charles Cres HP18 100 D4
Nicholas Gdns
High Wycombe HP13 173 D8
Slough SL1 204 E5
Nicholas Mead MK14 34 F8
Nicholas Winton Ct SL6 203 A8
Nicholls SL4 209 C4
Nicholls Wlk SL4 209 C4
Nicholson Gr MK8 45 E6
Nicholsons La SL6 202 F7
Nicholsons Sh Ctr 2 SL6 202 F7
Nickson Ct HP15 163 A3
Nicol Cl SL9 177 C2
Nicol End SL9 177 C2
Nicol Rd SL9 177 C2
Nielson Ct MK7 48 D5
Nigel Ct NN13 38 A5
Nightingale Cl
Hazelmere HP15 163 B5
Steeple Claydon MK18 63 E3
Nightingale Cres MK13 34 A7
Nightingale Ct
1 High Wycombe HP13 173 B7
6 Slough SL1 206 A3
Nightingale Ho HP11 174 A4
Nightingale La SL6 195 D3
Nightingale Lodge HP4 135 B4
Nightingale Pk SL2 197 F5
Nightingale Pl
Buckingham MK18 41 E1
Cookham Rise SL6 195 F7
Nightingale Rd
Aylesbury HP21 115 E6
2 Chesham HP5 144 B2
Wendover HP22 131 B5
Nightingales Cnr HP7 166 C7
Nightingales Ct HP8 166 C7
Nightingales La HP8 166 D4
Nightingale Way UB9 189 F5
Nightingale Wlk SL4 210 C4
Nijinsky Ho UB8 201 D3
Nine Acres SL1 204 F5
Nine Elms Ave UB8 208 D8
Nine Elms Cl UB8 208 D8
Nine Stiles Cl UB9 201 B6
Ninnings Rd SL9 177 F3
Ninnings Way SL9 177 F3
Niplands Cotts HP10 185 D2
Niven La MK4 45 E3
Nixey Cl SL1 206 A4
Nixons Cl MK6 46 E6
Noble Cl MK15 35 A7
Noble Cres HP18 100 D4
Noble Ct SL2 205 F5
Nocton Hall Dr HP22 131 E6
Noon Layer Dr MK10 35 E3
Norbrek MK8 33 E2
Norcott Farm La HP4 120 C1
NORCOTT HILL 120 D2
Norcott Hill
Cow Roast HP4 120 D1
Dudswell HP4 134 D8
Norcotts Kiln Cotts HP18 96 A1
Norden Cl SL6 202 C4
Norden Mdws SL6 202 C5
Norden Mead MK7 48 A5
Norden Rd SL6 202 C5
Norelands Dr SL1 197 C3
Norfolk Ave SL1 205 C8
Norfolk Ho 6 MK3 46 F1
Norfolk Park Cotts SL6 202 F8
Norfolk Rd
Maidenhead SL6 202 F8
Turvey MK43 8 E6
Uxbridge UB8 201 D6
Norfolk Terr HP20 101 E1
Norgrove Pk SL9 188 E7
Norjo-An Villas HP5 154 C6
Norland Dr HP10 185 C8
Norman Ave RG9 191 E1
Norman Cres MK10 35 E3
Normandy Dr HP4 135 B6
Normandy Way MK3 46 E2
Normans Cl UB8 208 F8
Normans Ct 5 HP13 173 F6
Normanstead RG9 191 D1
Normans The SL2 206 B7
Norman Way LU6 93 E8
Normill Terr HP22 117 A6
Norreys Dr SL6 202 D4
Norrington MK8 33 E3
Norris Ho SL6 202 E7
Norris Rd OX6 94 E8
NORTHALL 92 B5
Northall Cl LU6 92 D6
Northall Rd LU6 92 D6
Northampton Ave SL1 205 C7
Northampton Rd
Brackley NN13 26 A1
Cosgrove MK19 19 C1
Cosgrove MK19 32 C8
Grafton Regis NN12 9 C3
Lathbury MK16 22 D6
Lavendon MK46 7 F8
Yardley Hastings NN7 1 A6
Northborough Rd SL2 198 B1
Northbridge Rd HP4 135 A6
North Burnham Cl SL1 197 B3
NORTHCHURCH 134 E5
Northchurch La HP5 134 D2
North Cl
Beaconsfield HP9 186 B8
Drayton Parslow MK17 68 C8
Medmenham SL7 193 D7
Windsor SL4 209 F6
Northcliffe LU6 92 E6
Northcliffe Wy HP18 100 D5
North Common Rd UB8 201 D7
North Cotts SL2 198 C2
NORTH CRAWLEY 24 A6
North Crawley CE Sch MK16 24 B6
North Crawley Rd MK16 23 C4
Northcroft
Milton Keynes MK5 46 C6
Slough SL2 198 B1
Weedon HP22 87 C1
Wooburn Green HP10 185 F6
North Croft MK18 66 A4
Northdean 5 SL6 195 F1
Northdown Rd SL9 177 E4
North Dr
Aylesbury HP21 115 E5
Beaconsfield HP9 186 B8
High Wycombe HP13 173 E8
North Eastern Rd HP19 101 C2
North Eighth St MK9 34 E3
North Elder Rdbt MK9 34 C1
North Eleventh St MK9 34 E3
NORTHEND 168 E6
NORTH END
Stagsden 16 E8
Steeple Claydon 63 D3
Stewkley 68 D3
Northend MK46 5 E3
Northend Cl HP10 185 C7
Northend Ct 1 MK18 41 D1
North End Rd
Quainton HP22 85 A5
Steeple Claydon MK18 63 D3
Northend Sq 2 MK18 41 D1
Northend Workshops RG9 168 E5
Northern Hts SL8 185 B5
Northern Perimeter Rd (W) TW6 213 D6
Northern Rd
Aylesbury HP19 101 C2
Slough SL2 198 D1
Northern Woods HP10 185 C7
NORTHFIELD 35 F5
Northfield Barns Dr MK19 31 F4
Northfield Ct RG9 191 D3
Northfield Dr MK15 35 F5
Northfield End RG9 191 D3
Northfield Rd
Aylesbury HP20 116 B8
Eton Wick SL4 204 F2
Maidenhead SL6 195 F1
Princes Risborough HP27 139 C4
Tring HP23 119 F7
Northfield Rdbt MK10 36 A5
North Fifth St MK9 34 D2
North Fourteenth St MK9 34 F4
North Fourth St MK9 34 C2
North Gate MK2 47 C1
North Gn
3 Maidenhead SL6 195 F1
Slough SL1 205 E6
North Grafton Rdbt MK13 34 C2
North Hill
Dadford MK18 28 D2
Sarratt WD3 167 E8
North Hills HP18 96 A1
North La MK7 47 E7
Northlands Rd MK18 53 F1
NORTH LEE 130 A7
North Lee La
North Lee HP22 130 A6
Stoke Mandeville HP22 129 F7
Northleigh MK4 46 D2
North Links Rd HP10 174 B1
NORTH MARSTON 76 A2
North Marston CE Sch MK18 76 B2
North Marston La HP22 86 E7
Northmead Rd SL2 204 F8
Northmill HP27 138 F3
North Mill Rd HP27 138 A5
Northmoor Hill Wood Nature Reserve* UB9 189 F7
North Ninth St MK9 34 E3
Northolt Rd TW6 213 E6
North Orbital Rd
Denham Green UB9 189 F4
Rickmansworth WD3 178 E7
North Overgate Rdbt MK15 35 B5
North Pk
Gerrards Cross SL9 188 E8
Iver SL0 207 D3
North Rd
Amersham HP6 154 C3
Berkhamsted HP4 135 B4
Chorleywood WD3 167 D4
Cryers Hill HP15 162 D5
Maidenhead SL6 202 E7
West Drayton UB7 208 F3
North Ridge MK6 35 B1
North Row
Fulmer SL3 199 E8
Milton Keynes MK9 34 C2
North Saxon Rdbt MK14 34 D3
North Secklow Rdbt MK14 34 E3
North Second St MK9 34 C2
North Seventh St MK9 34 D2
North Sixth St MK9 34 D2
North Skeldon Rdbt MK9 35 A4
North Sq MK16 22 D5
North St
Castlethorpe MK19 19 F5
Milton Keynes, Bradville MK13 34 A7
Milton Keynes, Fenny Stratford MK2 47 C1
Thame OX9 125 F1
North Star La SL6 202 C6
North Tenth St MK9 34 E3
North Terr SL4 210 E7
North Third St MK9 34 C2
North Thirteenth St MK9 34 F3
NORTH TOWN 195 F1
North Town Cl 1 SL6 195 F1
North Town Mead 4 SL6 195 F1
North Town Moor SL6 195 F1
North Town Rd SL6 195 F1
North Twelfth St MK9 34 F3
Northumberland Ave HP21 116 B6
Northumberland Cl TW19 213 E1
Northumbria Rd SL6 202 B4
North View HP22 87 B3
North Way
Deanshanger NN12 31 E5
Potterspury NN12 18 E2
Uxbridge UB10 201 E5
NORTH WESTON 136 F8
Northwich MK6 47 D7
Northwick Rd MK10 35 F1
North Witan Rdbt MK13 34 D2
Northwood Rd TW6 213 D6
Nortoft Rd SL9 177 F5
Norton Leys MK7 48 C7
Norton Rd UB8 201 D2
Norton's Pl MK18 52 C8
Nortons The MK7 48 B3
Norvic Rd HP23 105 A1
Norway Dr SL2 206 B8
Norwich Ho
High Wycombe HP13 173 F8
Maidenhead SL6 202 E8
Norwood Cl HP20 101 F2
Norwood Ct 4 HP7 165 B7
Norwood La
Newport Pagnell MK16 22 C3
Uxbridge SL0 200 D1
Norwood Rd HP10 174 B2
Notley Farm HP18 126 A7
Nottingham Gr MK3 46 E2
Nottingham Ho 3 HP13 173 F7
Nottingham Rd WD3 167 C1
Nova Lodge MK4 46 B2
Novello Croft MK7 48 D4
Nugent Cl HP19 101 D4
Nugent Ct
Chesham HP5 144 A3
Marlow SL7 183 F3
Nuneham Gr MK4 45 F3
NUP END 89 B3
Nup End Cl HP22 89 B3
Nup End La HP22 89 B3
Nurseries The LU6 92 E6
Nursery Cl
2 Amersham HP7 165 E8
Aylesbury HP21 115 C5
Tylers Green HP10 174 C8
Nursery Ct HP12 172 D6
Nursery Dr HP14 171 B5
Nursery Gdns
Milton Keynes MK13 34 A4
Tring HP23 119 B4
Nursery La
Slough SL3 206 D5
Tylers Green HP10 174 C8
Nursery Pl SL4 211 B1
Nursery Rd SL6 204 B7
Nursery Way TW19 211 D1
Nursery Waye UB8 201 D4
Nursery Wlk SL7 183 B1
Nutfield La HP11 172 F8
Nuthatch 10 HP19 101 F3
Nutkins Way HP5 144 C2
Nutkin Wlk UB10 201 E5
Nutmeg Cl MK7 48 B5
Nye Way HP3 146 A3
Nymans Gate 8 MK4 45 F1

O

Oak Barn Cl MK43 25 A1
Oak Cres HP12 172 C4
Oak Ct MK9 34 E2
Oakdene HP9 175 E3
Oakdown Cres MK46 6 F3
Oak Dr HP4 135 D3
Oak End Dr SL0 200 C3
Oak End Way
Chinnor OX39 147 D5
Gerrards Cross SL9 188 F6
Oaken Gr SL6 195 C1
Oakengrove HP16 151 C5
Oakengrove Cl HP15 163 C6
Oakengrove La HP15 163 B3
Oakengrove Rd HP15 163 A3
Oaken Head MK4 46 C2
Oakeshott Ave HP14 161 D6
Oakfield WD3 167 F2
Oak Field HP5 144 B1
Oakfield Ave SL1 205 B5
Oakfield Cl HP6 154 C2
Oakfield Cnr HP6 154 C2
Oakfield Fst Sch SL4 210 B5
Oakfield Rd
Aylesbury HP20 116 A8
Bourne End SL8 185 A3
Oak Gn HP21 115 C7
Oak Green Sch HP21 115 C7
OAKGROVE 35 D2
Oakgrove L Ctr MK10 35 F2
Oakgrove Rdbt MK10 35 F2
Oakgrove Sch MK10 35 F2
Oakham Rise MK4 45 E1
OAKHILL 45 D4
Oakhill Cl
Maple Cross WD3 178 E6
Milton Keynes MK5 45 E6
Oakhill Rd
Maple Cross WD3 178 D6
Milton Keynes, Hazeley MK5 45 D5
Milton Keynes, Shenley Church End MK5 45 F6
Oakhill Rdbt MK5 45 D5
Oakhurst SL6 196 B4
Oakington Ave HP6 166 E8
Oak La
Buckland Common HP23 133 A2
Windsor SL4 210 A6
Oaklands HP4 135 A4
Oaklands Ct HP6 154 C1
Oakland Way HP10 174 A1
Oak Lawn HP23 119 A3
OAKLEY
Brill 109 D5
Chinnor 147 B5
Oakley HP10 185 F7
Oakley CE Comb Sch HP18 109 D4
Oakley Cres SL1 205 E6
Oakley Gdns MK15 35 B5
OAKLEY GREEN 209 B5
Oakley Green Rd SL4 209 B5
Oakley Hill Wildlife Reserve* OX39 147 D4
Oakley La OX39 147 B6
Oakley Rd
Brill HP18 110 A8
Chinnor OX39 147 C6
Horton-cum-S OX33 108 C5
Oak Rd HP27 139 C3
Oakridge MK4 46 E4
Oakridge Ct HP12 172 D6
Oakridge Pl SL2 198 C8
Oakridge Rd HP11 172 E7
Oakridge Sch HP11 172 E7
Oakside UB9 201 B6
Oaks Rd TW19 213 D2
Oak St HP11 173 C4
Oaks The HP4 135 A4
Oak Stubbs La SL6 203 F4
Oak Tree Ave SL7 183 D3
Oaktree Cl HP10 163 B2
Oak Tree Cl SL7 183 D3
Oak Tree Cotts HP18 83 B5
Oaktree Ct MK15 35 C7
Oak Tree Dr
Lane End HP14 171 C5
Slough SL3 207 B1
Oak Tree Rd SL7 183 D4
Oakview HP6 153 D4
Oak View
Great Kingshill HP15 162 D8
Towcester NN12 18 D3
Oakview Gdns SL3 206 F2
Oakway
Amersham HP6 154 B4
Winslow MK18 66 A4
Oakwell Cl LU6 93 F7
Oakwood HP10 174 A2
Oak wood HP4 134 F3
Oakwood Cl HP22 131 E6
Oakwood Dr MK2 58 E7
Oak Wood Pl SL9 188 F2
Oakworth Ave MK10 36 A4
Oat Cl HP21 115 C3
Oatlands Dr SL1 205 D7
Oban Ct SL1 205 D4
Oberon Way MK4 45 D2
Observatory Sh Ctr 4 SL1 205 F4
Ocean Cl MK10 36 D3
Ockwells Nature Reserve* SL6 202 E2
Ockwells Rd SL6 202 C2
Octagon Arc 10 HP11 173 A7
Octagon Par 6 HP11 173 A7
Octavian Dr MK13 33 F5
Octavian Way NN13 38 A7
Oddley La HP27 148 D8
Odds Farm Est HP10 186 B4
Odds Farm Park* HP10 186 B4
Oddy Hill
Tring HP23 119 C3
Oddy Hill *continued*
Wigginton HP23 119 C2
Odell Cl MK6 47 C8
Odencroft Rd SL2 198 A2
Odney La SL6 196 B7
Offas La MK18 66 B5
Ogilvie Cl 1 HP22 131 E6
Ogilvie Rd HP12 172 E7
O'Grady Way HP19 101 A3
Okeford Cl HP23 118 F4
Okeford Dr HP23 118 F4
Okeley La HP23 118 E3
Oldacres SL6 203 B7
Old Airfield Ind Est HP23 104 D6
Old Amersham Rd SL9 189 B3
Old Bakery Ct SL0 207 F7
Old Bakery The
Aston Abbotts HP22 88 D5
Lane End HP14 171 B4
Old Barn Cl MK18 52 A4
Old Bix Rd RG9 191 A6
Old Brewery Cl HP21 115 E7
Old Brewery La RG9 191 E2
OLDBROOK 46 E8
Oldbrook Bvd MK6 46 E8
Oldbrook Fst Sch MK6 46 E8
Old Bryers Cl HP18 124 C2
Old Burrs HP21 115 D3
Oldbury Gr HP9 175 D5
Oldcastle Croft MK4 46 A1
Old Chapel Cl HP17 129 E3
Old Coach Dr HP11 174 A4
Old Coal Yd LU7 78 E7
Old Common Rd WD3 167 D5
Old Court Cl SL6 202 B3
Old Dashwood Hill HP14 159 F2
Old Dean HP3 146 A4
Olde Bell Cl MK17 69 E7
Olde Bell La MK5 46 A7
Old End MK18 53 B2
Old English Cl MK17 44 C1
Oldershaw Mews SL6 202 B8
Old Farm LU7 105 D4
Old Farm Cl
Beaconsfield HP9 175 C5
Slapton LU7 91 A3
Worminghall HP18 123 E5
Old Farm La HP7 165 E6
OLD FARM PARK 48 E5
Old Farm Rd
High Wycombe HP13 161 E2
West Drayton UB7 208 D4
Old Ferry Dr TW19 211 D1
Old Field Cl HP6 166 E8
Oldfield Prim Sch SL6 203 B6
Oldfield Rd SL6 203 B7
Oldfield St HP19 100 F4
Old Fishery La HP1 146 F8
Old Fives Ct SL1 197 C2
Old Forge Cl
Maidenhead SL6 203 A3
Tingewick MK18 51 B6
Old Forge Gdns HP22 102 B4
Old Forge Rd HP10 174 C2
Old Forge The HP23 104 B4
Old Furlong The MK43 25 B2
Old Gaol Mus* MK18 41 D1
Old Garden Ctr The HP27 139 B3
Old Groveway MK6 47 D5
Oldham Rise MK5 45 E5
Oldhams Mdw 9 HP20 101 F2
Old Hardenwaye HP13 162 E1
Old Heatherdene Cotts HP15 162 D8
Old Horns La SL7 172 A3
Oldhouse Cl HP11 172 E3
Old House Ct SL3 206 D7
Old Kiln Rd
Flackwell Heath HP10 185 A8
Tylers Green HP10 163 C2
OLD LINSLADE 70 D2
Old Linslade Rd LU7 70 E3
Old Lodge Dr HP9 175 E1
Old Maltings The
Buckingham MK18 52 C7
Thame OX9 125 E1
Old Manor Cl
Askett HP27 139 C7
Whaddon MK17 45 B1
Old Manor Ct LU7 78 E8
Old Marsh La SL6 203 F4
Old Mead SL9 177 E4
Old Meadow Cl HP4 135 A2
Old Mews The MK46 6 F4
Old Mill Cl HP17 127 A6
Old Mill Furlong MK18 66 A5
Old Mill Gdns 12 HP4 135 D4
Old Mill La
Maidenhead SL6 203 D4
Uxbridge UB8 208 B8
Old Mill Pl TW19 212 B1
Old Mill Rd UB9 190 A1
Old Moor La HP10 185 E8
Old Nursery Ct SL2 187 C2
Old Oak Gdns HP4 134 E7
Old Orch
Henton OX39 137 E2
Iver SL0 207 F7
Old Orchard Mews 1 HP4 135 C4
Old Orchards HP22 102 A3
Old Orchard The HP15 151 D1
Old Oxford Rd HP14 160 C1

Old Palace Ct SL3......212 D6
Old Papermill Cl HP10....185 E8
Old Post Office La **11**
  SL6.................202 F7
Old Rd LU7.............80 E7
Old Rd The RG9........179 C8
Old Rectory Cl HP5.....65 F4
Old Rectory La UB9....189 E4
Old Risborough Rd
  HP22................130 A8
Old Saw Mill Pl
  Little Chalfont HP6....155 B1
  1 Little Chalfont HP6...166 B8
Old Sax La HP5........143 D4
Old School Cl HP22.....117 C1
Old School Cotts HP5...145 D5
Old School Ct
  1 Buckingham MK18.....52 C8
  Eaton Bray LU6........92 E6
Old School La MK17.....69 E8
Old School La The MK18..63 D3
Old School Rd UB8.....201 F1
Old School The HP10....185 D4
Old Shire La WD3......167 B3
Old Slade La SL0......207 F2
Old Springfields MK18...53 C2
Old Stable Yd MK19.....32 C7
Old Stable Yd The MK18..65 F4
Old Station Cl MK18.....66 A5
Old Station La TW19....212 A1
Old Station Way HP10...185 E5
Old Stoke Rd HP21.....115 D6
OLD STRATFORD........32 B7
Old Stratford Prim Sch
  MK19................32 B6
OLD TOWN.............38 A7
Old Town NN13........38 A7
Old Town Cl HP9.......175 D2
Old Town Farm HP16....152 A7
Old Union Way OX9.....125 E1
Old Uxbridge Rd WD3....178 E3
Old Watery La HP10....185 E8
Old Vicarage Way HP10..185 D4
Oldway La SL1.........204 D5
Old Windmill Way HP18..125 C7
OLD WINDSOR.........211 A1
OLD WOLVERTON.......33 D8
Old Wolverton Rd MK12...33 C8
Oliffe Cl HP20.........101 D3
Oliffe Way HP20.......101 D3
Oliver Rd MK2.........58 C8
Oliver Row **4** MK4....45 E3
Oliver's Paddock SL7...183 D5
Olivia Dr SL3.........206 F1
Olivier Way HP20......116 A8
Olleberrie La WD4......156 D7
OLNEY................6 E4
Olney Ind Est MK46.....6 F6
Olney Infant Acad MK46...6 E4
Olney Mid Sch MK46.....6 F5
Olney Rd
  Emberton MK46.......13 E8
  Lavendon MK46........7 E7
Olson Cotts HP14......158 F4
Olympic Ho UB8........201 F1
O'Neill Rd MK8........45 D6
One Pin La SL2........187 D1
One Pin Pl SL2........187 D1
One Tree La HP9.......175 E3
Onslow Ct MK7.........48 A4
Onslow Dr OX9.........126 B1
Onslow Gdns HP13......173 E7
Onslow Mills UB7......208 D6
Opal Ct SL3..........199 C1
Opal Dr MK15.........35 F4
Opal Mews HP18.......100 E3
Opecks Cl SL3.........199 B1
Opendale Rd SL1.......204 B8
Open University (Walton
  Hall) The MK7........47 F7
Oram Ct **3** SL7.....183 D2
Orbell Ct HP27........139 B3
Orbison Ct MK8........45 D7
Orchard Acad MK6......35 B2
Orchard Ave
  Berkhamsted HP4......135 A4
  Slough SL1..........204 D8
  Windsor SL4.........210 A6
Orchard Bglws SL2.....197 F5
Orchard Cl
  15 Aylesbury HP20...101 F3
  Beaconsfield HP9......175 D3
  Chorleywood WD3.....167 D5
  Cosgrove MK19.......19 E2
  Cranfield MK43.......25 A1
  Hughenden Valley HP14..162 A7
  Longwick HP27.......138 D7
  Maidenhead SL6......203 A3
  Milton Keynes MK3.....57 F7
  New Denham UB9.....201 B6
  Newton Longville MK17...57 C3
  Oakley HP18.........109 D4
  Slough SL1..........197 B1
  Stoke Mandeville HP22..116 B1
  Thornborough MK18....54 B7
  Upper Arncott OX25....94 D6
  Waddesdon HP18......99 A7
  Wendover HP22.......131 A5
  Wingrave HP22.......89 B3
  Yardley Gobion NN12....18 F6
Orchard Ct
  Aylesbury HP21.......115 F6
  Bovingdon HP3.......146 A4
  Harmondsworth TW6...213 C7

Orchard Ct continued
  Seer Green HP9.......176 C5
Orchard Dene MK18.....41 D1
Orchard Dr
  Aston Clinton HP22....117 E4
  Chorleywood WD3.....167 D5
  Hazelmere HP15.......163 A3
  Leighton Buzzard LU7...80 D6
  Uxbridge UB8.........201 D1
  Wooburn HP10........185 D4
Orchard End
  Edlesborough LU6......92 E4
  Hazelmere HP15.......163 B6
Orchard End Ave HP7...165 F8
Orchard Gate SL2......198 C7
Orchard Gdns HP23.....119 C5
Orchard Gn HP9.......186 E8
Orchard Gr
  Chalfont St Peter SL9..177 C2
  Flackwell Heath HP10...185 B7
  Maidenhead SL6......202 C7
Orchard Ho
  8 Bourne End SL8....185 A4
  Milton Keynes MK12....33 D6
Orchard La
  Amersham HP6.......154 D1
  Harrold MK43........3 F7
  Prestwood HP16......151 C6
  Stewkley LU7........78 E7
ORCHARD LEIGH.......145 B3
Orchard Leigh Villas
  HP5................145 A4
Orchard Lodge SL1.....204 E5
Orchard Mews HP9....176 D4
Orchard Mill SL8......185 B1
Orchard Pk HP15......163 C6
Orchard Pl
  Monks Risborough HP27..139 C5
  Uxbridge UB8.........201 D1
  Westbury NN13.......39 A4
Orchard Rd
  Beaconsfield HP9......175 F1
  Chalfont St Giles HP8..177 C8
  Loudwater HP13......174 A4
  Old Windsor SL4......211 B1
  Seer Green HP9.......176 C5
Orchard Rise MK46......6 F3
Orchard Row HP14.....171 A7
Orchards The
  Eaton Bray LU6.......92 E7
  Little Kingshill HP16...152 A2
  Slough SL3..........206 F5
  Tring HP23..........118 F3
Orchard The
  Aston Clinton HP22....117 E5
  Flackwell Heath HP10...185 B7
  Halton HP22.........131 C8
  Hazelmere HP15......163 A6
  Hillesden MK18.......63 A7
  Marlow SL7..........183 E3
  Pottersbury NN12.....18 C3
  Walter's Ash HP14....161 E6
Orchard View
  Hillesden MK18.......63 B7
  Uxbridge UB8.........201 D1
ORCHARDVILLE........197 B1
Orchardville SL1........197 B1
Orchard Way
  Aylesbury HP20......101 F2
  Bovingdon HP3.......146 A3
  Chinnor OX39........147 C5
  Cranfield MK43......25 A1
  East Claydon MK18....74 E6
  Eaton Bray LU6.......92 F5
  Holmer Green HP15...163 C6
  North Crawley MK16...24 A6
  Pitstone LU7.........105 E4
  Slough SL3..........206 F5
  Stoke Goldington MK16..12 B7
  Wing LU7............79 E2
Orchard Waye UB8.....201 D3
Orchard Wlk MK46......7 F7
Orchehill Ave SL9.....188 D7
Orchehill Cl SL9......188 E6
Orchehill Rise SL9.....188 E6
Oregano Cl UB7.......208 F6
Orford Ct MK5........46 B6
Oriel Cl MK12.........33 B6
Oriel Cotts MK18......63 D2
Orient Chase **1** MK10..36 B5
Orkney Cl
  Milton Keynes MK3....46 F2
  Stewkley LU7........78 E8
Orkney Ct SL6........196 E5
Ormesby Cl HP21......116 A5
Ormonde MK14.......34 D7
Ormond Rd OX9......126 A1
Ormsgill Ct MK13.....34 B5
Orne Gdns MK15......35 A7
Orpington Gr MK5.....46 B4
Ortensia Dr MK7......48 C7
Ortman Cl SL9.......188 E4
Orwell Cl
  Aylesbury HP21.......115 D4
  Newport Pagnell MK16..21 F5
  Windsor SL4.........210 D4
Orwell Dr HP21.......115 D4
Osborne Ct SL4......210 C5
Osborne Mews SL4....210 C5
Osborne Rd SL4......210 D4
Osborne St
  Milton Keynes MK2....58 C7
  Slough SL1..........205 F4
Osborne Way HP23....119 D5
Osborn Rd UB8.......201 C5
Osborn's Ct **5** MK46...6 F3
Osbourne St MK12....33 D6
Osier La MK5.........46 B4

Osier Way
  Aylesbury HP20......115 F8
  Buckingham MK18.....52 C6
Osmington Pl HP23.....118 F4
Osney Rd SL6........195 E2
Osprey Cl
  Milton Keynes MK6....47 B8
  West Drayton UB7....208 E4
Osprey The HP19......101 E4
Osprey Wlk
  Aylesbury HP19.......101 E4
  Buckingham MK18.....52 F7
Ossulbury La HP19.....101 C4
Osterley Cl MK16......22 C3
Ostler Gate SL6......195 C1
Ostlers Ct HP11......174 A4
Ostlers La MK11......32 D6
Otterburn Cres MK5....45 D5
Otter Cl MK3.........46 D1
Otterfield Rd UB7.....208 E6
Otters Brook MK18.....52 E7
Otter Wy UB7.........208 E5
Otway Cl HP21.......115 E3
Oulton Cl HP21.......116 A5
Our Lady of Peace RC Inf Sch
  SL1................204 C8
Our Lady of Peace RC Jun
  Sch SL1.............204 C8
Our Lady's RC Prim Sch
  HP6................154 B4
Ousebank Sch MK16....22 D5
Ousebank Way MK11....32 D5
Ousedale Sch
  Newport Pagnell MK16...22 B3
  Olney MK46.........6 E4
Ouseley Rd TW19......211 D1
Outfield Rd SL9......177 D3
Outlook Dr HP8......177 D7
Ouzel Cl MK3........46 E1
Oval The MK6........46 E7
Oval Way SL9........188 E7
Overdale Rd HP5......144 B3
Overdales HP15......162 F3
Overgate MK6, MK9, MK14..35 B4
Over Hampden HP16....151 C7
Overhills MK46........6 E4
Overn Ave MK18......41 C1
Overn Cl MK18.......41 D1
Overn Cres MK18.....41 C1
Overshot Ho HP10....174 C2
Over the Misbourne SL9..189 B5
Over the Misbourne Rd
  UB9................189 C5
Overton Dr OX9......126 B1
Oville Ct MK5........46 B5
Ovitts Cl MK18.......66 A5
Owen Cl **4** SL3.....206 F1
Owl Cl **5** HP19.....101 F3
Owlsears Cl HP9......175 D4
OWLSWICK...........128 C1
Oxendon Ct LU7......70 F2
Oxenhope Way MK10....36 A4
Oxfield Cl HP4.......135 A3
Oxfield Park Dr MK19...32 C8
Oxford Ave
  Burnham SL1........197 B3
  Slough SL1..........204 F8
Oxford Gdns UB9.....190 A1
Oxford Rd
  Aylesbury HP17, HP21...115 B7
  Denham UB9.........189 D2
  Gerrards Cross SL9...188 D5
  High Wycombe HP11...173 A7
  Marlow SL7..........183 D2
  Oakley HP18.........109 D5
  Piddington HP14......160 D1
  Stokenchurch HP14....158 D5
  Stone HP17..........114 C5
  Thame OX9..........125 E1
  Uxbridge UB8, UB9....201 B6
  Windsor SL4.........210 C6
Oxford Road E SL4....210 C6
Oxford St
  5 High Wycombe HP11..173 A7
  Lee Common HP16....142 A7
  Milton Keynes, Fenny Stratford
    MK2...............58 C8
  Milton Keynes, Stony Stratford
    MK11..............32 D5
  Milton Keynes, Wolverton
    MK12..............33 D6
Ox Gd HP18.........100 D4
Oxhouse Ct MK5......46 A3
Oxlade Dr SL1.......206 C2
OXLEY PARK..........45 E3
Oxley Park Rdbt MK5...45 F3
Oxleys MK46.........6 E4
Oxman La MK12......33 A5
Oxpen HP18.........100 D4
Oxwich Gr MK4......57 B8
Oxyard HP18.........100 D4

P

Pace Ctr The HP19.....101 B2
Packet Boat La UB8....208 C7
Packhorse Rd SL9.....188 E6
Pack & Prime La RG9...191 C4
PADBURY............53 B2
Padbury CE Sch MK18..53 C2

Padbury Oaks UB7.....213 B6
Padcroft Rd UB7......208 D5
Paddock Cl
  8 Aylesbury HP19....100 F1
  Castlethorpe MK19.....20 A5
  Maidenhead SL6......202 A2
  Milton Keynes MK14....34 E8
Paddock Cotts SL6.....202 A2
Paddocks Clinic The (BMI)
  HP27................139 C4
Paddocks End HP9.....176 C4
Paddocks The
  Amersham HP6.......154 F2
  Chorleywood WD3.....167 F5
  Flackwell Heath HP10...185 B8
  Haddenham HP17.....127 A5
  High Wycombe HP12....172 B3
  Leighton Buzzard LU7...80 F8
  Prestwood HP16......151 C5
  Steeple Claydon MK18..63 E3
  Wendover HP22.......131 B5
  Widmer End HP15.....162 E5
Paddock The
  Aylesbury HP21.......116 C7
  Chalfont St Peter SL9..177 E5
  Datchet SL3..........211 B6
  Emberton MK46......13 E8
  Maidenhead SL6......195 C2
  Maids Moreton MK18...41 E4
Paddock Way MK2.....47 D1
Padstow Ave MK6.....34 F1
Padstow Cl
  Aylesbury HP20......101 F1
  Slough SL3..........206 E3
PAGE HILL...........41 F2
Page Hill Ave MK18....41 E1
Pages Croft HP4......135 A6
Pages La MK18.......201 C6
Pages Wharf SL6......203 C8
Paget Cl SL7.........183 F4
Paget Ct UB7.........208 E4
Paget Dr SL6.........202 A4
Paget Rd SL3.........206 F2
Pagg's Ct MK16......22 D4
Pagoda Rdbt MK15.....35 C5
Pagoda The SL6......196 B1
Paignton Way **2** MK10..36 A3
Paines Orch LU7......105 A8
Pakenham Ct HP19....114 F8
Palace Cl SL1........204 F5
Palace Sq MK6.......46 F7
Palfreyman St HP19....101 D4
Pallatia Ct **2** HP13...162 A1
Palliser Rd HP8......177 B6
Palmer Ave
  Aylesbury HP19......115 C8
  Upper Arncott OX25....94 F8
Palmers Cl SL6.......202 A3
PALMERS MOOR.......201 A1
Palmers Moor MK18....54 A8
Palmer's Moor La SL0...201 A1
Palmers Rd MK46......7 A3
Palmerston Ave SL3....206 B3
Pankridge Dr HP16.....151 C7
Panleigh Cotts HP14...171 B3
Pannier Pl MK14......35 A5
Pann Mill HP13......173 C6
Panters Cl MK17......44 C1
Pantile Row SL3......207 A2
Pantile Wlk UB8......201 C5
Paprika Ct MK7......48 B5
Papworth Cl MK16....22 F3
Parade Ct **7** SL8....185 A4
Parade The
  Bourne End SL8......185 A3
  Farnham Common SL2..198 C6
  High Wycombe HP11...172 F6
  Uxbridge UB8.........208 C8
  Windsor SL4.........209 D6
Paradise MK17.......57 D4
Paradise Mews RG9....191 D2
Paradise Orchard HP18..150 D4
Paradise Rd RG9......191 C1
Parchment Cl HP6.....154 E2
Parish La SL2........187 C1
Parish Piece HP15.....163 C7
Park Ave
  Newport Pagnell MK16..22 B4
  Totternhoe LU6......93 B8
  Wraysbury TW19.....211 D3
Park Cl
  Cosgrove MK19.......19 F2
  Dunton MK18.........77 E5
  Lane End HP14.......171 C5
  Windsor SL4.........210 D5
Park Cnr SL4........209 E4
Park Ct UB8.........201 D4
Parker Cl MK13.......34 A6
Parker Gdns SL4......211 B1
Parker Knoll Way HP13..173 A7
Parker Wlk HP19......101 D3
Park Farm Rd HP12....161 B1
Park Farm Way HP14...171 C5
Parkfield WD3........167 F5
Parkfield Ave MK18....154 D2
Parkfield Rise HP27....139 B2
Parkgate SL1........197 C1
Park Gate LU7........79 E1
Park Gdns MK3......47 A1
Park Gr
  Beaconsfield HP9.....175 C7
  Little Chalfont HP8....166 D6
Park Hill OX33.......122 B1
Park Ho
  Berkhamsted HP4.....135 B5
  Gerrards Cross SL9...188 E7
  Maidenhead SL6......202 E6

Park House Bsns Ctr
  HP12................172 E8
Park House Dr MK5.....45 F6
Park La
  Beaconsfield HP9.....175 F1
  Burnham SL1........197 E7
  Eaton Bray LU6.......92 D6
  Hazelmere HP15......163 A4
  Horton SL3..........212 A4
  Lane End HP14.......171 D5
  Maidsgrove RG9.....179 D6
  Paulerspury NN12....17 B7
  Slough SL3..........206 B3
  Stokenchurch HP14....158 E6
Parkland Ave SL3......206 D2
Parklands MK14......21 D1
Park Lane Ct HP14.....158 E5
Park Lawn SL2.......198 C2
Park Lodge Ave UB7...208 F4
Park Manor Industries
  MK18................41 D3
Park Mdw HP27......139 A3
Parkminster MK10.....36 A1
Park Parade SL2......198 C3
Park Parade Ctr The
  HP15................163 A5
Park Pl
  Amersham HP6.......154 F1
  Seer Green HP9.......176 D5
Park Rd
  Amersham HP6.......154 F2
  Chesham HP5........154 B8
  Farnham Royal SL2....198 E3
  Granborough MK18....75 F6
  Grendon Underwood HP18.82 F8
  Hanslope MK19.......11 B1
  Hartwell NN7........10 C8
  Henley-on-Thames RG9..191 E1
  Milton Keynes MK11....32 D5
  Sherington MK16.....14 A2
  Stanwell TW19.......213 C1
  Tring HP23..........118 F2
  Uxbridge UB8.........201 E6
  Winslow MK18........65 F5
Park Rise HP4........134 E6
Park Road E UB10.....201 D3
Park Road S MK18.....65 F4
Parkside
  Gerrards Cross SL9...188 F7
  Henley-on-Thames RG9..191 C2
  Maidenhead SL6......195 E1
  Milton Keynes MK4....46 E3
  Naphill HP14........150 B3
Parkside Wlk SL1......206 A3
Park Sports Ctr OX33..122 B1
Park St
  Aylesbury HP20......115 F8
  Berkhamsted HP4.....135 B5
  High Wycombe HP11....173 D6
  Maidenhead SL6......202 F7
  Poyle SL3...........212 D6
  Princes Risborough HP27.139 B3
  Slough SL1..........205 F4
  Tring HP23..........119 A3
  Windsor SL4.........210 D6
Parkstone Lodge SL3...206 A3
Park Street Ind Est HP20.115 F8
Parkstone MK17......60 F7
Parkview
  Flackwell Heath HP10...185 B7
  Maidenhead SL6......202 F7
Park View
  Newport Pagnell MK16..22 D4
  West Drayton UB7....208 E6
Parkview Chase SL1...204 E7
Park View Ct
  Berkhamsted HP4.....135 B4
  High Wycombe HP12....172 E8
  4 Leighton Buzzard LU7..80 F7
Park View Rd
  Berkhamsted HP4.....135 B4
  Uxbridge UB8.........208 F7
Parkway
  Bow Brickhill MK17....48 D2
  Marlow SL7..........184 A3
  Woburn Sands MK17...49 A6
Parkway The SL0......200 C4
Parkwood HP14......150 A2
Park Wood, Gouldings Wood
  Nature Reserve★ SL6..194 E4
Parlaunt Park Prim Acad
  SL3................207 B3
Parlaunt Rd SL3......207 B3
Parliament Cl HP16....151 B7
Parliament La SL6, SL1..196 F5
Parliament Rd OX9....125 F1
Parmiter Cl HP19......115 B8
PARMOOR...........181 F7
Parmoor La RG9......170 E1
Parneleys MK10......35 F2
Parrin Dr HP22.......131 E6
Parrishs Piece HP22....87 B3
Parrock La MK10......36 A2
Parrot Cl HP21.......115 B6
Parrott's La HP23.....133 A4
Parrs Rd HP14.......158 E4
Parry Cotts SL9......177 C2
Parry Green N SL3....206 F2
Parry Green S SL3....207 A2
Parsley Cl
  Aston Clinton HP22....117 C5
  Walton MK7.........48 B5
Parslow Cl HP21......115 D3
Parslow Ct HP21......115 D3
Parsonage
  High Wycombe HP13...173 D7
  Tring HP23..........119 A4
Parsonage Ct **1** HP23..119 A3

Parsonage Farm HP22.... 89 B3
Parsonage Gdns SL7 .... 183 E1
Parsonage La
 Farnham Common SL2.... 198 D5
 Windsor SL4 .... 210 A6
Parsonage Pl HP7.... 165 C8
Parsonage Rd HP8.... 177 B7
Parson Cl MK18.... 65 F4
Parsons Cl LU7 .... 78 E8
Parsons Cres MK5 .... 46 C5
Parson's Fee HP20.... 115 D8
Parsons La HP22.... 102 B3
Parsons Rd SL3.... 206 F1
Parsons Wlk HP15 .... 163 C6
Parson's Wood La SL2 .. 198 D5
Parton Cl HP22 .... 131 A5
Parton Rd HP20.... 116 B8
Partridge Cl
 Buckingham MK18.... 52 F7
 Chesham HP5 .... 144 E3
 Leighton Buzzard LU7 .... 104 F7
Partridge Mead SL6.... 195 F2
Partridge Piece MK43 .... 25 C3
Partridge Way
 7 Aylesbury HP19 .... 101 F3
 High Wycombe HP13 .... 161 C2
Pascal Dr MK5.... 45 E5
Pascomb Rd LU6.... 93 F8
Passalewe La MK7 .... 48 D7
PASSENHAM.... 32 C4
Passmore MK6.... 47 D6
Pastern Pl MK14 .... 35 A5
Pastures The
 Aylesbury HP20 .... 102 B2
 Edlesborough LU6 .... 92 F3
 High Wycombe HP13.... 161 E1
Patch Cl UB10 .... 201 F4
Patches Field SL7.... 183 E5
Pateman Cl MK18.... 41 C1
Patemore La RG9.... 168 A1
Paterson Rd HP21.... 115 C6
Pathia Cl 7 MK10.... 36 C4
Patricia Cl SL1.... 204 E6
Patrick Haugh Rd OX25 .. 94 F7
Patricks La MK19 .... 31 F4
Patrick Way HP21.... 116 A4
Patrington Cl UB8 .... 201 C2
Patriot Dr MK13.... 34 B2
Patrons Way E UB9 .... 189 F5
Patrons Way W UB9.... 189 F5
Patterson Ct HP10 .... 185 E7
Patterson Rd HP5.... 144 B3
Pattison La MK15 .... 35 C3
PAULERSPURY.... 17 B7
Paulerspury CE Prim Sch
 NN12.... 17 B8
Pauls Hill HP10 .... 174 F6
Paul's Row HP11.... 173 B6
Pavers Ct HP21 .... 115 D3
Pavilion Cl HP20.... 116 A8
Pavilions The (Sh Ctr)
 UB8.... 201 C5
Pavilion Way HP6.... 166 C8
Paxton Ave SL1.... 205 C3
Paxton Cl MK46.... 6 F3
Paxton Cres MK5 .... 46 B5
Paxton Rd HP4.... 135 D4
Paynes Ct MK18.... 41 D1
Paynes Dr MK5 .... 46 A8
Paynes Field Cl HP4.... 134 D7
Payton Hos SL6.... 195 E6
Peace La SL6 .... 195 E6
Peace Rd SL0, SL3.... 200 A3
Peachey Cl UB8.... 208 D7
Peachey La UB8 .... 208 D8
Peach Tree Ave UB7 .... 208 F7
Peacock Hay MK4.... 46 C2
Peacock La HP19 .... 101 B4
Peacock Rd SL7 .... 184 A3
Peacocks Cl HP4.... 134 F6
Pea La HP4.... 134 D7
Pearce Cl
 Aylesbury HP21 .... 115 E4
 Maidenhead SL6 .... 195 F1
Pearce Ctyd HP18.... 109 E5
Pearce Dr SL6 .... 195 F7
Pearce Rd
 Chesham HP5 .... 144 B2
 Maidenhead SL6 .... 195 F1
Pearce's Orch RG9.... 191 D3
Pearl Cl MK18 .... 52 F6
Pearl Gdns SL1 .... 205 B5
Pearse Gr MK7.... 48 A4
Pearson Cl HP19.... 115 B6
Pear Tree Ave UB7.... 208 F7
Peartree Cl SL1.... 204 F5
Pear Tree Cl
 Amersham HP7 .... 165 F8
 Seer Green HP9.... 176 C4
Pear Tree Ct HP15 .... 163 C6
Pear Tree Farm Ind Units
 OX27.... 71 E2
Peartrees UB7.... 208 D6
Peascod Pl 12 SL4 .... 210 D6
Peascod St SL4.... 210 D6
Peascroft HP18.... 125 D6
Peatey Ct HP13 .... 173 D6
Pebble Brook Sch HP21. 115 C7
Pebble La
 Aylesbury HP20 .... 115 D8
 Brackley NN13.... 38 A7
Pebblemoor LU6.... 92 F3
Pebody Pl 10 MK46.... 6 F3
Peck Ct MK4.... 45 E3
Peckover Ct 8 MK8.... 33 F1
Pecks Farm Cl HP22.... 102 C4
Peddle Ct HP11.... 172 F7
Pednor Bottom HP5.... 143 B3
PEDNORMEAD END.... 154 A7
Pednormead End HP5... 154 B7
Pednor Rd HP5 .... 143 E2
Peebles Pl MK3.... 46 F3
Peel Cl SL4.... 210 B4
Peel Ct
 Monks Risborough HP27 .. 139 B4
 Slough SL1.... 205 B8
Peel Rd MK12.... 33 C6
Peel Way UB8 .... 208 E8
Peerless Dr UB9 .... 190 C7
Peers Dr MK17.... 49 E3
Peers La MK5.... 46 B6
Pegasus Wy HP17.... 126 D6
Peggs La HP22.... 117 F5
Pelham Ct SL6.... 202 E7
Pelham Pl MK14 .... 34 F5
Pelham Rd OX9.... 126 B1
Pelton Ct MK5 .... 46 C5
Pemberley Lodge SL4... 210 A4
Pemberton Cl HP21 .... 115 F5
Pemberton Rd SL2.... 197 E1
Pembridge Chase 4
 HP3 .... 146 A3
Pembridge Cl 3 HP3 ... 146 A3
Pembridge Gr MK4.... 45 E1
Pembridge Rd HP3.... 146 A3
Pembroke Ho
 2 Milton Keynes MK3 .... 46 F1
 7 Olney MK46 .... 6 F3
Pembroke Rd HP20 .... 101 F1
Pencarrow Pl MK6 .... 35 A1
Pendeen Ct SL1.... 205 A5
Pendennis Ct MK4 .... 57 A8
Pendles Paddocks HP14. 158 F2
Pendrill Ho 2 HP12.... 172 E7
Penfold HP22.... 116 F2
Penfold Cotts HP15 .... 163 D7
Penfold La
 Holmer Green HP15 .... 163 E8
 Hyde Heath HP7, HP15 ... 152 F1
Pengelly Ct 2 MK6 .... 35 A1
Penhale Cl MK4.... 57 B8
Penhow Rise MK4.... 45 E1
Penina Cl MK3.... 46 D1
Penington Rd HP9 .... 186 B8
Penlee Rise MK4.... 57 B8
Penley Cl OX39 .... 147 B6
Penling Cl SL6.... 195 E6
Penmon Cl MK10.... 35 F1
Penmoor Cl HP12.... 172 C8
PENN.... 174 E7
Penn Ave HP5 .... 144 A1
Penn Cl
 Chorleywood WD3.... 167 D3
 Uxbridge UB8.... 201 D1
Penn Ct
 14 Marlow SL7 .... 183 E2
 Tylers Green HP10.... 174 B8
Penn Dr UB9 .... 189 F5
Pennefather Ct 3 HP21. 115 E7
Penn Gaskell La SL9 .... 177 F5
Penn Gn HP9 .... 175 D4
Penn Haven SL9 .... 188 F6
Pennine Rd SL2.... 205 A8
Penning Cl MK14.... 21 C1
Pennings The HP22 .... 131 B5
Pennington Pl OX9.... 126 B1
Pennington Rd
 Chalfont St Peter SL9 .... 177 D3
 High Wycombe HP13.... 173 F6
Penningtons The HP6... 154 E2
Penn Mdw SL2.... 198 F4
Penn Mead HP10.... 174 F7
Penn Rd
 Aylesbury HP21 .... 115 D7
 Beaconsfield HP9 .... 175 C5
 Chalfont St Peter SL9 .... 177 D2
 Chorleywood WD3.... 167 F1
 Datchet SL3.... 211 D6
 Hazlemere HP15 .... 163 B3
 Milton Keynes MK2 .... 58 E8
 Slough SL2.... 198 D1
Penn Sch HP10 .... 174 D7
PENN STREET.... 164 B5
Penn Street Works Ind Est
 HP7.... 164 A4
Penn Way WD3 .... 167 D3
Penn Wood Prim Sch
 SL2 .... 198 D1
Penn Wood View HP7... 164 A4
Pennycress Way MK16 ... 21 F4
Pennycuik MK17.... 59 C1
PENNYLAND.... 35 A6
Pennylets Gn SL2 .... 199 A5
Penny Pk Rd MK16.... 22 F3
Pennyroyal MK7 .... 48 B7
Pennyroyal Dr UB7.... 208 F4
Penrith Cl UB8.... 201 D5
Penrith Way HP21.... 116 B7
Penryn Ave MK6 .... 35 A2
Penshurst Cl SL9.... 177 D1
Penshurst Cres MK6 .... 47 D4
Penshurst Rd SL6.... 202 D5
Pentewan Gate MK6 .... 34 F2
Pentland Rd
 Aylesbury HP21 .... 115 F6
 Slough SL2.... 205 A8
Pentlands MK11 .... 32 F4
Pentlands Ct HP13 .... 174 B4
Pentlands The HP13.... 174 B4
Penwood Ct SL6 .... 202 B7
Penwood La SL7.... 183 C1
Penyston Rd SL6.... 202 C7
Penzance Spur SL2 .... 198 B1
Peplar Way SL1.... 197 B2
Peplow Cl UB7.... 208 D5
Peppard Mdw HP16 .... 151 D5
Pepper Hill Sch MK13.... 34 A7
PEPPERSHILL.... 124 D6
Peppett's Gn HP5 .... 143 D8
Peppiatts The LU6 .... 92 B5
Pepys Cl SL3.... 212 B8
Pepys Dr HP16.... 151 C6
Perch Cl SL7.... 194 C8
Percheron Pl MK14 .... 34 F5
Perch Mdws HP22 .... 131 B8
Percy Bush Rd UB7 .... 208 F3
Percy Pl SL3.... 211 B6
Percy Terr HP8 .... 177 A7
Peregrine HP19.... 101 E3
Peregrine Bsns Pk HP13 174 A5
Peregrine Cl MK6 .... 47 B8
Perivale MK10 .... 35 E1
Perks La HP16 .... 151 C3
Permayne MK13 .... 34 A7
Perracombe MK4 .... 46 E3
Perran Ave MK6 .... 35 A1
Perrine Cl HP18.... 100 E5
Perrin Springs La RG9... 170 F1
Perrycroft SL4.... 209 F4
Perryfields Way SL1.... 197 B1
Perry Hill HP18 .... 73 A3
Perry Ho SL1 .... 197 B2
Perry La
 Bledlow HP27 .... 138 C2
 Sherington MK16.... 14 B2
Perryman Way SL2.... 197 F2
Perry Mead LU6 .... 92 E6
Perry St HP22.... 131 A5
Perrys The HP22 .... 131 B5
Pershore Croft 1 MK10 .. 36 A1
Pershore Wy HP18 .... 100 E3
Perth Ave SL1 .... 205 B7
Perth Cl MK3 .... 46 F2
Perth Rd HP13 .... 173 D8
Perth Trad Est SL1 .... 205 B8
Peterborough Ave 2
 HP13 .... 173 C7
Peterborough Gate MK15. 35 C6
Peterhead Mews SL3.... 207 A1
Peterhill Cl SL9.... 177 E5
Peterley Ave HP15, HP16 . 151 E3
Peterley La HP16.... 151 E3
Peter's Cl HP16 .... 151 C6
Petersfield HP22.... 116 C3
Petersfield Ave SL2 .... 206 A5
Petersfield Gn 5 MK9.... 34 E1
Petersham Cl MK16 .... 22 C2
Peters La HP27 .... 139 E4
Peter's Pl HP4.... 134 E6
Petronel Rd HP19.... 101 D4
PETSOE END.... 14 A7
Pettifer Way HP12 .... 172 D6
Pettingrew Cl MK7.... 48 B6
Petty Cross SL1.... 204 E7
Petworth MK8 .... 33 E1
Petworth Ct SL4 .... 210 B6
Petworth Ho 2 MK8 .... 33 F1
Pevensey Cl
 Aylesbury HP21 .... 116 B5
 Milton Keynes MK3 .... 57 E7
Pevensey Rd SL2.... 205 A8
Peverel Dr MK1.... 47 B3
Peveril Cl HP21 .... 116 B5
Pevers La MK46.... 6 A1
Pheasant Cl
 Berkhamsted HP4 .... 135 C3
 Tring HP23.... 119 B6
Pheasant Dr HP13.... 161 C1
Pheasant Hill HP8.... 177 C8
Pheasant Rise HP5.... 154 D6
PHEASANTS 181 E6
Pheasants Croft SL6 .... 202 A4
Pheasants Dr HP15.... 163 B5
PHEASANT'S HILL 181 D3
Pheasants Ridge SL7.... 183 C7
Pheasant Wlk SL9.... 177 E6
Phelps Rd MK2 .... 58 E6
Philbye Mews SL1 .... 204 F4
Philip Cotts SL8.... 185 C3
Philip Dr HP10.... 185 C7
Philip Rd HP13.... 173 D7
Philipshill Wood Reserve★
 WD3 .... 167 A2
Philips Rd HP19.... 115 A8
Phillimore Cl MK15 .... 35 B7
Phillip Ct MK5 .... 46 B6
Philpots Cl UB7.... 208 D6
Philps Cl HP14.... 171 C4
Phipps Cl
 Aylesbury HP20 .... 102 A2
 Maidenhead SL6 .... 202 A2
Phipps Rd SL1 .... 204 E8
Phoebe La MK17.... 48 E6
Phoebe's Orch MK17.... 69 E7
Phoenix Bsns Ctr 3 HP5 144 B1
Phoenix Ct SL6 .... 202 D4
Phoenix Dr MK6 .... 46 E6
Phoenix Ho 7 HP19.... 115 A8
Phoenix House Bsns Ctr
 HP12.... 172 E8
Phygtle The SL9 .... 177 E4
Phyllis Court Dr RG9.... 191 E3
Picasso Pl HP19 .... 100 F2
Piccadilly Mews MK18.... 66 A5
Pickering Dr MK4.... 46 B2
Pickford Dr SL3.... 207 A5
Pickfords Gdns SL1 .... 205 E5
Pickins Piece SL3.... 212 A5
Pickwick Terr SL2 .... 206 B6
Picton St MK4 .... 45 E1
Picts La HP27.... 139 A2
PIDDINGTON
 Blackthorn.... 95 E7
 High Wycombe.... 160 B1
PIDDINGTON *continued*
 Northamptonshire 4 B8
Piddington La HP14.... 171 B8
Piddington Rd HP18.... 96 A8
Piece Cl OX27 .... 71 F3
Pield Heath House Sch
 UB8.... 201 F1
Pield Heath Rd UB8.... 201 F1
Pierson Rd SL4 .... 209 D6
Pigeon Farm Rd HP14... 158 E5
Piggotts End 6 HP7 .... 165 B7
Piggott's Hill HP14.... 150 E1
Piggotts Orch HP7 .... 165 B7
Piggy La WD3.... 167 B3
Pightle Cres MK18 .... 41 D2
Pightle The
 Buckingham MK18.... 41 D1
 Maids Moreton MK18 .... 41 F4
 Oving HP22 .... 86 D7
 Pitstone LU7 .... 105 D3
Pigott Dr MK5 .... 46 A5
Pigott Orch HP22 .... 85 A5
Pike Cl
 Marlow SL7 .... 194 C8
 Uxbridge UB10.... 201 F4
Pike Cnr HP21 .... 116 C5
Pilch Field Wildlife
 Reserve★ MK17.... 54 B5
Pilch La MK17 .... 54 D4
Pilgrims Cl HP27.... 139 B5
Pilgrim St MK15 .... 35 A4
Pillow Wy MK18.... 52 F6
Pilots Pl HP17 .... 126 E6
Pilot Trad Est HP12.... 172 E8
PIMLICO 26 F6
Pimlico Ct 4 MK10 .... 35 F1
Pimms Cl HP13 .... 174 A6
Pimms Gr HP13.... 174 A5
Pimpernel Gr MK7 .... 48 B6
Pinchfield WD3.... 178 D5
Pinders Croft MK12 .... 33 B5
PINDON END.... 10 C4
Pineapple Rd HP7.... 165 F8
Pine Chase HP12.... 172 B3
Pine Cl
 Berkhamsted HP4 .... 135 B4
 Buckingham MK18.... 41 E3
 Hazelmere HP15 .... 163 B3
 Maidenhead SL6 .... 202 B7
Pine Crest Mews LU7 .... 80 E6
Pinecroft SL7.... 183 D4
Pine Ct HP5 .... 154 C8
Pine Gr MK17.... 49 A4
PINEHAM.... 35 E7
Pineham Rdbt MK15 .... 35 E5
Pine Hill HP15 .... 162 F3
Pinels Way HP11.... 172 E3
Piner Cotts SL4.... 209 E4
Pine Rd LU6 .... 106 F8
Pines Cl
 Amersham HP6 .... 154 B2
 Little Kingshill HP16 .... 152 B4
Pine St HP19 .... 115 A8
Pines The
 Felden HP3 .... 146 F7
 Slough SL3.... 206 F5
 Slough SL3.... 206 F5
 Tylers Green HP10.... 163 B1
Pinetree Cl SL9.... 177 C3
Pine Trees Dr UB10 .... 201 E8
Pine Wlk
 Berkhamsted HP4 .... 134 D7
 Hazelmere HP15 .... 163 B3
Pinewood Ave UB8.... 208 F7
Pinewood Cl
 Gerrards Cross SL9.... 188 E4
 Iver Heath SL0 .... 200 C5
Pinewood Dr MK2.... 58 E7
Pinewood Film Studios
 SL0 .... 200 B5
Pinewood Gn SL0.... 200 C5
Pinewood Mews TW19 .. 213 D1
Pinewood Rd
 High Wycombe HP12.... 172 C7
 Iver Heath SL0 .... 200 B4
Pinfold MK7 .... 48 B6
PINFOLDPOND.... 60 E6
Pinfold Yd MK18.... 51 B6
Pinglestone Cl UB7 .... 213 E7
Pinions Rd HP13 .... 173 E5
Pinkard Ct MK6.... 47 C8
Pink Hill HP27 .... 149 E8
Pink La SL1.... 197 B3
Pinkneys Dr SL6 .... 195 A1
PINKNEYS GREEN 195 A1
Pinkneys Rd SL6.... 202 A8
Pink Rd HP27 .... 149 E7
Pinks Cl MK5 .... 46 C8
Pinkworthy MK4 .... 46 D4
Pinn Cl UB8 .... 208 D7
Pinstone Way SL9.... 189 B2
Pintail Cl HP19.... 101 E4
Pintail Wy SL6 .... 203 B8
Pipard MK14.... 34 E7
Pipers Cl SL1 .... 197 C2
Pipers Corner Sch HP15. 162 D8
Pipers Croft LU6.... 93 F7
Pipers Ct SL1 .... 197 C2
Pipers La HP15 .... 162 C8
Pipers Wood Cotts HP7 . 153 C2
Pipit Gdns 7 HP19.... 101 E4
Pipit Wlk 6 HP19.... 101 E4
Pippin Cl MK16 .... 22 B3
Pippin Rd HP18 .... 100 E5
Pippins Cl UB7.... 208 D3
Pippins Sch SL3 .... 212 F6
Pippins The SL3 .... 206 F5
Pipston Gn
 Milton Keynes MK7 .... 48 B7
 Walton MK7.... 48 B6
PISHILL 179 D8
PISHILL BANK.... 168 B1
Pishill Bank RG9.... 168 B1
PISHILL BOTTOM.... 168 A1
Pistone Green Bsns Pk
 LU7.... 105 D2
Pistone Windmill★ LU7 . 105 F4
PITCHCOTT.... 86 B5
Pitchcott Rd HP22 .... 86 B6
Pitcher La MK5 .... 46 B8
Pitcher Wlk HP19 .... 115 A7
Pitchford Ave MK18.... 41 E2
Pitchford Wlk MK18.... 41 F1
PITCH GREEN.... 138 B3
Pitch Pond Cl HP9 .... 175 C5
Pitch The HP14 .... 159 D3
Pitfield MK11 .... 33 B3
PITSTONE.... 105 C4
Pitstone Green Farm Mus★
 LU7.... 105 D4
Pitters Piece HP18 .... 125 B7
Pitt Gn MK18 .... 41 F1
Pitts Rd SL1 .... 205 C5
Pixel Wy MK10.... 35 E2
Pixie Rd HP18 .... 100 E5
Place Farm Ho HP27 .... 139 B6
Place Farm Way HP27.... 139 B5
Plackett Way SL1 .... 204 D5
Plaines Cl SL1 .... 204 F5
Plaistow Cres MK10.... 35 F1
Plaiters Cl HP23 .... 119 B4
Plantain Ct MK7 .... 48 B6
Plantation Pl MK5.... 46 A4
Plantation Rd
 Amersham HP6 .... 154 E2
 High Wycombe HP13.... 174 A7
 Leighton Buzzard LU7 .... 70 F3
Plantation Way HP6.... 154 E2
Platt The HP7.... 165 B7
Playing Field Rd NN13.... 39 A4
Pleasant Cotts SL0.... 200 B2
Pleasant Pl WD3 .... 178 E3
Pleasaunce The HP22 .... 117 E5
Pleshey Cl MK5 .... 46 B6
Plested Ct HP22 .... 116 C2
Plomer Green Ave HP13 161 D2
Plomer Green La HP13 .. 161 D3
Plomer Hill HP13 .... 161 D1
Plough Cl HP21 .... 115 E3
Plough End HP22 .... 102 B4
Plough La
 Sarratt WD4.... 156 F6
 Wexham Street SL2.... 199 B4
Ploughlees La SL1 .... 205 E6
Ploughley Rd OX25.... 94 E8
Plover Cl
 1 Berkhamsted HP4 .... 135 C3
 Buckingham MK18.... 52 E7
 Newport Pagnell MK16 .... 22 F3
Plover The 4 HP19 .... 101 E4
Plover Wlk 3 HP19 .... 101 E4
Plowman Cl MK12.... 33 B5
Plumer Rd HP11 .... 172 E7
Plum Park La NN12 .... 17 D8
PLUMPTON END 17 C7
Plumstead Ave MK13.... 34 D3
Pluto Cl SL1 .... 204 E4
Pluto Way HP19.... 101 D4
Plym Cl HP21 .... 115 C5
Plymouth Gr MK4 .... 46 B1
Plymouth Rd SL1 .... 204 E8
Plysu Wy 1 MK17.... 49 A5
Pocketts Yd SL6 .... 196 B7
Pocock Ave UB7 .... 208 F3
Pococks La SL4.... 205 E1
Poets Chase HP21.... 115 F6
Points The SL6 .... 202 B3
Polar Pk UB7 .... 213 F7
Poles Hill
 Chesham HP5 .... 144 A2
 Sarratt WD4.... 156 E6
Police Hos SL9 .... 189 B3
Polidoris La HP15.... 163 C7
Polish Ave HP22 .... 131 E8
Pollard Ave UB9 .... 189 F5
Pollard Cl SL4 .... 211 B2
Pollards WD3.... 178 D5
Pollys Yd MK14 .... 22 D5
Pollywick Rd HP23.... 119 D1
Polmartin Ct 1 MK6 .... 35 A1
Polruan Pl
 Fishermead MK6 .... 47 A8
 Milton Keynes MK6 .... 35 A1
Polygon Bsns Ctr SL3 ... 212 F5
Pomander Cres MK7 .... 48 B7
Pomeroy Cl HP7 .... 165 D7
Pomeroy Ct HP18 .... 100 E5
Pond App HP15 .... 163 C7
Pond Cl
 Newton Longville MK17.... 57 C2
 Tring HP23.... 119 A4
 Winchmore Hill HP7 .... 164 C3
Pond Cotts HP14.... 171 B4
Pondecroft HP18.... 100 D4
Pondgate MK7.... 48 B8
Pond Gate MK14.... 21 F3
Pond La
 Chalfont St Peter SL9 .... 177 C2
 Little Gaddesden HP4 .... 121 E7
POND PARK 144 A2
Pond Park Rd HP5 .... 144 B2
Pondwicks HP7.... 165 B8

Pony Field The HP22 . . . . **116** D1
Poole Cl HP21 . . . . **115** E4
Pool La SL1 . . . . **205** E6
Poolmans Rd SL4 . . . . **209** D4
Pope Ct HP23 . . . . **118** F3
Popes Acre HP17 . . . . . . **126** F5
Popes Cl
  Amersham HP6 . . . . . . **154** F2
  Colnbrook SL3 . . . . **212** C7
Popes La SL6 . . . . **195** C7
Pope Way HP21 . . . . **115** E4
Poplar Ave UB7 . . . . **208** F6
Poplar Cl
  Aylesbury HP20 . . . . . . **102** A2
  Chesham HP5 . . . . **144** C3
  Milton Keynes MK6 . . . . **47** E5
  Poyle SL3 . . . . **212** E6
Poplar Ho SL3 . . . . **206** F1
Poplar Rd
  Aylesbury HP20 . . . . . . **102** A2
  New Denham UB9 . . . . . **201** C6
  Wooburn Green HP10 . . . **185** E7
Poplars Cl HP17 . . . . **114** C5
Poplars Gr SL6 . . . . **196** B2
Poplars Rd MK18 . . . . . . **52** D8
Poplars The HP22 . . . . . **131** C5
Poppy Ave MK10 . . . . . . **36** B4
Poppyfield Wy NN13 . . . **26** A2
Poppy Rd HP27 . . . . **139** A2
Porlock La MK4 . . . . **46** C4
Portal Cl UB10 . . . . **201** F5
Portal Rd HP22 . . . . **131** D6
Portchester Ct 1 MK8 . . **33** F1
Porter's Cl HP6 . . . . **31** E4
Porters Way UB7 . . . . . . **208** F4
Portfield Cl MK18 . . . . . . **52** E8
Port Field Farm MK16 . . **21** F5
Portfields Prim Sch MK16 **22** A5
Portfields Rd MK16 . . . . **22** B4
Portfield Way MK18 . . . . **52** E8
Porthcawl Gn MK3 . . . . . **57** C8
Porthleven Pl MK6 . . . . . **35** A2
Porthmellin Cl MK4 . . . . **57** D8
Portishead Dr MK4 . . . . . **56** F8
Portland Bsns Ctr SL3 . . **211** B6
Portland Cl SL2 . . . . **197** D1
Portland Ct MK14 . . . . . . **21** C1
Portland Dr MK15 . . . . . . **35** C7
Portland Gdns SL7 . . . . . **183** D1
Portland Ho HP13 . . . . . . **173** D8
Portland Pk SL9 . . . . **188** D5
Portland Rd HP11 . . . . . . **173** E4
Portlands Alley SL7 . . . . **183** D1
Portlands Mews 1 SL7 . . **183** D1
Port Line Rd MK10 . . . . . **36** C4
Portlock Rd SL6 . . . . **202** C7
Portman Mews HP19 . . . **114** F8
Portmarnock Cl MK3 . . . . **57** D8
Portnall Pl MK43 . . . . . . **25** B2
Portobello Cl HP5 . . . . . . **144** A2
Portobello Cotts
  Lacey Green HP27 . . . . . **149** E5
  Lewknor OX49 . . . . **157** C2
Portrush Cl MK3 . . . . **57** D8
Portsmouth Ct SL1 . . . . . **205** E6
Portway
  Milton Keynes, Bradwell
   Common MK5, MK9, MK13,
   MK14, MK15 . . . . **34** D2
  Milton Keynes, Shenley Church
   End MK8, MK5 . . . . . . **45** F4
  North Marston MK18 . . . **76** B1
  Stone HP17 . . . . **114** E4
Portway Dr HP12 . . . . . . **161** B1
Portway Rd
  Stone HP17 . . . . **114** E4
  Twyford MK18 . . . . **62** D1
Portway Rdbt MK5 . . . . . **34** B1
PORTWAYS **168** B8
Posting Ho HP23 . . . . . . **120** A5
Post Mdw SL0 . . . . **200** D2
Post Office Cotts SL2 . . . **199** A5
Post Office La
  Beaconsfield HP9 . . . . . **175** D3
  Hoggeston MK18 . . . . . **77** B7
  Slough SL3 . . . . **206** D7
  Whitchurch HP22 . . . . . **87** A6
Potash Cl HP17 . . . . **126** F5
Potash La HP23 . . . . **104** A5
Potkiln La HP9 . . . . **176** D1
Potter Row HP16 . . . . . . **142** C1
Potters Cl HP16 . . . . **151** B7
Potters Cross SL0 . . . . . **200** E2
Potters Cross Cres HP15 **162** C2
Potters Glen MK18 . . . . . **53** B1
Potters La MK11 . . . . **33** B4
POTTERSPURY **18** D2
Potterspury Lodge Sch
  NN12 . . . . **18** B6
Pottery Cl HP19 . . . . **115** A7
Pottery Ct HP19 . . . . **115** A7
Potts Pl 8 SL7 . . . . **183** D2
Poulcott TW19 . . . . **211** E1
Pound Cl
  Steeple Claydon MK18 . . **63** D1
  Wicken MK19 . . . . **31** B1
Pound Cres SL7 . . . . **183** C1
Poundfield La SL6 . . . . . **195** F7
Poundfield Rd NN12 . . . . **18** E2
Pound Hill MK17 . . . . **59** C1
Pound La
  Heath End HP5 . . . . . . **134** A1
  Little Marlow SL7 . . . . . **184** C4
  Marlow SL7 . . . . **183** D1
  North Crawley MK16 . . . **24** B7

Pound La continued
  Preston Bissett MK18 . . . **51** C1
POUNDON **71** E2
Pounds Cl MK43 . . . . **25** B1
Pound St HP22 . . . . **131** B4
Pound The
  Cookham Rise SL6 . . . . **195** F7
  Cookham SL6 . . . . **196** A7
  Slough SL1 . . . . **197** D1
  Syresham NN13 . . . . . . **27** B7
Powell Haven MK10 . . . . **35** E3
Powis Cl SL6 . . . . **202** B4
Powis La MK4 . . . . **45** F2
Powney Rd SL6 . . . . **202** C7
POYLE **212** E6
Poyle 14 Trad Est SL3 . . **212** E4
Poyle La SL1 . . . . **197** B3
Poyle New Cotts SL3 . . . **212** F5
Poyle Pk SL3 . . . . **212** E4
Poyle Rd SL3 . . . . **212** E5
Poyle Tech Ctr The SL3 . **212** E5
Poynings The SL0 . . . . . **207** F2
Pratt Ho HP6 . . . . **154** F1
Prebendal Ave HP21 . . . . **115** D7
Prebendal Cl 11 HP20 . . . **115** D8
Prebendal Ct 1 HP20 . . . **115** D8
PREBENDAL FARM **115** B7
Precedent Dr MK13 . . . . **34** B3
Precincts The SL1 . . . . . **197** C1
Premier Acad The MK2 . . **58** D6
Prentice Gr MK5 . . . . **46** B3
Prescott Rd SL3 . . . . **212** E5
Prescotts The UB9 . . . . . **189** F3
Presley Way MK8 . . . . . . **45** E7
Press Rd UB8 . . . . **201** D6
PRESTON BISSETT **62** B8
Preston Ct MK15 . . . . **35** B7
Preston Hill HP5 . . . . **144** D2
Preston Rd SL2 . . . . **206** C6
Prestwick Cl MK3 . . . . . . **57** D7
Prestwold Way HP19 . . . **115** A7
Prestwold Way HP19 . . . **115** A7
PRESTWOOD **151** D6
Prestwood SL2 . . . . **206** B7
Prestwood Cl HP12 . . . . . **172** C8
Prestwood Inf Sch HP16 **151** C7
Prestwood Jun Sch
  HP16 . . . . **151** C6
Prestwood Nature Reserve ★
  HP16 . . . . **151** B3
Prestwood Pl HP16 . . . . **151** C6
Pretoria Rd HP13 . . . . . . **173** C8
Priest End OX9 . . . . **125** E1
Priestland Gdns HP4 . . . **135** C6
Priestley Ct HP13 . . . . . . **173** D6
Priests Paddock HP9 . . . **175** B5
Prima Rd HP18 . . . . **100** E5
Primary Rd SL1 . . . . **205** D3
Primatt Cres MK5 . . . . . . **46** B6
Primrose Cotts HP14 . . . **150** E1
Primrose Ct HP21 . . . . . **115** B6
Primrose Dr
  Aylesbury HP21 . . . . . . **115** B5
  West Drayton UB7 . . . . . **208** D2
Primrose Gdns LU7 . . . . . **80** E7
Primrose Gn HP15 . . . . . **162** F6
Primrose Hill HP15 . . . . . **162** F6
Primrose La MK10 . . . . . **36** C3
Primrose Lea SL7 . . . . . . **183** D2
Primrose Rd MK13 . . . . . **34** A4
Primrose Terr HP18 . . . . **110** A8
Primrose Way MK18 . . . . **52** C7
Prince Albert's Wlk SL3,
  SL4 . . . . **211** B5
Prince Andrew Cl 1 SL6 **203** B8
Prince Andrew Rd SL6 . . **196** B1
Prince Consort Cotts
  SL4 . . . . **210** D5
Prince Consort's Dr SL4 . **210** B2
Prince Edward St HP4 . . . **135** C4
Prince Philip Ave MK43 . . **24** C2
Prince Rupert Dr HP19 . . **101** C4
Princes Cl
  Berkhamsted HP4 . . . . . **135** A6
  Chilton HP18 . . . . **111** B3
  Eton Wick SL4 . . . . **204** F1
Princes Ct
  Bourne End SL8 . . . . . . **185** C3
  Leighton Buzzard LU7 . . **80** F8
Princes Gate HP13 . . . . . **173** D6
Princes Gdns HP27 . . . . **139** B3
Prince's La HP16 . . . . . . **142** D5
Princes Pl HP27 . . . . **139** B1
Princes Rd SL8 . . . . **185** C3
Prince's Rd HP21 . . . . . . **115** E8
PRINCES RISBOROUGH . . **139** D4
Princes Risborough Sch
  Monks Risborough HP27 . **139** B5
  Princes Risborough HP27 **139** C2
Princes Risborough Sta
  HP27 . . . . **138** F2
Princess Ave SL4 . . . . . . **210** B4
Princess Gr HP9 . . . . **176** D6
Princess Margaret Hospl The
  (private) SL4 . . . . **210** D5
Princess St SL6 . . . . **202** F6
Princess St
  Piddington HP14 . . . . . **160** B1
  2 Slough SL1 . . . . **206** B4
Princes Terr SL8 . . . . . . **185** C3
Princes Way MK2 . . . . . . **58** C8
Princes Way Rdbt MK2 . . **58** B8
Printers End HP19 . . . . . **101** B1
Printers Piece HP17 . . . . **127** A6
Prior Gr HP5 . . . . **144** C1
Priors Cl
  Maidenhead SL6 . . . . . **203** B2
  5 Slough SL1 . . . . **206** A3

Priors Pk MK4 . . . . **46** D2
Priors Rd SL4 . . . . **209** D4
Priors Way SL6 . . . . **203** B2
Priors Way Ind Est SL6 . . **203** B2
Priory Ave
  High Wycombe HP13 . . . **173** B7
  South Harefield UB9 . . . **190** C7
Priory Cl
  Aylesbury HP19 . . . . . . **101** C2
  Denham UB9 . . . . **190** A1
  Horton-cum-S OX33 . . . **108** B5
  Newport Pagnell MK16 . . **22** C4
  South Harefield UB9 . . . **190** C7
Priory Common Sch
  MK13 . . . . **34** B4
Priory Cotts UB9 . . . . . . **190** C7
Priory Cres HP19 . . . . . . **101** C2
Priory Ct 2 HP4 . . . . . . **135** C4
Priory Farm Cotts OX27 . **71** E2
Priory Gdns
  Berkhamsted HP4 . . . . . **135** C4
  South Harefield UB9 . . . **190** C7
Priory Rd
  Gerrards Cross SL9 . . . . **188** D8
  High Wycombe HP13 . . . **173** B7
  Slough SL1 . . . . **204** C8
Priory Rise Sch MK4 . . . . **56** E7
Priory Sch SL1 . . . . **204** D8
Priory St MK16 . . . . **22** E4
Priory Way
  Datchet SL3 . . . . **211** B7
  Gerrards Cross SL9 . . . . **188** D8
  Harmondsworth UB7 . . . **213** D8
Pritchard Ct MK14 . . . . . **34** E8
Proctor Mews MK17 . . . . **58** B2
Proctor Rise MK8 . . . . . . **45** D6
Progress Bsns Ctr SL1 . . **204** D7
Progress Rd HP12 . . . . . **172** B7
Promenade SL4 . . . . **210** C7
Prospect Cl MK17 . . . . . . **68** D6
Prospect Cotts HP14 . . . **161** D6
Prospect Ct
  Lane End HP14 . . . . . . **171** B5
  Yardley Gobion NN12 . . . **18** F6
Prospect Pl
  Castlethorpe MK19 . . . . **19** F5
  Hurley SL6 . . . . **193** F3
  3 Windsor SL4 . . . . . . **210** D4
  Wing LU7 . . . . **79** E2
Prospect Rd
  Marlow SL7 . . . . **183** D2
  Milton Keynes MK11 . . . **32** C5
Prothero Cl HP21 . . . . . . **115** E4
Prothero Field MK7 . . . . **48** C5
Providence Pl
  9 Maidenhead SL6 . . . . **202** F7
  2 Milton Keynes MK3 . . **34** A4
Providence Rd UB7 . . . . . **208** F5
Provis Wharf HP20 . . . . . **102** B1
Prudential Bldgs 1 SL1 . **205** F4
PUDDS CROSS **145** E2
Pudseys Cl SL6 . . . . **195** B6
Puers Field HP9 . . . . **176** E4
Puers La HP9 . . . . **176** E4
Puffin Way HP19 . . . . . . **101** F3
Pulborough Cl MK3 . . . . **46** D1
Pulford Rd LU7 . . . . **80** F6
Pullfields HP5 . . . . **144** A1
Pulpit Cl HP5 . . . . **144** A2
Pulpit La HP22 . . . . **76** D1
Pulver Rd HP22 . . . . **102** C2
Pumpkin Hill SL1 . . . . . . **197** E6
Pump Lane N SL7 . . . . . . **183** F6
Pump Lane S SL7 . . . . . . **184** A4
Pump Mdw HP16 . . . . . . **152** A8
Pump Pl MK19 . . . . **32** B7
Pumpus Gn MK18 . . . . . . **66** A4
Punch Bowl La HP5 . . . . **154** C7
Purbeck MK13 . . . . **34** C6
Purbeck Cl HP21 . . . . . . **116** B5
Purcel Dr MK16 . . . . **22** C3
Purse La MK16 . . . . **11** F8
Pursers Ct SL1 . . . . **205** E7
Pursell Cl SL6 . . . . **202** A3
Pursell Pl HP27 . . . . **139** B5
Pursells Mdw HP14 . . . . **161** C7
Purton Cl SL2 . . . . **198** C5
Purton La SL2 . . . . **198** C5
PURY END **17** A7
Pury Rd
  Alderton NN12 . . . . **9** A2
  Paulerspury NN12 . . . . . **17** D8
Pusey Way HP14 . . . . . . **171** C5
Putlowes Dr HP18 . . . . . **100** C3
Putman Ho MK5 . . . . **46** C5
Putman Pl RG9 . . . . **191** E1
Putman St HP19 . . . . . . **101** C1
Putnams Dr HP22 . . . . . . **117** D5
PUTTENHAM **103** F2
Puttenham Ct HP23 . . . . **103** F2
PUXLEY **31** D7
Puxley Rd
  Deanshanger MK19 . . . . **31** D5
  Milton Keynes MK19 . . . **32** A5
Pye Bridge End MK10 . . . **36** A4
Pyebush La HP9 . . . . **187** A8
Pyghtles The HP22 . . . . . **85** B5
Pyghtle The
  Olney MK46 . . . . **6** F3
  Turvey MK43 . . . . **8** E6
Pyke Hayes MK8 . . . . . . **33** D3
Pymcombe Cl HP27 . . . . **139** B5
Pyms Stables MK16 . . . . **22** F2
Pym Wlk OX9 . . . . **125** F1
Pynefield Ho WD3 . . . . . **167** F2
Pyxe Ct MK7 . . . . **48** A4

Q

Quadrangle The HP13 . . **173** E7
Quadrans Cl MK15 . . . . . **35** A7
Quadrant The
  High Wycombe HP13 . . . **162** E1
  Maidenhead SL6 . . . . . **203** A6
QUAINTON **85** B5
Quainton CE Comb Sch
  HP22 . . . . **85** A5
QUAINTON HILL **75** B1
Quainton Rd
  North Marston MK18 . . . **76** A2
  Waddesdon HP18 . . . . . **99** A7
Quainton Road Sta ★
  HP22 . . . . **84** F2
Quainton Windmill ★
  HP22 . . . . **85** B5
Quaker's Mead HP22 . . . **116** F3
Quakers Mede HP17 . . . **127** A6
Quantock Cl SL3 . . . . . . **207** A1
Quantock Cres MK4 . . . . **46** D2
QUARRENDON **101** B3
Quarrendon Ave HP19 . . **101** B2
Quarrendon Rd HP7 . . . . **165** E7
Quarry Cl HP18 . . . . **125** C7
Quarry Ct LU7 . . . . **105** D2
Quarrydale Dr SL7 . . . . . **183** F2
Quarry Green Cl MK19 . . **31** B3
Quarry Rd LU7 . . . . **105** D2
Quarry Wood Rd SL6,
  SL7 . . . . **195** A8
Quaves Rd SL3 . . . . **206** C3
Quebec Rd HP13 . . . . . . **173** E6
Queen Alexandra Rd
  HP11 . . . . **173** A6
Queen Anne Royal Free CE
  Fst Sch The SL4 . . . . . . **210** D4
Queen Anne's Ct 10 SL4 . **210** C6
Queen Anne's Rd SL4 . . . **210** C3
Queen Anne St MK13 . . . **33** F7
Queen Catherine Rd
  MK18 . . . . **63** E2
Queen Charlotte St 10
  SL4 . . . . **210** D6
Queen Cl RG9 . . . . **191** E1
Queen Eleanor Prim Sch
  MK11 . . . . **32** F4
Queen Eleanor St MK11 . **32** E6
Queen Elizabeth's Wlk
  SL4 . . . . **210** F5
Queen Mother's Dr UB9 . **189** F5
Queens Acre
  High Wycombe HP13 . . . **173** D6
  Windsor SL4 . . . . **210** D3
Queen's Acre SL4 . . . . . **210** D3
Queen St Mews RG9 . . . **191** E1
Queens Ave MK16 . . . . . **22** C4
Queensbury La MK10 . . . **35** E1
Queens Cl OX9 . . . . **125** F2
Queen's Cl SL4 . . . . **211** A2
Queens Ct HP13 . . . . **173** C6
Queen's Ct SL1 . . . . **205** F6
Queen's Dr SL3 . . . . **199** F4
Queen's Dr The WD3 . . . **167** F2
Queensgate HP19 . . . . . **115** A8
Queen's Gate SL4 . . . . . **210** D3
Queensmead SL3 . . . . . . **211** B6
Queens Mead HP21 . . . . **116** C7
Queensmead Ho HP10 . . **174** C2
Queensmead Rd HP10 . . **174** C2
Queensmere Rd SL1 . . . **205** F4
Queensmere (Sh Ctr)
  SL1 . . . . **205** F4
Queens Park Arts Ctr
  HP21 . . . . **115** F8
Queen's Pk HP21 . . . . . . **115** F8
Queen Sq 8 HP11 . . . . . **173** A7
Queens Rd
  Berkhamsted HP4 . . . . . **135** C4
  1 Chesham HP5 . . . . . . **144** C1
  Eton Wick SL4 . . . . **204** F1
  High Wycombe HP13 . . . **173** C6
  Princes Risborough HP27 **139** C4
  Slough SL1 . . . . **205** F6
  West Drayton UB7 . . . . . **208** F4
Queen's Rd
  Datchet SL3 . . . . **211** B7
  Marlow SL7 . . . . **183** D2
  Uxbridge UB8 . . . . **201** C2
  Windsor SL4 . . . . **210** C5
Queen St
  Aylesbury HP20 . . . . . . **116** A8
  Henley-on-Thames RG9 . . **191** E1
  High Wycombe HP13 . . . **173** C7
  Leighton Buzzard LU7 . . **80** F8
  Maidenhead SL6 . . . . . **202** F7
  Milton Keynes MK11 . . . **32** E6
  Piddington HP14 . . . . . **160** B1
  Pitstone LU7 . . . . **105** D4
  Tring HP23 . . . . **119** A3
  Waddesdon HP18 . . . . . **98** F6
Queen's Terr 5 SL4 . . . . **210** D4
Queensway
  Bletchley MK2 . . . . **58** C8
  Hazelmere HP15 . . . . . **163** A4
  Maidenhead SL6 . . . . . **195** E2
  Milton Keynes MK2 . . . . **58** D8
Queensway The SL9 . . . . **188** D7
Queen Victoria Rd HP13 **173** B6
Queen Victoria's Wlk
  SL4 . . . . **210** F6
Quercetum Cl 3 HP19 . . **101** C1
Quickberry Pl HP7 . . . . . **165** C4
Quickley La WD3 . . . . . . **167** C3

Quickley Rise WD3 . . . . **167** B3
Quickly Brow WD3 . . . . . **167** B3
Quill Hall La HP6 . . . . . . **154** F2
Quilter Mdw MK7 . . . . . **48** D5
Quilters Way HP22 . . . . **130** D8
Quinbrookes SL2 . . . . . . **206** C7
Quince Cl MK7 . . . . **48** B5
Quinn Mdws MK4 . . . . . **45** E3
Quinton Dr MK13 . . . . . . **34** B3
Quintus Cl MK11 . . . . . . **33** A3
Quoitings Dr SL7 . . . . . **183** C2
Quoitings Gdns SL7 . . . **183** C2
Quoiting Sq SL7 . . . . . . **183** D2

R

Raans Rd HP6 . . . . **154** F1
Rabans Cl
  Aylesbury HP19 . . . . . . **100** E1
  Olney MK46 . . . . **6** E5
Rabans La HP19 . . . . **100** E1
Rabans Lane Ind Est
  HP19 . . . . **100** E1
Rabbsfarm Prim Sch
  UB7 . . . . **208** E6
Rabbs Mill Ho UB8 . . . . . **201** D3
Rachels Way HP5 . . . . . . **154** D5
Rackstraw Gr MK7 . . . . . **48** D5
Radcliffe Sch The MK12 . . **33** B6
Radcliffe St MK12 . . . . . **33** D6
RADCLIVE **51** E8
Radclive Rd MK18 . . . . . **51** F7
Radcot Ave SL3 . . . . **207** B3
Radcot Cl SL6 . . . . **195** E3
Radcote Lodge MK8 . . . . **33** E1
Radian Cl MK5 . . . . **46** C7
Radman Gr MK12 . . . . . . **33** B5
RADNAGE **159** C7
Radnage CE Inf Sch
  HP14 . . . . **159** D6
Radnage Common Rd
  HP14 . . . . **159** D5
Radnor Cl RG9 . . . . **191** E2
Radnor End HP20 . . . . . **101** E2
Radnor Way SL3 . . . . . . **206** E2
Radstock Cres MK10 . . . **36** A4
RADSTONE **26** A6
Radworthy MK4 . . . . **46** C3
Raeside Cl HP9 . . . . **176** C5
Raglan Dr MK4 . . . . **45** E1
Ragmans Cl SL7 . . . . . . **183** C8
Ragmans La HP10, SL7 . . **172** D1
Ragnall's La OX33 . . . . . **108** A6
Ragstone Rd SL1 . . . . . . **205** E3
Ragstones HP10 . . . . **174** A1
Railway Cotts
  Steeple Claydon MK18 . . **64** A1
  Wigginton HP23 . . . . . **119** F5
Railway St 2 HP20 . . . . **115** E8
Railway Terr SL2 . . . . . . **205** B5
Rainborough Gdns HP20 **101** E2
Rainbow Dr MK6 . . . . . . **46** F7
Rainbow Ind Est UB7 . . . **208** D6
Rainsborough MK14 . . . . **35** A4
Rainsborough Chase
  SL6 . . . . **202** B3
Rake Way HP21 . . . . **115** D3
Raleigh Cl SL1 . . . . **205** A5
Ralphs Retreat HP15 . . . **162** F4
Ralston Ct 20 SL4 . . . . . **210** D6
RAM ALLEY **12** B5
Ram Alley MK16 . . . . **12** B6
Rambler Cl SL6 . . . . **204** B7
Rambler La SL3 . . . . **206** C3
Ramsay Cl MK13 . . . . . . **34** B3
Ramsay View HP15 . . . . **163** A3
Ramscote La HP5 . . . . . . **143** F7
Ramsey Ct SL2 . . . . **197** D1
Ramsgill Ct MK13 . . . . . **34** C5
Ramsons Ave MK14 . . . . **34** E4
Ramsthorn Gr MK7 . . . . . **48** B6
Ramworth Way HP21 . . . **116** A6
Randall Ave MK19 . . . . . **45** D8
Randall Cl SL3 . . . . **206** F1
Randall Ct SL1 . . . . **211** A1
Randall Dr MK4 . . . . **45** D2
Randolph Cl MK13 . . . . . **34** A6
Randolph Rd SL3 . . . . . . **206** E3
Ranelagh Gdns MK16 . . . **22** C2
Rangers Ct MK8 . . . . **33** F1
Rannal Dr OX39 . . . . **147** C6
Rannoch Cl MK2 . . . . . . **58** D5
Rannock Gdns LU7 . . . . . **80** C7
Ranston Cl UB9 . . . . **189** F5
Rashleigh Pl MK6 . . . . . **46** E7
Ratcliffe Cl
  Old Stratford MK19 . . . . **32** B7
  Uxbridge UB8 . . . . **201** D2
Rathbone Cl MK8 . . . . . . **45** E7
Ravel Cl MK7 . . . . **48** D6
Raven Cl 3 HP19 . . . . . **101** F3
Raven Cres HP18 . . . . . . **98** C6
Raven Dr SL6 . . . . **203** A8
Raven Rd HP14 . . . . **158** F4
Ravensbourne Pl MK6 . . **35** B2
Ravensbourne Rd HP21 . **116** D4
Ravenscar Ct MK4 . . . . . **46** C2
Ravenscourt SL7 . . . . . . **184** A3
Ravenscroft Rd RG9 . . . **191** D2
Ravens Cl
  Berkhamsted HP4 . . . . . **135** C6
  High Wycombe HP13 . . . **161** E3
  Long Marston HP23 . . . . **104** B4
Ravens Field SL3 . . . . . . **206** D4
Ravensglass Croft 6
  MK10 . . . . **36** B3

Ravenshoe Cl SL8 . . . . 185 A3
Ravens La HP4 . . . . 135 D4
Ravensmead
  Chalfont St Peter SL9 . . . . 177 F5
  Chinnor OX39 . . . . 147 C6
RAVENSTONE 5 D2
Ravenstone Mill Rd MK46 . 12 E7
Ravens Wharf HP4 . . . . . 135 D4
Ravensworth Rd SL2 . . . . 198 A4
Ravigill Pl MK12 . . . . 33 D4
Rawcliffe Ho SL6 . . . . . . 203 A6
Rawlings Ct ML17 . . . . 60 F7
Rawlings La HP9 . . . . 176 D7
Rawlins Rd MK13 . . . . 34 A4
Ray Dr SL6 . . . . 203 B7
Ray Ho 5 SL8 . . . . 185 A4
Raylands Mead SL9 . . . . . 188 C6
Ray Lea Cl SL6 . . . . 203 B8
Ray Lea Rd SL6 . . . . 203 B8
Rayleigh Cl MK5 . . . . 46 B6
Raylens HP12 . . . . 172 B5
Ray Lodge SL6 . . . . 203 B7
Ray Lodge Mews SL6 . . . . 203 B7
Ray Mdw SL6 . . . . 196 A1
Ray Mead Cl SL6 . . . . 196 C1
Ray Mead Rd SL6 . . . . . . 203 C8
Ray Mill Road E SL6 . . . . . 196 B1
Ray Mill Road W SL6 . . . . 203 A8
Raymond Cl SL3 . . . . 212 E6
Raymond Rd
  Maidenhead SL6 . . . . . . 202 D7
  Slough SL3 . . . . 207 A3
Rayners Ave HP10 . . . . . . 174 B3
Rayners Cl
  Colnbrook SL3 . . . . 212 C2
  Loudwater HP10 . . . . . . 174 C3
Rayners La MK9 . . . . 35 E1
Ray Park Ave SL6 . . . . . . 203 B8
Ray Park La SL6 . . . . 203 B8
Ray Park Rd SL6 . . . . 203 B8
Rays Ave SL4 . . . . 209 F7
Rays Cl MK2 . . . . 58 E6
Ray's Hill HP5 . . . . 133 C2
Rays La HP10 . . . . 163 C1
Ray St SL6 . . . . 203 B7
Razzaq Pl HP12 . . . . 172 E7
Read Dr HP22 . . . . 102 C4
Reade Ct SL2 . . . . 198 C6
Read Ho HP19 . . . . 115 A7
Reading Cl HP19 . . . . 101 A3
Reading Rd RG9 . . . . 191 E1
Readings The WD3 . . . . . 167 F6
Reads La LU7 . . . . 78 D1
Recreation Rd SL8 . . . . . . 185 B3
Rectory Ave HP13 . . . . . . 173 C7
Rectory Cl
  Farnham Royal SL2 . . . . 198 C2
  Marsh Gibbon OX27 . . . . 71 F3
  Slapton LU7 . . . . 91 D6
  Windsor SL4 . . . . 210 A6
Rectory Ct
  2 Amersham HP7 . . . . . 165 B7
  3 High Wycombe HP13 . . 173 F5
  Lewknor OX49 . . . . 157 B8
  West Drayton UB7 . . . . . 208 E4
Rectory Dr HP18 . . . . 99 A6
Rectory Fields MK15 . . . . . 35 D3
Rectory Gdns HP8 . . . . . . 177 B7
Rectory Hill HP7 . . . . 165 B8
Rectory La
  Amersham HP7 . . . . . . 165 B7
  Berkhamsted HP4 . . . . . 135 C4
  Bix RG9 . . . . 179 D1
  Yardley Hastings NN7 . . . . 1 A7
Rectory Mdw OX39 . . . . . 147 D6
Rectory Orch MK46 . . . . . . 7 F8
Rectory Rd SL6 . . . . 196 E1
Rectory Terr SL2 . . . . 198 C3
Red Admiral St HP19 . . . . 101 C4
Redbourne Ct MK11 . . . . . 32 F5
Redbridge MK14 . . . . 34 D7
Redcliffe Wlk HP19 . . . . . 101 B2
Redcote Manor MK7 . . . . . 48 A4
Red Cottage HP23 . . . . . . 119 D1
Red Cottage Mews **6**
  SL3 . . . . 206 C3
Red Ct SL1 . . . . 205 E5
Redcurrant Ave HP18 . . . . 100 D5
Redding Ct HP17 . . . . 129 E2
Redding Dr HP6 . . . . 154 A2
Redding Gr MK8 . . . . 45 E6
Reddings Cl HP22 . . . . . . 131 B6
Reddington Dr SL3 . . . . . . 206 E2
Rede Cl HP19 . . . . 101 B4
Redfern Cl HP8 . . . . 201 C4
Redfield Cl LU6 . . . . 93 E8
Redford Way SL4 . . . . . . 209 D6
Red Friars Square Sh Ctr **21**
  HP20 . . . . 115 D8
Redgrave Dr **2** MK4 . . . . . 45 E3
Redgrave Pl SL7 . . . . 183 F3
Redhill UB9 . . . . 189 D2
Red House Cl
  Beaconsfield HP9 . . . . . 175 B4
  Newton Longville MK17 . . 57 B8
Redhuish Cl MK4 . . . . 46 D3
Red Kite Cl HP13 . . . . 161 D1
Red Kite View MK18 . . . . . 73 B5
Red Kite Wy HP13 . . . . . . 172 F8
Red Leaf Cl SL3 . . . . 206 F5
Red Leys UB10 . . . . 201 E5

Red Lion Cl MK43 . . . . 25 B1
Red Lion Cotts SL2 . . . . . 199 B1
Red Lion Ct HP14 . . . . . . 158 D5
Red Lion St HP5 . . . . 154 B7
Red Lion Way HP10 . . . . . 185 E6
Red Lodge Gdns HP4 . . . . 135 A3
Redman Rd HP12 . . . . . . 172 B3
REDMOOR 47 A4
Redmoor Ind Est MK6 . . . . 47 A4
Redpitch Pk HP10 . . . . . . 185 F6
Red Poll Wy MK19 . . . . 45 C8
Redriff Cl SL6 . . . . 202 D6
Red Roofs SL6 . . . . 203 C7
Redshaw Cl MK18 . . . . 41 E1
Redshots Cl SL7 . . . . 183 E4
Redvers Gate MK15 . . . . . . 35 F2
Redway Sch The MK6 . . . . . 47 C6
Red Wing HP20 . . . . 101 E3
Redwood SL1 . . . . 197 B1
Redwood Cl
  Hazlemere HP15 . . . . . 163 B3
  Wing LU7 . . . . 79 E2
Redwood Dr
  Aylesbury HP21 . . . . . . 115 E7
  Wing LU7 . . . . 79 E2
Redwood Gate MK5 . . . . . . 46 C4
Redwood Gdns SL1 . . . . . 205 D6
Redwood Glade LU7 . . . . . . 70 F3
Redwood Pl HP9 . . . . 175 D1
Redwoods The SL4 . . . . . 210 D4
Reed Cl SL0 . . . . 207 E7
Reeves Croft MK12 . . . . . . 33 C4
Reform Rd SL6 . . . . 203 B7
Reform Road Ind Est
  SL6 . . . . 203 B7
Regal Ct
  Maidenhead SL6 . . . . . . 203 B2
  14 Tring HP23 . . . . 119 A3
Regency Ct HP21 . . . . . . 116 B7
Regency Mews **2** MK17 . . 49 A5
Regent Ct
  3 Maidenhead SL6 . . . . 202 F7
  Slough SL1 . . . . 205 E2
  Windsor SL4 . . . . 210 D5
Regent Ho HP27 . . . . 139 B4
Regent Pk HP27 . . . . 138 F3
Regent Rd HP21 . . . . 116 B7
Regents Hall MK11 . . . . . . 32 E5
Regents Pl SL6 . . . . 202 D6
Regent St MK2 . . . . 58 C8
Regius Ct HP10 . . . . 174 D8
Reid Ave SL6 . . . . 202 E5
Reliance La MK9 . . . . 35 B3
Rembrandt End HP19 . . . . 100 F2
REMENHAM 192 A5
Remenham Church La
  RG9 . . . . 192 A4
REMENHAM HILL 192 C2
Remenham La
  Remenham Hill RG9 . . . . 191 F3
  Remenham RG9 . . . . . . 192 B5
Remenham Row RG9 . . . . 191 F2
Remenham Terr RG9 . . . . 192 C2
Remus Cl MK11 . . . . 32 F3
Remus Gate NN13 . . . . 38 A6
Rendlesham MK15 . . . . 35 C3
Rendlesham Way WD3 . . . 167 C3
Renfrew Way MK3 . . . . 46 F3
Rennie Cl HP13 . . . . 161 F1
Repton Cl SL6 . . . . 202 C3
Repton Pl HP7 . . . . 166 A8
Retreat The
  Little Chalfont HP6 . . . . . 166 E8
  Milton Keynes MK11 . . . . 32 D5
  Princes Risborough HP27 . 139 B4
Revel Rd HP10 . . . . 185 D8
Revesby Cl SL6 . . . . 202 D3
Reynard Cl MK11 . . . . 32 F3
Reynolds Cl
  Cranfield MK43 . . . . 24 E2
  High Wycombe HP13 . . . 173 E8
Reynolds Pl MK8 . . . . 45 D6
Reynolds Rd HP9 . . . . . . 175 D3
Reynolds Wlk HP5 . . . . . . 144 A4
Rhodes Pl MK6 . . . . 46 F7
Rhondda Cl MK1 . . . . 47 E1
Rhoscolyn Dr MK3 . . . . 57 C8
Rhuddlan Cl MK5 . . . . 45 F7
Rhymer Cl MK19 . . . . 10 F4
Ribble Cl MK16 . . . . 22 E4
Ribble Cres MK3 . . . . 57 D8
Ribstone Rd SL6 . . . . 202 B3
Ricardo Rd SL4 . . . . 211 B1
Richard Gdns HP13 . . . . . 173 E8
Richardson Pl **2** MK6 . . . . 34 E1
Richards Way SL1 . . . . . . 204 F5
Richborough MK13 . . . . . . 34 A6
RICHINGS PARK 207 E3
Richings Pl SL0 . . . . 207 E3
Richings Way SL0 . . . . . . 207 F3
Richmond Cl
  Amersham HP6 . . . . . . 154 F1
  Milton Keynes MK3 . . . . . 46 D1
Richmond Cres SL1 . . . . . 206 A5
Richmond Ct
  Dunstable LU6 . . . . 92 E6
  High Wycombe HP13 . . . 173 C7
Richmond Pl SL9 . . . . 188 C2
Richmond Rd HP20 . . . . . 116 C7
Richmond Way MK16 . . . . . 22 D3
Rickard Cl
  Aylesbury HP21 . . . . . . 115 D3
  West Drayton UB7 . . . . . 208 D3
Ricketts Cl HP17 . . . . 127 A6
Rickford's Hill HP20 . . . . . 115 D8
Rickley La MK3 . . . . 58 A8

Rickley Park Prim Sch
  MK3 . . . . 57 F8
Rickman's La SL2 . . . . . . 198 E6
RICKMANSWORTH 167 F1
Rickmansworth La SL9 . . . 177 F5
Rickmansworth Rd
  Amersham HP6 . . . . . . 154 C2
  Chorleywood WD3 . . . . . 167 F6
Rickman Wlk HP19 . . . . . 115 A7
Rickyard Cl
  1 Milton Keynes MK13 . . 34 A4
  Whitchurch HP22 . . . . . . 87 A7
Rickyard Gr HP18 . . . . 83 B5
Rickyard The MK46 . . . . 7 C3
Rick Yd The MK16 . . . . 13 F1
Riders Way OX39 . . . . . . 147 C6
Ride The LU6 . . . . 93 B6
Ridgebank SL1 . . . . 204 F6
Ridge
  Aylesbury HP21 . . . . . . 115 D3
  Lane End HP14 . . . . . . 171 C4
Ridge Cl SL4 . . . . 210 C4
Ridgemount End SL9 . . . . 177 E5
Ridge Side HP14 . . . . 160 A8
Ridge View HP23 . . . . 119 C5
Ridgeway
  Berkhamsted HP4 . . . . . 134 F4
  4 High Wycombe HP11 . . 173 A6
  Milton Keynes, Stony Stratford
    MK11 . . . . 32 F4
  Milton Keynes, Wolverton Mill
    MK12 . . . . 33 A3
  Wing LU7 . . . . 79 E3
Ridge Way
  High Wycombe HP13 . . . 162 C1
  Iver SL0 . . . . 207 F6
  Long Crendon HP18 . . . . 125 F4
Ridgeway Cl
  Chesham HP5 . . . . 144 B3
  Marlow SL7 . . . . 183 E4
Ridgeway Cotts MK17 . . . . 67 B3
Ridgeway Ct **3** HP20 . . . . 101 E1
Ridgeway Meads HP27 . . . 138 B2
Ridgeway Rd HP5 . . . . . . 144 B3
Ridgeway The
  Amersham HP6 . . . . . . 165 E7
  Gerrards Cross SL9 . . . . 188 D8
  Marlow SL7 . . . . 183 E4
Ridgeway Trad Est The
  SL0 . . . . 207 E6
Ridgewood RG9 . . . . 181 C1
Ridgmont MK19 . . . . 31 E5
Ridgmont Cl MK19 . . . . . . 31 E5
Ridgway MK17 . . . . 49 B6
Riding Court Rd SL3 . . . . 211 D7
Riding Ct SL3 . . . . 211 C8
Riding La HP9, HP10 . . . . 174 F3
Ridings Cotts HP15 . . . . . 163 B2
Ridings The
  Amersham HP6 . . . . . . 154 D4
  Iver SL0 . . . . 207 F2
  Latimer HP5 . . . . 155 F3
  Maidenhead SL6 . . . . . . 202 A7
Ridings Way LU7 . . . . 78 B1
Riding The MK13 . . . . 31 E5
Rigby Lodge SL1 . . . . 205 E7
Rigeway View LU7 . . . . . . 105 D4
Rignall Rd HP16 . . . . 151 E8
Riley Cl HP20 . . . . 115 C8
Riley Rd SL7 . . . . 183 D2
Rillington Gdns MK4 . . . . . 46 B3
Rimmington Way HP19 . . . 101 B1
Rimsdale Ct MK2 . . . . 58 D3
Ringlet Way HP19 . . . . . . 101 C4
Ring Rd HP10 . . . . 173 F2
Ring Road E MK7 . . . . 47 F7
Ring Road N MK7 . . . . 47 F7
Ring Road W MK7 . . . . 47 E7
RINGSHALL 107 B1
Ringshall Dr HP4 . . . . 121 C8
Ringshall Rd HP4 . . . . . . 107 B3
Ringstead Way HP21 . . . . 116 A5
Ripley Cl
  High Wycombe HP13 . . . 173 A8
  Milton Keynes MK4 . . . . . 45 E1
  Slough SL3 . . . . 206 E2
Ripley Rd **12** MK10 . . . . . 36 C3
Ripon Ho HP21 . . . . 115 F6
Ripon St HP20 . . . . 101 D1
Risborough Rd
  Great Kimble HP17,
    HP27 . . . . 139 E8
  Maidenhead SL6 . . . . . . 202 A8
  Stoke Mandeville HP17 . . 130 B7
Risborough Springs Swim &
  Fitness Ctr HP27 . . . . . 139 A4
Rise Hay Hill SL6 . . . . 204 F7
Riseley Rd SL6 . . . . 202 D7
Rise The
  Amersham HP7 . . . . . . 165 C8
  Gawcott MK18 . . . . 51 F4
  Hazlemere HP15 . . . . . 163 A5
  Loudwater HP13 . . . . . . 174 B4
  Uxbridge UB10 . . . . 201 F3
Risings The HP13 . . . . . . 162 B1
Riverbank Point UB8 . . . . 201 C6
Riverbank The SL4 . . . . . 210 B7
River Cl HP36 . . . . 22 D4
Rivercrest Rd MK19 . . . . . . 32 B6
River Ct SL6 . . . . 203 C7
River Gdns SL6 . . . . 203 D4
Rivermead **3** HP13 . . . . . 194 E8
Riverpark Dr SL7 . . . . 183 F1
River Park Ind Est HP4 . . . 135 A5
River & Rowing Mus★
  RG9 . . . . 191 F1
Riversdale SL8 . . . . 185 B1

Riversdale Cotts SL8 . . . . 185 B1
Riversdale Ct SL8 . . . . . . 185 A1
Rivers Edge
  Loudwater HP11 . . . . . . 174 A3
  Wooburn Green HP10 . . . 185 F5
River Side SL3 . . . . 183 D1
Riverside Cotts
  West Drayton UB7 . . . . . 208 C1
  Wooburn Green HP10 . . . 185 E8
Riverside Cvn Pk UB7 . . . 208 C3
Riverside Gdns HP4 . . . . . 135 A5
Riverside Mews MK18 . . . . 52 E8
Riverside Pk SL3 . . . . 212 E5
Riverside Pl TW19 . . . . . . 213 E1
Riverside Rd TW19 . . . . . 213 E1
Riverside Way SL6 . . . . . . 201 B4
River St SL4 . . . . 210 D7
Riverswood Gdns HP11 . . . 174 A3
River View HP10 . . . . 185 B7
Riverway SL4 . . . . 210 C7
River Wlk UB9 . . . . 201 C7
Riverwood Ave SL7 . . . . . 184 A1
Riverwoods Dr SL7 . . . . . 184 A1
Rivets SL1 . . . . 115 E6
Rivett Cl MK46 . . . . 6 E4
Rivington Gdns HP4 . . . . . 134 D7
Rixband Cl MK7 . . . . 48 B4
Rixman Cl SL6 . . . . 202 D5
Rixon Cl SL3 . . . . 206 E7
Rixons Mdw HP19 . . . . . . 115 B7
Roade Hill NN7 . . . . 9 F8
Roald Dahl Mus & Story Ctr★
  HP16 . . . . 152 A7
Robert Rd SL2 . . . . 187 D2
Roberts Cl
  Deanshanger MK19 . . . . 31 E4
  Stanwell TW19 . . . . . . 213 C1
  West Drayton UB7 . . . . . 208 E5
Robert's Dr HP19 . . . . . . 101 D2
Roberts La SL9 . . . . 178 B5
Robertson Cl MK5 . . . . 45 F7
Robertson Rd **6** HP4 . . . 135 D4
Roberts Rd
  Haddenham HP17 . . . . . 127 B6
  High Wycombe HP13 . . . 173 B8
Roberts Ride HP15 . . . . . 163 A5
Roberts Wood Dr SL9 . . . . 177 F5
Robeson Pl MK8 . . . . 45 E8
Robin Cl
  Aylesbury HP19 . . . . . . 101 F3
  Buckingham MK18 . . . . . 52 F7
  Great Kingshill HP15 . . . . 151 D1
Robin Ho HP4 . . . . 135 C3
Robin Ho HP11 . . . . 174 A4
Robin Hood Cl SL1 . . . . . 204 F5
Robin Par **2** SL2 . . . . . . 198 C7
Robins Cl
  High Wycombe HP12 . . . 172 D3
  Uxbridge UB8 . . . . 208 C8
Robins Hill MK6 . . . . 47 A6
Robinson Cl HP19 . . . . . . 100 F3
Robinson Ct SL6 . . . . 202 E4
Robinson Rd HP13 . . . . . 174 B4
Robins Orch SL9 . . . . 177 E4
Robins Platt OX39 . . . . . . 147 B6
Robins St HP22 . . . . 102 C2
Robinswood Ct
  Beaconsfield HP9 . . . . . 175 C5
  Leighton Buzzard LU7 . . . 70 F2
Robinwood Gr UB8 . . . . . 201 F1
Roblin Cl HP21 . . . . 115 E4
Robson Cl **4** HP16 . . . . . 152 A8
Roche Gdns MK3 . . . . 58 A8
Rochester Ct MK5 . . . . 46 A5
Rochester Mews LU7 . . . . . 80 E6
Rochester Pl HP19 . . . . . 115 B8
Rochfords MK6 . . . . 46 F6
Rochfords Gdns SL2 . . . . 206 C5
Rochford Way SL6 . . . . . . 204 A7
Rockall Ct SL3 . . . . 207 B3
Rock Cl LU7 . . . . 80 C6
Rockingham Cl
  Pitstone LU7 . . . . 105 D3
  Uxbridge UB8 . . . . 201 C4
Rockingham Dr MK14 . . . . 34 E6
Rockingham Par UB8 . . . . 201 C5
Rockingham Pl HP9 . . . . . 175 F1
Rockingham Rd UB8 . . . . 201 B4
Rockingham Wharf UB8 . . 201 B4
Rock La LU7 . . . . 80 D7
Rockleigh Ct **3** LU7 . . . . . 80 E7
Rockspray Gr MK7 . . . . . . 48 B5
ROCKWELL END 181 F5
Rodney Way SL3 . . . . 212 E6
Rodwell Gdns MK7 . . . . . . 48 D4
Rodwell Yd **3** HP23 . . . . . 119 A3
Roebuck Ave HP13 . . . . . 173 F6
Roebuck Gn SL1 . . . . 204 E5
Roebuck Mews LU6 . . . . . 92 E6
Roebuck Way MK5 . . . . . . 46 C6
Roeburn Cres MK4 . . . . . . 46 C1
Rogers Croft MK6 . . . . 47 D7
Rogers La
  8 Buckingham MK18 . . . 41 E3
  Stoke Poges SL2 . . . . . 198 A4
Rogers Wy MK18 . . . . 65 E4
Roker Park Ave UB10 . . . . 201 E8
Rokesby Rd SL2 . . . . 197 F2
Rolfe Cl
  Beaconsfield HP9 . . . . . 175 D1

Rolfe Cl continued
  Winslow MK18 . . . . 65 F4
Rolls La HP16 . . . . 150 F5
Rolvenden Gr MK7 . . . . . . 48 B7
Roman Lea SL6 . . . . 195 F7
Roman Pl SL6 . . . . 202 C6
Roman Rdbts MK1 . . . . 47 C2
Romans Field Sch MK3 . . . 46 E1
Roman Way
  Aylesbury HP19 . . . . . . 115 B8
  Bourne End SL8 . . . . . . 185 B4
  Brackley NN13 . . . . 38 A7
Romar Ct MK1 . . . . 47 C2
Romney Ct **3** SL7 . . . . . . 183 F3
Romney Lock Rd SL4 . . . . 210 D7
Romney Rd HP21 . . . . . . 115 E4
Romney Wy MK8 . . . . 33 D1
Romsey Cl SL3 . . . . 206 F3
Romsey Dr SL2 . . . . 187 D1
Romsey Way HP11 . . . . . 173 B4
Romulus Way NN13 . . . . . . 38 A6
Ronald Rd HP9 . . . . 175 F2
Ronaldsay **1** MK18 . . . . . 41 E3
Ronaldsay Spur SL1 . . . . . 205 E8
Rookery Ct SL7 . . . . 183 D2
Rookery Mdw HP15 . . . . . 163 C7
Rookery Wlk MK18 . . . . . . 63 F3
Rook Rd HP10 . . . . 185 D4
ROOKSLEY 34 B2
Rooksley Rdbt MK13 . . . . . 34 B3
Rooks Terr UB7 . . . . 208 E4
Rook Tree Farm Ind Est
  MK17 . . . . 37 F3
Rook Wood Way HP16 . . . . 152 B5
Ropa Ct **6** LU7 . . . . 80 F7
Roperies The HP11 . . . . . 173 E6
Ropley Way **3** MK10 . . . . . 36 B3
Rosamund's Cotts HP18 . . 83 B3
Rosary The HP15 . . . . . . 163 C7
Roseary Cl UB7 . . . . 208 C2
Rose Ave
  Aylesbury HP19 . . . . . . 101 C2
  Hazlemere HP15 . . . . . 163 B2
Rosebank Cl SL6 . . . . 195 E7
Rosebank Cotts HP10 . . . . 174 B3
Rosebarn La HP23 . . . . . . 104 D1
Rosebay Cl MK7 . . . . 48 B5
Rosebery Ave
  High Wycombe HP13 . . . 173 E5
  Leighton Buzzard LU7 . . . 80 E7
Rosebery Ct **4** LU7 . . . . . . 80 F7
Rosebery Mews LU7 . . . . . 90 D4
Rosebery Rd HP22 . . . . . 117 F5
Rosebery Way HP23 . . . . 119 B5
Rose Cnr HP14 . . . . 158 E5
Rosecomb Pl MK5 . . . . . . 46 A4
Rose Cotts SL6 . . . . 202 C3
Rose Ct
  Amersham HP6 . . . . . . 154 E2
  Chesham HP5 . . . . 154 D6
  Eaton Bray LU6 . . . . 92 D6
  3 Olney MK46 . . . . 6 F3
Rose Dr HP5 . . . . 154 D7
Rosehill HP4 . . . . 135 B4
Rose Hill SL1 . . . . 197 A5
Rosehill Cres MK18 . . . . . . 62 D1
Rosehill Ct SL1 . . . . 206 A3
Rose Ind Est SL7 . . . . . . 183 D5
Rose La RG9 . . . . 193 A1
Roseleigh Cl SL6 . . . . 202 A7
Rosemary Cl
  Buckingham MK18 . . . . . 52 F6
  High Wycombe HP12 . . . 161 B1
Rosemary Ct
  High Wycombe HP12 . . . 161 B1
  3 Walton MK7 . . . . 48 A5
Rosemary La HP17 . . . . . 127 A7
Rosemead HP22 . . . . 117 E1
Rosemoor Mews HP19 . . . 114 F8
Rosemullion Ave MK4 . . . . 57 B8
Rosery The **5** SL8 . . . . . . 185 A3
Roses Cl LU7 . . . . 78 B1
Roses La SL4 . . . . 209 D5
Rose Terr HP18 . . . . 99 A6
Rosetree Cl HP16 . . . . . . 151 C6
Rose Wlk SL2 . . . . 205 B8
Rosewood Gdns HP12 . . . 172 C4
Rosewood Way SL2 . . . . . 198 C2
Rosken Gr SL2 . . . . 198 B3
Roslyn Ct MK15 . . . . 35 D7
Rossal Pl MK12 . . . . 33 D4
Rossendale MK14 . . . . 34 D7
Rossetti Pl HP15 . . . . 163 C7
Rossini Pl MK7 . . . . 48 D5
Rossiter Cl SL3 . . . . 206 E2
Ross Rd
  Aston Abbotts HP22 . . . . 88 D5
  Maidenhead SL6 . . . . . . 202 E4
Ross Way MK3 . . . . 46 F2
Rossway La HP4 . . . . 134 A7
Rostrevor Gdns SL0 . . . . . 200 D3
Rothersthorpe MK14 . . . . . 35 A8
Rothersay Ct HP20 . . . . . 101 E1
Rothesay Cl HP4 . . . . 135 A4
Rothesay Ct HP4 . . . . 117 E5
Rothschild Pl **19** HP23 . . . 119 A3
Rothschild Rd
  Leighton Buzzard LU7 . . . 80 F8
  Wing LU7 . . . . 79 E2
ROTTEN ROW 181 F2
Rotten Row MK17 . . . . 59 C2
Roughwood La HP8 . . . . . 166 F5
Roundhead Dr OX9 . . . . . 125 F1
Roundheads End HP9 . . . . 175 B4
Round Hill HP17 . . . . 114 D5

Roundhill Ct HP17 . . . . . 126 E8
Roundhouse Cl HP22 . . . . 117 F4
Roundlands HP27 . . . . . . 149 E5
Roundwood Prim Sch (Inf)
 MK18 . . . . 51 B6
Roundwood Prim Sch (Jun)
 MK18 . . . . 51 F4
Roundwood Rd HP12 . . . . 172 C7
Round Wood Rd HP6 . . . . 154 F2
Rouse Ct SL9 . . . . 188 F6
Routs Gn HP14 . . . . 148 D2
ROUT'S GREEN 148 D2
Roveley Ct MK11 . . . . 32 F5
Rowan Ave HP13 . . . . 173 D8
Rowan Cl
 Aylesbury HP21 . . . . 115 E4
 Beaconsfield HP9 . . . . . . 175 B1
 Hazlemere HP15 . . . . 163 A3
Rowan Dr MK19 . . . . 20 D2
Rowan Gdns SL0 . . . . 200 C3
Rowan Ho 1 SL8 . . . . 185 A4
Rowanhurst Dr SL2 . . . . . 198 C7
Rowan Pl HP6 . . . . 154 F1
Rowan Rd UB7 . . . . 208 E2
Rowans The SL9 . . . . 188 D8
Rowan Way SL2 . . . . 205 B8
Rowan Wlk HP5 . . . . 144 B1
Rowborough Rd HP22 . . . 131 D7
Rowditch Furlong MK14 . . 21 F3
Rowland Cl SL4 . . . . 209 D4
Rowland Ho HP9 . . . . 175 F1
Rowlands Cl MK2 . . . . 58 E8
Rowland Way HP19 . . . . . 115 B7
Rowle Cl MK14 . . . . 34 E7
Rowley Furrows LU7 . . . . . 80 D8
Rowley La SL3 . . . . 199 D4
Rowlheys Pl UB7 . . . . 208 E3
Rowliff Rd HP12 . . . . 172 C6
ROWSHAM 102 D8
Rowsham Dell MK14 . . . . . 21 F2
Rowsham Rd HP22 . . . . . . 102 C5
Row The
 Cholesbury HP5 . . . . 133 D2
 Cold Brayfield MK46 . . . . . 8 B4
 Lane End HP14 . . . . 171 B4
 Newton Blossomville MK43 . . 8 B3
 Winchmore Hill HP7 . . . . . 164 C3
Rowton Heath MK5 . . . . . . 45 C5
Roxburgh Way MK3 . . . . . . 46 F3
Roxhill Rd MK43 . . . . 25 F3
Roxwell Cl SL1 . . . . 204 E5
Roxwell Path 5 HP20 . . . . 101 F2
Royal Buckinghamshire
 Hospl HP19 . . . . 101 D1
Royal Cl UB7, UB8 . . . . . . 208 F7
Royal Cotts SL6 . . . . 195 C2
Royal Cotts HP7 . . . . 164 C2
Royal Ct HP23 . . . . 120 A5
Royal Free Ct 13 SL4 . . . . 210 D6
Royal Gram Sch The
 HP13 . . . . 162 C1
Royal La UB8 . . . . 201 F1
Royal Latin Sch The
 MK18 . . . . 52 D7
Royal Mansions RG9 . . . . 191 E1
Royal Mead HP17 . . . . . . 130 C5
Royal Windsor Racecourse
 SL4 . . . . 209 F2
Royce Cl LU6 . . . . 93 F7
Royce Rd MK43 . . . . 24 D3
Royle Cl SL9 . . . . 177 F3
Royston Way SL1 . . . . 204 D8
Rubbra Cl MK7. . . . . 48 C5
Rubens Cl HP19 . . . . 100 F2
Ruby Cl SL1 . . . . 205 A4
Ruckles Way HP7 . . . . . . 165 C7
Rudchesters MK13 . . . . . . 33 F5
Ruddlesway SL4 . . . . 209 D6
Rudds Cl MK18 . . . . 66 A5
Rudd's La HP17 . . . . 127 A7
Rudsworth Cl SL3 . . . . . . 212 D7
Ruffle Cl UB7 . . . . 208 E4
Rugby Rise HP11 . . . . 174 A3
Rugwood Rd HP10 . . . . . . 173 F2
Rumptons Paddock HP18 . 82 F6
Runford Ct MK5 . . . . 46 C5
Run Furrow HP17 . . . . . . 127 A7
Runnymede MK14 . . . . 21 F2
Runrig Hill HP6 . . . . 154 E4
Rupert Ave HP12 . . . . 172 E4
Rupert Cl RG9 . . . . 191 E3
Rupert House Sch RG9 . . . 191 E2
Rupert's La 191 E3
Rupert Way OX9 . . . . 126 A1
Ruscombe Gdns SL3 . . . . 211 A7
Ruscote HP4 . . . . 135 A3
Rushall Rd OX9 . . . . 126 A1
Rushbeds Wood Wildlife
 Reserve★ HP18 . . . . 96 D4
Rushbrooke Cl HP13 . . . . 162 F2
Rushburn HP10 . . . . 185 F6
Rushendon Furlong LU7 . . 105 E5
Rushes Mead UB8 . . . . . . 201 C4
Rushes The
 Maidenhead SL6 . . . . . . 203 C6
 Marlow SL7 . . . . 194 C8
Rushfields Cl 12 MK4 . . . . 45 F1
RUSH GREEN 200 E5
Rushington Ave SL6 . . . . 202 F5
Rushleys Cl MK5 . . . . 46 A8
RUSHMERE 70 E4
Rushmere Cl MK41 . . . . . . 48 D2
Rushmere La HP5 . . . . . . 145 B3
Rushmere Ret Pk MK1 . . . 47 D2
Rushmoor Ave HP15 . . . . 163 B3

Rushton Ct 5 MK8 . . . . . . 45 F8
Ruskin Ct MK16 . . . . 22 C2
Rusland Cir MK4 . . . . 46 C2
Russel Ct HP14 . . . . 161 C8
Russell Ave HP21 . . . . . . 115 C6
Russell Cl
 Little Chalfont HP6 . . . . . 166 D8
 Tylers Green HP10 . . . . . 163 B1
Russell Ct
 Aylesbury HP21 . . . . 115 E6
 Chesham HP5 . . . . 144 D2
 Maidenhead SL6 . . . . . . 202 F7
 Wendover HP22 . . . . 131 B5
Russell Dr TW19 . . . . 213 D1
Russell Ho 4 SL8 . . . . . . 185 A4
Russell Sch The WD3 . . . . 167 B5
Russell St
 Milton Keynes MK11 . . . . . 32 D5
 Windsor SL4 . . . . 210 D6
 Woburn Sands MK17 . . . . 49 B4
Russell Street Sch MK11 . . 32 D5
Russet Cl TW19 . . . . 212 F1
Russet Rd SL6 . . . . 202 C3
Russets The SL9 . . . . 177 D1
Russett Hill SL9 . . . . 188 E8
Russwell La MK17 . . . . 59 C6
Rustics Cl MK18 . . . . 73 B5
Rustlings Gate HP14 . . . . 171 C5
Rutherford Cl
 Uxbridge UB8 . . . . 201 F1
 Windsor SL4 . . . . 209 F6
Rutherford Gate MK5 . . . . 46 C5
Rutherford Rd HP21 . . . . 115 E4
Ruthven Cl MK2. . . . . 58 C4
Rutland Ave
 High Wycombe HP12 . . . . 172 D6
 Slough SL1 . . . . 205 C8
Rutland Ct 2 HP11 . . . . . 173 A6
Rutland Gate SL6 . . . . . . 202 C6
Rutland Ho 3 MK3. . . . . . . 46 F1
Rutland Pl SL6 . . . . 202 C6
Rutland Rd SL6 . . . . 202 D6
Rutland St HP11 . . . . 173 A6
Ryans Mount SL7 . . . . . . 183 C2
Rycote La OX9 . . . . 136 B4
Rycote Lane Ind Est OX9 136 C4
Rycroft
 Milton Keynes MK4 . . . . . . 46 E3
 Windsor SL4 . . . . 209 F4
Rydal Way
 High Wycombe HP12 . . . . 172 B5
 Milton Keynes MK2 . . . . . . 58 D5
Ryder Cl HP3 . . . . 146 A4
Rydings SL4 . . . . 209 F4
Ryding The MK5 . . . . 46 A4
Rye The
 Aylesbury HP21 . . . . 115 D4
 Maidenhead SL6 . . . . . . 202 A4
Rye Ct 9 SL1 . . . . 206 A4
Ryefield Terr SL3 . . . . . . 212 D7
Ryeland MK11 . . . . 32 E6
Ryeland Cl UB7 . . . . 208 E7
Ryeland Croft MK14 . . . . . 21 C1
Ryemead Way HP11 . . . . 173 F4
Rye The LU6, LU7 . . . . 92 B8
Rye View HP13 . . . . 173 C7
Rylstone Cl
 Maidenhead SL6 . . . . . . 202 C3
 Milton Keynes MK13 . . . . . 34 B3
Ryman Ct WD3 . . . . 167 C3
Rymill Cl HP3 . . . . 146 A3
Rynn Cl 1 HP13 . . . . 162 A1
Ryton Pl MK4 . . . . 46 C3
Ryvers End SL3 . . . . 206 F3
Ryvers Prim Sch SL3 . . . . 206 D3
Ryvers Rd SL3 . . . . 206 F3

S

Sabina Cl HP12 . . . . 172 E6
Sacred Heart RC Prim Sch
 RG9 . . . . 191 D1
Saddington MK6 . . . . 47 D6
Saddlers Pl MK14 . . . . 35 A5
Sadleirs Gn MK17 . . . . 49 B5
Sadlers Mews SL6 . . . . . . 203 B7
Saffron Cl SL3 . . . . 211 B6
Saffron Ct HP13 . . . . 173 C6
Saffron Rd HP13 . . . . 173 C6
Saffron Rise LU6 . . . . 92 E6
Saffron St MK2 . . . . 58 D7
Saham Croft Cl MK18. . . . . 65 E4
Sailing Club Rd SL8 . . . . . 185 A3
St Abbs Ct MK4 . . . . 56 F8
St Adrian's Cl SL6 . . . . . . 202 B4
St Agnes Gate HP22 . . . . 131 A5
St Aidan's Cl MK3 . . . . 57 E6
St Albans Ct 7 SL4 . . . . . 210 D6
St Alban's Rd MK18 . . . . . 65 E4
St Alban's St SL4 . . . . . . 210 D6
St Andrew's Ave SL4 . . . . 209 F5
St Andrew's CE Inf Sch
 MK14 . . . . 34 E8
St Andrew's CE Prim Sch
 Chinnor OX39 . . . . 147 C7
 Uxbridge UB8 . . . . 201 D4
St Andrew's Cl
 High Wycombe HP13 . . . . 162 F1
 Old Windsor SL4 . . . . . . 211 A1
 Wraysbury TW19 . . . . . . 211 E1
St Andrews Cotts 1 SL4 . 210 A5
St Andrews Cres SL4 . . . . 209 F5
St Andrews Ct
 Colnbrook SL3 . . . . 212 D7
 2 Slough SL1 . . . . 205 E8

St Andrews Ho OX39 . . . . 147 C6
St Andrew's Rd
 Chinnor OX39 . . . . 147 C5
 Milton Keynes MK3 . . . . . . 57 E7
 Uxbridge UB10 . . . . 201 E5
St Andrews Way SL1 . . . . 204 D6
St Andrews Way Ind Est 6
 HP19 . . . . 101 C1
St Anne's Cl
 Henley-on-Thames RG9 . . 191 D1
 Wendover HP22 . . . . 131 B5
St Ann's Rd
 Aylesbury HP19 . . . . 115 B8
 South Harefield UB9 . . . . 190 C8
St Ann's Ct HP10 . . . . . . 174 C2
St Anthony's Cl HP19 . . . 115 B8
St Anthony's Ct HP9 . . . . 186 C5
St Anthony's Pl MK4 . . . . . 57 B8
St Augustus Cl MK3 . . . . . 57 E7
St Bartholomews MK10 . . . 36 A1
St Bartholomew's CE Sch
 HP23 . . . . 119 D1
St Bees MK10 . . . . 36 A1
St Bernadette's RC Prim Sch
 MK10 . . . . 47 F8
St Bernards Ct HP13 . . . . 173 C6
St Bernard's Prep Sch
 SL1 . . . . 206 B4
St Bernard's RC Gram Sch
 SL3 . . . . 206 C4
St Bernards Rd SL3 . . . . . 206 C3
St Birinus HP10 . . . . 174 A2
St Botolphs 2 MK10 . . . . . 36 B1
St Brides Cl MK6 . . . . 35 C2
St Catherine RC Prim Sch
 UB7 . . . . 208 D4
St Catherine's Ave MK3 . . 57 D6
St Catherines Ct 3 SL4 . 210 A5
St Catherine's Ct HP19 . . 115 B8
St Chad's Rd SL6 . . . . . . 202 B4
St Christopher Rd UB8 . . . 208 D8
St Christopher's Cl HP16 152 B3
St Christophers Ct WD3 . . 167 D5
St Clement Cl UB8 . . . . . . 208 D7
St Clement Danes Sch
 WD3 . . . . 167 D7
St Clement's Dr MK3 . . . . 57 D6
Saint-Cloud Way SL6 . . . . 203 A7
St Columba's Cl SL6 . . . . 202 B4
St Cuthburt La UB8 . . . . . 208 D7
St David Cl UB8 . . . . 208 D8
St David's Cl
 Iver Heath SL0 . . . . 200 D4
 Maidenhead SL6 . . . . . . 202 A4
St David's St NN13 . . . . . . 38 A8
St David's Par SL0 . . . . . . 200 D4
St David's Rd MK3 . . . . . . 57 E6
St Dunstans MK6. . . . . 47 A6
St Dunstans Ct HP27 . . . . 139 C6
St Edmund Campion RC Prim
 Sch SL4 . . . . 202 B5
St Edmunds HP4 . . . . 135 C3
St Edmund's Cl HP19 . . . . 115 B8
St Edwards Ct MK14 . . . . . 34 F7
St Edward's RC Fst Sch
 SL4 . . . . 210 A6
St Edward's RC Jun Sch
 HP21 . . . . 116 A7
St Edward's Royal Free
 Middle Sch SL4 . . . . 210 A6
St Elmo Cl SL2 . . . . 198 D1
St Elmo Cres SL2 . . . . . . 198 D1
St Ethelbert's RC Prim Sch
 SL2 . . . . 206 A7
St Faith's Cl MK17 . . . . . . 57 D3
St Francis Cl HP4 . . . . . . 135 A5
St Francis Rd
 Beacon's Bottom HP14 . . 159 D3
 Denham Green UB9 . . . . . 189 F5
 Highway SL6 . . . . 202 B7
St George's CE Inf Sch 4
 HP7 . . . . 165 E8
St George's Cl
 High Wycombe HP13 . . . . 173 D7
 Windsor SL4 . . . . 209 E6
St Georges Cres SL1 . . . . 204 D6
St Georges Ct 2 HP12 . . . 172 D8
St George's Dr UB10 . . . . 190 F1
St Georges Ind Est HP7 . . 165 E8
St Georges Lodge SL6. . . 196 B7
St George's Rd MK3 . . . . . 57 E6
St George's Sch SL4 . . . . 210 D7
St Georges Way 33 D7
St Giles Mews MK11 . . . . . 32 D6
St Giles St MK13 . . . . 33 F7
St Govans Cl MK4 . . . . 57 B8
St Helena Ave MK3. . . . . . 58 C3
St Helen Cl UB8. . . . . 208 D8
St Helens Gr MK10 . . . . . . 47 F8
St Hilda's Ct HP19 . . . . . 115 B8
St Hilda's Way HP10 . . . . 174 A2
St Huberts Cl SL9 . . . . . . 188 E2
St Huberts Cotts SL9 . . . . 188 E4
St Huberts La SL9 . . . . . . 188 F2
St Hugh's Ave HP13 . . . . 173 F6
St Hugh's Cl HP14 . . . . . 158 F4
St Hugh's Pl HP14 . . . . . 158 F4
St Ives Cres MK4 . . . . 57 B8
St Ives Rd SL6 . . . . 203 A7
St James Cl MK19 . . . . 11 A2
St James Ctyd 8 SL7 . . . 183 E2
St James Pl SL1 . . . . 204 C7
St James & St John CE Prim
 Sch Infant Site MK18 . . . 41 B4
St James & St John CE Prim
 Sch Junior Site MK18 . . . 41 B4
St James St MK13 . . . . . . 33 F7

St James Way HP22 . . . . 102 B3
St James Wlk SL0 . . . . . . 207 E4
St John's Ave HP10 . . . . . 174 B8
St John's CE Comb Sch
 HP27 . . . . 149 F4
St Johns Cl HP10 . . . . . . 163 B1
St John's Cl UB8 . . . . 201 B4
St John's Cres MK12 . . . . . 33 D5
St Johns Dr
 Stone HP17 . . . . 114 B5
 Windsor SL4 . . . . 210 A5
St Johns La MK18 . . . . 75 F2
St John's La MK19 . . . . 31 B4
St John's Manor Ho
 HP15 . . . . 162 E2
St Johns Rd
 Slough SL2 . . . . 206 A6
 Tylers Green HP10 . . . . . 163 B1
 Windsor SL4 . . . . 210 A5
St John's Rd
 4 Aylesbury HP20 . . . . . 101 E1
 Hazlemere HP15 . . . . . . 162 F2
 Milton Keynes MK3 . . . . . . 57 E6
 Uxbridge UB8 . . . . 201 B4
St John's St HP20 . . . . . . 101 E1
St John St MK16 . . . . 22 D4
St John's Terr MK16 . . . . . 22 D4
St John's Well Ct HP4 . . . 135 B5
St John's Well La HP4 . . . 135 B5
St Josephs Cl MK46 . . . . . . 6 F4
St Josephs Mews HP9 . . . 175 F2
St Joseph's RC High Sch
 SL2 . . . . 206 A7
St Joseph's RC Inf Sch
 HP21 . . . . 116 A7
St Joseph's RC Prim Sch
 SL9 . . . . 188 C8
St Katherine's Way HP4 . . 134 F7
St Laurence Cl UB8 . . . . . 208 C8
St Laurence Rd MK18 . . . . 65 F4
St Laurence Way SL1. . . . 206 A3
St Lawrence Cl HP3 . . . . . 146 A4
St Lawrence View MK13 . . 34 A4
St Leger Ct MK14 . . . . 34 E8
St Leger Dr MK14 . . . . 34 E7
ST LEONARDS 132 E3
St Leonard's Ave 2 SL4 . 210 C5
St Leonard's Hill SL4. . . . 209 E4
St Leonards Rd HP6 . . . . 154 E4
St Leonard's Rd
 Oakley Green SL4 . . . . . 209 D1
 Windsor SL4 . . . . 210 C4
St Leonard's Way LU6 . . . . 92 E1
St Leonards Wlk SL0 . . . . 207 F3
St Louis RC Prim Sch 15
 HP20 . . . . 101 F2
St Lucia Cres MK17 . . . . . . 58 B3
St Luke Cl UB8 . . . . 208 D7
St Luke's CE Prim Sch 2
 SL6 . . . . 202 F8
St Luke's Rd
 Maidenhead SL6 . . . . . . 202 F8
 Old Windsor SL4 . . . . . . 211 A1
 Uxbridge UB10. . . . . 201 E5
St Margaret Ct MK2. . . . . . 58 E8
St Margarets Cl MK16 . . . . 22 E4
St Margaret's Cl
 Berkhamsted HP4 . . . . . 135 D3
 Iver Heath SL0 . . . . 200 D3
 Tylers Green HP10 . . . . . 174 C8
St Margaret's Ct SL0 . . . . 200 D3
St Margaret's Gate SL0. . 200 D3
St Margarets Gr HP15 . . . 151 E1
St Margaret's Rd SL6 . . . 202 A7
St Margaret Way SL1 . . . 204 F4
St Marks Cl HP13 . . . . . . 173 D7
St Mark's Cres SL6 . . . . . 202 B7
St Mark's Pl SL4 . . . . 210 C5
St Mark's Rd
 Aylesbury HP21 . . . . 115 C7
 Henley-on-Thames RG9 . . 191 E1
 Maidenhead SL6 . . . . . . 202 D7
 Windsor SL4 . . . . 210 C5
St Martin Cl UB8 . . . . 208 D7
St Martin's Cl UB7 . . . . . 208 D3
St Martin's Prim Sch
 UB7 . . . . 208 E2
St Martin's Rd UB7 . . . . . 208 D3
St Martin's St MK2 . . . . . . 58 C8
St Mary & All Saints CE Prim
 Sch HP9 . . . . 175 E3
St Mary Magdalene RC Prim
 Sch MK12 . . . . 33 A5
St Mary & St Giles CE Jun
 Sch MK11 . . . . 32 E6
St Mary's Ave
 Berkhamsted HP4 . . . . . 134 D6
 Milton Keynes MK3 . . . . . . 57 E7
 Milton Keynes, Stony Stratford
 MK11 . . . . 32 E6
St Mary's CE Prim Sch
 Amersham HP7 . . . . 165 A8
 Berkhamsted HP4 . . . . . 134 C6
 Slough SL1. . . . . 206 A3
St Mary's CE Sch HP19 . . 115 A8
St Marys Cl
 East Claydon MK18 . . . . . 74 F8
 Mursley MK17 . . . . 67 D6
St Mary's Cl
 Lee Common HP16 . . . . . 142 D5
 Maidenhead SL6 . . . . . . 203 A7
 South Harefield UB9 . . . . 190 B8
 Wavendon MK17 . . . . 48 E7
St Mary's Ct MK18 . . . . . . 51 B7
St Mary's Farnham Royal CE
 Prim Sch SL2. . . . . 198 C2
St Mary's Glebe LU6 . . . . 92 E4

St Mary's RC Prim Sch
 Maidenhead SL6 . . . . . . 195 F2
 Uxbridge UB8. . . . . 201 C4
St Marys Rd MK18. . . . . . . 74 F7
St Mary's Rd
 Denham Green UB9 . . . . . 189 F5
 Slough SL3. . . . . 206 E4
 South Harefield UB9 . . . . 190 B8
St Mary's Row 7 HP20 . . 115 D8
St Mary's Sch SL9 . . . . . . 188 E7
St Mary's Sq 3 HP20 . . . 115 D8
St Mary St
 High Wycombe HP11 . . . . 173 B6
 Milton Keynes MK13 . . . . . 33 F7
St Mary's Wavendon CE Prim
 Sch MK17 . . . . 48 E7
St Mary's Way
 Chalfont St Peter SL9 . . . 177 D1
 Chesham HP5 . . . . 154 B8
 Leighton Buzzard LU7 . . . . 80 D7
St Mary's Wlk 10 SL6 . . . 202 F7
St Matthew Cl UB8 . . . . . 208 D7
St Matthew's CE Prim Sch
 UB7 . . . . 208 E5
St Matthews Ct MK3 . . . . . 57 E6
St Michael's Catholic Sch
 HP11 . . . . 173 A4
St Michael's CE Comb Sch
 LU7 . . . . 68 C1
St Michaels Cl
 Edgcott HP18. . . . . 72 F2
 Halton HP22 . . . . 131 C8
 Stewkley LU7 . . . . 68 E1
St Michael's Cl HP22 . . . . 117 C1
St Michael's Ct
 Ashton NN7 . . . . 9 F8
 Slough SL2 . . . . 197 D1
St Michaels Dr
 Milton Keynes MK7 . . . . . . 47 F6
 Walton MK7 . . . . 47 E7
St Michael's Gn HP9 . . . . 175 E3
St Michaels Way MK18 . . . 63 E3
St Monica's RC Prim Sch
 MK14 . . . . 34 F6
St Nicholas CE Comb Sch
 SL6 . . . . 196 E1
St Nicholas Cl
 Cublington LU7 . . . . 78 B1
 Little Chalfont HP7 . . . . . 166 B8
 Uxbridge UB8. . . . . 208 D7
St Patrick's Cl SL6 . . . . . 202 B4
St Patrick's Way MK3 . . . . 57 E6
St Paul Cl UB8 . . . . 208 D8
St Pauls Ave SL2 . . . . . . 206 A3
St Paul's CE Comb Sch
 HP10 . . . . 185 D4
St Pauls Ct MK11. . . . . 32 D6
St Paul's Ct SL6 . . . . 202 F6
St Pauls Gdns SL6 . . . . . 202 B8
St Pauls RC Sch MK6. . . . . 46 F7
St Paul's Rd MK3 . . . . 57 E6
St Pauls Yd MK16 . . . . 22 D4
St Peter's Ave HP19 . . . . 101 C3
St Peter's CE Mid Sch
 SL4 . . . . 210 F1
St Peter's CE Sch SL1 . . . 197 B2
St Peters Cl
 Loudwater HP11 . . . . . . 174 B1
 Speen HP27 . . . . 150 C4
St Peter's Cl
 Burnham SL1 . . . . 197 B1
 Old Windsor SL4 . . . . . . 211 A2
St Peter's Ct SL1 . . . . . . 177 E2
St Peter's Gate NN13 . . . . 38 A7
St Peters Hill HP23 . . . . . 119 A4
St Peter's RC Prim Sch
 SL7 . . . . 183 D3
St Peter's Rd
 Brackley NN13 . . . . 38 A4
 Maidenhead SL6 . . . . . . 195 D2
 Uxbridge UB8. . . . . 208 D3
St Peter St SL7 . . . . 183 E1
St Peters Way
 Chorleywood WD3 . . . . . 167 B5
 Milton Keynes MK13 . . . . . 34 A8
St Pirans Sch SL6. . . . . . 195 E1
St Rumbold's La 3 MK18. 52 D4
St Stephens Dr MK15. . . . . 35 B7
St Stephen's Rd UB7 . . . . 208 D5
St Teresa's Cl HP27 . . . . 139 D4
St Teresa's Sch HP27 . . . 139 D4
St Thomas Aquinas Catholic
 Prim Sch MK3 . . . . 57 E7
St Thomas Ct MK4 . . . . . . 45 F1
St Thomas More RC Prim
 Sch HP4 . . . . 135 A4
St Thomas Wlk SL3 . . . . . 212 D7
St Vincents MK17 . . . . 49 C4
Sakura Wlk MK15 . . . . 35 C6
Salcey Forest Trail★ MK16. 4 C2
SALCEY GREEN 11 B7
SALDEN 67 F8
Salden Cl
 Drayton Parslow MK17 . . . 68 C6
 Milton Keynes MK5 . . . . . . 46 B6
SALFORD 37 C3
Salford Rd MK17 . . . . 49 D7
Salisbury Ave SL2 . . . . . . 205 C8
Salisbury Cl
 Amersham HP7 . . . . 165 E8
 Princes Risborough HP27 . 139 C3
Salisbury Ct SL6 . . . . 202 E5
Salisbury Gr MK14 . . . . . . 21 F2
Salisbury Mews SL2. . . . . 198 C1
Salisbury Rd
 High Wycombe HP13 . . . . 162 D1
 Uxbridge UB8. . . . . 201 B3
Sallowsprings LU6 . . . . . . 93 F2

Salmons La HP16 151 D6
Salop Ho MK3 46 F2
Saltash Cl HP13 174 B4
Salters Cl
 Ludgershall HP18 96 C8
 Maidenhead SL6 203 A7
Salter's Cl HP4 134 F6
Salters La HP18 96 C8
Salters Mews MK14 34 F6
Salters Rd SL6 203 B7
Salters Row HP10 186 A4
SALT HILL 205 D5
Salt Hill Ave SL1 205 C5
Salt Hill Cl UB8 201 E7
Salt Hill Dr SL1 205 C5
Salt Hill Mans SL1 205 C5
Salt Hill Way SL1 205 D5
Salton Link MK4 46 B2
Saltwood Ave MK4 45 E1
Samian Wy HP22 117 D8
Samphire Ct MK7 48 A6
Sampsons Gn SL2 197 F2
Sampsons Hill HP7 164 E2
Samuel Cl MK16 22 F3
San Andres Dr MK3 58 B4
Sanctuary Rd HP15 163 B5
Sandage Rd HP14 171 B5
Sandal Ct MK5 46 A5
Sandbrier Cl MK7 48 B6
Sandbrook La HP23 104 C1
Sandels Way HP9 175 D4
Sandelswood End HP9 175 D5
Sanders La NN12 18 D3
Sanderson Rd UB8 201 C6
Sandford Gdns HP11 173 B4
SANDHILL 64 E2
Sandhill Rd
 Buckingham MK18 64 C4
 East Claydon MK18 74 F8
Sandhill Way HP19 115 A8
Sandholme MK18 63 E2
Sandhurst Dr MK18 52 C7
Sandisplatt Rd SL6 202 A6
Sandlers End SL2 198 B1
Sandles The SL4 205 B1
Sandleswood Cl HP9 175 D4
Sandmartin Cl MK18 41 E1
Sandon Cl HP23 118 F4
Sandown Ct
 8 High Wycombe HP12 172 E7
 Milton Keynes MK3 57 D6
Sandown Rd SL2 204 F8
Sandpiper 1 HP19 101 E4
Sandpipers Pl SL6 195 E6
Sandpit Hill MK18 50 F6
Sandpit Hill Cotts HP23 133 B2
Sandpit La HP27 138 B4
Sandpits La HP10 174 C7
Sandringham Ct
 8 High Wycombe HP13 173 B7
 Newport Pagnell MK16 22 B3
 Slough SL1 204 D7
Sandringham Pl MK2 58 C8
Sandringham Rd
 Maidenhead SL6 195 E2
 Stanwell TW6 213 E2
SANDS 172 B7
Sands Bank Nature Reserve★
 HP12 172 A7
Sandsdown Cl HP12 172 C8
Sands Farm Dr SL1 197 C1
Sands Ind Est HP12 172 B7
Sandstone Cl MK18 73 B5
Sandwell Ct MK8 33 C2
Sandy Cl
 Buckingham MK18 52 F8
 Milton Keynes MK14 34 D8
Sandycroft Rd HP6 155 C1
Sandygate Cl SL7 183 D3
Sandygate Rd SL7 183 D3
Sandy La
 Aspley Heath MK17 49 B2
 Leighton Buzzard LU7 70 F3
 Long Crendon HP18 125 B6
Sandy Mead SL6 203 C1
Sandy Rd MK18 73 B5
Sandy Rise SL9 177 E2
Sandywell Dr MK15 35 A6
San Remo Rd MK17 49 F4
Santa Cruz Ave MK17 58 A3
Santa Maria La MK17 58 B2
Santen Gr MK2 58 D4
Saracens' Wharf MK2 47 E1
Sargeant Cl UB8 201 D2
SARRATT 156 F4
Sarum Complex UB8 201 B3
Satis Ho SL3 211 C7
Saunders Cl MK7 48 D6
Saunders Ct 1 HP13 173 F6
Saunders End HP6 153 C5
Saunders Pl HP19 115 A7
Saunders Rd UB10 201 F4
Saunders Wood Copse
 HP14 158 F4
SAUNDERTON
 Bledlow Ridge 149 C1
 Princes Risborough 138 E1
SAUNDERTON LEE 149 A4
Saunderton Sta HP14 149 C1
Saunderton Vale HP14 149 C1
Savage Croft MK10 35 E3
Savay Cl UB9 190 A4
Savay La UB9 190 A5
Savernake Rd HP19 101 D3
Savill La MK4, MK5 45 F2
Savill Way SL7 183 F2
Savoy Cres MK9 34 F3
Savoy Ct SL6 195 F1
Sawley Ho 5 MK3 46 F1
Sawmill Cotts SL3 199 F2
Sawmill Rd HP27 138 D7
Sawpit Hill HP15 163 B5
Sawyers Cl SL6 202 A2
Sawyer's Cl SL4 209 E7
Sawyers Cres SL6 202 A2
Saxeways Bsns Ctr HP5 143 E3
Saxhorn Rd HP14 171 C4
Saxon Cl
 Amersham HP6 154 D1
 Dunstable LU6 93 E8
 Milton Keynes MK19 11 B2
 Slough SL3 206 F4
 Uxbridge UB8 208 E8
Saxon Ct
 High Wycombe HP12 172 D8
 Stanwell TW19 213 A2
Saxon Gate MK9 34 E2
Saxon Gdns SL6 196 D1
Saxonia Bvd MK16 36 B5
Saxon Lodge SL1 204 F5
Saxon Park Ind Est MK1 47 D2
Saxon St
 Milton Keynes, Ashland MK1,
 MK6 47 C4
 Milton Keynes, Heelands MK6,
 MK13, MK14 34 C5
 Milton Keynes MK2 58 C8
Saxon Way
 Harmondsworth UB7 213 C8
 Old Windsor SL4 211 B1
Saxon Way Trad Ctr UB7 213 C8
Sayers Ct MK4 56 F8
Sayers Gdns HP4 135 A6
Saye & Sele Cl HP18 82 F6
Sayward Cl HP5 144 D2
Scafell Rd SL2 204 F8
Scaldwell Pl HP21 115 F4
Scarborough Way SL1 205 B4
Scardale MK13 34 C5
Scarlett Ave HP22 131 E6
Scatterdells La WD4 146 F1
Scatterill Cl MK13 34 A4
Scholars Way HP6 154 F1
Scholars Wlk
 Chalfont St Peter SL9 177 E4
 Slough SL3 207 A4
School Cl
 Asheridge HP5 143 E5
 Brackley NN13 39 A4
 Cryers Hill HP15 162 C6
 High Wycombe, Downley
 HP13 161 D2
 High Wycombe HP11 173 A4
 Holmer Green HP15 163 C7
 Ickford HP18 124 A3
School Dr MK17 57 C3
School End
 Chetwode MK18 61 D8
 Great Horwood MK17 55 A3
School Hill
 Charndon OX27 73 A6
 North Marston MK18 76 B2
School Ho TW19 213 C1
School La
 Amersham HP7 165 A8
 Buckingham MK18 52 C8
 Castlethorpe MK19 19 F5
 Chalfont St Giles HP8 177 B7
 Chalfont St Peter SL9 177 D1
 Cookham Dean SL6 195 B7
 Cookham SL6 196 B7
 Dinton HP17 113 F2
 Eaton Bray LU6 92 F6
 Leighton Buzzard LU7 68 E1
 Little Marlow SL7 184 C5
 Maidenhead SL6 195 E1
 Medmenham SL7 193 B6
 Milton Keynes MK5 46 B8
 Oakley HP18 109 D5
 Penn Street HP7 164 B5
 Preston Bissett MK18 62 B8
 Seer Green HP9 176 D4
 Shabbington HP18 124 D3
 Sherington MK16 14 A2
 Slough SL2 205 F6
 Turville RG9 169 F3
 Twyford MK18 62 D2
 Upper Winchendon HP18 99 A1
 Waddesdon HP18 99 A6
 Weston Turville HP22 116 F1
 Wexham Street SL2 199 B5
 Yardley Gobion NN12 18 E6
School Rd
 Harmondsworth UB7 213 D8
 Tylers Green HP10 174 D8
 Wooburn Green HP10 185 E6
School St MK13 33 F7
School The HP23 118 C8
School Way HP11 174 B2
Schorne La MK18 76 B2
Schumann Cl MK7 48 C4
Scotch Firs MK7 48 C6
Scotlands Dr SL2 198 B6
Scotney Gdns MK3 57 E8
Scotsgrove Cotts OX9 126 A4
Scotsgrove Hill OX9 126 A3
Scotswood Cl HP9 175 D5
Scott Cl
 Farnham Common SL2 198 C7
 West Drayton UB7 208 F2
Scott Dr MK16 22 A5
Scott End HP19 100 F2
Scott Evans Ct MK18 66 A5
Scotts Cl
 Marsh Gibbon OX27 72 A3
 Stoke Hammond MK17 69 E8
Scotts Cnr NN13 39 A4
Scotts Farm Cl MK18 41 E4
Scotts La
 Adstock MK18 53 F1
 Buckingham MK18 41 E3
 Marsh Gibbon OX27 71 E2
Scriven Ct MK15 35 E7
Scriveners La NN12 17 A8
Scrubb's La HP14 160 B7
Seabrooke Ct MK8 45 D6
Seacourt Rd SL3 207 B2
Seaford Rd TW6 213 D2
Seagrave Ct MK7 48 A4
Seagrave Rd HP9 175 C4
Sears The LU6 92 B5
Seaton Dr HP21 115 D4
Seaton Gr MK10 36 A4
Secklow Gate MK9 34 F3
Second Ave MK1 47 C2
Second Cres SL1 205 C8
Second St HP11 173 C4
Sedgemere MK8 33 D2
Sedgemoor Dr OX9 126 A1
Sedgmoor Cl HP10 185 A7
Sedgmoor Gdns HP10 185 A8
Sedgmoor La HP10 185 B7
Sedgmoor Rd HP10 185 A8
Sedley Gr UB9 190 C7
SEDRUP 114 F3
Sedrup La HP17 114 F4
Seebeck Cl MK5 46 C7
Seechfield HP22 85 A3
Seeleys Cl HP9 175 C4
Seeleys Ct HP9 175 D3
Seeleys La HP9 175 D3
Seeleys Rd HP9 175 C4
SEER GREEN 176 D4
Seer Green CE Comb Sch
 HP9 176 C4
Seer Green & Jordans Sta
 HP9 176 C3
Seer Green La HP9 176 E3
Seer Mead HP9 176 D4
Sefton Cl SL2 198 F4
Sefton Paddock SL2 199 A5
Sefton Park Cotts SL2 199 A4
Sefton Way UB8 208 C7
Selbourne Ave MK3 57 F7
Selbourne Ho 10 SL8 185 A4
Selby Gr MK5 46 B5
Selim Ct 4 SL1 206 B4
Selkirk Ave HP19 101 D2
Selkirk Dr
 Stantonbury MK13 34 B8
 Stantonbury MK14 21 C1
Selkirk Gr MK3 46 F2
Selwood Cl TW19 213 C1
Selwood Gdns TW19 213 C1
Selwood Way HP13 161 E2
Selworthy MK4 46 D3
Selwyn Cl SL4 209 E5
Selwyn Ct HP21 116 B6
Selwyn Gr MK3 58 B8
Selwyn Pl SL1 204 F6
September Ct UB10 201 D3
Serjeants Gn MK14 34 F6
Serles Cl MK6 47 A6
Sermed Ct SL2 206 C5
Serpentine Ct MK2 58 D5
Serpentine The HP19 115 C8
Servite Ho SL6 203 B8
Seven Acre Ho HP10 174 C2
Seven Acres HP18 125 B7
Seven Gables MK18 65 D6
Sevenhills Rd SL0 200 C6
Severalls Ave HP5 144 C2
Severn Cres SL3 207 B1
Severn Dr MK16 22 E4
Severn Ho HP13 173 F7
Severn Way MK3 57 D8
Sewell Cl HP19 100 F2
Seymour Cl
 Flackwell Heath HP10 173 F2
 Maidenhead SL6 202 B3
Seymour Court La SL7 183 B5
Seymour Court Rd SL7 183 C4
Seymour Ct
 Berkhamsted HP4 134 E6
 Tring HP23 119 A4
Seymour Ho
 High Wycombe HP12 172 E4
 Slough SL3 206 E4
Seymour Park Rd SL7 183 D3
Seymour Plain SL7 183 C5
Seymour Rd
 Berkhamsted HP4 134 E6
 Chalfont St Giles HP8 177 C6
 Slough SL1 205 D4
SHABBINGTON 124 D3
Shackerstone Cl MK10 36 B4
Shackleton Ct 6 TW19 213 E1
Shackleton Pl MK6 34 E1
Shackleton Rd
 High Wycombe HP12 172 E5
 Slough SL1 205 F6
Shaftesbury Cres MK3 47 A1
Shaftesbury Ct
 Maidenhead SL6 202 E5
 6 Slough SL1 205 E4
 Winslow MK18 65 F5
Shaftesbury Ho HP21 116 C7
Shaftesbury St HP11 172 F8
Shaggy Calf La SL2 206 A6
Shakespeare Cl MK16 22 A5
Shakespeare Lodge SL1 204 F5
Shakespeare Orch HP18 82 F6
Shakespeare Way HP20 116 A8
Shallowford Gr MK4 46 D4
SHALSTONE 39 E6
Shamaa Ho 13 SL1 205 F4
Shamrock Cl MK7 48 B6
Shannon Ct
 Chesham HP5 144 C1
 Milton Keynes MK14 35 A6
Shantock Hall La HP3 145 E1
Shantock La HP3 145 E1
Shantung Pl HP5 154 C6
Shardeloes HP7 164 D8
Sharkham Ct MK4 46 B1
Sharman Row 8 SL3 206 F1
Sharman Wlk MK13 34 A3
Sharney Ave SL3 207 B3
Sharp Cl HP21 115 E5
Sharp's Cl HP18 99 B6
Sharrow Vale HP12 172 E7
Shaw Cl
 Aylesbury HP20 116 A8
 Newport Pagnell MK16 22 A5
Shaw Ct
 Aylesbury HP21 115 E3
 Old Windsor SL4 211 A2
Shawfield Ct UB7 208 E3
Shaw Gdns 11 SL3 206 F1
Shaw Savill Wy MK10 36 C4
Shaws Cl HP16 151 D5
Shaw The SL6 195 E6
Shearmans MK11 33 A4
Sheehy Way SL2 206 B6
Sheelin Gr MK2 58 D4
Sheepcoat Cl MK5 46 A5
Sheepcote Cl HP9 175 C4
Sheepcote Dell Rd HP15 163 E7
Sheepcote Gdns UB9 190 A5
Sheepcote La HP10, SL1 186 A2
Sheepcote Rd
 Eton Wick SL4 205 A1
 Windsor SL4 209 E5
Sheepfold La HP7 165 D7
Sheephouse Rd SL6 196 B2
Sheeplane MK17 60 C2
SHEEPRIDGE 184 E7
Sheepridge La SL7, SL8 184 E7
Sheep St MK18 66 A4
Sheep Wy MK14 21 F3
Sheer Croft HP5 143 F2
Sheering Gr MK13 34 B8
Sheerness Ct MK4 57 A8
Sheerstock HP17 126 E5
Sheerwater HP19 101 E4
Sheet St SL4 210 D6
Sheet Street Rd SL4 210 C2
Sheffield Dr HP21 115 E6
Sheffield Rd SL1 205 C7
Shelburne Ct HP12 172 E4
Shelburne Rd HP12 172 E4
Sheldon Ct MK8 33 F1
Sheldon Rd HP18 124 A3
Sheldon Way HP4 135 A5
Shelduck Cl 3 HP19 101 E3
Shelley Cl
 Medmenham SL7 193 D7
 Newport Pagnell MK16 22 B4
 Slough SL3 206 F1
 Wooburn Green HP10 185 E8
Shelley Dr MK3 57 F7
Shelley Rd
 Chesham HP5 144 B2
 High Wycombe HP11 172 F5
 12 Marlow SL7 183 F3
Shellfield Cl TW19 213 A2
Shelsley Ave MK6 47 C5
Shelsmore MK14 35 A8
Shelton Ct
 Slough SL3 206 C3
 Woburn Sands MK17 49 B4
SHENLEY BROOK END 46 A2
Shenley Brook End Sch
 MK5 46 A2
SHENLEY CHURCH END 45 E6
Shenley L Ctr MK5 46 A7
SHENLEY LODGE 46 C5
Shenley Rd
 Milton Keynes, Bletchley
 MK3 46 E1
 Milton Keynes, Loughton
 MK5 46 A7
 Whaddon MK17 56 C8
Shenley Rdbt MK5 46 A5
SHENLEY WOOD 45 F4
Shenston Ct 13 SL4 210 C6
Shenstone Dr SL1 197 D1
Shenstone Hill HP4 135 E5
Shenton MK10 36 C3
Shepherd Cl HP20 102 A2
Shepherds MK11 33 A4
Shepherds Cl
 Beaconsfield HP9 175 F1
 Hurley SL6 193 F3
 Uxbridge UB8 201 C1
Shepherds Ct SL4 209 E5
Shepherds Fold HP15 163 D8
Shepherds Gate HP16 152 A2
Shepherds Hey MK14 21 C1
Shepherds La
 Beaconsfield HP9 175 F1
 Hazlemere HP15 162 F5
 Hurley SL6 193 E4
Shepherd's La WD3 167 E2
Shepherds Row MK18 66 A4
Shepherds Way HP5 154 D6
Shepherdswell Acad MK6 35 B2
Sheppards Cl MK16 22 C4
Shepperds Cl MK18 76 A2
Shepperds Gn MK5 45 F6
Shepperton Cl MK19 19 F5
Sheraton Dr HP13 162 D1
Sheraton Ho WD3 167 C5
Sherborne Cl SL3 212 E6
Sherborne Ct SL6 202 E5
Sherbourne Dr
 Bow Brickhill MK7 48 B4
 Maidenhead SL6 202 C3
 Windsor SL4 209 F3
Sherbourne Wlk SL2 198 C8
Shereway HP19 115 B8
Shergold Way SL6 195 F6
Sheridan Cl HP21 115 D3
Sheridan Ct
 High Wycombe HP12 172 C3
 Maidenhead SL6 203 B8
 Slough SL1 204 E6
Sheridan Gr MK4 45 D2
Sheriff Cl HP19 115 B8
Sheringham Ct SL6 202 E7
SHERINGTON 14 A2
Sherington CE Fst Sch
 MK16 14 A2
Sherington Rd MK16 22 E7
Sherman Rd SL1 205 E8
Shernfold MK7 48 B7
Sherriff Cotts HP18 99 A7
Sherwood Cl SL3 206 E3
Sherwood Ct
 Colnbrook SL3 212 D7
 10 Slough SL3 206 F1
Sherwood Dr
 Maidenhead SL6 202 A6
 Milton Keynes MK1, MK2,
 MK3 47 B1
Shetland 1 MK18 41 D3
Shetland Mdws MK17 58 A3
Shields Ct HP10 163 B1
Shifford Cres SL6 195 E3
Shilling Cl MK15 35 A7
Shillingridge Pk SL7 182 E5
Shinfield Cl MK18 63 D2
Ship Hill SL1 186 E4
Ship La LU7 105 D3
Shiplake Ho SL8 185 B4
Shipley Rd MK16 22 B4
Shipman Ct MK15 35 B7
Ship Rd LU7 80 E6
Ship St HP11 173 A7
Shipton MK18 66 B3
Shipton Hill MK13 34 B6
SHIPTON LEE 84 D7
Shipton Rd UB10 201 F8
Shire Ct MK14 35 A5
Shire La
 Chalfont St Peter HP8,
 SL9 178 B6
 Cholesbury HP23 133 B4
 Chorleywood WD3 167 C4
 North Crawley MK16 24 E4
Shires Bsns Pk The NN13 38 A6
Shires Rd NN13 38 A6
Shirley Ave SL4 209 F6
Shirley Cl HP20 101 D2
Shirley Moor MK7 48 B8
Shirley Rd SL6 202 C5
Shirwell Cres MK4 46 D5
Shogmoor La RG9 170 C1
Shootacre Cnr HP27 149 A8
Shootacre La HP27 149 A8
SHOOTERSWAY 134 E4
Shootersway HP4 134 E4
Shootersway La HP4 134 F4
Shootersway Pk HP4 134 F3
Shop La NN7 1 B6
Shoppenhanger's Rd
 SL6 202 E4
Shoredich Cl UB10 190 F1
Shoreham Rise SL2 197 D1
Shoreham Road (E) TW6 213 E2
Shoreham Road (W)
 TW6 213 E2
Shorham Rise MK8 33 E2
Shortborough Ave HP27 139 B5
Short Ditch HP17 127 A7
Shortfern SL2 206 C7
Short Hale LU7 105 D3
Shorthorn Dr MK8 45 D7
Short Massey MK46 6 E5
Short Rd TW6 213 E1
Short St HP11 172 F7
Shortway
 Amersham HP6 154 D2
 Chesham HP5 144 B2
Shotfield Rd HP14 171 C4
Shothanger Way HP3 146 D6
Shouler Cl MK5 46 A5
SHREDING GREEN 207 C7
Shrewsbury Cl MK10 36 A2
Shrimpton Cl HP9 175 D6
Shrimpton Rd
 Beaconsfield HP9 175 D6
 High Wycombe HP12 172 B3
Shropshire Ct MK3 46 E1
Shrubbery Cl HP13 173 B8
Shrubbery Rd HP13 173 B8
Shrublands Ave HP4 135 A4
Shrublands Rd HP4 135 A5
Shucklow Hill MK17 55 E3
Shugars Gn HP23 119 B5
Shupp's La HP18 112 B1
Shutlanger Rd NN12 9 A8
Shuttleworth Gr MK7 48 D6
Siareys Cl OX39 147 C6
Sibleys Rise HP16 152 D8
Siddington Dr HP18 100 E5
Side Rd UB9 189 D4

Sidings Ind Est The NN13 . 38 A8
Sidings The
Loudwater HP11 . 174 B3
Milton Keynes MK2 . 47 E1
Sidlow Ct MK11 . 32 F4
Sidney Cl UB8 . 201 C5
Sidney Ho HP14 . 171 C5
Sidney Rd SL4 . 209 C4
Sidney Terr HP22 . 131 B5
Sierra Dr HP19 . 100 F4
Sierra Rd HP11 . 173 E5
Silbury Arc MK9 . 34 E3
Silbury Bvd MK9 . 34 D2
Silbury Rdbt MK9 . 34 C1
Silchester Ho SL6 . 203 B8
Silco Dr SL6 . 202 E6
Silicon Ct MK5 . 46 C5
Silk Mill Way HP23 . 119 A5
Silk St HP18 . 99 A6
Silkwood Ct SL1 . 205 F6
Sillswood MK46 . 6 E4
Silsden Cres HP8 . 177 D7
Silverbeck Way TW19 . 213 A2
Silver Birch Cl UB10 . 201 E8
Silver Birch Dr HP27 . 149 E5
Silverbirches La MK17 . 49 A2
Silver Birch Way HP22 . 116 B4
Silver Cl SL6 . 202 A5
Silverdale Cl
4 Aylesbury HP20 . 101 D1
Tylers Green HP10 . 163 A1
Silver End MK46 . 7 A3
Silver Hill HP8 . 177 B8
Silverhill Ct SL1 . 205 C8
Silvermead HP18 . 123 D5
Silver St
20 Aylesbury HP20 . 115 D8
Cublington LU7 . 78 B1
Milton Keynes MK11 . 32 D5
Newport Pagnell MK16 . 22 D4
Silverstone Mews SL6 . 202 C4
Silverstone Motor Racing Circuit* MK18 . 28 F8
Silvertrees Dr SL6 . 202 A5
Silverweed Ct MK7 . 48 B5
Simatt Ho HP10 . 174 C2
Simdims MK43 . 25 A1
Simmons Cl SL3 . 207 A2
Simmons Ct
Aylesbury HP21 . 115 E4
High Wycombe HP12 . 172 E7
Simmons Rd RG9 . 191 D3
Simmons Way
Lane End HP14 . 171 C4
Thame OX9 . 125 F1
Simms Croft MK10 . 36 A2
Simnel MK6 . 47 B6
Simon Dean HP3 . 146 A4
Simonsbath MK4 . 46 D2
Simons Lea MK13 . 34 B4
Simon's Way MK18 . 39 E7
Simpson Cl SL6 . 203 B8
Simpson Dr MK6 . 47 E5
Simpson Pl HP21 . 115 F5
Simpson Rd MK1, MK2, MK6 . 47 E3
Simpson Rdbt MK6 . 47 D5
Simpsons Way SL1 . 205 E5
Sinatra Dr MK4 . 45 E3
Sinclair Ct MK1 . 47 B3
Sinclair Rd SL4 . 210 C4
Singers La RG9 . 191 E1
SINGLEBOROUGH . 54 F5
Singleborough La MK17 . 54 F3
Singleton Dr MK8 . 45 D6
Singleton Way 8 HP19 . 115 A8
Singret Pl UB8 . 201 C1
Sion Terr MK18 . 51 B6
Sipson Rd UB7 . 208 F3
Sipthorp Cl MK7 . 48 C6
Sir Henry Floyd Gram Sch HP21 . 115 C7
Sir Henry Lee Cres
Aylesbury HP18 . 100 D3
Aylesbury HP18 . 100 E3
Sir Henry Peakes Dr SL2 . 198 A6
Sir Herbert Leon Acad MK2 . 58 C5
Sir Peter's Way HP4 . 107 E6
Sir Robert Mews SL3 . 207 A1
Sir Sydney Camm Ho SL4 . 210 B6
Sir Thomas Fremantle Sch MK18 . 65 F5
Sir William Borlase's Gram Sch SL7 . 183 C1
Sir William Ramsay Sch HP15 . 163 A3
Sissinghurst Dr MK4 . 45 E2
Sitwell Cl MK16 . 21 F5
Six Cotts MK18 . 29 E5
Sixth St HP11 . 173 C4
Sixty Acres Rd HP16 . 151 C6
Skeats Wharf MK15 . 35 A7
Skeldon Gate MK14 . 35 A4
Skeldon Rdbt MK9 . 35 A4
Skelton Cl HP9 . 186 A8
Skelton Rd 7 MK18 . 41 E3
Skene Cl MK2 . 58 C4
Skerries Ct SL3 . 207 A2
Skimmers Cl HP15 . 163 C6
Skimmers End HP15 . 163 C6
Skimmers Field HP15 . 163 C6
Skinner Rd HP19 . 101 B4
Skinners Cl MK14 . 21 F3
Skip La UB9 . 190 E3
Skipper Cl HP19 . 101 C4
Skippon Way OX9 . 125 F2
Skipton Cl MK15 . 35 C6
SKIRMETT . 170 A1
Skirmett Rd RG9 . 181 C1
Skittle Gn HP27 . 138 A2
SKITTLE GREEN . 138 A3
Skydmore Path SL2 . 197 F1
Skye Cres MK17 . 58 C3
Skye Lodge SL1 . 205 E5
Skylark Rd UB9 . 189 C3
Skyline Mews HP12 . 172 C4
Skyport Dr UB7 . 213 D7
Skyway 14 Trad Est SL3 . 212 F4
Slade Hill
Aylesbury HP19 . 115 A7
Mixbury NN13 . 38 D1
Slade La MK11 . 33 A4
Slade Oak La UB9 . 189 C5
Slade Rd HP14 . 158 E4
Slade The MK17 . 57 D3
Slad La HP27 . 149 F3
SLAPTON . 91 C5
Slapton La LU6 . 91 F6
Slated Row MK12 . 33 B7
Slated Row Sch MK12 . 33 A7
Slatepits Croft MK46 . 6 E5
Slater St HP13 . 173 C6
Slattenham Cl HP19 . 115 B7
Slave Hill HP17 . 126 F5
Slayter Rd HP14 . 171 C4
Slickett's La LU6 . 92 F3
Slipe The LU7 . 105 A7
SLOUGH . 205 D5
Slough & Eton CE Bsns & Enterprise Coll SL1 . 205 D3
Slough Gram Sch SL3 . 206 B3
Slough Ice Arena SL1 . 205 D4
Slough Interchange Ind Est SL2 . 206 A5
Slough La HP14 . 160 C6
Slough Rd
Datchet SL3 . 211 B8
Iver Heath SL0 . 200 E3
Slough SL4 . 205 E2
Slough Sta SL1 . 205 F5
Slough Trad Est SL1 . 205 B7
Sly Corner HP16 . 142 E4
Smabridge Wlk MK15 . 35 D7
SMAE Inst The SL6 . 202 B6
Smallbrook MK43 . 25 B2
Small Cres MK18 . 52 F8
Smalldean La HP27 . 149 E2
Smarden Bell MK7 . 48 B8
Smeaton Cl
Aylesbury HP19 . 101 A1
Blakelands MK14 . 22 A2
Smewin Ct HP11 . 172 E7
Smith Cl HP20 . 116 B7
Smith Ctr The RG9 . 191 B5
Smithergill Ct MK13 . 34 C5
Smithfield End MK17 . 66 F4
Smithfield Rd SL6 . 202 A3
Smith's La
Waterperry Common OX33 . 122 F7
Windsor SL4 . 209 E6
Smithsons Pl MK9 . 35 B3
Smithy The MK19 . 31 E4
Snaith Cres MK5 . 46 B7
Snakeley Cl HP10 . 174 C1
Snakemoor Nature Reserve* HP17 . 126 D6
Snape Spur SL1 . 205 E7
Snells La HP7 . 166 C7
Snells Wood Ct HP7 . 166 C7
SNELSHALL EAST . 57 B7
Snelshall St MK4 . 56 F8
SNELSHALL WEST . 57 A7
Snowball Hill SL6 . 202 A1
Snowberry Cl MK12 . 33 D5
Snowden Cl SL4 . 209 D3
Snowdon Dr MK6 . 46 D7
Snowdrop Way HP15 . 162 F7
Snowhill Cotts HP5 . 144 F7
Snowshill Ct MK14 . 21 F2
Soames Cl MK46 . 7 F7
Soane Wlk HP13 . 173 A8
Soho Cres HP10 . 185 D4
Soho Mills Ind Est HP10 . 185 D4
Sokeman Cl MK12 . 33 A5
Solar Ct MK14 . 21 E1
Solesbridge Cl WD3 . 167 F6
Solesbridge La WD3 . 167 F6
Somerford Cl SL6 . 203 B8
Somerford Pl HP9 . 175 D3
Somerlea SL6 . 196 C3
Somersby Cres SL6 . 202 E3
Somerset Cl MK3 . 46 F1
Somerset Lodge 3 SL6 . 202 F6
Somerset Way SL0 . 207 F4
Somerset Wlk MK10 . 36 D3
Somers Lees 13 HP19 . 115 A8
Somerville Rd SL4 . 205 C1
Somerville Way HP19 . 115 B8
Sophie Gdns SL3 . 206 D4
Sorensen Ct MK5 . 45 E4
Sorrell Dr MK16 . 21 F4
Soskin Dr MK14 . 34 D6
Sospel Ct SL2 . 198 C3
SOULBURY . 69 E3
Soulbury LU7 . 69 E2
Soulbury Rd
Burcott LU7 . 79 D4
Leighton Buzzard LU7 . 80 D7
Stewkley LU7 . 68 F1
Sounding Arch Wy SL6 . 202 D5
Southampton Road E TW6 . 213 F1
Southampton Road W TW6 . 213 E1
South Bank NN13 . 38 C7
South Bank Rd HP4 . 134 F6
Southbourne 1 HP13 . 173 C7
Southbourne Dr SL8 . 185 A3
Southbridge Gr MK7 . 48 A7
South Cl
Medmenham SL7 . 193 D7
Slough SL1 . 204 D6
West Drayton UB7 . 208 F3
Southcliffe Dr SL9 . 177 E5
South Common Rd UB8 . 201 E6
Southcote Way HP10 . 163 B1
South Cottage Dr WD3 . 167 F4
South Cottage Gdns WD3 . 167 F4
Southcott Lower Sch LU7 . 80 D8
Southcott Village LU7 . 80 D6
Southcott Way MK6 . 47 D5
SOUTHCOURT . 115 D6
Southcourt Ave LU7 . 80 D6
Southcourt Ho LU7 . 80 D7
Southcourt Rd LU7 . 80 D7
Southcroft SL2 . 198 B1
South Dr
Beaconsfield HP9 . 186 B8
High Wycombe HP13 . 173 D8
South Eighth St MK9 . 34 E2
SOUTHEND . 180 C8
SOUTH END
Leckhampstead . 42 E7
Stewkley . 78 E8
South End HP17 . 126 F5
South End La LU6 . 92 B4
South Enmore Rdbt MK6 . 35 B3
Southern Cotts TW19 . 213 A2
Southern Perimeter Rd TW6, TW19 . 213 D2
Southern Rd
Aylesbury HP19 . 101 C1
Thame OX9 . 125 E1
Southern Way MK12 . 33 D5
Southfield Cl MK15 . 35 E7
South Field Cl SL4 . 204 C3
Southfield Cotts HP17 . 130 C3
Southfield Dr HP15 . 163 A6
Southfield Gdns SL1 . 204 B8
Southfield Rd
Aylesbury HP20 . 116 B8
Flackwell Heath HP10 . 174 A1
High Wycombe HP13 . 161 D1
Princes Risborough HP27 . 139 C3
South Fifth St MK9 . 34 E1
South Fourth St MK9 . 34 D1
Southgate Ho SL6 . 202 F8
South Gn SL1 . 205 E6
South Hall MK18 . 41 E3
SOUTH HAREFIELD . 190 D6
SOUTH HEATH . 152 E8
South Hills HP18 . 96 A1
South Ho MK1 . 47 D3
South La LU7 . 78 E7
Southland Dr MK2 . 58 E6
Southlands Rd UB9 . 189 F1
South Lawne MK3 . 57 F8
Southlea Rd SL3, SL4 . 211 B5
South Maundin HP14 . 162 A7
South Meadow La SL4 . 210 C8
South Ninth St MK9 . 34 F2
South Overgate Rdbt MK6 . 35 B3
South Park Ave WD3 . 167 F4
South Park Cres SL9 . 188 F7
South Park Ct SL9 . 188 E6
South Park Dr SL9 . 188 E7
South Park Gdns HP4 . 135 B5
South Park View SL9 . 188 F7
South Path SL4 . 210 C5
South Pk SL9 . 188 F6
South Pl SL7 . 183 E1
South Rd
Amersham HP6 . 154 C3
Chorleywood WD3 . 167 C4
Maidenhead SL6 . 202 E6
West Drayton UB7 . 208 F3
South Row
Fulmer SL3 . 199 E8
Milton Keynes MK9 . 34 E1
Milton Keynes MK9 . 46 D8
South Saxon Rdbt MK9 . 34 F1
South Secklow Rdbt MK6 . 34 F2
South Second St MK9 . 34 D1
South Seventh St MK9 . 34 E1
South Side SL9 . 188 D8
South Sixth St MK9 . 34 E1
South St
Castlethorpe MK19 . 19 F5
Wendover HP22 . 131 B4
South Tenth St MK9 . 34 F2
South Terr
Milton Keynes MK2 . 58 C8
Windsor SL4 . 210 E6
South Vale NN7 . 1 A5
South View
Cookham Rise SL6 . 195 E7
Eton SL4 . 205 B1
High Wycombe HP13 . 161 D2
Wooburn Green HP10 . 185 D8
Southview Rd SL7 . 183 E4
South View Rd SL9 . 188 D7
South Way HP9 . 186 A8
Southwick Ct MK8 . 45 F8
South Witan Rdbt MK6 . 34 E1
Southwold Cl HP21 . 116 A6
Southwold Cres MK10 . 36 C3
Southwold Spur SL3 . 207 C4
Southwood Gdns SL6 . 195 E5
Southwood Rd SL6 . 195 E5
Southwood Sch MK14 . 34 E5
Sovereign Beeches SL2 . 198 B6
Sovereign Cl
Granborough MK18 . 75 F7
5 Linslade LU7 . 80 F8
Sovereign Ct
Aylesbury HP19 . 101 D1
High Wycombe HP13 . 173 D6
Sovereign Dr MK15 . 35 A7
Sovereign Hts SL3 . 212 A8
Sovereign Lodge MK15 . 35 A7
Spackmans Way SL1 . 205 D3
Spa Cl HP18 . 110 B8
Spade Oak Farm SL8 . 184 E3
Spade Oak Mdw SL8 . 184 E4
Spark Way MK16 . 21 F5
Sparrow Cl HP19 . 101 F3
Sparrow Hall Bsns Pk LU6 . 92 D3
Sparrow Hall Farm LU6 . 92 D3
Sparsholt Cl 5 MK4 . 46 C2
Spartlet Mews HP18 . 100 E4
Spearing Rd HP12 . 172 C7
Spearmast Ind Est HP12 . 172 B6
Spearmint Cl MK7 . 48 B5
Specklands MK5 . 46 A8
Speedbird Way UB7 . 213 B7
Speedwell Pl MK14 . 34 E4
SPEEN . 150 C4
Speen CE Sch HP27 . 150 B4
Speen Rd HP14, HP16, HP27 . 150 D2
Speldhurst Ct MK7 . 48 B7
Spencer MK14 . 34 C8
Spencer Cl UB8 . 201 C2
Spencer Gdns OX27 . 72 E5
Spencer Rd SL3 . 206 F3
Spencers Cl SL6 . 202 D8
SPENCERSGREEN . 132 C7
Spencers La SL6 . 195 E6
Spencers Rd SL6 . 202 D8
Spencer St MK13 . 33 F7
Spencer Villas SL1 . 204 F5
Spenlows Rd MK3 . 47 A3
Spens SL6 . 202 F8
Spenser Ho HP21 . 115 F6
Spenser Rd HP21 . 115 F6
Sperling Rd SL6 . 195 F1
Spicers Yd HP17 . 127 A6
Spickett's La HP18 . 113 A3
Spier's La OX27 . 71 F2
Spiert The HP17 . 114 D5
Spindle Cl HP15 . 163 A3
Spindle Ct HP12 . 172 E7
Spindle Mews MK18 . 52 F6
Spinfield La SL7 . 183 B2
Spinfield Lane W SL7 . 183 C1
Spinfield Mount SL7 . 183 B1
Spinfield Pk SL7 . 183 C1
Spinfield Sch SL7 . 183 B2
Spinners Wlk
Marlow SL7 . 183 C1
Stantonbury MK14 . 21 C1
Windsor SL4 . 210 C6
Spinney SL1 . 205 B5
Spinney Bglws LU7 . 91 C6
Spinney Cl
Steeple Claydon MK18 . 63 E2
West Drayton UB7 . 208 E6
Spinney Cotts OX33 . 123 B1
Spinney Cres LU6 . 93 F8
Spinney Hill Rd MK46 . 6 E3
Spinney La MK17 . 49 F4
Spinney The
Beaconsfield HP9 . 175 E1
Berkhamsted HP4 . 134 F3
Chesham HP5 . 144 D2
Gerrards Cross SL9 . 188 D3
High Wycombe HP11 . 173 A4
Holmer Green HP15 . 163 D7
Milton Keynes MK13 . 34 A4
Winslow MK18 . 66 A6
Spire Thames Valley SL3 . 199 C4
Spire View TW19 . 213 D1
SPITAL . 210 B3
Spitfire Cl SL3 . 207 A2
Spittal St SL7 . 183 D2
Spoondell LU6 . 93 F7
Spoonley Wood MK13 . 33 E5
Sportsman Cl MK18 . 63 D3
Spout La TW19 . 213 A3
Spout Lane N TW19 . 213 B3
SPRIG'S ALLEY . 147 F1
Sprigs Holly La HP14 . 159 B8
Springate Field SL3 . 206 E4
Springbank Ct MK16 . 12 B7
Spring Cl
High Wycombe HP13 . 173 F7
Latimer HP5 . 155 D3
Maidenhead SL6 . 195 F2
Milton Keynes MK17 . 55 A2
Spring Coppice HP14 . 171 F5
Spring Coppice La HP27 . 150 D5
Springdale Cotts SL8 . 185 B2
Springett Pl HP6 . 154 F2
SPRINGFIELD . 35 B2
Springfield SL1 . 206 A3
Springfield Bvd MK6 . 35 B2
Springfield Cl
Aylesbury HP21 . 115 C8
Chesham HP5 . 154 C7
Windsor SL4 . 210 B5
Springfield Ct
1 Leighton Buzzard LU7 . 80 E7
1 Maidenhead SL6 . 203 B7
Springfield Ct *continued*
Milton Keynes MK6 . 35 B2
Springfield Gdns
Chinnor OX39 . 147 C7
Deanshanger MK19 . 31 E4
Springfield Hollow HP14 . 158 E5
Springfield Pk SL6 . 203 C1
Springfield Rd
Chesham HP5 . 154 C7
Dunstable LU6 . 93 D5
Leighton Buzzard LU7 . 80 E7
Olney MK46 . 6 F4
Slough SL3 . 212 B7
Stokenchurch HP14 . 158 F4
Windsor SL4 . 210 B5
Spring Field Rd HP4 . 135 A6
Springfield Rdbt MK6 . 35 A2
Springfields
Amersham HP6 . 154 C2
Padbury MK18 . 53 C1
Tylers Green HP10 . 163 C2
Springfields Cl MK18 . 53 C2
Springfields Ct MK18 . 53 C1
Springfield Way MK43 . 25 C2
Spring Gardens Rd HP13 . 173 E5
Spring Gdn La HP4 . 134 D5
Spring Gdns
Bourne End SL8 . 185 A4
Marlow SL7 . 183 E3
Newport Pagnell MK16 . 22 C4
Wooburn Green HP10 . 185 E8
Spring Gr MK17 . 49 B5
Spring Hill SL6 . 202 E3
Springhill Rd HP18 . 83 A8
Spring Ho SL7 . 183 E3
Spring La
Alderton NN12 . 9 A2
Clifton Reynes MK46 . 7 C3
Cookham Dean SL6 . 195 C5
Farnham Common SL2 . 198 C5
Flackwell Heath HP10 . 173 F3
Great Horwood MK17 . 55 A2
Olney MK46 . 6 F3
Slough SL1 . 204 F5
Spring Mdw HP18 . 97 A1
Springs Cl HP17 . 130 B2
Springside 2 LU7 . 80 E7
Springs La HP17 . 130 B3
Spring Valley Dr HP14 . 162 A7
Springwater Mill HP11 . 173 E4
Springwood HP27 . 150 C4
Sprinters L Ctr HP16 . 151 A7
Sproggit Ind Est TW19 . 213 F1
Spruce Ct 7 SL1 . 205 F3
Spruce Dene HP15 . 162 F2
Spruce Rd 1 HP19 . 100 F1
SPURGROVE . 170 E2
Spurgrove La RG9 . 170 E2
SPURLANDS END . 163 A8
Spurlands End Rd HP15 . 163 A8
Spur The SL1 . 204 D8
Spurt St HP18 . 112 F3
Square Close Cotts RG9 . 169 F3
Square The
Akeley MK18 . 41 F8
Aspley Guise MK17 . 49 E4
Brill HP18 . 110 A8
Great Missenden HP16 . 152 B7
Harmondsworth UB7 . 213 B6
Long Crendon HP18 . 125 C6
Milton Keynes MK12 . 33 D6
Preston Bissett MK18 . 62 B8
Waddesdon HP18 . 99 A6
Yardley Hastings NN7 . 1 A6
Squires Cl MK6 . 47 A6
Squirrel La HP12 . 172 C5
Squirrel Rise SL7 . 183 D6
Squirrels Way MK18 . 52 E7
Stablebridge Rd HP22 . 117 F3
Stable Cl MK18 . 50 C7
Stable Cotts SL7 . 194 C5
Stable La HP9 . 176 C4
Stable Rd HP22 . 131 E7
Stables Ct SL7 . 183 B1
Stables The MK19 . 20 F3
Stacey Ave MK12 . 33 D6
STACEY BUSHES . 33 E4
Stacey Bushes Trad Ctr MK12 . 33 E4
Stacey Ho HP12 . 172 E4
Stacey's Ct HP8 . 177 C8
Staddle Stones HP27 . 139 B4
Stadium App HP21 . 115 E4
Stadium MK (MK Dons FC) MK1 . 47 C3
Stafferton Way SL6 . 203 A6
Stafford Ave SL2 . 198 C1
Stafford Cl SL6 . 204 B7
Stafford Gr MK5 . 46 B6
Stafford Keep HP19 . 115 A8
Stag Ct WD3 . 167 C5
Stag La
Berkhamsted HP4 . 135 B5
Chorleywood WD3 . 167 C3
Great Kingshill HP15 . 151 D1
STAGSDEN WEST END . 16 F4
Stagshaw Gr 5 MK4 . 46 B2
Stainby Cl UB7 . 208 E3
Stainton Dr MK13 . 34 C4
Stamford Ave MK6 . 35 B2
Stamford Rd SL6 . 202 C6
Stanbridge Cl HP17 . 127 A7
Stanbridge Ct MK11 . 32 F5
Stanbridge Rd HP17 . 127 B6
Stanbrook Pl MK10 . 36 A1
Standfield Cl HP19 . 115 A8

Standing Way
Milton Keynes, Coldharbour
  Spinney MK3, MK4 . . . . . . **46** E3
Milton Keynes, Kingston
  MK10 . . . . **36** C1
Milton Keynes, Peartree Bridge
  MK10, MK4, MK6 . . . . **47** C7
Milton Keynes, Snelshall East
  MK4 . . . . **57** B7
Standring Pl HP20 . . . . . . **101** F2
Stanhope Cl HP22 . . . . . . **131** B7
Stanhope Heath TW19 . . . **213** C1
Stanhope Rd
  Aylesbury HP20 . . . . **116** A8
  Slough SL1 . . . . **204** D7
Stanhope Way TW19 . . . . **213** C1
Stanier Rise HP4 . . . . **134** F7
Stanier Sq ⑤ MK2 . . . . **58** C8
Stanley Ave HP5 . . . . **154** B8
Stanley Cl
  Marlow SL7 . . . . **183** F3
  Uxbridge UB8 . . . . **201** D3
Stanley Cotts SL2 . . . . . . **205** F5
Stanley Ct MK46 . . . . **6** F3
Stanley Gdns HP23 . . . . . **118** F3
Stanley Green E SL3 . . . . **206** F2
Stanley Green W SL3 . . . . **206** F2
Stanley Hill HP7 . . . . **165** E7
Stanley Hill Ave HP7 . . . . **165** E8
Stanley Ho SL4 . . . . **211** A2
Stanley Rd HP12 . . . . **172** C7
Stanley Spencer Gall★
  SL6 . . . . **196** B7
Stanmore Gdns MK16 . . . . **22** B2
Stanstead Pl HP7 . . . . **165** C8
Stanton Ave MK13 . . . . **34** A6
STANTONBURY **34** D7
Stantonbury Campus
  MK14 . . . . **34** C7
Stantonbury Campus L Ctr
  MK14 . . . . **34** C7
Stantonbury Cl MK13 . . . . . **34** A8
Stanton Gate MK13 . . . . . . **34** D8
Stanton Sch MK13 . . . . **34** B7
Stanton Way SL3 . . . . **206** C2
Stanway Cl MK15 . . . . **35** B6
STANWELL **213** C1
Stanwell Cl TW19 . . . . **213** C1
Stanwell Fields CE Prim Sch
  TW19 . . . . **213** E1
Stanwell Gdns TW19 . . . . **213** D1
STANWELL MOOR **212** D1
Stanwell Moor Rd TW6, TW19,
  UB7 . . . . **213** B4
Stanwell Rd SL3 . . . . **212** C4
Stanwyck La ④ MK4 . . . . . . **45** D2
Stapeley Ct ① MK4 . . . . **45** F1
Stapleford Mill★ LU7 . . . . . **70** B5
Staple Hall Rd MK1 . . . . **47** E1
Stapleton Cl SL7 . . . . **183** F4
Starling Cres SL1 . . . . . . **206** C2
Starling Mews HP19 . . . . . **114** E8
Stars La HP17 . . . . **113** E2
Startins La SL6 . . . . **195** C8
STARTOP'S END **104** F1
Starveall Cl UB7 . . . . **208** F3
Starwood Ct ① SL3 . . . . . . **206** C3
Staters Pound MK15 . . . . . . **35** A7
Statham Pl MK6 . . . . **46** F8
Station App
  Amersham HP6 . . . . **154** C1
  Chorleywood WD3 . . . . **167** D5
  Denham UB9 . . . . **189** D4
  Gerrards Cross SL9 . . . . . . **188** E6
  Great Missenden HP16 . . . . **152** A4
  Little Chalfont HP7 . . . . . . **166** D8
  Maidenhead SL6 . . . . **202** F6
  Marlow SL7 . . . . **183** E2
  Wendover HP22 . . . . **131** B4
  West Drayton UB7 . . . . **208** E5
Station Bvd HP20 . . . . **115** D8
Station Cotts
  Denham UB9 . . . . **190** A4
  Winslow MK18 . . . . **66** A5
Station Hill SL6 . . . . **195** F7
Station Par
  Beaconsfield HP9 . . . . **175** D3
  Cookham Rise SL8 . . . . **195** F6
  Denham Green UB9 . . . . . . **190** A4
Station Rd
  Aldbury HP23 . . . . **120** B5
  Amersham HP7 . . . . **165** C8
  Beaconsfield HP9 . . . . **175** E2
  Berkhamsted HP4 . . . . **135** D4
  Blackthorn OX25 . . . . **81** A4
  Bourne End SL8 . . . . **185** A3
  Bow Brickhill MK17 . . . . **48** C2
  Buckingham MK18 . . . . **52** E7
  Cactlethorpe MK19 . . . . **19** F5
  Cheddington LU7 . . . . **91** A1
  Chesham HP5 . . . . **154** C8
  Chinnor OX39 . . . . **147** C6
  Cookham Rise SL6 . . . . **195** F7
  Gerrards Cross SL9 . . . . . . **188** E6
  Haddenham HP17 . . . . **126** C5
  Henley-on-Thames RG9 . . . **191** E1
  High Wycombe HP13 . . . . . **173** C6
  Ivinghoe LU7 . . . . **105** E5
  Leighton Buzzard LU7 . . . . . **80** E7
  Little Kimble HP17 . . . . **129** E2
  Long Marston HP23 . . . . . . **104** B4
  Loudwater HP10 . . . . **174** C2
  Marlow SL7 . . . . **183** E1
  Marsh Gibbon OX27 . . . . **71** F3
  Mursley MK17 . . . . **67** B7
  Newport Pagnell MK16 . . . . **22** C4
  Padbury MK18 . . . . **53** B1

Station Rd continued
  Princes Risborough HP27 . **139** A2
  Quainton HP22 . . . . **85** A4
  Slough, Langley SL3 . . . . . . **207** A4
  Slough SL1 . . . . **204** E7
  Stoke Mandeville HP22 . . . **116** B2
  Swanbourne MK17 . . . . **67** A4
  Taplow SL6 . . . . **203** F7
  Tring HP23 . . . . **119** D4
  Uxbridge UB8 . . . . **201** D1
  West Drayton UB7 . . . . **208** E4
  Winslow MK18 . . . . **66** A5
  Woburn Sands MK17 . . . . . . **49** B5
  Wraysbury TW19 . . . . **212** A1
Station Rd Ind Est MK18 . . **66** A5
Station Rise SL7 . . . . **183** E2
Station Sq MK9 . . . . **34** C1
Station Terr
  Buckingham MK18 . . . . **52** C7
  Milton Keynes MK14 . . . . . . **21** E2
Station Way E HP20 . . . . . **115** D7
Station Way W HP20 . . . . . **115** D7
Staunton Ho MK17 . . . . **60** F7
Staunton Rd SL2 . . . . **205** D8
Staveley Cl HP21 . . . . **116** C6
Staverton Gr MK10 . . . . **36** B2
Stavordale ② MK10 . . . . . . **36** A1
Stayning La MK14 . . . . **34** F6
Steeple Cl MK4 . . . . **57** A8
STEEPLE CLAYDON **63** C3
Steeple Claydon Sch
  MK18 . . . . **63** E3
Steinbeck Cres MK4 . . . . . . **56** F7
Stephenson Cl
  Aylesbury HP19 . . . . **115** B7
  High Wycombe HP13 . . . . . **161** F1
  Leighton Buzzard LU7 . . . . . **80** E6
Stephenson Ct ⑫ SL1 . . . . **205** F4
Stephenson Dr SL4 . . . . . . **210** B7
Stepnells HP23 . . . . **105** A1
Steppingstones LU6 . . . . . . **93** F8
Sterling Bus Pk MK18 . . . . **52** D6
Sterling Cl MK15 . . . . **35** A6
Stevens Cl
  Holmer Green HP15 . . . . . . **163** D3
  Prestwood HP16 . . . . **151** D5
Stevens Field MK7 . . . . **48** D6
Stevens Ho ⑧ HP7 . . . . . . **165** B7
Stevenson Rd SL2 . . . . **187** D2
Stevens Wy HP7 . . . . **165** B7
Stewart Ave SL1 . . . . **205** F8
Stewarts Dr SL2 . . . . **198** B7
Stewarts Way SL7 . . . . **183** D7
STEWKLEY **68** E2
STEWKLEY DEAN **68** B1
Stewkley Rd
  Cublington LU7 . . . . **78** C1
  Hollingdon LU7 . . . . **69** C2
  Wing LU7 . . . . **79** B3
Stilebrook Rd MK46 . . . . **6** F6
Stile Mdw HP9 . . . . **175** E3
Stile Rd SL3 . . . . **206** D3
Stilliters Farm Rd MK43 . . . **37** E8
Stilton Cl ④ HP19 . . . . **101** C1
Stilwell Dr UB8 . . . . **201** F1
Stirling Ave HP20 . . . . **101** E1
Stirling Cl
  Uxbridge UB8 . . . . **201** C2
  Windsor SL4 . . . . **209** D5
Stirling Gr SL6 . . . . **202** A8
Stirling Ho
  ② High Wycombe HP13 . . **173** F7
  Milton Keynes MK3 . . . . **57** D7
Stirling Mews ② MK10 . . . . **36** C3
Stirling Rd
  High Wycombe HP12 . . . . . **172** D5
  Slough SL1 . . . . **205** A8
  Stanwell TW6 . . . . **213** F1
Stockaway HP22 . . . . **87** C1
Stockdale MK13 . . . . **34** C5
Stockdales Rd SL4 . . . . . . **204** F2
Stocken Cl MK46 . . . . **6** E4
Stock Field HP15 . . . . **163** B3
Stockfields Pl HP14 . . . . . **158** D5
Stockgrove Ctry Pk★ LU7 . . . **70** F7
Stockgrove Park Ho LU7 . . **70** F8
Stockhall Cres LU7 . . . . **68** D2
Stocking Green Cl MK19 . . . **11** A3
Stocking La HP14 . . . . **161** E7
Stock La MK17 . . . . **45** D1
Stocklake
  Aylesbury HP20 . . . . **101** F1
  Aylesbury HP22 . . . . **102** B1
Stocklake Ind Est HP20 . . **101** F1
Stocklake Park Sch
  HP20 . . . . **101** F1
Stocklands Way HP16 . . . . **151** D5
Stockley Academy UB8 . . **208** F7
Stuckleys La MK18 . . . . **51** B6
Stockport Rd WD3 . . . . **167** C2
Stocks Cl MK18 . . . . **65** F4
Stocks Rd HP23 . . . . **120** C7
Stocks The MK19 . . . . **19** E2
Stockwell HP17 . . . . **127** A6
Stockwell Furlong HP17 . . **127** A6
Stockwell La
  Longwick HP17 . . . . **139** A8
  Wavendon MK17 . . . . **48** D7
Stockwells SL6 . . . . **196** B1
STOKE BRUERNE **9** B8
Stoke Bruerne CE Prim Sch
  NN12 . . . . **9** A8
Stoke Common Rd SL2,
  SL3 . . . . **199** B8
Stoke Court Dr SL2 . . . . . . **198** F4
Stoke Farm La HP21 . . . . . **115** E3

Stoke Gdns SL1 . . . . **205** F5
Stoke Gn SL2 . . . . **199** A1
STOKE GOLDINGTON **12** A6
Stoke Goldington CE Fst Sch
  MK16 . . . . **12** B6
STOKE GREEN **199** B1
STOKE HAMMOND **69** E8
Stoke Ho ② SL1 . . . . **205** F3
Stoke La MK17 . . . . **59** C1
Stoke Leys Cl HP21 . . . . . . **115** E3
STOKE MANDEVILLE **116** A2
Stoke Mandeville Comb Sch
  HP22 . . . . **116** A1
Stoke Mandeville Hospl
  HP21 . . . . **115** F4
Stoke Mandeville Sta
  HP22 . . . . **116** B2
STOKENCHURCH **158** E5
Stokenchurch Pl MK13 . . . . **34** C3
Stokenchurch Prim Sch
  HP14 . . . . **158** E5
Stoke Park Ave SL2 . . . . . **198** C2
Stoke Pk Pavilions★ NN12 . . . **9** A6
STOKE POGES **198** F4
Stoke Poges La SL1 . . . . . **205** E7
Stoke Poges Sch The
  SL2 . . . . **198** F5
Stoke Rd
  Ashton NN7 . . . . **9** E8
  Aylesbury HP21 . . . . **115** E6
  Leighton Buzzard LU7 . . . . . **70** D1
  Milton Keynes MK2 . . . . **58** E5
  Newton Longville MK17 . . . . **57** F3
  Slough SL2 . . . . **205** F7
Stokesay SL2 . . . . **205** F6
Stokesay Ct MK4 . . . . **45** E2
Stokes Croft HP17 . . . . . . **127** A6
Stokes End HP17 . . . . **127** A7
Stokes La HP17 . . . . **127** A7
Stokesley Rise HP10 . . . . . **185** E8
Stoke View SL1 . . . . **205** F5
Stoke Wood SL2 . . . . **198** F8
Stolford Rise MK4 . . . . **46** B1
Stompits Rd SL6 . . . . **203** C1
Stomp Rd SL1 . . . . **204** B8
STONE **114** C5
STONEBRIDGE **33** F7
Stonebridge Field SL4 . . . . **205** B1
Stonebridge Gr MK10 . . . . . **35** C1
Stonebridge Rd HP19 . . . . **101** B3
Stonebridge Rdbt MK13 . . . **33** E8
Stone CE Comb Sch
  HP17 . . . . **114** D5
Stonechat HP19 . . . . **101** E3
Stone Cl UB7 . . . . **208** F5
Stonecroft HP6 . . . . **153** C4
Stone Croft HP17 . . . . **114** D5
Stonecroft Ave SL0 . . . . . . **207** E7
Stonecrop PL MK14 . . . . **34** E4
Stone Ct MK46 . . . . **13** E8
Stonefield Pk SL6 . . . . **202** C7
Stonefield Rd HP14 . . . . . . **161** C8
Stonegate MK13 . . . . **34** A5
Stonehaven Rd HP19 . . . . . **101** B2
Stone Hill MK8 . . . . **33** D1
Stone House La SL6 . . . . . **184** C1
Stoneleigh Ct MK4 . . . . **45** E1
Stonemasons Cl ⑪ MK46 . . . **6** F3
Stone Pit Cl MK46 . . . . **6** E3
Stonepitts Rd HP18 . . . . . . **111** B3
Stones Row HP11 . . . . **173** F4
Stones Way MK17 . . . . **68** C6
Stone View HP22 . . . . **86** D7
Stoney Cl HP4 . . . . **134** F6
Stoneycroft HP23 . . . . **120** C5
Stoneyfield SL9 . . . . **188** C3
Stoney Furlong HP18 . . . . **112** B2
Stoney Gr HP5 . . . . **144** C1
Stoney Grove HP5 . . . . **144** C1
Stoney La
  Berkhamsted HP1 . . . . **146** B8
  Bovingdon HP3 . . . . **146** C5
  Chipperfield WD4 . . . . **146** F1
  Cholesbury HP5 . . . . **133** F1
  East Burnham SL2 . . . . **198** A4
Stoney Meade SL1 . . . . . . **205** B5
Stoney Ware SL7 . . . . **194** E8
STONOR **179** F6
Stonor Ho & Gdns★ RG9 **180** A7
Stony Dean Sch HP7 . . . . . **165** F8
STONY GREEN **151** A4
Stony Hill NN12 . . . . **17** C8
Stony La
  Little Chalfont HP6 . . . . . . **155** F1
  Little Kingshill HP16 . . . . . **152** C3
Stookslade HP22 . . . . **89** A3
Stopps Orch HP27 . . . . **139** C5
Stork Cl ② HP19 . . . . **101** F3
Stornaway Rd SL3 . . . . **207** C2
Stotfold Ct MK11 . . . . **32** E4
Stour Cl
  Aylesbury HP21 . . . . **115** C4
  Milton Keynes MK3 . . . . **57** D8
  Newport Pagnell MK16 . . . . **22** E3
  Slough SL1 . . . . **205** B3
Stourhead Gate MK4 . . . . . . **45** E2
Stovell Rd SL4 . . . . **210** B7
Stowe Ave MK18 . . . . **41** B3
Stowe Castle Bsns Pk
  MK18 . . . . **41** B7
Stowe Cl MK18 . . . . **41** C1
Stowe Cl MK14 . . . . **34** C8
Stowe Landscape Gdns★
  MK18 . . . . **40** F7
STOWE PARK **40** F7
Stowe Rd SL1 . . . . **204** E6
Stowe Rise MK18 . . . . **41** C1

Stowe Sch MK18 . . . . **40** F7
Stowe View MK18 . . . . **51** A7
Straight Bit HP10 . . . . **185** B8
Straight Mile Rd OX33 . . . **108** A5
Straight Rd SL4 . . . . **211** B1
Strande Pk SL6 . . . . **195** F5
Strande View Wlk SL6 . . . **195** F5
Strand La SL6 . . . . **195** F5
Strand The HP22 . . . . **85** B5
Strangers La MK18 . . . . **51** A6
Strangford Dr MK2 . . . . **58** C4
Stranraer Gdns SL1 . . . . . **205** E5
Stranraer Rd TW19 . . . . . . **213** E1
Stranraer Way ① TW6 . . . . **213** E1
Stratfield Rd
  Maidenhead SL6 . . . . **203** B8
  Milton Keynes MK8 . . . . **33** F1
Stratfield Rd SL1 . . . . **206** A4
Stratford Arc MK11 . . . . **32** D6
Stratford Ave UB10 . . . . . . **201** F3
Stratford Cl
  Aylesbury HP22 . . . . **117** C5
  Slough SL2 . . . . **197** D1
Stratford Dr
  Aylesbury HP21 . . . . **115** B6
  Wooburn HP10 . . . . **185** D4
Stratford Gdns SL6 . . . . . . **202** C4
Stratford Rd
  Buckingham MK18 . . . . **41** E1
  Cosgrove MK19 . . . . **19** D1
  Deanshanger MK19 . . . . **31** F4
  Maids Moreton MK18 . . . . . **42** C2
  Milton Keynes MK12 . . . . . . **33** C7
  Nash MK17 . . . . **44** C1
  Old Stratford MK19 . . . . **32** B5
  Whaddon MK17 . . . . **45** A2
Stratfords Way MK17 . . . . **127** A6
Strathcona Cl HP10 . . . . . . **185** C7
Strathcona Way HP10 . . . . **185** C7
Strathnaver Pl MK12 . . . . . . **33** D4
Strathspey Gate MK10 . . . . **36** C3
Stratton Chase Dr
  Chalfont St Giles HP8 . . . . **177** B8
  Chalfont St Peter HP8 . . . . **177** A8
Stratton La HP21 . . . . **116** B6
Stratton Rd
  Beaconsfield HP9 . . . . **175** B2
  Princes Risborough HP27 . **139** A3
Stratus Pk MK10 . . . . **48** C7
Strauss Gr MK7 . . . . **48** C4
Strawberry Cl HP16 . . . . . . **151** D5
Strawberry Fields MK17 . . . **70** B6
Straws Hadley Ct HP22 . . . . **89** B2
Streamside SL1 . . . . **204** F5
Streamside Wlk HP21 . . . . **115** C6
Streatham Pl MK13 . . . . **34** C2
Stretton Cl HP10 . . . . **174** C8
Stretton Pl HP6 . . . . **154** F1
Stringers Cotts ① SL9 . . . **177** D2
Stringfellow Cl MK43 . . . . . . **24** E2
Stroma Ct SL1 . . . . **204** D6
Stroud Cl SL4 . . . . **209** D4
Strudwick Dr MK6 . . . . **46** F8
Stuart Cl
  Milton Keynes MK2 . . . . **47** D1
  Windsor SL4 . . . . **209** F5
Stuart Ct HP6 . . . . **154** F1
Stuart Rd HP13 . . . . **173** C6
Stuart Way
  Thame OX9 . . . . **126** A1
  Windsor SL4 . . . . **209** F5
Stubble Hill HP19 . . . . **115** A8
Stubbles La SL6 . . . . **195** B6
Stubbs End Cl HP6 . . . . . . **154** E2
Stubbs Field MK5 . . . . **46** A3
Stubbs Wood HP6 . . . . **154** E3
Stuchbury Cl HP19 . . . . . . **115** A8
Studdridge Ct HP14 . . . . . **158** C4
Studham La HP4 . . . . **107** D4
Studland Ct HP21 . . . . **116** B5
STUDLEY GREEN **159** E3
Studley Knapp
  Milton Keynes MK7 . . . . **48** B5
  Walnut Tree MK7 . . . . **48** B7
Studridge La HP27 . . . . . . **150** B4
Sturdy La MK17 . . . . **49** A5
Sturges Cl MK7 . . . . **48** A5
Sturman Ho MK6 . . . . **154** C2
Stylecroft Rd HP8 . . . . **177** D8
Styles Cl OX27 . . . . **71** E2
Styles Ct HP18 . . . . **99** A7
Sudbury Chase MK10 . . . . . **35** C1
Sudgrove Ho MK15 . . . . **35** A6
Suffield Rd HP11 . . . . **172** F6
Suffolk Cl
  Maidenhead SL6 . . . . **202** F8
  Marsh Gibbon OX27 . . . . . . **71** F3
Suffolk Ho HP10 . . . . **185** E6
Suffolk Rd SL6 . . . . **202** D4
Sulby Cl HP21 . . . . **115** C5
Sulgrave Cres HP23 . . . . . **119** C5
Sulgrave Ct ③ MK8 . . . . **45** F8
Sullivan Cres MK7 . . . . **48** C5
Sumatra Cres MK3 . . . . **58** B3
Sumburgh Way SL1 . . . . . . **205** B8
Summer Dr LU7 . . . . **80** D7
Summerfield Sch MK13 . . . . **34** C3
Summergill Ct MK13 . . . . . . **34** C5
Summerhayes MK14 . . . . . . **34** F7
Summerhouse La UB7 . . . . **213** D6
Summerleaze Rd SL6 . . . . **196** B1
Summerlea SL1 . . . . **205** B5
Summerleys LU6 . . . . **92** E4
Summerleys Rd HP27 . . . . **138** F4

Summerlin Dr MK17 . . . . . . **49** B5
Summersby Ct SL1 . . . . . . **206** C1
Summerson Ct MK6 . . . . . . **46** F5
Summerson Rd
  Bleak Hall MK6 . . . . **47** A5
  Milton Keynes MK6 . . . . **46** F5
Summers Rd SL1 . . . . **197** C2
SUMMERSTOWN **72** B2
Summit Ctr UB7 . . . . **213** D7
Sumner Ct MK5 . . . . **46** A8
Sunbury Cl MK13 . . . . **34** A6
Sunbury Ct SL4 . . . . **210** D8
Sunbury Rd SL4 . . . . **210** D8
Sun Cl SL4 . . . . **210** D8
Sun Cres HP18 . . . . **109** D5
Sunderland Ct
  Milton Keynes MK4 . . . . **45** F1
  ⑪ Stanwell TW19 . . . . . . **213** E1
Sunderland Rd SL6 . . . . . . **202** B8
Sun La SL6 . . . . **202** F7
Sunningdale Cl HP12 . . . . . **172** B5
Sunningdale Way MK3 . . . . . **57** D8
Sunnybank SL7 . . . . **183** D4
Sunny Bank
  Cheddington LU7 . . . . **104** F7
  Hazlemere HP15 . . . . **162** F6
Sunny Brook Cl HP22 . . . . **117** D6
Sunny Croft HP13 . . . . **161** C2
Sunnyhill Rd WD3 . . . . **178** D4
SUNNYMEADS **211** E4
Sunnymeads Sta TW19 . . . **211** E4
Sunnymede Ave HP5 . . . . . **144** E3
Sunnymede Cotts SL6 . . . . **196** B1
Sunnyside Cotts HP5 . . . . **145** A5
Sunnyside Rd HP5 . . . . . . **144** C1
Sunny View NN7 . . . . **1** B6
Sun Pas ⑯ SL4 . . . . **210** D6
Sunray Ave UB7 . . . . **208** D4
Sunridge Cl MK16 . . . . **22** C3
Sunrise Parkway MK14 . . . . **34** E6
Sunset Cl MK2 . . . . **58** C7
Sunset Wlk MK9 . . . . **34** E2
Sunters End HP12 . . . . **172** A7
Sunters Wood Cl HP12 . . . **172** B5
Surly Hall Wlk SL4 . . . . . . **209** F6
Surrey Ave SL2 . . . . **198** C1
Surrey Pl
  Milton Keynes MK3 . . . . **46** F2
  Tring HP23 . . . . **119** A3
Surrey Rd MK3 . . . . **46** F2
Sussex Cl
  Aylesbury HP19 . . . . **101** A3
  Chalfont St Giles HP8 . . . . **177** B8
  High Wycombe HP13 . . . . . **162** D1
  Slough SL1 . . . . **206** B4
Sussex Ho SL2 . . . . **198** C6
Sussex Keep ⑦ SL1 . . . . . **206** B4
Sussex Lodge ⑦ SL6 . . . . **202** F6
Sussex Pl SL1 . . . . **206** B4
Sussex Rd MK3 . . . . **46** F1
Sutcliffe Ave MK6 . . . . **34** E1
Sutherland Gr MK3 . . . . **46** F3
Sutherland Grange SL4 . . **209** F7
Sutherland Grange Nature
  Reserve★ SL4 . . . . **209** D7
Sutherland Wlk HP21 . . . . **115** F5
Sutleye Ct MK5 . . . . **46** A5
SUTTON **207** C1
Sutton Ave SL3 . . . . **206** C4
Sutton Cl
  Cookham SL6 . . . . **196** B7
  Maidenhead SL6 . . . . **202** C5
  Tring HP23 . . . . **119** B6
Sutton Ct MK4 . . . . **46** C1
Sutton La SL3 . . . . **207** B1
Sutton Pl SL3 . . . . **212** B8
Sutton Rd SL6 . . . . **196** B6
Swabey Rd SL3 . . . . **207** A2
Swains Cl UB7 . . . . **208** E4
Swains La HP10 . . . . **174** A1
Swains Mkt HP10 . . . . **174** A1
Swakeleys Dr UB10 . . . . . . **201** F8
Swakeleys Rd UB10 . . . . . . **201** E8
Swaledale End MK14 . . . . . . **21** C1
Swale Rd HP21 . . . . **115** C5
Swallow Cl MK18 . . . . **52** E7
Swallowdale SL0 . . . . **200** D2
Swallow Dr HP15 . . . . **163** B5
Swallowfield MK8 . . . . **33** E1
Swallowfield Lower Sch
  MK17 . . . . **49** B5
Swallow Fields SL0 . . . . . . **200** D1
Swallow Ho SL7 . . . . **184** A2
Swallow La
  Aylesbury HP19 . . . . **114** F8
  Stoke Mandeville HP22 . . . **116** A1
Swallow St
  Iver Heath SL0 . . . . **200** D1
  Iver SL0 . . . . **207** D8
Swallowtail Wlk HP4 . . . . . **134** F7
SWANBOURNE **67** B3
Swanbourne CE Sch
  MK17 . . . . **67** A3
Swanbourne House Sch
  MK17 . . . . **66** F3
Swanbourne Rd MK17 . . . . . **67** D4
Swanbrook Cl SL6 . . . . **203** A2
Swan Bsns Pk MK18 . . . . . . **52** C6
Swan Cl
  Aylesbury HP19 . . . . **101** F3
  Blackthorn OX25 . . . . **81** A3
  Buckingham MK18 . . . . **52** E7
  Chesham HP5 . . . . **144** B4
  Ivinghoe Aston LU7 . . . . . . **92** A1
  Whitchurch HP22 . . . . **87** B5

Swan Cotts HP17. . . . . . . .129 D1
Swan Ct
  Buckingham MK18. . . . . . . .65 F5
  Chorleywood WD3. . . . . . .167 C5
  Datchet SL3. . . . . .211 B6
  Leighton Buzzard LU7. . . . .80 E6
  Olney MK46. . . . . .7 A4
  West Drayton UB7. . . . . . .208 D4
Swan Hill HP18. . . . . .112 F3
Swan Hill Cotts HP18. . . .112 F3
Swan Hunter Cl 8 MK10 . 36 C4
Swan La
  Lee Gate HP16. . . . . .142 C8
  Marsh Gibbon OX6 . . . . . . .72 A3
Swan Mews HP22 . . . . . . .131 B5
Swannells Wk WD3 . . . . .167 F2
Swann Rd HP22. . . . . .131 D8
Swan Pool & L Ctr MK18 . 52 D7
Swan Rd
  Iver SL0. . . . . .207 F7
  West Drayton UB7. . . . . . .208 D4
Swanson Dr MK4. . . . . .45 D3
Swansons LU6. . . . . .92 F3
Swan Terr
  Milton Keynes MK11 . . . . . .32 D5
  Windsor SL4. . . . . .210 A7
Swan Wharf Bsns Ctr
  UB8. . . . . .201 C3
Swanwick La MK10. . . . . . .36 B3
Swayne Rise MK10 . . . . . . .36 A2
Sweetcroft La UB10 . . . . .201 F6
Sweetlands Cnr MK7. . . . . .48 B8
Swift Cl
  Aylesbury HP19. . . . . .101 F3
  Newport Pagnell MK16 . . . .22 A5
Swift Ho SL7. . . . . .184 B2
SWILLET THE 167 B3
Swimbridge La MK4. . . . . . .46 D4
Swinden Ct MK13 . . . . .34 B4
Swing Gate Fst Sch HP4 135 D3
Swing Gate La HP4. . . . . .135 D2
Swinnerton Ho RG9 . . . . . .191 E3
Switchback Cl SL6 . . . . . . .195 D2
Switchback Office Pk
  SL6. . . . . .195 D2
Switchback Road N SL6 .195 D3
Switchback Road S SL6 .195 D2
Switchback The SL6 . . . . .195 D2
Swithland 8 MK10. . . . . . .36 C3
Sycamore Ave MK2 . . . . . . .58 C8
Sycamore Cl
  Amersham HP6 . . . . .154 D2
  3 Bourne End SL8 . . . . . .185 B3
  Buckingham MK18. . . . . . . .52 F7
  Chalfont St Giles HP8 . . . .177 A7
  Long Crendon HP18. . . . . .125 C6
  Maidenhead SL6 . . . . .202 C4
  Stewkley LU7. . . . . .68 D2
  West Drayton UB7. . . . . . .208 F6
Sycamore Cnr HP6. . . . . . .154 D2
Sycamore Ct
  Aylesbury HP19. . . . . .101 D1
  High Wycombe HP12. . . . .172 C4
  Windsor SL4. . . . . .210 C4
Sycamore Dene HP5 . . . . .144 D3
Sycamore Dr
  Marlow Bottom SL7. . . . . .183 D5
  Tring HP23. . . . . .119 D4
Sycamore Ho
  Amersham HP6 . . . . .154 D2
  Princes Risborough HP27 . 139 B3
Sycamore Leys MK18. . . . . .63 E3
Sycamore Pl HP6 . . . . . . .154 C1
Sycamore Rd
  Amersham HP6 . . . . .154 D2
  Chalfont St Giles HP8 . . . .177 A7
  High Wycombe HP12 . . . . .172 C4
Sycamore Rise
  Berkhamsted HP4 . . . . . . .135 D3
  Chalfont St Giles HP8 . . . .177 A7
Sycamores The HP4. . . . . .146 F8
Sycamore Way HP15 . . . . .163 A3
Sycamore Wlk SL3. . . . . . .206 E7
Sydney Gr SL1. . . . . .205 C2
Sygnus Ct 8 SL6. . . . . . . .202 F7
Syke Cl SL0 . . . . .207 E4
Syke Ings SL0. . . . . .207 E4
Sykes Croft MK4 . . . . .46 C1
Sykes Rd SL1. . . . . .205 B8
Sylvana Cl UB10 . . . . .201 F4
Sylvania Gdns 1 MK16. . . .36 C4
Sylvester Rd SL6. . . . . . . .195 E2
Sylvia Cl HP16. . . . . .152 B4
Symington Ct MK5 . . . . . . .46 B5
Syon Gdns MK16 . . . . .22 C2
SYRESHAM 27 B8
Syresham St James CE Prim
  Sch NN13 . . . . .27 C8

T

Tabard Gdns MK16 . . . . . . .22 C2
Tachbrook Rd UB8. . . . . . .201 C3
Tacknell Dr MK5. . . . . .46 A4
Tacks La HP17. . . . . .126 F6
Tadmarton MK15. . . . . .35 A6
Tadmere MK8. . . . . .33 D1
Tadros Ct HP13 . . . . .173 D6
Tahiti Row MK17. . . . . .58 A3
Talbot Ave
  High Wycombe HP13. . . . .161 D2
  Slough SL3. . . . . .206 F4
Talbot Ct
  Milton Keynes MK15 . . . . . .35 C1

Talbot Ct continued
  Windsor SL4 . . . . .210 B4
Talbot Pl SL3. . . . . .211 C6
Talbot Rd HP22. . . . . .117 E5
Talbots Dr SL6. . . . . .202 B6
Talbots Hyde MK46. . . . . .6 E4
Talland Ave MK6. . . . . .34 F1
Tallis La MK7. . . . . .48 C5
Tall Oaks HP6. . . . . .154 D2
Tall Pines LU7. . . . . .70 F2
Tall Trees SL3. . . . . .212 E6
Tamar Cl
  Aylesbury HP21. . . . . .115 C4
  Loudwater HP13 . . . . .174 B4
Tamar Ho
  High Wycombe HP13 . . . . .173 F7
  Milton Keynes MK3 . . . . . . .46 C1
Tamarisk Ct MK7. . . . . .48 B5
Tamarisk Way
  Aylesbury HP22. . . . . .116 C4
  Slough SL1. . . . . .205 B5
Tamar Way SL3. . . . . .207 B2
Tamworth Stubb MK7. . . . . .48 A5
Tancred Rd HP13. . . . . . . .162 A1
Tandra MK6. . . . . .47 B5
Tandy Rise MK8. . . . . .45 D6
Tandys Cl MK43. . . . . .8 E5
Tanfield La MK10 . . . . .36 A3
Tangier Ct SL4. . . . . .210 D8
Tangier La SL4. . . . . .210 D8
Tankard Cl MK16. . . . . .22 C4
Tank House Rd MK18. . . . . .66 B6
Tanners Dr MK14 . . . . .22 A2
Tannery Rd HP13 . . . . .174 A4
Tannery Road Ind Est
  HP13. . . . . .174 A4
Tannery The MK18. . . . . . . .65 F4
Tansley La MK17. . . . . .49 B5
Tansman La MK7. . . . . .48 D5
Tanton Ho HP16 . . . . .151 F8
Tapestries Hall SL4. . . . . .211 A2
Tapestries The SL4. . . . . .211 A2
Taplin Way HP10. . . . . .163 C1
TAPLOW 196 E1
Taplow Common Rd SL1 197 A3
Taplow Rd SL6. . . . . .204 A7
Taplow Sta SL6. . . . . .203 F7
Tapping Rd HP14 . . . . .171 C5
Taranis Cl MK7. . . . . .48 C7
Tarbay La SL4. . . . . .209 B5
Tarbert Cl MK2. . . . . .58 C5
Tarmac Way UB7 . . . . .213 B7
Tarnbrook Cl 6 MK4. . . . . .46 B2
Tarragon Cl
  Milton Keynes MK7 . . . . . . .48 B6
  Walton MK7. . . . . .48 A6
Tarry Ct MK13. . . . . .34 B6
Taskers Row LU6. . . . . .92 F4
Taskers Row Cotts LU6. . . .92 F4
Task The MK46. . . . . .7 A4
Tasmania Gr MK3. . . . . .58 C4
Tatchbrook Cl SL6. . . . . . .203 A8
Tate Rd SL9. . . . . .177 F5
TATHALL END 11 E2
TATLING END 189 B3
Tatling Gr MK7. . . . . .48 A6
Tattam Cl MK15. . . . . .35 C2
Tattams La MK17. . . . . .67 B3
TATTENHOE 57 A8
Tattenhoe La MK3. . . . . .57 D8
Tattenhoe Pavilion MK5. . .57 A8
Tattenhoe St MK5. . . . . .45 E4
Tattershall Cl MK5. . . . . . . .46 A6
Tattlers Hill HP22. . . . . .89 B3
Taunton Deane MK4 . . . . . .46 D2
Taurus Cl MK18. . . . . .63 D2
Tavelhurst MK8. . . . . .33 E1
Taverner Ct MK7. . . . . .48 D5
Tavistock Cl
  Maidenhead SL6 . . . . .202 A8
  Woburn Sands MK17. . . . . .49 B6
Tavistock Mews HP12 . . . .172 E2
Tavistock Rd UB7 . . . . .208 D5
Tavistock St MK2. . . . . .47 D1
Tavistock Wlk HP20 . . . . . .101 E2
Taylor Cl MK18. . . . . .63 C2
Taylor Rd HP21. . . . . .115 D5
Taylors Cl SL7. . . . . .183 E2
Taylors Cnr HP18 . . . . .99 A7
Taylors Ct SL6. . . . . .202 B8
Taylors La
  Little Missenden HP7 . . . .153 A3
  Stewkley LU7. . . . . .78 E7
  St Leonards HP23 . . . . . . .132 C3
Taylors Mews MK14. . . . . . .34 F6
Taylors Rd HP5. . . . . .144 D2
Taylor's Ride LU7. . . . . .70 F2
Taylors Turn HP13 . . . . . . .161 D3
Taymouth Pl MK9. . . . . .35 B3
Tay Rd MK3. . . . . .46 E1
Teale Cl OX25. . . . . .94 E7
Teal Ho HP11. . . . . .173 C6
Teasel Ave MK14. . . . . .34 E5
Tedder Cl UB10 . . . . .201 F5
Tedder Rd HP22. . . . . .131 D5
Teesdale Rd SL2. . . . . .204 F8
Tees Rd HP21. . . . . .115 C5
Teeswater 3 MK18 . . . . . . .41 D2
Teeswater Wy MK8. . . . . . . .33 D1
Tees Way MK3. . . . . .46 D1
Teign Cl MK16. . . . . .22 D4
Teikyo Sch UK SL2. . . . . . .199 D5
Telford Dr SL1. . . . . .205 A4
Telford Way
  High Wycombe HP13. . . . .162 A1
  Milton Keynes MK14 . . . . . .22 B1
Telston Cl SL8. . . . . .185 A5

Temperance Terr MK11 . . .32 C6
Templars Pl 2 SL7 . . . . . .183 E1
TEMPLE 194 C5
Temple MK14 . . . . .34 C7
Temple Cl
  Buckingham MK18. . . . . . . .41 D2
  Milton Keynes MK3 . . . . . . .57 D7
Temple Cres MK4. . . . . .45 D3
Templecroft Terr HP17. . . .114 A2
Temple End HP13 . . . . .173 A8
Temple Gate HP13 . . . . . . .173 A7
Temple Ho RG9 . . . . .191 E3
Temple La SL7. . . . . .194 D6
Templemead SL7 . . . . .188 C3
Temple Mill Cotts SL7. . . .194 C5
Temple Mill Island SL7. . .194 C5
Temple Orch HP13 . . . . . . .173 B7
Temple Pk SL6. . . . . .193 C5
Temple Rd SL4 . . . . .210 D5
Templeside Gdns HP12. . . .172 E8
Temple Sq 17 HP20 . . . . . .115 D8
Temple St
  Aylesbury HP20. . . . . .115 D8
  Brill HP18 . . . . .96 B1
Temple Way SL2. . . . . .198 C4
Templewood HP14. . . . . . . .150 B1
Templewood Gate SL2. . . .198 C7
Templewood La SL2 . . . . . .198 E8
Tenby Gr MK4. . . . . .45 D1
Tene Acres MK5. . . . . .45 F6
Tennant Cl MK8. . . . . .45 D6
Tennis La MK18. . . . . .66 A3
Tennyson Dr MK16 . . . . .22 A4
Tennyson Gr 1 MK3 . . . . . .57 F7
Tennyson Rd
  Aylesbury HP21. . . . . .115 F6
  High Wycombe HP11 . . . . .173 A5
Tennyson Way SL2. . . . . . .197 E1
Tenor Cl MK18. . . . . .52 C8
Tenterden Cres MK7 . . . . . .48 B7
Tenzing Dr HP13 . . . . .173 C6
Terrace The
  Aspley Guise MK17. . . . . . .49 E5
  Bray SL6 . . . . .203 C3
  7 Tring HP23 . . . . .119 A3
Terrent Ct SL4. . . . . .210 A5
TERRICK 130 C5
Terrick Row HP17. . . . . . . .130 B5
TERRIERS 162 D2
Terrington Hill SL7. . . . . . .183 B2
Terry Dr HP19. . . . . .101 C3
Terryfield Rd HP13. . . . . . .173 E6
Terry Orch HP13 . . . . .173 C6
Terry Pl UB8. . . . . .208 C8
Terry Rd HP13 . . . . .173 C6
Terry's La SL6. . . . . .195 F8
Testwood Rd SL4 . . . . .209 D6
TETCHWICK 82 F2
Tetherdown HP16. . . . . . . .151 C5
Tewkesbury La 1 MK10 . . .35 F1
TEW'S END 17 C8
Tews End La NN12 . . . . .17 B8
Texel Cl MK13. . . . . .34 B8
Thackeray End HP19 . . . . .100 F2
THAME 125 E2
Thame Ho 5 HP13. . . . . . .173 B7
Thame Rd
  Aylesbury HP17. . . . . .127 C2
  Aylesbury HP21. . . . . .115 D7
  Blackthorn OX25 . . . . .81 A3
  Brill HP18 . . . . .110 B7
  Chilton HP18 . . . . .111 B3
  Chinnor OX39. . . . . .147 B8
  Haddenham HP17 . . . . . . .126 D5
  Long Crendon HP18, OX9 .125 D4
  Longwick HP27 . . . . .138 E6
  Piddington OX25 . . . . .95 D6
  Thame OX9 . . . . .136 C7
Thame Road S HP21. . . . . .115 B6
Thames Ave SL4. . . . . .210 D7
Thames Bank SL6. . . . . . . .203 C7
Thamesbourne Mews 3
  SL8. . . . . .185 A3
Thames Cl
  Bourne End SL8 . . . . .185 A4
  Milton Keynes MK3 . . . . . . .57 E8
Thames Cres SL6 . . . . .196 B2
Thames Dr MK16. . . . . .22 E3
Thamesfield Gdns SL7 . . .183 E1
Thames Ho
  Datchet SL3. . . . . .211 B6
  Henley-on-Thames RG9 . . .191 E3
Thames Ind Est SL7. . . . . .183 F2
Thames Mead SL4 . . . . . . .209 E6
Thames Rd SL3 . . . . .207 B3
Thames Reach SL7. . . . . . .193 D6
Thames Side
  Henley-on-Thames RG9. . .191 E2
  Windsor SL4 . . . . .210 D7
Thames St SL4. . . . . .210 D7
Thames Valley Athletics Ctr
  SL4 . . . . .205 E1
Thane Ct MK14 . . . . .34 C7
Thanestead Copse HP10.174 C2
Thanestead Ct HP10. . . . . .174 C2
Thatcher Ct UB7. . . . . .208 E4
Thatchers Dr SL6. . . . . . . .202 A5
Theatre Wlk MK9 . . . . .34 F3
thecentre 3 Milton
  Keynes. MK9 34 F3
Thellusson Way WD3. . . . .167 F2
Theseus Terr 4 MK17 . . . . .36 B5
Theydon Ave MK17. . . . . . . .49 B4
Thicket The
  Tylers Green HP10. . . . . . .163 A1
  West Drayton UB7. . . . . . .208 E7
Thimble Cl MK18. . . . . .52 F6

Third Ave
  Marlow SL7. . . . . .183 F2
  Milton Keynes MK1 . . . . . . .47 B2
Third Cres SL1. . . . . .205 C8
Third St HP11. . . . . .173 B4
Thirkleby Cl SL1. . . . . .205 C5
Thirlby La MK5. . . . . .46 A6
Thirlmere Ave
  Milton Keynes MK2 . . . . . . .58 D6
  Slough SL1. . . . . .204 C8
Thirsk Gdns MK3. . . . . .57 C6
Thistle Cl HP21. . . . . .115 C5
Thomas Bourne Ho 1
  HP4 . . . . .135 D4
Thomas Coram CE Sch The
  HP4. . . . . .135 D2
Thomas Ct
  Berkhamsted HP4 . . . . . . .134 E6
  Maidenhead SL6 . . . . .202 A2
Thomas Dr
  Newport Pagnell MK16 . . . .22 A6
  Uxbridge UB10. . . . . .201 E6
Thomas Gdns HP23 . . . . . .119 B4
Thomas Harding Jun Sch
  HP5. . . . . .154 B7
Thomas Hickman Sch
  HP19. . . . . .101 A3
Thomas Rd HP10. . . . . .185 D4
Thomas Valentine Ho
  HP8 . . . . .177 B7
Thompkins La SL2 . . . . . . .198 A5
Thompson Cl SL3. . . . . . . .207 A2
Thompson Rd UB10 . . . . . .201 E5
Thompson St MK13 . . . . . . .34 A7
Thomson Cl HP21. . . . . . . .115 B6
Thomson Wlk HP21. . . . . . .115 B6
Thornaby Pl HP10. . . . . . . .185 E8
Thornbank CT TW19 . . . . . .213 A2
THORNBOROUGH 54 A8
Thornborough Inf Sch
  MK18 . . . . .54 A8
Thornborough Rd MK17. . . .55 B8
Thornbridge Rd SL0. . . . . .200 C5
Thornbury MK6. . . . . .47 B4
Thorncliffe MK8. . . . . .33 D1
Thorndike SL2. . . . . .205 B8
Thorn Dr SL3. . . . . .206 E7
Thorne Rd HP14 . . . . .171 C4
Thorne Way
  Aston Clinton HP22 . . . . . .118 A4
  Aylesbury HP20. . . . . .101 F2
THORNEY 208 B3
Thorneycroft La MK15. . . . .35 B5
Thorney Ctry Pk★ UB7 .208 B3
Thorney Lane N SL0. . . . . .207 F6
Thorney Lane S SL0. . . . . .207 F5
Thorney Mill Rd SL0, UB7 208 B3
Thornhill MK18. . . . . .54 B8
Thornhill Cl HP7. . . . . .165 B7
Thornhill Rd UB10 . . . . . . .201 F8
Thornlea Croft MK46. . . . . . .6 F3
Thornley Cl HP18 . . . . .100 E4
Thornley Croft MK4. . . . . . .46 C2
Thorns Cl HP27. . . . . .139 D5
Thorns La HP27. . . . . .139 E5
THORNTON 43 C4
Thornton Ave UB7 . . . . . . .208 F3
Thornton Chase MK14. . . . .34 E6
Thornton Cl UB7 . . . . .208 F3
Thornton Coll MK17. . . . . . .43 C5
Thornton Cres HP22. . . . . .131 A5
Thornton Rd MK17. . . . . . . .44 A1
Thorntree Dr HP23. . . . . . .118 F4
Thorpe Cl HP21. . . . . .116 A4
Thorpe House Pre-Prep Sch
  SL9 . . . . .188 E7
Thorpe House Senior Sch
  SL9 . . . . .188 E7
Thorpeness Croft MK4 . . . .56 F8
Thorwold Pl MK5. . . . . .46 B6
Thrasher Rd HP21. . . . . . . .115 D5
Threads La MK18. . . . . .52 F6
Three Close La HP4 . . . . . .135 C4
Three Gables HP9. . . . . . . .175 E2
Three Horseshoes Cl
  HP18 . . . . .83 A6
THREE HOUSEHOLDS 176 F7
Three Households HP8. . . .176 F6
Three Oaks Cl UB10 . . . . . .190 F1
Three Points La MK18. . . . .74 A6
Thresher Gr MK12. . . . . . . .33 A5
Thrift La SL6. . . . . .202 D1
Thrift View MK43. . . . . .25 C2
Thrupp Cl MK19. . . . . .20 A6
Thrush Cl
  6 Aylesbury HP19 . . . . . .101 F3
  High Wycombe HP12. . . . .172 C4
Thurlby Way SL6. . . . . .202 D3
Thurley Cotts SL2. . . . . . . .199 B3
Thurne CT MK16. . . . . .22 E3
Thursby Cl MK15. . . . . .35 D7
Thurston Rd SL1. . . . . .205 E7
Thyme Cl MK16. . . . . .21 F5
Tibbys La HP18 . . . . .112 F3
Tiberius Dr MK11. . . . . .33 A3
Ticehirst Cl MK7. . . . . .48 B7
Ticehurst Cl MK7. . . . . .48 B7
Tichborne WD3. . . . . .178 D5
Tickford Arc MK16. . . . . . . .22 D4
TICKFORD END 22 F4
Tickford Park Prim Sch
  MK16. . . . . .22 D3
Tickford St MK16. . . . . .22 E4
Tiddington 136 A7

Tierney 5 MK4. . . . . .45 D2
Tierney Ct 3 SL7 . . . . .183 E1
Tiffany Cl MK17. . . . . .58 D6
Tiggywinkles Wildlife
  Hospl★ HP17. . . . . .127 A4
TILBROOK 48 C3
Tilbrook Ind Est MK7. . . . . .48 B3
Tilbrook Rdbt MK7. . . . . . . .48 B2
Tilbury Wlk SL3. . . . . .207 A2
Tilburywood Cl HP13. . . . . .161 C2
Tilebarn Cl RG9. . . . . .191 C1
Tilecotes Cl SL7 . . . . .183 C2
Tilehouse Comb Sch
  UB9. . . . . .189 F5
Tilehouse La UB9. . . . . . . .189 E6
Tilehouse Way UB9. . . . . . .189 F4
Tilers Rd MK11. . . . . .33 B2
Tilling Cres HP13. . . . . . . .174 A7
Tillman Cl MK12 . . . . .33 C5
Tillson Square HP21. . . . . .115 F4
Tilstone Ave SL4. . . . . .204 E2
Tilstone Cl SL4. . . . . .204 E1
Tilsworth Rd HP9. . . . . . . .175 C1
Timber La MK17. . . . . .60 F7
Timberley La HP16. . . . . . .142 A8
Timberscombe MK4. . . . . . .46 D3
Timbers Wlk SL6. . . . . .202 B5
Timber Way OX39. . . . . . . .147 C6
Timberwood SL2. . . . . .187 D1
Timbold Dr MK7. . . . . .48 A7
Timor Cl MK11. . . . . .32 D6
Timothy's Cl MK12 . . . . . . .33 C7
Timpson Ct HP15 . . . . .162 D8
Timpson La MK46. . . . . .7 C3
Timpsons Row MK46. . . . . . .7 A3
Tindal Rd HP20. . . . . .101 E2
TINGEWICK 51 B7
Tingewick Rd
  Buckingham MK18. . . . . . . .52 B8
  Radclive MK18. . . . . .51 E7
Tingewick Road Ind Est
  MK18 . . . . .52 B8
TINKERS BRIDGE 47 D6
Tinkers Dr MK18. . . . . .65 F3
TINKERS END 65 F3
Tinkers La
  Berkhamsted HP23 . . . . . .134 A6
  Windsor SL4. . . . . .209 D5
Tinkers Wood Rd HP13 . . .161 E1
Tintagel Cl MK6. . . . . .47 A8
Tintagel Ho SL1. . . . . .205 C5
Tintern Cl SL1. . . . . .205 C3
Tinterne Cl HP21. . . . . .116 C6
Tippet Cl MK7. . . . . .48 D4
Tiree Ct MK3. . . . . .58 C3
Tiree Ho SL2. . . . . .205 B8
Titchmarsh Ct MK6. . . . . . .46 E8
Tithe Barn Dr SL6. . . . . . . .203 E1
Tithe Cl SL6. . . . . .203 C1
Tithe Cl SL3. . . . . .207 A2
Tithe La TW19 . . . . .212 A1
Tithe Mdw HP23. . . . . .51 A6
Titmus Rd HP22. . . . . .131 E2
Titus Ct MK11. . . . . .32 F3
Tiverton Cres
  Aylesbury HP19. . . . . .101 C3
  Milton Keynes MK4 . . . . . . .45 E1
Tobago Dr MK3. . . . . .58 B3
Tobermory Cl SL3. . . . . . . .206 E2
Tockley Rd SL1. . . . . .197 B2
Todd Cl
  Aylesbury HP21. . . . . .115 B6
  Holmer Green HP15 . . . . . .163 B6
Tofield Cl HP19. . . . . .101 D3
Tolcarne Ave MK6 . . . . .35 A1
Tolkien Mdws MK4. . . . . . . .56 F8
Toll Bar Cnr HP27. . . . . . . .138 D7
Tollgate SL6. . . . . .202 A6
Tollgate Cl WD3 . . . . .167 C3
Tollgate St MK18. . . . . .51 B6
Tolman Ct HP21. . . . . .115 B6
Tomlin Rd SL2 . . . . .197 E1
Tomo Ind Est UB8. . . . . . . .208 C7
Tompion Rd HP19. . . . . . . .100 F1
Tompkins Cl
  Aston Clinton HP22 . . . . . .117 F4
  Milton Keynes MK5 . . . . . . .46 B3
Tompkins La OX27 . . . . .71 E2
Tom Scott Ho HP5 . . . . . . .144 B2
Toms Hill Cl HP23. . . . . . . .120 D5
Toms Hill Rd HP23 . . . . . . .120 D5
Toms Turn HP15 . . . . .162 F5
TONGWELL 35 C8
Tongwell Ind Est MK15 . . .35 B8
Tongwell La MK15, MK16. . .22 C2
Tongwell Rdbt MK15. . . . . .35 D8
Tongwell St
  Milton Keynes, Broughton
    MK10. . . . . .36 A3
  Milton Keynes, Northfield
    MK15. . . . . .35 F5
  Milton Keynes, Pineham
    MK15. . . . . .35 E7
  Walnut Tree MK7. . . . . .48 C6
Toot Hill Cl MK5. . . . . .46 A5
Top Angel MK18. . . . . .52 D5
Topaz Cl SL1. . . . . .205 B5
Top Fair Furlong MK14. . . . .21 F7
Top Farm Cl HP9. . . . . .175 A1
Top Fox Wy MK14. . . . . .21 F3
Topland Rd SL9. . . . . .177 D3
Top Mdw
  Bow Brickhill MK7. . . . . . . .48 B3
  Milton Keynes MK3 . . . . . . .47 B3
Topping La UB8. . . . . .201 D2
Top Pk SL9. . . . . .188 C5
Top Station Rd NN13. . . . . .38 A8

Top Station Road Ind Est
NN13. 38 A8
Torbay HP22. . . . . 85 B4
Tornay Ct LU7. . . . . 91 D6
Torquay Spur SL2. . . . . 198 B2
Torre Cl MK3. . . . . 47 A2
Torridge Rd
  Aylesbury HP21. . . . . 115 D4
  Slough SL3. . . . . 212 B8
Torridon Ct MK2. . . . . 58 D4
Torrington Rd HP4. . . . . 135 B4
Tortoiseshell Way
  Aylesbury HP19. . . . . 101 C4
  Berkhamsted HP4. . . . . 134 F6
Torwood Cl HP4. . . . . 134 F4
TOTTERIDGE. 173 F8
Totteridge Ave HP13 . . . . 173 D6
Totteridge Common Cotts
  HP13 . . . . 173 F8
Totteridge Dr HP13. . . . . 162 E1
Totteridge Ho HP13. . . . . 173 E8
Totteridge La HP13. . . . . 162 E1
Totteridge Par HP13 . . . . 173 E8
Totteridge Rd HP13 . . . . 173 D7
TOTTERNHOE. 93 B7
Totternhoe Knolls & Quarry★
  LU6. 93 B8
Totternhoe Lower Sch
  LU6. 93 B7
Totternhoe Rd
  Dunstable LU6. . . . . 93 E7
  Eaton Bray LU6. . . . . 92 D7
TOUCHBRIDGE 95 E1
Towan Ave
  Fishermead MK6. . . . . 47 A8
  Milton Keynes MK6. . . . . 35 A1
Towcester Dr NN12 . . . . 18 B3
Towcester Rd
  Buckingham MK18. . . . . 41 E4
  Old Stratford MK19 . . . . 32 B7
TOWERAGE. 171 F8
Tower Cl
  Berkhamsted HP4. . . . . 135 A3
  Emberton MK16. . . . . 13 C5
  Flackwell Heath HP10 . . . . . 185 C7
Tower Cres MK14. . . . . 34 F6
Tower Ct HP27. . . . . 139 B3
Tower Dr MK14. . . . . 34 F7
Towergate Cl UB8 . . . . 201 E7
TOWER HILL 146 F2
Tower Hill WD4. . . . . 146 F1
Tower Hill Bsns Pk OX27 . 71 D7
Tower Ho
  Iver SL0. . . . . 207 E7
  4 Slough SL1. . . . . 205 E4
Toweridge La
  High Wycombe HP12 . . . . . . 172 C8
  West Wycombe HP14 . . . . . . 160 F1
Tower Rd HP7 . . . . 165 A4
Towersey Way HP21. . . . . . . 115 B7
Towers Lea HP13 . . . . 173 C7
Tower St HP13. . . . . 162 D2
Town Bridge Ct HP5 . . . . 154 B7
Town Cl MK18 . . . . 50 D6
TOWN END. 159 C8
Town End Cres MK16. . . . . 12 B5
Town End Rd HP14. . . . . 159 C8
Town Farm LU7. . . . . 105 A7
Town Farm Barns HP27 . . . 139 B3
Town Farm Cl OX49 . . . . 157 B8
Townfield HP5. . . . . 154 C4
Town Field La HP8. . . . . 177 C7
Townfield Rd 5 HP13 . . 173 C7
Town La
  Stanwell TW19. . . . . 213 D1
  Wooburn HP10 . . . . 185 D4
Townlands Meml Hospl
  RG9. 191 D2
TOWNSEND. 71 D2
  Haddenham. 127 A7
  North Marston. 76 B2
TOWN'S END. 71 D2
Townsend
  Haddenham HP17 . . . . 127 A7
  Marsh Gibbon OX27. . . . . . . 71 E2
  Quainton HP22. . . . . 85 A5
Townsend Cl MK43. . . . . 37 F8
Townsend Cotts
  Great Horwood MK17. . . . . . . 55 B3
  Middle Claydon MK18 . . . . . . 74 C8
Townsend Gate HP4. . . . . . . 135 E3
Townsend Gr MK13. . . . . 34 B8
Townsend La OX27 . . . . 71 E2
Townsend Piece HP19. . . . . 101 C1
Townsend Rd HP5 . . . . 144 C1
Townside
  Edlesborough LU6 . . . . 92 F3
  Haddenham HP17 . . . . 126 F5
Town Sq 8 SL1. . . . . 205 F4
Tozer Wlk SL4. . . . . 209 D4
Tracy Ave SL3. . . . . 206 F1
Tracy Way 3 MK4. . . . . 45 E3
Trafalgar Ave MK3. . . . . 46 E2
Trafalgar Cl HP21. . . . . 115 F6
Trafalgar Dr MK16. . . . . 36 B5
Trafford Cl HP16. . . . . 152 A6
Trafford Rd HP16. . . . . 152 A7
Tram Hill HP18 . . . . 96 B2
Tranlands Brigg MK13. . . . . . 34 B4
Transcend 10 SL4. . . . . 210 C5
Trapp's Ct HP5. . . . . 154 C6
Trapp's La HP5 . . . . 154 C6
Travell Ct MK13. . . . . 34 B3
Travic Rd SL2. . . . . 197 F2
Travis Ct SL2. . . . . 198 B2
Travis Gr MK3. . . . . 58 A8
Treacher's Cl HP5 . . . . 154 B8

Treadaway Bsns Ctr
  HP10. . . . . 174 C1
Treadaway Hill HP10 . . . . . . 174 B1
Treadaway Rd HP10. . . . . . . 174 B1
Trebah Sq HP19. . . . . 114 F8
Treborough MK4. . . . . 46 D2
Tredington Gr MK7 . . . . 48 A4
Treefields MK18. . . . . 52 E8
Treehanger Cl HP23. . . . . . . 119 B4
Trees Ave HP14. . . . . 162 A6
Treeside Cl UB7 . . . . 208 D2
Treesmill Dr SL6. . . . . 202 C3
Trees Rd
  Bourne End SL8. . . . . 185 B3
  Hughenden Valley HP14 . . . 162 A6
Trelawney Ave SL3. . . . . 206 E3
Tremayne Ct MK6. . . . . 47 A8
Trenchard Ave HP22. . . . . . . 131 D6
Trenchard St HP19. . . . . 115 A8
Trenches La SL3. . . . . 207 A6
Trengothal Ct NN13. . . . . 26 D4
Trent Dr MK16. . . . . 22 D4
Trentishoe Cres MK4. . . . . . . 46 D3
Trent Rd
  Milton Keynes MK3. . . . . 46 E1
  Slough SL3. . . . . 212 B8
Trent Villas Est SL3. . . . . . . 211 B6
Tresco Rd HP4. . . . . 134 F5
Tresham Ct MK5. . . . . 46 A7
Tressell The SL6. . . . . 202 D6
Trevelyan Mid Sch SL4 . . . . 210 C3
Trevelyan Way HP4 . . . . 135 B6
Treves Gn HP21. . . . . 115 E5
Trevithick La MK5. . . . . 46 B5
Trevone Ct MK6. . . . . 47 A8
Trevor Ct TW19. . . . . 213 A2
Trevose Ho SL2. . . . . 198 B1
Trewarden La SL0 . . . . 200 D3
Triangle Bsns Pk HP22. . . . . 130 D8
Trident Ind Est SL3. . . . . 212 E4
TRING. 119 C3
Tring Bsns Ctr HP23. . . . . . . 118 E4
Tring Ford Rd HP23. . . . . . . 119 A7
Tring Hill HP23. . . . . 118 C3
Tring Park Sch for the
  Performing Arts HP23. . . . 119 B3
Tring Rd
  Aylesbury HP21. . . . . 116 B7
  Berkhamsted HP4. . . . . 134 D7
  Dunstable LU6. . . . . 93 E7
  Edlesborough LU6. . . . . 106 E8
  Long Marston HP23. . . . . . . 104 C3
  Wendover HP22. . . . . 131 C5
  Wilstone HP23. . . . . 104 C1
  Wingrave HP22. . . . . 89 C1
Tring Reservoirs (Wildlife
  Trust Reserves)★
  HP23. . . . . 118 E7
Tring Sch HP23. . . . . 119 B4
Tring Sta HP23. . . . . 120 A5
Trinidad Gr MK17. . . . . 58 A3
Trinity Ave SL7. . . . . 183 D3
Trinity CE Prim Sch RG9 191 D1
Trinity Cl
  Old Stratford MK19 . . . . 32 B7
  Stanwell TW19. . . . . 213 C1
Trinity Ct
  Aylesbury HP19. . . . . 101 D1
  Chesham HP5. . . . . 154 C7
  Marlow SL7. . . . . 183 D3
Trinity Ho SL8. . . . . 195 F6
Trinity Pl SL4. . . . . 210 C5
Trinity Rd
  Hazlemere HP15 . . . . 162 F3
  Marlow SL7. . . . . 183 D2
  Milton Keynes MK12 . . . . 33 B7
Trinity St Stephen CE Fst Sch
  SL4. 210 B6
Tripps Hill Cl HP8. . . . . 177 A7
Trispen Ct MK6. . . . . 47 A8
Trooper Rd HP23. . . . . 120 C5
Troutbeck MK6. . . . . 47 C8
Troutbeck Cl SL2. . . . . 206 A6
Trout Cl SL7. . . . . 194 C8
Trout Hollow HP27. . . . . 148 E8
Trout La UB7. . . . . 208 C5
Trout Rd UB7. . . . . 208 D6
Trubys Gdn MK6. . . . . 47 A7
Trueman Pl MK6. . . . . 46 F8
Truesdale Dr UB9. . . . . 190 C7
Trumper Way
  Slough SL1. . . . . 204 F5
  Uxbridge UB8. . . . . 201 C4
Trumpton La MK7. . . . . 48 C7
Trunk Furlong MK17 . . . . 49 D6
Truro Cl SL6. . . . . 202 A7
Trust Cotts HP4. . . . . 107 A1
Trustees Cl UB9 . . . . 189 F5
Tubwell Rd SL2. . . . . 199 B4
Tucker Cl HP13 . . . . 173 C6
Tuckers Dr HP15. . . . . 163 C7
Tudeley Hale MK7. . . . . 48 B8
Tudor Ct
  Amersham HP6 . . . . 154 D1
  5 Leighton Buzzard LU7. . . 80 F7
  Maidenhead SL6. . . . . 196 C2
  Piddington HP14 . . . . 160 C1
Tudor Dr HP10. . . . . 185 D7
Tudor Gdns
  Milton Keynes MK11 . . . . 32 E4
  Slough SL3. . . . . 204 C8
  Steeple Claydon MK18. . . . . . 63 D3
Tudor Mill HP10. . . . . 185 E6
Tudor Orch HP4. . . . . 134 E6
Tudor Pk HP6. . . . . 154 D2
Tudor Rd HP15. . . . . 163 C3

Tudors Cl MK18. . . . . 73 B4
Tudor Way SL4. . . . . 209 E6
Tuffnell Cl MK15. . . . . 35 E7
Tuffnell Gn MK10. . . . . 35 E1
Tulip Way UB7. . . . . 208 D2
Tulkers Cl HP16. . . . . 151 D5
Tulla Ct MK2. . . . . 58 C4
Tummel Way MK2. . . . . 58 C6
Tunbridge Gr MK7. . . . . 48 B8
Tunmers Ct SL9 . . . . 177 C2
Tunmers End SL9 . . . . 177 C2
Tunmers Ho SL9. . . . . 177 C2
Tunnel Way LU7. . . . . 105 C2
Tuns La
  Henley-on-Thames RG9 . . . 191 E2
  Slough SL1. . . . . 205 C4
Turks Head Ct SL4 . . . . 210 C7
Turnberry Cl MK3. . . . . 57 D7
Turner Cl HP20 . . . . 101 F3
Turner Rd SL3. . . . . 206 C4
Turners Dr HP13 . . . . 173 E8
Turners Field HP13. . . . . 161 E3
Turner's Mdw HP22. . . . . 117 B6
Turners Mews MK14. . . . . 34 F6
Turners Pl HP15. . . . . 163 C6
Turners Wlk 4 HP5. . . . . . . 144 C1
Turners Wood Dr HP8. . . . . . 177 D7
Turner Wlk 12 HP20. . . . . . 101 F3
Turneys Dr MK12. . . . . 33 A6
Turneys Orch WD3. . . . . 167 D4
Turnfields HP18 . . . . 124 A3
Turnfurlong HP21. . . . . 115 F7
Turnfurlong Inf Sch
  HP21. . . . . 116 A6
Turnfurlong Jun Sch
  HP21. . . . . 116 A6
Turnfurlong La HP21. . . . . . . 116 A6
Turnfurlong Row HP21. . . . . 116 A6
Turnham Row HP19 . . . . 115 B7
Turnmill Ave MK6. . . . . 35 B2
Turnmill Ct MK6 . . . . 35 B2
Turnoak Pk SL4. . . . . 209 E3
Turnpike Ct MK17. . . . . 49 A5
Turnpike End HP21 . . . . 115 F6
Turnpike La UB10. . . . . 201 E3
Turnpike Rd HP12. . . . . 172 D4
Turnpike The HP18. . . . . 109 D5
Turnpike Way HP12. . . . . 172 C4
Turnpin Cl MK6. . . . . 52 F6
Turnside St MK18 . . . . 52 F6
Turnstone Way HP19. . . . . . 101 E3
Turpins Gn SL6. . . . . 202 A5
Turpyn Ct MK6. . . . . 47 D8
Turton Way SL1. . . . . 205 D3
TURVEY. 8 F6
Turvey Ct MK2. . . . . 117 E5
Turvey Lower Sch MK43. . . . . 8 E6
Turvey Mill MK43. . . . . 8 D5
Turvey Rd
  Astwood MK16. . . . . 15 F5
  Turvey MK43. . . . . 3 E2
TURVILLE. 169 F3
TURVILLE HEATH. 169 A3
Turvill End MK5. . . . . 46 B8
Turville Rd HP21. . . . . 116 C6
TURWESTON. 38 C8
Turweston Rd NN13 . . . . 26 A1
Tuscans MK18. . . . . 73 B5
Tweeddale Cl MK17. . . . . 67 C2
Tweed Cl HP4. . . . . 135 B5
Tweed Dr MK3. . . . . 46 D1
Tweed Rd SL3. . . . . 212 B8
Tweenways HP5. . . . . 144 C1
Twelve Leys HP22. . . . . 89 B3
Twickenham CI 2 MK4. 41, 41 E3
Twinches La SL1. . . . . 205 B5
Twinflower MK7. . . . . 48 B6
Twist The HP23. . . . . 119 D2
Twitchell La HP22. . . . . 117 E5
Twitchell Rd HP16. . . . . 152 A7
Twitchell's La HP9. . . . . 176 F5
Twitchen La MK4. . . . . 46 D3
Twizel Cl MK13. . . . . 33 E4
Two Dells La
  Ashley Green HP5 . . . . 145 A4
  Chesham HP5. . . . . 155 B8
Two Gates La HP5 . . . . 143 D7
TWO MILE ASH. 33 E1
Two Mile Ash Sch MK8. . . . 33 E1
Two Mile Dr SL1. . . . . 204 E4
Two Ponds La HP4. . . . . 134 C7
TWYFORD. 62 C1
Twyford CE Sch MK18. . . . . . 62 C2
Twyford La MK7. . . . . 48 C5
Twynham Rd SL6. . . . . 202 B5
Tyburn Ave MK6. . . . . 35 B2
Tyhurst MK10. . . . . 36 A2
Tyle Pl SL4. . . . . 211 A2
Tylers Cres HP15. . . . . 163 B2
Tylers Gn MK13. . . . . 34 D3
TYLERS GREEN. 163 D1
Tylers Green Fst Sch
  HP10. . . . . 174 D8
Tylers Green Mid Sch
  HP10. . . . . 174 B8
Tylers Hill Rd HP5. . . . . 154 F8
Tylers Rd HP15. . . . . 163 B2
Tyler Wlk 3 SL3. . . . . 206 F1
Tylsworth Cl HP6. . . . . 154 D1
Tyndale Mews SL1. . . . . 205 B4
Tyneham Cl HP21. . . . . 116 B4
Tynemouth Rise 3 MK10. 36 A1
Tyne Rd HP21. . . . . 115 D4
Tyne Sq MK3. . . . . 46 D1
Tyrell Cl
  Buckingham MK18. . . . . 52 C7
  Milton Keynes MK19 . . . . 20 A5
Tyrell Gdns SL4. . . . . 209 F4

Tyrells Gdns MK17 . . . . 69 E8
Tyrells Rd MK17. . . . . 69 E8
Tyrill MK14. . . . . 34 C7
TYRINGHAM. 12 F2
Tyson Pl MK6. . . . . 46 E8
Tyson Rd HP18. . . . . 100 E4
Tythe Cl LU7. . . . . 78 E8
Tythe Gdns LU7. . . . . 78 E8
Tythe Mews LU6. . . . . 92 E3
Tyzack Rd HP13. . . . . 162 F1

U

Ufton Court Yd SL8. . . . . 185 B4
Ufton Ct SL8. . . . . 185 B4
Ullswater Cl SL1. . . . . 204 C8
Ullswater Dr LU7. . . . . 80 C7
Ultra Ave MK3. . . . . 47 A1
Ulverscroft MK10. . . . . 36 B2
Ulverston Cres MK10 . . . . . . 36 B2
Ulyett Pl MK6. . . . . 46 E8
Umberville Way SL2. . . . . . . 197 E2
Underhill MK6. . . . . 202 E6
Underwood Cotts HP7. . . . . . 164 C2
Underwood Pl MK6 . . . . 46 E8
Underwood Rd HP13. . . . . . . 173 D8
Union Bldgs UB8. . . . . 201 B2
Union Bsns Pk UB8 . . . . 201 B5
Union Castle Row 9
  MK10. . . . . 36 C4
Union Ct 11 HP4 . . . . 135 D4
Union Ind Est HP12 . . . . 172 A7
Union St MK16. . . . . 22 D5
Univ Campus Aylesbury Vale
  6 HP21. . . . . 115 E9
University Way MK43. . . . . . . 24 D1
Univ of Buckingham (Hunter
  St) The MK18. . . . . 52 C8
Univ of Buckingham The
  (Chandos Rd) MK18. . . . . . 52 C7
Univ of Buckingham The
  (Verney Pk) MK18. . . . . 52 E7
Up Corner HP8. . . . . 177 C8
Up Corner Cl HP8. . . . . 177 B8
Upcroft SL4. . . . . 210 B4
UP END. 24 A8
Upende HP18. . . . . 100 D4
Upland Ave HP5 . . . . 144 B3
Uplands SL7. . . . . 183 D6
Uplands Cl
  Gerrards Cross SL9 . . . . 188 E3
  High Wycombe HP13 . . . . . . 173 E8
Uplands Ct SL9. . . . . 144 C1
Uplands The SL9. . . . . 188 E2
Upminster Cl MK10 . . . . 35 E1
Upper Abbotts Hill HP19. 115 A7
UPPER ARNCOTT. 94 E7
Upper Ashlyns Rd HP4 . 135 B3
Upper Barn Farm HP18. . . . 84 B1
Upper Belmont Rd HP5. . 144 B3
Upper Bourne End La
  HP1. 146 B7
Upper Bray Rd SL6. . . . . 203 C3
Upper Church St HP18 . . 112 F3
Upper Coombe LU7. . . . . 80 E5
Upper Dr HP9. . . . . 175 D5
UPPER DUNSLEY. 119 C4
Upper Fifth St MK9. . . . . 34 D2
Upper Fourth St MK9. . . . . . 34 D2
Upper George St HP5 . . . . . 144 C1
Upper Gladstone Rd 2
  HP5. 144 C1
Upper Green St HP11. . . . . . 172 E7
Upper Hall Pk HP4 . . . . 135 E2
Upper Hartwell HP17. . . . . . 114 E5
Upper Hollis HP16 . . . . 151 F7
Upper Hundreds Way
  HP20. . . . . 115 E8
Upper Icknield Way
  Askett HP27. . . . . 139 E7
  Halton HP22 . . . . 117 F2
  Monks Risborough HP27. . 139 D6
  Pitstone HP23, LU7 . . . . 105 E7
  Princes Risborough HP27. 139 B2
  Saunderton HP27 . . . . 148 F7
Upper Lees Rd SL2. . . . . 198 A2
Upper Lodge La HP15. . . . . 162 F6
UPPER
  MAIDENSGROVE. 179 A7
Upper Mdw 2 MK9. . . . . . . 144 B1
UPPER NORTH DEAN. 150 E2
UPPER POLLICOTT. 111 E8
Upper Ray Mdws Wildlife
  Reserve★ OX25. . . . . 81 D4
Upper Rd UB9. . . . . 189 D4
Upper Riding HP9. . . . . 175 B2
Upper Second St MK9. . . . . . 34 D1
Upper St
  Quainton HP22. . . . . 85 A5
  Tingewick MK18 . . . . 51 B6
Upper Stonehayes MK14. . 34 F8
Upper Thames Way SL8 . 184 F3
Upper Third St MK9. . . . . 34 D1
Upper Tring Pk HP23. . . . . . 119 D1
Upper Ventnor Cotts
  SL6. 195 C8
Upper Way MK17. . . . . 59 C2
Upper Weald MK19. . . . . 45 A8
UPPER WINCHENDON. 99 B1
Upperwood Cl 1 MK5. . . . . 46 A3
Upper Wood Cl 4 MK5. . . . . 45 F3
UPTON
  Slough. 206 B3
  Stone. 114 A4
Upton Cl
  Henley-on-Thames RG9 . . . 191 E1
  5 Slough SL1. . . . . 205 F3

Upton Court Rd SL3. . . . . . . 206 B2
Upton Gr MK5. . . . . 46 C4
Upton Hospl SL1. . . . . 205 F4
Upton House Sch SL4 . . . . . 210 C5
UPTON LEA. 206 A7
Upton Lea Par SL2. . . . . 206 B6
UPTON PARK. 205 F3
Upton Pk SL1. . . . . 205 F3
Upton Rd
  Dinton HP17. . . . . 114 A3
  Slough SL3. . . . . 206 A3
Upton Terr HP17. . . . . 114 A3
Upway SL9. . . . . 177 C2
Ushercombe View MK18. . 50 D6
UXBRIDGE. 201 E5
Uxbridge Coll UB8 . . . . 201 E6
Uxbridge High Sch UB8 . . . 201 D3
Uxbridge Ind Est UB8 . . . . . 201 B3
UXBRIDGE MOOR. 201 B4
Uxbridge Rd
  Iver Heath SL0, SL3. . . . . . . 200 B2
  Rickmansworth WD3. . . . . . 178 F7
  Slough SL1, SL3. . . . . 206 C2
  Uxbridge UB10. . . . . 201 F2
  5 Wendover HP22. . . . . 131 E6
Uxbridge U Sta UB8. . . . . . . 201 D5

V

Vache La
  Chalfont St Giles HP8. . . . . 177 C8
  Milton Keynes MK5. . . . . 45 F6
Vale Cl SL9 . . . . 177 D2
Vale Gr SL1. . . . . 205 E3
Vale House HP19. . . . . 115 C8
Vale Ind Ctr The HP19 . . . . 101 C1
Valens Cl MK8. . . . . 45 E7
Valentine Ct MK8. . . . . 45 E7
Valentine Way HP8. . . . . 177 D7
Vale Park Dr HP20 . . . . 115 C8
Vale Rd
  Aylesbury HP20. . . . . 101 E2
  Chesham HP5. . . . . 144 C4
  Windsor SL4. . . . . 209 F6
Vale Ret Pk HP20 . . . . 115 E8
Valerian Pl MK16. . . . . 21 F4
Vale Rise HP5. . . . . 144 C3
Vale The SL9. . . . . 177 D2
Valley Cl
  Brackley NN13. . . . . 38 A8
  Whipsnade HP4. . . . . 107 E7
Valley Cres NN13. . . . . 38 A8
Valley Ctr The HP13 . . . . . . 173 C6
Valley End SL3. . . . . 199 C1
Valley Rd
  Berkhamsted HP4. . . . . 134 F6
  Brackley NN13. . . . . 38 A8
  Buckingham MK18. . . . . 52 F8
  Finmere MK18. . . . . 50 F8
  Henley-on-Thames RG9 . . . 191 C1
  Hughenden Valley HP14 . . . 162 A5
  Uxbridge UB10. . . . . 201 E3
Valley Rise MK13. . . . . 33 A8
Valley View HP5. . . . . 144 B2
Valley Way SL9. . . . . 188 D5
Valor Dr HP18. . . . . 100 E3
Valpy Cl HP23. . . . . 119 C1
Van Der Bilt Ct MK13. . . . . . 33 F6
Van Diemens Cl OX39 . . . . 147 C7
Vandyke Cl MK17. . . . . 49 B6
Vane Rd OX9. . . . . 126 B1
Vanguard Cl HP12. . . . . 172 D7
Vanguard Ho 5 TW19. . . . . 213 E1
Vansittart Rd
  Bisham SL7. . . . . 194 E7
  Windsor SL4. . . . . 210 A6
Vantage Cl MK16. . . . . 22 F3
Vantage Rd SL1. . . . . 205 B5
Vantage St HP22. . . . . 117 F4
Vanwall Bsns Pk SL6. . . . . . 202 C5
Vanwall Rd SL6. . . . . 202 C4
Varnell Terr RG9. . . . . 181 C2
Vaughan Copse SL4. . . . . . . 205 D2
Vaughan Gdns SL4. . . . . 204 F2
Vaughan Way SL2. . . . . 197 E1
Vauxhall MK13. . . . . 34 B6
Vaynol Cl MK19. . . . . 45 C8
Vector Wlk MK10. . . . . 35 E2
Vellan Ave MK6. . . . . 35 B1
Venables La MK15. . . . . 35 B7
Vendeen Ct MK11. . . . . 21 C1
Venetian Ct MK7. . . . . 48 C7
Ventfield Cl OX33 . . . . 108 A5
Venus Cl SL2. . . . . 197 F1
VENUS HILL. 156 B8
Venus Hill HP3. . . . . 156 A8
Verbena Cl UB7. . . . . 208 D1
Verdi Cl MK7. . . . . 48 C5
Verdon Ct SL2. . . . . 198 B2
Verdon Dr MK15. . . . . 35 B7
Verity Pl MK6. . . . . 34 F1
Verley Cl MK6. . . . . 47 C8
Verley Way SL9. . . . . 144 C4
Vermont Pl MK15. . . . . 22 C1
Vermont Rd SL2. . . . . 197 F1
Verney Ave HP12. . . . . 172 D4
Verney Cl
  Berkhamsted HP4. . . . . 134 F5
  6 Buckingham MK18. . . . . . 41 D8
  Marlow SL7. . . . . 183 D2
  Tring HP23. . . . . 119 C5
Verney Farm Cl MK18 . . . 74 F8
Verney Junc Bsns Pk
  MK18. . . . . 64 E3

VERNEY JUNCTION 64 F4
Verney Rd
　Slough SL3 . . . . 207 A2
　Winslow MK18 . . . . 65 E4
Verney Wlk HP21 . . . . 115 D6
Vernier Cres MK5 . . . . 45 E5
Vernon Bldg 7 HP11 . . . . 172 F7
Verona Cl UB8 . . . . 208 C7
Verwood Rd HP20 . . . . 101 E2
Veryan Pl MK6 . . . . 35 B1
Vicarage Cl
　Cookham SL6 . . . . 196 B7
　Seer Green HP9 . . . . 176 D3
　Steeple Claydon MK18 . . . . 63 D2
　Wendover HP22 . . . . 131 B5
Vicarage Ct
　Hanslope MK19 . . . . 11 B2
　Steeple Claydon MK18 . . . . 63 D3
Vicarage Dr SL6 . . . . 203 C4
Vicarage Flats SL4 . . . . 210 D8
Vicarage Gdns
　Leighton Buzzard LU7 . . . . 80 E6
　Marsworth HP23 . . . . 105 A2
　3 Milton Keynes MK13 . . . 34 A4
Vicarage La
　Bovingdon HP3 . . . . 146 B4
　Ivinghoe LU7 . . . . 105 F5
　Piddington OX25 . . . . 95 E6
　Steeple Claydon MK18 . . . . 63 D2
　Wing LU7 . . . . 79 E2
Vicarage Mews 2 SL6 . . 202 D6
Vicarage Rd
　Aylesbury HP21 . . . . 115 D5
　Henley-on-Thames RG9 . . 191 E1
　Leighton Buzzard LU7 . . . . 80 E6
　Maidenhead SL6 . . . . 202 F8
　Milton Keynes, Bradwell
　　MK13 . . . . 34 A4
　Milton Keynes, Fenny Stratford
　　MK2 . . . . 58 E8
　Milton Keynes, Stony Stratford
　　MK13 . . . . 32 B4
　Pitstone LU7 . . . . 105 D2
　Whaddon MK17 . . . . 56 B8
　Wigginton HP23 . . . . 119 D1
　Winslow MK18 . . . . 65 F4
　Yardley Gobion NN12 . . . . . 18 E6
Vicarage St MK17 . . . . 49 C4
Vicarage Way
　Colnbrook SL3 . . . . 212 D7
　Gerrards Cross SL9 . . . . . 188 F5
Vicarage Wlk MK11 . . . . . . 32 D6
Vickers Ct 9 TW19 . . . . . 213 E1
Vickery Cl HP21 . . . . 115 E5
Vickery Way HP21 . . . . . . 115 E5
Victor Cl SL6 . . . . 202 B8
Victoria CE Fst Sch
　Berkhamsted HP4 . . . . 135 C4
Victoria Cotts SL6 . . . . . . 195 C6
Victoria Cres SL0 . . . . . . 208 A6
Victoria Ct
　Henley-on-Thames RG9 . . 191 E1
　High Wycombe HP11 . . . . . 172 F8
　4 Marlow SL7 . . . . 183 E2
　Slough SL1 . . . . 205 E5
　21 Windsor SL4 . . . . 210 D6
Victoria Dr SL1, SL2 . . . . 197 F6
Victoria Gdns
　High Wycombe HP11 . . . . . 172 F4
　Marlow SL7 . . . . 183 E2
Victoria Ho SL4 . . . . 211 A2
VICTORIA PARK 116 B8
Victoria Rd
　Berkhamsted HP4 . . . . 135 C4
　Chesham HP5 . . . . 144 C1
　Eton Wick SL4 . . . . 204 F1
　Farnham Common SL2 . . . 198 C6
　Leighton Buzzard LU7 . . . . 80 E6
　Marlow SL7 . . . . 183 E2
　Milton Keynes MK2 . . . . . . 47 E1
　Slough SL2 . . . . 206 B5
　Uxbridge UB8 . . . . 201 C5
Victoria Row MK18 . . . . . . 52 D8
Victoria St
　Aylesbury HP20 . . . . 115 F8
　High Wycombe HP11 . . . . . 172 F7
　Milton Keynes MK12 . . . . . 33 D6
　9 Slough SL1 . . . . 205 F4
　Windsor SL4 . . . . 210 D6
Victor Rd SL4 . . . . 210 C4
Victory Ave MK16 . . . . 36 B5
Victory Ct MK1 . . . . 47 B2
Victory Rd
　Berkhamsted HP4 . . . . 135 A5
　Steeple Claydon MK18 . . . . 63 D2
　Wendover HP22 . . . . 131 B5
Vienna Gr MK13 . . . . 33 E6
Village Cl MK16 . . . . 13 F2
Village Cl The OX25 . . . . . . 94 D7
Village Ct LU7 . . . . 80 D6
Village La SL2 . . . . 187 D4
Village Mews 2 HP3 . . . . 146 A4
Village Rd
　Coleshill HP7 . . . . 164 F3
　Denham UB9 . . . . 190 A2
　Dorney SL4 . . . . 204 B3
Village Way HP7 . . . . 166 D7
Villa Park (Mobile Home Pk)
　MK43 . . . . 37 F7
Villiers Bldgs 8 HP20 . . 115 D8
Villiers Cl MK18 . . . . 41 E2
Villiers Cres SL4 . . . . 210 A2
Villiers Rd SL2 . . . . 205 D8
Villier St UB8 . . . . 201 D3
Vimy Ct LU7 . . . . 80 F7

Vimy Rd LU7 . . . . 80 F7
Vincent Ave MK8 . . . . 45 F8
Vincent Dr MK18 . . . . 201 F4
Vincent Rd HP19 . . . . 101 A3
Vincents Way HP14 . . . . . 161 D6
Vine Cl
　Hazlemere HP15 . . . . 163 A3
　Stanwell TW19 . . . . 213 A2
Vine Ct SL2 . . . . 199 A6
Vine Gr UB10 . . . . 201 F5
Vine La UB10 . . . . 201 F4
Vine Rd SL2 . . . . 198 F6
Vine Row MK43 . . . . 8 E6
Vine St UB8 . . . . 201 C4
Vine The HP18 . . . . 124 D3
Vinetrees HP22 . . . . 131 B4
Vineyard Dr SL8 . . . . 185 A5
Vineyards The HP27 . . . . 138 A2
Viney La HP19 . . . . 114 F8
Vinlake Ave UB10 . . . . 190 F1
Vintners Mews MK14 . . . . . 34 F6
Violet Ave UB8 . . . . 208 F8
Violet Cl HP27 . . . . 149 D6
Violets Cl MK16 . . . . 24 B6
Virage HP22 . . . . 117 F4
Virginia MK6 . . . . 47 A7
Virginia Gdns HP14 . . . . . 159 F8
Viridian Sq HP21 . . . . 115 E7
Viscount Cl 13 HP20 . . . . 101 F2
Viscount Ct 12 SL4 . . . . . 210 C6
Viscount Ind Est SL3 . . . 212 E4
Viscount Way MK2 . . . . 47 C1
Vitalograph Bsns Pk
　MK18 . . . . 41 F4
Vivaldi Ct MK7 . . . . 48 D5
Vivien Cl SL6 . . . . 195 F6
Volta Rise MK5 . . . . 46 C4
Vyne Cres MK8 . . . . 33 F1
Vyners Sch UB10 . . . . 201 F8

W

Waborne Rd SL8 . . . . 185 B4
WADDESDON 99 B7
Waddesdon CE Sch HP18 . 99 A6
Waddesdon Cl 8 MK8 . . . . 45 F8
Waddesdon Green HP21 . . 115 E4
Waddesdon Hill HP18 . . . . 99 C3
Waddesdon Manor★
　HP18 . . . . 98 E5
Waddesdon Manor Flats
　HP18 . . . . 98 E6
Waddesdon Village Prim Sch
　HP18 . . . . 99 A6
Wade Dr SL1 . . . . 205 A5
Wadesmill La MK7 . . . . 48 A4
Wadhurst La MK10 . . . . 36 B1
Wadworth Holme MK10 . . . 35 E3
Waglands Gdn MK18 . . . . . 52 D7
Wagner Cl MK7 . . . . 48 C4
Wagstaff Way 12 MK46 . . . . 6 F3
Waine Cl MK18 . . . . 52 D7
Wainers Croft MK12 . . . . . . 33 B4
Wainwrights HP18 . . . . . . 125 D6
Waivers Way HP21 . . . . . . 116 A5
Wakefield Cl MK14 . . . . 34 F7
Wakefield Cres SL2 . . . . . 198 F6
Wakelins End SL6 . . . . . . 195 E7
Wakeman Rd SL8 . . . . 185 A3
Walbank Gr 5 MK5 . . . . . . 46 A3
Walbrook Ave MK6 . . . . 35 B3
Waldeck Rd SL6 . . . . 203 A7
Waldeck Rd SL6 . . . . 203 A7
Walden Croft MK6 . . . . 47 E4
Waldens Cl 4 SL8 . . . . . . 185 A3
Walducks Cl LU7 . . . . 78 E8
Walford Rd UB8 . . . . 201 D3
Walgrave Dr MK13 . . . . 34 B4
Walker Ave MK12 . . . . 33 A6
Walker Cres SL3 . . . . 206 F1
Walker Ct SL6 . . . . 202 D7
Walker Rd SL6 . . . . 203 A4
Walkers Rd MK27 . . . . 138 D7
Walkham Cl HP13 . . . . 174 B4
Walkhampton Ave MK13 . . 34 C3
Walk House Cl MK43 . . . . . 25 B1
Walk The
　Eton Wick SL4 . . . . 205 A1
　Winslow MK18 . . . . 65 F4
Walkwood End HP9 . . . . . . 175 C1
Walkwood Rise HP9 . . . . . 186 C8
Wallace Cl
　Marlow SL7 . . . . 183 F4
　Uxbridge UB10 . . . . 201 E3
Wallace Dr LU6 . . . . 92 E6
Wallace End HP21 . . . . . . 116 A6
Wallace Mews LU6 . . . . 92 E6
Wallace St MK13 . . . . 33 E7
Wallace Wlk SL4 . . . . 205 F1
Wallbridge Cl HP19 . . . . . 115 B7
Wall Brown Way HP19 . . . 101 C4
Waller Rd HP9 . . . . 175 F2
Waller Wy HP5 . . . . 144 D3
Wallinger Dr MK5 . . . . 46 A3
Wallingford MK13 . . . . 34 B5
Wallingford Gdns HP11 . . 173 B4
Wallingford Rd HP18 . . . . 201 B2
Wallington Rd HP5 . . . . . . 144 B1
Wallis Cl SL1 . . . . 206 A3
Wallis Rd TW6 . . . . 213 B5
Wallmead Gdns MK5 . . . . . 46 B7
Walmer Wy MK4 . . . . 56 E8
Walney Pl MK4 . . . . 45 F1
Walnut Cl
　Great Missenden HP16 . . . 152 A7
　Long Crendon HP18 . . . . . 125 C7
　Newport Pagnell MK16 . . . 22 A3

Walnut Cl continued
　Stoke Mandeville HP22 . . . 116 C2
Walnut Cres HP27 . . . . . . 138 D7
Walnut Dr
　Maids Moreton MK18 . . . . . 41 F4
　Milton Keynes MK2 . . . . . . 58 E8
　Wendover HP22 . . . . 131 B6
Walnut Gr HP10 . . . . 185 E6
Walnut Lodge SL1 . . . . . . 205 D4
Walnuts Sch The
　Milton Keynes MK3 . . . . . . 46 F1
　Milton Keynes MK8 . . . . . . 45 D5
WALNUT TREE 48 C6
Walnut Tree Cl
　Bourne End SL8 . . . . 185 B2
　High Wycombe HP12 . . . . . 172 C8
　Uxbridge UB10 . . . . 201 E8
　Winslow MK18 . . . . 65 F4
Walnut Tree Ct HP22 . . . . 116 C3
Walnut Tree Ho HP11 . . . . 174 B3
Walnut Tree La HP27 . . . . 138 D6
Walnut Tree Rdbt MK7 . . . 48 C7
Walnut Way
　Bourne End SL8 . . . . 185 B2
　Hyde Heath HP6 . . . . 153 C4
Walpole Rd SL1 . . . . 204 D7
Walsh's Manor MK14 . . . . . 34 D7
Walsingham Gate HP11 . . 173 A4
WALTER'S ASH 150 C1
Waltham Dr MK10 . . . . 36 A1
Waltham Ho 4 MK3 . . . . . . 46 F1
WALTON
　Aylesbury 115 F7
　Milton Keynes 47 F5
Walton Cl HP13 . . . . 162 E1
WALTON COURT 115 C5
Walton Court Ctr HP21 . . . 115 C5
Walton Dene HP21 . . . . . . 115 F7
Walton Dr
　High Wycombe HP13 . . . . . 162 E1
　Walton MK7 . . . . 47 F6
Walton End MK7 . . . . 48 C6
Walton Gn HP21 . . . . 115 E7
Walton Gr HP21 . . . . 115 E7
Walton Heath MK5 . . . . 57 D7
Walton High Brooklands
　Campus MK10 . . . . 36 D4
Walton High Sch MK7 . . . . 48 C6
Walton La SL2 . . . . 197 F3
WALTON MANOR 48 A6
WALTON PARK 48 A4
Walton Park Rdbt MK7 . . . 48 B4
Walton Pl HP22 . . . . 116 F3
Walton Rd
　Aylesbury HP21 . . . . 115 F7
　Caldecotte MK7 . . . . 48 B3
　Milton Keynes MK10 . . . . . 36 A2
　Walton MK7 . . . . 48 B6
　Wavendon MK10, MK17 . . . 48 D7
Walton St HP21 . . . . 115 E7
Walton Terr HP21 . . . . 115 E7
Walton Way HP21 . . . . 116 A7
Wandlebury MK14 . . . . 35 A8
Wandsworth Pl MK13 . . . . . 34 D3
Wannamaker Gdns MK4 . . . 45 E3
Wannions Cl HP5 . . . . 145 A1
Wantage Cl LU7 . . . . 79 E3
Wantage Cres LU7 . . . . 79 E3
Wappenham Rd NN13 . . . . . 27 B8
Wapping HP18 . . . . 125 D6
Wapseys La SL2 . . . . 187 F4
Warbler Cl HP19 . . . . 114 F8
Warburg Nature Reserve★
　RG9 . . . . 179 B5
Ward Cl SL0 . . . . 207 F7
Wardes Cl HP16 . . . . 151 C5
Ward Gdns SL1 . . . . 204 E5
Wardle Pl MK6 . . . . 46 E8
Ward Pl HP7 . . . . 165 B7
Ward Rd
　Brackley NN13 . . . . 38 A5
　Milton Keynes MK1 . . . . . . 47 E3
Wardrobes La HP27 . . . . . 149 D8
Ward Royal 6 SL4 . . . . . . 210 C6
Ward Royal Parade 3
　SL4 . . . . 210 C6
Wards Dr WD3 . . . . 156 F3
Wardstone End MK4 . . . . . . 46 B2
Ware Leys Cl OX27 . . . . 71 E3
Wargrave Rd RG9 . . . . 191 F1
Warmington Gdns MK15 . . 35 B5
Warmstone Cl HP18 . . . . . . 99 B6
Warmstone La HP18 . . . . . . 99 B6
Warneford Ave HP22 . . . . . 131 D5
Warner Cl SL1 . . . . 204 E5
Warners Cl MK17 . . . . 59 D1
Warners Hill SL6 . . . . 195 D8
Warners Rd MK17 . . . . 57 D3
Warren Bank MK6 . . . . 47 E5
Warren Cl
　Buckingham MK18 . . . . 52 E7
　Slough SL3 . . . . 206 E3
　Stone HP17 . . . . 114 B5
Warren Ct
　Farnham Common SL2 . . . 198 C2
　Little Horwood MK17 . . . . . 55 F5
Warrendene Rd HP14 . . . . 162 A8
Warrender Rd MK5 . . . . . . 144 E2
Warren Farm Cotts MK18 . 50 A7
Warren Field SL0 . . . . 200 C3
Warren Ho HP19 . . . . 101 B1
Warren Nature Reserve★
　HP10 . . . . 185 E5
Warren Parade SL2 . . . . . 206 C5
Warren Rd
　Ickenham UB10 . . . . 201 F8
　Little Horwood MK17 . . . . . 55 F5
　Yardley Gobion NN12 . . . . . 18 F6

Warren The
　Aylesbury HP18 . . . . 100 D4
　Chalfont St Peter SL9 . . . 177 F3
　Chartridge HP5 . . . . 143 E3
　Hazlemere HP15 . . . . 163 A5
Warren Wood Dr HP11 . . . 173 C5
Warren Yd MK12 . . . . 33 A6
WARRINGTON 2 B1
Warrington Ave SL1 . . . . . 205 C7
Warrington Rd MK46 . . . . . . 7 B7
Warwick Ave
　High Wycombe HP12 . . . . . 172 B6
　Milton Keynes MK10 . . . . . 36 C3
　Slough SL3 . . . . 198 C1
Warwick Cl
　Aston Clinton HP22 . . . . . 117 E5
　Maidenhead SL6 . . . . 202 B4
Warwick Ct
　Beaconsfield HP9 . . . . 175 D3
　Chorleywood WD3 . . . . . . 167 F6
　7 Windsor SL4 . . . . 210 C5
Warwick Dr LU7 . . . . 79 E2
Warwick Ho 7 HP13 . . . . . 173 F7
Warwick Pl
　Milton Keynes MK3 . . . . . . 57 E7
　Uxbridge UB8 . . . . 201 C5
Warwick Rd
　Beaconsfield HP9 . . . . 175 D3
　Hanslope MK19 . . . . 11 A3
　Milton Keynes MK3 . . . . . . 57 F7
　Pitstone LU7 . . . . 105 D2
　West Drayton UB7 . . . . . . 208 E5
Warwick Row HP20 . . . . . . 102 A1
Washfield MK4 . . . . 46 D3
Wash Hill HP10 . . . . 185 E3
Wash Hill Lea HP10 . . . . . 185 E4
Wash Hill Mobile Home Pk
　HP10 . . . . 185 E3
Washingleys MK43 . . . . 25 C2
Washington Ct SL7 . . . . . . 184 A3
Washington Dr
　Slough SL1 . . . . 204 D6
　Windsor SL4 . . . . 209 E4
Washington Row HP7 . . . . 165 C7
Wastel MK6 . . . . 47 B5
Watchcroft Dr MK18 . . . . . . 41 E2
Watchet Ct MK4 . . . . 46 D3
Watchet La
　Holmer Green HP15 . . . . . 163 B7
　Little Kingshill HP16 . . . . 152 C1
Waterbeach Cl SL1 . . . . . 205 D7
Waterbeach Rd SL1 . . . . . 205 D7
Waterborne Wlk LU7 . . . . . 80 F7
Water Cl MK19 . . . . 32 B7
Watercress Way MK10 . . . . 36 B3
WATER EATON 58 D5
Water Eaton Ind Est MK2 . 58 C6
Water Eaton Rd MK2, MK3 . 58 C7
WATEREND 159 C5
Water End Rd
　Beacon's Bottom HP14 . . . 159 D3
　Beacon's Bottom, Waterend
　　HP14 . . . . 159 C5
Waterfield WD3 . . . . 167 C2
Waterford Cl MK3 . . . . 46 E1
Waterford Ho UB7 . . . . 208 C3
Water Gdns The HP15 . . . . 162 E2
Waterglades The HP9 . . . . 175 C6
Water Hall Prim Sch MK2 . 58 D4
Waterhouse Cl MK16 . . . . . 22 D4
Water La
　Berkhamsted HP4 . . . . 135 C4
　Bovingdon HP3 . . . . 146 B1
　Ford HP17 . . . . 128 B7
　Leighton Buzzard LU7 . . . . 80 F7
　Sherington MK16 . . . . 13 E1
　Speen HP27 . . . . 150 C4
Waterlily 5 HP19 . . . . 101 E4
Waterloo Ct MK3 . . . . 46 E2
Waterloo Rd
　Leighton Buzzard LU7 . . . . 80 E6
　Uxbridge UB8 . . . . 201 C4
Waterlow Cl MK16 . . . . 22 C2
Waterman Ct SL1 . . . . 204 E5
Water Mdw HP5 . . . . 154 B7
WATERMEAD 101 F4
Watermead HP19 . . . . 101 E4
Watermeadow HP19 . . . . . . 101 F3
Water Meadow Way
　HP22 . . . . 131 B6
Watermill Way HP22 . . . . . 116 F2
WATERPERRY 123 B1
Waterperry OX33 . . . . 123 B1
WATERPERRY
　COMMON 122 F8
Waterperry Gdns★ OX33 . 123 B1
Waterperry Mews HP19 . . 114 F8
Waterperry Rd HP18 . . . . . 123 D5
WATERSIDE 154 C6
Waterside
　Berkhamsted HP4 . . . . 135 C4
　Chesham HP5 . . . . 154 D6
　Edlesborough LU6 . . . . 92 F4
　Milton Keynes MK6 . . . . . . 47 C8
　Uxbridge UB8 . . . . 208 C8
　Wooburn Green HP10 . . . . 185 E7
Waterside Comb Sch
　HP5 . . . . 154 D6
Waterside Ct HP5 . . . . 154 C7
Waterside Dr SL3 . . . . 207 B4
Waterside Lodge SL6 . . . . 203 C8
Waterside Pk MK12 . . . . . . 33 C7
Waterslade Pens HP17 . . . 126 F6
Waters Reach SL6 . . . . . . 196 A1
WATER STRATFORD 40 A1
Water Stratford Rd MK18 . 51 A7
Water Tower Cl UB8 . . . . . 201 E7

Watery La
　Beachampton MK19 . . . . . . 44 B6
　Brackley NN13 . . . . 38 A7
　Marsworth HP23 . . . . 104 F1
　Turville RG9 . . . . 170 A2
　Wooburn Green HP10 . . . . 185 E8
Watling St
　Bletchley MK2 . . . . 47 D1
　Bow Brickhill MK17 . . . . . . 58 F8
　Granby MK6 . . . . 47 A3
　Milton Keynes, Kiln Farm MK8,
　　MK11 . . . . 33 B2
　Milton Keynes, Shenley Lodge
　　MK6 . . . . 46 C6
　Potterspury NN12 . . . . 18 C3
Watling Terr MK2 . . . . 47 E1
Watlington Ct HP16 . . . . . 152 A8
Watlington Rd OX49 . . . . . 157 A7
Watling Way Pool MK11 . . 32 F4
Watlow Gdns MK18 . . . . . . 41 E2
Watson Cl MK8 . . . . 45 D6
Watten Ct MK2 . . . . 58 E4
Wattleton Rd HP9 . . . . 175 E1
Watts Cl MK19 . . . . 11 A3
Wavell Ct MK15 . . . . 35 B7
Wavell Gdns SL2 . . . . 197 F2
Wavell Rd
　Beaconsfield HP9 . . . . 176 B1
　Maidenhead SL6 . . . . 202 B6
WAVENDON 48 E7
Wavendon Fields MK17 . . . 48 D6
WAVENDON GATE 48 D6
Wavendon Gate Sch MK7 . 48 D6
Wavendon House Dr
　MK17 . . . . 49 B8
Wavendon Rd MK17 . . . . . . 37 C2
Waveney Cl MK16 . . . . 22 E3
Waverley Croft MK10 . . . . . 36 A1
Waverley Rd SL1 . . . . 205 C8
Waverley Wlk HP20 . . . . . . 101 D2
Waxwing Cl HP19 . . . . 101 E3
Wayfarer Rd TW6 . . . . 213 B5
Wayfarers Pk HP4 . . . . . . 134 F4
Waylands TW19 . . . . 211 E1
Wayside
　High Wycombe HP13 . . . . . 173 D7
　Speen HP27 . . . . 150 C4
Wayside Cl HP6 . . . . 154 C1
Wayside Gdns SL9 . . . . . . 188 A4
Wayside Mews SL6 . . . . . . 202 F8
Wealdstone Pl MK6 . . . . . . 35 A4
Weasel La MK3 . . . . 57 C6
Weatherby LU6 . . . . 93 E8
Weathercock Cl MK17 . . . . 49 B5
Weathercock Gdns
　HP15 . . . . 163 C7
Weathercock La MK17 . . . . 49 C4
Weavers Cl MK18 . . . . 52 F6
Weavers End MK19 . . . . . . 11 B2
Weavers Hill MK11 . . . . 33 A4
Weavers La MK14 . . . . 21 C1
Weavers Rd HP23 . . . . 118 E4
Webb Cl
　Chesham HP5 . . . . 144 B1
　Slough SL3 . . . . 206 D2
Webber Heath MK7 . . . . 48 D4
Webber Independent Sch
　The MK14 . . . . 34 D7
Webbs Home Cl MK10 . . . . 36 A2
Webbs Wharf HP19 . . . . . . 115 A8
Webster Cl
　Maidenhead SL6 . . . . 202 A5
　Thame OX9 . . . . 125 F1
Webster Rd HP21 . . . . 116 A6
Websters Mdw MK4 . . . . . . 46 C1
Wedgewood St HP19 . . . . 115 A8
Wedgwood Ave MK14 . . . . . 22 A1
Wedgwood Dr HP14 . . . . . 162 A6
WEEDON 87 D3
Weedon Cl SL9 . . . . 177 B2
Weedon Hill HP6 . . . . 153 D4
Weedon La HP6 . . . . 154 A3
Weedon Rd HP19 . . . . 101 C2
Weekes Dr SL1 . . . . 205 B4
Weill Rd HP21 . . . . 116 A4
Weir La
　Blackthorn OX25 . . . . 81 A4
　East Claydon MK18 . . . . . . 74 E5
　Whitchurch HP22 . . . . 86 F6
Weirside Gdns UB7 . . . . . 208 D5
Welbeck Ave HP21 . . . . . . 116 C6
Welbeck Cl MK10 . . . . 35 F1
Welbeck Rd SL6 . . . . 202 D5
Welburn Ar MK4 . . . . 46 B2
Welby Cl SL6 . . . . 202 A4
Welden SL2 . . . . 206 C7
Welders La
　Chalfont St Giles SL9 . . . . 177 A3
　Seer Green SL9 . . . . 177 B3
Weldon Rise MK5 . . . . 46 B6
Welford Way HP18 . . . . . . 112 F3
Welland Cl SL3 . . . . 212 B8
Welland Dr MK16 . . . . 22 E3
Welland Ho MK3 . . . . 57 E8
Welland Rd
　Aylesbury HP21 . . . . 115 C5
　Longford TW6 . . . . 213 D6
Wellbank SL6 . . . . 196 E1
Wellbrook Mews HP23 . . . 119 B4
Wellcroft LU7 . . . . 105 F5
Wellcroft Rd SL1 . . . . 205 B5
WELL END 184 F5
Well End Cotts SL8 . . . . . 184 F5
Weller Cl HP6 . . . . 154 C1
Weller Ct LU6 . . . . 93 C7
Weller Rd HP6 . . . . 154 C2
Wellesbourne Cres
　HP13 . . . . 162 C3

Wellesbourne Gdns
  HP13 . . . . .162 D2
Welles La MK4 . . . . 45 D3
Wellesley Ave SL0 . . . . . .207 F4
Wellesley Ct SL0 . . . . .207 F4
Wellesley Ho SL4 . . . . . . .210 B6
Wellesley Path SL1 . . . . .206 A4
Wellesley Rd SL1 . . . . . . .206 A4
Welles Rd HP13 . . . . .173 F7
Welley Ave TW19 . . . . . . .211 E3
Welley Rd SL3, TW19 . . . .211 E3
Wellfield HP15 . . . . .163 B3
Wellfield Ct MK15 . . . . . . .35 D8
Wellfield Rd HP14 . . . . . .171 B8
Wellhayes MK14 . . . . .34 F8
WELL HEAD 93 D5
Well Head Rd LU6 . . . . . . .93 C6
Wellhouse Rd SL6 . . . . . .195 E2
Wellhouse Way HP46 . . . .161 E6
Wellingborough Rd MK46 . .6 F5
Wellington Ave HP27 . . . .139 B4
Wellington Cl ⬛ SL6 . . . .202 B8
Wellington Pl
  Aylesbury HP21 . . . . . . .115 E4
  Milton Keynes MK3 . . . . .58 B7
Wellington Rd
  Aylesbury HP21 . . . . . . .115 E4
  High Wycombe HP12 . . . .172 E4
  Maidenhead SL6 . . . . . . .202 D7
  Uxbridge UB8 . . . . .201 C4
Wellington St SL1 . . . . . .206 A4
Well La LU7 . . . . .80 A1
Well Mdw HP19 . . . . .101 D4
Wells Cl SL4 . . . . .210 A7
Well St MK18 . . . . .52 D8
Welsh La MK18 . . . . .40 C5
Welsummer Gr MK5 . . . . . .46 A3
Welton Rd HP21 . . . . .116 B7
WENDOVER 131 C4
Wendover CE Jun Sch
  HP22 . . . . .131 B6
WENDOVER DEAN 141 C5
Wendover Hts HP22 . . . . .131 C6
Wendover Rd
  Bourne End SL8 . . . . . . .185 A5
  Burnham SL1 . . . . .204 B8
  Ellesborough HP17 . . . . .130 D3
Wendover St HP11 . . . . . .172 F7
Wendover Sta HP22 . . . . .131 B4
Wendover Way
  Aylesbury HP21 . . . . . . .115 F6
  High Wycombe HP11 . . . .173 B6
Wendover Woods (Forest
  Wlks)⋆ HP23 . . . . .131 F6
Wenford MK10 . . . . .36 C3
Wenlack Cl UB9 . . . . .190 A1
Wenning La MK4 . . . . .46 B2
Wensleydale Cres MK14 . . .21 C1
Wentworth Ave SL4 . . . . .198 A2
Wentworth Cl HP13 . . . . .173 C8
Wentworth Cres SL4 . . . .202 C6
Wentworth Dr TW6 . . . . .213 B4
Wentworth Way MK3 . . . . .57 C7
Wenwell Cl HP22 . . . . . . .118 A3
Werner Ct HP21 . . . . .115 E4
Werner Terr MK18 . . . . . . .73 B6
Werth Dr MK17 . . . . .49 B2
Wescott Way UB8 . . . . . .201 C3
Wesley Cl HP20 . . . . .102 A2
Wesley Dene ⬛ HP13 . . . .173 B7
Wesley Hill ⬛ HP5 . . . . . .144 B1
Wessex Ct
  ⬛ Stanwell TW19 . . . . . .213 E1
  ⬛ Windsor SL4 . . . . .210 C6
Wessex Rd SL8 . . . . .185 B2
Wessex Road Ind Est
  SL8 . . . . .185 B2
Wessex Way SL6 . . . . . . .202 B4
Wessons Hill SL6 . . . . . . .195 C7
West Acres HP7 . . . . .165 D7
Westanley Ave HP7 . . . . .165 D8
West Ave HP10 . . . . .163 C1
Westborne Ct MK13 . . . . . .34 A6
Westborough St SL6 . . . . .202 C6
Westborough Rd SL6 . . . .202 C6
Westbourne St ⬛ HP11 . .172 F7
Westbrook End MK17 . . . . .57 C3
Westbrook Hay Prep Sch
  HP1 . . . . .146 D7
WESTBURY 39 B4
Westbury Cl
  Bicester OX27 . . . . .71 E2
  Newport Pagnell MK16 . . .22 B4
Westbury Court Bsns Ctr
  OX27 . . . . .71 C4
Westbury Farm Studios
  MK5 . . . . .45 F4
Westbury Ho ⬛ HP20 . . .101 D1
Westbury La MK16 . . . . . . .22 A5
Westbury Mill HP13 . . . . . .38 F4
Westbury Terr OX27 . . . . . .71 E2
West Cl SL7 . . . . .193 D7
Westcliffe MK8 . . . . .33 C2
Westcoign Ho SL6 . . . . . .203 B8
West Comm SL9 . . . . . . .188 D6
West Common Cl SL9 . . . .188 E6
West Common Rd UB8 . . .201 D6
WESTCOTT 98 C2
Westcott CE Sch HP18 . . . .98 A7
Westcott Venture Pk
  HP18 . . . . .98 A6
West Cres SL4 . . . . .209 F6
WESTCROFT 45 E2
Westcroft
  Slough SL2 . . . . .198 B1
  Tring HP23 . . . . .119 A3
Westcroft Rdbt MK4 . . . . . .46 A2

Westcroft Stables⋆
  HP27 . . . . .150 B3
West Ct
  Bray SL6 . . . . .203 C4
  High Wycombe HP13 . . . .161 D3
West Dales MK13 . . . . .34 C5
West Dean SL6 . . . . .202 F8
Westdean La SL6 . . . . . . .143 C3
Westdown Gdns LU6 . . . . .93 F7
West Dr HP13 . . . . .173 D8
WEST DRAYTON 208 D3
West Drayton Park Ave
  UB7 . . . . .208 E4
West Drayton Prim Sch
  UB7 . . . . .208 E4
West Drayton Sta UB7 . . .208 E5
West Edge OX27 . . . . .71 E2
WEST END 63 C2
West End HP22 . . . . .116 E2
West End Cl MK18 . . . . . . .63 C2
West End Ct SL2 . . . . .198 F4
West End La SL2 . . . . .198 E4
West End Pl HP22 . . . . . . .116 E2
West End Rd
  Cheddington LU7 . . . . . .104 F7
  High Wycombe HP11 . . . .172 F7
West End St HP11 . . . . . . .172 F7
Western Ave
  Buckingham MK18 . . . . . .41 C1
  New Denham UB9 . . . . . .201 D8
Western Dene HP15 . . . . .163 A5
Western Dr
  Hanslope MK19 . . . . .11 A3
  Wooburn Green HP10 . . .185 E5
Western House Prim Sch
  SL1 . . . . .204 F5
Western La MK18 . . . . .65 F3
Western Link Rd HP18 . . .100 E4
Western Perimeter Rd
  TW6 . . . . .213 B4
Western Perimeter Road
  Rdbt TW19 . . . . .213 C2
Western Rd
  Great Horwood MK17 . . . .55 A3
  Milton Keynes, Fenny Stratford
    MK2 . . . . .47 D1
  Milton Keynes, Wolverton
    MK12 . . . . .33 C6
  Tring HP23 . . . . .118 F3
West Farm Way MK46 . . . .13 E8
Westfield
  Aylesbury HP21 . . . . . . .115 E3
  Hyde Heath HP6 . . . . . . .153 C4
Westfield Ave MK19 . . . . . .31 D5
Westfield Bglws SL7 . . . . .192 F5
Westfield Cotts SL7 . . . . .192 F5
Westfield Fst Sch HP4 . . . .134 F5
Westfield Rd
  Beaconsfield HP9 . . . . . .175 C1
  Berkhamsted HP4 . . . . . .134 E6
  Dunstable LU6 . . . . .93 F8
  Maidenhead SL6 . . . . . . .202 B7
  Milton Keynes MK2 . . . . .58 C7
  Pitstone LU7 . . . . .105 C3
  Slough SL2 . . . . .198 B1
  Wheatley OX33 . . . . .122 A1
Westfields
  Buckingham MK18 . . . . . .52 C8
  Princes Risborough HP27 .139 D4
Westfield St SL8 . . . . .185 A3
Westfield Wlk HP13 . . . . .172 D6
West Furlong MK18 . . . . . .53 A1
Westgate Cres SL1 . . . . . .204 F6
Westgate Ret Pk SL1 . . . .205 A6
Westgate Sch The SL1 . . .205 A5
Westhill MK14 . . . . .34 D8
West Hill MK17 . . . . .49 D4
Westhorpe Rd SL7 . . . . . .183 F3
WEST HYDE 178 E3
West Hyde La SL9 . . . . . .178 A4
West La
  Bledlow HP27 . . . . .138 B1
  Emberton MK46 . . . . .13 E8
  Henley-on-Thames RG9 . .191 D2
Westland Cl TW19 . . . . . .213 E1
Westlands Ave SL1 . . . . . .204 C7
Westlands Cl SL1 . . . . . . .204 C7
Westlands Rd HP27 . . . . .149 E5
WEST LEITH 118 F2
West Leith HP23 . . . . .118 F1
WESTLINGTON 113 E1
Westlington La HP17 . . . .113 E1
Westlington Lea HP17 . . .113 E2
Westmead
  Monks Risborough HP27 . .139 B5
  Windsor SL4 . . . . .210 B4
West Mead SL6 . . . . .195 F2
Westminster Cl
  Brackley NN13 . . . . .38 A7
  High Wycombe HP11 . . . .173 B4
Westminster Cres NN13 . . .38 A7
Westminster Dr
  Aylesbury HP21 . . . . . . .115 F6
  Milton Keynes MK3 . . . . .47 A2
Westmorland Ave HP21 . .116 B6
Westmorland Ho MK3 . . . .46 F2
Westmorland Rd SL6 . . . .202 D6
Westmount Ave HP7 . . . .165 C8
Weston Ct HP21 . . . . .117 C5
Weston La OX9 . . . . .136 F8
Weston Rd
  Aston Clinton HP22 . . . . .117 C5
  Lewknor OX49 . . . . .157 A8
  Olney MK46 . . . . .6 C1
  Ravenstone MK46 . . . . . . .5 C2
  Slough SL1 . . . . .204 F8
WESTON TURVILLE 116 E3

Weston Turville CE Sch
  HP22 . . . . .116 E3
Weston Turville Resr Wildlife
  Reserve⋆ HP22 . . . . . . .130 F8
WESTON UNDERWOOD . . .6 B1
Weston Way HP22 . . . . . .116 A2
Weston Way Ind Est
  HP22 . . . . .116 A2
Westover Ct HP13 . . . . . . .161 D1
Westover Rd HP13 . . . . . .161 D2
West Pas ⬛ HP23 . . . . . .119 A3
Westpits MK46 . . . . .13 E8
West Point SL1 . . . . .204 D5
West Puxley Cl MK19 . . . . .31 C5
West Rd
  Berkhamsted HP4 . . . . . .135 A5
  Cranfield MK43 . . . . .24 D2
  Maidenhead SL6 . . . . . . .202 E7
  West Drayton UB7 . . . . . .208 F3
  Woburn Sands MK17 . . . . .49 B5
West Richardson St ⬛
  HP11 . . . . .172 F7
Westrick Walk HP16 . . . . .151 C5
West Ridge SL8 . . . . .185 B4
Westridge Cl HP5 . . . . . . .144 A1
Westron Gdns HP23 . . . . .119 B4
Westside La MK16 . . . . . . .12 B6
West Side Rise MK46 . . . . .6 F4
West Spur Rd UB8 . . . . . .201 D2
West Sq SL0 . . . . .207 F7
West St
  Adstock MK18 . . . . .53 F1
  Aylesbury HP19 . . . . . . .101 C1
  Buckingham MK18 . . . . . .41 C1
  Dunstable LU6 . . . . .93 F7
  Henley-on-Thames RG9 . .191 D2
  Leighton Buzzard LU7 . . . .80 F7
  Maidenhead SL6 . . . . . . .202 F7
  Marlow SL7 . . . . .183 D1
  Olney MK46 . . . . .6 F4
  Steeple Claydon MK18 . . . .63 D2
West View
  Chesham HP5 . . . . .144 D2
  Hardwick HP22 . . . . .87 B3
West Way High Wycombe HP13 . . .173 B8
West Way HP9 . . . . .174 F1
West Waye HP13 . . . . . . .162 C2
West Well Cl MK18 . . . . . . .51 A6
West Well La MK18 . . . . . . .51 A6
Westwood HP12 . . . . .172 B3
Westwood Cl
  Little Chalfont HP6 . . . . .166 D8
  Milton Keynes MK8 . . . . .45 F8
Westwood Dr HP6 . . . . . . .166 D8
Westwood Gn SL6 . . . . . .195 F6
Westwood Rd SL7 . . . . . . .183 C1
Westwood Wlk ⬛ HP20 . .101 F2
WEST WYCOMBE 160 F2
West Wycombe Comb Sch
  HP14 . . . . .160 F2
West Wycombe Park⋆
  HP14 . . . . .161 A1
West Wycombe Rd HP12 .161 C1
West Yard Ind Est HP14 . .160 C8
Wetherby Gdns MK3 . . . . .57 D6
Wethered Pk SL7 . . . . . . .183 D1
Wethered Rd
  Burnham SL1 . . . . .204 B8
  Marlow SL7 . . . . .183 D2
Wexford Ct ⬛ SL6 . . . . . .203 B7
Wexham Court Prim Sch
  SL3 . . . . .206 C8
Wexham Park Hospl SL3 .199 C1
Wexham Park La SL3 . . . .199 C1
Wexham Pl 199 D6
Wexham Rd SL1, SL2 . . . .206 B6
Wexham Sch Sports Coll
  SL2 . . . . .206 C8
WEXHAM STREET 199 C4
Wexham Woods SL3 . . . . .206 C8
Weybourne Rd ⬛ MK10 . .36 A4
Wey La HP5 . . . . .154 B7
WHADDON 45 A1
Whaddon CE First Sch
  MK17 . . . . .56 B8
Whaddon Chase HP19 . . .101 D2
Whaddon Hall MK17 . . . . . .45 B2
Whaddon Rd
  Milton Keynes, Shenley Brook
    End MK5 . . . . .46 A3
  Mursley MK17 . . . . .56 C3
  Nash MK17 . . . . .44 D2
  Newport Pagnell MK16 . . .22 B3
  Newton Longville MK17 . . .57 D3
Whaddon Way MK3 . . . . . .46 F2
Whales La OX27 . . . . .71 E2
Whalley Dr MK3 . . . . .47 A2
Wharf Cl
  Old Stratford MK19 . . . . . .32 B7
  Wendover HP22 . . . . . . .131 B5
Wharf Ct UB8 . . . . .201 C1
Wharfe La RG9 . . . . .191 E2
Wharf La
  Berkhamsted HP4 . . . . . .134 C8
  Bourne End SL8 . . . . . . .185 A3
  Old Stratford MK19 . . . . . .32 C7
Wharf Rd HP22 . . . . .131 B5
Wharf Row HP22 . . . . . . .118 B4
Wharfside MK2 . . . . .47 E1
Wharfside Pl MK18 . . . . . .41 E1
Wharf The
  Leighton Buzzard LU7 . . . .80 E6
  Milton Keynes, Giffard Park
    MK14 . . . . .21 E2
  Milton Keynes MK2 . . . . .58 E6
Wharf View MK18 . . . . .41 E1

WHARLEY END 24 D1
Wharton Ho ⬛ HP20 . . . .101 D1
Whatmore St TW19 . . . . .213 A1
Wheatbutts The SL4 . . . . .204 F2
Wheat Cl HP21 . . . . .115 E3
Wheatcroft Cl MK6 . . . . . . .47 A5
Wheatfield OX39 . . . . .147 E8
Wheatfield Cl SL6 . . . . . . .202 A4
Wheatlands LU6 . . . . .92 D7
Wheatlands Rd SL3 . . . . .206 C3
WHEATLEY 122 A1
Wheatley Cl MK4 . . . . .46 C2
Wheatley Park Sch OX33 .122 B2
Wheatley Rd OX33 . . . . . .122 A3
Wheatley Way SL9 . . . . . .177 E4
Wheatsheaf Ho HP10 . . . .185 E7
Wheatsheaf Par SL4 . . . . .211 A2
Wheatstone Cl SL3 . . . . . .206 A3
Wheeler Ave HP10 . . . . . .174 C8
Wheeler Cl HP20 . . . . . . .116 B8
WHEELER END 171 B6
Wheeler Pl
  Beaconsfield HP9 . . . . . .175 F2
  ⬛ Buckingham MK18 . . . .41 E3
Wheelers End OX39 . . . . .147 C6
Wheelers Flats HP10 . . . .174 D8
Wheelers La MK13 . . . . . . .34 A6
Wheelers Orch SL9 . . . . .177 E4
Wheelers Pk HP13 . . . . . .173 D7
Wheelers Yd HP16 . . . . . .152 A7
Wheelwright Mews MK14 . .34 F6
Wheelwright Rd HP27 . . . .138 D7
Wheelwrights HP22 . . . . .116 F2
Wheelwrights Pl SL3 . . . .212 C7
Wheelwrights Way MK3 . . .32 C7
Wheelwrights Yd HP22 . . .85 A5
WHELPLEY HILL 145 D5
Whelpley Hill Pk HP5 . . . .145 D5
Whet Stone Cl MK3 . . . . . .34 B4
Whichcote Gdns HP5 . . . .154 D6
Whichert Cl HP9 . . . . .175 C6
Whichford MK14 . . . . .22 A1
Whielden Cl HP7 . . . . .165 B7
Whielden Gate HP7 . . . . .164 E4
Whielden Gn HP7 . . . . . . .165 B7
Whielden Hts HP7 . . . . . .165 A7
Whielden La
  Coleshill HP7 . . . . .164 E5
  Winchmore Hill HP7 . . . .164 D3
Whielden St HP7 . . . . .165 B7
Whinchat HP19 . . . . .101 E3
Whincup Cl HP11 . . . . . . .172 F4
Whinneys Rd HP10 . . . . . .174 C3
Whipass Hill HP9 . . . . . . .176 A5
WHIPSNADE 107 F8
Whipsnade Park Homes
  LU6 . . . . .93 F1
Whipsnade Rd LU6 . . . . . . .93 F6
Whipsnade Tree Cathedral⋆
  LU6 . . . . .93 F1
Whiskin La HP21 . . . . .115 F4
Whitby Cl MK3 . . . . .47 A2
Whitby Rd SL1 . . . . .205 C6
WHITCHURCH 87 B6
Whitchurch Cl
  Maidenhead SL6 . . . . . . .195 E3
  Westcott HP18 . . . . .98 B7
Whitchurch Comb Sch
  HP22 . . . . .86 E7
Whitchurch Ho ⬛ SL6 . . .202 F7
Whitchurch La HP22 . . . . .86 D8
Whitchurch Rd LU7 . . . . . .78 B1
Whiteacres Dr SL6 . . . . . .203 B1
White Alder MK12 . . . . . . .33 E5
Whitebaker Ct MK14 . . . . .34 F6
Whitebeam Cl HP22 . . . . .116 C3
Whitebrook Pk SL6 . . . . . .196 C4
Whitchurch Cl HP17 . . . . .114 C5
White Cl
  High Wycombe HP13 . . . .161 D1
  Slough SL1 . . . . .205 D5
White Cotts MK18 . . . . . . .29 D4
White Cres HP22 . . . . .131 D7
Whitecross Green Wood
  Wildlife Reserve⋆ OX5 . . .94 C2
Whitecross Rd HP17 . . . . .126 F5
Whitefield La HP16 . . . . . .152 A6
Whiteford Rd SL2 . . . . . . .205 E8
Whitegate Ct MK6 . . . . . . .47 B6
Whitehall SL6 . . . . .196 B1
Whitehall Ave MK10 . . . . . .36 D1
Whitehall Cl UB8 . . . . .201 D4
Whitehall Inf Sch UB8 . . .201 C4
Whitehall Jun Sch UB8 . . .201 C4
Whitehall La TW19 . . . . . .212 A1
Whitehall Rd UB8 . . . . . . .201 D3
Whitehall St ⬛ HP20 . . . .101 D1
White Hart Cl
  Chalfont St Giles HP8 . . .177 A7
  Ludgershall HP18 . . . . . . .96 B8
White Hart Field HP22 . . . .85 B4
White Hart La HP7 . . . . . .127 A5
White Hart Mdw HP9 . . . .175 E1
White Hart Rd
  ⬛ Maidenhead SL6 . . . . .202 F7
  Slough SL1 . . . . .205 D3
White Hart St ⬛ HP11 . . .173 A4
Whitehaven SL1 . . . . .205 D3
Whitehaven Cl ⬛ MK10 . . .36 A4
Whitehead Way HP21 . . . .115 D6
Whitehead W MK18 . . . . . .41 D3
White Hermitage SL4 . . . .211 C4
Whitehill
  Berkhamsted HP4 . . . . . .135 D5
  Olney MK46 . . . . .6 E5
White Hill
  Ashley Green HP4, HP5 . . .145 C7

White Hill continued
  Beaconsfield HP9, HP10 . .185 F8
  Chesham HP5 . . . . .144 D1
  High Wycombe HP13 . . . .162 B2
  Remenham Hill RG9 . . . . .192 A2
White Hill Cl
  Chesham HP5 . . . . .144 D1
  Marlow Bottom SL7 . . . . .183 C6
Whitehill Cl MK4 . . . . .135 D5
Whitehill La LU7 . . . . .105 D3
White Hill La LU7 . . . . . . .105 D3
White Horse Ct HP6 . . . . .154 C2
White Horse Dr MK4 . . . . . .46 C2
White Horse La HP22 . . . . .87 A6
White Horse Rd SL4 . . . . .209 D5
Whitehorse Yd MK11 . . . . .32 D5
White Hos 50 D6
Whitehouse Cl HP10 . . . . .174 E1
White House La HP22 . . . .174 E2
Whitehouse Prim Sch
  NK19 . . . . .45 C8
Whitehouse Way
  Iver Heath SL0 . . . . .200 D2
  Slough SL3 . . . . .206 D3
Whitelands Ave WD3 . . . .167 C5
Whitelands Rd HP12 . . . . .172 D7
Whitelands Way HP22 . . .172 D7
WHITELEAF 139 D5
Whiteleaf Ctr The HP20 . .101 F1
Whiteleaf Hill Nature
  Reserve⋆ HP27 . . . . . . .139 E4
Whiteleaf Way HP27 . . . . .139 D5
Whiteley SL4 . . . . .209 E7
Whiteley Cres MK3 . . . . . . .57 F6
White Lilies Island SL4 . . .210 B7
White Lion Cl HP7 . . . . . . .166 A8
White Lion Rd HP7 . . . . . .166 B8
Whitelock Ho RG9 . . . . . .191 E3
White Lodge Cl SL7 . . . . .183 C6
White Paddock SL6 . . . . . .202 A2
Whitepit La HP10 . . . . . . .185 D7
White Rock SL6 . . . . .196 B1
Whites Cl MK18 . . . . .63 D3
Whites Croft MK6 . . . . .46 F6
Whites La SL3 . . . . .211 B8
White Spire Sch MK3 . . . . .46 F1
Whitethorn Ave MK7 . . . .208 F6
Whitethorn Cl HP22 . . . . .130 A8
Whitethorn Pl UB7 . . . . . .208 F5
Whitethorns MK16 . . . . . . .22 B3
White View ⬛ HP20 . . . . .101 F3
Whitewood Rd HP4 . . . . . .135 A4
WHITFIELD 26 D3
Whitfield Rd HP14 . . . . . . .162 A6
Whitfield Way WD3 . . . . . .167 F1
Whitley Cl TW19 . . . . .213 E1
Whitley Ct HP21 . . . . .115 E4
Whitmees Cl MK46 . . . . . . .6 E4
Whitney Rdbt MK4 . . . . . . .45 E2
Whitsun Pasture MK15 . . . .35 B7
Whittaker Rd SL2 . . . . . . .197 E1
Whittenham Cl SL2 . . . . . .206 A5
Whittingham Ave HP22 . .131 D6
Whittington Chase MK4 . . .45 E1
Whittle Ct MK5 . . . . .46 C7
Whittle Parkway SL1 . . . .204 D7
Whitton Way MK16 . . . . . .22 C3
Whitworth La MK5 . . . . . . .46 B7
Whurley Way SL6 . . . . . . .195 E2
Whybrow Gdns HP4 . . . . .135 E6
Whyteladyes La SL6 . . . . .195 E2
Whytingham Rd HP23 . . . .119 C4
WICKEN 31 B3
Wicken Park Rd MK19 . . . .31 B2
Wicken Rd MK18 . . . . .30 E1
Wickets The SL6 . . . . .202 C7
Wicket The SL1 . . . . .205 E3
Wickham Cl HP19 . . . . . . .101 E2
Wick Rd HP23 . . . . .133 D8
Wickstead Ave MK8 . . . . . .45 D6
Widbrook Rd SL6 . . . . . . .196 B3
Widdenton View HP14 . . .171 C5
Widecroft Rd SL0 . . . . . . .207 E7
Widgeon Ho HP11 . . . . . .173 C6
Widgeon Rd TW6 . . . . . . .213 B4
Widmere Field HP16 . . . . .151 C5
Widmere La SL7 . . . . .183 A6
WIDMER END 162 E6
Widmer End Com Comb Sch
  HP15 . . . . .162 F6
WIDMOOR 185 E3
Widmore Cl HP5 . . . . .143 E5
Widnell La OX25 . . . . .95 C7
Wigan's La HP14 . . . . .148 C6
Wiggington Ho SL4 . . . . . .210 D7
WIGGINTON 119 D1
WIGGINTON BOTTOM . . .133 D8
Wigginton Bottom HP23 . .133 E8
Wiggles La HP23 . . . . .110 F7
Wigmore Ct HP19 . . . . . . .101 A2
Wigmore Rd HP19 . . . . . .101 A2
Wigwell Gdns MK15 . . . . . .55 A2
Wilberforce Mews ⬛
  SL6 . . . . .202 F7
Wildacre Rd MK5 . . . . .46 A4
Wilderness The HP4 . . . . .135 C4
Wildgreen N SL3 . . . . .207 A2
Wildgreen S SL3 . . . . .207 A2
Wilds Cross MK14 . . . . . . .21 F3
Wildwood Ct WD3 . . . . . . .167 F5
Wilford Cl MK15 . . . . .35 C2
Wilford Rd SL3 . . . . .206 F2
Wilfrids Wood Cl HP10 . . .185 B6

Wilkie Ct **8** MK17 . . . . 49 A5
Wilkinson Cl MK3 . . . . 58 A8
Wilks Croft MK5 . . . . 45 F7
WILLEN 35 D7
Willen La MK14 . . . . 34 F8
WILLEN PARK 35 C6
Willen Park Ave MK15 . . . 35 B6
Willen Prim Sch MK15 . . . 35 C7
Willen Rd
  Milton Keynes MK10 . . . . . . 35 F3
  Newport Pagnell MK16 . . . 22 D3
Willets Rise MK5 . . . . 46 A5
Willetts La UB9 . . . . 200 F7
Willey Ct MK11 . . . . 32 F4
William Bandy Cl LU7 . . . . 79 F3
William Burt Cl HP21 . . . . 116 F1
William Ellis Cl SL4 . . . . . 211 A1
William Fiske Ho **4** HP4 135 C4
William Harding HP21 115 E7
William Harding Comb Sch
  HP21 . . . . 116 A5
William Hartley Yd SL3 . . 199 B1
William Hill Dr HP22 . . . . 102 C4
William Ho **4** HP13 . . . . 173 F5
William Moulder Ct HP5 . 144 B3
Williams Circ MK7 . . . . . . 48 A4
Williams Cl
  Aylesbury HP19 . . . . 101 D1
  Hanslope MK19 . . . . 10 F3
William Shakman Ho
  HP8 . . . . 177 B8
William Smith Cl MK15 . . 35 C3
William St
  Berkhamsted HP4 . . . . . . 135 D4
  Slough SL1 . . . . 205 F5
  Windsor SL4 . . . . 210 D6
William Sutton Ho MK5 . . 46 A6
Williams Way HP27 . . . . . 138 D6
Willis Pl SL1 . . . . 206 C1
Willis Rd HP17 . . . . 127 A6
Willmott Cl HP19 . . . . 101 D4
Willoners SL2 . . . . 205 A8
Willoughby Ave UB10 . . . 201 E3
Willoughby Rd SL3 . . . . . 207 B3
Willoughby's Wlk HP13 . . 161 D2
Willow Ave
  High Wycombe HP12 . . . . 172 B4
  New Denham UB9 . . . . . . 201 C6
  West Drayton UB7 . . . . . . 208 F6
WILLOWBANK 201 C7
Willow Bank SL7 . . . . 183 D5
Willowbank Terr **6**
  HP21 . . . . 115 E8
Willowbrook
  Slough SL1 . . . . 205 D2
  Wendover HP22 . . . . 131 B4
Willow Chase
  Chesham HP5 . . . . 144 B1
  Hazlemere HP15 . . . . 162 E3
Willow Cl
  Chalfont St Peter SL9 . . . 177 E1
  Colnbrook SL3 . . . . 212 C7
  Flackwell Heath HP10 . . . 185 C6
  Maidenhead SL6 . . . . 195 D1
  Moulsoe MK16 . . . . 36 E8
Willow Crescent E UB9 . . 201 C7
Willow Crescent W UB9 . 201 C7
Willow Ct
  2 Aylesbury, Quarrendon
  HP19 . . . . 101 A2
  Aylesbury, Walton Court
  HP21 . . . . 115 C6
  High Wycombe HP11 . . . . 173 E4
  Walter's Ash HP14 . . . . . 161 C8
Willow Dr
  Buckingham MK18 . . . . . . 52 F7
  Maidenhead SL6 . . . . 203 B2
Willow End HP22 . . . . 116 F2
Willowford MK13 . . . . 33 E5
Willow Gr MK19 . . . . 32 B6
Willow Herb HP19 . . . . . . 101 E4
Willow Ho LU7 . . . . 80 E7
Willow La
  Amersham HP7 . . . . 165 F6
  Milton Keynes MK11 . . . . . 32 C5
Willowmead HP17 . . . . . . 114 F5
Willowmead Cl **10** SL7. . 183 D3
Willowmead Gdns SL7 . . 183 D3
Willowmead Rd **8** SL7. . 183 D3
Willowmead Sq **9** SL7 . 183 D3
Willow Parade SL3 . . . . . 207 A3
Willow Pk SL2 . . . . 199 A5
Willow Pl SL4 . . . . 210 C8
Willow Prim Sch SL2 . . . 206 B6
Willow Rd
  Aylesbury HP19 . . . . 101 D1
  Brackley NN13 . . . . 38 A6
  Chinnor OX39 . . . . 147 C6
  Great Horwood MK17 . . . . 55 A3
  Poyle SL3 . . . . 212 E5
  Thame OX9 . . . . 125 F1
Willow Rise HP17 . . . . 127 A7
Willows Rd SL8 . . . . 185 B4
Willows Riverside Pk The
  SL4 . . . . 209 C7
Willows Sch The MK6 . . . . 35 A2
Willows The
  Amersham HP6 . . . . 154 B4
  4 Bourne End SL8 . . . . 185 B3
  Edlesborough LU6 . . . . 92 F3
  High Wycombe HP12 . . . . 172 E8
  Longwick HP27 . . . . 138 E6
  Windsor SL4 . . . . 209 D7
Willow Way
  Loudwater HP11 . . . . 174 B2

Willow Way continued
  Milton Keynes MK2 . . . . . . 58 C7
  Princes Risborough HP27 . 139 A3
  Wing LU7 . . . . 79 E3
Willow Wlk HP15 . . . . 163 A3
Willow Wood Cl SL1 . . . . 197 B3
Willow Wren MK14 . . . . . . 21 F2
Wilmar Cl UB8 . . . . 201 D5
Wilmin Gr MK5 . . . . 46 B7
Wilmot Rd SL1 . . . . 197 B2
Wilsley Pound MK7 . . . . . . 48 B8
Wilson Ct MK8 . . . . 45 F7
WILSTONE 104 D1
WILSTONE GREEN 118 D8
Wilstone Resr ★ HP22,
  HP23 . . . . 118 C7
Wilton Ave MK3 . . . . 58 A8
Wilton Cl UB7 . . . . 213 D8
Wilton Cres
  Beaconsfield HP9 . . . . . . 175 E3
  Windsor SL4 . . . . 209 D4
Wilton Hollow HP9 . . . . . 175 F3
Wilton La HP9 . . . . 176 E4
WILTON PARK 176 B1
Wilton Rd HP9 . . . . 175 E3
Wiltshire Ave SL2 . . . . . . 198 C1
Wiltshire Lodge **2** SL6 . 202 F6
Wiltshire Rd **2** SL7 . . . . 183 F3
Wiltshire Way MK3 . . . . . . 46 E1
Wimbledon Pl MK13 . . . . . 34 D3
Wimblington Dr MK6 . . . . . 47 A4
Wimborne Cres MK4 . . . . . 45 F2
Wimpole Rd UB7 . . . . 208 D5
Winbury Ct SL6 . . . . 202 E7
Winbury Pl SL6 . . . . 203 B3
Wincanton Hill MK3 . . . . . 57 C6
Winchbottom La
  High Wycombe HP10 . . . . 173 B1
  Little Marlow SL7, HP10 . . 184 B7
Winchcombe Mdws
  Stantonbury MK14 . . . . . . 21 C1
  Stantonbury MK14 . . . . . . 34 C8
Winchester Circ MK10. . . . 36 B1
Winchester Cl
  Amersham HP7 . . . . 165 E8
  Poyle SL3 . . . . 212 E6
Winchester Ct HP11. . . . . 174 B3
Winchester Dr SL6 . . . . . 202 B3
Winchester Ho HP21 . . . . 115 F6
WINCHMORE HILL 164 D2
Winch Terr SL4 . . . . 209 D5
Windermere Cl
  Aylesbury HP21 . . . . 116 B6
  Chorleywood WD3 . . . . . . 167 D4
Windermere Dr MK2 . . . . . 58 D5
Windermere Gdns LU7 . . . 80 C7
Windermere Way
  Slough SL1 . . . . 204 C7
  West Drayton UB7 . . . . . . 208 E5
Windmill Cl
  Aylesbury HP19 . . . . 115 B8
  Buckingham MK18 . . . . . . 41 F1
  Ivinghoe LU7 . . . . 105 F5
  Windsor SL4 . . . . 210 B5
Windmill Dr HP15 . . . . . . 162 F6
Windmill Hill
  Chipperfield WD4. . . . . . . 156 F7
  Coleshill HP7 . . . . 164 F2
  Princes Risborough HP27 . 139 B2
Windmill Hill Dr MK3. . . . . 57 D7
Windmill Hill Rdbt MK4 . . 46 C1
Windmill La HP15 . . . . . . 162 F6
Windmill Par HP15 . . . . . 162 F6
Windmill Rd
  Chalfont St Peter SL9 . . . 177 D3
  Cookham Rise SL6 . . . . . . 195 E6
  Fulmer SL3. . . . . 199 D7
  Haddenham HP17 . . . . . . 126 F6
  Slough SL1 . . . . 205 D5
  Thame OX9 . . . . 126 E1
Windmill St HP18 . . . . 96 A1
Windmill Way
  Cranfield MK43 . . . . 25 C3
  Tring HP23 . . . . 118 F4
Windmill Wood HP6 . . . . 154 A2
Windrush Ave SL3 . . . . . . 207 B3
WINDSOR 210 E6
Windsor Ave
  Leighton Buzzard LU7 . . . . 80 F7
  Newport Pagnell MK16 . . . 22 C4
Windsor Boys' Sch The
  SL4 . . . . 210 B6
Windsor Bsns Ctr SL4 . . . 210 C6
Windsor Castle ★ SL4. . . . 210 E7
Windsor Cl
  Bovingdon HP3 . . . . 146 A3
  Burnham SL1 . . . . 197 C1
Windsor Cres HP10 . . . . . 174 C2
Windsor Ct HP6 . . . . 154 D1
Windsor Dr HP13 . . . . 162 D1
Windsor End HP9 . . . . . . 186 F8
Windsor & Eton Central Sta
  SL4 . . . . 210 D6
Windsor & Eton Riverside Sta
  SL4 . . . . 210 D7
Windsor Girls' Sch SL4 . . 210 A4
Windsor Great Pk ★ SL4 . 210 B2
Windsor Hall SL4 . . . . . . 210 F4

Windsor Hill
  Monks Risborough HP27 . . 139 C5
  Wooburn Green HP10 . . . 185 F5
Windsor Ho **4** SL1. . . . . 205 F3
Windsor La
  Burnham SL1 . . . . 197 C1
  Little Kingshill HP16 . . . . 152 C3
Windsor Rd
  Aylesbury HP21 . . . . 116 A7
  Chesham HP5 . . . . 144 B3
  Datchet SL3 . . . . 211 A7
  Gerrards Cross SL9 . . . . . 188 C3
  Maidenhead SL6 . . . . 203 C2
  Oakley Green SL4 . . . . . . 209 A7
  Pitstone LU7 . . . . 105 C3
  Slough SL1 . . . . 205 E4
  Wraysbury TW19 . . . . . . 211 E1
Windsor Royal Sta **1**
  SL4 . . . . 210 D6
Windsor St
  Milton Keynes MK2 . . . . . . 58 C7
  Milton Keynes, Wolverton
  MK12 . . . . 33 C6
  Uxbridge UB8 . . . . 201 C5
Winemar Cl MK19 . . . . 11 A3
Winfold La MK4 . . . . 46 B1
WING 79 F2
Wingate Ave HP13 . . . . . . 173 E7
Wingate Circ MK7 . . . . . . 48 A4
Wingate Cl HP13 . . . . 173 E7
Wingate Wlk HP20 . . . . . . 116 A7
Wingbury Ctyd Bsns Village
  HP22 . . . . 89 D5
Wing Cl SL7 . . . . 183 C1
Wingfield Gr MK10 . . . . . . 36 A2
WINGRAVE 89 C3
Wingrave CE Comb Sch
  HP22 . . . . 89 A3
Wingrave Cross Rds HP22 88 F4
Wingrave Rd
  Aston Abbotts HP22 . . . . . 88 E4
  Long Marston HP23 . . . . . 104 D1
  Tring HP23 . . . . 119 B5
Wing Rd
  Cublington LU7 . . . . 78 C1
  Leighton Buzzard LU7 . . . . 80 D5
  Stewkley LU7 . . . . 78 F6
Winkers Cl SL9 . . . . 177 F2
Winkers La SL9 . . . . 177 F3
Winkfield La SL4 . . . . 209 A1
Winkfield Rd SL4 . . . . 209 E2
Winnock Rd UB7 . . . . 208 D5
Winsford Hill MK4 . . . . 46 E3
WINSLOW 66 B4
Winslow CE Comb Sch
  MK18 . . . . 66 A5
Winslow Field HP16 . . . . . 151 E8
Winslow Gdns HP13 . . . . 174 A7
Winslow Rd
  Granborough MK18 . . . . . . 75 F7
  Great Horwood MK17 . . . . 54 F1
  Little Horwood MK17. . . . . 55 D1
  Nash MK17 . . . . 55 C8
  Swanbourne MK17 . . . . . . 66 F3
  Wingrave HP22 . . . . 89 B3
Winstanley La MK5. . . . . . . 46 C6
Winston Ct SL6 . . . . 202 A8
Winstone Cl HP6. . . . . 154 B5
Winston Gdns HP4 . . . . . . 134 F4
Winston Ho HP11 . . . . 174 A4
Winston Mews HP18 . . . . 100 E5
Winterburn MK13 . . . . 34 B5
Winter Ct **6** SL7 . . . . . . 183 E2
Wintergreen Bvd **1** UB7 208 F4
WINTERHILL 46 D8
Winter Hill SL6 . . . . 184 C1
Winter Hill Rd SL6 . . . . . . 195 A4
Winters Acre SL1 . . . . . . 204 B8
Winters Way HP15 . . . . . . 163 D7
Winterton Dr HP21 . . . . . 115 E4
Wintoun Path SL2. . . . . . . 197 E1
Winvale SL1 . . . . 205 E3
Winwood
  Slough SL2. . . . . 206 C7
  Windsor SL4 . . . . 209 F6
Winwood Cl MK19. . . . . . . 31 E5
Winwood Dr HP22 . . . . 85 A5
Wirecut Rise **3** MK17 . . . 49 A5
Wirethorn Furlong HP17 . 126 E6
Wise La HP27 . . . . 208 D2
Wisewood Rd MK4, MK5 . . 45 E4
Wishart Gn MK7 . . . . 48 E5
Wisley Ave MK13 . . . . 34 D3
Wistmans MK4. . . . . 46 D4
Witan Ct MK9 . . . . 34 D2
Witan Gate MK9 . . . . 34 D1
Witchell MK17 . . . . 131 B4
Witham Ct MK3 . . . . 46 D1
Witham Way HP21 . . . . . . 115 C4
Witheridge La HP9, HP10. 175 B7
Withey Cl SL4 . . . . 209 E6
Withington MK13 . . . . 34 A5
Withycombe MK4 . . . . 46 D4
Withycroft SL3. . . . . 206 E7
Witney Cl UB10 . . . . 201 F8
Wittington Cotts SL7. . . . 193 D6
Wittmills Oak MK18 . . . . . 41 E1
Witton Ho WD3 . . . . 167 D4
Wivelsfield LU6. . . . . 92 E6
Wixon Path HP19 . . . . . . 115 A8
Wizard Wy MK10 . . . . 35 E2
Wker Pl HP21 . . . . 115 E5
Woad La MK14 . . . . 34 E8
WOBURN 60 F7
Woburn Ave MK12 . . . . . . 33 C6
Woburn Ct LU7 . . . . 80 E6
Woburn La MK17 . . . . 49 E4
Woburn Lower Sch MK17. 60 F7

Woburn Rd
  Aspley Heath MK17 . . . . . 49 C2
  Little Brickhill MK17 . . . . . 59 E6
  Sheeplane MK17, LU7. . . . 60 C1
WOBURN SANDS 49 A5
Woburn Sands Rd MK17. . 48 D3
Woburn Sands Sta MK17 . 49 A5
Wodehouse Wlk MK16 . . . 22 A5
Wolf La SL4 . . . . 209 E4
Wolfscote La MK4. . . . . . . 46 B3
Wolseley Cl NN13 . . . . 26 A1
Wolsey Gdns MK13. . . . . . 34 A4
Wolstan Cl UB9 . . . . 190 A1
Wolston Mdw MK10 . . . . . 35 F3
WOLVERTON. 33 C5
WOLVERTON MILL 33 A6
Wolverton Park Rd MK12. 33 D8
Wolverton Rd
  Castlethorpe MK19 . . . . . . 20 B5
  Milton Keynes, Giffard Park
  MK16 . . . . 21 E2
  Milton Keynes, Stony Stratford
  MK11 . . . . 32 E6
  Milton Keynes, Wolverton MK12,
  MK19 . . . . 33 E8
  Newport Pagnell MK16 . . . 22 B4
Wolverton Sta MK12 . . . . 33 E7
WOOBURN 185 D4
Wooburn Common Rd HP10,
  SL1. . . . . 186 A2
Wooburn Grange HP10 . . 185 D3
WOOBURN GREEN 185 F7
Wooburn Green La HP9 . 186 A8
Wooburn Manor Pk
  HP10 . . . . 185 E5
Wooburn Mead HP10. . . . 185 E6
Wooburn Mews HP10 . . . 185 E5
WOOBURN MOOR 174 C1
Wooburn Town HP10. . . . 185 D4
Woodall Cl MK10. . . . . 35 E3
Woodbank Ave SL9 . . . . . 188 D5
Woodbank Dr HP8 . . . . . . 177 D7
Woodbine Cl HP27 . . . . . . 138 E5
Woodbine Cotts SL9 . . . . 188 D8
Woodbridge Ho UB8 . . . . 201 C5
WOODBURN COMMON . . 186 B3
Woodbury Cl SL3 . . . . . . 185 C3
Woodchester Pk HP9 . . . 175 C6
Wood Cl SL4. . . . . 210 C3
Woodcock Ave HP14 . . . . 161 B8
Woodcote SL6 . . . . 202 D6
Woodcote Gn HP13 . . . . . 161 D2
Woodcote Lawns HP5 . . . 144 A4
Woodcroft Rd HP5 . . . . . 144 D3
WOOD END
  Little Horwood MK17. . . . . 55 E2
  Nash 55 C8
Wood End
  Little Horwood MK17. . . . . 55 E2
  Nash MK17 . . . . 55 C8
Wood End Cl SL2 . . . . . . 187 D1
Wood End Fst Sch MK14. . 34 D8
Wood End La MK16 . . . . . 23 E1
Woodfield HP27 . . . . 149 D6
Woodfield Dr SL6 . . . . . . 202 A6
Woodfield Pk HP6 . . . . . . 154 B5
Woodfield Rd HP27 . . . . . 139 C4
Woodford Cl HP19 . . . . . . 115 B7
Woodford Way SL2 . . . . . 198 A2
Wood Gn MK10 . . . . 47 F8
WOOD GREEN 27 F2
Woodhall Cl UB8. . . . . 201 D7
WOODHAM 83 E1
Woodhill Ave SL9 . . . . . . 189 A5
Woodhill Ct
  Amersham HP6 . . . . 154 D2
  Gerrards Cross SL9. . . . . . 188 E4
Woodhouse Ct MK14 . . . . 34 D6
Woodhurst Dr UB9 . . . . . 189 F6
Woodhurst Rd SL6 . . . . . 196 B1
Woodhurst South SL6. . . 196 C1
Wood La
  Aspley Guise MK17 . . . . . 49 D4
  Iver SL0. . . . . 207 C3
  Milton Keynes MK14 . . . . . 34 E8
  Slough SL1 . . . . 205 A4
  South Heath HP16 . . . . . . 152 E8
  Tingewick MK18 . . . . 51 B6
  Weston Underwood MK46. . . 6 A2
Woodland Ave
  Leighton Buzzard LU7 . . . . 70 F2
  Slough SL1 . . . . 205 D6
  Windsor SL4 . . . . 209 F3
Woodland Cl
  High Wycombe HP12 . . . . 172 C6
  Marlow SL7 . . . . 183 E4
  Tring HP23 . . . . 118 F2
Woodland Glade SL2. . . . 187 D1
Woodland Grange SL0 . . 207 E3
Woodland La WD3 . . . . . . 167 D6
Woodland Pl WD3 . . . . . . 167 F5
Woodland Rd WD3. . . . . . 178 D5
Woodlands SL9 . . . . 188 F5
Woodlands Ave HP4 . . . . 135 D4
Woodlands Bsns Pk
  Maidenhead SL6 . . . . 202 A2
  Milton Keynes MK14 . . . . . 34 C6
Woodlands Cl
  Buckingham MK18. . . . . . . 41 E2
  Gerrards Cross SL9. . . . . . 189 A5
  Holmer Green HP15 . . . . . 163 C6
Woodlands Cotts **1** SL2. 198 C7
Woodlands Cres MK18 . . . 41 D2
Woodlands Dr
  Beaconsfield HP9 . . . . . . 175 C4
  Walter's Ash HP14 . . . . . 161 C8
Woodlands Farm SL6 . . . 195 C6

Woodlands Glade HP9 . . 175 C4
Woodlands Hill HP9. . . . . 186 E5
Woodlands Park Ave
  SL6. . . . . 202 A2
Woodlands Park Prim Sch
  SL6. . . . . 202 A1
Woodlands Park Rd SL6. 202 A3
Woodlands The
  Amersham HP6 . . . . 154 C4
  Tylers Green HP10. . . . . . 162 F3
Woodlands View HP13 . . 174 A7
Woodland View
  Chesham HP5 . . . . 154 D6
  Milton Keynes MK12 . . . . . 33 D5
Woodland Way
  Marlow SL7 . . . . 183 E4
  Woburn Sands MK17. . . . . 49 A4
Woodlane Cl HP10 . . . . . . 173 F1
Wood Lane Cl
  Flackwell Heath HP10. . . . 173 F1
  Iver Heath SL0 . . . . 200 B2
Woodlane Gdns HP10 . . . 174 A1
Woodley Ct HP7 . . . . 165 D8
Woodley Headland MK6. . 47 C7
Woodley Hill HP5 . . . . . . 154 D5
Woodman Cl LU7 . . . . 79 F3
Woodmans Cl MK19 . . . . . 31 E4
Woodmans Croft HP19 . . 115 A8
Woodmoor End SL6. . . . . 196 B7
Woodpiece Rd OX25 . . . . 94 C7
Woodpits La MK46. . . . . . . 7 F7
Wood Pond Cl HP9. . . . . . 176 C4
Wood Rd MK43 . . . . 3 F7
WOODROW 164 D5
Woodruff Ave MK14 . . . . . 34 E4
Woodrush Cl MK6 . . . . 47 B4
Woodside
  Aspley Guise MK17 . . . . . 49 D3
  Eaton Bray LU6 . . . . 92 E6
  Flackwell Heath HP10. . . . 185 C6
  Milton Keynes MK11 . . . . . 32 E6
Woodside Ave
  Amersham HP6 . . . . 154 D3
  Beaconsfield HP9 . . . . . . 175 C4
  Flackwell Heath HP10. . . . 185 C7
Woodside Cl
  Amersham HP6 . . . . 154 D1
  Beaconsfield HP9 . . . . . . 175 C3
  Chalfont St Peter SL9 . . . 177 E1
  Loudwater HP11 . . . . 174 B2
Woodside Hill SL9 . . . . . . 177 E1
Woodside Jun Sch HP6 . 154 E1
Woodside Rd
  Amersham HP6 . . . . 154 D1
  Beaconsfield HP9 . . . . . . 175 C4
  High Wycombe HP13 . . . . 174 A8
Woodside Way
  Leighton Buzzard LU7 . . . . 80 D6
  Tylers Green HP10. . . . . . 174 C8
Woods La NN12 . . . . 18 E3
Woods Pl
  13 Tring HP23 . . . . 119 A3
  Wendover HP22 . . . . 131 B4
Woodspring Ct **2** MK10. . 35 F1
Wood St
  Milton Keynes MK13 . . . . . 33 F7
  Waddesdon HP18 . . . . . . 99 A7
  Woburn Sands MK17. . . . . 49 B4
Woodstock Ave SL3 . . . . 206 D2
Woodstock Cl
  Aylesbury HP21 . . . . 116 B6
  Maidenhead SL6 . . . . 195 F1
Woodstock Ct MK13. . . . . 34 B7
Woodstock Dr UB10. . . . . 201 F8
Woodview Cl HP12 . . . . . 161 B2
Wood View Cotts HP5 . . . 144 B7
Woodview Dr HP16 . . . . . 150 C5
Woodville OX39 . . . . 147 C5
Woodville Cres NN12. . . . . 18 E6
Woodward Ho **4** MK2. . . 58 C8
Woodward Pl MK8 . . . . . . 34 A1
Woodway HP27 . . . . 149 D6
Wood Way HP9 . . . . 174 F1
Woodway Farm Ind Est
  HP18. . . . . 124 F8
Woodways HP17 . . . . 127 A6
Wood White Dr HP19. . . . 101 B4
Woodwicks WD3 . . . . 178 D5
Woollerton Cres HP22. . . 131 D5
Woollerton Ct HP27 . . . . 139 B4
Woolmans MK11 . . . . 33 A4
Woolpack Grange MK14. . 21 C1
Woolrich Gdns MK11 . . . . 32 E5
WOOLSTONE. 35 D3
Wooster Rd HP9 . . . . 175 D4
Wooton Ct MK15. . . . . 33 F8
WOOTTON BOURNE END . 25 E8
Wootton Dr HP10. . . . . . . 185 E8
Wootton Gn OX27. . . . . . . 72 E6
Wootton La HP17 . . . . . . 113 E1
Wootton Way SL6. . . . . . . 202 C6
Worcester Cl
  Maidenhead SL6 . . . . 202 D3
  Newport Pagnell MK16 . . . 22 A3
Worcester Gdns SL1 . . . . 205 D4
Worcester Ho MK3. . . . . . 46 F2
Worcester Rd UB8 . . . . . 208 D4
Wordsworth Ave MK16. . . 22 A4
Wordsworth Dr MK3 . . . . 58 A7
Wordsworth Rd
  High Wycombe HP11 . . . . 173 A5
  Slough SL2. . . . . 197 D1
Wordsworth Way UB7. . . 208 E2
WORLD'S END 130 F7
World's End La HP22 . . . . 130 F8
Worley Pl HP9 . . . . 176 D5
WORMINGHALL 123 E6

Worminghall Rd
Ickford HP18 . . . . **123** F4
Oakley HP18 . . . . **109** D4
Wormsley Cres HP14. . . . **158** C4
WORMSTONE **99** C5
Wornal Pk HP18 . . . . **123** C7
Wornal Pk HP18 . . . . **123** C8
Worple The TW19. . . . . . **211** F1
Worrelle Ave MK10. . . . . . **36** A3
Worster Rd SL6 . . . . . **195** E6
Worth Ct MK10 . . . . **36** B1
Worthies The HP7 . . . . **165** B7
Worthington Rd HP18 . . . . . . **93** F8
Wotton End HP18 . . . . . . **96** C7
Wotton Path HP21 . . . **115** E3
Wotton Rd HP18 . . . . . . **97** E1
WOTTON UNDERWOOD . . . **97** C4
Woughton L Ctr MK6. . . . . **46** F7
WOUGHTON ON THE
   GREEN **47** D8
WOUGHTON PARK **47** E6
Wraxall Way MK6 . . . . . . **47** D5
Wray Ct MK4 . . . . **46** A2
WRAYSBURY **211** E1
Wraysbury Dr UB7 . . . . . . **208** D6
Wraysbury Prim Sch
   TW19 . . . . **211** E1
Wraysbury Sta TW19 . . . . **212** A1
Wren Cl MK18 . . . . **52** F7
Wren Ct SL3 . . . . **207** A3
Wren Dr UB7 . . . . **208** D3
Wren Path HP19 . . . . **114** F8
Wren Rd HP16 . . . . **151** C5
Wrensfield SL7 . . . . **183** C2
Wrens Pk MK10 . . . . **36** B2
Wren Vale HP13 . . . . . . **173** A8
Wren Wlk LU6 . . . . . **92** E4
Wreschner Cl MK19 . . . . . . **31** F4
Wright SL4 . . . . **209** C4
Wrights Cl HP14 . . . . . **171** B5
Wright's La HP16 . . . . . . **151** C5
Wrights Mdw Rd HP11 . . **173** F4
Wright Sq SL4 . . . . **209** C4

Wrights Yd HP16. . . . . . . **152** A7
Wright Way SL4. . . . . **209** C4
Wroughton Rd 4 HP22. . **131** E6
Wroxton Ct MK4 . . . . **45** F2
Wyatt Cl HP13 . . . . **172** F8
Wyatt Rd SL4 . . . . **209** D4
Wyatt's Rd WD3 . . . . **167** F5
Wyatt Wy HP18 . . . . **100** D4
Wychwood HP16. . . . . . . **152** B4
Wychwood Gdns HP12 . . **172** C6
Wychwood Rise HP16 . . . **152** B4
Wyclands Ho HP12 . . . . . **161** B2
Wycombe Abbey Sch
   HP11 . . . . **173** A6
Wycombe Air Pk SL7. . . . **171** F2
Wycombe Cl HP21 . . . . . . **116** B4
Wycombe End HP9. . . . . . **175** E1
Wycombe High Sch
   HP11 . . . . **172** F4
Wycombe Hospl HP11. . . . **173** A6
Wycombe Ind Mall HP11 . . **172** F7
Wycombe La HP10 . . . . . . **185** E7
WYCOMBE MARSH **173** F4
Wycombe Mus* HP13. . . . **173** B7
Wycombe Mus & Gdn 18
   HP13. . . . . **173** B7
Wycombe Rd
   Beacon's Bottom HP14 . . . **159** D3
   Holmer Green HP15 . . . . . **163** B6
   Lacey Green HP14. . . . . . **149** B4
   Marlow Bottom SL7. . . . . **183** E6
   Marlow SL7 . . . . **183** E4
   Prestwood HP15 . . . . **151** C5
Wycombe Ret Pk HP11. . . **173** F4
Wycombe Sp Ctr HP11 . . **172** F3
Wycombe Swan Theatre
   HP11. . . . . **173** B6
Wycombe View HP10. . . . **174** A2
Wye Cl
   Aylesbury HP21 . . . . **115** C5
   Milton Keynes MK3 . . . . . . **46** E1
Wye Ct 2 SL8 . . . . **185** A3
Wye Est HP11. . . . . **173** E5

Wye Gdns HP12. . . . . **172** D8
Wye Rd HP10 . . . . **185** D8
Wye River Bsns Ctr 8
   HP11. . . . . **172** F7
Wye Valley Sch The SL8 . **185** B4
Wykeham Gate HP17 . . . . **126** F5
Wykeham Rise OX39 . . . . **147** D6
Wykeham Way HP17 . . . . **126** F6
Wykeridge Cl HP5 . . . . . . **144** B4
Wylands Rd SL3. . . . . **207** A2
Wylie End MK13. . . . . **34** A7
WYMBUSH **33** F2
Wymbush Ind Est MK8 . . . **33** E3
Wymering Rd HP21 . . . . . **116** C6
Wymers Cl SL1 . . . . **197** B3
Wymers Wood Rd SL1. . . **197** A3
Wymondham MK10 . . . . . . **36** B1
Wynbury Dr HP13 . . . . . . **162** E1
Wyndale Cl RG9. . . . . **191** E1
Wyndham Ave HP13 . . . . **161** F2
Wyndham Cres SL1 . . . . . **197** B3
Wyness Ave MK17. . . . . . . **59** E5
Wynford Gn HP21 . . . . . . **115** F6
Wyngates LU7 . . . . **80** E5
Wyngrave Pl HP9 . . . . . . **175** C5
Wynne-Jones Ctr HP21 . . **115** F8
Wynn Gr HP15 . . . . **163** B3
Wynnstay Gdns SL7 . . . . **183** E5
Wynnswick Rd HP9 . . . . . **176** C5
Wynyard Ct MK6 . . . . **46** E7
Wyre Cl HP17. . . . . **127** A5
Wyvern Sch MK12. . . . . . . **33** C6
Wyvern Way UB8 . . . . . . **201** C4

X

Xscape* MK6 . . . . **34** F2

Y

Yalts Brow MK4. . . . . **46** B2

Yardley Ave LU7 . . . . **105** D4
Yardley Gn HP20. . . . . . . **101** F2
YARDLEY GOBION **18** E5
Yardley Gobion CE Prim Sch
   NN12. . . . . **18** E6
YARDLEY HASTINGS **1** B6
Yardley Hastings Prim Sch
   NN7. . . . . **1** A7
Yardley Rd
   Cosgrove MK19 . . . . **19** D2
   Olney MK46 . . . . **6** E6
   Potterspury NN12 . . . . **18** F4
Yarmouth Rd SL1 . . . . . . **205** C6
Yarrow Pl MK14. . . . . **34** E4
Yarrowside HP7 . . . . **166** B7
Yeates Cl
   Thame OX9 . . . . **125** F1
   Winslow MK18. . . . . **65** F4
Yeats Cl MK16 . . . . **21** F5
Ye Meads SL6 . . . . **203** E5
Ye Meads Cotts SL6 . . . . **203** E5
Ye Meads Ho SL6 . . . . . . **203** E5
Yeomans Cl NN13 . . . . **38** A8
Yeomans Dr MK14 . . . . . . **22** B1
Yeovil Ent Ctr SL1. . . . . . **204** F8
Yeovil Rd SL1. . . . . **204** E8
Yew Ave UB7 . . . . **208** E6
Yewtree Cl LU7 . . . . **105** E5
Yew Tree Cl
   Beaconsfield HP9 . . . . **175** F1
   Botley HP5. . . . . **145** A1
   Eaton Bray LU6 . . . . **92** F5
   Maidenhead SL6 . . . . **202** E8
   Newton Longville MK17. . . . **57** C3
   Stoke Mandeville HP22 . . . **116** A1
Yew Tree Dr
   Bovingdon HP3 . . . . **146** B3
   Hazlemere HP15 . . . . **162** F6
Yew Tree Rd
   Slough SL1. . . . . **206** A3
   Uxbridge UB10. . . . . **201** F4
Yew Wlk HP15 . . . . **163** A3
Yiewsley Ct UB7 . . . . . . **208** E5

Yolsum Cl HP17. . . . . **126** E6
Yonder Slade MK18 . . . . . . **52** D6

York Ave
   Slough SL1. . . . . **205** C7
   Windsor SL4 . . . . **210** B5
York Cl HP7 . . . . **165** F8
York Ct 3 LU7. . . . . **80** F7
Yorke Cl HP22 . . . . **117** E5
York Ho
   High Wycombe HP13 . . . . . **173** F8
   Milton Keynes MK3 . . . . . . **57** E7
York Pl HP21 . . . . **115** D7
York Rd
   Henley-on-Thames RG9 . . . **191** D2
   Maidenhead SL6 . . . . **203** A7
   Marlow SL7 . . . . **183** D2
   Milton Keynes MK11 . . . . . . **32** D5
   Uxbridge UB8. . . . . **201** D5
   Windsor SL4 . . . . **210** B5
Yorkshire Cl MK3 . . . . **46** F1
York Way HP12 . . . . **172** C4
Youens Rd HP12 . . . . . . **172** C5
Young Cl HP21. . . . . **116** A6
Young People's Acad
   UB7. . . . . **208** E6

Z

Zealand Ave UB7. . . . . . . **213** E7
Zetland Ct SL6. . . . . **203** B8
Zodiac Bsns Pk UB8. . . . . **208** D7
ZSL Whipsnade Zoo*
   HP4. . . . . **107** E8